★ MARCO POLO Highlights

NORDKAPPLATÅET

ⓓ Sommernächte, in denen die Sonne kaum das Meer berührt – unvergesslich!

ⓖⓑ Unforgettable summer nights where the sun barely touches the sea!

ⓕ Des nuits d'été quand le soleil touche à peine la mer – inoubliable!

② OSLO ⓝ

ⓓ Kleine Hauptstadt – tolles Umland: Vom Oslofjord geht's hinauf bis zum Holmenkollen.

ⓖⓑ A small capital at the head of the Oslofjord, surrounded by stunning countryside.

ⓕ Petite capitale – magnifique environnement: de l'Oslo-Fjord on grimpe au Holmenkollen.

③ HELSINKI ⓕⓘⓝ

ⓓ Felsenkirche und Senats-platz, dazu das Weltkulturerbe Suomenlinna sind die Attraktionen.

ⓖⓑ Major attractions include the Rock Church, carved into a hillside of solid granite, the massive Senate Square, and the island fortress of Suomen-linna, now a World Cultural Heritage Site.

ⓕ L'église construite dans les rochers et la place du sénat avec le patrimoine culturel mondial Suomenlinna sont les attractions ici.

④ САНКТ-ПЕТЕРБУРГ · SANKT-PETERBURG ⓡⓤⓢ

ⓓ Weiße Nächte, Zarenpracht – die Stadt an der Newa ist einmalig schön.

ⓖⓑ The former capital of the Tsars has a unique architectural heritage.

 11 DUBLIN (IRL)

ⅅ National Gallery, Old Library und das Szeneviertel Temple Bar – Dublin ist toll!

⅁⅀ Boasting the National Gallery, Old Library and the Temple Bar – the place to go for night life – Dublin is outstanding.

ⅆ National Gallery, Old Library et Temple Bar – Le quartier de la vie nocturne – Dublin est fantastique!

 12 LONDON (GB)

ⅅ Big Ben, Tower Bridge und British Museum sind nur drei der vielen Top-Ziele in London.

⅁⅀ Big Ben, Tower Bridge and the British Museum are just three of the top attractions in London.

ⅆ Pour ne nommer que trois des nombreux attractions de Londres: Big Ben, Tower Bridge, British Museum.

ⅆ Des nuits blanches, la gloire des tsars – la ville située sur la rivière Neva est exceptionnellement belle.

 5 STOCKHOLM (S)

ⅅ Altstadt Gamla Stan, Nobelquartier, Museen, Schären... das „Venedig des Nordens" lädt ein.

⅁⅀ The 'Venice of the north' offers the old town of Gamla Stan, the prestigious Strandvägen quarter, museums, and countless small islands of the coast.

ⅆ La vieille ville Gamla Stan, le quartier noble, les musées, les archipels... la «Venise du Nord» vous invite.

 6 TALLINN (EST)

ⅅ Quirlige Metropole, in der Mittelalter und Moderne verschmelzen.

⅁⅀ Lively metropolis in which Middle Age architecture and modern culture form a perfect blend.

ⅆ Métropole vivante dans laquelle fusent le Moyen Age et la Moderne.

 7 GRAMPIAN MOUNTAINS (GB)

ⅅ Fantastische Bergwelt mit weiten Moor- und Heidelandschaften im mittleren Schottland.

⅁⅀ Awe-inspiring mountain range with expansive moors and heathland in central Scotland.

ⅆ Des montagnes fantastiques avec de vastes paysages de marécages et de landes au centre de l'Écosse.

8 BLÅVAND, VEJERS STRAND, HENNE STRAND (DK)

ⅅ Nichts als Sand, Dünen, Wind und Meer – auf vielen Kilometern.

⅁⅀ Nothing but sand, dunes, wind and sea – as far as the eye can see.

ⅆ Rien d'autre que sable, dunes, vent et mer – à perte de vue.

 9 RĪGA (LV)

ⅅ Riga ist ein Jugendstiljuwel – aber auch die Altstadt mit dem Dom ist eine Attraktion.

⅁⅀ Riga is noted for its Art Nouveau architecture, but also its 17th century centre and beautiful cathedral.

ⅆ Riga est un joyau du style d'Art Nouveau – mais aussi sa vieille ville avec la cathédrale sont des attractions.

 10 MOCKBA · MOSKVA (RUS)

ⅅ Die Hauptstadt glänzt mit dem Kreml und großartiger Kultur.

⅁⅀ The capital of Russia is known for its cultural heritage and architectural masterpieces, like the Kremlin.

ⅆ La capitale doit son rayonnement au Kremlin et à sa riche vie culturelle.

---

 13 AMSTERDAM (NL)

ⅅ Rijksmuseum, Van-Gogh-Museum, Nieuwmarkt und Grachtenring... Amsterdam hat viele Highlights!

⅁⅀ Boasting the Rijksmuseum, Van-Gogh-Museum, Nieuwmarkt and Canal Ring area, Amsterdam has many attractions for visitors.

ⅆ Rijksmuseum, Van-Gogh-Museum, Nieuwmarkt et le quartier des canaux concentriques du 17ème siècle... Amsterdam a tant d'attraits!

 14 BERLIN (D)

ⅅ Museumsinsel, Schlösser und Parks, Historisches und Berliner Moderne: eine Weltmetropole.

Ⓓ Fantastisch: Eiffelturm und Louvre, jenseits der Péripherique La Défense und Versailles.

ⒼⒷ The visitor to Paris is spoilt for choice: the Eiffel Tower and the Louvre, and on the outskirts La Défense and Versailles.

Ⓕ Fantastique: La Tour Eiffel et le Louvre, de l'autre côté du périphérique La Défense et Versailles.

⭐ 19 **PRAHA** Ⓒⓩ

Ⓓ Über der Moldaumetropole, dem „Goldenen Herz Mitteleuropas", thront der Hradschin.

ⒼⒷ The Hradčany, the 'Golden Heart of Central Europe', sits enthroned above the city on the banks of the Vltava river.

Ⓕ Au-dessus de la métropole au bord de la rivière Vltava, «le cœur

ⒼⒷ The 'Museum Island', castles and parks, and historical buildings alongside modern architecture in the world metropolis of Berlin.

Ⓕ L'île aux Musées, des châteaux et des parcs, des temps anciens et modernes à Berlin – une métropole.

⭐ 15 **WARSZAWA** ⓅⓁ

Ⓓ Alter Markt, Kulturpalast und Königsschloss sind Highlights der Weichselmetropole.

ⒼⒷ The Polish capital sits astride the Vistula River and boasts highlights such as the Old Market, the Palace of Culture and the Royal Palace.

Ⓕ Les attraits de la capitale aux berges de la Vistule sont le vieux marché, le palace de la culture et le palace royal.

⭐ 16 **BRUSSEL · BRUXELLES** Ⓑ

Ⓓ Atomium, Manneken Pis, Sitz der EU – die „Hauptstadt Europas" lohnt einen Besuch.

ⒼⒷ The Atomium, Manneken Pis, and headquarters of the EU alone make the 'capital of Europe' well worth a visit.

Ⓕ Atomium, Manneken Pis, siège de la UE – la «capitale de l'Europe» vaut le détour.

⭐ 17 **КИЇВ · KYJIV** ⓊⒶ

Ⓓ „Mutter der russischen Städte", „Jerusalem des Ostens", „Heldenstadt" – Kiew hat viele Facetten.

ⒼⒷ A city of many names, Kiev has been called the 'Mother of Russian Cities', the 'Jerusalem of the East', and the 'City of Heroes'.

Ⓕ «La mère de toutes les villes russes», «Jérusalem de l'Est», «la ville des héros» – Kiev a beaucoup de facettes.

doré de l'Europe centrale», trône le Hradschin.

20 KRAKÓW (PL)

ⓓ Tuchhallen und Hauptmarkt, Nationalmuseum und Burgberg muss man gesehen haben.

ⓖⓑ The Main Market, Cloth Halls, National Museum and the Castle Hill are a 'must see' for visitors to the city.

ⓕ Il faut absolument voir les Halles aux Draps, le marché principal, le musée national et la colline du château.

 21 BODENSEE ⓓ

ⓓ Das „Schwäbische Meer" mit tollen Uferstrecken, zwei Welterbestätten und einer Blumeninsel.

ⓖⓑ The 'Swabian Sea' with wonderful trails along the shore, world heritage sites and the garden island of Mainau.

ⓕ La «mer Souabe» avec de superbes chemins longeant le bord, deux sites classés patrimoine mondial et une île pleine de fleurs.

22 WIEN ⓐ

ⓓ Habsburgerpracht, Stephansdom und das atemberaubende Museumsareal – einfach ein Muss!

ⓖⓑ Wien is a must see for any visitor, combining the glory of the Habsburg monarchy, St Stephen's Cathedral, and breathtaking museums.

ⓕ La gloire de la monarchie des Habsbourg, la Cathédrale Saint Étienne de Vienne et la zone des musées belle à couper le souffle – c'est un «must»!

 23 BRATISLAVA (SK)

ⓓ Viel Kunst, Kultur und Geschichte auf engem Raum, im Umland die Burgen Devín und Castá.

ⓖⓑ The area around the castles of Devín and Castá concentrate an astonishing collection of important art, historical and cultural artefacts in one place.

ⓕ Beaucoup d'art, culture et histoire dans un espace réduit, dans le voisinage les châteaux de Devín et Castá.

 24 BUDAPEST ⓗ

ⓓ Ungarns Hauptstadt verzaubert mit ihrer Pracht, der Donau … und den Kaffeehäusern.

ⓖⓑ The Hungarian capital is packed with important works of art and historical monuments.

ⓕ La capitale hongroise attire avec une multitude d'œuvres d'art et de monuments historiques.

 25 MATTERHORN (CH)

ⓓ Vom Gornergrat hat man den besten Ausblick auf den weltbekannten Berg.

ⓖⓑ The summit of the Gornergrat offers the best views of this world-famous mountain.

ⓕ Depuis le Gornergrat on a la meilleure vue sur cette montagne connue mondialement.

26 VRŠIČ (SLO)

ⓓ Die atemberaubende Passstraße führt in 40 spitzen Kehren von Krajnska Gora nach Süden.

ⓖⓑ From Krajnska Gora this breathtaking mountain road climbs up the mountainside in 40 hairpin bends to reach the summit.

ⓕ La vertigineuse route de montagne se tortille en 40 virages étroits de Krajnska Gora vers le Sud.

 27 SIGHIŞOARA (RO)

ⓓ Das Siebenbürger Städtchen klebt wie eine mittelalterliche Puppenstube an seinem Berg.

ⓖⓑ The little medieval town clings to the Transylvanian hillside like a collection of dolls houses.

ⓕ La petite ville de la Transylvanie colle à sa colline comme une maison de poupées du Moyen Âge.

28 БЕОГРАД · BEOGRAD (SRB)

ⓓ Festung und Dom sind nur zwei der vielen Highlights, die das „Tor zum Balkan" bietet.

Ⓖ A dream of rolling hills, broad beaches and the cities of Florence, Siena, Pisa, and Lucca.

Ⓕ Des douces collines, de larges plages et Florence, Siena, Pisa, Lucca – un vrai rêve!

⭐ 31 DUBROVNIK Ⓗⓡ

Ⓓ Die Königin der östlichen Adria mit Wehrmauern, Palazzi, Kirchen und Museen.

Ⓖ The queen of the Eastern Adriatic with palaces, churches, museums, and ancient fortified walls.

Ⓕ La reine de la mer Adriatique de l'Est avec murs fortifiés, palais, églises et musées.

Ⓕ Une métropole au pied du massif montagneux Vitocha – une des villes les plus anciennes d'Europe.

⭐ 34 İSTANBUL Ⓣⓡ

Ⓓ Die Metropole am Goldenen Horn lockt mit orientalischem Charme und weltstädtischem Flair.

Ⓖ The metropolis on the Golden Horn combines oriental charm and cosmopolitan flair.

Ⓕ La métropole située sur la Corne d'Or attire les visiteurs avec charme oriental et ambiance cosmopolite.

Ⓖ The 'Gateway to the Balkans' boasts architecture from different eras, along with a bohemian and artists quarter.

Ⓕ Le château et la cathédrale sont seulement deux des points forts qui offre «la porte aux Balkans».

⭐ 29 CÔTE D'AZUR Ⓕ

Ⓓ Azurblaues Meer, spektakuläre Küste und glamouröse Städte wie Nizza und Cannes.

Ⓖ The glamorous towns of Nice and Cannes lie on this spectacular coastline by the azure blue sea.

Ⓕ Une mer d'azur, une côte spectaculaire et des villes de glamour comme Nice et Cannes.

⭐ 30 TOSCANA Ⓘ

Ⓓ Sanfte Hügel, breite Strände, dazu Florenz, Siena, Pisa, Lucca – einfach ein Traum!

⭐ 32 TARA Ⓜⓝⓔ

Ⓓ Die tiefste Schlucht Europas, der zweittiefste Canyon der Welt.

Ⓖ The deepest gorge in Europe, and second deepest canyon of the world.

Ⓕ La gorge la plus profonde d'Europe, le canyon le secon profond du monde.

⭐ 33 СОФИЯ · SOFIJA Ⓑⓖ

Ⓓ Metropole am Fuße des Witoscha-Gebirges – eine der ältesten Städte Europas.

Ⓖ This bustling metropolis at the bottom of the Vitosha mountain massif is also one of the most ancient settlements in Europe.

⭐ 35 LISBOA Ⓟ

Ⓓ Die weiße Stadt am Tejo ist das Herz Portugals; Strände, Cabo da Roca und Sintra sind nahe.

Ⓖ The white town on the Tejo river is the heart of Portugal and has beaches, the Cabo da Roca and Sintra are close by.

Ⓕ La ville blanche au bord de la rivière Tejo est le cœur du Portugal; les plages, Cabo da Roca et Sintra sont proches.

⭐ 36 MADRID Ⓔ

Ⓓ Die Hauptstadt Spaniens – und der marcha, des nimmermüden Nachtlebens.

Ⓖ The capital of Spain – and the endless night life that is the Marcha.

Ⓕ La capitale de l'Espagne – et de la marcha, la vie nocturne qui n'arrête pas.

⭐ 37 BARCELONA Ⓔ

Ⓓ Gaudís Jugendstilbauten, Altstadt, Hafen und Rambla, dazu das Meer und jede Menge Flair …

ⒼⒷ Gaudí's Art Nouveau buildings, the old town, port and Rambla, combine with stunning coastline to give Barcelona a unique atmosphere.

Ⓕ Les bâtiments Art Nouveau de Gaudí, vieille ville, port et rambla, avec cela la mer et beaucoup d'ambiance …

⭐ 38 ROMA Ⓘ

Ⓓ Die „Ewige Stadt" mit dem größten Dom, dem kleinsten Staat und vielem mehr.

ⒼⒷ The 'Eternal City' with the world's smallest state, the world's largest cathedral, and much more.

Ⓕ La «Ville éternelle» avec la plus grande cathédrale, le plus petit état et tant d'autres choses à voir.

⭐ 39 ANDALUCÍA Ⓔ

Ⓓ Kulturelle Schätze in Granada, Sevilla, Córdoba, Cádiz, Sonne und Meer – gibt es Schöneres?

ⒼⒷ Cultural treasures in Granada, Sevilla, Córdoba, Cádiz, sun and sea. Destinations don't get better than this.

Ⓕ Des trésors culturels à Granada, Sevilla, Córdoba, Cádiz, du soleil, la mer – y aurait-il mieux?

⭐ 40 SICILIA Ⓘ

Ⓓ Griechische Tempel und römische Mosaiken, stille Strände und prunkvolle Städte.

ⒼⒷ Greek temples and Roman mosaics, quiet beaches and magnificent cities.

Ⓕ Des temples grecs et des mosaïques romains, des plages tranquilles et des villes somptueuses.

⭐ 41 I AKRÓPOLI TIS AΘÍNAS · AKROPOLIS Ⓖⓡ

Ⓓ Vier Tempel auf einem Fels über Athens Altstadt haben Griechenlands antiken Glanz bewahrt.

ⒼⒷ The four temples dominating the old city of Athens bear witness to the glory of ancient Greece.

Ⓕ Les quatre temples sur un rocher dominant la vieille ville d'Athènes ont gardé l'ancien éclat de la Grèce.

⭐ 42 ΣΑΝΤΟΡΙΝΗ · SANTORINI Ⓖⓡ

Ⓓ Per Schiff in den Vulkankrater, dazu antike Stätten – einzigartig!

ⒼⒷ A unique experience: boat trips across a massive volcanic caldera, ringed by ancient towns and villages.

Ⓕ Unique: en bateau dans le cratère du volcan et des sites antiques.

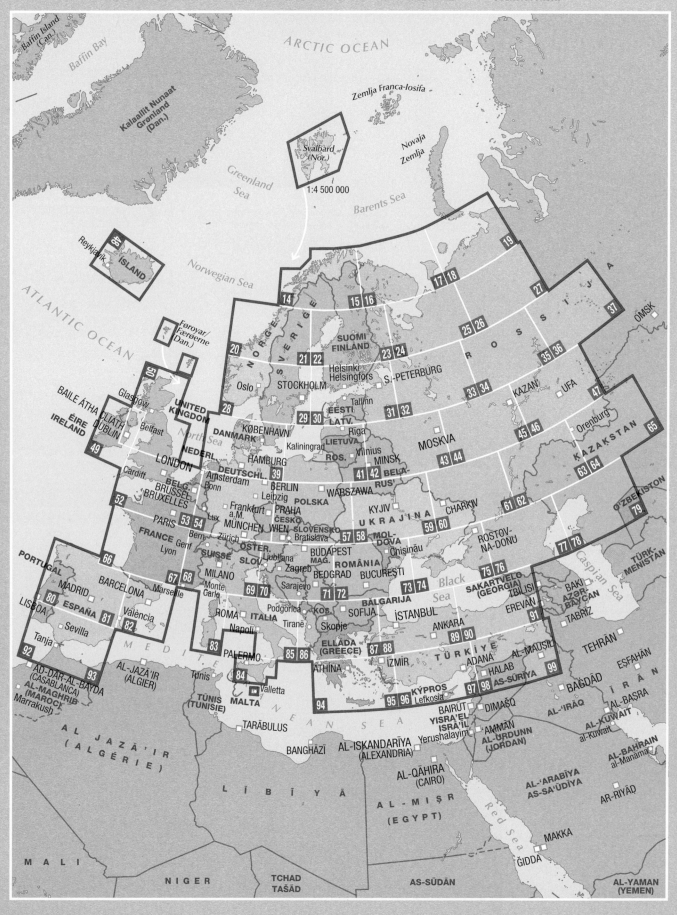

1:2 000 000

KLAD MAPOVÝCH LISTŮ	BLATTÜBERSICHT	KEY MAP	CARTE D'ASSEMBLAGE
QUADRO D' UNIONE	ÍNDICE DE MAPA	MAPA ÍNDICE	OVERZICHTSKAART
SKOROWIDZ ARKUSZY	KLAD MAPOVÝCH LISTOV	ÁTTEKINTŐTÉRKÉP	OVERSIGTSKORT

1 : 2 000 000

Zeichenerklärung
Legend

Légende
Segni convenzionali

D **F**
GB **I**

Autobahn - Autobahn in Bau Motorway - Motorway under construction		Autoroute - Autoroute en construction Autostrada - Autostrada in costruzione
Autobahnähnliche Schnellstraße - in Bau Dual carriageway with motorway characteristics - under construction		Chaussée double de type autoroutier - en construction Doppia carreggiata di tipo autostradale - in costruzione
Fernverkehrsstraße - in Bau Trunk road - under construction		Route à grande circulation - en construction Strada di grande communicazione - in costruzione
Hauptstraße Main road		Route principale Strada principale
Nebenstraße Secondary road		Route secondaire Strada secondaria
Fahrweg, Piste Practicable rnad, track		Chemin carrossable, piste Strada carrozzabile, pista
Entfernungen in Kilometer Distances in kilometers	**227** 130 97	Distances en kilomètres Distanze in chilometri
Höhe in Meter - Pass Height in meters - Pass	1365	Altitude en mètres - Col Altitudine in metri - Passo
Eisenbahn - Eisenbahnfähre Railway - Railway ferry		Chemin de fer - Ferry-boat Ferrovia - Traghetto ferroviario
Autofähre - Schifffahrtslinie Car ferry - Shipping route		Bac pour automobiles - Ligne de navigation Traghetto auto - Linea marittima
Wichtiger Flughafen Important airport	✈	Aéroport important Aeroporto importante
Flughafen - Flugplatz Airport - Airfield	✈ ✈	Aéroport - Aérodrome Aeroporto - Aerodromo
Internationale Grenze - Provinzgrenze International boundary - Province boundary		Frontière internationale - Limite de Province Confine internazionale - Confine di Provincia
Unbestimmte Grenze Undefined boundary		Frontière d'État non définie Confine di Stato indefinito
Zeitzonengrenze Time zone boundary	••••••••••••••	Limite de fuseau horaire Limite fuso orario
Hauptstadt eines souveränen Staates National capital	**LISBOA**	Capitale nationale Capitale di stato sovrano
Hauptstadt eines Bundesstaates State capital	**MURMANSK**	Capitale d'un état fédéral Capitale dello stato federale
Sperrgebiet Restricted area		Zone interdite Zona vietata
Nationalpark - Naturpark National park - Nature park		Parc national - Parc naturel Parco nazionale - Parco naturale
Besonders sehenswert: Kultur - Natur Of particular interest: culture - nature	**SIRACUSA** *Mývatn*	Très intéressant: culture - nature Molto interessante: cultura - natura
Sehenswerter Ort Place of interest	**Alba Iulia**	Localité intéressante Località interessante
Sehenswert: Kultur - Natur Of interest: culture - nature	✷ Blair Castle ✷ *Drachenfels*	Intéressant: culture - nature Interessante: cultura - natura
Landschaftlich schöne Strecke Route with beautiful scenery		Parcours pittoresque Percorso pittoresco
MARCO POLO Highlight MARCO POLO Highlight	★	MARCO POLO Highlight MARCO POLO Highlight
Ausgrabungs- oder Ruinenstätte Archaeological excavation or ruins	∴	Site archéologique ou ruines Scavo o rovine
Brunnen Well		Puits Pozzo
Vulkan Volcano	•	Volcan Vulcano

1:2 000 000

0   20   40   60   80   100 km

0   10   20   30   40   50   60 miles

1 : 2 000 000

Signos convencionales
Sinais convencionais

Vysvětlivky
Objaśnienia znaków

E
P

CZ
PL

Autopista - Autopista en construcción Auto-estrada - Auto-estrada em construção		Dálnice - Dálnice ve stavbě Autostrada - Autostrada w budowie
Autovía - en construcción Vía rápida de faixas separadas - em construção		Dvouproudá silnice dálnicového typu - ve stavbě Droga szybkiego ruchu - w budowie
Ruta de larga distancia - en construcción Itinerário principal - em construção		Dálková silnice - ve stavbě Droga dalekobieżna - w budowie
Carretera principal Estrada principal		Hlavní silnice Droga główna
Carretera secundaria Estrada secundária		Vedlejší silnice Droga drugorzędna
Camino vecinal, pista Caminho, pista		Vozová cesta, vyježděná cesta Droga bita, szlaka
Distancias en kilómetros Distâncias em quilómetros	**227** 130 97	Vzdálenosti v kilometrech Odległości w kilometrach
Altura en metros - Puerto de montaña Altura em metros - Passagem	1365	Výška v metrech - Průsmyk Wysokości w metrach - Przełęcz
Ferrocarril - Transbordador para ferrocarriles Linha ferroviária - Comboios balsa		Železnice - Vlakový trajekt Kolej - Prom kolejowy
Ferry - Ruta marítima Balsa de carro - Linha de navegação		Říční přívoz pro auta - Lodní linka Prom samochodowy - Linia żeglugowa
Aeropuerto importante Aeroporto principal	✈	Důležité letiště Ważny port lotniczy
Aeropuerto - Aeródromo Aeroporto - Aeródromo	✈ ✈	Dopravní letiště - Přistávací plocha Port lotniczy - Lotnisko
Frontera internacional - Frontera provincial Fronteira internacional - Fronteira provincial		Mezinárodní hranice - Hranice provincie Granica międzynarodowa - Granica prowincji
Frontera indeterminada Fronteira indeterminada		Neurčitá hranice Granica nieustalona
Límite del huso horario Limite de fuso horário	·················	Hranice časového pásma Granica strefy czasowej
Capital de un estado soberano Capital de estado soberano	**LISBOA**	Hlavní město suverenního států Stolica państw niezależnych
Capital de estado Capital de estado federal	**MURMANSK**	Hlavní město spolkového států Stolica stanów federalnych
Zona prohibida Área proibida		Zakázaný prostor Obszar zamknięty
Parque nacional - Parque natural Parque nacional - Parque natural		Národní park - Přírodní park Park narodowy - Park krajobrazowy
De interés especial: cultura - natura De interesse especial: cultura - natureza	**SIRACUSA** Mývatn	Turisticky pozoruhodný: kultura - příroda Szczególnie interesujący: kultura - przyroda
Población de interés Povoação interessante	**Alba Iulia**	Turisticky zajímavá lokalita Miejscowość interesująca
De interés: cultura - natura Interessante: cultura - natureza	✱ Blair Castle ✱ Drachenfels	Zajímavý: kultura - příroda Interesujący: kultura - przyroda
Ruta pintoresca Itinerário pitoresco		Úsek silnice s pěknou scenérií Droga piękna widokowa
MARCO POLO Highlight MARCO POLO Highlight	★	MARCO POLO Highlight MARCO POLO Highlight
Excavación o ruinas historicas Sítio de escavações ou ruinas	∴	Archeologické naleziště nebo ruiny Wykopalisko albo ruina
Fuente Poço	∪	Studny Studnie
Volcán Vulcão	●	Sopka Wulkan

1 : 2 000 000

```
0        20       40       60       80      100 km

0      10      20      30      40      50    60 miles
```

1 : 2 000 000

Objašnjenja   **Jelmagyarázat**
Legenda   **Tegnforklaring**

HR / SLO   H / DK

Autocesta - Autocesta u izgradnji Avtocesta - Avtocesta v gradnji	Autópálya - épités alatt Motorvej - Motorvej under bygning
Četverotračna brza cesta - u izgradnji Hitra cesta - v gradnji	Gyorsforgalmi út autópályahoz hasonlóan - épités alatt Motortrafikvej med to vejbaner - under bygning
Magistralna cesta - u izgradnji Magistralna cesta - v gradnji	Távolsági összekötő út - épités alatt Fjerntrafikvej - under bygning
Glavna cesta Glavna cesta	Főútvonal Hovedvej
Lokalna cesta Stranska cesta	Mellékút Bivej
Provozni put, stazu Vozna pot, pobočja	Közlekedési út, ösvény Mindre vej, bane
Udaljenosti u kilometrima Razdalje v kilometrah	**227** 130 97	Kilométertávolság Afstænder i kilometer
Visina u metrima - Prijevoj Višina v metrih - Prelaz	1365	Magasság méterben - Szoros Højde i meter - Pas
Željeznička pruga - Dereglija za prevoženje vozova Železniška proga - Železniški trajekt	Vasútvonal - Vasúti komp Jernbanelinie - Jernbanefærge
Trajekt za automobile - Brodska pruga Trajekt za avtomobile - Ladijska proga	Autószallító komp - Hajózási vonal Bilfærge - Skibsrute
Važna zračna luka Pomembno mednarodno letališče	✈	Fontos repülőtér Vigtig lufthavn
Zračna luka - Uzletište Mednarodno letališče - Letališče	✈ ✈	Közlekedési repülőtér - Egyéb repülőtér Lufthavn - Flyveplads
Međunarodna granica - Pokrajina granica Mednarodna meja - Provinca meja	Nemzetközi határ - Körzethatár International grænse - Provinsgrænse
Neodređeno granica Nedoločen meje	Bizonytalan határ Ubestemt grænse
Ograničenje vremenske zone Časovni pas mejo	Időzónahatár Tidszonegrænse
Glavni grad suverene države Glavno mesto suverena država	**LISBOA**	Önálló állam fővárosa Suveræn stats hovedstad
Glavni grad savezne države Glavno mesto stanje	**MURMANSK**	Szövetsegi állam fővárosa Forbundsstats hovedstad
Zabranjeno područje Zaprto območje	Zárt terület Afspærret omrade
Nacionalni park - Prirodni park Narodni park - Naravni park	Nemzeti park - Természeti park Nationalpark - Naturpark
Osobito znamenito: kultura - priroda Posebej zanimivo: kultura - priroda	**SIRACUSA** *Mývatn*	Különleges látványosság: kultúra - természet Særlig seværdig: kultur - natur
Znamenito naselje Zanimivo naselje	**Alba Iulia**	Látványos település Seværdig by
Znamenito: kultura - priroda Zanimivo: kultura - priroda	∗ *Blair Castle* ∗ *Drachenfels*	Látványos: kultúra - természet Seværdig: kultur - natur
Cesta u lijepom krajoliku Slikovita cesta	Természetileg szép szakasz Landskabelig smuk vejstrækning
MARCO POLO Highlight MARCO POLO Highlight	★ 1	MARCO POLO Highlight MARCO POLO Highlight
Najidišč ali razvaline Najidišča ali razvaline	∴	Régészeti asatások és romhely Udgravnings- eller ruinsted
Vodnjak Vodnjak	⌣	Kút Brønd
Vulkan Vulkan	●	Vulkán Vulkan

1 : 2 000 000

0	20	40	60	80	100 km

0	10	20	30	40	50	60 miles

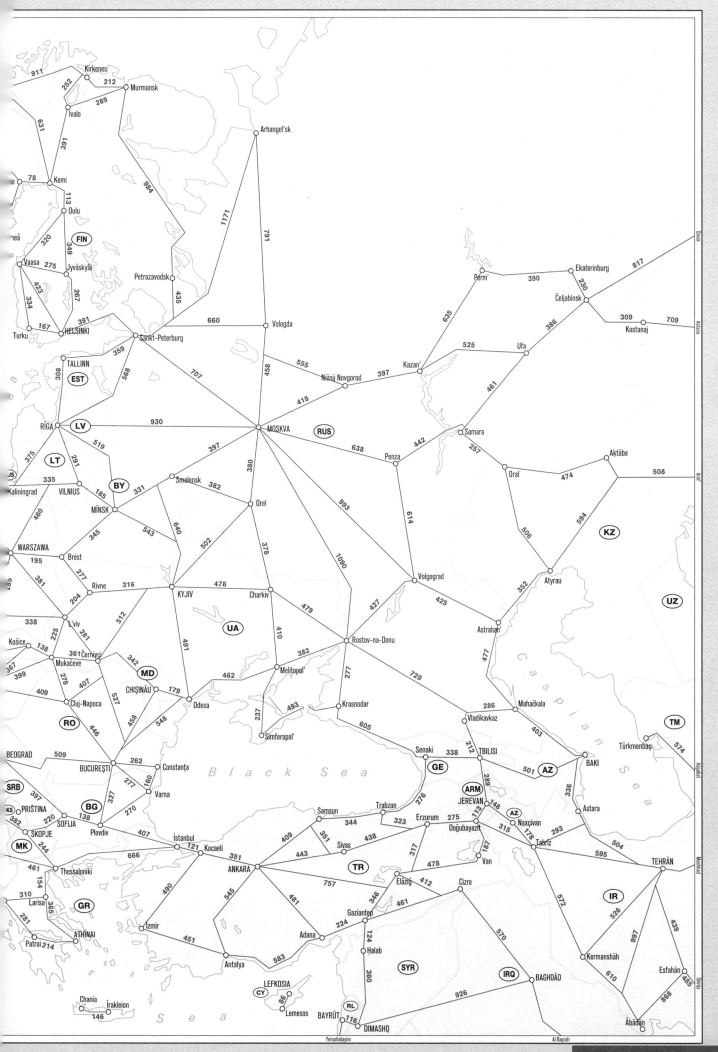

I Svalbard 1:4 500 000

Svalbard (Nor.)

Danskøya
Albert I
Land
Reinsdyr
Øya
Haakon VII
Land
Fuglehuken
Grampianfjella 1084
Prins Karls
Forland
nasjonalpark
Ny Ålesund
Forland
Daudmannsodden
Isfjord Radio
Lågneset
Barentsburg
Longyearbyen
Grumantbyen
Nordenskiöld
Land
Gustavfjellet
Heer
Sveagruva
Nathorst Land
Van Mijenfjorden
Wedel
Jarlsberg
Land
Oscar II
Land
Spitsbergen
Andrée
Land
Dickson
Land
Pyramiden
Olav V
Land

Verlegen-
huken
Phippsøya
Sjuøyane
Nordkapp
Parryøya
Martensøya
Kapp
Platen
Storsteinhalvøya
Gustav
V Land
Prins
Oscars Land
Foynøya
Storøya
Kvitøya
(Nor.)
Nordaust-Svalbard
nat-res
Nordaustlandet
Wahlbergøya
Gustav Adolf nat-res
Von
Otterøyane
Willefmøya
Erik Eriksenstretet
Nordaust-Svalbard
nat-res
Kongsøya
Abeløya
Svenskøya
Kong Karls Land
Friesland
Wahlbergøya
Barentsøya
Freemansundet
Edgeøya
Stonepynten
Tjuvfjorden
Hornsund
Hornsundtind
Sørkapp
Land
Øyrlandsodden
Sørkappøya
Halvmåneøya
Tusenøyane

Storfjorden

Norwegian Sea

Vesterålen

Nordkvaløy
Vannareid
Fugløya
Vanna
Arnøy
Arviksand
Lauksletta
Rebbenesøy
Helgøy
Mikkelvik
Kågen
Russelv
Nordkjosen
Uløya
Måsvik
Komagvik
Ringvassøy
Reinøy
Nordneidet
Finnkroken
Tromvik
Blåmannen
Oldervik
Svensby
Kvaløy
Kvaløysletta
Tromsø
Jøvik
Lyngseidet
Sandneshamn
Bakke-
jord
Fågernes
Jiekkevarrebreen
Skibotn
Berg
Fjordgård
Vikran
Furuflaten
Kåfjord

Senja
Gryllefjord
Gibostad
Lunneborg
Seljelvnes
Oteren
Bleik
Kaldfarnes
Silsand
Finnsnes
Moen
Nordkjos-botn
Rognli
Nordmela
Ånderdalen
nasjonalpark
Sørreisa
Brøstadbotn
Andselv
Øvergård
Andøya
Sjursnes
Bjarkøy
Stong-
landet
Dyrøya
Løksa
Setermoen
Bjørkås
Høgstadgård
Risøyhamn
Åse
Grøtavær
Andørja
Sjøvegan
Innset
Øvre Dividal
nasjonalpark
Myre
Grytøya
Rolla
Myrlandshaug
Tennevoll
Fossbakken
Langøya
Harstad
Ibestad
Grovfjord
Straumsjøen
Borkenes
Sørrollnes
Tjeldøya
Steine
Sørland
Sigerfjord
Kilbotn
Steinsland
Bjerkvik
Stokmarknes
Hadseløya
Moysalen
np.
Moysalen
Fiskebøl
Kaljord
Melbu
Fjordbotn
Ramnes
Narvik
Bjørkliden
Austvågøy
Kongselva
Tjeldøya
Bogen
Beisfjord
Abisko
nat-p.
Abisko
Vestvågøy
Svolvær
Ytterstad
Lødingen
Kjeldebotn
Ballangen
Skjomen
Katterjåkk
Torneträsk
Leknes
Kabelvåg
Digermulen
Storsten-
fjellet
Flakstadøya
Stamsund
Henningsvær
Hamarøy
Ulvsvåg
Kjøpsvik
Tornehamn
Flakstad
Ballstad
Tranøy
Skutvik
Finnøya
Kuolasjaure
Moskenesøya
Reine
Sørvågen
Engeløya
Ålstad
Singistugorna
Kebnekaise
Nikkaluokta
Kurravaara
Kiruna
Værøy
Sørland
Hellnessund
Nordfold
Hellemobotn
Kebne-
kaisefjällst.
Kiirunavaara
Holmajärvi
Røst
Helligvær
Kråktinden
Mørsvikbotn
Vaisaluokta-
stugan
V. Ritjemjåkk
Kalixfors
Landegode
Gammelt
handelssted
Helldalisen
Gåskačokka
Kisurisstugan
Stora Sjöfallets
n.p.
Sjaunja naturreservat
Bliksvær
Tårnvik
Styrksvik
Rosvik
Akkavare
Akkajaure
Vietas
Fjällåsen
Bodø
Festvåg
Loding
Straumen
Padjelanta
national-
Stortoppen
Sareks
Ruokto
Sitojaure-
stugorna
Sandhornøy
Lekanger
Skjerstad
Fauske
Sulitjelma
park
Staloluokta-
stugorna
nationalpark
Inndyr
Bejarn
Monus
Sulitjelma
Pårtefjällen
Malmberget
Fugløya
Vesterli
Rognan
Gällivare
Ørnes
Høgtind
Pieskehaure-
stugan
Kvikkjokk
Ålloluokta
Porjus
Amøya
Glomfjord
Storjord
Riepentjåkkå
Tjåmotis
Muddus
nationalpark
Nesøya
Vågaholmen
Svartisen
Kilvik
Ölfjellet
Mavas-
jaure
Randijaur
Karats
Kvikkjokk
Trænstaven
Reppen
Melfjordbotn
Svartisen
Saltfjellet
Kaisetjåkkå
Karatj
Jokkmokk
Kilboghamn
Grønli-
grotten
Stødi
Fierras
Ballasviken
Tjeggelvas
Stokkvågen
Høgtuvbreen
Stor-
forshei
Nasarfjället
Sådva-
jaure
Stenudden
Lovund
Lunderøy
Mo i Rana
Toftlia
Rieljekaise
nationalpark
Vuonatj-
viken
Arctic Circle
Nausta
Tomma
Storakers
vatnet
Adolfström
Lövnäs
Vuollerim
Rølvåg
Nesna
Hemnes

0　10　20　30　40　50 km
0　10　20　30 miles

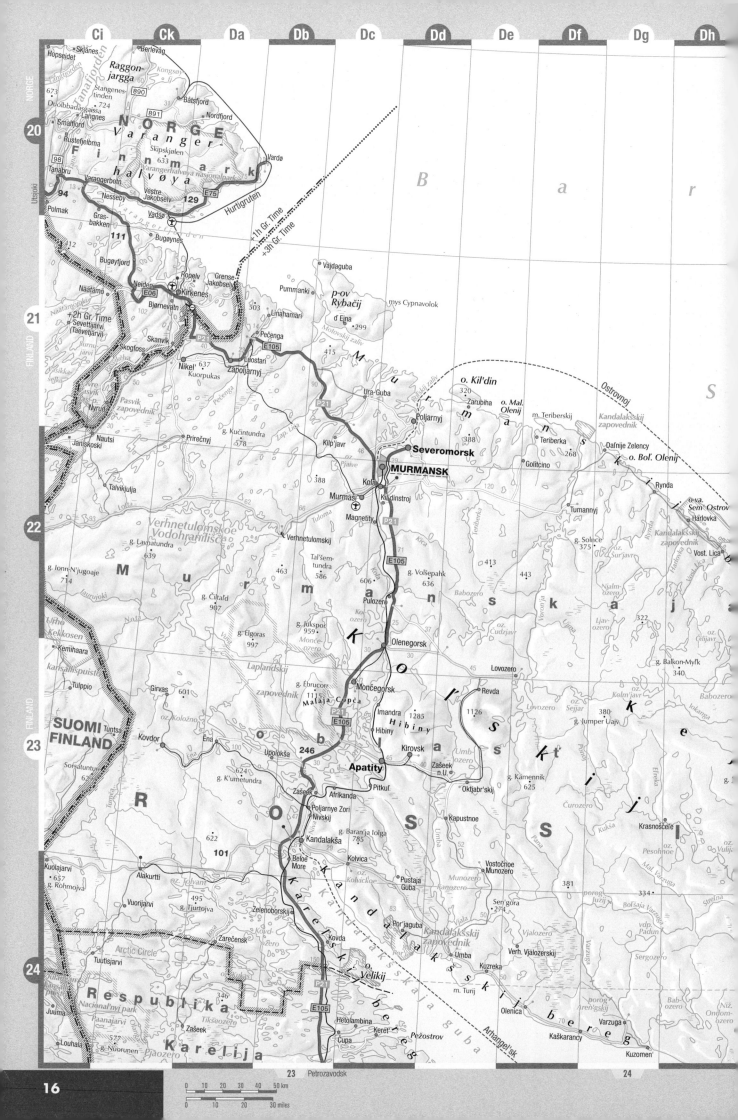

e　n　t　s

e　a

m. Kanin Nos
Kanin Nos

K　a　n　i　n

204
g. Korytova

m. Lajdennyj
o. Korga
o-va Kambal'nickie
Koški

o. Nokuev
Varzino

·283

zeёo

m. Svjatoj Nos

p-ov Svjatoj Nos

Svjatonosskij
zaliv
Ostrovnoj

242
g. Mohovaja

Rybnaja

Mesna

K　a　m　e　n　'

225

Iokanga

Lyljok

Lumbovskij zaliv

o. Lumbovskij

303

Lumbovka

Vyhča

Turta
6

Lumbovka

Kolmak

Kačkovka

Kačkovskij zaliv

e　Šojnskaja guba
Šojna

Sojna

Kija

74

oz.
Sučej

Neneckij

m. Mikulkin

b　e　r　e　g

K　a　n　i　n

p　-　o　v

m. Zapadnyj
Ludovatyj Nos

Čésskaja

guba

Čiža

m　o　r

J

g. Manjuk
342

Lebjaž'ja

Aterjok

Losinga

p

Kanevka

por.
Kolmackij

O

Purnač

V

Ponoj

A

Orlovskij zaliv
m. Orlovskij

b　e　r　e　g

Ponoj

o. Gorjainov

m. Konušin

Čiža

avtonomnyj

Jažma

k　a　n　i　n　s　k　a　j　a

Čésa

Perepusk

Vižas

Oma

Oma

302

Pjalka

oz.
Bab'e

sosnovka

Sosnovka

o. Moržovec

Pjalica

Pulonga

o. Sosnovec

T　e　r　s　k　i　j

Verh.
Ondom-
ozero

Stečna

Čapoma

Pjalica

Pulonga

k　a　n　i　n　s　k　i　j　　b　e　r　e　g

m. Mihailovskij

Nes'

m. Voronov

Arctic Circle
M　e　z　e　n　s　k　a　j　a

m. Abramov

Kojda

Niža

Majda

Kojda

b

e

l

guba

Vižas

t　u　n　d　r　a

91

okrug

oz. Vižas

147

Niž. Mgla

Konušinskij

Nes'

Sёmža

Semža

A　r　h　a　n　g　e　l　'　s　k　a　j　a　　o　b　l　a　s　t　'

20

21

22

23

24

ROSSIJA

m. Kostin Nos

p-ov Mučnoj

Krasino

192

B a r e n t s

S e a

Pečorsko

o. Kolguev

Pesčanka

Pesčanoe

oz.

Gubistaja

g. Paarkov
Sarlopy
166

kosa Vost. Tonkie (Ploskie) Koški

Bugrino

kosa Zap. Tonkie (Ploskie) Koški

p-ov Russkij
Zavorot

m. Russkij
Zavorot

Hodovariha

Kuzneckaja guba

o. Dolgij

P o m o r s k i j   p r o l i v

o. Sengejskij

Tobseda

oz.
Pesčanoe

Kolokolkova
guba

Pečorskaja guba

m. Lajdennyj
o. Korga
o-va Kambaľnickie
Koški

Sengejskij
proliv

Sengejskij

T i m a n s k i j

b e r e g

Korovinskaja
guba

Nosovaja

Rybnaja

p-ov Kanin

M a l o z e m e ľ s k a j a   t u n d r a

138

Neruta

Neneckaja grjada

R

O

Jušino

225

g. Tenja Seda
182

m. Sv. Nos

Gornostaľja
guba

Jett

Seľjacha

oz. Golodnaja
Guba

Andeg

Pečora

Neruta

m. Mikulkin

Indiskaja
guba

Kuja

Indiga

Kamenka

Oksino

Nar'jan-Mar

T i m a n

m. Barmin Nos

Vyučeskij

Indigskie
ozëra

Labožskoe

Pylemec

a

v

t

o

Č ë s s k a j a   g u b a

Černaja

Velikaja

Indiga

oz.
Urdjužskoe

31

Seľjacha

Kuja

Čajcynskij kamen'

g. Pron'kina
256

M a l o z e m e ľ s k i j

Sula

Tošviska

m. Suvojnyj Nos

Velikaja

g. Kovriga
303

Kotkino

Š

Volonga

Volonga

226

Sula

Sula

Leždug

Sčuja

Timanskij kamen'

Beluš'e

Bol. Jangyra

Sula

Ërmica

B

o

l

Egorovo

Nižnjaja Peša

Bol. Pula

Novyj Bor

Šapkina

R

e

s

Snopa

N

e

Kosma

Nalimja

Verhnjaja Peša

Snopa

Oma

Bezmošcica

vozž

Kosminskij kamen'

Arctic Circle

Tarasovo

Volokovaja

Volok

Medvežka

Sozva

Jurjaga

Elbej

n

Peľno

e

c

k

i

j

k r j a ž

o

b y s s k a j a

Toby

Myla

Robdina

Snopa

oz. Vars

oz.
Kosminskoe

Krestovka

Okunev Nos

167

ROSSIJA

26

0 10 20 30 40 50 km
0 10 20 30 miles

Novaja Zemlja

m. Menšikova'
65
Rusanovo
guba Sahanina
ina

proliv Karskie Vorota
m. Bolvanskij Nos
Guba Dolgaja
171

+5h Gr.Time

+3h Gr.Time

o. Vajgač

m. Bol. Ljamčin Nos
Varnek
Amderma

pr. Jugorskij Šar

Jugorskij

Bol. Oju
Talotajaha
467
p - o v

o. Matveev

o. Dolgij

Tab'ju
Sopčaju

g. Bol'šaja Padeja
428

m. Bel'kovskij Nos
o. Bol. Zelenec

m. Medynskij Zavorot
Osuha Perezoznaja

Karatajka

a Guljaevskie Koški
o. Pesjakov
Varandej
oz. Pil'nja
Hejjaha

Čornaja
Alekseevka
Pahančeskaja guba

Hajpudyrskaja guba
70
Talotajaha
214
Korotaiha

Hyl'cuju
205
Cornaja
Naul'jaha
212

Vašutkiny ozero

S   S   I   J   A
n   d   r   a

Uret'jaha
More-Ju
k   t   r   u   g

n   o   m   n   y   j   j   a   j   a
s   e   v   a
226

Šapkina
oz. Oškoto
176
k
Adz'va
Severnyj
Promyšlennyj
Vorgašor
Komsomol'skij
Mul'da

VORKUTA

oz. Lajato
m   e   l'
Horej-Ver
Kolvavis

Hanovej

324
Laja
z   e   m
e
Hosedaju
Bol. Rogovaja
Čym
Ošvor
Ust'-Vorkuta

242
Serc'jaha
Adz'va
211
Č   e   r   n
208
Sivomaskinskij

+3h Gr.Time

p   u   b   l   i   k   a   k   o   m   i
b   r   j   a   d   a
Adz'vavom
Usa
Abez'
Arctic Circle

Petrun'
Usa

Poljarnyj Ural

191
Usa
Kolva
Laja
92
Denisovka
Ščel'jabož

Vojkalsvvinskij massiv
1137
+5h Gr.Time

ATLANTIC

OCEAN

Norwegian

Sea

Vega
Brø
Leka
Solsem
Vikna
Valøya
Børvik
Kolver
Hurtigruten
Foldefjorden
Jøa
Otter-
øya
Brekksilla
Sør-
Flatanger
766
Namsos
769
Bangsund
Jøssund
Solem
Sundet
Sjøåsen
715
Snåsav
Harsvik
540
Finnvollheia
123
17 Tr
Stokksund
Sprova
Malm
Sunna
Afjord
Follafoss
Steinkjer
Lysøysund
81
Beitstadfj
Sparbu
Botngard
715 516
Fosna
Verdalsøra
Brekstad
710
Husbysjøen
720 755 Ytterøy Vuk
Frøya
Hellesvik
Leksvik
Skogn
Levanger 72
Titran
Flatval
601
93
Fjellværøya
Frøyfjorden 55
Fillan
Rissa
29 Frosta E06 Mørkabygd 48
Hitra
710
Vanvikan
Trondheimsfj.
Veidholmen
Sandstad
714
Skatval
Stjørdalshalsen
Kvenvæ
Forsnes
369
38
Selbekken
Malvik Hommelvik E14 Mer
Hopen
713
TRONDHEIM
35 Koppera
Dyrnes
Storoddan
Heimdal
og Rotldalen
Smøla
669
Kyrksæterøra
Elistranda
Melhus Selbu Stordal n.p.
680
Aure
Orkanger Fannrem
Reinsfjell 705 Fongen
Ertvågøya
E39 144 51 833
E06
Storerikvoller
Leira
Rute
933 Sør-
Tømmervåg
.905
Enge
Løkken 36
Tjustna
Halsa
Rindal
700 Meldal
96 Støren Lauvun Østby
Kristiansund
70
63 65
65 54
1219 Soknedal Singsås 30 1322
Storbakken
Tingvoll
670
1667 Todal
Rennebu
Berkåk Ålen 1322
Bud
64 1020 E39 Kleive 70
Snøta
Trøndelag Stuguda
Elnesvågen
66 Eidsvåg
Innset 1264
Gossa
Hjellset 198 Sunndalsøra
Gaudalen
1332
Steinshamn
1095
Møre Isfjorden Sunndalen 70 Oppdal Glåmos
Midsund 64 Grøa (600) 1621 Brekk
Nordøyane Molde og Andalsnes Dovrefjell- E06 104 Os 1199
Austnes 9 233 24 Sunndalsfjella 31
Roald Brattvåg Romsdal NORGE 1633 Røros
Alnes 67 E136 92 Høggia 1229 Narbuvoll
Sørøyane Vestnes 1229 30 Fem
Ålesund 650 Tresfjord 1795 N O R G E
Kvalsvik Langevåg Sykkylven Trolltinden 180 Snøhetta Tynset
Fosnavåg Stordal 1739 Bjørli Dovrefjell (1025) 1604 1591
Sandøy Ulsteinvik 104 Vartdal 63 Marstein Lesjaskog 1660 Holøydal 1604
Larsnes Stranda Liabygd E136 Hjerkinn Alvdal
Stadlandet 1307 Romsdal Valldal Lora Lesja Follldal 26
Leikanger Ørsta Eidsdal Pyttegga Dombås 29 41
Nord- Fiskå 113 Voldal Slogen 1597 Reinheimen Store Barkald
Vågsøy 54 Sæbø Eide n.p. nasjonalpark Storhø Sølnkletten Hedmark
Måløy 7 Systre (624) 1713 1827 Isteren
15 Selje Helldsetra 63 Tverrfjelli Oppland Dovre 27
57 Starheim Sunnmøre E39 Geirangerfjorden 1926 Rond fjele Store Øvre
Bremanger- 614 Grodås 15 Norberg Rondslottet Sølnkletten 1755 Rendal
pollen Nordfjordeid Pollfoss 1833 2178 Atnbrua Rendal
Bremanger- 60 227 n.p. Barkald 30 Sølen
landet Utvik Breheimen Ottadalen Vågåmo 47 217
Kalvåg Oppstryn n.p. Garmo 15 Hanestad Otnes
Sogn og Olden (630) Sandane Lom 29
Svelgen 1632 Hyen 2083 Bøverdal Jotunheimen Bjølstad Otta 219
Norddal 615 Jostedalsbreen Breheimen Glittertinden Åkrestrømmen
5 68 Jostedalen Jotunheimen 2470
Floro 69 Eikefjord Fjordane 102 Jostedalen Galdhøpiggen P

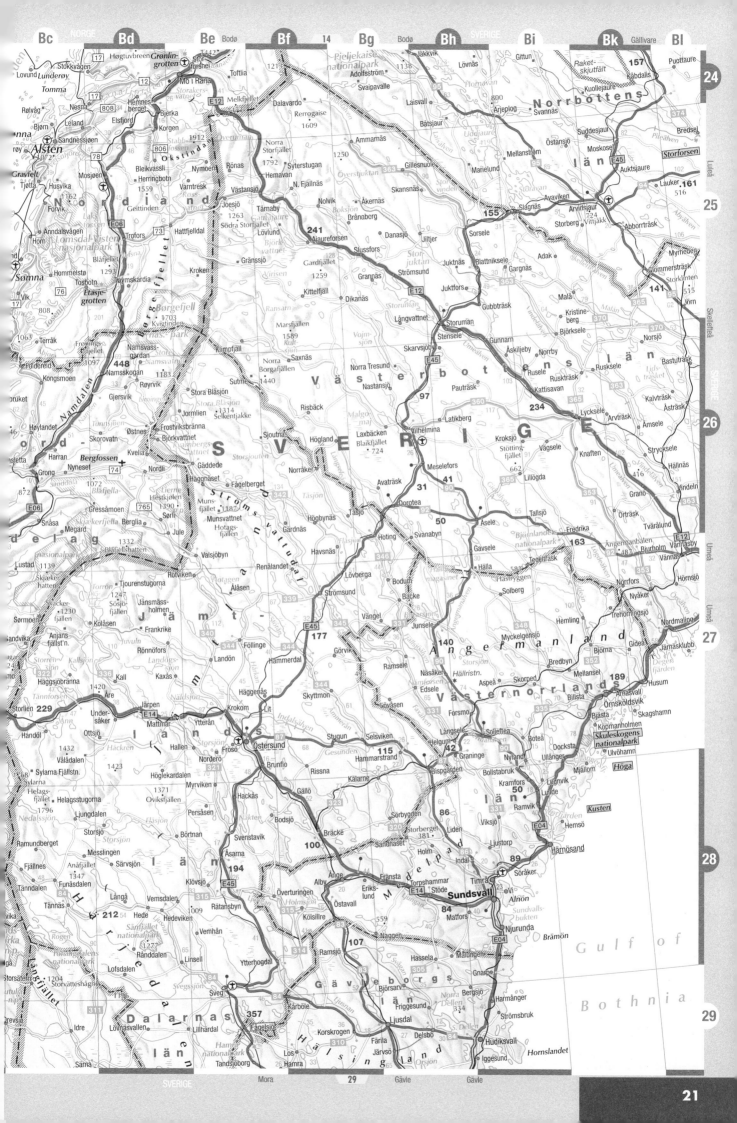

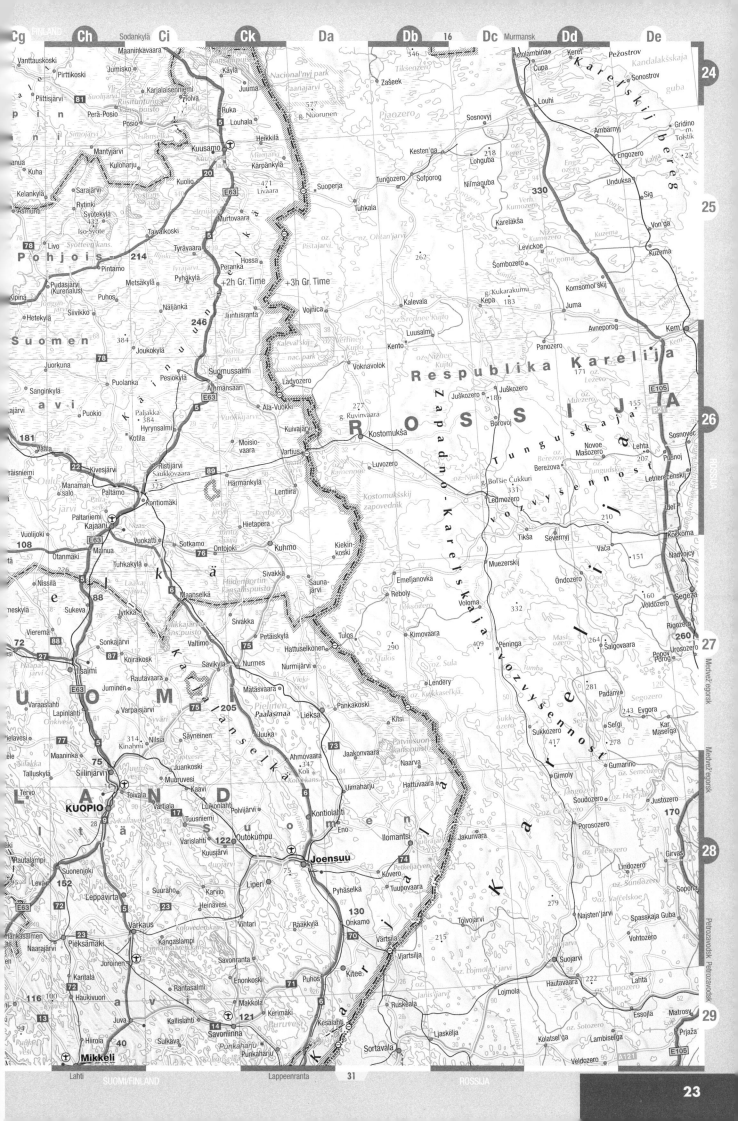

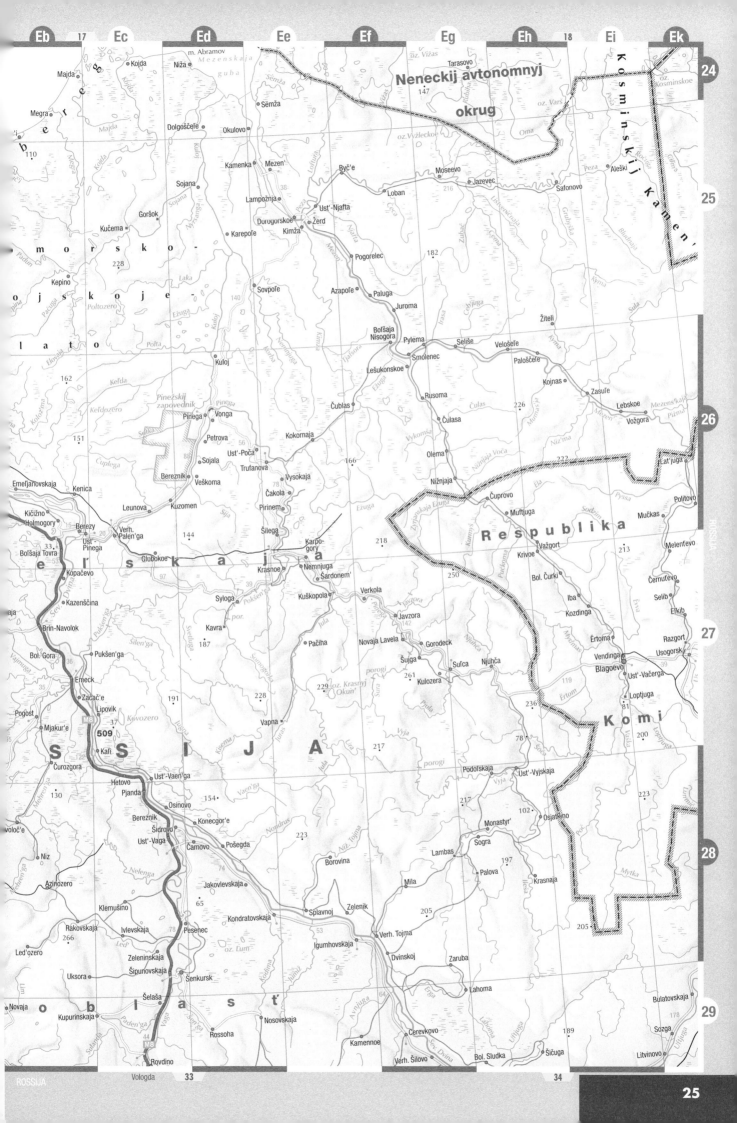

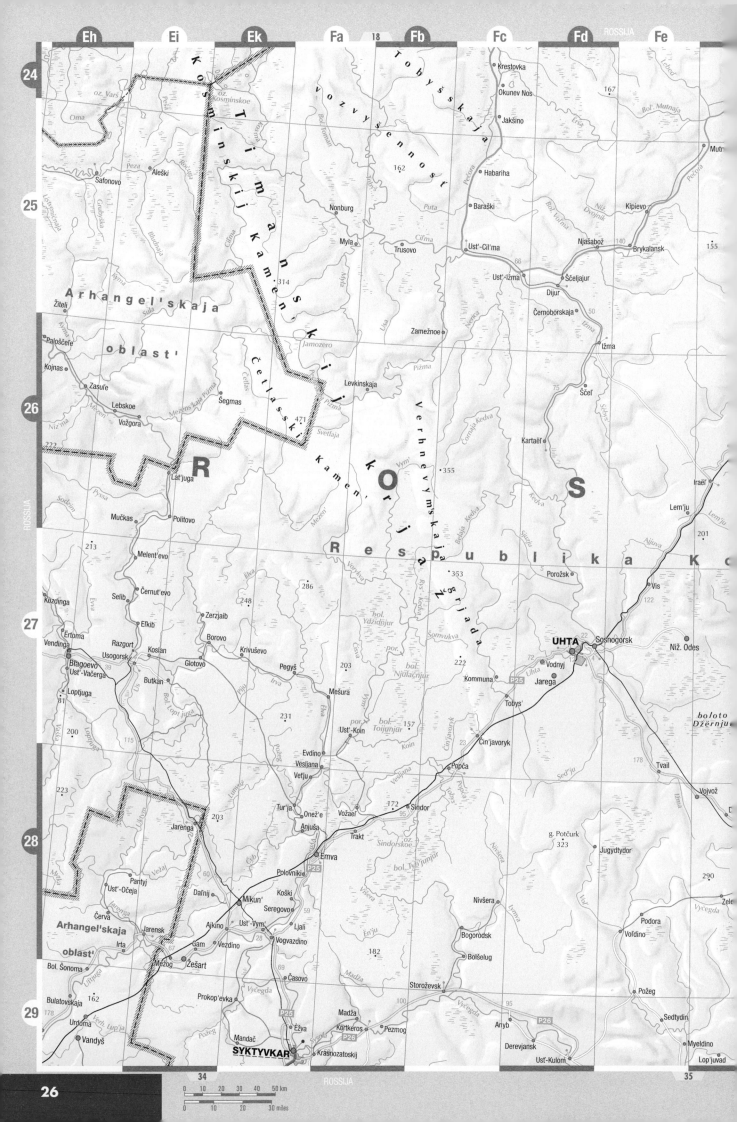

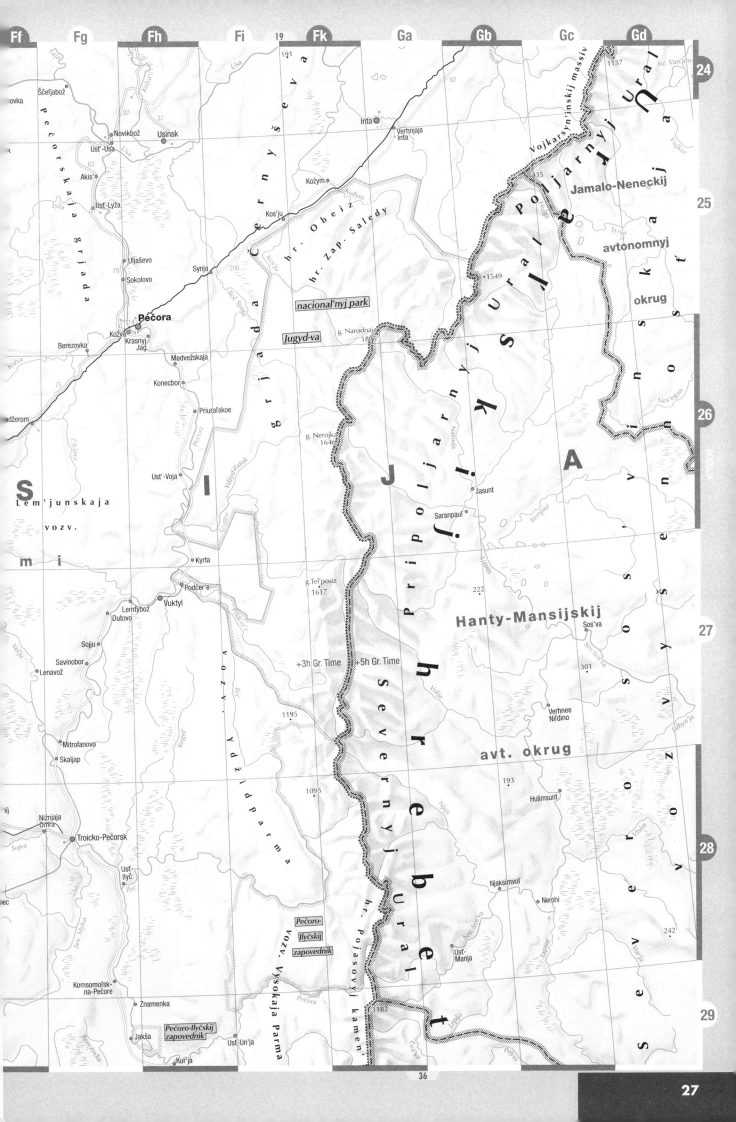

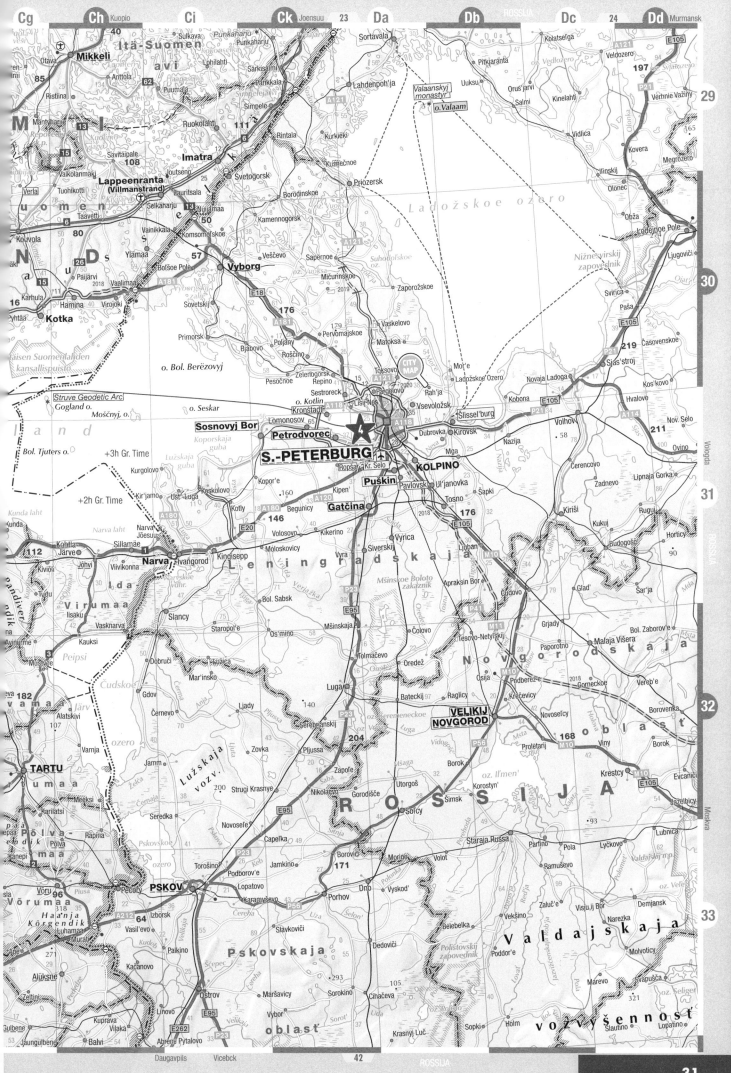

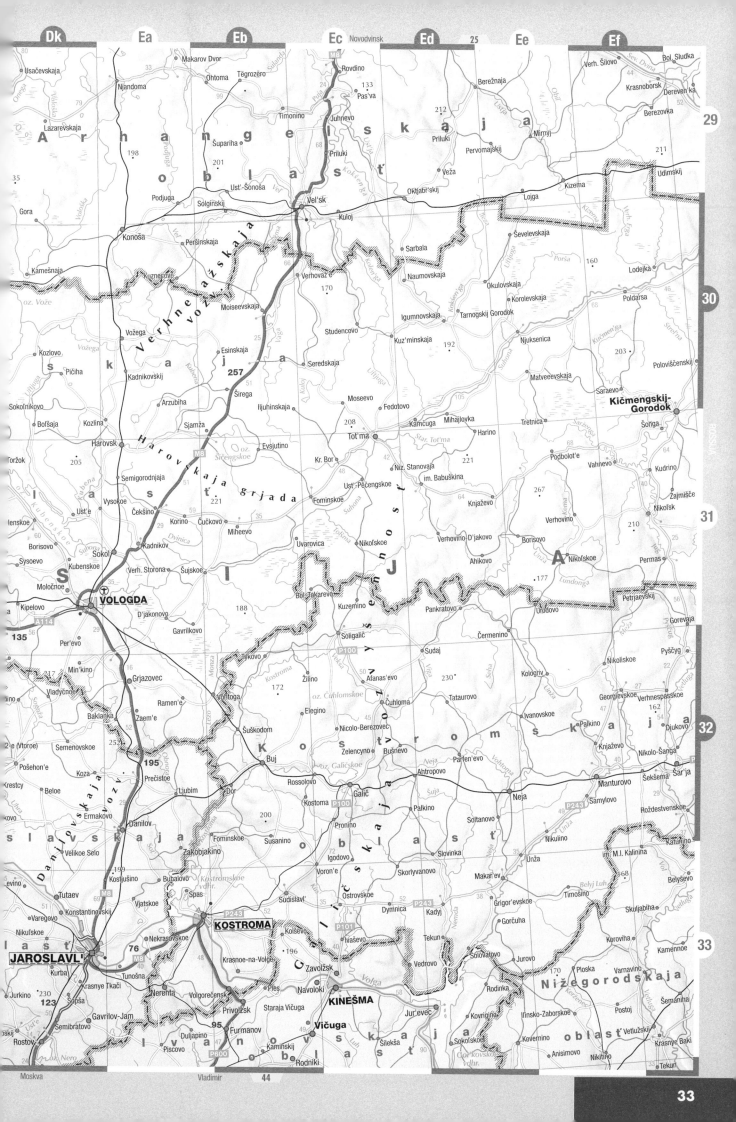

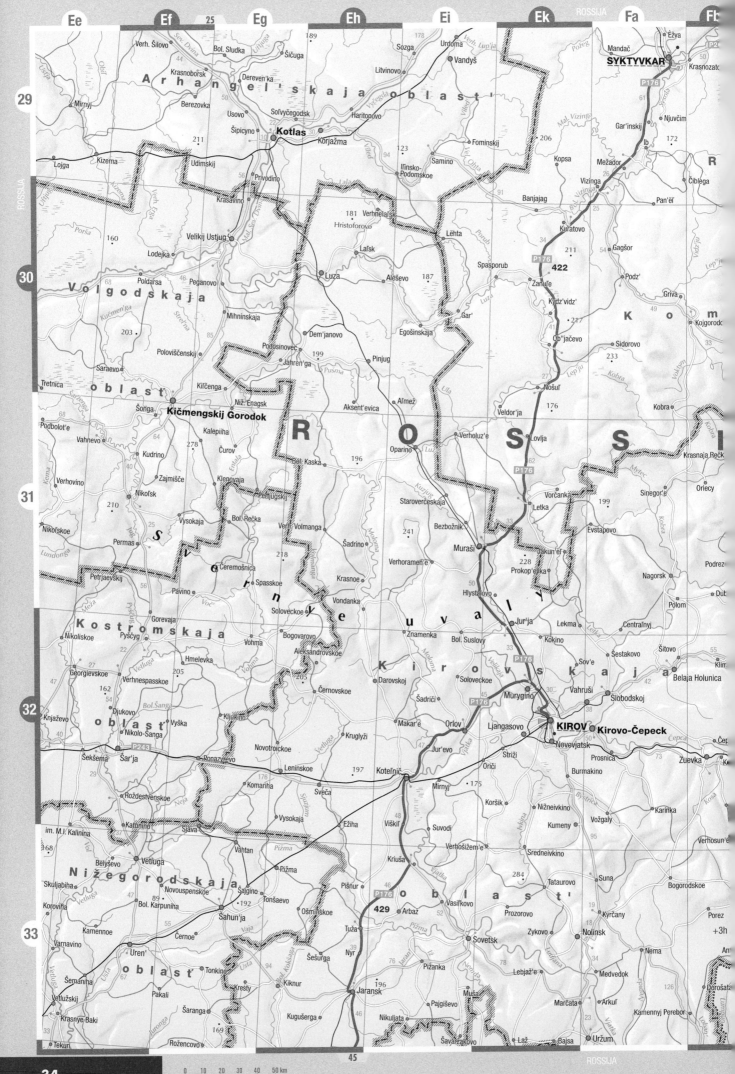

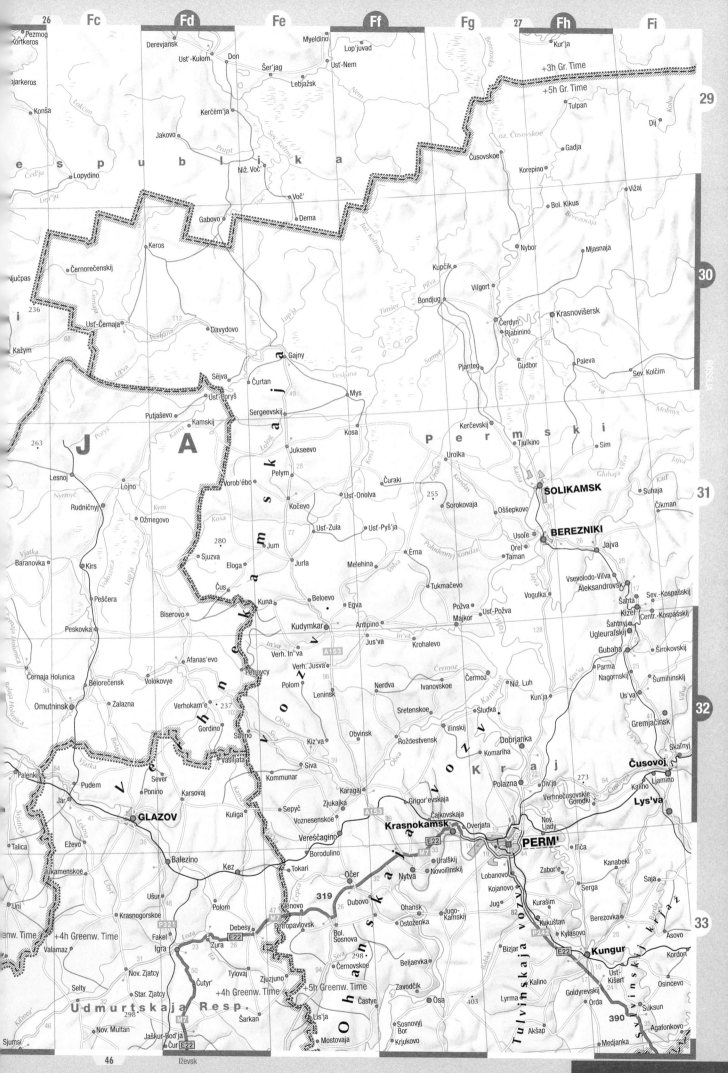

Pezmog
Kortkeros
ojarkeros
Konša
Čed'ju
Njučpas
i 236
Kažym
Lopydino
Čed'ju
Leb'ju
Lokčim
Derevjansk
Ust'-Kulom
Don
Šer'jag
Myeldino
Lop'juvad
Usť-Nem
Kerčëm'ja
Jakovo
Niž. Voč'
Voč'
Gabovo
Dema
Keros
Usť-Černaja
Davydovo
112
68

Kur'ja
+3h Gr. Time
+5h Gr. Time
Tulpan
Čusovskoe
oz. Čusovskoe
Gadja
Korepino
Vižaj
Bol. Kikus
Nybor
Mjasnaja

Čërnorečenskij
Njučpas
263
Lesnoj
Rudničnyj
Ožmegovo
Nyrmyč
Lojno
Vjatka
Baranovka
Kirs
Peščera
Peskovká
Čërnaja Holunica
Belorečensk
Volokovye
Beloreča Holunica
34
Omutninsk
Zalazna
Gordino
Verhokam'e
237
103
Satino
Vasiljata
Sever
Ponino
Karsovaj
Pudem
Jar
Palenki
54
GLAZOV
Kuliga
Sepyč
Talica
Ežëvo
Balezino
Kez
36
41
Jukamenskoe
Ušur
48
Uni
Krasnogorskoe
Polom
Valamaz
+4h Greenw. Time
Fakel
P321
Igra
Selty
Nov. Zjatcy
Star. Zjatcy
Čutyr'
Zura
Debesy
E22
Tylovaj
Zjuzjuno
50
23
26
Klenovo
Petropavlovsk
M7
Bol. Sosnova
Loza
Ila
Sarkan
Lis'ja
Tyloja
Mostovaja
298
Krjukovo

J A
Sëjva
Čurtan
Usť-Boryš
Putjaševo
Kamskij
Sergeevskij
Vorob'ëvo
Pelym
Kočevo
Usť-Zula
Jukseevo
Kosa
Gajny
Mys
Lolog
Kudymkar
In'va
Verh. In'va
A153
Verh. Jusva
Polom
Leninsk
Petrovcy
Jus'va
Krohalevo
Antipino
Egva
Beloevo
Kuna
Jum
Eloga
Jurla
Čus
Sjuzva
Afanas'evo
Biserovo
280
77
Usť-Onolva
Usť-Pyš'ja
Čuraki
255
Sorokovaja
Oššepkovo
Urolka
Melehina
Nerdva
Ivanovskoe
Čermoz
Čermoz
Sretenskoe
Sludka
Niž. Luh
Kun'ja
Obvinsk
Roždestvensk
Il'inskij
Dobrjanka
Komariha
Karagaj
Zjukajka
Grigor'evskaja
Voznesenskoe
Čajkovskaja
Overjata
A153
Krasnokamsk
39
E22
Borodulino
M7
Očer
319
Dubovo
Nytva
Ohansk
Novoil'inskij
Ostoženka
Jugo-Kamskij
Lobanovo
Kojanovo
Jug
Kurašim
Zabor'e
Serga
PERM'
Il'iča
Kanabeki
Saja
Kukuštan
82
P242
Bizjar
Kalino
Kylasovo
Kungur
E22
Ust'-Kišert'
Goldyrevskij
Orda
Suksun
390
Agafonovo
Medjanka
Akšap
Lyrma
Zavodčik
Osa
403
Beljaevka
Častye
Černovaja
Siva
94
298
Sosnovyj Bor

Permski
Kerčevskij
Urolka
SOLIKAMSK
BEREZNIKI
Usol'e
Orel
Taman
Jajva
Vsevolodo-Vil'va
Aleksandrovsk
Vogulka
Požva
Usť-Požva
Majkor
128
Šanta
Kizel
Sev.-Kospašskij
Šantnyj
Centr.-Kospašskij
Ugleural'skij
Gubaha
Parma
Nagornskij
Širokovskij
Šumihinskij
Us'va
Gremjačinsk
Skal'nyj
Čusovoj
Kalino
Ljamino
Div'ja
273
94
Verhnečusovskie Gorodki
Polazna
Nov. Ljady
Lys'va
Vjaznik
Čerdyn'
Rjabinino
29
32
Pjanteg
Gudbor
Sev. Kolčim
Paleva
Krasnovišersk
Bondjug
Vil'gort
Kupčik
Tjul'kino
Sim
Gluhaja Vil'va
Suhaja
Čikman
Kad'
Jajva
Bol. Kikus
ROSSIJA

Vjatka
Belaja Holunica
Belaja
Kama
Kosa
Lupja
Obva
Inva
Kama
Kamskoe vozv.
vozv.
Kraj
Permskij kraj
Tulvinskaja vozv.
Sylvinskij kraj

Udmurtskaja Resp.
+4h Greenw. Time
+5h Greenw. Time
Nov. Multan
Sjumsi
Kilmez
46
Jaškur-Bod'ja
M7
Čur
E22

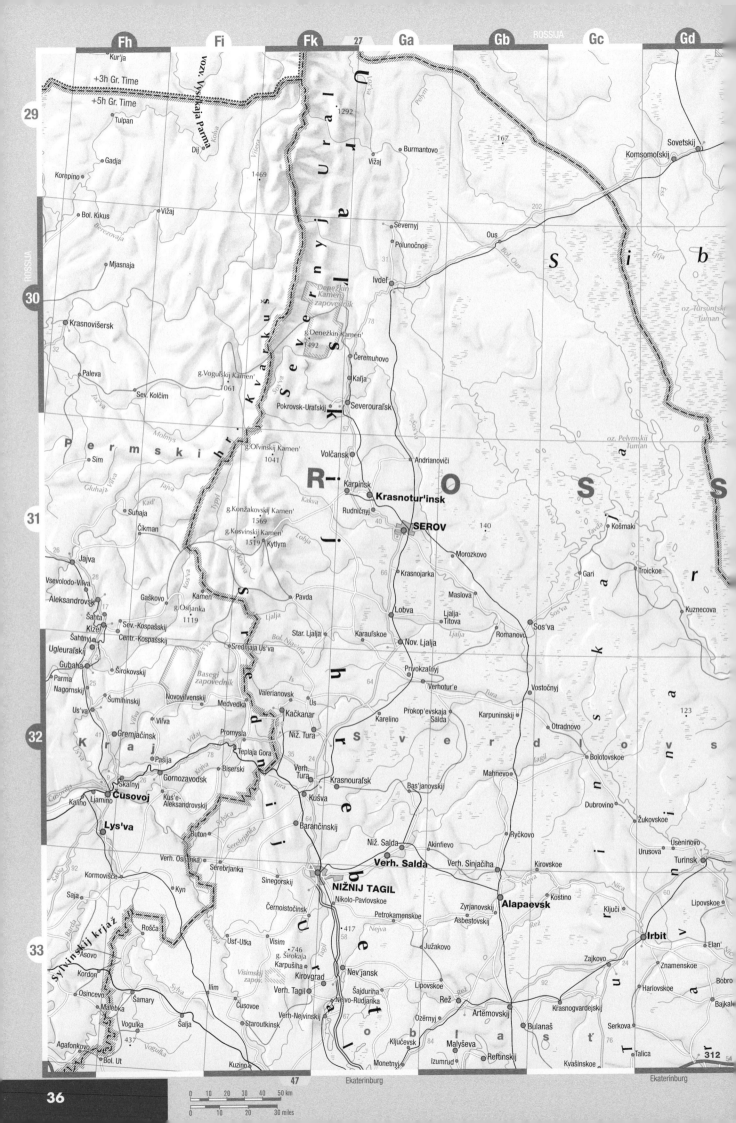

29

ROSSIJA

30

31

32

33

+3h Gr. Time
+5h Gr. Time

vozv. Vysškaja Parma

Kur'ja
Tulpan
Dij
Gadja
Korepino
Bol. Kikus
Vižaj
Mjasnaja
Krasnovišersk
Paleva
Sev. Kolčim

Berezovaja
Visera
Kolva

Burmantovo
Vižaj
Severnyj
Polunočnoe
Ivdeľ

Denežkin Kamen'
zapovednik
g.Denežkin Kamen'
1492
Čeremuhovo
Kaľja
Pokrovsk-Uraľskij
Severouraľsk

U r a l

Severnyj

1292

167

Burmantovo

Ous
Bol. Ous

Ejfja

Sovetskij
Komsomoľskij

oz. Tūrsūntskij
Tuman

S i b

g.Voguľskij Kamen'
1061

P e r m s k i

Sim

Sim
Suhaja
Čikman

Molmys

Gluhaja
Vilva
Jajva

Kad'

g.Oľvinskij Kamen'
1041
Volčansk
Karpinsk
Krasnotur'insk
Rudničnyj
SEROV
40
57

R i

O

Andrianoviči

S S

Severnyj Kvarkuš

Severnyj ural'

Ural'

g.Konžakovskij Kamen'
1569
g.Kosvinskij Kamen'
1519 Kytlym

Morozkovo
140
Krasnojarka
66
Lobva
Maslova
Ljalja-
Titova
Nov. Ljalja
Sos'va
Romanovo

Košmaki
Gari
Troickoe
Kuznecova
123

s k a j a

o z. P e l y m s k i j
T u m a n

31

Jajva
Vsevolodo-Vilva
Aleksandrovsk
Šahta
Kizel
Šahtnyj
Ugleuraľskij
Gubaha
Parma
Nagornskij
Us'va
Gremjačinsk
Pašija
Skaľnyj
Kalino Ljamino
Čusovoj
Lys'va
Buton

26
28
17

Gaškovo
Kamen'
g.Osljanka
1119
Sev.-Kospašskij
Centr.-Kospašskij
Srednjaja Us'va

Basegi
zapovednik
Novovilvenskij
Medvedka
Vilva
Promysla
Teplaja Gora
Biserski
Gornozavodsk
Kuš'e-
Aleksandrovskij

Kosva
Ljalja
Star. Ljalja
Bol. Njav'ma
Valerianovsk
Us
Kačkanar
Niž. Tura
Verh.
Tura
Kušva
Barančinskij

Pavda
Lobja
Karauľskoe
Prokop'evskaja
Salda
Karelino
Krasnouraľsk
Bas'janovskij

Ljalja
Privokzaľnyj
Verhotur'e
Karpuninskij
Vostočnyj
Mahnevo
Otradnovo
Bolotovskoe
Dubrovino
Žukovskoe

64
66
35 24
78
9
26

S v e r d l o v s k a j a

T a g i l
Tura
Tavda
Sos'va
Sos'va
Lozva
Tura

32

Kraj

Perm

Vilva
Kos'va
41

Us'va

Šumihinskij
Širokovskij

Srednij ural'hreb
Is

Zapadnyj ural'

Niž. Salda
Akinfievo
Verh. Salda
Verh. Sinjačiha
Kirovskoe
Ryčkovo
Usёninovo
Urusova
Turinsk
60

Nica
Rež

Tavda

Turinsk Tavda

33

Sylvinskij krjaž

Asovo
Kordon
Osincevo
Malebka
Vogulka
Agafonkovo
Bol. Ut

437

Barda
Saja
Kormovišče
Kyn
Rošča
Usť-Utka
Karpušiha
Kirovgrad
Verh. Tagil
Čusovoe
Staroutkinsk
Kuzino

92
746
g. Širokaja

Visimskij
zapov.
Visim

Sinegorskij
Serebrjanka
Verh. Osljanka
Černoistočinsk
Nikolo-Pavlovskoe
NIŽNIJ TAGIL
Petrokamenskoe
Asbestovskij
Zyrjanovskij
Južakovo

417
58

Nejva

Nev'jansk
Šajduriha
Nejvo-Rudjanka
Verh-Nejvinskij
Ozёrnyj
Ključevsk
Monetnyj
Izumrud

Rež
Reftinskoe
Malyševa
Kvašinskoe

Zapadnyj ural'

U s t'

o b l a s t'

Artёmovskij
Bulanaš
Asovo
Zajkovo
Krasnogvardejskij

Sylva
Sylvica
Sylva
Syha
Serebrjanka
Čusovaja
Tura
Tagil
Nejva
Rež

Irbit
Elan'
Znamenskoe
Lipovskoe
Bobro
Bajkal

Harlovskoe
Serkova
Talica
312
54

Kostino
Ključi
24
76
92

84

47
Ekaterinburg

Ekaterinburg

0 10 20 30 40 50 km
0   10   20   30 miles

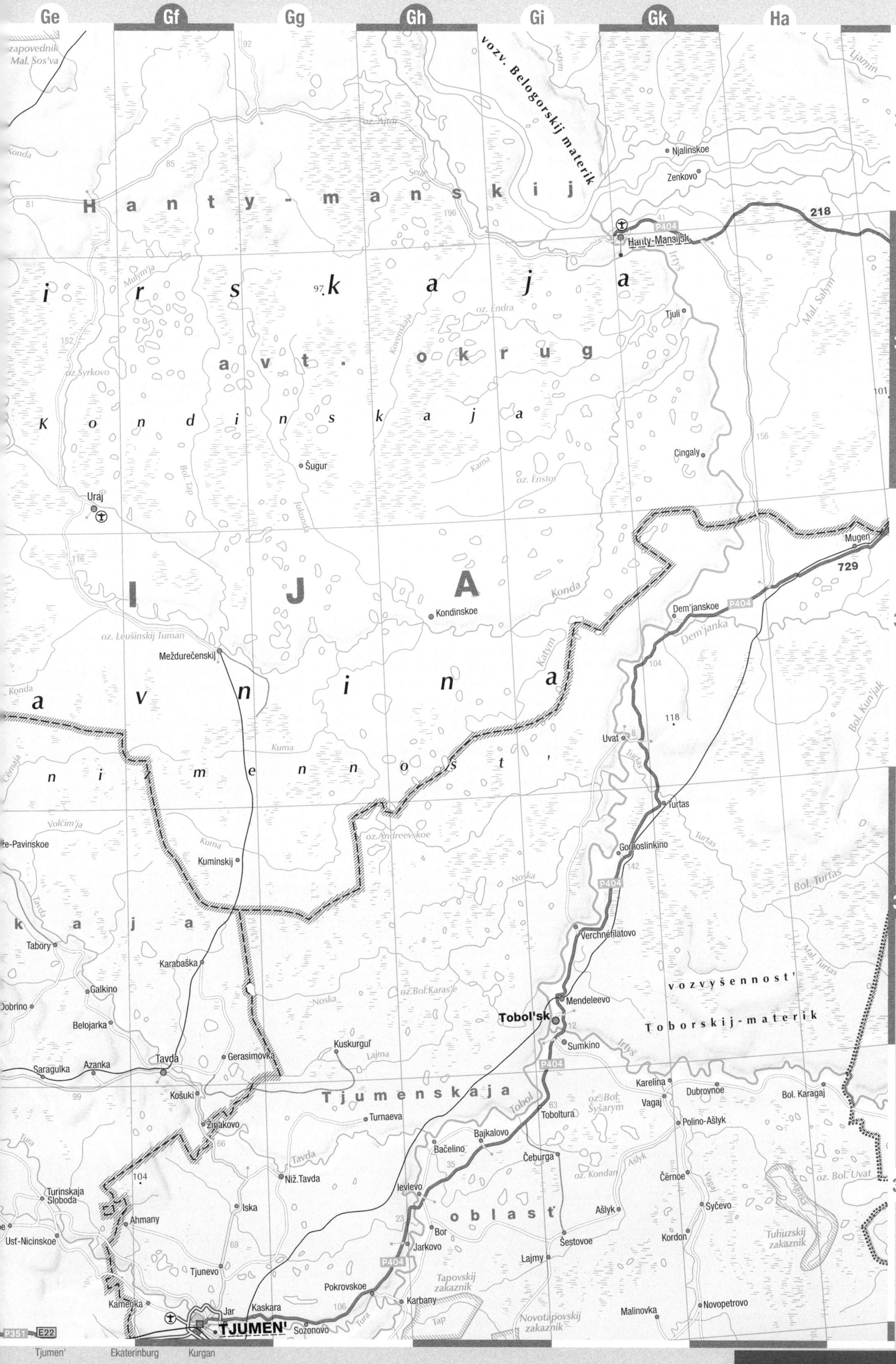

zapovednik
Mal. Sos'va

Konda

vozv. Belogorskij materik

Nazym

Njalinskoe

Zenkovo

218

Surgut

H a n t y - m a n s k i j

Muhm'ja

97

196

41 P404

Hanty-Mansijsk

Irtyš

Mal. Salym

Tjuli

i   **r**   **s**   **k**   **a**   **j**   **a**

oz. Endra

152

ROSSIJA

30

101

oz. Syrkovo

a   **v**   **t**   **.**   **o**   **k**   **r**   **u**   **g**

Bol. Tap

Kama

oz. Enstor

Čingaly

156

K   **o**   **n**   **d**   **i**   **n**   **s**   **k**   **a**   **j**   **a**

Šugur

Jukonda

Surgut

Uraj

116

Mugen

729

I   **J**   **A**

Konda

Dem'janskoe   P404

31

Dem'janka

oz. Leušinskij Tuman

Kondinskoe

104

Meždurečenskij

a   **v**   **n**   **i**   **n**   **a**

Katym

118

Černaja

Kuma

n   **i**   **m**   **e**   **n**   **n**   **o**   **s**   **t'**

Uvat

8

Turtas

Volčim'ja

Kuma

oz. Andreevskoe

Noska

Turtas

Turtas

e-Pavinskoe

Kuminskij

Gornoslinkino

142

k   **a**   **j**   **a**

Tavda

P404

Bol. Turtas

32

Tabory

Verchnéfilatovo

Mal. Turtas

Karabaška

v o z v y š e n n o s t'

Galkino

oz. Bol. Karas'e

Noska

Mendeleevo

T o b o r s k i j - m a t e r i k

Dobrino

Belojarka

Tobol'sk

12

Kuskurguľ

Lajma

Sumkino

Irtyš

Saragulka   Azanka   Tavda   Gerasimovka

99

Tura

Košuki

T j u m e n s k a j a

Tobol

Karelina   Dubrovnoe   Bol. Karagaj

Tobol

oz. Bol. Sыšarym

Vagaj

Toboltura

63

Žirjakovo

Polino-Ašlyk

66

Turnaeva

Bajkalovo

Čeburga

Černoe

Vagaj

oz. Bol. Uvat

Turinskaja   Sloboda

104

Tavda

Bačelino

35

oz. Kondan

Ašlyk

Syčevo

Tuhúzskij zakaznik

Iska

Niž.Tavda

o b l a s t'

Ievlevo

23

Ašlyk

Kordon

Ahmany

69

Bor

Šestovoe

Lajmy

Usť-Nicinskoe

Jarkovo

Malinovka   Novopetrovo

Tjunevo

P404

Tapovskij zakaznik

Kamenka

Jar   Kaskara

Pokrovskoe

106

Karbany

Novotapovskij zakaznik

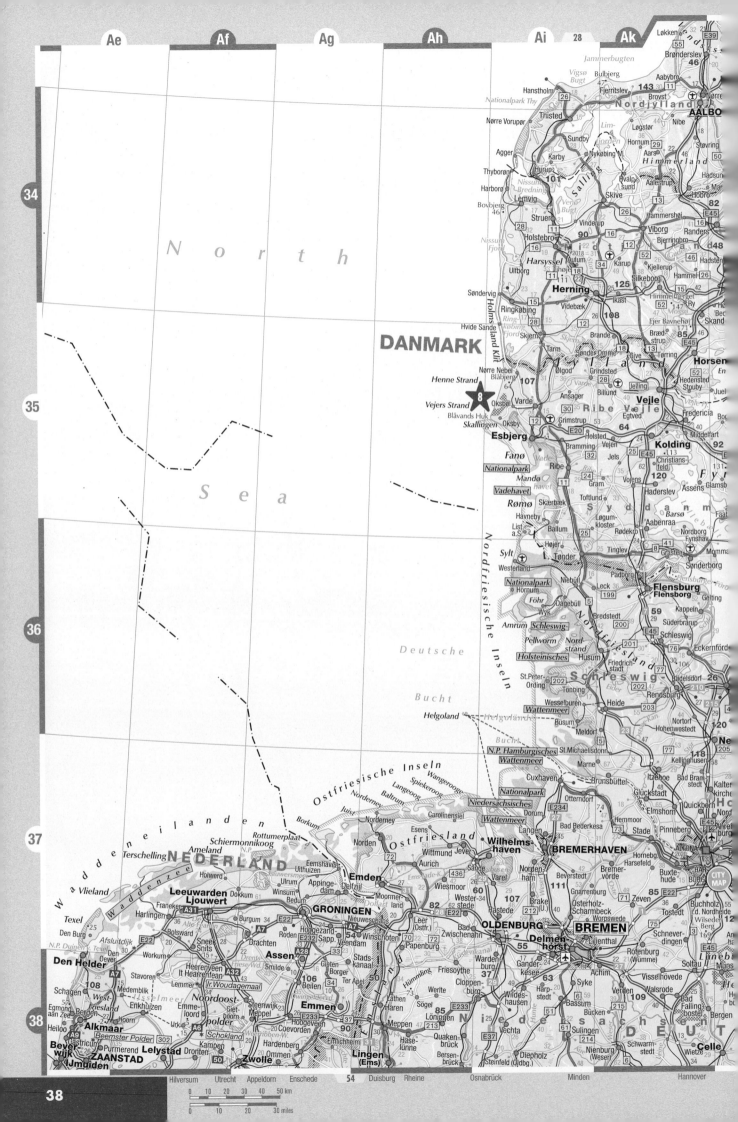

Jönköping
Växjö
SVERIGE
Kalmar län
Blekinge län
Malmö

Bläjungfrun nat. park
Runnö
Öland
Ölands södra udde

Gotlands län
Gotland
Burgsvik
Faludden
Hoburgen

Ventspi
Liepāja · Grobiņa
Priekl
Bārta
Rucava
Salanta
Medze
Durbe
Pāvilosta
Alsu

Helsinki, S.-Peterburg

KLAIPĖDA · Gargžda
Kuršių nerija
Juodkrantė
Priekulė
Kuršių Nerijos nac. parkas
Nida · Rusne
Šilutė
Kuršskaja kosa
Nac. p. Kuršskaja kosa

+1h Gr. Time · +2h Gr. Time

Svetlogorsk · Pionerskij · Zelenogradsk
Jantarnyj
Primorsk
Baltijsk
KALININGRAD
Svetlyj
Gdan'skij zaliv
ROS
Gvardejsk · Znamensk
Nivenskoe
Kaliningradskaja oblas
Ladušin · Mamonovo · Bagrationovsk · Pravdinsk
Branievo
Tolkmicko · Pakosze · Górowo Iławeckie · Bartoszyce · Barciany
Frombork · Wzniesienia
Pieniężno
ELBLĄG · Pasłęk · Wilczęta · Górowskie Warmińskie · Lidzbark Warmiński · Reszel · Kętrzyn
Malbork · Miłakowo · Orneta · Dobre Miasto · Biskupiec · Mrągowo
Sztum · Dzierzgoń · Morąg · Jeziorany
Zalewo · Łukta · OLSZTYN · Barczewo · warmińsko-mazurski
Prabuty · Ostróda · Olsztynek · Szczytno · Rozogi
Iława · Lubawa · warmińsko-mazurskie
Nowe Miasto Lubawskie · Nidzica · Chorzele
Brodnica · Działdowo · Mława · Przasnysz
Ciechanów · Maków Macowiecki · Różan
Glinojeck · Parcele-Przewodowo · Pułtusk
Płońsk · Nasielsk · Wyszków

Poznań · 56 · Łódź · Łódź · Łódź Warszawa · Warszawa · Warszawa · Warszawa

0 10 20 30 40 50 km
0 10 20 30 miles

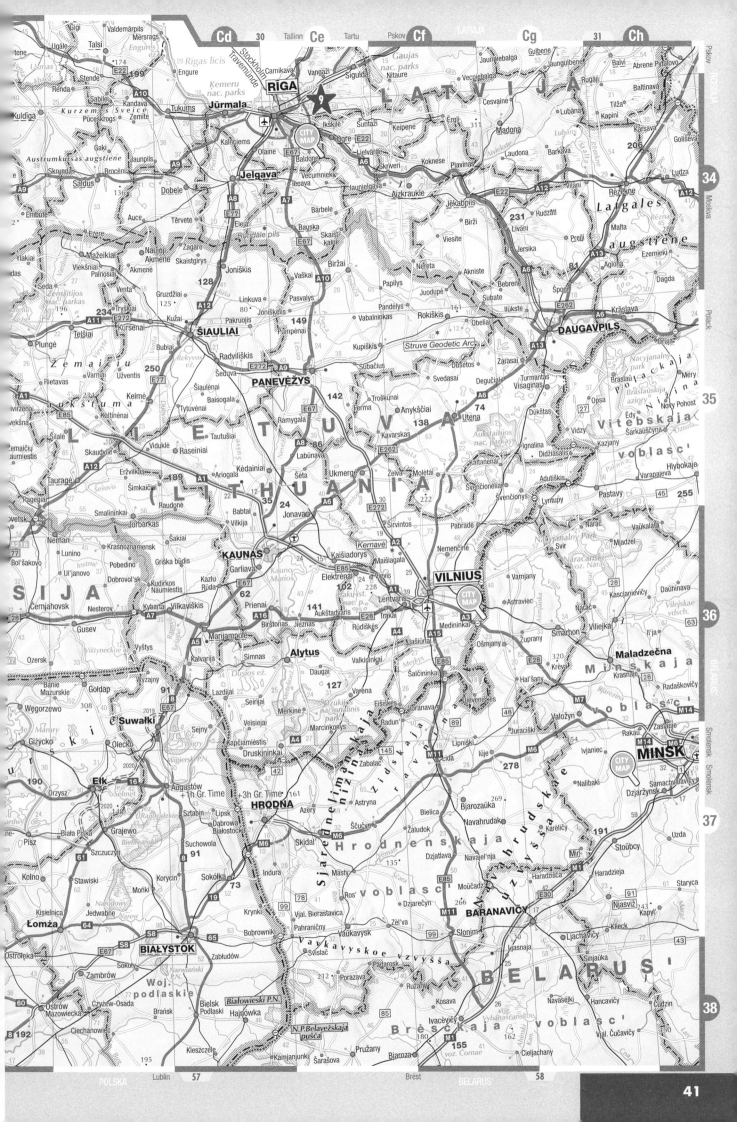

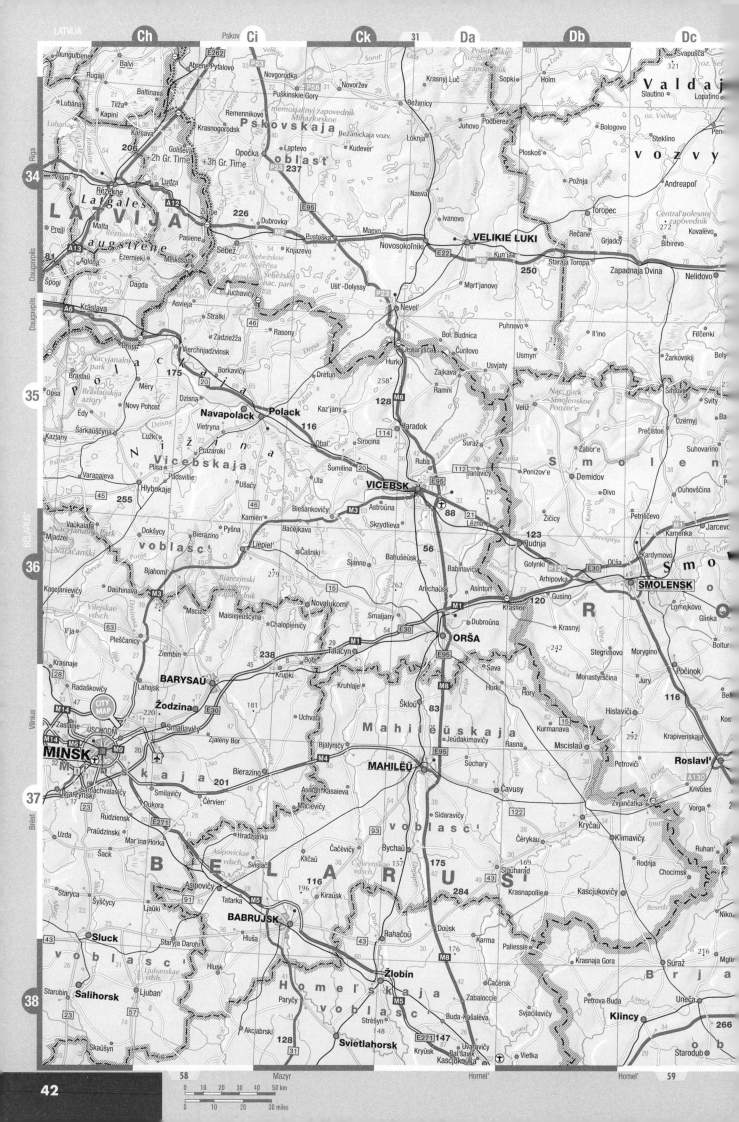

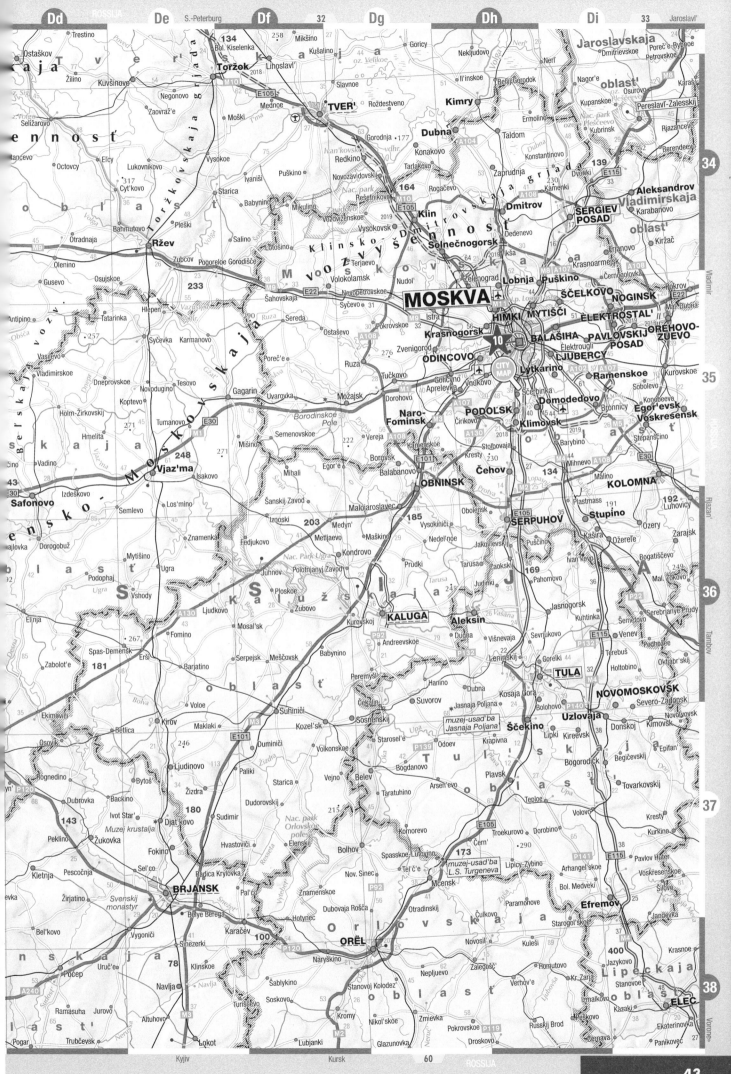

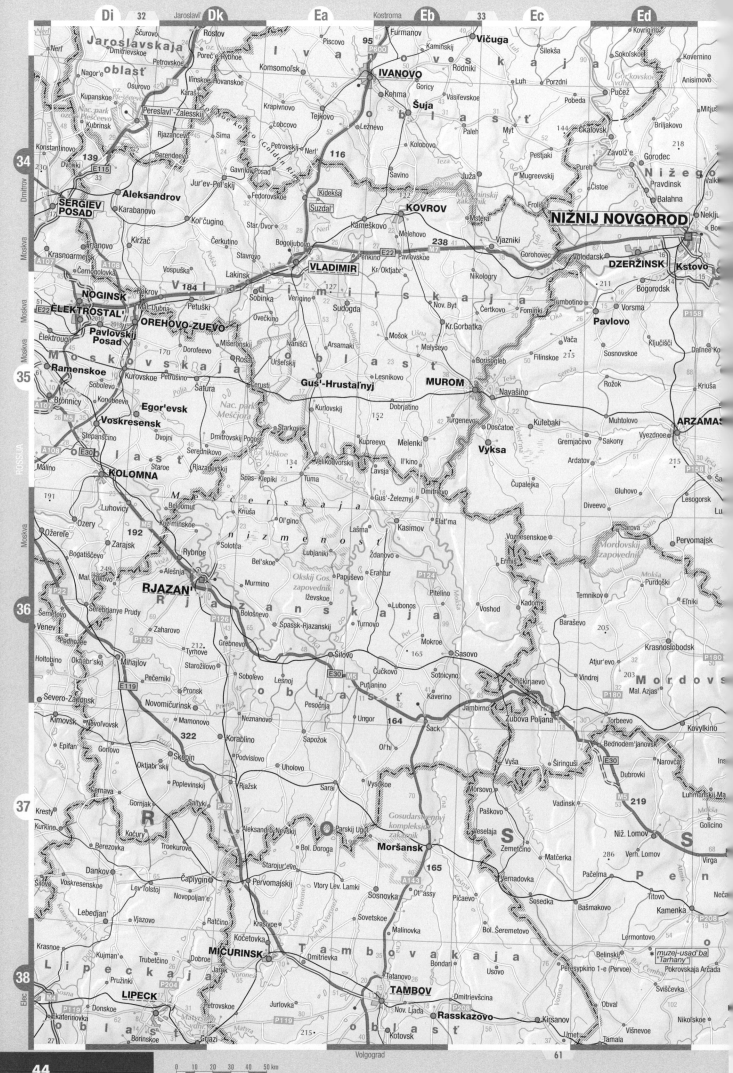

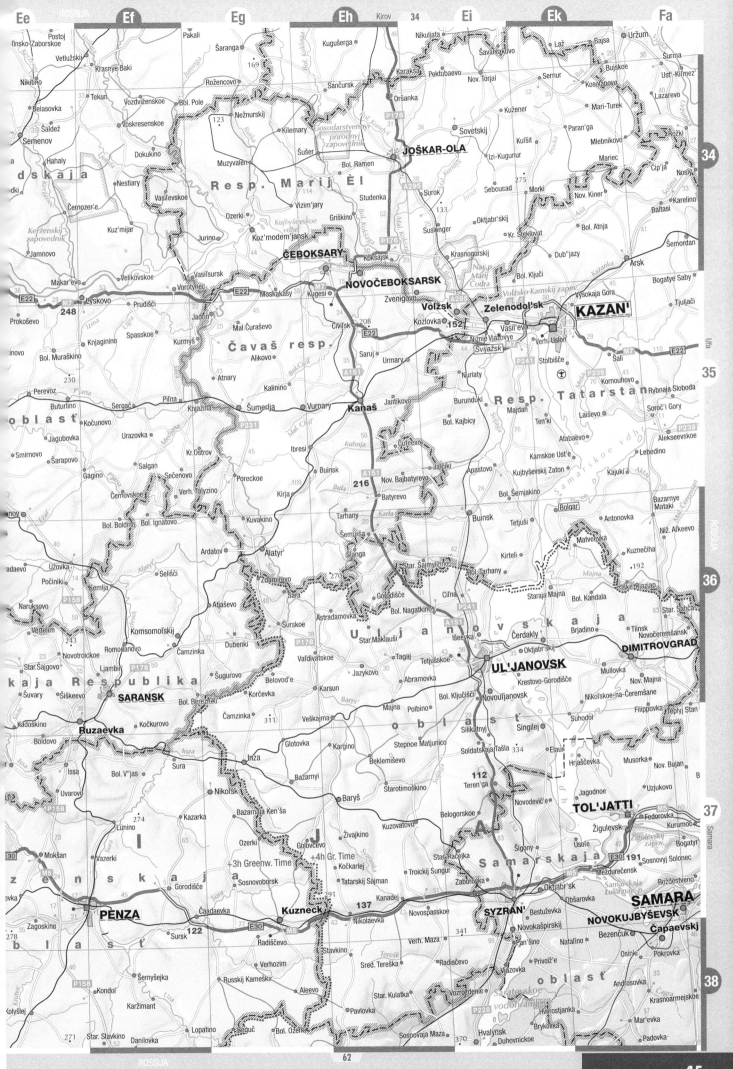

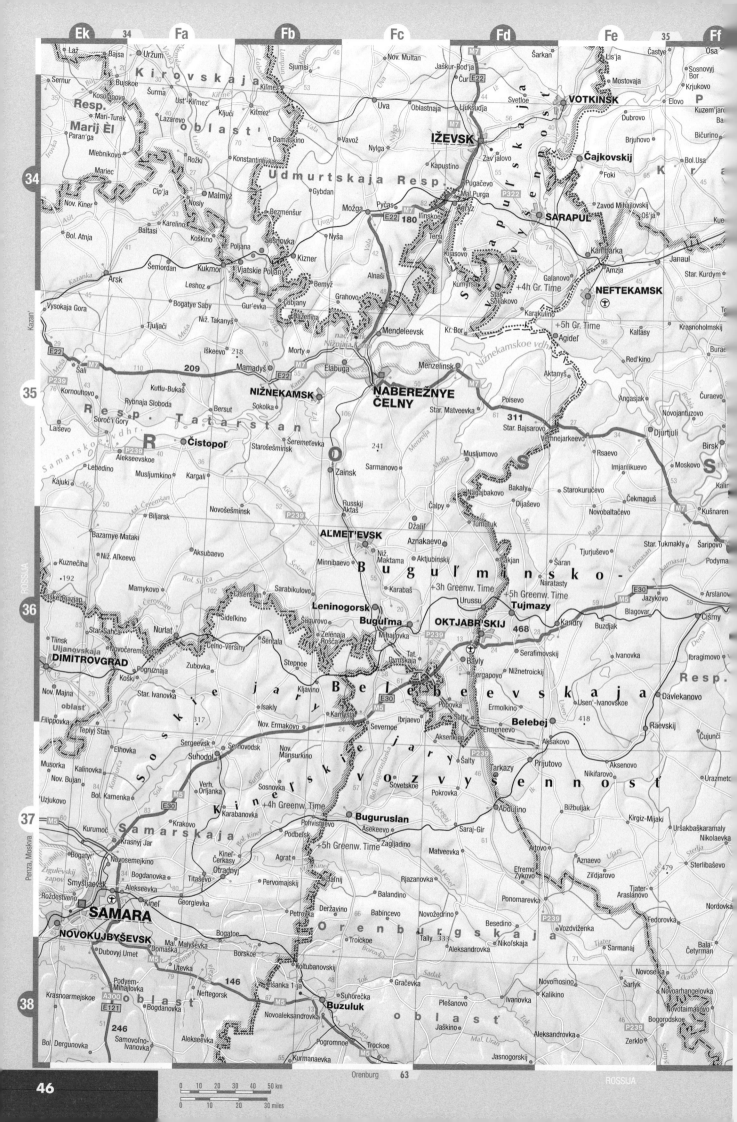

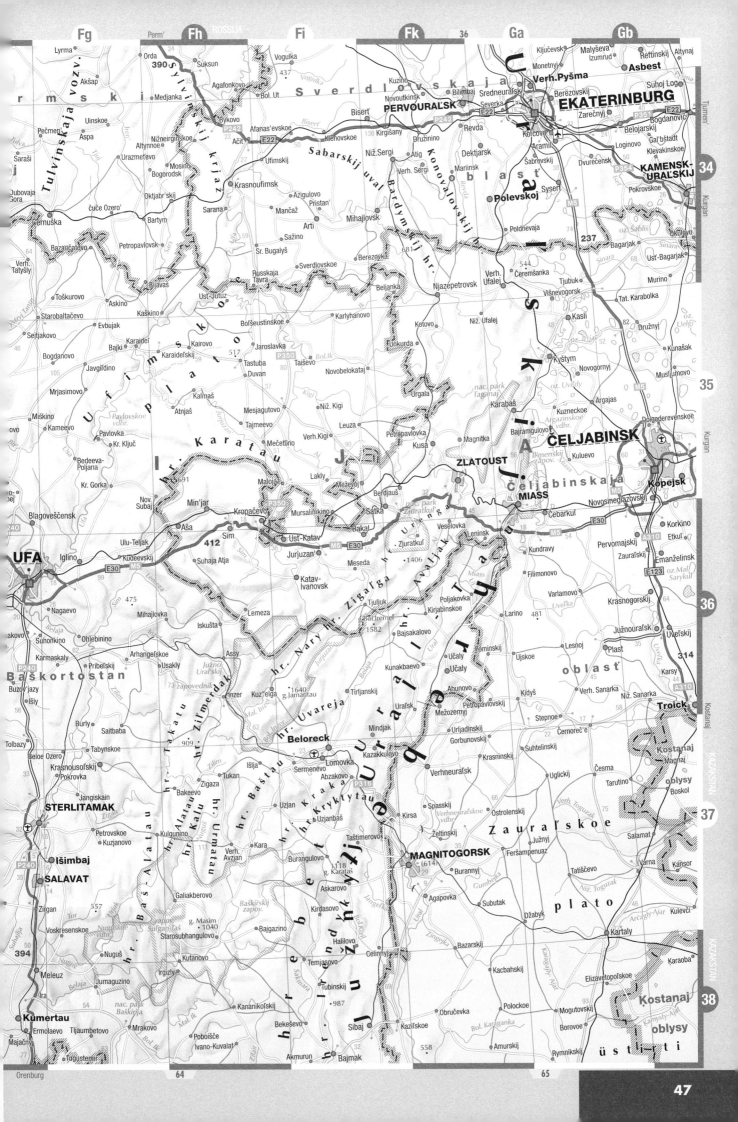

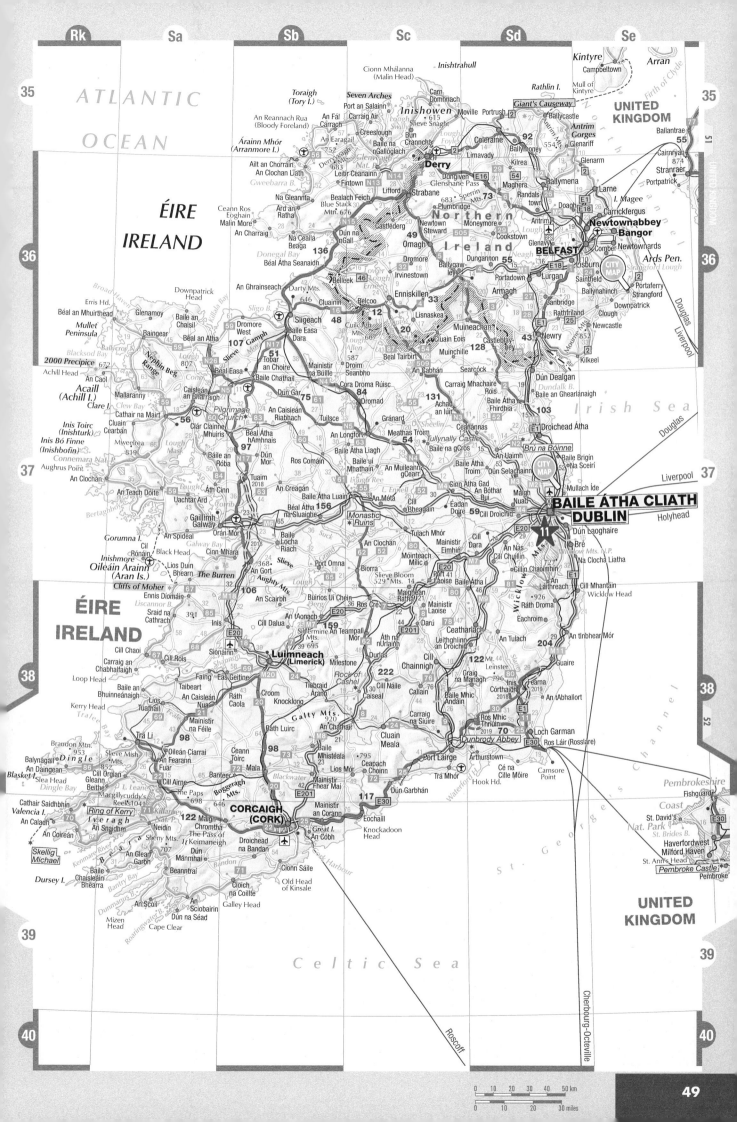

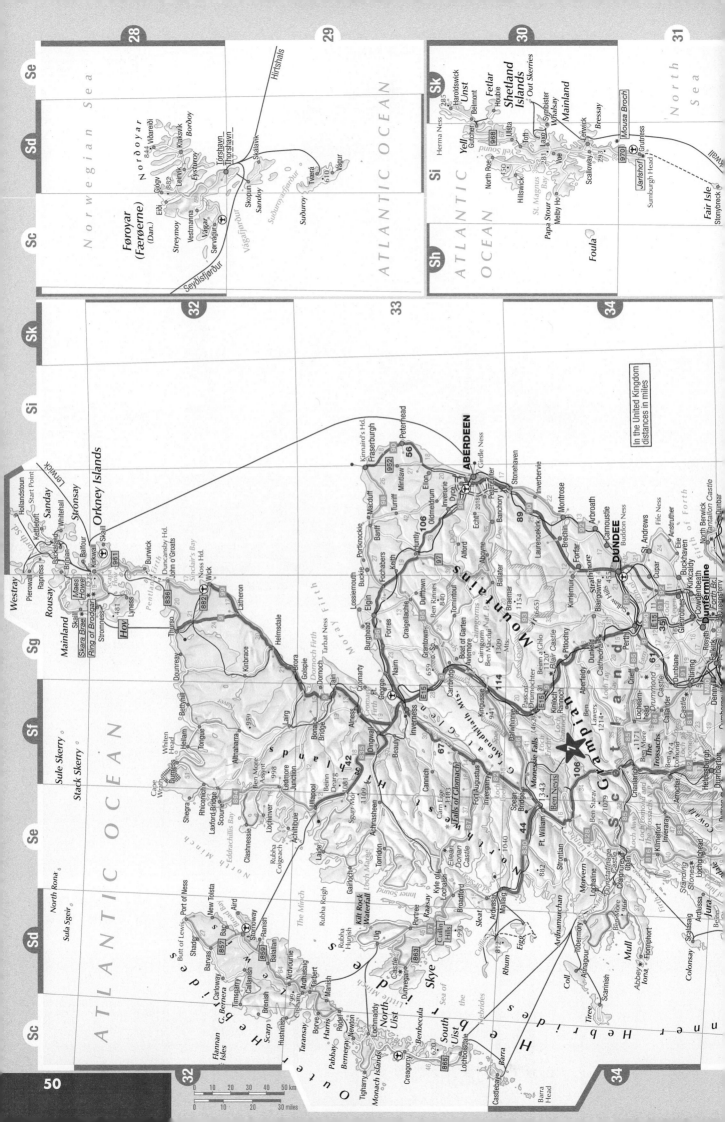

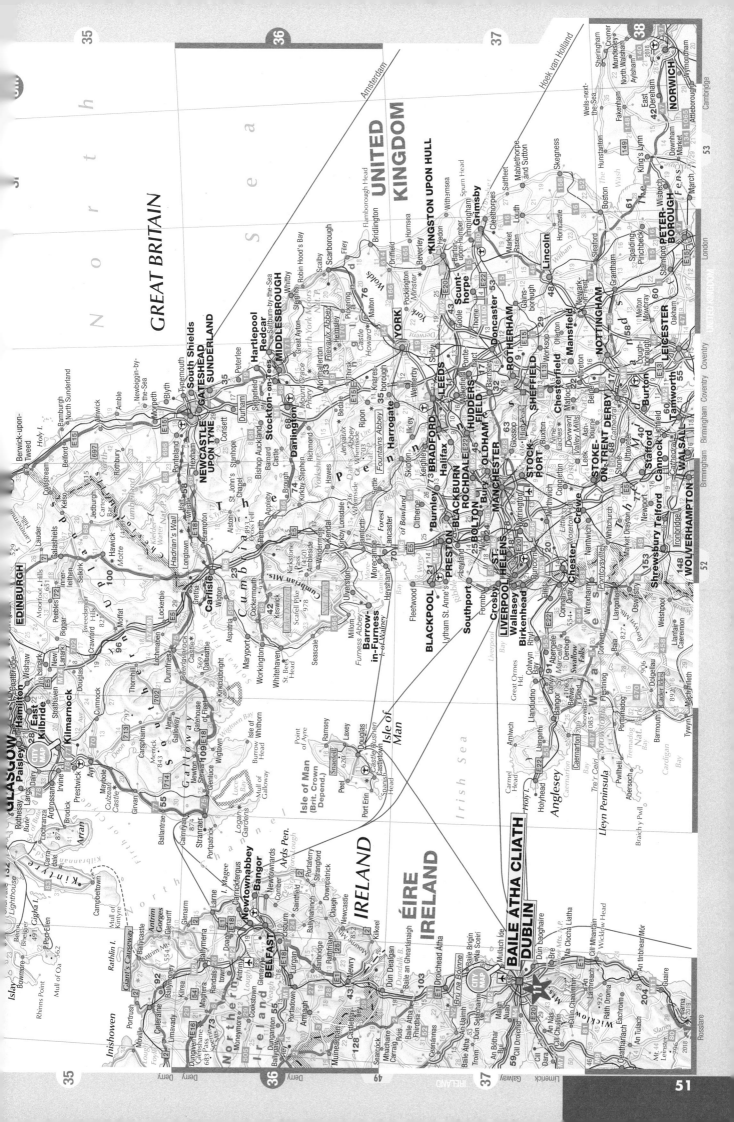

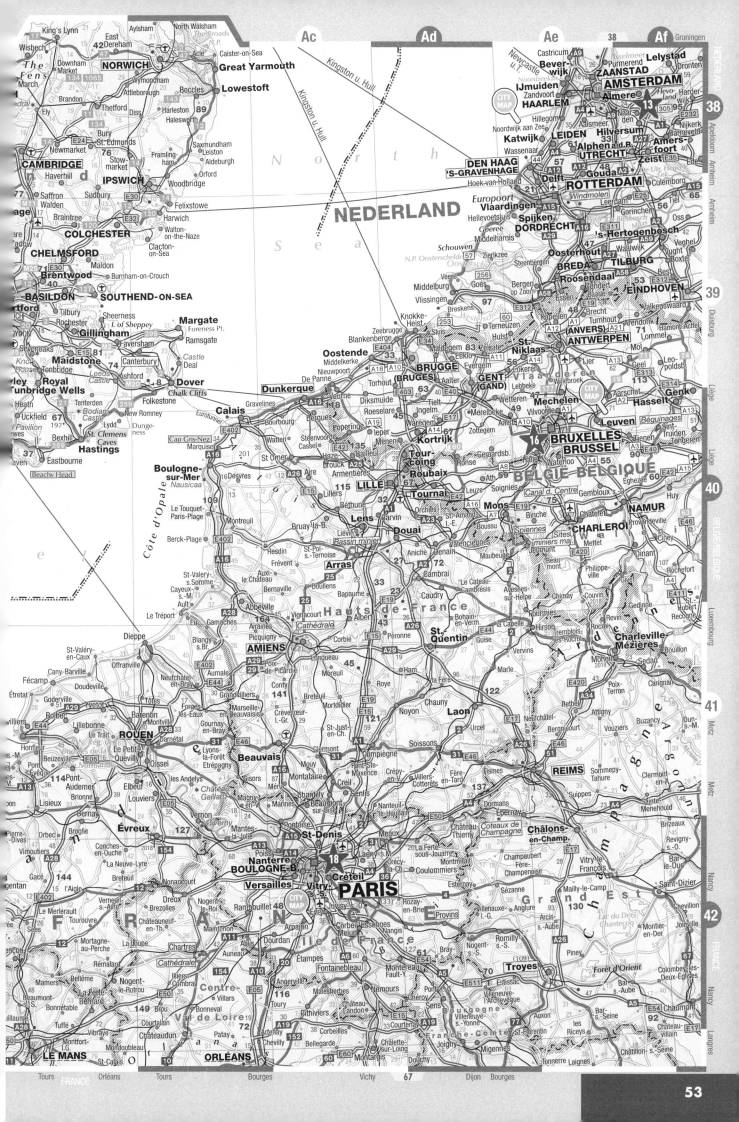

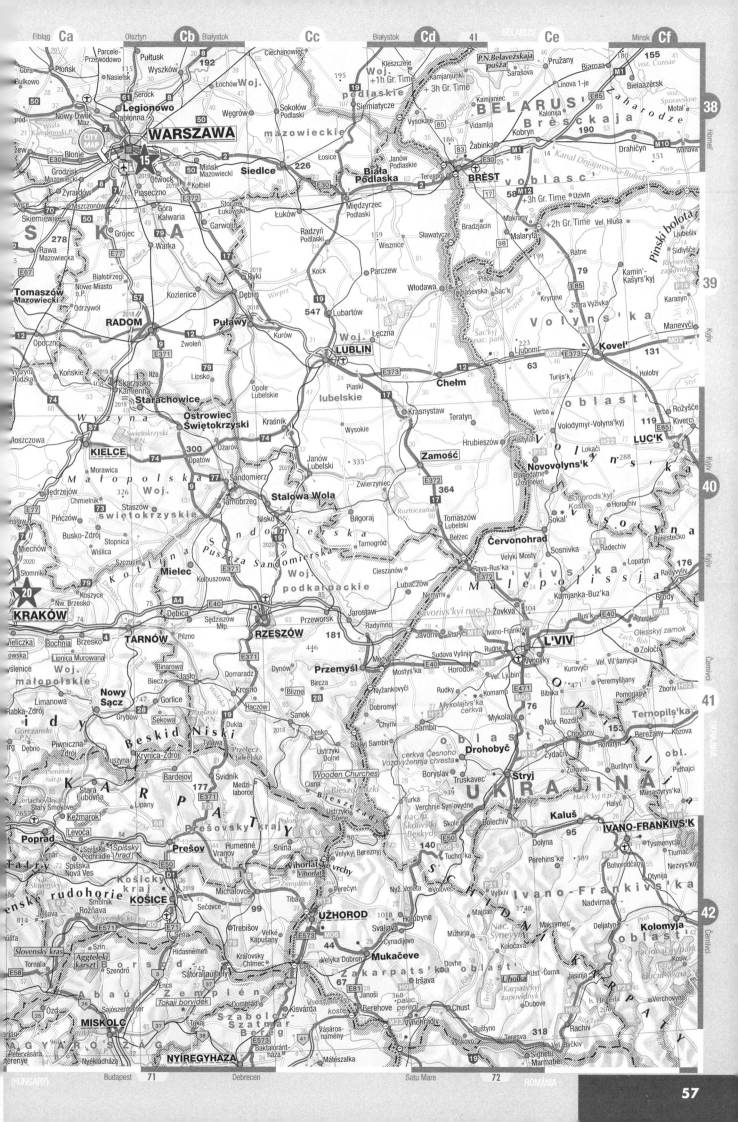

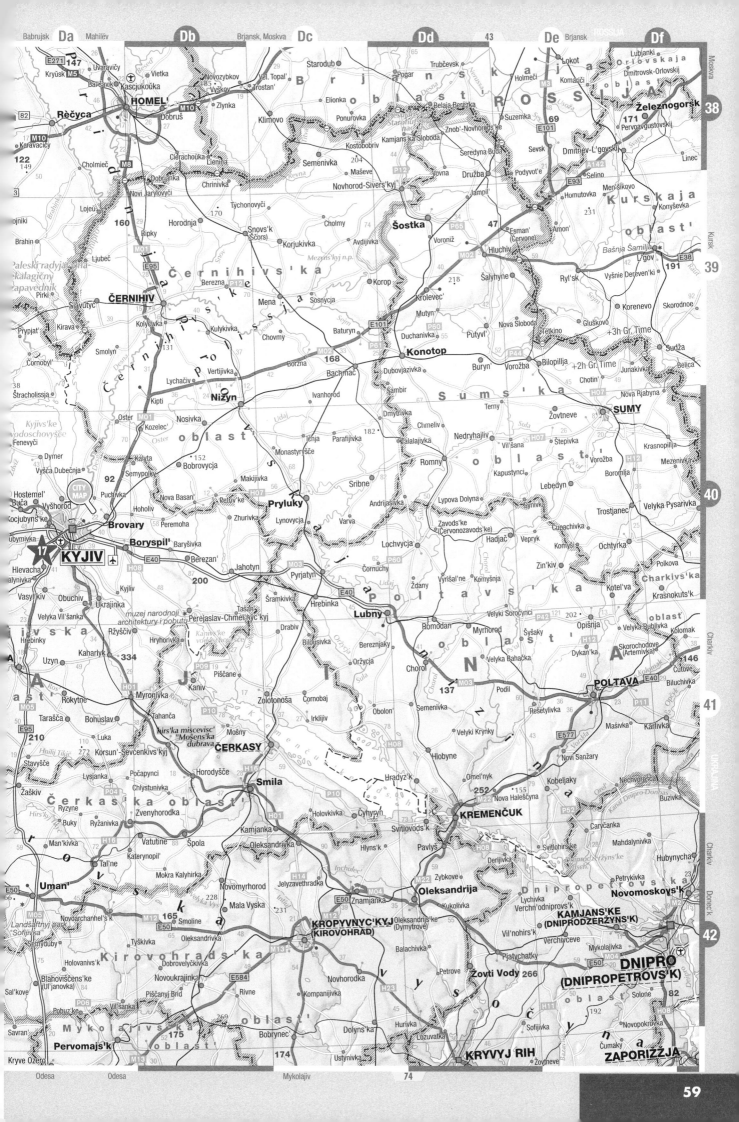

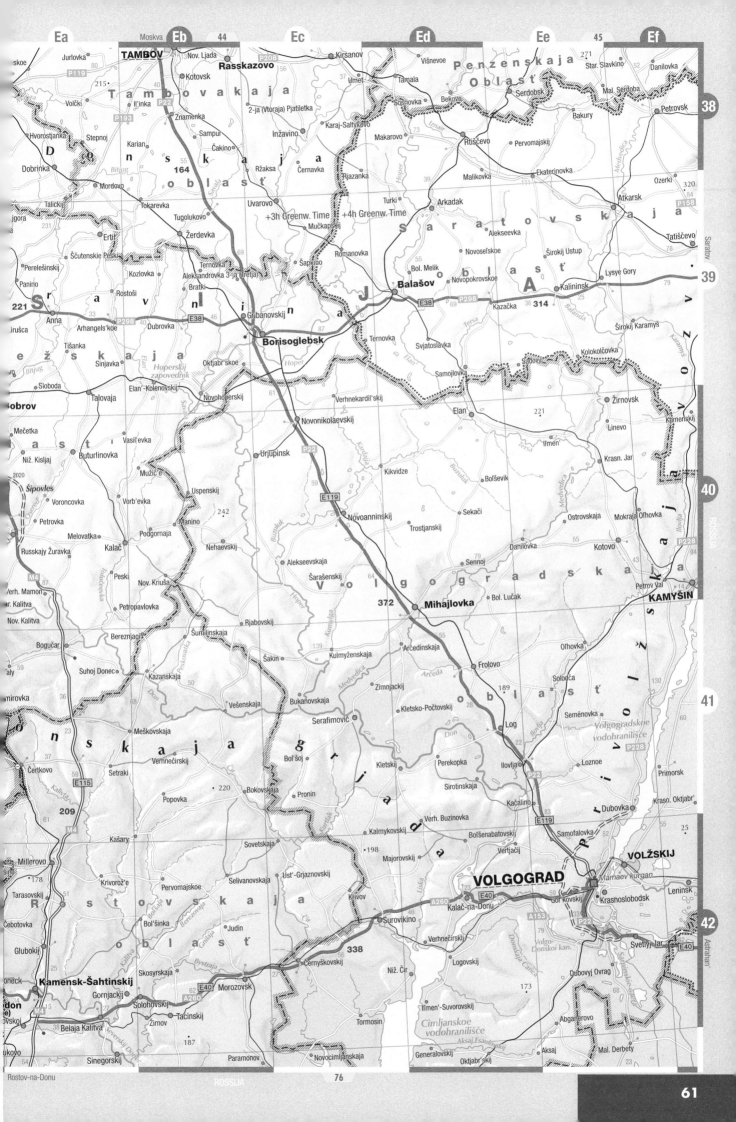

38

271
Lopatino
Pavlovka
Androsovka
Star. Slavkino
52
Beguč
Bol. Ozerki
Hvorostjanka
Mar'evka
Danilovka
P158
Jakovlevka
Sosnovaja Maza
Brykovka
Padovka
Mal. Serdoba
+3h Greenw. Time
Hvalynsk
Pestrav
Bakury
Baltaj
Čerkasskoe
Belogornoe
Duhovnickoe
+4h Greenw. Time
Saratovskoe
Petrovsk
vodohranilišče
Podsnežnoe
Bazarnyi Karabulak
Ivanteevka
45
Ekaterinovka
Kulikovka
Gorjainovka
Nadeždinka
P158
Nov. Burasy
Vjazovka
Šennoj
Šihany
Nikolaevka
Ozerki
56
Sokur
Arjaš
Sinodskoe
Bol. Tavoložka
Atkarsk
320
Vol'sk
Tersa
BALAKOVO
P226
84
89
280
Pugačev
Rahmanovka
Balašov
Širokij Ustup
Tatiščevo
Elšanka
P228
P226
160
Davydovka
Gračev Ku
78
12
Mal. Bykovka
Sulak
87
Dubki
Marks
Novopolevodino
Rukopol'
Karlovka
Ljubickoe
SARATOV
Gornyj
Nov. Porub

39
Kaliñinsk
Lysye Gory
22
ENGEL'S
Klincovka
314
79
Pervomajskoe
Rimsko-Korsakovka
Žestjanka
Širokij Karamyš
67
Bezymjannoe
Stepnoe
Romanovka
62
Lipovskij
Pigari
E38
Zolotaja Step'
46
35
423
Pervomajskij
P236
P236
Volgogradskoe
Puškino
Mokrous
Eršov
102
vodohranilišče
Privolžskoe
Ždanovka
Dergači
Dem'jas
Ozinki
P228
Krasnyj Kut
Novorepnoe
Altata
Žirnovsk
Borisoglebovka
Krasnoarmejsk
Orlov Gaj
Novožizevka
Šyža 2-i
Kamenskij
19
Krivojar
Komsomol'skoe
Novotulka
Linevo
Rovnoe
Kurilovka
Kčevo
Šil'naja Balka
Kajrat
Krasn. Jar
Piterka
Pograničnoe

40
Ilovatka
Mal. Uzen
Žumaly
Mokraja Ol'hovka
Star. Poltavka
Talovka
Novouzensk
Kotovo
Nov. Poltavka
Gmelinka
Petropavlovka
Kanavka
Bogatyrevo
P228
Berezino
Taldyküdyk
Petrov Val
Savinka
Borsyk
Aleksandrov Gaj
KAMYŠIN
Pallasovka
Port-Artur
Nikolaevsk
Kaztalovka
Saryküdyk
Baranovka
Kamysty
Ašbaj
Furmanovo
Bykovo
Eršov
Kajsackoe
Bostandyk
Krasnoselec
Prudentov
Kajrat
Kökterek
Žuldyz

41
Soldatsko-Stepnoe
Volgogradskoe
Visnevka
Ak-oba
vodohranilišče
Žanybek
Primorsk
Majak Oktjabrja
Üzynköl
Dubovka
Elton
Önege
Saralžynköl
Krasn. Oktjabr'
oz. Elton
Saralžyn
+5h Greenw. Time

42
+3h Greenw. Time
VOLŽSKIJ
Zarja
Žermenke
Bisen
Žetibaj
Terenküdyk
Žaña Kazan
Leninsk
Sajkyn
+4h Greenw. Time
Orda
Žualyoj
Kapustin Jar
Seitkali
E40
Svetlyj Jar
Pologoe Zajmišče
Pokrovka
E119
Solodniki
Vjazovka
Stupino
Torgaj
Astrahanskaja
Starica
Ahtubinsk
Sujindik
P22
Verh. Baskunčak
Resp. Kalmykija
Černyj Jar
Novonikolaevka
Taldyapan
Hal'mg- Tangč
Iki-Manlan
Solënoe Zajmišče
oblast'
Voshod
Sokrutovka

62

Astrahan'
0 10 20 30 40 50 km
0   10   20   30 miles
77

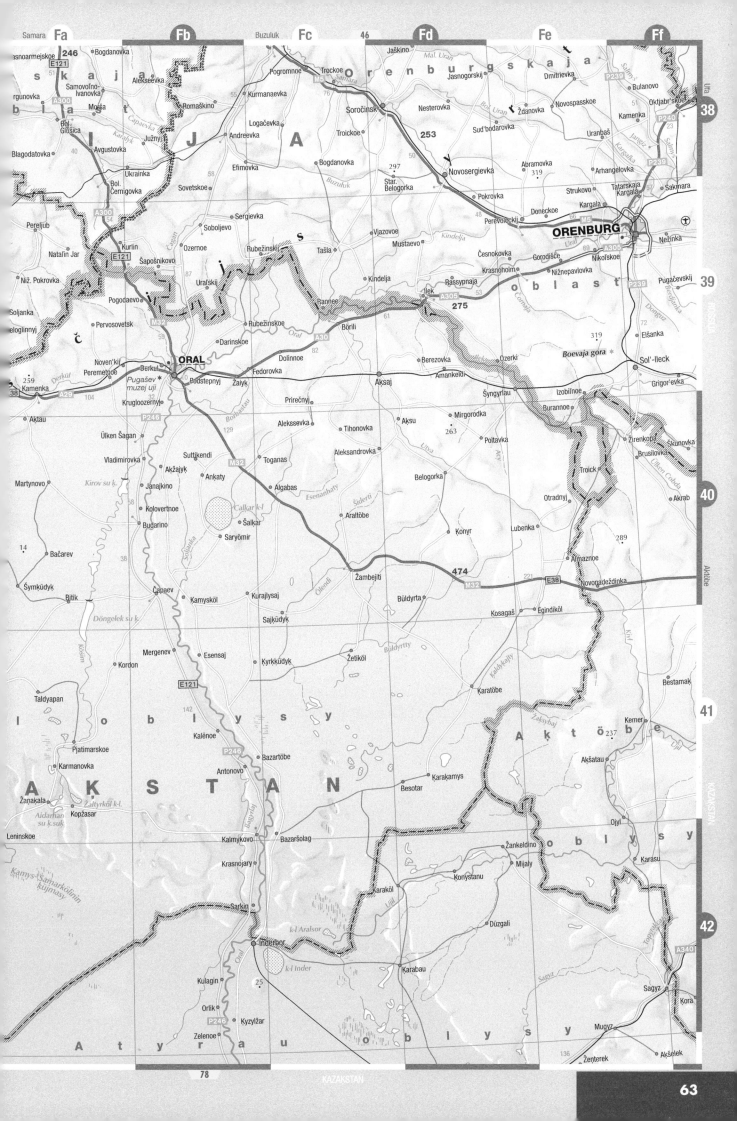

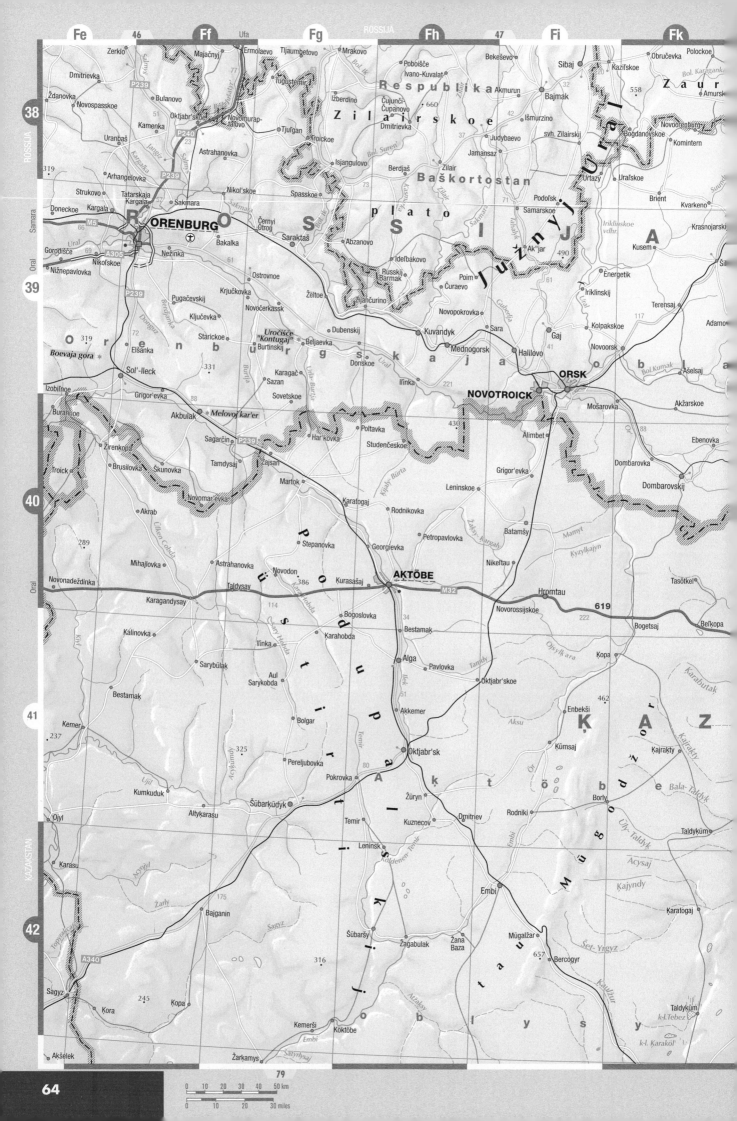

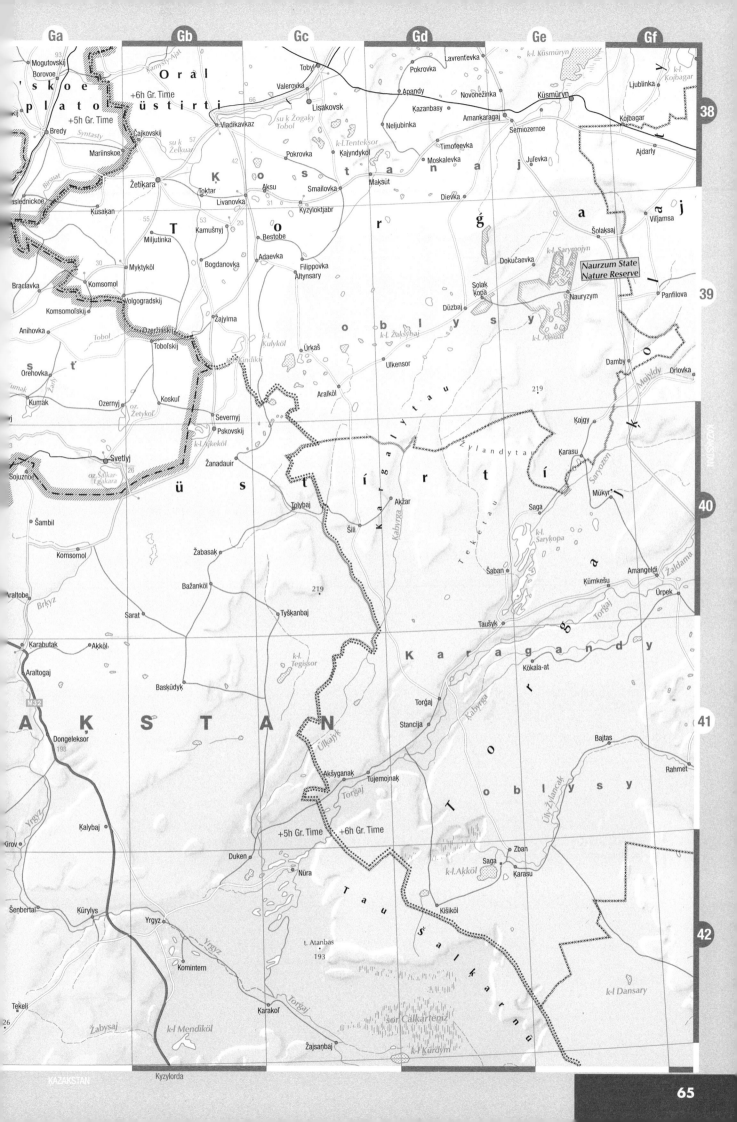

38

39

40

41

42

Mogutovskij
Borovoe
'skoe
plato
+6h Gr. Time
üstirti
+5h Gr. Time
Bredy   Syntasty
Mariinskoe
Žetikara
Toktar
Küsakan
T   Kamušnyj
Miljutinka
Myktyköl
Braclavka
Komsomol
Komsomoľskij
Anihovka
Volgogradskij
Džeržinskij
Tobol   Tobolskij
s   ť
Orehovka
Kumak   Žaty
Kumak
Ozernyj   oz. Žetykoľ   Koskuľ
Severnyj
Pskovskij
Šambil
Komsomol
Žabasak
Bažanköl
Sarat
Karabutak   Akköl
Araltogaj
M32
AĶSTAN
Dongeleksor
198
Kalybaj
Kirov
Šenbertal   Kürylys
Tekeli
26

Oral
Kamyšy-Ajat
Tobyl
Valerovka
Lisakovsk   su k Žogaky Tobol
Vladikavkaz   66
Čajkovskij   57
su k Želkuar
Ķ   o   s   t   a   n   a   j
Pokrovka   42
Aksu   Smailovka
Livanovka   31   Kyzyloktjabr
53   20
Kamušnyj   Bestobe
Adaevka
Bogdanovka   Filippovka
Altynsary
Zajylma
k-l. Kulyköl
Ürkaš
Severnyj   Kindikli
k-l. Ajkeköl
Žanadauir   26
Tolybaj
Šili
Akžar
Tyškanbaj   219
k-l. Tegissor
Basküdyk
N
Ülkajyk
Akšyganak   Tujemojnak
Torgaj
+5h Gr. Time   +6h Gr. Time
Duken
Nüra
Yrgyz
Yrgyz
Komintern
Karakoľ   Torgaj
k-l Mendiköl
Žabysaj
Žajsanbaj
Kyzylorda

Lavreňevka   k-l. Küsmüryn
Pokrovka
Apandy   Novonežinka   Küsmüryn
Kazanbasy
Neljubinka   Amankaragaj   Kojbagar
Semiozernoe
Timofeevka
Moskalevka   Jurevka
Dievka   o   r   ǵ   a   j   Viľjamsa
Šolaksaj
Dokučaevka   k-l. Sarymojyn   Naurzum State Nature Reserve
Solak kopa   Nauryzym   Panfilova
Düzbaj
o   b   l   y   s   y
k-l. Žaksybaj   Damby   Orlovka
Ulkensor   Kajgy   k
219   Karasu
Zylandytau   Saga   Mükyr
k-l. Sarykopa   Amangeldi   Žaldama
Šaban   Kümkešu   Ürpek
Teketau   Taušyk   Torgaj
K   a   r   a   g   a   n   d   y
Kökala-at
Torgaj
Stancija   Kabyrga   Bajtas
T   o   b   l   y   s   y
Uly-Žylanšak   Rahmet
Zban
Saga
k-l. Akköl   Karasu
Kišiköl
t. Atanbas   193
T   a   u   Šalkarnu
šor Calkarteniz   k-l Dansary
k-l Kürdym

Aralköl   k-l. Tenteksor   Küsakan   Mŭksüt   219

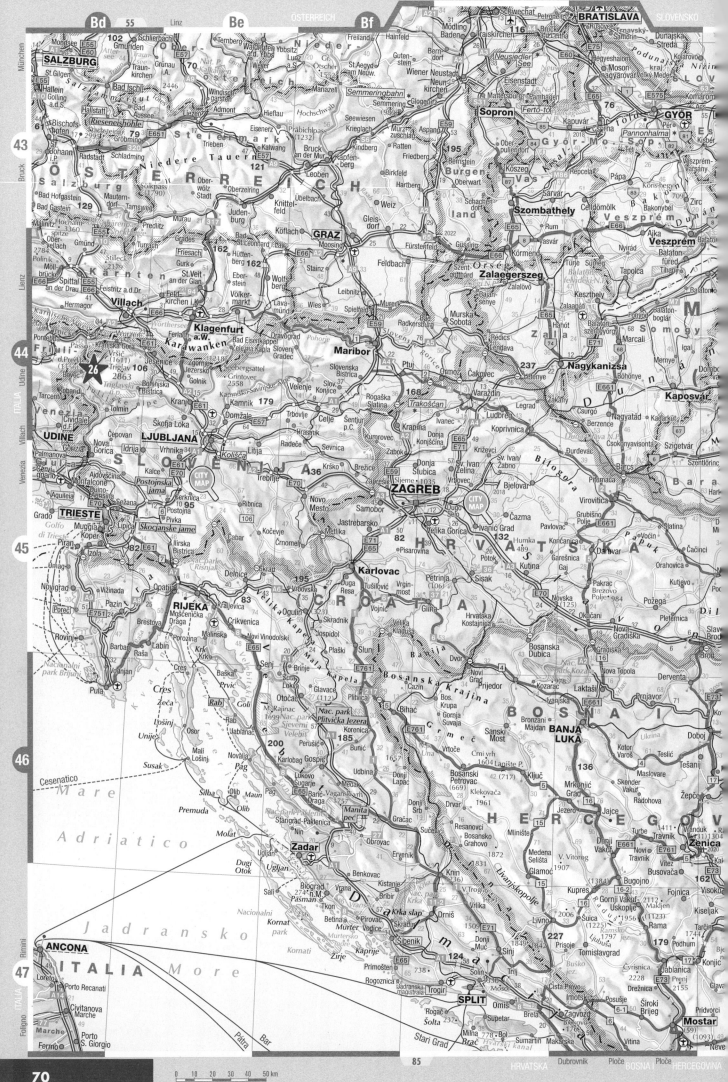

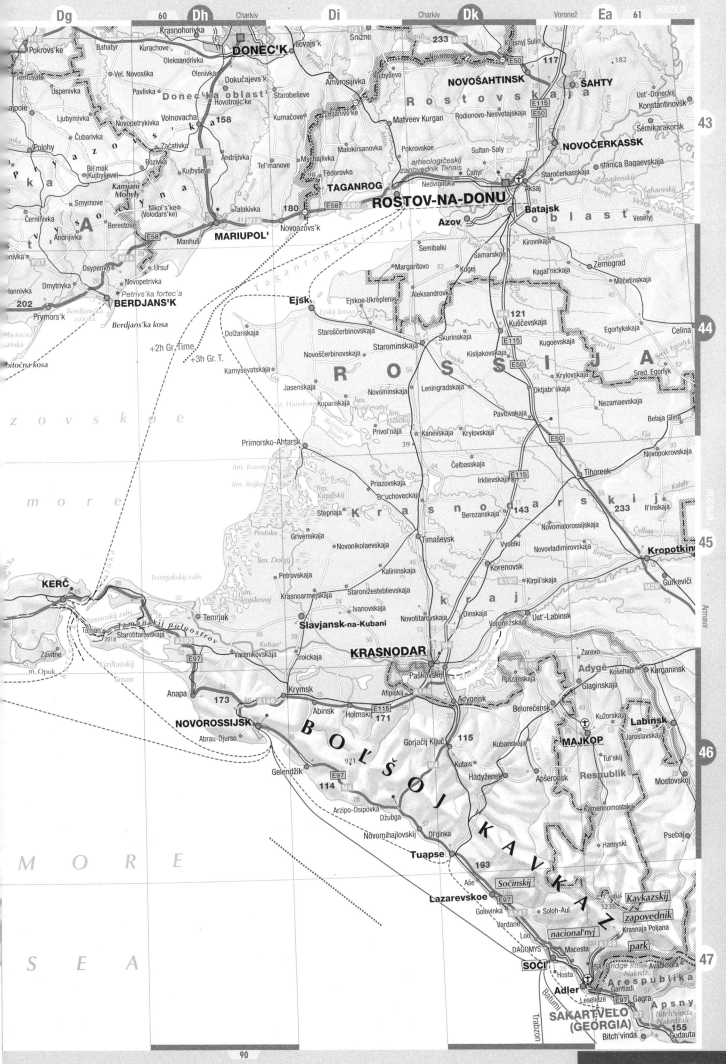

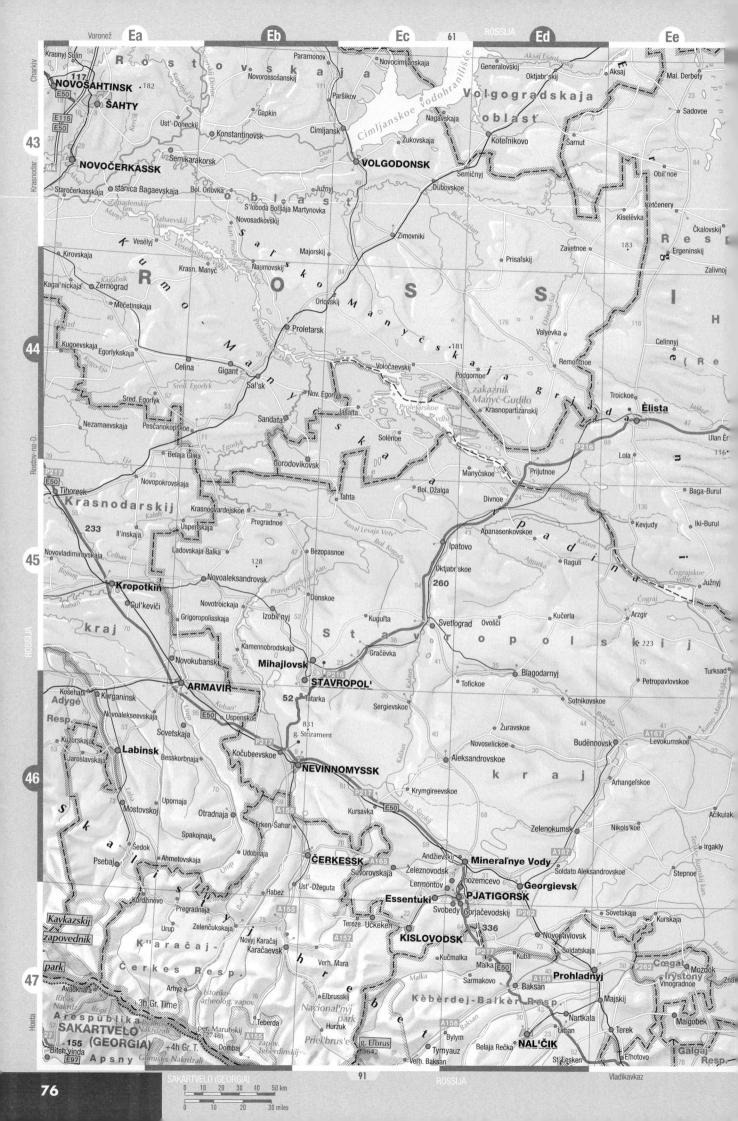

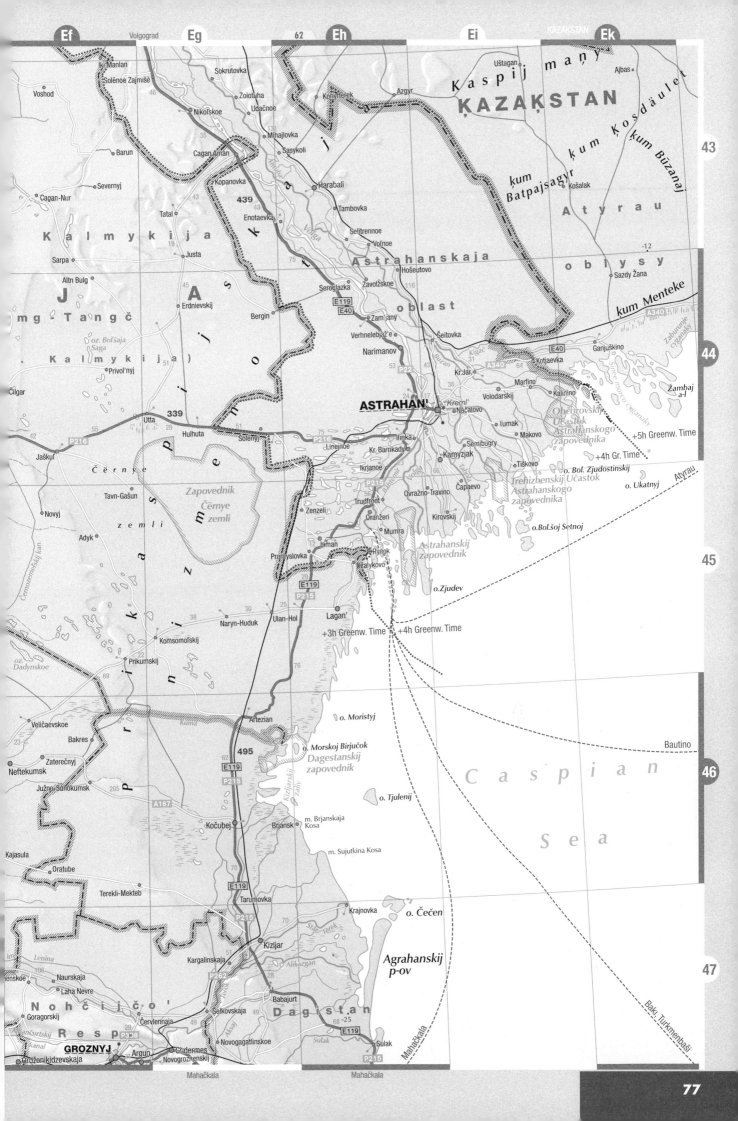

Uštagan
Ajbas
A t y r a u   o b l y s y
kum Kosdäulet
kum Büzanaj
Košalak
kum
Batpajsagyr
kum Menteke
-12
Sazdy Žana
Žaňakamys
Zaburun'e
E40   A340

43

K a s p i j   m a ň y
166
Sarytogaj
Mahambet
k-l Žaltyr
Bykožek
Tandaj
Balsaj
70
Sarajšyk
Kyzylúj
Novobogat
Redut
60   A340
Akkystau
92   A340
Talkajran
Tamyrly
Kyzylbas
ATYRAU
Kyzylbalyk
Šumysker
Böget
t-k Pečnoj
a-l Nordvestinskij

s i n e k l i z a s y
P246
35   Makat
Dossor
Sakyz
Kockar   Bekbe
Eskene   Bajconas   Komsomol!
Tehtek sor
27   k-l Bartylaakt!
Kossagyl
Embi
K
sor Oli
Karaton

44

Ganjuškino
Zaburunje cyganaky
Sinee morco cyganaky
Žambaj a-l
Občorovskij
Učastok
Astrahanskogo
zapovednika   +5h Greenw. Time
+4h Gr. Time
Bol. Zjudostinskij
o. Ukatnyj
Oranžeri

C a s p i a n
S e a

45

Prorva   Sarykamys
a-l Durnev
ovlk Komsomol
m-i Buryncyk
Kalamkas
Ülken sor
Tubek
Büzačy

Tjulender
a-l Kulandy   a-l Morskoj
araly
a-l Podgornyj
a-l Rybacij
cyganak
Mankyclaks
Kijakty
-44
Šeber   Kyzan
Karakečuor kajdak

Oranžeri
m-i Tubkaragan
Bautino
Fort-Ševčenko
Tubek
Karaton
Tub-Karagan
Taušyk
taulary Mangystau
Karatau
Kujbyžev
Šetre
Žarmyš
128
tau Soltau
229   Saj-Utjés
35

46

Mahačkala
m-i Sakyndyk
tau Bescoky
556
M a ň k y s
Uštagan
tau Kölbaj
321

47

Mangyčlak
AKTAU
m-i Melovoj
-132
vpad.
Karagije
Kyzylkum
70
72
Žetybaj
Münajšy
üstírtí
M a ň k y s t a u   B o s t a n k u m
Ozen
Senek
Novyj Uzen   o b l y

0   10   20   30   40   50 km
0   10   20   30 miles

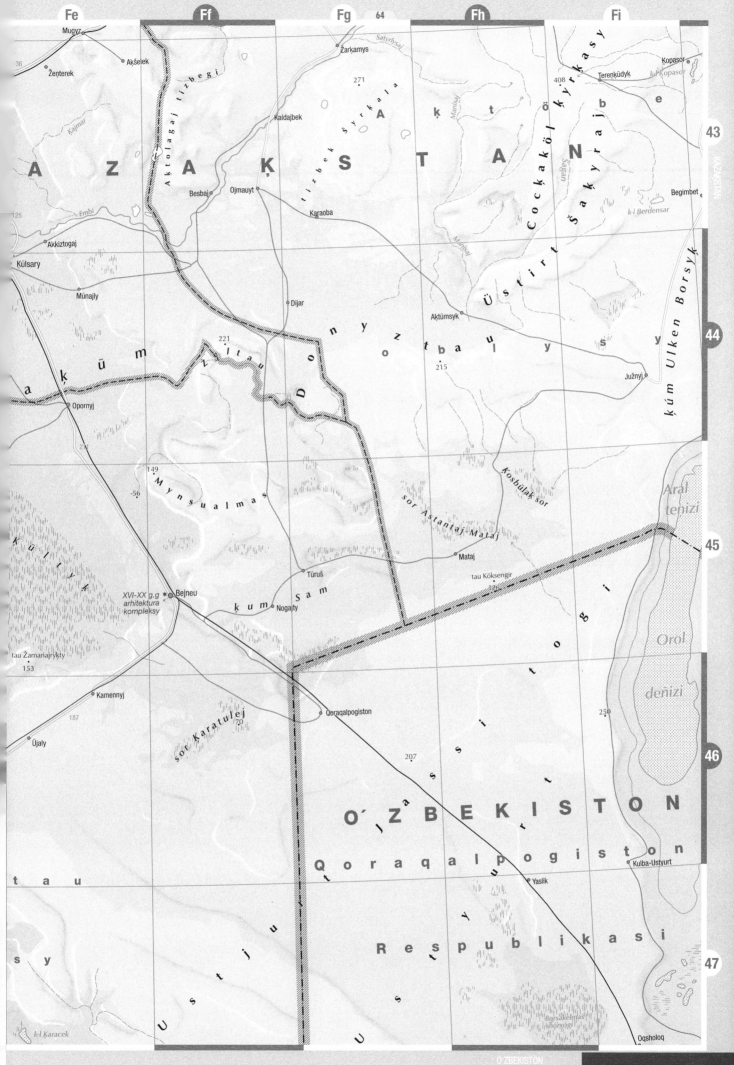

43

44

45

46

47

Mugyz

Akšelek

Žeņterek

36

Kajmar

125

Embi

Akkiztogaj

Külsary

Münajly

A Ķ S T A N

Aktolagaj tizbegi

Besbaj

Ojmauyt

Karaoba

Žarkamys

Satyrlysaj

Kaldajbek

271

A tizbek šyrķala ķ t

Dijar

Manisaj

Sagan

Cockaköl ķyrkasy

408

Terenķüdyk

Kopasor

k-l Kopasor

Begimbet

k-l Berdensar

Üstirt Šaķyraj b

e

KAZAKSTAN

a ķ ū m

Zaltau

221

D o n y z t b a u l y

Aķtümsyk

215

ķ ū m Ulken Borsyķ

y

Južnyj

Opornyj

2

Küldyk

149

-56

M y n s u a l m a s

sor Astantaj-Mataj

Kosbūlaķ sor

Orol

Aral teņizi

tau Žamanajrykty

153

XVI-XX g.g
arhitektura
kompleksy

Bejneu

ķ u m S a m

Tūruš

Nogajty

Mataj

tau Köksengir

120

U s t i o g i

deñizi

Kamennyj

187

Üjaly

sor Ķaratulej

70

Qoraqalpogiston

207

250

Kulba-Ustyurt

tau

s y

k-l Karacek

U s t j u s

Yaslik

O´ Z B E K I S T O N

Qoraqalpogiston

Respublikasi

Borsäkelmäs
šorxögi

Ogsholoq

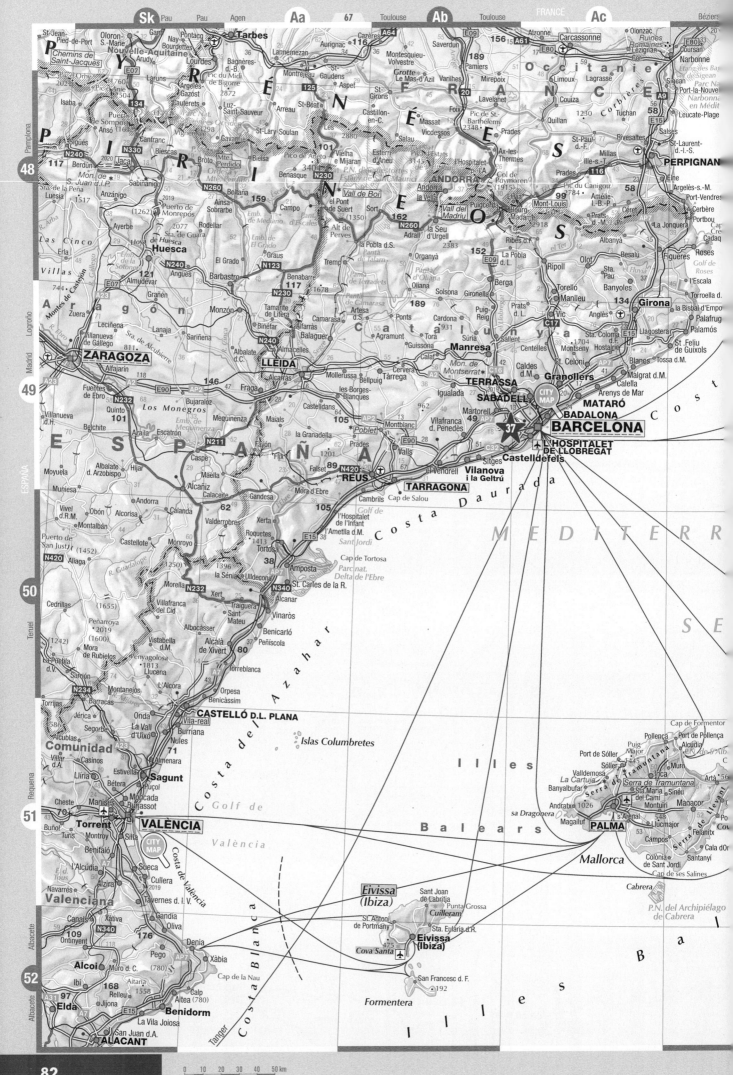

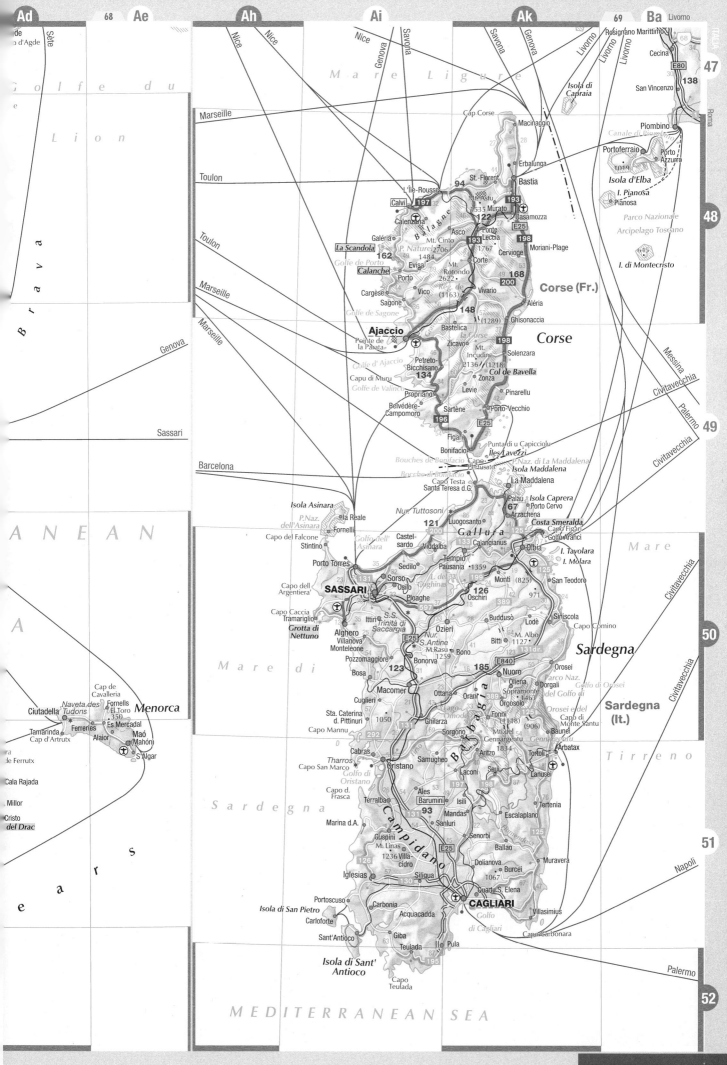

Golfe du Lion

B r a v a

Sète
d'Agde
o d'Agde

Marseille
Toulon
Toulon
Marseille
Marseille
Marseille
Genova
Sassari
Barcelona

Mare Ligure

Nice
Nice
Nice
Savona
Savona
Genova
Genova
Livorno
Livorno
Livorno
Livorno

ITALIA
Livorno
Rosignano Marittimo
Cecina
San Vincenzo
Piombino
Portoferraio
Porto Azzurro
Isola d'Elba
Isola di Capraia
I. Pianosa
Piānosa
Parco Nazionale
Arcipelago Toscano
I. di Montecristo
E80
E25
138
Roma

Cap Corse
Macinaggio
Erbalunga
St.-Florent
Bastia
L'Île-Rousse
Calvi 197
94
Murato 193
122
Casamozza
Calenzana
Balagne
Asco Ponte Leccia 198
Galéria
Mt. Cinto 193
Moriani-Plage
La Scandola
2706 1767
Corte
162
Evisa 1484
Mt. Rotondo
2622
Cervione
Calanche
Porto
Vico Reg. de (1163)
168
Cargèse
Vivario
200
Corse (Fr.)
Sagone
148
Aléria
Golfe de Sagone
Ghisonaccia
Ajaccio
Bastelica (1289)
Corse
Pointe de la Parata
Zicavoe 198
Mt. Incudine
Solenzara
Petreto-Bicchisano 2136 (1218)
134 Col de Bavella
Capu di Muru
Zonza
Golfe de Valinco
Levie Pinarellu
Propriano
Belvédère-Campomoro
Sartène Porto-Vecchio
196 E25
Figari
Bonifacio Punta di u Capicciolu
Îles Lavezzi
Bouches de Bonifacio Capo P.Naz. di La Maddalena
Bocche di Bonifacio Pertusato
Capo Testa Isola Maddalena
Santa Teresa d.G. La Maddalena
Isola Asinara Palau Isola Caprera
P.Naz. la Reale Nur. Tuttosoni 67 Porto Cervo
dell'Asinara Fornelli Arzachena
Golfo dell' Luogosanto Costa Smeralda
Capo del Falcone Asinara 121 Capo Figari
200 Gallura Golfo Aranci
Stintino Castel- Calangianus 125
sardo Viddalba I. Tavolara
Porto Torres Sedilo Tempio I. Molara
35 Pausania 1359
131 Sorso L. del 199 Monti (825)
SASSARI Osilo Coghinas San Teodoro
Ploaghe Oschiri 126 971
597 Capo Comino
Capo dell' S.S. Ozieri 389 Buddusò
Argentiera' Trinità di Lodè Siniscola
Capo Caccia Ittiri Saccargia Bitti M. Albo
Tramariglio Nur. 131dir. Sardegna
Grotta di Alghero S.Antine 1127
Nettuno Villanova E25 M.Rasu Bono E840 Orosei
Monteleone 1259 131
Pozzomaggiore Bonorva 185 Nuoro Parco Naz.
123 Oliena del Golfo di
Bosa Dorgali Orosei
Macomer Ottana Orani Sopramonte Golfo di Orosei
Mare di Cuglieri Orgosolo 1463 Sardegna
Lago- Fonni Orosei e del (It.)
Sta. Caterina Omodeo Ghilarza Mti. del (1118) Capo di
d. Pittinuri 1050 Sorgono Barbagia Gennargentu Monte Santu
Capo Mannu Aritzo 1834 Gennargentu (906) Baunei
292 131 Seui Arbatax
Cabras 0 Laconi Tortolì Tirreno
Tharros Samugheo Lanusei
Capo San Marco Oristano 197 198
Golfo di 87
Oristano Ales Isili
Capo d. Terralba Barumini Tertenia
Frasca 93 Mandas Escalaplano
Sardegna Marina d.A. Sanluri
131 Senorbi 125
Guspini Ballao
M. Linas Dolianova
1236 Villa- Burcei
126 cidro 1067
Iglesias Siliqua Quartu S. Elena
130 CAGLIARI
Portoscuso Carbonia Villasimius
Isola di San Pietro Acquacadda Golfo Capo Carbonara
Carloforte di Cagliari
Sant'Antioco Giba Pula
Teulada
Isola di Sant' 195
Antioco Capo
Teulada

Mare Tirreno

Messina
Civitavecchia
Palermo
Civitavecchia
Civitavecchia
Civitavecchia
Napoli
Palermo

Cap de Cavalleria
Fornells
Naveta des Tudons El Toro
Ciutadella 350
Ferreries Es Mercadal Menorca
Tamarinda Alaior Maó
Cap d'Artrutx Mahón
S'Algar
de Ferrutx
Cala Rajada
Millor
Cristo del Drac

A N E A N
A
e a r s

M E D I T E R R A N E A N S E A

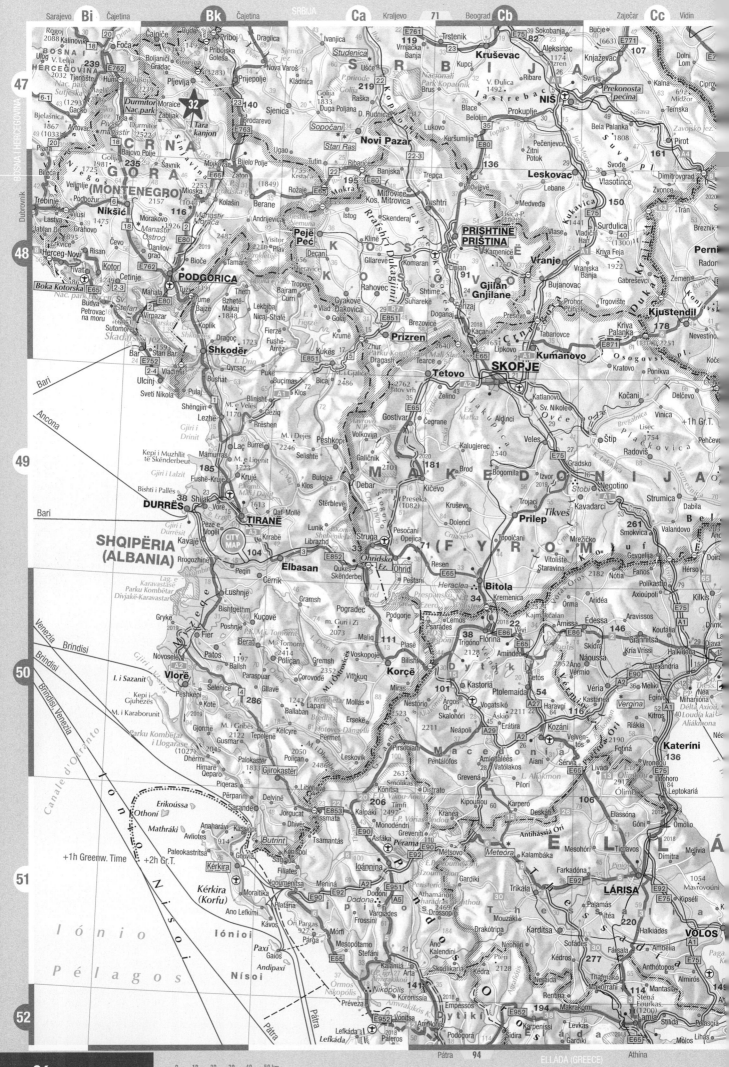

47

48

49

50

51

52

O E M O R E

A C K S E A

A R A D E N İ Z

İnceburun

Kızılabalı   (18)   **Sinop** (310)

Sinop Br.

Kerempe Br.   Doğanyurt   İnebolu   Abana   Çatalzeytin   Ayancık   58   Kabalı

Akbayır   Bozkurt   Türkeli   **158**   Şerefiye   Erfelek (1370)   010   Gerze

Çide   96   Dikmen D. 1471   Küre (1240)   Çangal D. 1605   Çiçekyaylâ 2019   Yenikonak   Bürnük   Dranoz   Bafra Br.   Kürtler

Şenpazar   88   **169**   69   Yakakent   **Bafra**   Harız   Ovası

Küre Dağları Milli Parkı   Meydan   Sabiban   Karaçam   g (1440)   Dikman   Alaçam   **Bafra**   Ondokuzmayıs

Amasra   Ant   Şahin   **152**   Yaralıgöz Dağı   Çuhalı   Boyabat   Durağan   Boğazkaya 1300

İnkumu   Bartın   Azdavay   Seydiler   Devrekâni   030   Çakırçay   Pelitbükü   Esençay

Hisarönü   Pınarbaşı   Çerçiler   70   Sargın

Kilimli   010   (1550)   Daday   44   Taşköprü   Sarayiçik Dağı   Saraydüzü   Türkmen   Yunddağı

ULDAK (5)   Çaycuma   58   Kozcağız   Kumluca   Eflâni   Daday Çayı   14   Akkaya   106   Mezraa   1783   Çakıralan

utçuk   Kozlu   38   Gökçebey   Karapınar   (798)   **Kastamonu** 775   Çiftlikçy   Kargı   Kâmil   785   Vezirköprü

74   Beycuma   **KARABÜK**   Safranbolu   İğdir   Araç   Kuzyaka   68   Hacıhamza   Köprübaşı   (940)

Ormanlı   Devrek   Yenice   030   Çavuşlar   İhsangazi   64   Kırık 2587   Ada Dağı   Sarayiçik (960)   Hayza   030

Dağları   Dorukhan   Ovacık   Boyalı   Nıf Dağı Milli Parkı   39   43   Gümüşhacıköy   14   Lâdik

Egerci   025   Eskipazar   Soğanlı   Ilgaz Dağı   Tosya   **228**   Osmancık   785   E80   **Merzifon**

1615   Mengen   Pazarköy   İsmetpaşa   Bayramören   Ilgaz   36   100   Harun   175   Hamamözü   795   Sarı-buğday

Yedigöller Milli Parkı   Gökçesu   **135**   Çerkeş   E80   Kurşunlu   Devrez Çayı   75   Kargın   97   Lâçin   **Amasya**

29   Gerede   Karamürgen Dağı   64   Atkaracalar   Belören   Yapraklı   Asarcık   Doğantepe   E80

Bolu (725)   O-4   Dörtdivan   Kavacık   Işık D. 2015   Sakaevi   54   Korgun   İkizören   İskilip   **ÇORUM**   180   Kalekö

E89   (1570)   Güvem   Orta   ğ   **187**   **Çankırı**   Bayat   Seydim   16   Mecitözü   Gediksaray

2378   Köroğlu T.   Çamlıdere   Kızılcahamam   Eldivan   Kuzu   84   Uğurludağ   1791   İbek   Göynücek   Zile

Seben   Kıbrıscık   Bayındır   Balcılar   Karagöl   Şabanözü   21   Bozkır   Sağpazar   1198   Cemilbey   785   39   Ortaköy   İğdir   **190**

R   Karaşar   Soğuksu Milli P.   Çeltikçi   750   **135**   Çubuk Brj.   Karamusa   Kızılırmak   Demirşeyh   40   Alaca   Çöplü   Boztepe

K   Karaköy   115   **138**   Pazar   45   Çandır   Sulakyurt   Kavak   Karaçay   Alacahöyük   190   Aydıncık   74

I   Güdül   Kazan   **Çubuk** (1365)   Sungurlu   Çekerek   Devrez Dağ

Çayırhan   Beypazarı   96   Sirkeli   **140**   Kalecik   190   Tasarı Milli Parkı   Eymir   **805**   Kadışehri

anyar   Ayaş   CITY MAP   KEÇİÖREN   58   İdris D. 1985   Balışeyh   200   Boğazkale   1689 Hattuşaş   Deremahal   Beyyurdu

Koyunağıl   Kırbaşı   İçmeces   SİNCAN   ALTINDAĞ   O-20   Delice   Salmanlı   Musabeyli   Yanık

Mihalıççık   Sarıoba   Polatlar   21   MAMAK   **74**   Elmadağ   E88   46   Sorgun   Doğanlı

Sarayköy   (18) (850)   **ANKARA**   ÇANKAYA   1862   Yahşihan   1742   Sekili   795   40

Poyraz   Gölbaşı   Hacılar   **KIRIKKALE**   **136**   37   **Yozgat**   200   Saraykent   **228**

Biçer   Şabanözü   44   O-20   **29**   (700)   Dinek D.   Çamlık Milli Parkı   E88   Oluközü

OS   Temelli   Koparan   260   Süleymanlı   Keskin   Takâzlı   Yerköy   Osmanpaşa   Alcı   67   Hasbek   Akçakışla

Sarıköy   Sazılar   Karaâli   753   Karakeçili   Akçakent   Saray   Gelingüllü Brj.

İğdecik   **130**   Kayabaşı   56   İkizce   E90   Çiçekdağı   Şefaatli   Yenipazar   Sarıkaya

Yassıhöyük (Gordion)   Polatlı   750   Balâ   **158**   260   Göllü   785   Çamalak   **805**

E90   200   Şeyhali   Oyaca   26   Çelebi   Akpınar   B   Çayıralan   2272

Sivrihisar   Günyüzü   Çimşit   Kaman   757   Çoğun   o   Çandır

Arayıt D. 1820   Yenimehmetli   Haymana   42   Boztepe   z   Seyfe G.   Karahasanlı   o   Boğazlıyan   Oğulcuk

Ertuğrulköy   İlıca   Yamak   **68**   Odunboğazı   753   Aydınlar   1808   Seyfeköy   Fakılı   Felâhiye

İlyaspaşa   Yenice Yaylâsı   Çeltikli   Hırfanlı Brj.   1724   Toklumân (978)   **KIRŞEHİR**   Kozaklı   Akpınar   Büyüköz   Tuzla

Çeltik   Yeşilöz   Karaca D.   Akın   Kaçarlı   Mucur   Kaldağ   Yamula Barajı   İncesu

Yarıkkaya   Adatoprakpınar   Emirler   Kozanlı   Kulu   Şereflikoçhisar   Kesikköprü Hanı   27   **126**   Kızıl Dağı   Güneşli   Gesi

Yunak   Hacıfatlı   Sülüklü   Yenieoba   Tavşançalı   Tuzyaka   61   Hacıbektaş   765   Çalligedik Geç   Himmetdede   Özkonak   Erkilet   **KAYSERİ**

Cihanbeyli   107   750   Ağaçören   Bozkır   Gümüşkent   64   260   Boğazköprü   260

Tuz Gölü   E90

Samsun   Taşova   Tokat   TÜRKİYE   Sivas   Bünyan

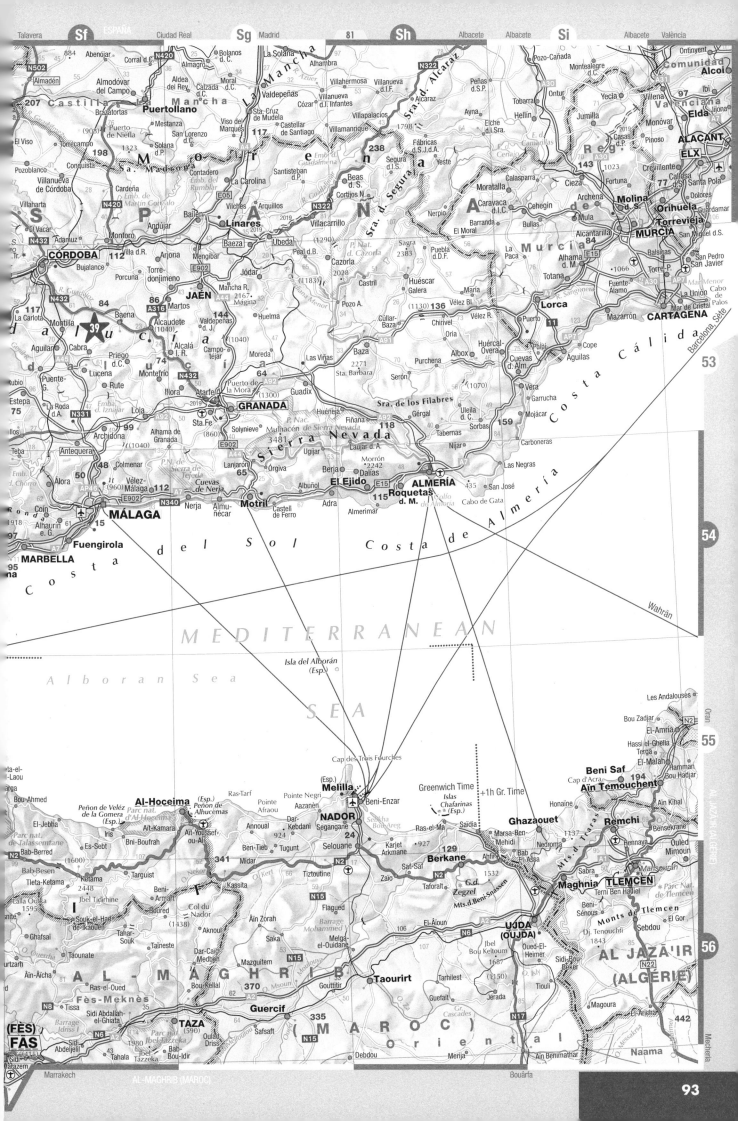

Óri Pargas
927
Frossiní
Mórfi
Várgiades
Mouzáki
30
Palamás
Itéa
220
Kipséli
Kanália
Makriráhi
Mourési

51

Párga
Gaïos
Mesopótamo
Stefáni
Ano
Kalendíni
Drakótripa
Kardítsa
Sofádes
Halkiádes
VOLOS

Andípaxi
Venezía
E55
Arta
Kalamiá
Néoheri
Kédros
Fálsala
277
Ambélia
Anthótopos
Argalastí

Órmos
Nikópolis
Nikópolis
Skoulikariá
Kédra
Pteri
2128
Thafmakó
Almirós
Skiathos
Loútráki

Préveza
Empessós
Neraida
Makrakómi
Mantasiás
Ahillio
Skiathos
Skópelos
Alónnisos

194
E952
38
Levkas
Stená
Fourkas
Agriovótano
Glifa

Lefkáda
Vónitsa
Amfilohía
Podogorá
Sidira
Karpeníssi
Gardíki
Lamía
Stilida
Istiéa
Kokinómblea

Elatí
Nidri
Paleros
Proússós
Dolmiáná
Mólos
Xiró
Strofiliá

Meganíssi
Fíties
Paúliani
Brálos
Konstantínos
Arkitsa
Limni

Kálamos
Astakós
Levkaditi
215
Zélio
Atalánti
150
Evoïkós

51
Sevgarákio
A5
Trichonís
85
E.Dr.Parnassós
Orhomenós
Akréfnio

Neohóri
Kapsorráhi
Amfissa
27
Parnassós
Livadiá
178
Movrikí

Messolóngi
Delfi
2457
Itéa
Óssios
Kiriáki

PÁTRA
A5
Río
91
Erátini
Akra Agia
Agia Ana
Thiva

Araxos
Panahaïkó
E65
Halandrítsa
Akráta
Perahóra
Megara
Salamína
ATHÍNA

130
Kaláyrita
Xilókastro
Kiáto
Kórinthos
PIREÁS

53

226
Andrítsena
Levídi
85
E65
Argos
Nafplio
Epídauros

Tripolí
Giokaréika
Astros
Kranídi
Spétses

175
Leonídio
Pláka
Ídra

Kalamáta
Spárti
Mistra
Geráki
Paralia

Pílos
Likódimo
2407
Skála
Niáta

Methóni
Koróni
Arna
Githio
Monemvassía

0 10 20 30 40 50 km
0   10   20   30 miles

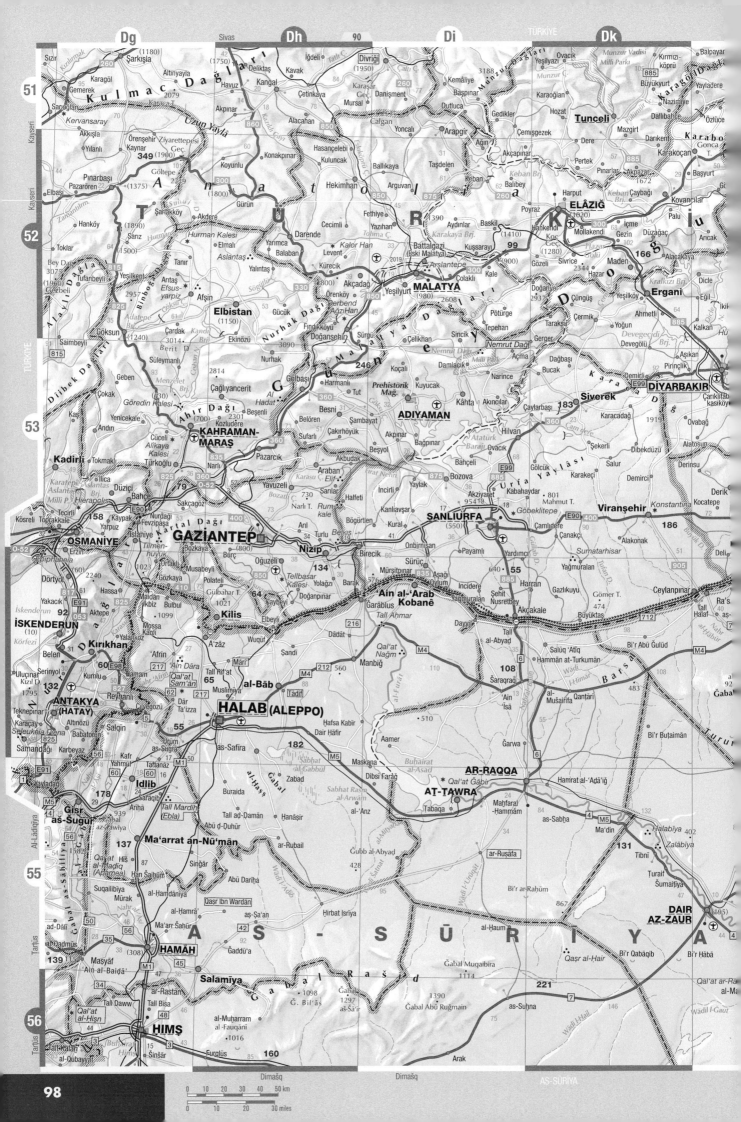

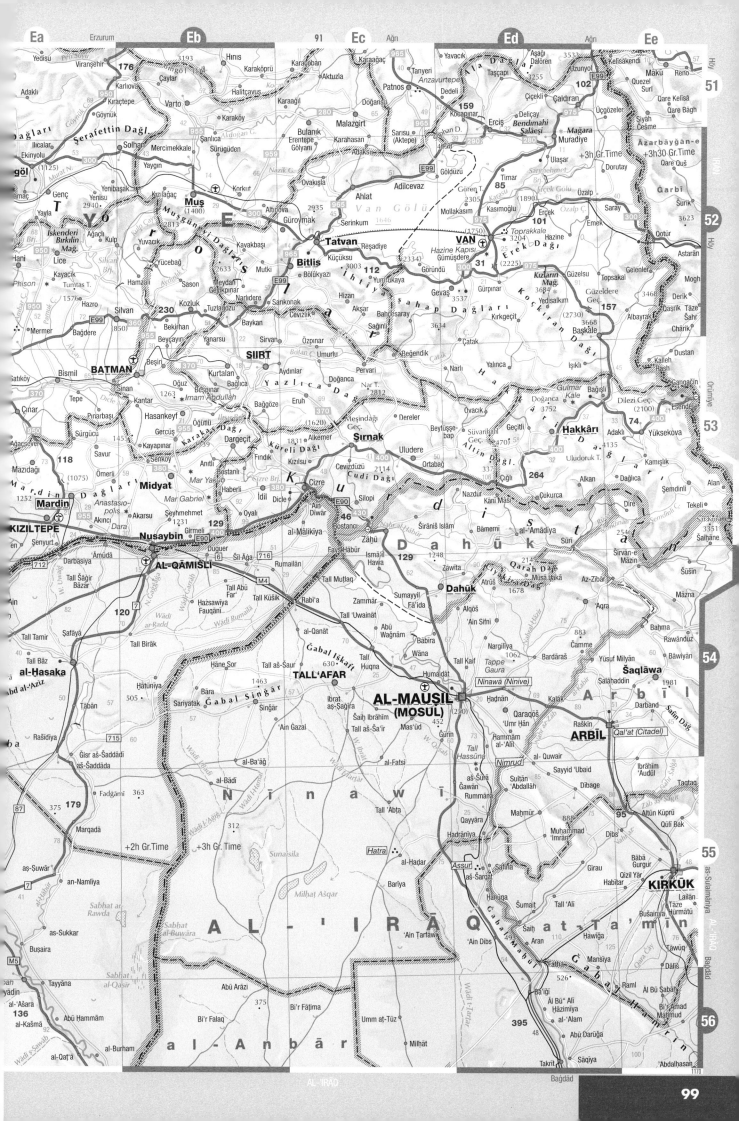

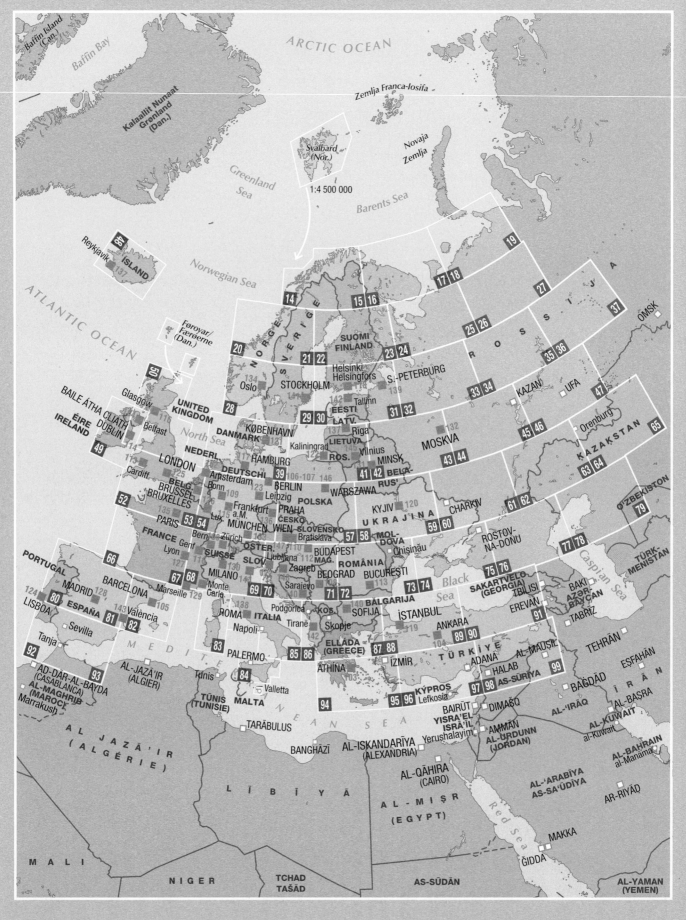

1:20 000

KLAD MAPOVÝCH LISTŮ   BLATTÜBERSICHT   KEY MAP   CARTE D'ASSEMBLAGE
QUADRO D' UNIONE   ÍNDICE DE MAPA   MAPA ÍNDICE   OVERZICHTSKAART
SKOROWIDZ ARKUSZY   KLAD MAPOVÝCH LISTOV   ÁTTEKINTŐTÉRKÉP   OVERSIGTSKORT

1 : 20 000

Zeichenerklärung Vysvětlivky (D)	Legend Objaśnienia znaków (GB)	Légende Objasit znakova (F)	Segni convenzionali Legenda (I)	Signos convencionales Jelmagyarázat (E)	Sinais convencionais Tegnforklaring (P)
Autobahn	Motorway	Autoroute	Autostrada	Autopista	Auto-estrada
Vierspurige Straße	Road with four lanes	Route à quatre voies	Strada a quattro corsie	Carretera de cuatro carriles	Estrada com quatro faixas
Durchgangsstraße	Thoroughfare	Route de transit	Strada di attraversamento	Carretera de tránsito	Estrada de trânsito
Hauptstraße	Main road	Route principale	Strada principale	Carretera principal	Estrada principal
Sonstige Straßen	Other roads	Autres routes	Altre strade	Otras carreteras	Outras estradas
Einbahnstaße - Fußgängerzone	One-way street - Pedestrian zone	Rue à sens unique - Zone piétonne	Via a senso unico - Zona pedonale	Calle de dirección única - Zona peatonal	Rua de sentido único - Zona de peões
Information - Parkplatz	Information - Parking place	Information - Parking	Informazioni - Parcheggio	Información - Aparcamiento	Informação - Parque de estacionamento
Hauptbahn mit Bahnhof	Main railway with station	Chemin de fer principal avec gare	Ferrovia principale con stazione	Ferrocarril principal con estación	Linha principal ferroviária com estação
Sonstige Bahn	Other railway	Autre ligne	Altra ferrovia	Otro ferrocarril	Linha ramal ferroviária
U-Bahn	Underground	Métro	Metropolitana	Metro	Metro
Straßenbahn	Tramway	Tramway	Tram	Tranvía	Eléctrico
Park+Ride	Park+Ride	Park+Ride	Park+Ride	Park+Ride	Park+Ride
Polizeistation - Postamt	Police station - Post office	Poste de police - Bureau de poste	Posto di polizia - Ufficio postale	Comisaria de policia - Correos	Esquadra da polícia - Correios
Krankenhaus - Jugendherberge	Hospital - Youth hostel	Hôpital - Auberge de jeunesse	Ospedale - Ostello della gioventù	Hospital - Albergue juvenil	Hospital - Pousada da juventude
Kirche	Church	Église	Chiesa	Iglesia	Igreja
Fernsehturm - Leuchtturm	TV tower - Lighthouse	Tour de télévision - Phare	Torre televisiva - Faro	Torre de televisión - Faro	
Denkmal - Turm	Monument - Tower	Monument - Tour	Monumento - Torre	Monumento - Torre	Monumento - Torre
Bebaute Fläche, öffentliches Gebäude	Built-up area, public building	Zone bâtie, bâtiment public	Caseggiato, edificio pubblico	Zona edificada, edificio público	Área urbana, edifício público
Industriegelände	Industrial area	Zone industrielle	Zona industriale	Zona industrial	Zona industrial
Park, Wald	Park, forest	Parc, bois	Parco, bosco	Parque, bosque	Parque, floresta

(CZ)	(PL)	(HR)	(SLO)	(H)	(DK)
Dálnice	Autostrada	Autocesta	Avtocesta	Autópálya	Motorvej
Čtyřstopá silnice	Droga o czterech pasach ruchu	Četiri traka ceste	Štiripasovna cesta	Négysávos út	Firesporet vej
Průjezdní silnice	Droga przelotowa	Prolaz	Tranzitna cesta	Átmenő út	Genemmfartsvej
Hlavní silnice	Droga główna	Glavna cesta	Glavna cesta	Főút	Hovedvej
Ostatní silnice	Drogi inne	Ostale ceste	Druge ceste	Egyéb utak	Andre mindre vejen
Jednosměrná ulice - Pěší zóna	Ulica jednokierunkowa - Strefa ruchu pieszego	Jednosmjerna ulica - Pješačka zona	Enosmerna cesta - Površine za pešce	Egyirányú utca - Sétáló utca	Gade med ensrettet kørsel - Gågade
Informace - Parkoviště	Informacja - Parking	Informacije - Parkiranje	Informacije - Parkirišče	Információ - Parkolóhely	Information - Parkeringplads
Hlavní železnice s stanice	Kolej główna z dworcami	Glavni željeznički kolodvor s	Glavna železniška proga z	Fővasútvonal állomással	Hovedjernbanelinie med station
Ostatní železnice	Kolej drugorzędna	Drugi vlak	Druga železniška proga	Egyéb vasútvonal	Anden jernbanelinie
Metro	Metro	Metro	Podzemska železnica	Földalatti vasút	Underjordisk bane
Tramvaj	Linia tramwajowa	Tramvaj	Tramvaj	Villamos	Sporvej
Park+Ride	Park+Ride	Park+Ride	Park+Ride	Park+Ride	Park+Ride
Policie - Poštovní úřad	Komisariat - Poczta	Policijska stanica - Pošta	Policijska postaja - Pošta	Rendőrség - Postahivatal	Politistation - Posthus
Nemocnice - Ubytovna mládeže	Szpital - Schronisko młodzieżowe	Bolnica - Hostel	Bolnišnica - Mladinski hotel	Kórház - Ifjúsági szálló	Sygehus - Vandrerhjem
Kostel	Kościół	Crkva	Cerkev	Templom	Kirke
Televizní věž - Maják	Wieża telewizyjna - Laternia morska	Televizijski toranj - Svjetionik	Televizijski stolp - Svetilnik	Vagy tévétorony - Világítótorony	Telemast - Fyrtårn
Pomník - Věž	Pomnik - Wieża	Spomenik - Kula	Spomenik - Stolp	Emlékmű - Torony	Mindesmærke - Tårn
Zastavěná plocha, veřejná budova	Obszar zabudowany, budynek użyteczności publicznej	Izgrađenom dijelu, Javna zgrada	Stanovanjske zgradbe, Javna zgradba	Beépítés, középület	Bebyggelse, offentlig bygning
Průmyslová plocha	Obszar przemysłowy	Poslovni park	Industrijske zgradbe	Iparvidék	Industriområde
Park, les	Park, las	Park, šuma	Park, gozd	Park, erdő	Park, skov

Ankara

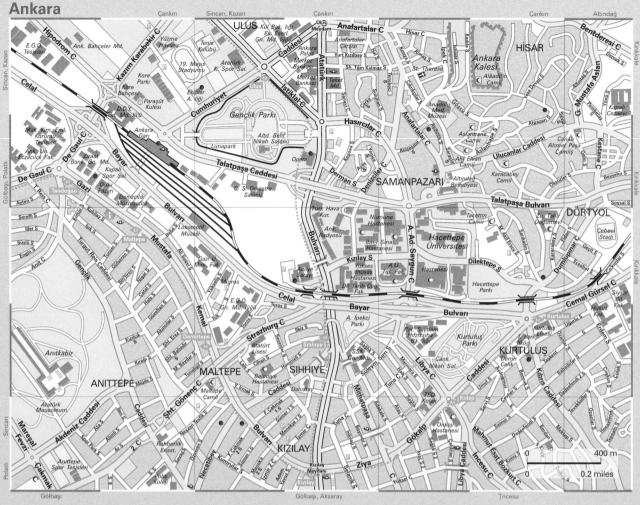

Belfast

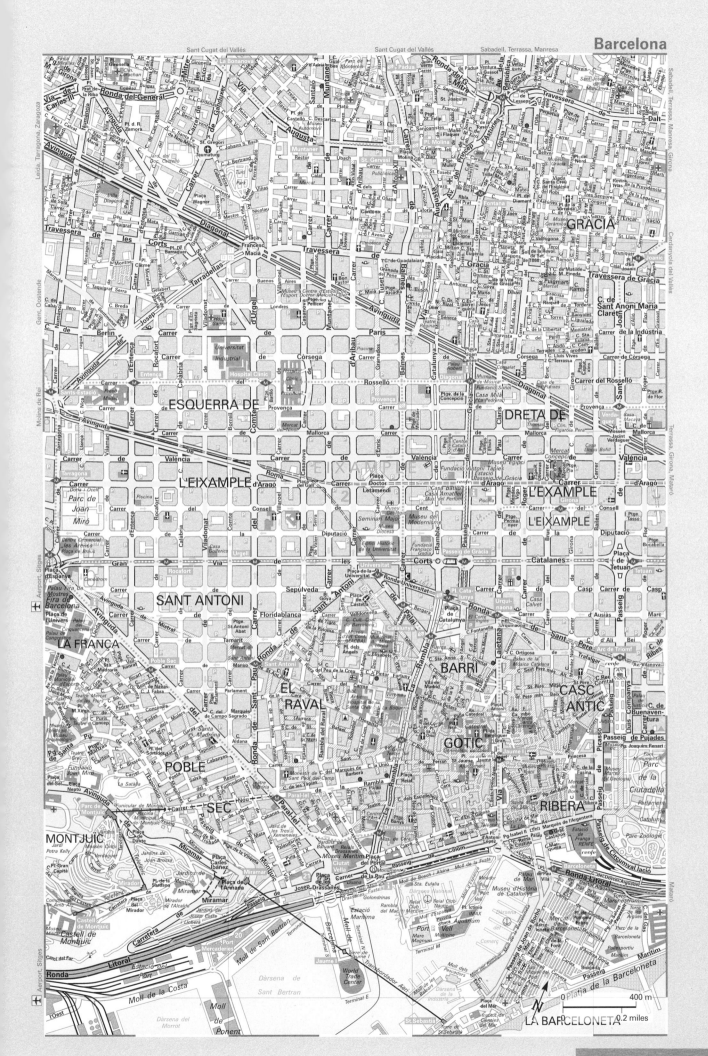

Beograd

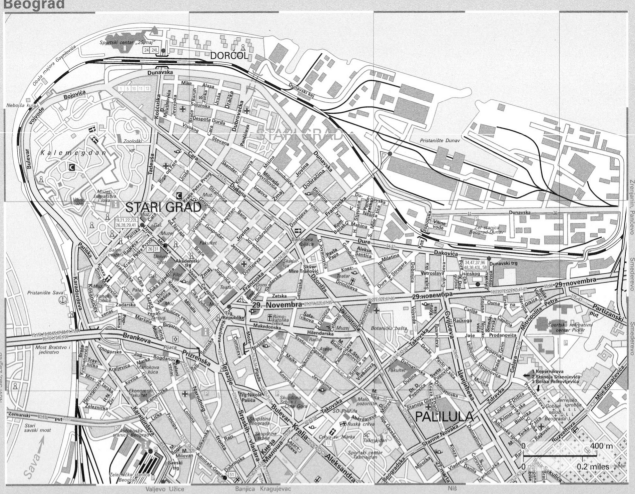

Bern

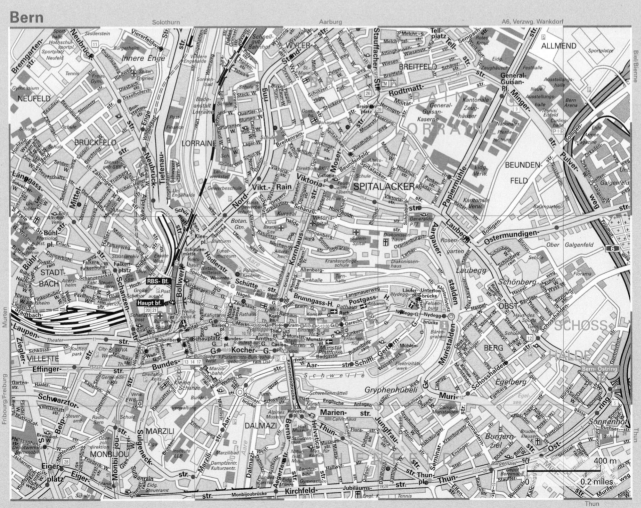

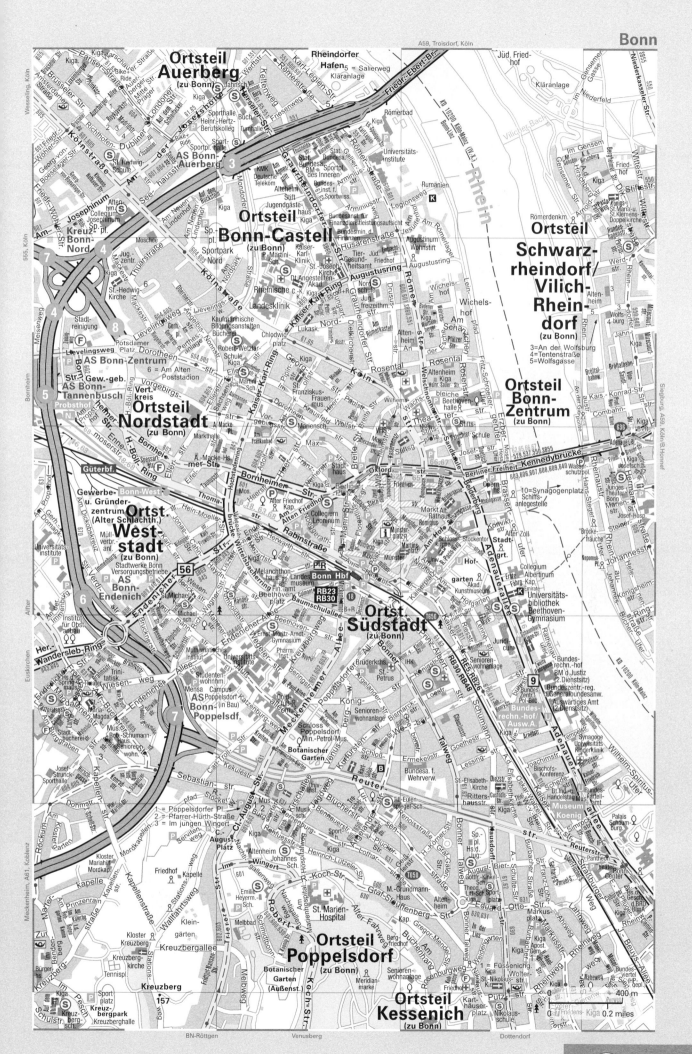

Bratislava

400 m

0.2 miles

Budapest

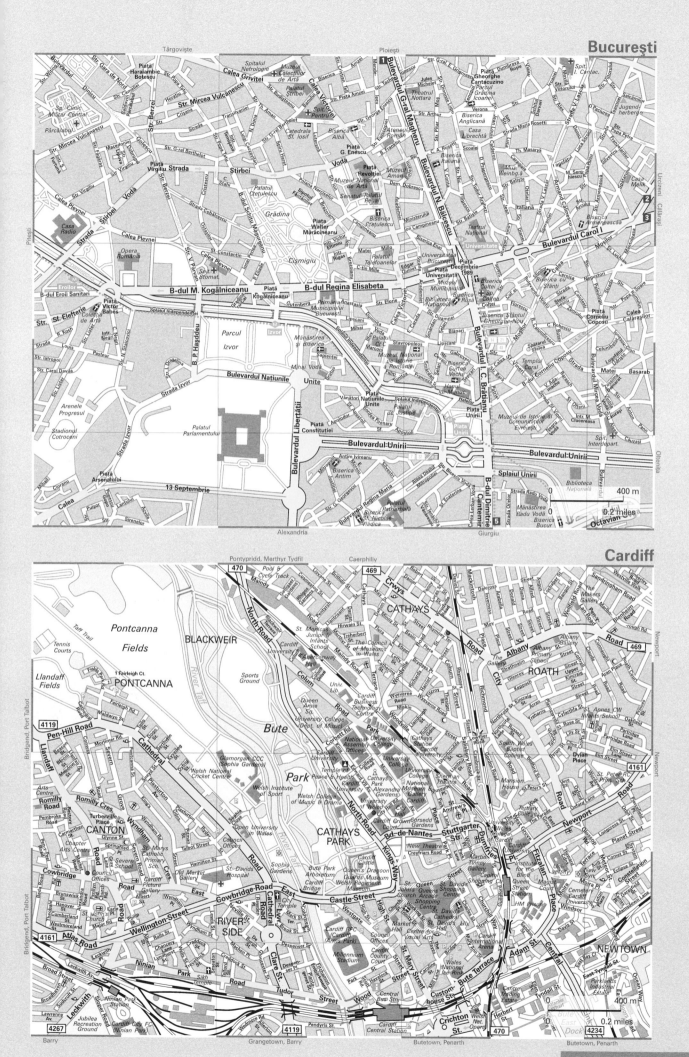

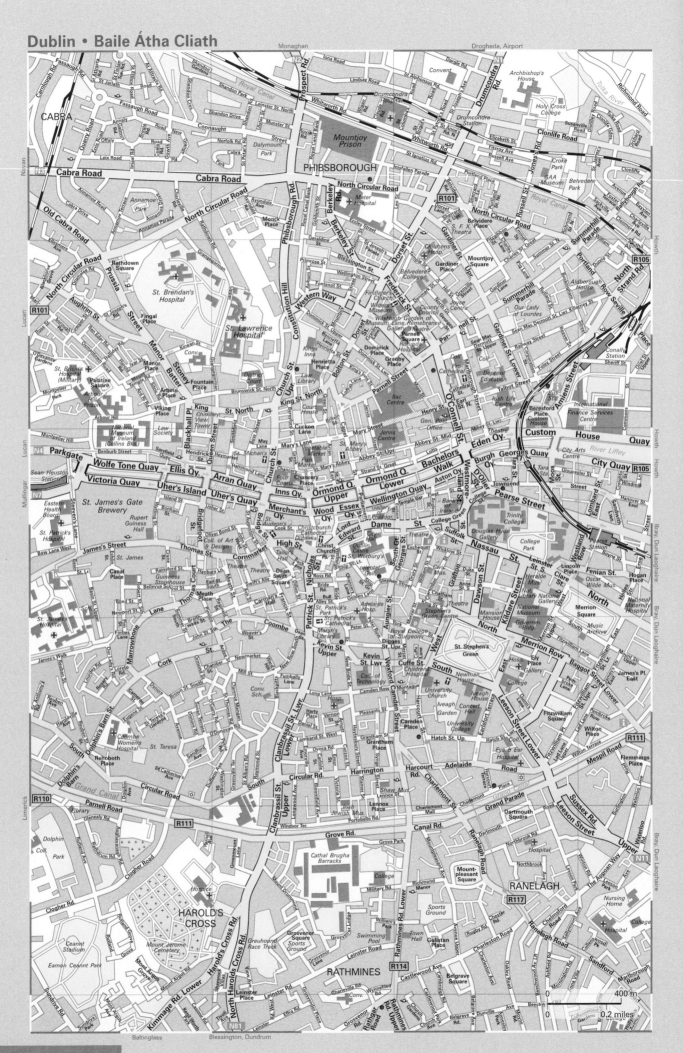

Dublin • Baile Átha Cliath

Genève

Glasgow

400 m
0.2 miles

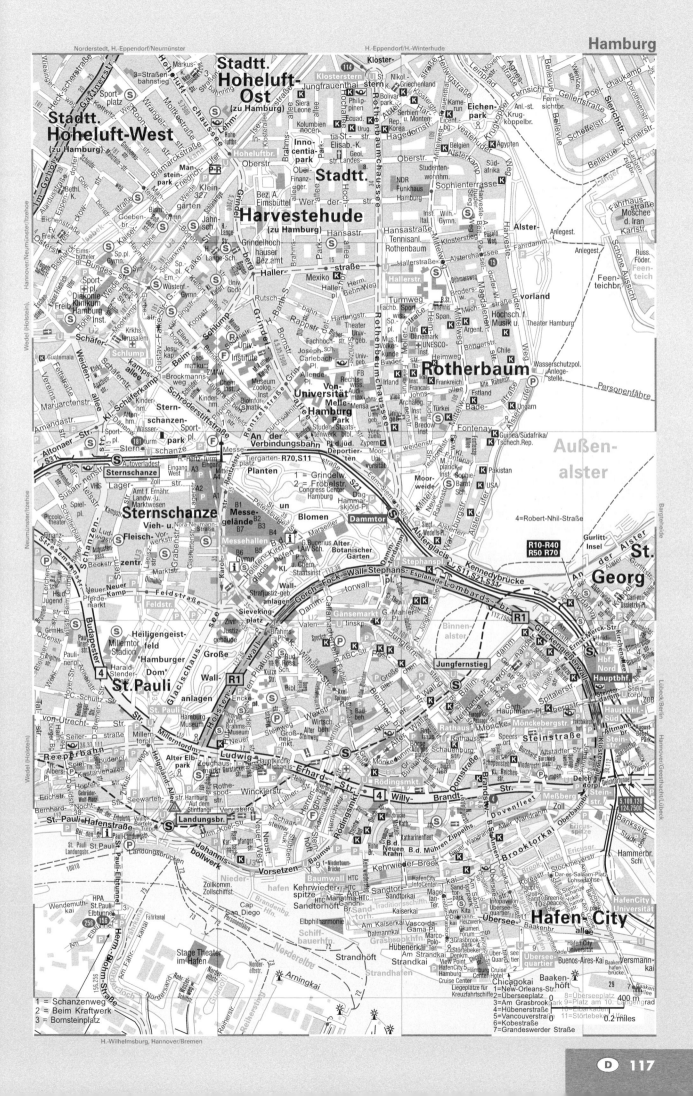

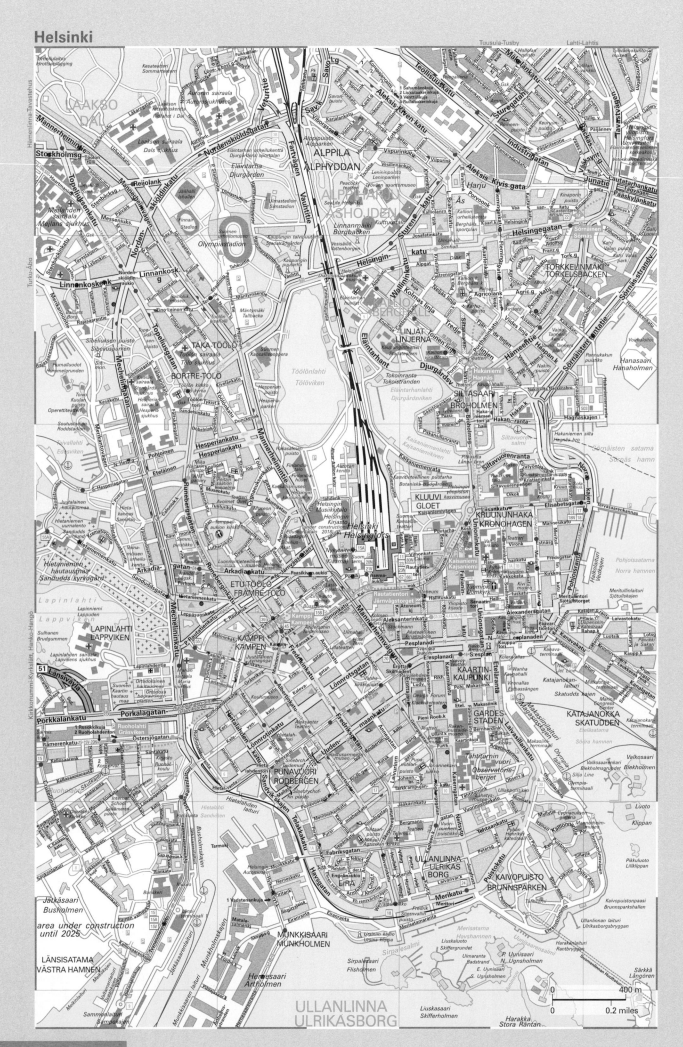

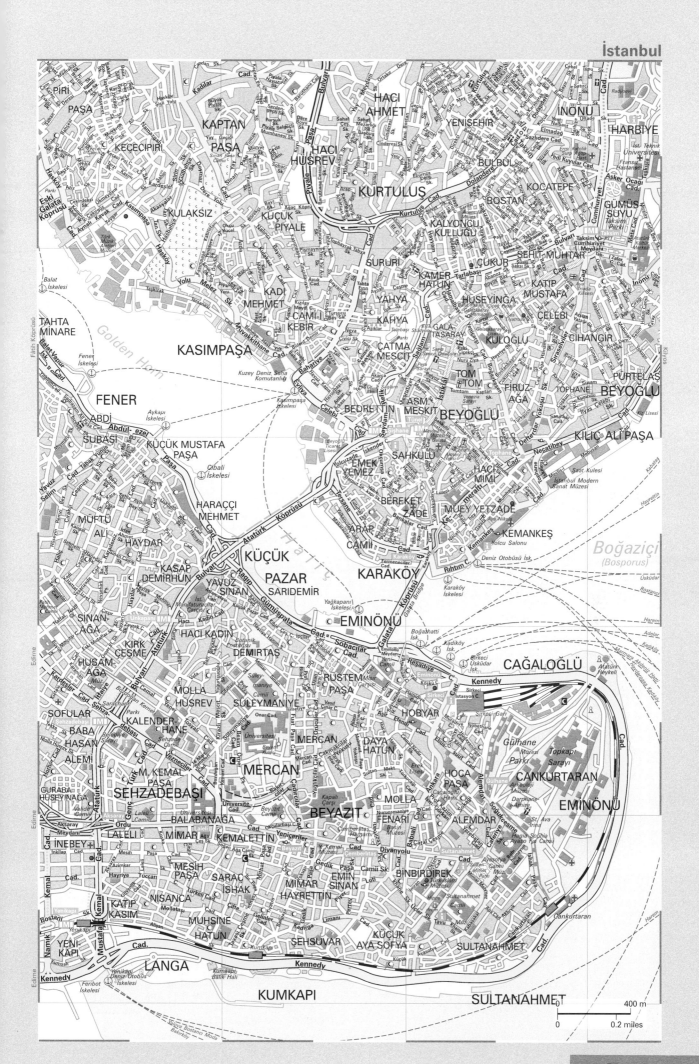

İstanbul

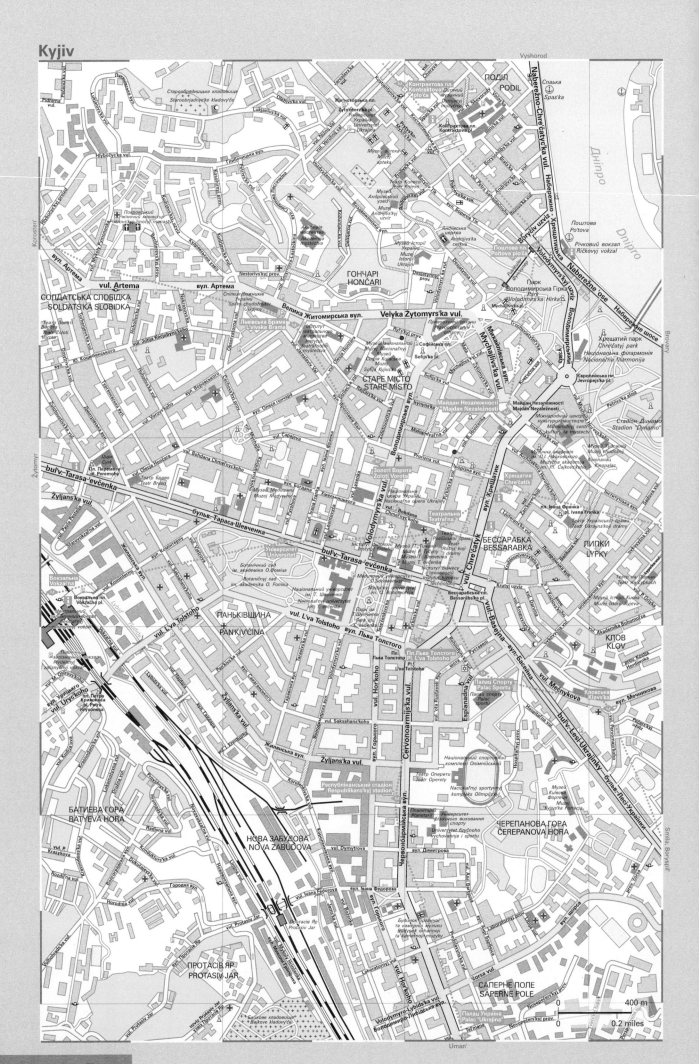

Kyjiv

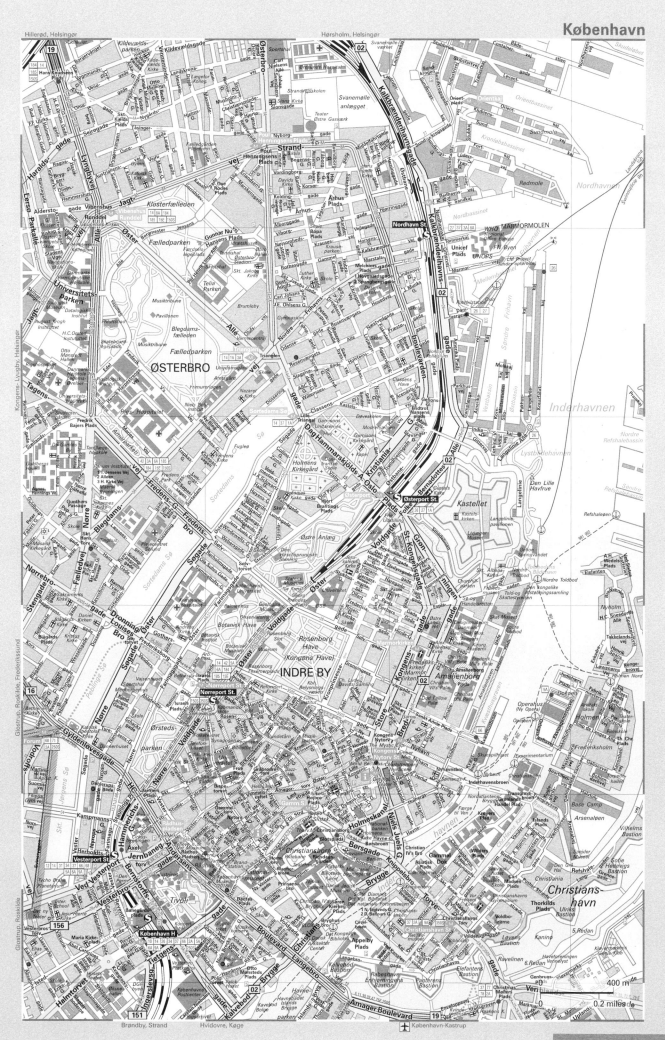

Kaliningrad

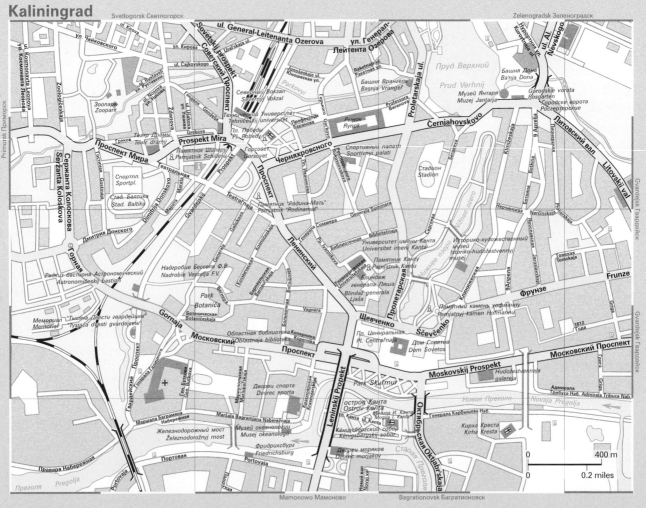

Ljubljana

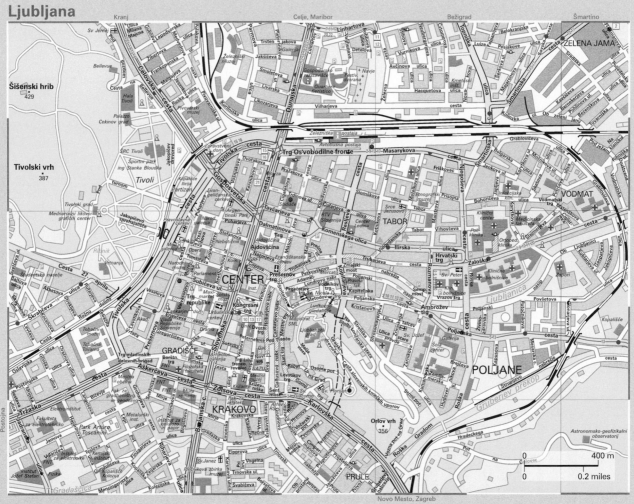

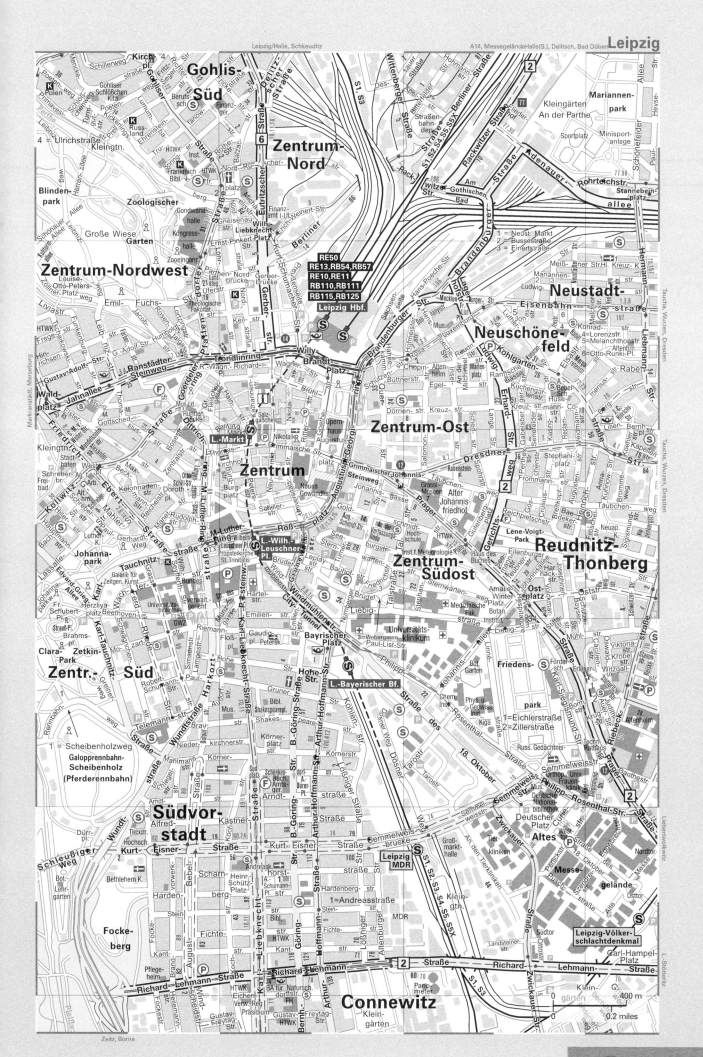

Aeroporto, Porto

FONTE DO LOURO

da Bela Vista

Centro Social

CHELAS

ARMADOR

OLAIAS

AREEIRO

CAMPO PEQUENO

PICHELEIRA

ARCO DO CEGO

SALDANHA

ALTO DO PINA

MADRE DE DEUS

ESTEFÂNIA

PENHA DE FRANÇA

BAIRRO LOPES

Parque Eduaardo VII

Marquês de Pombal

ANJOS

GRAÇA

CAMINHOS DE FERRO

ALFAMA

MOURARIA
Castelo de São Jorge

RESTAURADORES

ROSSIO

SOCORRO

Santa Apolónia

BAIRRO ALTO

Baixa-Chiado

CHIADO

SANTA CATARINA

Terreiro do Paço

BAIXA

Rio Tejo

Cais do Sodré

0		400 m
0		0.2 miles

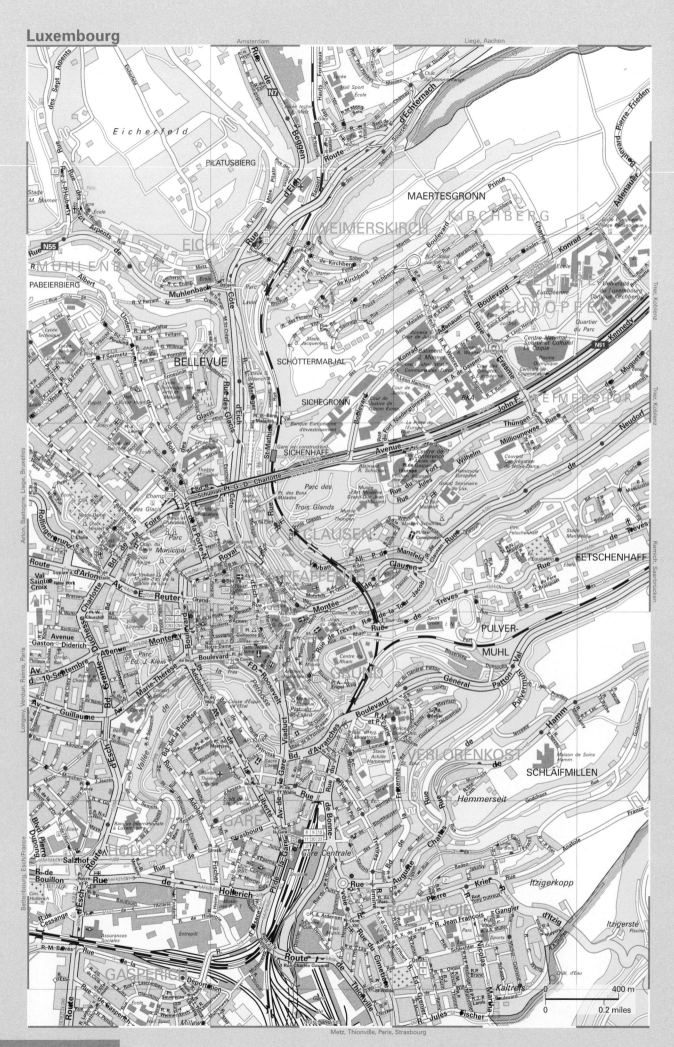

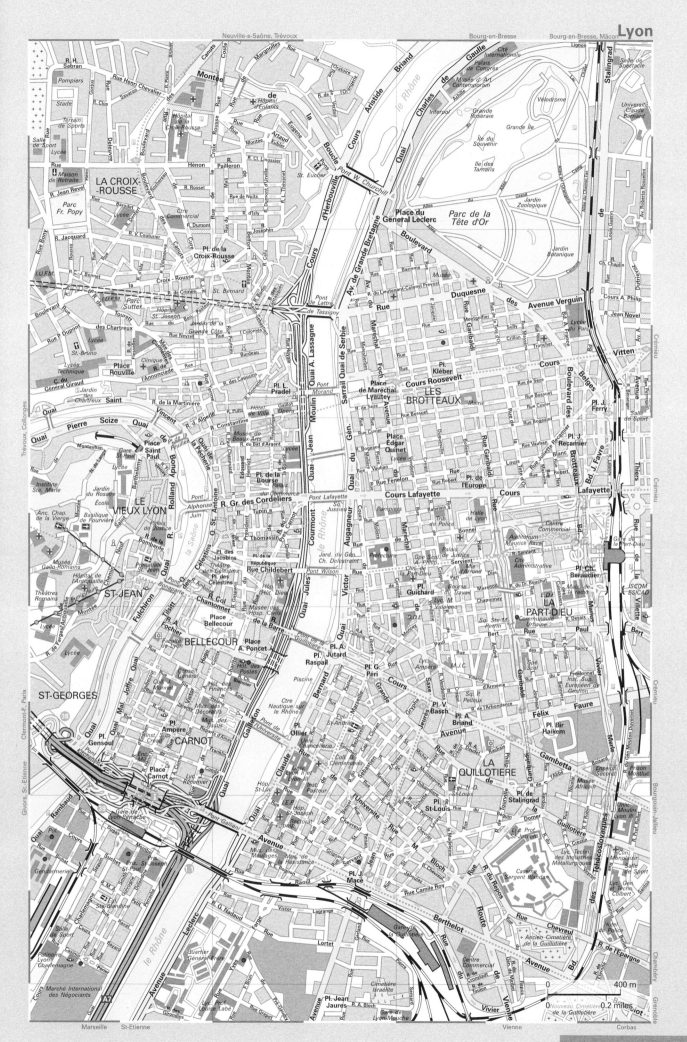

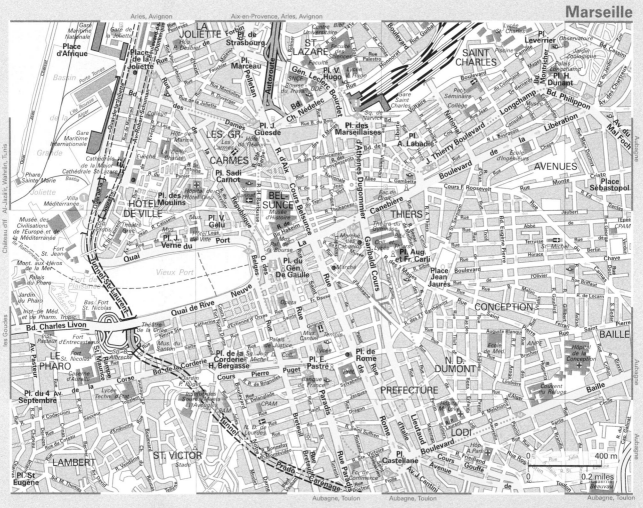

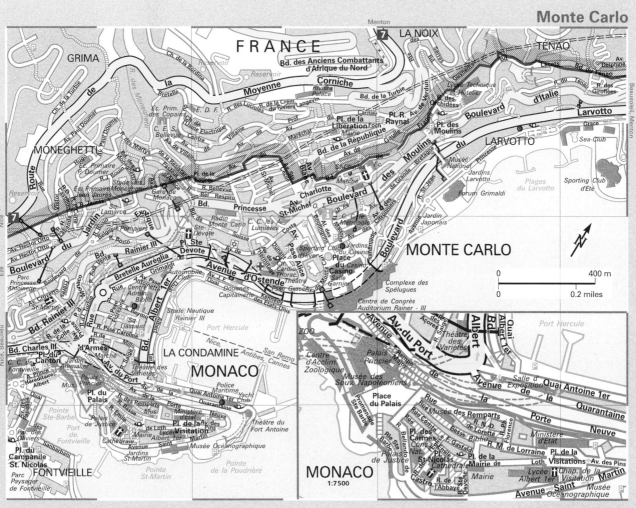

Minsk

Oslo

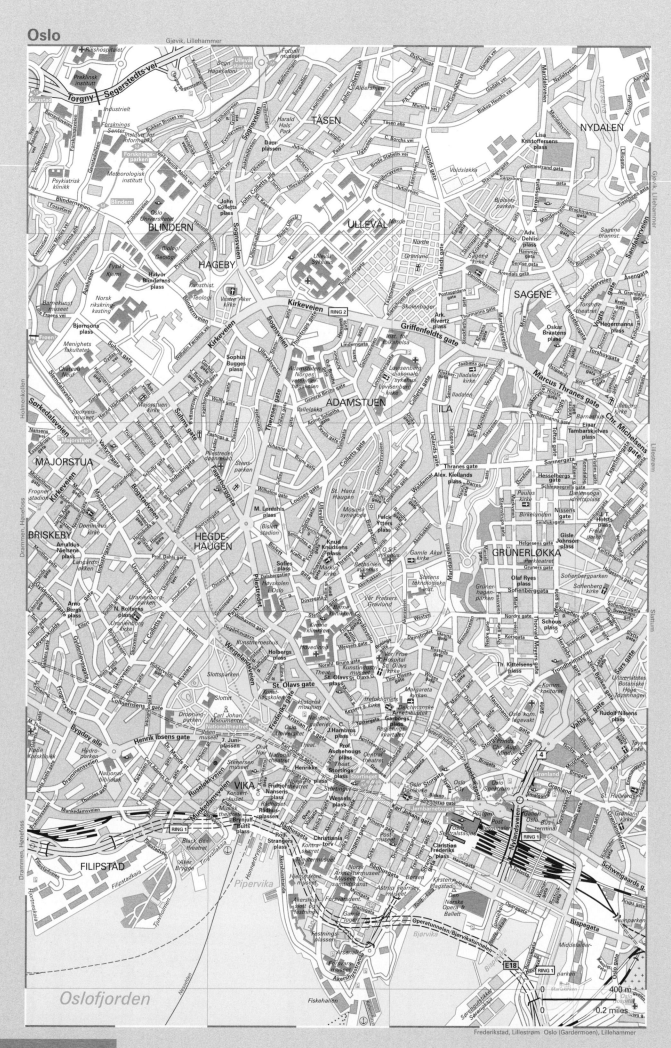

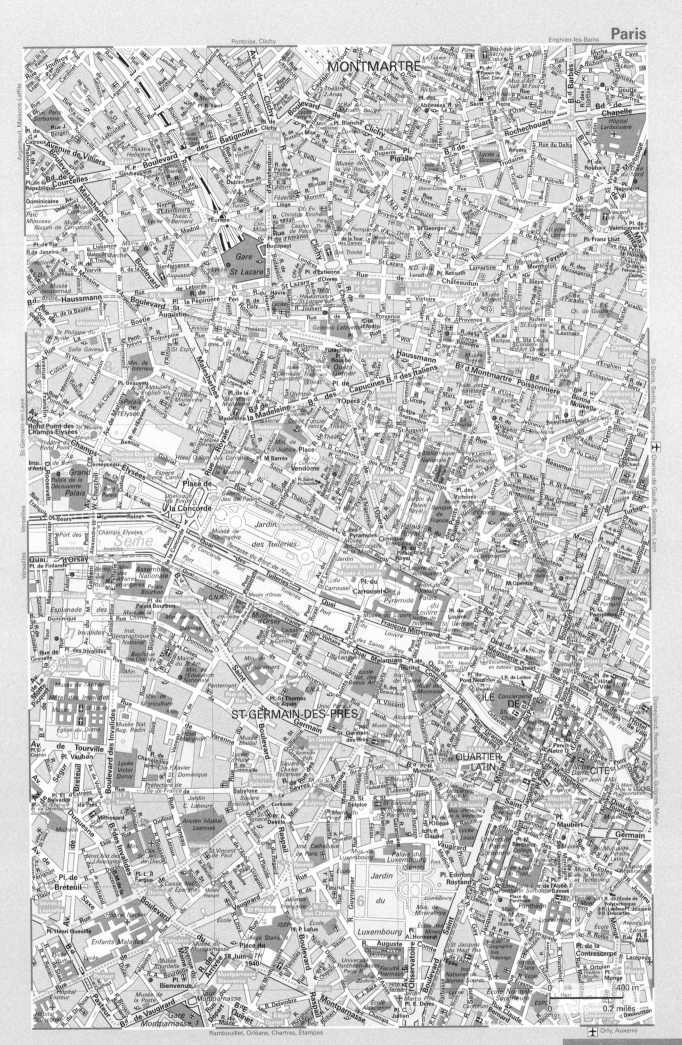

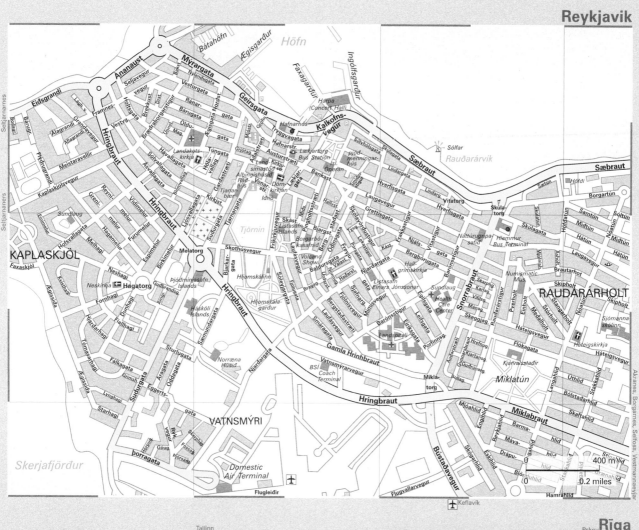

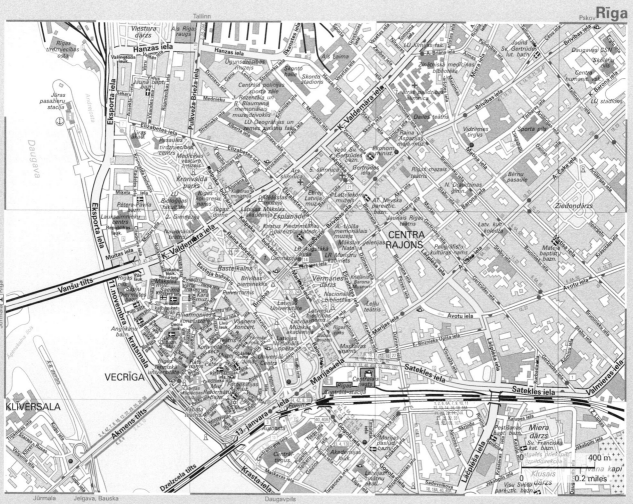

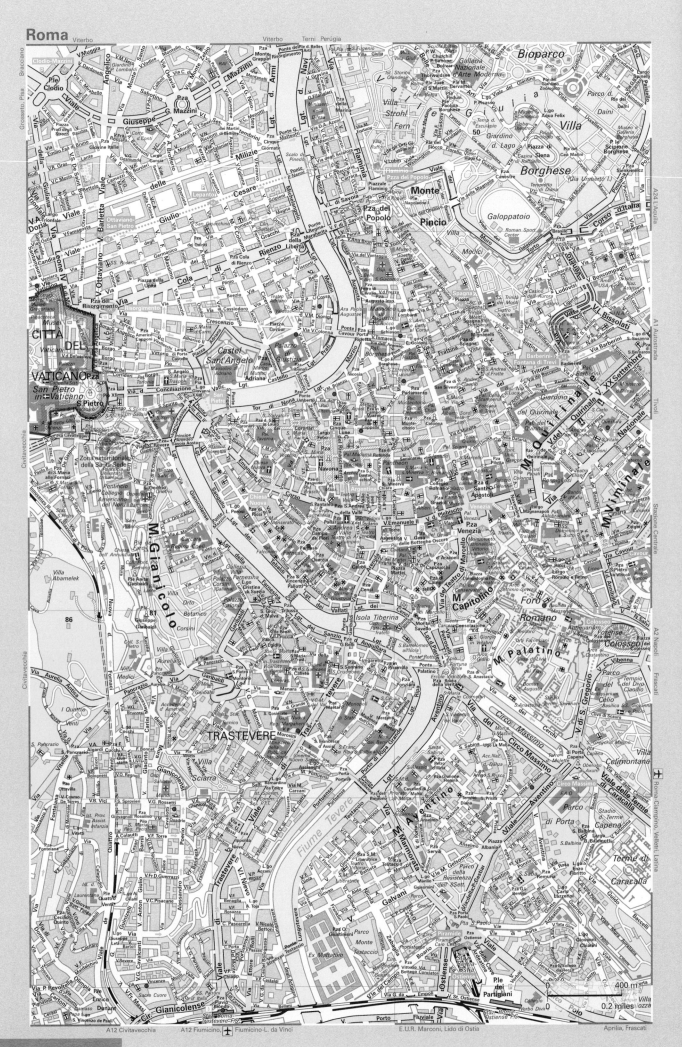

Roma

Sarajevo

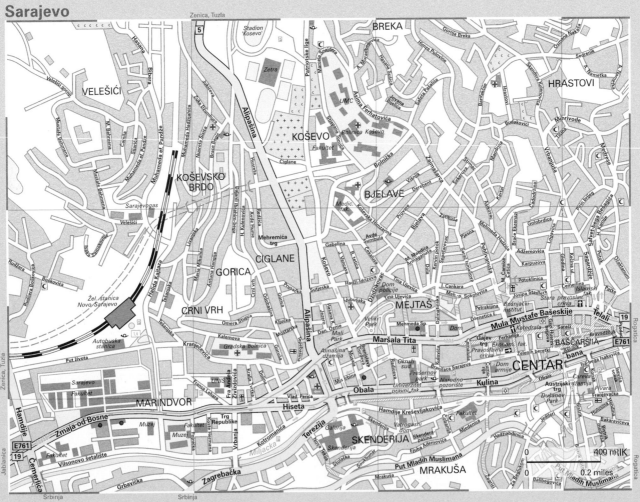

Sofija

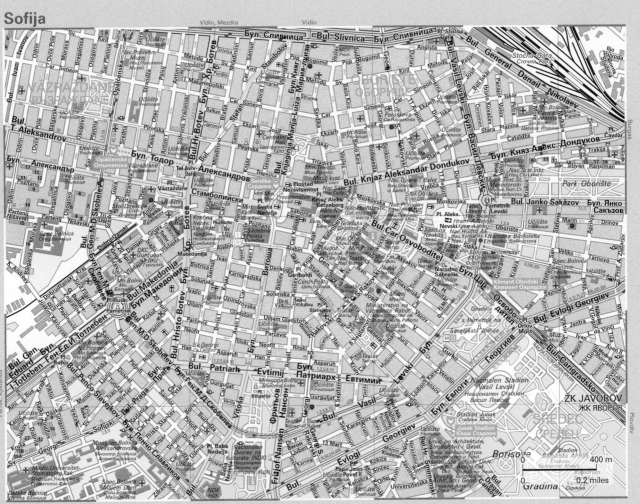

Tallinn

Tiranë

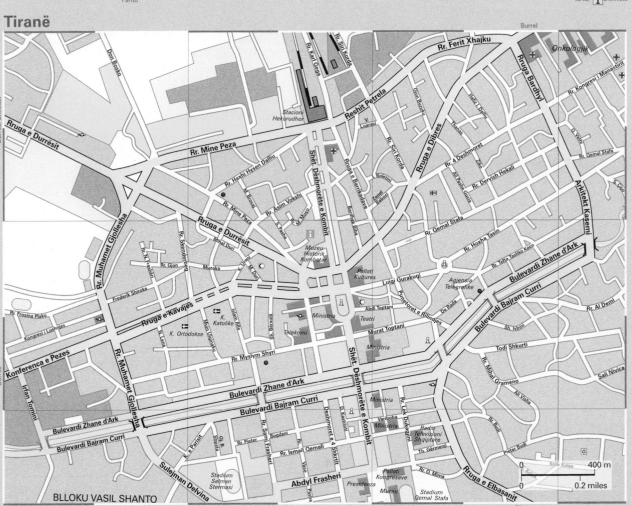

València

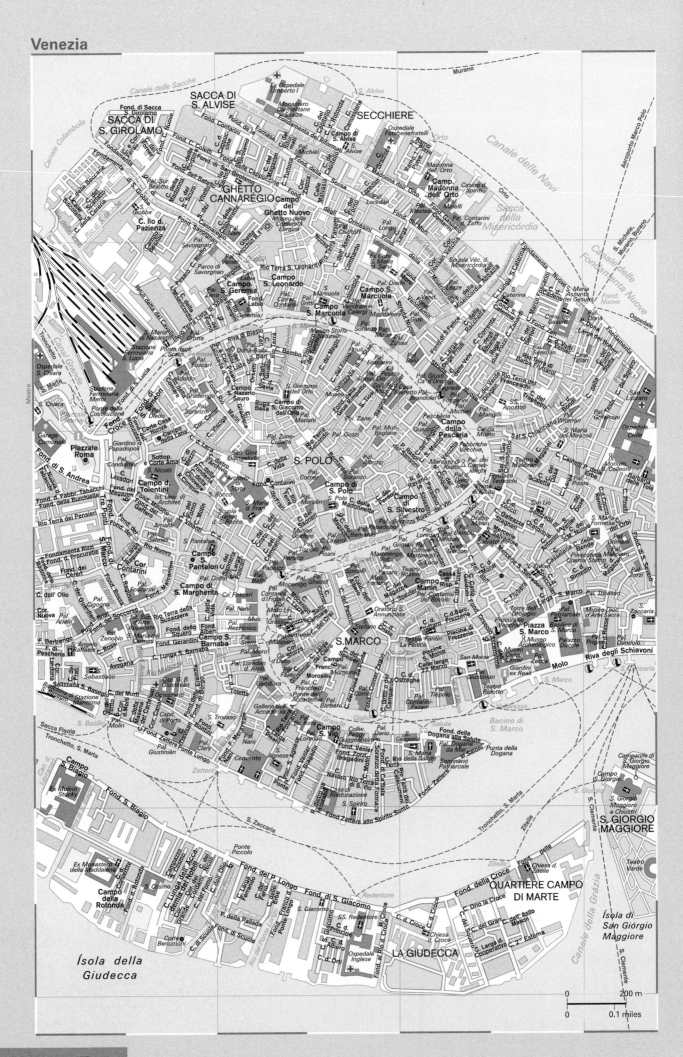

Zagreb

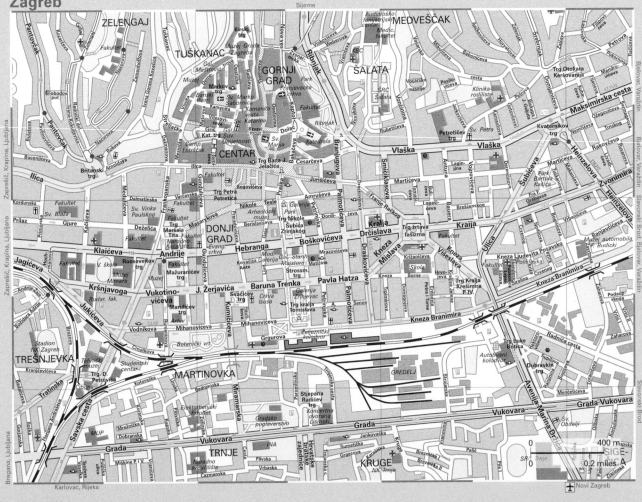

Zürich

Österreich (A)

■ 83 879 km² · 8 500 000 · Wien 1 800 000
+1h Gr. Time · GER · ☎ +43 · 1 Euro (EUR) = 100 Cent
Österreich Werbung Wien, +43 0800 40 02 00 00, www.austria.info

Belarus' (BY)

■ 207 595 km² · 9 500 000 · Minsk 1 900 000
+3h Gr. Time · BLR, RUS · ☎ +375
1 Rubel' (BYR) = 100 Kapejek
Nacional'noe agenstvo po turizmu NAT, +375 17 2 26-99 00, www.belarustourism.by

Danmark (DK)

■ 43 098 km² · 5 600 000 · København 570 000
+1h Gr. Time · DNK · ☎ +45 · 1 Krone (dkr) = 100 Øre
Visitdenmark, +45 32 88 99 00, www.visitdenmark.com

Shqipëria (Albania) (AL)

■ 28 748 km² · 2 800 000 · Tiranë 420 000
+1h Gr. Time · ALB · ☎ +355 · 1 Lek (ALL) = 100 Qindarka
National Tourist Organisation, +355 4 27 37 78

Schweiz · Suisse · Svizzera · Svizra (CH)

■ 41 285 km² · 8 100 000 · Bern 126 000
+1h Gr. Time · GER, FRA, ITA · ☎ +41
1 Franken (sfr) = 100 Rappen
Schweiz Tourismus, +41 800 10 02 00-29, www.myswitzerland.com

España (E)

■ 504 645 km² · 46 600 000 · Madrid 3 200 000
+1h Gr. Time · ESP · ☎ +34 · 1 Euro (EUR) = 100 Cent
Instituto de Turismo de España – Turespaña, +34 91 3 43 35 00, www.tourspain.es

Andorra (AND)

■ 468 km² · 79 000 · Andorra la Vella 22 500
+1h Gr. Time · CAT · ☎ +376 · 1 Euro (EUR) = 100 Cent
Ministeri de Turisme e Medi Ambient, +376 87 57 02, www.visitandorra.com

Kýpros (CY)

■ 58 966 km² · 885 041 · Lefkosia 276 400
+2h Gr. Time · GRC, TUR · ☎ +357
1 Euro (EUR) = 100 Cent
Kypriakós Organismós Tourismoú, +357 22 69 11 00, www.visitcyprus.com

Eesti (EST)

■ 45 227 km² · 1 300 000 · Tallinn 430 000
+2h Gr. Time · EST · ☎ +372 · 1 Euro (EUR) = 100 Cent
EAS Turismiarenduskeskus, +372 6 27 97 70, www.puhkaeestis.ee

België · Belgique (B)

■ 32 545 km² · 11 200 000 · Brussel (Bruxelles) 1 200 000 · +1h Gr. Time · NLD, FRA, GER · ☎ +32 · 1 Euro (EUR) = 100 Cent
Toerisme Vlaanderen, +32 2 5 04 03 00, www.toerismevlaanderen.be I Tourisme de Wallonie, +32 70 22 10 21, www.opt.be

Kuzey Kıbrıs (CY)

■ 3 355 km² · 294 906 · Lefkoşa 276 400
+3h Gr. Time · TUR · ☎ +90 392
1 Lira (TL) = 100 Kuruş
Nord Zypern Tourismus, +49 30 889 294 84, www.nordzypern-touristik.de

France (F)

■ 543 965 km² · 66 000 000 · Paris 2 200 000
+1h Gr. Time · FRA · ☎ +33 · 1 Euro (EUR) = 100 Cent
ATOUT France, +33 1 42 96 70 00, int.rendezvousenfrance.com

Bălgarija (BG)

■ 110 994 km² · 7 300 000 · Sofija 1 300 000
+2h Gr. Time · BGR · ☎ +359 · 1 Lew (Lw) = 100 Stotinki
Dăržavna Agencija po Turizăm, +359 2 9 33 58 11, www.bulgariatravel.org

Česko (CZ)

■ 78 866 km² · 10 500 000 · Praha 1 200 000
+1h Gr. Time · CSK · ☎ +420 · 1 Koruna (Kč) = 100 Haléřů
Česká centrála cestovního ruchu – CzechTourism, +420 221 58 01 11, www.czechtourism.com

Suomi · Finland (FIN)

■ 338 144 km² · 5 400 000 · Helsinki · Helsingfors 620 000 · +2h Gr. Time · FIN, SWE · ☎ +358
1 Euro (EUR) = 100 Cent
Visit Finland, +358 29 46 956 50, www.visitfinland.com

Bosna i Hercegovina (BIH)

■ 51 197 km² · 3 800 000 · Sarajevo 290 000
+1h Gr. Time · BIH, HRV, SRB · ☎ +387
1 Konvertibilna Marka (BAM) = 100 Feninga
Turistička zajednica Federacije B & H, +387 33 58 09 99, www.bhtourism.ba

Deutschland (D)

■ 357 168 km² · 80 700 000 · Berlin 3 400 000
+1h Gr. Time · GER · ☎ +49 · 1 Euro (EUR) = 100 Cent
Deutsche Zentrale für Tourismus e. V. (DZT), +49 69 97 46 40, www.deutschland-tourismus.de

Liechtenstein (FL)

■ 160 km² · 37 000 · Vaduz 5 372 · +1h Gr. Time · GER · ☎ +423 · 1 Euro (EUR) = 100 Cent
Liechtenstein Tourismus, +423 2 39 63 63, www.tourismus.li

United Kingdom (GB)

- 242 910 km² | 64 100 000 | London 8 400 000
- Gr. Time | GBR | ☎ +44 | 1 Pound Sterling (£) = 100 Pence
- Visit Britain, +44 020 75 78 10 00, www.visitbritain.com

Ísland (IS)

- 103 000 km² | 323 000 | Reykjavik 120 000
- –1h Gr. Time | ISL | ☎ +354 | 1 Króna (ikr) = (ehemals) 100 Aurar
- Skrifstofur Ferðamálastofu Ísland, +354 535 55 00, www.ferdamalastofa.is

Moldova (MD)

- 33 800 km² | 3 600 000 | Chişinău 674 500
- +2h Gr. Time | ROU | ☎ +373 | 1 Leu (MDL) = 100 Bani
- Agenţia Turismului a Republicii Moldova, +373 22 22 66 34, www.turism.gov.md

Elláda (Greece) (GR)

- 131 957 km² | 11 000 000 | Athína 665 000
- +2h Gr. Time | GRC | ☎ +30 | 1 Euro (EUR) = 100 Cent
- Greek National Tourism Organisation, +30 210 33 10 392, www.visitgreece.gr

Lëtzebuerg · Luxembourg (L)

- 2586 km² | 543 000 | Luxembourg 107 000
- +1h Gr. Time | GER, FRA, LUX | ☎ +352
- 1 Euro (EUR) = 100 Cent
- Office National du Tourisme, +352 42 82 82 10, www.visitluxembourg.com

Makedonija (F.Y.R.O.M.) (MK)

- 25 713 km² | 2 100 000 | Skopje 491 000
- +1h Gr. Time | MKD | ☎ +389 | 1 Denar (Den) = 100 Deni
- Exploring Macedonija, +389 230 80 111, www.exploringmacedonia.com

Magyarország (Hungary) (H)

- 93 030 km² | 9 900 000 | Budapest 1 700 000
- +1h Gr. Time | HUN | ☎ +36 | 1 Forint (Ft) = 100 Fillér
- Magyar Turizmus Zárt részvénytársaság, +36 1 4 48 87 00, www.itthon.hu

Lietuva (Lithuania) (LT)

- 65 301 km² | 3 000 000 | Vilnius 537 000
- +2h Gr. Time | LTU | ☎ +370 | 1 Euro (EUR) = 100 Cent
- Vilniaus Turizmo Informacijos Centras, +370 52 62 96 60, www.vilnius-tourism.lt

Crna Gora (Montenegro) (MNE)

- 13 812 km² | 625 000 | Podgorica 187 000
- +1h Gr. Time | MNE | ☎ +382 | 1 Euro (EUR) = 100 Cent
- Nacionalna turistička organizacija Crne Gore, +382 77 100 001, www.montenegro.travel

Hrvatska (Croatia) (HR)

- 56 542 km² | 4 200 000 | Zagreb 790 000
- +1h Gr. Time | HRV | ☎ +385 | 1 Kuna (kn) = 100 Lipa
- Croatian national tourist board, +385 1 46 99 333, www.croatia.hr

Latvija (LV)

- 65 589 km² | 2 000 000 | Rīga 700 000
- +2h Gr. Time | LVA | ☎ +371 | 1 Euro (EUR) = 100 Cent
- Latvijas Tūrisma attīstības valsts aģentūra, +371 67 22 99 45, www.latvia.travel

Norge (N)

- 323 759 km² | 5 100 000 | Oslo 624 463
- +1h Gr. Time | NOR | ☎ +47 | 1 Krone (nkr) = 100 Øre
- Innovasjon Norge, +47 22 00 25 00, www.visitnorway.com

Italia (I)

- 301 336 km² | 60 100 000 | Roma 2 800 000
- +1h Gr. Time | ITA | ☎ +39 | 1 Euro (EUR) = 100 Cent
- Agenzia nazionale del turismo ENIT, +39 06 49 711, www.enit.it

Malta (M)

- 316 km² | 423 000 | Valetta 7 650 | +1h Gr. Time | GBR, MLT | ☎ +356 | 1 Euro (EUR) = 100 Cent
- Malta Tourism Authority, +356 22 91 50 00, www.visitmalta.com

Nederland (NL)

- 41 526 km² | 16 800 000 | Amsterdam 810 937
- +1h Gr. Time | NLD | ☎ +31 | 1 Euro (EUR) = 100 Cent
- Koninklijke Nederlandse Toeristenbond (ANWB), +31 88 269 71 47, www.anwb.nl

Éire · Ireland (IRL)

- 70 273 km² | 4 600 000 | Baile · Dublin · Átha Cliath 525 000 | Gr. Time | GBR, IRL | ☎ +353
- 1 Euro (EUR) = 100 Cent
- Tourism Ireland, +353 1 8 84 77 00, www.tourismireland.com

Monaco (MC)

- 2 km² | 38 000 | Monaco Ville 1 100
- +1h Gr. Time | FRA | ☎ +377 | 1 Euro (EUR) = 100 Cent
- Direction du Tourisme et des Congres de la Principauté de Monaco, +377 92 16 61 16, www.visitmonaco.com

Portugal (P)

- 92 345 km² | 10 400 000 | Lisboa 547 700
- Gr. Time | PRT | ☎ +351 | 1 Euro (EUR) = 100 Cent
- Turismo de Portugal, +351 211 14 02 00, www.turismodeportugal.pt

Polska (PL)

■ 312 685 km² 38 500 000 ♔ Warszawa 1 700 000 ⏱ +1h Gr. Time POL ☎ +48
1 Złoty (Zł) = 100 Groszy
Polska Organizacja Turystyczna, +48 22 536 70 70, www.pot.gov.pl

Rossija (RUS)

■ 17 075 400 km² 143 500 000 ♔ Moskva 11 800 000 ⏱ +2h, 3h, 4h Gr. Time RUS ☎ +7
1 Rubl' (Rbl) = 100 Kopeek
Rossijskij nacional'nyj turističeskij ofis, +7 495 623 79 78, www.russia-travel.com

Srbija (SRB)

■ 77 474 km² 7 200 000 ♔ Beograd 1 200 000 ⏱ +1h Gr. Time SRB ☎ +381 1 Dinar (RSD) = 100 Para
Turistička organizacija Srbije, +381 11 6557 100, www.srbija.travel

Kosovë · Kosovo (RKS)

■ 10 887 km² 1 800 000 ♔ Prishtinë · Priština 207 000 ⏱ +1h Gr. Time ALB, SRB ☎ +381
1 Euro (EUR) = 100 Cent
Ministria e tregtisë dhe industrisë Departamenti i Turizmit, +381 38 200 36 042, www.mti-ks.org

Sverige (S)

■ 449 964 km² 9 600 000 ♔ Stockholm 897 700 ⏱ +1h Gr. Time SWE ☎ +46 1 Krone (skr) = 100 Øre
VisitSweden, +46 63 12 81 37, www.visitsweden.com

Türkiye (TR)

■ 779 452 km² 76 900 000 ♔ Ankara 5 100 000 ⏱ +2h Gr. Time TUR ☎ +90 1 Lira (TL) = 100 Kuruş
Türkiye Cumhuriyeti Kültür ve Turizm Bakanlığı, +90 312 309 08 50, www.kultur.gov.tr

România (RO)

■ 238 391 km² 20 000 000 ♔ Bucureşti 1 900 000 ⏱ +2h Gr. Time ROU ☎ +40 1 Leu (L) = 100 Bani
Autoritatea Nationala pentru Turism, +40 21 314 99 33, www.turism.gov.ro

Slovensko (SK)

■ 49 034 km² 5 400 000 ♔ Bratislava 417 400 ⏱ +1h Gr. Time SVK ☎ +421 1 Euro (EUR) = 100 Cent
Slovenská agentúra pre cestovný ruch, +421 48 413 61 46, www.sacr.sk

Ukrajina (UA)

■ 603 700 km² 45 500 000 ♔ Kyïv 2 800 000 ⏱ +2h Gr. Time UKR, RUS ☎ +380
1 Hryvnja (UAH) = 100 Kopiyok
International Travel Agency „Ukraine-Rus‴, +380 44 483 23 74, www.ukraine-rus.kiev.ua

San Marino (RSM)

■ 61 km² 31 000 ♔ San Marino 4 124 ⏱ +1h Gr. Time ITA ☎ +378 1 Euro (EUR) = 100 Cent
Ufficio di Stato per il Turismo, +378 549 88 29 14, www.visitsanmarino.com

Slovenija (SLO)

■ 20 253 km² 2 100 000 ♔ Ljubljana 227 554 ⏱ +1h Gr. Time SVN ☎ +386 1 Euro (EUR) = 100 Cent
Slovenska turistična organizacija, +386 1 589 85 50, www.slovenia.info

Civitas Vaticana · Città del Vaticano (V)

■ 0,44 km² 842 ♔ Vatikanstadt 842 ⏱ +1h Gr. Time ITA, LAT ☎ +39 1 Euro (EUR) = 100 Cent
Ufficio Informazioni Pellegrini e Turisti, +39 06 69 88 23 50, www.vaticanstate.va

		🚓	✚☎	SOS	🛣️	%‰	🚗	🦺	🚗⚠	🔧📱
A		112	112	112	✓ Vignette	0,5‰	✓	✓	✓	120 ÖAMTC
AL		129	127	128	✗	0,1‰	✗	✓	✓	+355 42 262 263 ACA
AND		110	116	118	✗	0,5‰	✗	✗	✓	+376 80 34 00 Automòbil Club d'Andorra
B		101	112	100	✗	0,5‰	✗	✓	✓	+32 70 34 47 77 Touring Club Belgium
BG		166	150	160	✓ Vignette	0,5‰	✓	✓	✓	+359 2 911 46 Union of Bulgarian Motorists
BIH		122	124	123	✓	0,3‰	✓	✓	✓	+387 33 12 82 BIHAMK
BY		02	03	01	✓	0,0‰	✓	✓	✓	116 BKA
CH		112/117	112/144	112/118	✓ Vignette	0,5‰	✓	✗	✓	0800 140 140 TCS
CY		112	112	112	✗	0,5‰	✗	✓	✓	22 31 31 31 CAA
Kıbrıs		155	112	199	✗	0,0‰	✗	✗	✓	22 31 31 31 CAA
CZ		112	112	112	✓ Vignette	0,0‰	✓	✓	✓	12 30 ÚAMK
D		110	112	112	✗	0,5‰	✗	✓	✓	22 22 22 ADAC
DK		112	112	112	✗	0,5‰	✓	✗	✓	+45 70 13 30 40 FDM
E		112	112	112	✓	0,5‰	✗	✓	✓	+34 900 11 22 22 RACE
EST		110/112	112	112	✗	0,2‰	✓	✓	✓	1888 EAK
F		112/17	112/17	112/18	✓	0,5‰	✗	✓	✓	0800 08 92 22 AIT
FIN		112	112	112	✗	0,5‰	✓	✓	✓	0200 80 80 AL
FL		117	144	118	✗	0,8‰	✗	✗	✓	0800 140 140 TCS
FO		112	112	112	✗	0,5‰	✓	✗	✓	+45 70 13 30 40 FDM
GB		112	112	112	✗	0,8‰	✗	✗	✓	0800 82 82 82 RAC
GBZ		199	199	190	✗	0,5‰	✗	✓	✓	+34 900 11 22 22 RACE
GR		112/100	112/166	112/199	✓	0,5‰	✗	✗	✓	10 400 ELPHA
H		112/107	112/104	112/105	✓ Vignette	0,0‰	✓	✓	✓	188 MAK
HR		112/192	112/94	112/93	✓	0,5‰	✓	✓	✓	+385 1 1987 HAK
I		112	112	112	✓	0,5‰	✓	✓	✓	803 116 ACI

		🚓	✚📞	SOS	🛣️	🍷‰	🚗	🦺	🚗📞	🔧📱
IRL		112	112	112	✗	0,5‰	✗	✗	✓	1800 66 77 88 AA
IS		112	112	112	✗	0,5‰	✓	✗	✓	+354 511 21 12 FIB
L		112/113	112	112	✗	0,5‰	✗	✓	✓	+352 260 00 ACL
LT		112	112	112	✗	0,4‰	✓	✓	✓	1888 LAS
LV		112	112	112	✗	0,5‰	✓	✓	✓	1888 LAMB
M		112	112	112	✗	0,8‰	✗	✓	✓	+356 21 24 22 22 RMF
MC		112	112	112	✗	0,5‰	✗	✓	✓	0800 08 92 22 AIT
MD		902	903	901	✗	0,0‰	✓ XI–III	✓	✓	+373 6 91 43 724 ACM
MK		192	194	193	✓	0,5‰	✓	✓	✓	196 AMSM
MNE		112	112	112	✗	0,3‰	✓	✓	✓	+382 198 07 AMSCG
N		112	113	110	✗	0,2‰	✓	✓	✓	08 505 NAF
NL		112	112	112	✓ Vignette	0,5‰	✗	✗	✓	+31 88 269 28 88 ANWB
P		112	112	112	✓	0,5‰	✗	✓	✓	707 509 510 ACP
PL		112	112	112	✓	0,2‰	✓	✗	✓	19637 PZM
RKS		92	94	93	✗	0,5‰	✓	✗	✓	+385 1 1987 HAK
RO		112	112	112	✓	0,0‰	✓	✓ Fahrzeuge > 3,5 t	✓	+40 21 222 22 22 ACR
RSM		112	112	112	✗	0,5‰	✓	✓	✓	803 116 ACI
RUS		02	03	01	✗	0,0‰	✓	✗	✓	8 800 505 08 66 AKAR
S		112	112	112	✗	0,2‰	✓	✓	✓	+46 771 91 11 11 M
SK		112	112	112	✓	0,0‰	✓	✓	✓	18 124 SATC
SLO		112	112	112	✓ Vignette	0,5‰	✓	✓	✓	19 87 AMZS
SRB		92	94	93	✓	0,3‰	✓	✓	✓	1987 AMSS
TR		155	112	110	✓	0,5‰	✗	✗	✓	+90 212 3 47 90 45 TTOK
UA		02	03	01	✗	0,0‰	✓	✓	✓	+380 9 76 68 38 30 112UA
V		112	118	115	✗	0,5‰	✓	✓	✓	803 116 ACI

km/h	🏍				🚗				🚗🚐			
A	50	100	100	130	50	100	100	130	50	70 100	80 100	80 100
AL	40	80	90	110	40	80	90	110	35	70	70	80
AND	50	90	–	–	50	90	–	–	50	90	–	–
B	50	90	120	120	50	90	120	120	50	90	120	120
BG	50	80	80	100	50	90	90	130	50	70	70	100
BIH	50	80	100	130	50	80	100	130	50	80	80	80
BY	60	90	90	110	60	90	90	110	60	70	70	90
CH	50	80	100	120	50	80	100	120	50	80	80	80
CY	50	65	80	100	50	65	80	100	50	65	80	100
Kıbrıs	45	65	100	–	45	65	100	–	45	65	100	–
CZ	50	90	130	130	50	90	130	130	50	80	80	80
D	50	100	130	130	50	100	130	130	50	80	80	80 100
DK	50	80	80	130	50	80	80	130	50	70	70	80
E	50	90	100	120	50	90	100	120	50	70	80	80 90
EST	50	90	100 120	–	50	90	100 120	–	50	70	90	–
F	50	90	110	130	50	90	110	130	50	90	110	130
FIN	50	80 100	100	120	50	80 100	100	120	50	80	80	80
FL	50	80	100	–	50	80	100	–	50	80	80	–
FO	50	80	–	–	50	80	–	–	50	80	–	–
GB	48	96	112	112	48	96	112	112	48	80	96	96
GBZ	50	–	–	–	50	–	–	–	50	–	–	–
GR	40	70	70	90	50	90	110	130	50	80	80	80
H	50	90	110	130	50	90	110	130	50	70	70	80
HR	50	90	110	130	50	90	110	130	50	80	80	90
I	50	90	110	130	50	90	110	130	50	70	80	80

🚐				🚌				🚚				
50	70	70	80	50	80	80	100	50	70	70	80	(A)
35	70	70	80	35	60	70	80	35	60	70	80	(AL)
50	80	–	–	50	80	–	–	50	70	–	–	(AND)
50	90	90	90	50	75	90	90	50	60	90	90	(B)
50	70	70	100	50	80	80	100	50	70	80	100	(BG)
50	80	80	80	50	80	80	100	50	80	80	100	(BIH)
60	70	70	90	60	70	70	90	60	70	70	90	(BY)
50	80	70	100	50	80	100	100	50	80	80	80	(CH)
50	65	80	100	50	65	80	100	50	65	80	100	(CY)
45	65	100	–	45	65	100	–	45	65	100	–	Kıbrıs
50	80	80	80	50	90	100	100	50	80	80	80	(CZ)
50	60	80	100	50	80	80	100	50	60	80	80	(D)
50	70	80	80	50	80	80	80	50	70	70	80	(DK)
50	80	90	100	50	80	90	100	50	70	80	90	(E)
50	70	90	–	50	70	70	–	50	70	70	–	(EST)
50	80	100	110	50	90	90	90	50	80	80	80	(F)
50	80	80	80	50	80	80	80	50	80	80	80	(FIN)
50	80	100	–	50	80	90	–	50	80	80	–	(FL)
50	80	–	–	50	80	–	–	50	80	–	–	(FO)
48	80	96	112	48	80	96	112	48	64	80	96	(GB)
50	–	–	–	50	–	–	–	50	–	–	–	(GBZ)
50	80	80	80	50	80	80	90	50	80	80	80	(GR)
50	70	70	80	50	70	70	100	50	70	70	80	(H)
50	80	80	90	50	80	80	100	50	70	70	70	(HR)
50	80	80	100	50	80	80	100	50	70	70	80	(I)

km/h	🏍				🚗				🚗🚐			
	🏘	🌲	🛣	🛤	🏘	🌲	🛣	🛤	🏘	🌲	🛣	🛤
IRL	50	80	60 100	120	50	80	60 100	120	50	80	60 80	80
IS	50	80 90	90	–	50	80 90	90	–	50	80	80	–
L	50	90	90	130	50	90	90	130	50	75	75	90
LT	50	70 90	100 110	110 130	50	70 90	100 110	110 130	50	70 90	90	90
LV	20 50	90	90 110	–	20 50	90	90 110	–	20 50	80	90	–
M	50	80	–	–	50	80	–	–	50	80	–	–
MC	50	–	–	–	50	–	–	–	50	–	–	–
MD	60	90	110	–	60	90	110	–	50	90	90	–
MK	50	80	100	120	50	80	100	120	50	80	80	80
MNE	50	80	100	–	50	80	100	–	50	80	80	–
N	50	80	90 100	90 100	50	80	90 100	90 100	50	80	80	80
NL	50	80	100	130	50	80	100	130	50	80	90	90
P	50	90	100	120	50	90	100	120	50	70	80	100
PL	50 60	90	100 120	140	50 60	90	100 120	140	50 60	70	80	80
RKS	50	80	110	130	50	80	110	130	50	80	80	80
RO	50	90	100	130	50	90	100	130	50	70	80	90
RSM	50	90	–	–	50	90	–	–	50	70	–	–
RUS	60	90	90	110	60	90	90	110	60	70	70	90
S	30 60	70 100	90 110	110 120	30 60	70 100	90 110	110 120	30 60	80	80	80
SK	50	90	90	130	50	90	90	130	50	90	90	90
SLO	50	90	100	130	50	90	100	130	50	80	80	80
SRB	50	80	100	120	50	80	100	120	50	80	80	80
TR	50	70	70	80	50	90	90	120	40	80	70 80	80 110
UA	60	80	80	80	60	90	110	130	60	80	80	80
V	30	–	–	–	30	–	–	–	30	–	–	–

🚐				🚌				🚚				
50	80	60 80	80	50	80	60 80	80	50	80	60 80	80	IRL
50	80 90	90	–	50	80	90	–	50	80	80	–	IS
50	75	75	90	50	75	70	90	50	70	70	90	L
50	70 90	80	90	50	70	70	100	50	70	80	90	LT
20 50	90	90 100	–	20 50	90	90	–	20 50	80	80	–	LV
50	80	–	–	50	80	–	–	50	80	–	–	M
50	–	–	–	50	–	–	–	50	–	–	–	MC
50	70	90	–	50	90	90	–	50	70	70	–	MD
50	80	80	80	50	80	80	80	50	70	70	70	MK
50	80	80	–	50	80	80	–	50	80	80	–	MNE
50	80	80	80	50	80	80	80	50	80	80	80	N
50	80	80	80	50	80	80	100	50	80	80	80	NL
50	80	90	110	50	80	90	90	50	80	80	80	P
50 60	70	80	80	50 60	70	80	80	50 60	70	80	80	PL
50	80	110	130	50	80	80	80	50	70	70	80	RKS
50	80	90	110	50	80	90	110	50	70	80	90	RO
50	80	–	–	50	80	–	–	50	70	–	–	RSM
60	70	70	90	60	90	90	90	60	70	70	90	RUS
30 60	80	80	110 120	30 60	90	90	100	30 60	70	80	90	S
50	80	80	80	50	90	90	100	50	80	80	80	SK
50	80	80	80	50	80	100	100	50	70	70	70	SLO
50	80	80	80	50	80	80	100	50	70	70	70	SRB
50	80	80	90	50	80	80	80	50	80	80	90	TR
60	80	80	80	60	70	70	90	60	70	70	90	UA
30	–	–	–	30	–	–	–	30	–	–	–	V

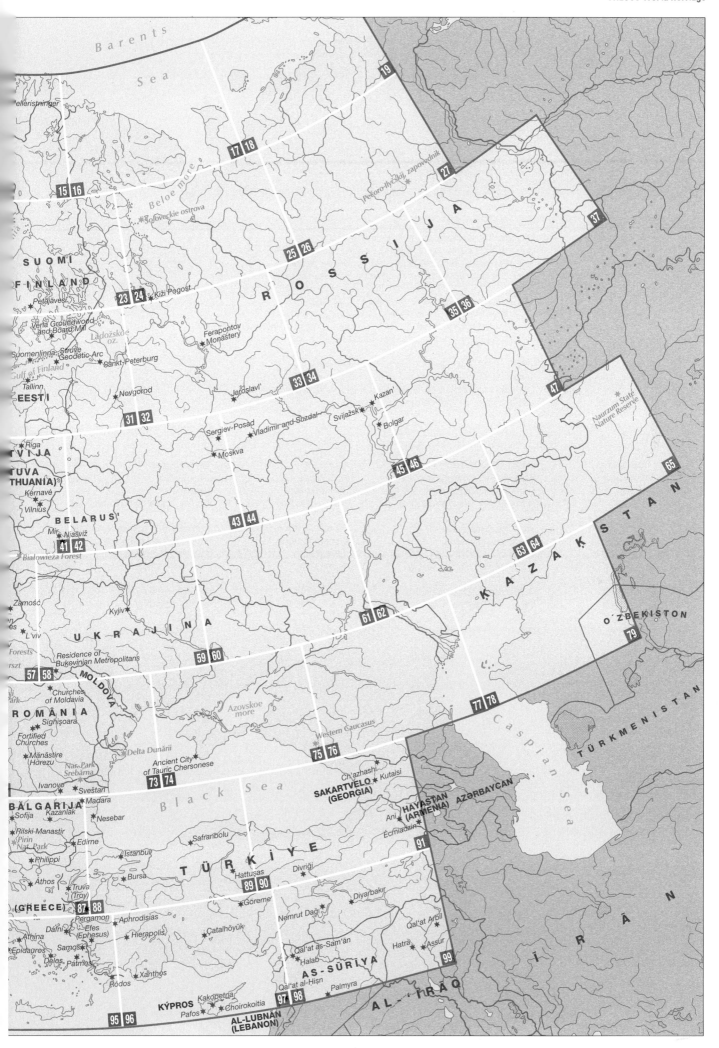

Barents
Sea

*elleristninger

Beloe more

SUOMI
FINLAND

R O S S I J A

Soloveckie ostrova

Pečoro-Ilyčskij. zapovednik

Petäjävesi

*Kiži Pogost

Verla Groundwood
and Board Mill

Ladožskoe
oz.

Ferapontov
Monastery

Naurzum State
Nature Reserve

Suomenlinna Struve
Geodetic Arc

Sankt-Peterburg

Jaroslavl'

Kazan'

Tallinn

EESTI

Novgorod

Svijažsk

Bolgar

*Riga

VIJA

TUVA
THUANIA)

Sergiev-Posad

Vladimir and Suzdal'

*Kernavė

*Vilnius

*Moskva

K A Z A K S T A N

BELARUS'

*Mir
Njasviž

*Białowieža Forest

O'ZBEKISTON

Zamość

*Kyjiv

U K R A J I N A

L'viv

Forests

Residence of
Bukovinian Metropolitans

rszt

MOLDOVA

Churches
of Moldavia

Azovskoe
more

ROMÂNIA

Sighişoara

Caspian Sea

Fortified
Churches

Delta Dunării

TÜRKMENISTAN

Mănăstire
Horezu

Nat.Park
Srebârna

Western Caucasus

Ancient City
of Tauric Chersonese

Ivanovo

Sveštari

SAKARTVELO
(GEORGIA)

Ch'azhashi

Kutaisi

BĂLGARIJA

Madara

Black Sea

Sofija

Kazanlâk

Nesebar

HAYASTAN
(ARMENIA)

AZƏRBAYCAN

Rilski-Manastir

Ani

Pirin
Nat.Park

Edirne

Safranbolu

Ečmiadzin

Philippi

Istanbul

TÜRKIYE

Divriği

Athos

Bursa

Hattuşaş

Diyarbakır

Truva
(Troy)

Qal'at Arbil

(GREECE)

Pergamon

Göreme

Nemrut Dağı

Dáfni

Efes
(Ephesus)

Aphrodisias

Hierapolis

Çatalhöyük

Qal'at as-Sam'ân

Hatra

Assur

Athina

Epidauros

Samos

İ R Â N

Delos
Patmos

Xanthos

Qal'at al-Hişn

Palmyra

Ródos

AS-SÜRIYA

KÝPROS

Kakopetuá

AL - 'IRÂQ

Pafos

Choirokoitia

AL-LUBNÂN
(LEBANON)

15 16
17 18
19
23 24
25 26
27
31 32
33 34
35 36
37
41 42
43 44
45 46
47
57 58
59 60
61 62
63 64
65
73 74
75 76
77 78
79
87 88
89 90
91
95 96
97 98
99

Ortsnamenverzeichnis · Index of place names · Index des localités · Elenco dei nomi di località
Índice de topónimos · Índice dos toponímicos · Rejstřík sídel · Skorowidz miejscowości
Gradski imena · Kazalo naselij · Helységnévjegyzék · Stednavnsfortegnelse

①	②	③	④	⑤
1009*	Luxembourg	Ⓛ	54	Ag 41
72300	Palékastro	ⒼⓇ	95	Cg 55
9170	Longyarbyen	Ⓝ	14	I Svalbard

①

*

Ⓓ	Postleitzahl	Niedrigste Postleitzahl bei Orten mit mehreren Postleitzahlen
ⒼⒷ	Postal code	Lowest postcode number for places having several postcodes
Ⓕ	Code postal	Code postal le plus bas pour les localités à plusieurs codes posteaux
Ⓘ	Codice postale	Codice di avviamento postale riferito a città comprendenti più codici di avviamento postale
Ⓔ	Código postal	Código postal más bajo en lugares con varios códigos postales
Ⓟ	Código postal	Código postal menor em caso de cidades com vários códigos postais
ⒸⓏ	Poštovní směrovací číslo	Nejnižší poštovní směrovací číslo v městech s vicenásobnými poštovními směrovacími čísly
⒫Ⓛ	Kod pocztowy	Najniższy kod pocztowy w przypadku miejscowości z wieloma kodami pocztowymi
ⒽⓇ	Poštanski broj	Najniži poštanski broj u mjestima sa više poštanskih brojeva
⒮ⓁⓄ	Poštna številka	Najmanjša poštna številka v mestih z več poštnimi številkami
Ⓗ	Irányítószám	Több irányítószámmal rendelkező helységeknél a legalacsonyabb irányítószám
ⒹⓀ	Postnummer	Laveste postnummer ved byer med flere postnumre

	②	**③**	**④**	**⑤**
Ⓓ	Ortsname	Internationale Autokennzeichen	Seitenzahl	Suchfeldangabe
ⒼⒷ	Place name	Motor vehicle nationality letters	Page number	Grid reference
Ⓕ	Localité	Plaques de nationalité	Numéro de page	Coordonnées
Ⓘ	Località	Targhe automobilistiche internazionali	Numero di pagina	Riquadro nel quale si trova il nome
Ⓔ	Topónimo	Matrículas internacionales	Número de página	Coordenadas de la casilla de localización
Ⓟ	Topónimo	Matrículas internacionals	Número da página	Coordenadas de localização
ⒸⓏ	Jméno obcí	Poznávací značky aut	Číslo strany	Údaje hledacího čtverce
⒫Ⓛ	Nazwa miejscowości	Międzynarodowe znaki rejestracyjne	Numer strony	Współrzędne skorowidzowe
ⒽⓇ	Ime naselje	Međunarodne registarske oznake	Broj stranica	Koordinatna podjela
⒮ⓁⓄ	Ime naselja	Mednarodne registrske tablice	Številka strani	Položajna koordinata
Ⓗ	Helységnév	Nemzetközi autójelzések	Oldalszám	Keresőadat
ⒹⓀ	Stednavn	Nationalitetsbetegnelser	Sidetal	Kvadratangivelse

|

Ⓓ	Nebenkarte
ⒼⒷ	Inset map
Ⓕ	Carton intérieur
Ⓘ	Inserto cartografico
Ⓔ	Cartela
Ⓟ	Inserto
ⒸⓏ	Vedlejší mapa
⒫Ⓛ	Mapa boczna
ⒽⓇ	Dodatnu karticu
⒮ⓁⓄ	Priložena karta
Ⓗ	Melléktérkép
ⒹⓀ	Bikort

Internationale Autokennzeichen · Motor vehicle nationality letters · Plaques de nationalité · Targhe automobilistiche internazionali
Matrículas internacionales · Matrícules internacionals · Poznávací značky aut · Międzynarodowe znaki rejestracyjne
Međunarodne registarske oznake · Mednarodne registrske tablice · Nemzetközi autójelzesek · Nationalitetsbetegnelser

(A)
Österreich
Austria

(AL)
Shqipëria
Albania

(AND)
Andorra

(AX)
Åland / Ahvenanmaa
Åland Islands

(B)
België / Belgique
Belgium

(BG)
Bălgarija
Bulgaria

(BIH)
Bosna i Hercegovina
Bosnia and Herzegovina

(BY)
Belarus'

(CH)
Schweiz / Suisse / Svizzera / Svizra
Switzerland

(CY)
Kýpros / Kıbrıs
Cyprus

(CZ)
Česko
Czechia

(D)
Deutschland
Germany

(DK)
Danmark
Denmark

(E)
España
Spain

(EST)
Eesti
Estonia

(F)
France

(FIN)
Suomi / Finland

(FL)
Liechtenstein

(FO)
Føroyar
Faroe Islands

(GB)
United Kingdom

(GBA)
Alderney

(GBG)
Guernsey

(GBJ)
Jersey

(GBM)
Isle of Man

(GBZ)
Gibraltar

(GR)
Elláda
Greece

(H)
Magyarország
Hungary

(HR)
Hrvatska
Croatia

(I)
Italia
Italy

(IRL)
Éire / Ireland

(IS)
Ísland
Iceland

(L)
Lëtzebuerg / Luxembourg / Luxemburg

(LT)
Lietuva
Lithuania

(LV)
Latvija
Latvia

(M)
Malta

(MC)
Monaco

(MD)
Moldova

(MK)
Makedonija (F.Y.R.O.M.)
Macedonia (F.Y.R.O.M.)

(MNE)
Crna Gora
Montenegro

(N)
Norge
Norway

(NL)
Nederland
Netherlands

(P)
Portugal

(PL)
Polska
Poland

(RKS)
Kosovë / Kosovo

(RO)
România
Romania

(RSM)
San Marino

(RUS)
Rossija
Russia

(S)
Sverige
Sweden

(SK)
Slovensko
Slovakia

(SLO)
Slovenija
Slovenia

(SRB)
Srbija
Serbia

(TR)
Türkiye
Turkey

(UA)
Ukrajina
Ukraine

(V)
Civitas Vaticana / Città del Vaticano
Vatican City

A

6200 Aabenraa (DK) 38 Ak 35
9440 Aabybro (DK) 28 Ak 33
52062* Aachen (D) 54 Ag 40
9000* Aalborg (DK) 28 Ak 33
73430* Aalen (D) 55 Ba 42
1430* Aalsmeer (NL) 53 Ae 38
3800 Aalst (B) 53 Ae 40
7120* Aalten (NL) 54 Ag 39
9880 Aalter (B) 53 Ad 39
44150 Äänekoski (FIN) 22 Cf 28
Aapua (S) 15 Cd 24
5000* Aarau (CH) 68 Ai 43
Aareavaara (S) 15 Cd 23
8000* Aarhus (DK) 39 Ba 34
3200 Aarschot (B) 53 Ae 40
27730 Abadín (E) 80 Sc 47
35031 Abano Terme (I) 69 Bb 45
Abaş (TR) 88 Ck 51
53021 Abbadia San Salvatore (I) 84 Bb 48
27404 Abbekås (S) 39 Bd 35
80100* Abbeville (F) 53 Ab 40
Abbeyfeale = Mainistir na Féile (IRL) 49 Sa 38
Abbeyleix = Mainistir Laoise (IRL) 49 Sc 38
93082 Abborrträsk (S) 22 Bk 25
Abdulino (RUS) 46 Fd 37
42146 Abejar (E) 81 Sh 49
13180 Abenójar (E) 93 Sf 52
Åbenrå = Aabenraa (DK) 38 Ak 35
SA46 Aberaeron (GB) 52 Sf 38
CF44 Aberdâr = Aberdare (GB) 52 Sg 39
CF44 Aberdare (GB) 52 Sg 39
SA73 Aberdaugleddau = Milford Haven (GB) 52 Se 39
AB16 Aberdeen (GB) 50 Sh 33
PH15 Aberfeldy (GB) 50 Sg 34
NP7 Abergavenny (GB) 52 Sg 39
LL22 Abergele (GB) 51 Sg 37
LD3 Aberhonddu = Brecon (GB) 52 Sg 39
LL42 Abermaw = Barmouth (GB) 51 Sf 38
LL53 Abersoch (GB) 51 Sf 38
SA1 Abertawe = Swansea (GB) 52 Sg 39
SA43 Aberteifi = Cardigan (GB) 52 Sf 38
SY23 Aberystwyth (GB) 52 Sf 38
Abez' (RUS) 19 Gb 24
Abganerovo (RUS) 61 Ee 42
17900 Abide (TR) 87 Cg 50
17900 Abide (TR) 96 Ck 52
CB1 Abington (GB) 51 Sg 35
Abinsk (RUS) 75 Di 46
98107 Abisko (S) 14 Bi 22
78660 Ablis (F) 53 Ab 42
20002* Åbo = Turku (FIN) 30 Cc 30
2740 Abony (H) 71 Ca 43
AB34 Aboyne (GB) 50 Sh 33
Abramovka (RUS) 45 Eh 36
Abramovka (RUS) 63 Fe 38
2200-001* Abrantes (P) 80 Sb 51
Abrau-Djurso (RUS) 75 Dh 46
Abrene = Pytalovo (LV) 41 Ch 33
38490 Abrets, les (F) 68 Af 45
05460 Abriès (F) 68 Ag 46
515100 Abrud (RO) 72 Cd 44
9100 Åbybro = Aabybro (DK) 28 Ak 33
93047 Åbyn (S) 22 Cb 25
Abzakovo (RUS) 47 Fi 37
Abzanovo (RUS) 64 Fg 39
12021 Acceglio (I) 68 Ag 46
Achad an Iúir (IRL) 49 Sc 37
IV26 Achiltibuie (GB) 50 Se 32
28832 Achim (D) 38 Ak 37
IV22 Achnasheen (GB) 50 Se 33
50140 Acıgöl (TR) 97 De 52
Ačikulak (RUS) 76 Ee 46
20800* Acıpayam (TR) 96 Ck 53
19500 Acıpınar (TR) 97 Dd 52
95024 Acireale (I) 84 Bf 53
Ačit (RUS) 47 Fh 34
NR13 Acle (GB) 53 Ab 38
Açma (TR) 98 Di 52
05021 Acquasparta (I) 84 Bc 48
15011 Acqui Terme (I) 68 Ai 46
87041 Acri (I) 85 Bg 51
2941 Ács (H) 71 Bi 43
24430 Ada (SRB) 86 Bk 49
Adaevka (RUS) 65 Gc 39
93072 Adak (S) 21 Bi 25
Adaklı (TR) 91 Ea 51
Adaklı (TR) 99 Ee 53
Adaksu (TR) 99 Ec 52
907010 Adamclisi (RO) 73 Ch 46
14430 Adamuz (E) 93 Sf 52
01000* Adana (TR) 97 Df 54
Adapazarı = Sakarya (TR) 88 Da 50
Adatoprakpınar (TR) 89 Dc 51
3715 Adelboden (CH) 68 Ah 44
70010 Adelfia (I) 85 Bg 50
13500 Adilcevaz (TR) 99 Ec 52
70820 Adiller (TR) 96 Dc 54
02000* Adıyaman (TR) 98 Di 53
625100 Adjud (RO) 73 Ch 44
Adler (RUS) 75 Dk 47
8911* Admont (A) 70 Be 43
Adolfsström (S) 14 Bg 24
08626 Adorf (D) 55 Bc 40
25797 Adrall (E) 82 Ab 48
95031 Adrano (I) 84 Be 53
45011 Adria (I) 69 Bc 45
087005 Adunaţii-Copăceni (RO) 72 Cg 46
18039 Adutiškis (LT) 41 Cg 35
Adygejsk (RUS) 75 Dk 46
Adyk (RUS) 77 Ef 45
74501 Aegviidu (EST) 30 Cf 31
30004 Aetós (GR) 86 Cb 50
Afanas'evo (RUS) 33 Ec 32
Afanas'evo (RUS) 35 Fd 32
Afanas'evskoe (RUS) 47 Fi 34
85103 Afándou (GR) 96 Ci 54
Afipinskij (RUS) 75 Dk 45
Afipskij (RUS) 75 Di 46
7170 Åfjord (N) 20 Ba 27
Afrikanda (RUS) 16 Dc 23
Afşar (TR) 89 Dd 51
46500 Afşin (TR) 98 Dg 52
077010 Afumaţi (RO) 72 Cg 46
03000* Afyon (TR) 96 Da 52
18600 Ağaca (TR) 89 Dc 50
64810 Ağaçbeyli (TR) 96 Ck 52
21920 Ağaçlı (TR) 99 Ea 52
68600 Ağaçören (TR) 97 Dd 52
Ağaçsever (TR) 99 Ea 53
Agafonkovo (RUS) 35 Fh 33
Agapovka (RUS) 47 Fk 37
34300* Agde (F) 67 Ad 47
47000* Agen (F) 66 Aa 46
7770 Agger (DK) 38 Ai 34
Agia Ána (GR) 94 Cc 52
Agia Déka (GR) 94 Ce 55
9610 Agia Eirini (CY) 96 Dc 55
70200 Agía Galíni (GR) 94 Ce 55
35101 Agía Marína (GR) 95 Cg 53
5330 Agia Napa (CY) 97 Dd 56
71001 Agía Pelagía (GR) 94 Cc 54
73005 Agía Rouméli (GR) 94 Cd 55
14565 Ágias Triás Parnithos (GR) 94 Cd 52
21055 Agía Triáda (GR) 94 Cb 53
Agidel' (RUS) 46 Fe 35
827236 Agighiol (RO) 73 Ci 45
23960 Ağın (TR) 98 Di 52
Ágios Amvrosios 97 Dd 55
Ágios Apóstoli (GR) 94 Cd 54
81400 Ágios Efstrátios (GR) 87 Ce 51
69400 Ágios Harálambos (GR) 87 Cf 50
Ágios Kírikos (GR) 95 Cg 53
Ágios Konstantínos (GR) 94 Cc 52
Agios Nikólaos (GR) 95 Cf 55
31082 Ágios Pétros (GR) 94 Ca 52
Ágios Theódori (GR) 94 Cd 53
94011 Agira (I) 84 Be 53
15800 Ağlasun (TR) 96 Da 53
5304 Aglona (LV) 41 Cg 34
555100 Agnita (RO) 72 Ce 45
86081 Agnone (I) 85 Be 49
50230 Agon-Coutainville (F) 52 Si 41
25310 Agramunt (E) 82 Ab 49
Agrat (RUS) 46 Fb 37
04000* Ağrı (TR) 91 Ed 51
92100 Agrigento (I) 84 Bd 53
30100 Agrínio (GR) 94 Cb 52
34200 Agriovótano (GR) 87 Cd 51
84043 Agropoli (I) 85 Be 50
Agryz (RUS) 46 Fd 34
13410 Agudo (E) 81 Sf 52
3750-101* Águeda (P) 80 Sb 50
33619 Aguilar (E) 93 Sf 53
34800 Aguilar de Campoo (E) 81 Sf 48
30880 Águilas (E) 93 Si 53
34991 Ağva (TR) 88 Ck 49
Ahat (TR) 96 Ck 52
48683 Ahaus (D) 54 Ah 38
Ahikovo (RUS) 33 Ed 31
37007 Ahíllio (GR) 86 Cc 51
06940 Ahillones (E) 92 Se 52
42180 Ahırlı (TR) 96 Dc 53
62300 Ahladohóri (GR) 87 Cd 49
29700 Ahlainen (FIN) 30 Cb 29
13400 Ahlat (TR) 99 Ec 52
39000 Ahlatlı (TR) 91 Eb 50
17419 Ahlbeck (D) 39 Be 37
88524 Ahlen (D) 54 Ah 39
Ahmany (RUS) 37 Ge 33
39770 Ahmetbey (TR) 88 Ch 49
Ahmetli (TR) 95 Ch 52
Ahmetli (TR) 98 Dk 52
Ahmetovskaja (RUS) 76 Eb 46
83950 Ahmovaara (FIN) 23 Ck 27
23623 Ahrensbök (D) 39 Ba 36
22926 Ahrensburg (D) 39 Ba 37
Ahrotiri (CY) 96 Dc 56
53474 Ahrweiler, Bad Neuenahr- (D) 54 Ah 40
63701 Ähtäri (FIN) 22 Ce 28
Ahtarsk, Primorsko- (RUS) 75 Di 44
41541 Ahtme, Jõhvi- (EST) 31 Ch 31
8280 Ahtopol (BG) 88 Ch 48
Ahtropovo (RUS) 33 Ec 32
Ahtubinsk (RUS) 62 Eg 42
23150 Ahun (F) 67 Ac 44
Ahunovo (RUS) 47 Fk 36
29600 Åhus (S) 39 Be 35
98630 Ahvenselkä (FIN) 15 Ci 24
50004 Aianí (GR) 86 Cb 50
83043 Aibling, Bad (D) 69 Bc 43
86551 Aichach (D) 55 Bb 42
Aiddejavrre Fjellstue (N) 15 Cd 22
4160* Aigen im Mühlkreis (A) 55 Bd 42
Aigialousa 97 De 55
1860 Aigle (CH) 68 Ag 44
61300 Aigle, l' (F) 53 Aa 42
Aigósthena (GR) 94 Cd 52
16140 Aigre (F) 66 Aa 45
73220 Aiguebelle (F) 68 Ag 45
30220 Aigues-Mortes (F) 67 Ae 47
47190 Aiguillon (F) 66 Aa 46
36140 Aigurande (F) 67 Ab 44
89110 Aillant-sur-Tholon (F) 67 Ad 43
Ailt an Chorráin (IRL) 49 Sb 36
4035 Ainaži (LV) 30 Ce 33
Ainsa-Sobrarbe (E) 82 Aa 48
80270 Airaines (F) 53 Ab 41
HS2 Aird (GB) 50 Sd 32
50680 Airel (F) 52 Si 41
40800* Aire-sur-l'Adour (F) 66 Sk 47
62120 Aire-sur-la-Lys (F) 53 Ac 40
6780 Airolo (CH) 68 Ai 44
79600 Airvault (F) 66 Sk 44
Aitovo (RUS) 46 Fe 37
515200 Aiud (RO) 72 Cd 44
18220 Aix-d'Angillon, les (F) 67 Ac 43
13080* Aix-en-Provence (F) 68 Af 47
73100* Aix-les-Bains (F) 68 Af 45
85190 Aizenay (F) 66 Si 44
3456 Aizpute (LV) 40 Cb 34
20000 Ajaccio (F) 83 Ai 49
Ajaureforsen (S) 21 Bf 25
Ajdar (RUS) 60 Di 40
5270 Ajdovščina (SLO) 69 Bd 45
8400* Ajka (H) 70 Bh 43
Ajkino (RUS) 26 Ek 28
8500 Ajtos (BG) 88 Ch 48
Akarsu (TR) 90 Di 51
Akarsu (TR) 99 Eb 53
95901 Äkäsjokisuu (FIN) 15 Cd 23
95970 Äkäslompolo (FIN) 15 Ce 23
Akbaba (TR) 91 Ed 50
Akbaş (TR) 96 Dc 52
Akbelenli (TR) 96 Da 53
Akbıyıklı (TR) 89 De 51
Akbudak (TR) 98 Dh 53
Akbulak (RUS) 64 Ff 39
Akburun (TR) 96 Db 53
61300 Akçaabat (TR) 90 Dk 49
42705 Akçabelen (TR) 96 Db 53
44600 Akçadağ (TR) 98 Dh 52
Akçagöze (TR) 98 Dh 53
Akçakale (TR) 90 Dk 49
Akçakale (TR) 98 Di 54
Akçakent (TR) 89 De 51
66660 Akçakışla (TR) 89 Df 51
58420 Akcakışla (TR) 90 Dg 51
14700 Akçakoca (TR) 88 Db 49
41620 Akçaova (TR) 88 Ck 49
41620 Akçaova (TR) 96 Ci 53
17600 Akçapınar (TR) 98 Di 52
Akçaşehir (TR) 97 Dd 53
21560 Akçay (TR) 91 Ed 50
21560 Akçay (TR) 96 Ck 54
Akçayazı (TR) 97 Dd 53
Akcjabrski (BY) 58 Ci 38
66300 Akdağmadeni (TR) 90 Df 51
33940 Akdere (TR) 96 Ck 52
33940 Akdere (TR) 98 Dg 52
06385 Aken (Elbe) (D) 55 Bc 39
Åkernäs (S) 21 Bg 25
18400* Åkersberga (S) 29 Bi 31
29650* Akhisar (TR) 95 Ch 52
06965 Akın (TR) 89 Dd 51
Akıncı (TR) 99 Ea 53
02420 Akıncılar (TR) 90 Di 50
02420 Akıncılar (TR) 98 Di 53
33630 Akıne (TR) 96 Dc 54
Akinfievo (RUS) 36 Gb 32
Åkirkeby (DK) 39 Be 35
Ak"jar (RUS) 64 Fi 39
06840 Akkaya (TR) 89 De 49
20710 Akkent (TR) 96 Ck 52
38830 Akkışla (TR) 90 Dg 51
Akkoç (TR) 90 Dh 51
Akköprü (TR) 96 Ci 54
38800 Akköy (TR) 95 Ch 53
38800 Akköy (TR) 96 Ck 53
Akkuş (TR) 90 Dh 50
85022 Akmenė (LT) 41 Cc 34
85001 Akmenė, Naujoji (LT) 41 Cc 34
Akmeşe (TR) 88 Da 50
Akmurun (RUS) 64 Fi 38
Akniste (LV) 41 Cf 34
Akören (TR) 96 Dc 53
33700 Akova (TR) 97 Dd 54
62810 Akpazar (TR) 98 Dk 52
Akpınar (TR) 88 Da 51
Akpınar (TR) 89 Dd 51
Akpınar (TR) 89 De 50
Akpınar (TR) 90 Dh 51
Akpınar (TR) 96 Ck 52
Akpınar (TR) 98 Di 53
4276 Åkrahamn-Vedavågen (N) 28 Af 31
300 Akranes (IS) 48 Qh 26
25006 Akráta (GR) 94 Cc 52
32200 Akréfnio (GR) 94 Cd 52
2480 Åkrestrømmen (N) 28 Bb 29
Aksaj (RUS) 75 Dk 43
Aksaj (RUS) 76 Ed 43
10245 Aksakal (TR) 88 Ci 50
Aksakovo (RUS) 46 Fe 36
Akšap (RUS) 35 Fg 33
Akşar (TR) 91 Ec 50
Akşar (TR) 99 Ec 52
68000* Aksaray (TR) 97 De 52
17200 Aksaz (TR) 96 Ck 52
42550* Akşehir (TR) 96 Db 52
37400 Akseki (TR) 96 Db 53
Aksenkino (RUS) 46 Fd 36
Aksenovo (RUS) 46 Fe 37
Aksent'evica (RUS) 34 Eh 30
25430 Aksu (TR) 96 Da 54
25430 Aksu (TR) 96 Db 53
Aksubaevo (RUS) 46 Fa 36
Aktanyš (RUS) 46 Fe 35
Aktarsk (RUS) 61 Ee 39
Aktaş (TR) 90 Dg 50
Aktepe (TR) 91 Ec 51
Aktepe (TR) 98 Dg 54
Aktjubinskij (RUS) 46 Fc 36
48920 Aktur (TR) 95 Ch 54
49430 Aktuzla (TR) 91 Ec 51
600* Akureyri (IS) 48 Rb 25
Akyaka (TR) 91 Ed 50
Akyaka (TR) 97 Dd 54
Akyazı (TR) 88 Da 50
06750 Akyurt (TR) 89 Dd 50
Akžarskoe (RUS) 64 Fk 39
63180 Akziyaret (TR) 98 Di 53
3570 Ål (N) 28 Ai 30
Ala (S) 29 Bi 33
25500 Alaca (TR) 89 De 50
25500 Alaca (TR) 91 Ea 51
58910 Alacahan (TR) 90 Dh 51
23410 Alacakaya (TR) 98 Dk 52
34886 Alacalı (TR) 88 Ck 49
Alacami (TR) 96 Dc 54
03001 Alacant (E) 93 Sk 52
Alaçatı (TR) 95 Cg 52
01720 Aladağ (TR) 96 Dc 53
01720 Aladağ (TR) 97 Df 53
47510 Alaejos (E) 80 Se 49
Alagir (RUS) 91 Ee 48
62375 Alahärmä (FIN) 22 Cc 27
07730 Alaior (E) 83 Ae 51
62901 Alajärvi (FIN) 22 Cd 28
63700 Alakonak (TR) 98 Dk 53
Alakurtti (RUS) 16 Da 24
Alan (TR) 99 Ee 53
06840 Alange (E) 92 Sd 52
41380 Alanís (E) 92 Se 52
07400 Alanya (TR) 96 Dc 54
Alanyurt (TR) 88 Da 51
Alapaevsk (RUS) 36 Gb 33
67850 Alaplı (TR) 88 Db 49
37312 Alaraz (E) 80 Se 50
45600 Alaşehir (TR) 95 Ci 52
83060 Ålåsen (S) 21 Be 27
Alassio (I) 68 Ai 46
Alatosun (TR) 99 Ea 53
03011 Alatri (I) 84 Bd 49
60201 Alatskivi (EST) 31 Ch 32
Alatyr' (RUS) 45 Eg 36
85201 Alavieska (FIN) 22 Ce 26
89830 Ala-Vuokki (FIN) 23 Ck 26
63301 Alavus (FIN) 22 Cd 28
Alayurt (TR) 88 Da 51
12051 Alba (I) 68 Ai 46
517005 Albac (RO) 71 Cc 44
02001* Albacete (E) 93 Si 52
37800 Alba de Tormes (E) 80 Se 50
6740 Ålbæk (DK) 28 Ba 33
000510* Alba Iulia (RO) 72 Cd 44
22534 Albalate de Cinca (E) 82 Aa 49
44540 Albalate del Arzobispo (E) 82 Sk 49
19117 Albalate de Zorita (E) 81 Sh 50
81250 Alban (F) 67 Ac 47
Albanyà (E) 82 Ac 48
65610 Albayrak (TR) 99 Ee 52
17031 Albenga (I) 68 Ai 46
37624 Alberca, La (E) 80 Sd 50
3850-001* Albergaria-a-Velha (P) 80 Sb 50
7800-601 Albernoa (P) 92 Sc 53
80300 Albert (F) 53 Ac 40
73200 Albertville (F) 68 Ag 45
81000* Albi (F) 67 Ac 47
Albocásser (E) 82 Aa 50
9100 Ålborg = Aalborg (DK) 28 Ak 33
04800 Albox (E) 93 Sh 53
72458* Albstadt (D) 54 Ak 42
06170 Albuera, La (E) 92 Sd 52
8200-001* Albufeira (P) 92 Sb 53
18700 Albuñol (E) 93 Sg 54
Albuquerque (E) 80 Sc 51
84144 Alby (S) 21 Bf 28
7580-001* Alcácer do Sal (P) 92 Sb 52
7090-010* Alcáçovas (P) 92 Sb 52
12570 Alcalá de Chivert = Alcalá de Xivert (E) 82 Aa 50
41500 Alcalá de Guadaira (E) 92 Se 53
28801 Alcalá de Henares (E) 81 Sg 50
12570 Alcalá de Xivert (E) 82 Aa 50
23680 Alcalá la Real (E) 93 Sg 53
Alcamo (I) 84 Bc 53
43530 Alcanar (E) 82 Aa 50
2025-030* Alcanede (P) 80 Sb 51
49500 Alcañices (E) 80 Sd 49
44600 Alcañiz (E) 82 Sk 49
10980 Alcántara (E) 80 Sd 51
02489 Alcantarilla (E) 93 Si 53
14480 Alcaracejos (E) 93 Sf 52
25180 Alcarràs (E) 82 Aa 49
23660 Alcaudete (E) 93 Sf 53
45662 Alcaudete de la Jara (E) 81 Sf 51
13600 Alcázar de San Juan (E) 81 Sg 51
Alčevs'k (UA) 60 Di 42
66700 Alcı (TR) 89 Df 51
Alçı (TR) 96 Ck 53
Alçıören (TR) 90 Dh 51
13116 Alcoba (E) 81 Sf 51
2460-001* Alcobaça (P) 80 Sb 51
03800 Alcoi (E) 82 Sk 52
13107 Alcolea de Calatrava (E) 93 Sf 52
06131 Alconchel (E) 92 Sc 52
Alcora (E) 82 Sk 50
28921 Alcorcón (E) 81 Sg 50
44550 Alcorisa (E) 82 Sk 50
2000-791 Alcoutim (P) 92 Sc 53
03800 Alcoy = Alcoi (E) 93 Sk 52
46172 Alcublas (E) 82 Sk 51
07400 Alcúdia (E) 82 Ad 51
37250 Aldeadávila de la Ribera (E) 80 Sd 49
13380 Aldea del Rey (E) 93 Sg 52
10740 Aldeanueva del Camino (E) 80 Se 50
IP15 Aldeburgh (GB) 53 Ab 38
GU11 Aldershot (GB) 52 Sk 39
1052 Aldinci (MK) 86 Cb 49
Aleevo (RUS) 45 Eg 38
Alëhovščina (RUS) 32 Dd 30
7555 Alekovo (BG) 73 Ch 47
Aleksandrija = Oleksandrivka (UA) 59 Dd 42
Aleksandro-Nevskij (RUS) 44 Ea 37
Aleksandrov (RUS) 43 Di 34
37230 Aleksandrovac (SRB) 71 Cb 47
Aleksandrov Gaj (RUS) 62 Ei 40
Aleksandrovka (RUS) 46 Fd 37
Aleksandrovka (RUS) 46 Fe 38
Aleksandrovka (RUS) 60 Dk 41
Aleksandrovka (RUS) 75 Di 44
Aleksandrovka Tret'ja (RUS) 61 Eb 39
Aleksandrovsk (RUS) 35 Fh 31
Aleksandrovskij (RUS) 60 Dg 39
Aleksandrovskij, Kus'e- (RUS) 36 Fi 32
Aleksandrovskoe (RUS) 34 Eh 32
Aleksandrovskoe (RUS) 76 Ec 46
Aleksandrovskoe (RUS) 76 Ed 46
95-070 Aleksandrów Łódzki (PL) 56 Bk 39
Alekseevaka (RUS) 60 Di 40
Alekseevka (RUS) 46 Fa 37
Alekseevka (RUS) 61 Ed 39
Alekseevka (RUS) 63 Fb 38
Alekseevka (RUS) 19 Fg 22
Alekseevskaja (RUS) 61 Ec 40
Alekseevskaja, stanica = Alekseevskaja (RUS) 61 Ec 40
Alekseevskoe (RUS) 46 Fa 35
Aleksin (RUS) 43 Dh 36
18220 Aleksinac (SRB) 71 Cb 47
38402 Ålem (S) 40 Bg 34
19300 Alembeyli (TR) 89 De 50
Alemdar (TR) 88 Ck 49
7380 Ålen (N) 20 Bb 28
61000* Alençon (F) 53 Aa 42
2580-012* Alenquer (P) 80 Sa 51
Aleria (F) 83 Ak 48
30100* Alès (F) 67 Ae 46
09091 Ales (I) 83 Ai 51

162 | Aabenraa

79150 Argenton-Château (F) 66 Sk 44
36200 Argenton-sur-Creuse (F) 67 Ab 44
18410 Argent-sur-Sauldre (F) 67 Ac 43
Argıthanı (TR) 96 Db 52
21201 Árgos (GR) 94 Cc 53
52200 Árgos Orestikó (GR) 86 Cb 50
28100 Argostóli (GR) 94 Ca 52
Argun (RUS) 77 Ef 47
Arhangelovka (RUS) 63 Fe 38
Arhangel'sk (RUS) 24 Ea 26
Arhangel'skoe (RUS) 43 Dh 37
Arhangel'skoe (RUS) 47 Fg 36
Arhangels'koe (RUS) 61 Ea 39
Arhangel'skoe (RUS) 76 Ee 46
08200 Arhavi (TR) 91 Eb 49
Arhipo-Osipovka (RUS) 75 Di 46
Arhipovka (RUS) 42 Db 36
8000* Århus = Aarhus (DK) 39 Ba 34
Arhyz (RUS) 76 Eb 47
83031 Ariano Irpino (I) 85 Bf 49
23510 Arıcak (TR) 99 Ea 52
58400 Aridéa (GR) 86 Cc 50
Arıkören (TR) 96 Dc 53
Arıl (TR) 98 Dh 53
31230 Arilje (SRB) 71 Ca 47
PA78 Arinagour (GB) 50 Sd 34
60019 Ariogala (LT) 41 Cd 35
24015 Aristoménis (GR) 94 Cb 53
46540 Arıtaş (TR) 98 Dg 52
08031 Aritzo (I) 83 Ak 51
67201 Årjäng (S) 29 Bc 31
Arjaš (RUS) 62 Eg 39
93087 Arjeplog (S) 21 Bh 24
23760 Arjona (E) 93 Sf 53
Arkadak (RUS) 61 Ed 39
85700 Arkássa (GR) 95 Ch 55
Arkesíni (GR) 95 Cf 54
Arkul' (RUS) 34 Fa 33
63220 Arlanc (F) 67 Ad 45
Arlanzón (E) 81 Sg 48
13200* Arles (F) 67 Ae 47
6700 Arlon (B) 54 Af 41
BT60 Armagh (GB) 49 Sd 36
Armavir (RUS) 76 Eb 45
Armavir (RUS) 76 Eb 46
37500 Arméni (GR) 94 Ce 55
09215 Armentia (E) 81 Sh 48
59116 Armentières (F) 53 Ac 40
Armjans'k 74 Dd 44
Armutçuk (TR) 88 Db 49
Armutlu (TR) 88 Ci 50
Armutlu (TR) 98 Dh 53
10700 Armutova (TR) 87 Cg 51
23054 Arna (GR) 94 Cc 54
89155 Arnäsvall (S) 21 Bi 27
21230 Arnay-le-Duc (F) 67 Ae 43
63074 Arnéa (GR) 87 Cd 50
39596 Arneburg (D) 39 Bc 38
Årnes (N) 28 Bb 30
6800* Arnhem (NL) 54 Af 38
58002 Árnissa (GR) 86 Cb 50
85110 Arnsberg (D) 54 Ai 39
99310 Arnstadt (D) 55 Ba 40
97450 Arnstein (D) 54 Ak 41
34454 Arolsen (D) 54 Ak 39
7050 Arosa (CH) 69 Ak 44
4540-098* Arouca (P) 80 Sb 50
Arøysund (N) 28 Ba 31
36730 Arpaçay (TR) 91 Ed 50
Arpacık (TR) 96 Ck 54
91290 Arpajon (F) 53 Ac 42
Arpalı (TR) 91 Ed 50
95590 Arpela (FIN) 22 Ce 24
03033 Arpino (I) 84 Bd 49
63043 Arquata del Tronto (I) 84 Bd 48
23230 Arquillos (E) 93 Sg 52
7040-010* Arraiolos (P) 92 Sc 52
62000* Arras (F) 53 Ac 40
Arrasate-Mondragón (E) 81 Sh 47
65240 Arreau (F) 82 Aa 48
69300 Arrianá (GR) 87 Cf 49
33540 Arriondas (E) 80 Se 47
G83 Arrochar (GB) 50 Sf 34
7340-001* Arronches (P) 80 Sc 51
10900 Arroyo de la Luz (E) 80 Sd 51
Års (DK) 38 Ak 34
Arsamaki (RUS) 44 Ea 35
Arsen'evo (RUS) 43 Dg 37
61900 Arsin (TR) 90 Dk 50
Arsk (RUS) 45 Ek 34
Árskogssandur (IS) 48 Rb 25
33000 Arslanköy (TR) 97 De 53
Arslanovo (RUS) 46 Ff 36
81022 Årsunda (S) 29 Bg 30
07570 Artà (E) 82 Ad 51
47101 Árta (GR) 86 Ca 51
Artemivka (UA) 60 Df 41
Artemivs'k = Bachmut (UA) 60 Di 42
Artëmovskij (RUS) 36 Gb 33
45410 Artenay (F) 53 Ab 42
25730 Artesa de Segre (E) 82 Ab 49
Artezian (RUS) 77 Eg 46
Arthurstown (IRL) 49 Sd 38
Arti (RUS) 47 Fi 34
60670* Artova (TR) 90 Dg 50
08000 Artvin (TR) 91 Eb 49
64260 Arudy (F) 82 Sk 47
93301 Arvidsjaur (S) 22 Bk 25
67101* Arvika (S) 29 Bc 31
9195 Årviksand (N) 14 Ca 20
92101 Arvträsk (S) 22 Bk 26
07021 Arzachena (I) 83 Ak 49
Arzamas (RUS) 44 Ed 35
Arzgir (RUS) 76 Ee 45
36071 Arzignano (I) 69 Bb 45
Arzipo Osipovka (RUS) 75 Di 46
56640 Arzon (F) 66 Sh 43
15810 Arzúa (E) 80 Sb 48
Arzubiha (RUS) 33 Ea 30
3665 As (B) 54 Af 39
352 01 Aš (CZ) 55 Bc 40
Aša (RUS) 47 Fh 35
Aså = Asaa (DK) 28 Ba 33
Asaa = Aså (DK) 28 Ba 33
Aşağıasarcık (TR) 90 Dh 50
42620 Aşağıçiğil (TR) 96 Db 52
Aşağı Dalören (TR) 91 Ed 51
Aşağı İrmaklar (TR) 91 Ec 49
Aşağı Karacasu (TR) 91 Ec 50
Aşağı Katırlı (TR) 91 Ed 51
Aşağıköy (TR) 98 Di 52
Aşağı Oylum (TR) 98 Di 54
Aşağı Pınarbaşı (TR) 96 Dc 52
19400 Asarcık (TR) 89 De 50
19400 Asarcık (TR) 90 Dg 49
84031 Åsarna (S) 21 Be 28
Asbest (RUS) 47 Gb 33
Asbestovskij (RUS) 36 Gb 33
84046 Ascea (I) 85 Bf 50
63739* Aschaffenburg (D) 54 Ak 41
06449 Aschersleben (D) 55 Bb 39
20276 Asco (F) 83 Ak 48
63100 Ascoli Piceno (I) 84 Bd 48
Åse (N) 14 Bf 21
Aše (RUS) 75 Dk 47
36070 Åseda (S) 29 Bf 33
Asekeevo (RUS) 46 Fc 37
91060 Åsele (S) 21 Bh 26
Ašelsaj (RUS) 64 Fk 39
Åsen (S) 29 Bd 29
4230* Asenovgrad (BG) 87 Ce 48
4540 Åseral (N) 28 Ah 32
Aševo (RUS) 31 Ck 33
45500 Asfáka (GR) 86 Ca 51
3179 Åsgårdstrand (N) 28 Ba 31
DE6 Ashbourne (GB) 51 Si 37
LE65 Ashby-de-la-Zouch (GB) 51 Si 38
TN23 Ashford (GB) 53 Aa 39
Aşıkan (TR) 98 Dk 53
Asintorf (BY) 42 Da 36
Asipovičy (BY) 42 Ci 37
5307 Ask (N) 28 Af 30
99550 Aska (FIN) 15 Cg 23
Aşkale (TR) 91 Ea 51
Askanija-Nova (UA) 74 Dd 44
Askarovo (RUS) 47 Fi 37
Askeaton = Eas Geitine (IRL) 49 Sb 38
1383* Asker (N) 28 Ba 31
69601 Askersund (S) 29 Be 32
92195 Åskiljeby (S) 21 Bh 26
1807* Askim (N) 28 Bb 31
Askino (RUS) 47 Fg 34
Äsköping (S) 29 Bg 31
57016 Askós (GR) 87 Cd 50
Askøy (N) 28 Af 30
51050 Aşlama (TR) 97 Df 52
43210 Aslanapa (TR) 88 Ck 51
Ašlyk (RUS) 37 Gi 33
Ašlyk, Polino- (RUS) 37 Gk 33
Asman-Kasaeva (BY) 42 Ck 37
Ašmjany (BY) 41 Cf 36
93190 Asmunti (FIN) 22 Cg 25
46041 Asola (I) 69 Ba 45
Asovo (RUS) 35 Fh 33
Aspa (RUS) 47 Fg 34
CA15 Aspatria (GB) 51 Sg 36
89597 Aspeå (S) 21 Bh 27
31160 Aspet (F) 82 Aa 47
Aspres-sur-Buëch (F) 68 Af 46
9400* Assen (NL) 38 Ag 37
9550 Assens (DK) 38 Ak 35
9550 Assens (DK) 39 Ba 34
06081 Assisi (I) 84 Bc 47
Ássos (GR) 94 Ca 52
Assy (RUS) 47 Fh 36
47220 Astaffort (F) 66 Aa 46
30006 Astakós (GR) 94 Cb 52
5720 Asten (NL) 54 Af 39
14100 Asti (I) 68 Ai 46
39610 Astillero,El (E) 66 Sg 47
85900 Astipálea (GR) 95 Cg 54
24700 Astorga (E) 80 Sd 48
26501 Åstorp (S) 39 Bc 34
Astradamovka (RUS) 45 Eh 36
Astrahan' (RUS) 77 Eh 44
Astrahanovka (RUS) 64 Ff 38
93061 Asträsk (S) 22 Bk 26
Astravec (BY) 41 Cf 36
2722 Astromeritis (CY) 97 Dd 55
22001 Ástros (GR) 94 Cc 53
Astrovna (BY) 42 Ck 35
Astryna (BY) 41 Ce 37
Asveja (BY) 42 Ci 34
Atabaevo (RUS) 45 Ek 35
32670 Atabey (TR) 96 Da 53
35200 Atalánti (GR) 94 Cc 52
18230 Atarfe (E) 93 Sg 53
Atça (TR) 96 Ci 53
66041 Atessa (I) 85 Be 48
7800 Ath (B) 53 Ad 40
Áth Cinn (IRL) 49 Sa 37
10678* Athína (GR) 94 Cd 52
Athlone = Baile Átha Luain (IRL) 49 Sc 37
Áth na nUrlainn (IRL) 49 Sc 38
Athy = Baile Átha Í (IRL) 49 Sd 38
19270 Atienza (E) 81 Sh 49
Atig (RUS) 47 Fk 34
Atış Poligonu (TR) 97 Dd 53
Atjaševo (RUS) 45 Eg 36
Atjur'evo (RUS) 44 Ed 36
18310 Atkaracalar (TR) 89 Dd 50
Atlant (TR) 96 Dc 52
Atnary (RUS) 45 Eg 35
2580 Atnbrua (N) 20 Ba 29
Atnjaš (RUS) 47 Fh 35
31061 Åtran (S) 29 Bc 33
64032 Atri (I) 84 Bd 48
08130 Attigny (F) 53 Ae 41
59700 Åtvidaberg (S) 29 Bg 32
13400* Aubagne (F) 68 Af 47
07200 Aubenas (F) 67 Ae 46
18700 Aubigny-sur-Nère (F) 67 Ac 43
12110 Aubin (F) 67 Ac 46
23200 Aubusson (F) 67 Ac 45
3708 Auce (LV) 41 Cc 34
32000* Auch (F) 66 Aa 47
29770 Audierne (F) 52 Sf 42
25400 Audincourt (F) 68 Ag 43
88301 Audru (EST) 30 Ce 32
57319 Aue (D) 55 Bc 40
39040 Auer = Ora (I) 69 Bb 44
08209 Auerbach (Vogtland) (D) 55 Bc 40
91275 Auerbach in der Oberpfalz (D) 55 Bb 41
Aughrim = Eachroim (IRL) 49 Sd 38
86150* Augsburg (D) 55 Ba 42
96011 Augusta (I) 84 Bf 53
16-300* Augustów (PL) 41 Cc 37
21034 Aukštadvaris (LT) 41 Ce 36
Auktsjaure (S) 22 Bk 25
84031 Auletta (I) 85 Bf 50
17470 Aulnay (F) 66 Sk 44
80460 Ault (F) 53 Ab 40
76390 Aumale (F) 53 Ab 41
48130 Aumont-Aubrac (F) 67 Ad 46
14260 Aunay-sur-Odon (F) 52 Sk 41
28700 Auneau (F) 53 Ab 42
8963 Auning (DK) 39 Ba 34
21381 Aura (FIN) 30 Cc 30
56400* Auray (F) 66 Sh 43
2910 Aurdal (N) 28 Ak 30
6690 Aure (N) 20 Ai 27
26603* Aurich (Ostfriesland) (D) 38 Ah 37
31420 Aurignac (F) 82 Aa 47
15000 Aurillac (F) 67 Ac 46
5743 Aurlandsvangen (N) 28 Ah 30
2000 Aursmoen (N) 28 Bb 31
33058 Ausa-Corno (I) 69 Bd 45
2224 Austmarka (N) 29 Bc 30
6293 Austnes (N) 20 Ag 28
5943 Austrheim (N) 28 Ae 30
71400* Autun (F) 67 Ae 44
89000* Auxerre (F) 67 Ad 43
62390 Auxi-le-Château (F) 53 Ac 40
10130 Auxon (F) 53 Ad 42
21130 Auxonne (F) 68 Af 43
23700 Auzances (F) 67 Ac 44
4262 Avaldsnes (N) 28 Af 31
89200* Avallon (F) 67 Ad 43
93010 Avan (S) 22 Cb 25
50500 Avanos (TR) 97 De 52
91701 Avaträsk (S) 21 Bg 26
Avaviken (S) 21 Bi 25
Avcılar (TR) 97 Df 53
Avdijivka (UA) 59 Dc 39
3800-002* Aveiro (P) 80 Sb 50
83100 Avellino (I) 85 Be 50
81031 Aversa (I) 85 Be 50
59440 Avesnes-sur-Helpe (F) 53 Ad 40
77401* Avesta (S) 29 Bg 30
67051 Avezzano (I) 84 Bd 48
64910 Avgan (TR) 96 Ck 52
Avgustovka (RUS) 63 Fa 38
PH22 Aviemore (GB) 50 Sg 33
85021 Avigliano (I) 85 Bf 50
84000* Avignon (F) 67 Ae 47
Ávila de los Caballeros (E) 81 Sf 50
33400 Avilés (E) 80 Se 47
42101 Avinurme (EST) 30 Cg 32
Avio (I) 69 Ba 45
7480-101* Avis (P) 80 Sc 51
Avliotes (GR) 86 Bk 51
Avlum (DK) 38 Ai 34
Avneporog (RUS) 23 Dd 25
Avnjugskij (RUS) 34 Ef 29
96012 Avola (I) 84 Bf 54
Avradsberg (S) 29 Bd 30
50300* Avranches (F) 52 Si 42
9135 Avren (BG) 87 Cf 49
555200 Avrig (RO) 72 Ce 45
Avtovac (BIH) 85 Bi 47
99801 Avvil = Ivalo (FIN) 15 Ch 22
61400 Axioúpoli (GR) 86 Cc 50
09110 Ax-les-Thermes (F) 82 Ab 48
Axmar bruk (S) 29 Bh 29
63700 Ayaklı (TR) 98 Dk 53
21400 Ayamonte (E) 92 Sc 53
33730 Ayas (TR) 89 Dc 50
06710 Ayaş (TR) 89 Dc 50
06840 Ayaş İçmecesi (TR) 89 Dc 50
52500 Aybastı (TR) 90 Dh 50
53400 Ayder Kablıca (TR) 91 Eb 50
Aydın (TR) 95 Ch 53
05040 Aydınca (TR) 90 Dg 50
33840 Aydıncık (TR) 89 Df 50
33840 Aydıncık (TR) 97 Dd 54
42280 Aydınkent (TR) 96 Db 53
Aydınlar (TR) 89 Dd 51
Aydınlar (TR) 98 Di 52
Aydınlar (TR) 99 Ec 53
69500 Aydıntepe (TR) 91 Ea 50
22800 Ayerbe (E) 82 Sk 48
HP19 Aylesbury (GB) 52 Sk 39
40520 Ayllón (E) 81 Sg 49
NR11 Aylsham (GB) 51 Ab 38
KA7 Ayr (GB) 51 Sf 35
Ayrancı (TR) 97 Dd 53
Ayrıtepe (TR) 96 Db 52
55550 Ayvacık (TR) 87 Cg 51
55550 Ayvacık (TR) 90 Dg 50
60700 Ayvalı (TR) 91 Eb 50
Ayvalık (TR) 87 Cg 51
32960 Ayvalıpınar (TR) 96 Db 53
44590 Azaila (E) 82 Sk 49
Azanka (RUS) 37 Ge 32
Azapol'e (RUS) 25 Ef 25
7005-100* Azaruja (P) 92 Sc 52
Azaryčy (BY) 58 Ck 38
37190 Azay-le-Rideau (F) 66 Aa 43
Azëry (BY) 41 Ce 37
Azigulovo (RUS) 47 Fi 34
Azinozero (RUS) 25 Eb 28
Aznaevo (RUS) 46 Fe 37
Aznakaevo (RUS) 46 Fd 36
Azov (RUS) 75 Dk 43
20730 Azpeitia (E) 66 Sh 47
06920 Azuaga (E) 92 Se 52

B

27371 Baamonde (E) 80 Sc 47
2387 Baarle-Nassau (B) 53 Ae 39
825100 Babadag (RO) 73 Ci 46
20480 Babadağ (TR) 96 Ci 53
39200 Babaeski (TR) 88 Ch 49
Babaevo (RUS) 32 Df 31
31000 Babatorun (TR) 97 Dg 54
87727 Babenhausen (D) 55 Ba 42
457020 Băbeni (RO) 72 Ce 46
11-710 Babięta (PL) 40 Cb 37
37330 Babilafuente (E) 80 Se 50
Babinavičy (BY) 42 Da 36
Babincevo (RUS) 46 Fc 37
Babrujsk (BY) 42 Ck 37
54059 Babtai (LT) 41 Cd 35
18330 Babušnica (SRB) 71 Cc 47
Babynino (RUS) 43 Df 34
Babynino (RUS) 43 Df 36
HS2 Bac (GB) 50 Sd 32
21420 Bač (SRB) 71 Bk 45
000600* Bacău (RO) 72 Cg 44
54120 Baccarat (F) 54 Ag 42
Bačějkava (BY) 42 Ck 35
Bačelino (RUS) 37 Gh 33
737050 Băceşti (RO) 73 Ch 44
Bachčysaraj 74 Dd 46
Bachmač (UA) 59 Dc 39
Bachmut (UA) 60 Di 42
KW17 Backaland (GB) 50 Sh 31
21400* Bačka Palanka (SRB) 71 Bk 45
24300* Bačka Topola (SRB) 71 Bk 45
88050 Backe (S) 21 Bg 27
66840 Bäckefors (S) 29 Bc 32
Bäckhammar (S) 29 Be 31
Backino (RUS) 43 Dd 37
71522 Backnang (D) 54 Ak 42
6430 Bácsalmás (H) 71 Bk 44
83043 Bad Aibling (D) 69 Bc 43
06001* Badajoz (E) 92 Sd 52
08910* Badalona (E) 82 Ac 49
8990* Bad Aussee (A) 69 Bd 43
27624 Bad Bederkesa (D) 38 Ai 37
48455 Bad Bentheim (D) 54 Ah 38
76887 Bad Bergzabern (D) 54 Ah 41
99438 Bad Berka (D) 55 Bb 40
57319 Bad Berleburg (D) 54 Ai 39
29549 Bad Bevensen (D) 39 Ba 37
07422 Bad Blankenburg (D) 55 Bb 39
24576 Bad Bramstedt (D) 38 Ak 37
18209 Bad Doberan (D) 39 Bb 36
04849 Bad Düben (D) 55 Bc 39
06231 Bad Dürrenberg (D) 55 Bc 39
Bademli (TR) 87 Cf 50
Bademli (TR) 95 Ci 52
56130 Bad Ems (D) 54 Ah 40
2500* Baden (A) 70 Bg 43
5400* Baden (CH) 68 Ai 43
76530* Baden-Baden (D) 54 Ai 42
29683 Bad Fallingbostel (D) 38 Ak 38
06567 Bad Frankenhausen (Kyffhäuser) (D) 55 Bb 39
16259 Bad Freienwalde (Oder) (D) 39 Be 38
74177 Bad Friedrichshall (D) 54 Ak 41
5640* Bad Gastein (A) 69 Bd 43
94086 Bad Griesbach im Rottal (D) 55 Bd 42
38667 Bad Harzburg (D) 55 Ba 39
36251 Bad Hersfeld (D) 54 Ak 40
5630* Bad Hofgastein (A) 69 Bd 43
61348* Bad Homburg vor der Höhe (D) 54 Ai 40
53604 Bad Honnef (D) 54 Ah 40
4820* Bad Ischl (A) 69 Bd 43
97688 Bad Kissingen (D) 55 Ba 40
23996 Bad Kleinen (D) 39 Bb 37
97631 Bad Königshofen im Grabfeld (D) 55 Ba 40
06628 Bad Kösen (D) 55 Bb 39
93444 Bad Kötzting (D) 55 Bc 41
55543* Bad Kreuznach (D) 54 Ah 41
57334 Bad Laasphe (D) 54 Ai 40
37431 Bad Lauterberg im Harz (D) 55 Ba 39
04924 Bad Liebenwerda (D) 55 Bd 39
07356 Bad Lobenstein (D) 55 Bb 40
32805 Bad Meinberg, Horn- (D) 54 Ai 39
97980 Bad Mergentheim (D) 54 Ak 41
53474 Bad Neuenahr-Ahrweiler (D) 54 Ah 40
97616 Bad Neustadt an der Saale (D) 55 Ba 40
32545* Bad Oeynhausen (D) 54 Ai 38
23843 Bad Oldesloe (D) 39 Ba 37
63619 Bad Orb (D) 54 Ak 40
31812 Bad Pyrmont (D) 54 Ak 39
8490 Bad Radkersburg (A) 70 Bf 44
83435 Bad Reichenhall (D) 69 Bc 43
49214 Bad Rothenfelde (D) 54 Ai 38
31162 Bad Salzdetfurth (D) 55 Ba 38
32105* Bad Salzuflen (D) 54 Ai 38
36433 Bad Salzungen (D) 55 Ba 40
9462 Bad Sankt Leonhard im Lavanttal (A) 70 Be 44
01814 Bad Schandau (D) 55 Be 40
06905 Bad Schmiedeberg (D) 55 Bc 39
88427 Bad Schussenried (D) 54 Ak 42
23611 Bad Schwartau (D) 39 Ba 37
23795 Bad Segeberg (D) 39 Ba 37
55566 Bad Sobernheim (D) 54 Ah 41
18334 Bad Sülze (D) 39 Bc 36
83646 Bad Tölz (D) 69 Bb 43
88339 Bad Waldsee (D) 69 Ak 43
34537 Bad Wildungen (D) 54 Ak 39
19336 Bad Wilsnack (D) 39 Bb 38
26160 Bad Zwischenahn (D) 38 Ai 37
LL29 Bae Colwyn = Colwyn Bay (GB) 51 Sg 37
14850 Baena (E) 93 Sf 53
23440 Baeza (E) 93 Sg 53
Baga-Burul (RUS) 76 Ee 45
Bagaevskij = stanica Bagaevskaja (RUS) 76 Ea 43
35690 Bağarası (TR) 95 Ch 53
Bagarjak (RUS) 47 Gb 34
Bagarjak, Ust'- (RUS) 47 Gb 34
Bağbaşı (TR) 96 Dc 53
Bağdaşan (TR) 91 Ec 49
21560 Bağdere (TR) 99 Ea 52
5935 Bagenkop (DK) 39 Ba 36
Bağgöze (TR) 99 Eb 53
30100 Bağışlı (TR) 99 Ee 53
32410 Bağkonak (TR) 96 Db 52
Bağlama (TR) 97 De 52
73600 Bağlıca (TR) 99 Eb 53
73600 Bağlıca (TR) 99 Ec 53
06840 Bağlium (TR) 89 Dc 50
2930 Bagn (N) 28 Ak 30
65200* Bagnères-de-Bigorre (F) 82 Aa 47
47021 Bagno di Romagna (I) 69 Bb 47

164 | **Argenton-Château**

30200 Bagnols-sur-Cèze (F) 67 Ae 46
Bağpınar (TR) 98 Di 53
Bagrationovsk (RUS) 40 Ca 36
35204 Bagrdan (SRB) 71 Cb 46
Bahatyr (UA) 75 Dg 43
Bahçe (TR) 98 Dg 53
Bahçecik (TR) 88 Ck 50
Bahçecik (TR) 97 Df 52
Bahçeli (TR) 98 Di 53
65710 Bahçesaray (TR) 99 Ec 52
Bahmutovo (RUS) 43 De 34
547055 Bahnea (RO) 72 Ce 44
317381 Baia (RO) 73 Ci 46
225100 Baia de Aramă (RO) 71 Cc 46
000430* Baia Mare (RO) 72 Cd 43
435100 Baia Sprie (RO) 72 Cd 43
105200 Băicoi (RO) 72 Cf 45
117065 Băiculeşti (RO) 72 Ce 45
Baile an Bhuinneánaight (IRL) 49 Sa 38
Baile an Chaisil (IRL) 49 Sa 36
BT54 Baile an Chaistil = Ballycastle (GB) 49 Sd 35
Baile an Ghearlánaigh (IRL) 49 Sd 37
Báile an Róba (IRL) 49 Sa 37
Baile Átha Cliath = Dublin (IRL) 49 Sd 37
Baile Átha Fhirdhia = Ardee (IRL) 49 Sd 37
Baile Átha Í (IRL) 49 Sd 38
Baile Átha Liagh (IRL) 49 Sc 37
Baile Átha Luain = Athlone (IRL) 49 Sc 37
Baile Átha Troim = Trim (IRL) 49 Sd 37
Baile Brigín = Balbriggan (IRL) 49 Sd 37
Baile Chaisleáin Bhéarra = Castletown Bearhaven (IRL) 49 Rl 39
Baile Chathail = Charlestown (IRL) 49 Sb 37
Baile Easa Dara = Ballycadare (IRL) 49 Sb 36
325200 Băile Herculane (RO) 71 Cc 46
Baile Locha Riach = Loughrea (IRL) 49 Sb 37
Baile Mhic Andáin (IRL) 49 Sc 38
Baile Mhistéala = Mitchelstown (IRL) 49 Sb 38
23710 Bailén (E) 93 Sg 52
Baile na gCros (IRL) 49 Sc 37
Baile na nGallóglach (IRL) 49 Sc 35
205100 Băileşti (RO) 72 Cd 46
Baile uí Mhathaín (IRL) 49 Sc 37
59270 Bailleul (F) 53 Ac 40
7313 Baimaclia (MD) 73 Ci 44
35470 Bain-de-Bretagne (F) 66 Si 43
Baingear (IRL) 49 Sa 36
Baio Grande (E) 80 Sb 47
36300 Baiona (E) 80 Sb 48
53160 Bais (F) 52 Sk 42
82025 Baisogala (LT) 41 Cd 35
6500* Baja (H) 71 Bi 44
9944 Bajánsenye (H) 70 Bg 44
Bajgazino (RUS) 47 Fh 37
31250 Bajina Bašta (SRB) 71 Bk 47
Bajkalovo (RUS) 37 Gh 33
Bajki (RUS) 47 Fg 35
Bajmak (RUS) 64 Fi 38
Bajmok (SRB) 71 Bk 45
81 432 Bajovo Polje (MNE) 86 Bi 47
Bajram Curri (AL) 86 Ca 48
Bajramgulovo (RUS) 47 Ga 35
Bajsa (RUS) 45 Ek 33
Bajsakalovo (RUS) 47 Fk 36
Bakacak (TR) 88 Ch 50
Bakal (RUS) 47 Fi 36
Bakalka (RUS) 64 Ff 39
Bakaly (RUS) 46 Fd 35
Bakeevo (RUS) 47 Fh 37
Bakırdağı (TR) 97 Df 52
Bakirköy (TR) 88 Ci 49
685 Bakkafjörður (IS) 48 Rf 24
Bakkejord (N) 14 Bi 21
Bakko (N) 28 Ai 31
20770* Baklan (TR) 96 Ck 52
Baklanka (RUS) 33 Ea 32
8427 Bakonybél (H) 70 Bh 43
Bakres (RUS) 77 Ef 46
Baksan (RUS) 76 Ed 47
4561 Baktalórántháza (H) 57 Cc 43
Bakury (RUS) 61 Ee 38
LL23 Bala (GB) 51 Sg 38
06720 Balâ (TR) 89 Dd 51
61450 Balaban (TR) 98 Dh 52
807010 Bălăbăneşti (RO) 73 Ch 44
Balabanovo (RUS) 43 Dg 35
Bala-Četyrman (RUS) 46 Ff 37
Balachivka (UA) 59 Dd 42
147005 Balaci (RO) 72 Ce 46
227040 Bălăciţa (RO) 72 Cd 46
927040 Balaciu (RO) 72 Cg 46
25600 Balaguer (E) 82 Aa 49
Balahna (RUS) 44 Ed 34
Balaklija (UA) 60 Dg 41
Balakovo (RUS) 62 Eh 38
HS2 Balallan (GB) 50 Sd 32
Balandino (RUS) 46 Fc 37
Balašiha (RUS) 43 Dh 35
Balašov (RUS) 61 Ed 39
Balassagyarmat (H) 56 Bk 42
Balatonboglár (H) 70 Bh 44
Balatonföldvár (H) 70 Bh 44
Balatonfüred (H) 70 Bh 44
8175 Balatonfűzfő (H) 71 Bi 43
8710 Balatonszentgyörgy (H) 70 Bh 44
547100 Bălăuşeri (RO) 72 Ce 44
02320 Balazote (E) 81 Sh 52
Balbriggan = Baile Brigín (IRL) 49 Sd 37
245400 Bălceşti (RO) 72 Cd 46
18320 Balcı (TR) 97 De 52
9600 Balčik (BG) 73 Ci 47
06890 Balcılar (TR) 87 Cg 50
06890 Balcılar (TR) 89 Dc 50
06890 Balcılar (TR) 96 Dc 54
2125 Baldone (LV) 41 Ce 34
4000* Bâle = Basel (CH) 68 Ah 43
6899 Balestrand (N) 28 Ag 29
Balezino (RUS) 35 Fd 33
KW17 Balfour (GB) 50 Sh 31
8110 Bălgarovo (BG) 88 Ch 48
Bălgarska Poljana (BG) 87 Cg 48
Balí (GR) 94 Ce 55
Balıbey (TR) 98 Di 52
10000* Balıkesir (TR) 88 Ch 51
17270 Balıklıçeşme (TR) 88 Ch 50
72336 Balingen (D) 54 Ai 42
307005 Balinţ (RO) 71 Cb 45
71520 Balışeyh (TR) 89 Dd 51
Ballaban (AL) 86 Ca 50
8540 Ballangen (N) 14 Bg 22
KA26 Ballantrae (GB) 51 Se 35
09040 Ballao (I) 83 Ak 51
370 Ballará (IS) 48 Qh 25
Ballasviken (S) 14 Bg 24
AB35 Ballater (GB) 50 Sg 33
14490 Balleroy (F) 52 Sk 41
59800 Ballı (TR) 88 Ch 50
73600 Ballıca (TR) 90 Di 50
Ballık (TR) 96 Ck 54
73600 Ballıkaya (TR) 98 Di 52
Ballina = Béal an Atha (IRL) 49 Sa 36
Ballinasloe = Béal Átha na Sluaighe (IRL) 49 Sb 37
Ballinrobe = Báile an Róba (IRL) 49 Sa 37
Ballsh (AL) 86 Bk 50
8373 Ballstad (N) 14 Bd 22
Ballum (DK) 38 Ai 35
Ballybofey = Bealach Feich (IRL) 49 Sc 36
Ballybunnion = Baile an Bhuinneáight (IRL) 49 Sa 38
Ballycadare (IRL) 49 Sb 36
BT54 Ballycastle (GB) 49 Sd 35
Ballycastle = Baile an Chaisil (IRL) 49 Sa 36
BT70 Ballygawley (GB) 49 Sc 36
Ballyhaunis = Béal Átha hAmhnais (IRL) 49 Sb 37
Ballymahon = Baile uí Mhathaín (IRL) 49 Sc 37
BT42 Ballymena (GB) 49 Sd 36
BT53 Ballymoney (GB) 49 Sd 35
BT24 Ballynahinch (GB) 49 Se 36
Ballyshannon = Béal Átha Seanaidh (IRL) 49 Sb 36
48800 Balmaseda (E) 66 Sg 47
4060 Balmazújváros (H) 71 Cb 43
97240 Bálojávri = Palojärvi (FIN) 15 Cd 22
Balpayam (TR) 91 Ea 51
235100 Balş (RO) 72 Ce 46
Bal'šavik (BY) 59 Da 38
227030 Balta (RO) 71 Cc 46
Balta (UA) 73 Ck 43
Baltaj (RUS) 62 Eg 38
Baltalin (TR) 89 Dc 51
34240 Baltanás (E) 81 Sf 49
Baltasi (RUS) 46 Fa 34
3100 Bălţi (MD) 73 Ch 43
Baltijsk (RUS) 40 Bk 36
Baltimore = Dún na Séad (IRL) 49 Sa 39
4594 Baltinava (LV) 42 Ch 34
4501 Balvi (LV) 31 Ch 33
10840 Balya (TR) 88 Ch 51
Balynagall (IRL) 49 Rk 38
96047* Bamberg (D) 55 Ba 41
NE69 Bamburgh (GB) 51 Si 35
24746 Baña, La (E) 80 Sd 48
59010 Banarlı (TR) 88 Ch 49
64500 Banaz (TR) 96 Ck 52
BT32 Banbridge (GB) 49 Sd 36
OX16 Banbury (GB) 52 Si 38
AB31 Banchory (GB) 50 Sh 33
32840 Bande (E) 80 Sc 48
4941 Bandholm (DK) 39 Bb 36
10200* Bandırma (TR) 88 Ch 50
83150 Bandol (F) 68 Af 47
Bandon = Droichead na Bandan (IRL) 49 Sb 39
087010 Băneasa (RO) 72 Cg 46
087010 Băneasa (RO) 73 Ch 46
24750 Bañeza, La (E) 80 Se 48
AB45 Banff (GB) 50 Sh 33
BT3 Bangor (GB) 49 Se 36
BT3 Bangor (GB) 51 Sf 37
Bangor = Baingear (IRL) 49 Sa 36
7822 Bangsund (N) 20 Bb 26
74-100 Banie (PL) 39 Be 37
19-520 Banie Mazurskie (PL) 41 Cc 36
8239 Banja (BG) 87 Ce 48
8239 Banja (BG) 88 Ch 48
Banjajag (RUS) 34 Ek 30
15316 Banja Koviljača (SRB) 71 Bk 46
78000* Banja Luka (BIH) 70 Bh 46
14214 Banjani (SRB) 71 Bk 46
Banjska (RKS) 86 Ca 48
56420 Bankeryd (S) 29 Be 33
29380 Bannalec (F) 66 Sg 43
04150 Banon (F) 68 Af 46
Banovići (BIH) 71 Bi 46
17429 Bansin (D) 39 Be 37
947 01 Banská Bystrica (SK) 56 Bk 42
969 01 Banská Štiavnica (SK) 56 Bi 42
2770 Bansko (BG) 87 Cd 49
Banteer (IRL) 49 Sb 38
Bantry = Beanntraí (IRL) 49 Sa 39
07191 Banyalbufar (E) 82 Ac 51
17820 Banyoles (E) 82 Ac 48
62450* Bapaume (F) 53 Ac 40
85 000 Bar (MNE) 86 Bk 48
Bar (UA) 58 Ch 41
16460 Barajas de Melo (E) 81 Sh 50
11460 Barajevo (SRB) 71 Ca 46
Barak (TR) 98 Dh 54
Barakaldo (E) 66 Sh 47
Baraklı (TR) 96 Ck 52
Baranavičy (BY) 41 Cg 37
Barančinskij (RUS) 36 Fk 32
Baranivka (UA) 58 Ch 40
Baranoviči = Baranavičy (BY) 41 Cg 37
Baranovka (RUS) 34 Fb 31
Baranovka (RUS) 62 Eg 41
Baranykivka (UA) 60 Dk 41
525100 Baraolt (RO) 72 Cf 44
Baraševo (RUS) 44 Ec 36
Baraški (RUS) 26 Fc 25
Barban (HR) 69 Bd 45
Barbantes (E) 80 Sb 48
59020 Barbaros (TR) 88 Ch 50
22300 Barbastro (E) 82 Aa 48
Barbate de Franco (E) 92 Se 54
3905 Bārbele (LV) 41 Ce 34
16300 Barbezieux-Saint-Hilaire (F) 66 Sk 45
207331 Bârca (RO) 72 Cd 47
6440-071 Barca de Alva (P) 80 Sd 49
06160 Barcarrota (E) 92 Sd 52
08001* Barcelona (E) 82 Ac 49
04400 Barcelonnette (F) 68 Ag 46
4750-100* Barcelos (P) 80 Sb 49
Bárcena de Pie de Concha (E) 66 Sf 47
11-410 Barciany (PL) 40 Cb 36
88-190 Barcin (PL) 40 Bh 38
88-190 Barcino (PL) 40 Bg 36
05600 Barco de Ávila, El (E) 80 Se 50
7570 Barcs (H) 70 Bh 45
11-010 Barczewo (PL) 40 Ca 37
Barda (RUS) 46 Ff 34
25500 Bardakçı (TR) 88 Da 51
085 01 Bardejov (SK) 57 Cb 41
10052 Bardonecchia (I) 68 Ag 45
76360 Barentin (F) 53 Aa 41
9178 Barentsburg (N) 14 I Svalbard
55051 Barga (I) 69 Ba 46
Bârgăului, Mureşenii (RO) 72 Ce 43
CF82 Bargoed (GB) 52 Sg 39
70100* Bari (I) 85 Bg 49
Barić-Draga (HR) 70 Bf 46
67021 Barisciano (I) 84 Bd 48
48000 Barjac (F) 67 Ae 46
Barjatino (RUS) 43 De 36
83670 Barjols (F) 68 Ag 47
2560 Barkald (N) 20 Ba 29
4834 Barkava (LV) 41 Cg 34
32530 Barla (TR) 96 Da 52
000731* Bârlad (RO) 73 Ch 44
55000* Bar-le-Duc (F) 54 Af 42
70051 Barletta (I) 85 Bg 49
74-320 Barlinek (PL) 39 Bf 38
LL42 Barmouth (GB) 51 Sf 38
DL12 Barnard Castle (GB) 51 Si 36
3770* Barneveld (NL) 54 Af 38
50270 Barneville-Carteret (F) 52 Si 41
S70 Barnsley (GB) 51 Si 37
EX31 Barnstaple (GB) 52 Sf 39
67140 Barr (F) 54 Ah 42
12420 Barracas (E) 82 Sk 50
94012 Barrafranca (I) 84 Be 53
7875-051 Barrancos (P) 92 Sd 52
30412 Barranda (E) 93 Si 52
2830-445 Barreiro (P) 92 Sa 52
04330 Barrême (F) 68 Ag 47
CF62 Barri = Barry (GB) 52 Sg 39
LA14 Barrow-in-Furness (GB) 51 Sg 36
CF62 Barry (GB) 52 Sg 39
Barsaniha (RUS) 32 Df 32
30890 Barsinghausen (D) 54 Ak 38
10200 Bar-sur-Aube (F) 53 Ae 42
10110 Bar-sur-Seine (F) 53 Ae 42
3482 Bārta (LV) 40 Cb 34
18356 Barth (D) 39 Bc 36
DN18 Barton-upon-Humber (GB) 51 Sk 37
11-200 Bartoszyce (PL) 40 Ca 36
Bartym (RUS) 47 Fg 34
09021 Barumini (I) 83 Ak 51
Barun (RUS) 77 Ef 43
15837 Baruth (D) 55 Bd 38
HS2 Barvas (GB) 50 Sd 32
76450 Barville, Cany- (F) 53 Aa 41
Barvinkove (UA) 60 Dg 42
78-460 Barwice (PL) 40 Bg 37
Barybino (RUS) 43 Dh 35
Baryš (RUS) 45 Eh 37
Barysav (BY) 42 Ci 36
Baryšivka (UA) 59 Db 40
23316 Bašaid (SRB) 71 Ca 45
905100 Basarabi (RO) 73 Ci 46
25530 Başbağlar (TR) 91 Eb 50
4000* Basel (CH) 68 Ah 43
Başgedikler (TR) 91 Ed 50
Başharman (TR) 97 Dd 53
SS16 Basildon (GB) 53 Aa 39
Başin (TR) 97 Dd 53
RG23 Basingstoke (GB) 52 Si 39
Bas'janovskij (RUS) 36 Ga 32
Baška (HR) 70 Be 46
25530 Başkale (TR) 99 Ee 52
23800 Baskil (TR) 98 Di 52
Başköy (TR) 90 Dk 51
Başköy (TR) 91 Ea 50
Başköy (TR) 91 Ea 51
Başköy (TR) 99 Ec 53
42820 Başkuyu (TR) 96 Dc 52
Başlar (TR) 96 Db 53
Başmakçı (TR) 96 Da 53
Bašmakovo (RUS) 44 Ed 37
Başpınar (TR) 90 Di 51
Başpınar (TR) 96 Da 53
36061 Bassano del Grappa (I) 69 Bb 45
Bassella (E) 82 Ab 48
Bassevuovdde (N) 15 Cf 22
32320 Bassoues (F) 66 Aa 47
27211 Bassum (D) 38 Ai 38
26901 Båstad (S) 39 Bc 34
Baštanka (UA) 74 Dc 43
20119 Bastelica (F) 83 Ak 48
6600 Bastenaken = Bastogne (B) 54 Af 40
20200 Bastia (F) 83 Ak 48
48250 Bastide-Puylaurent, la (F) 67 Ad 46
6600 Bastogne (B) 54 Af 40
93061 Bastuträsk (S) 22 Ca 26
Bastyn' (BY) 58 Cg 38
23610 Başyurt (TR) 98 Dk 52
Batajnica (SRB) 71 Ca 46
Batajsk (RUS) 75 Dk 43
5228 Batak (BG) 87 Ce 49
7140 Bátaszék (H) 71 Bi 44
Bateckij (RUS) 31 Da 32
BA1 Bath (GB) 52 Sh 39
72000* Batman (TR) 99 Eb 53
34220 Batočina (SRB) 71 Cb 46
9990 Båtsfjord (N) 15 Ck 20
Båtsjaur (S) 21 Bh 24
Battalgazi = Eskimalatya (TR) 98 Di 52
Battipaglia (I) 85 Be 50
5830 Battonya (H) 71 Cb 44
Baturino (RUS) 42 Dc 35
Baturyn (UA) 59 Dc 39
Batyrevo (RUS) 45 Eh 35
56150 Baud (F) 66 Sg 43
49150 Baugé (F) 66 Sk 43
71110 Baugy (F) 67 Ac 43
Baule-Escoublac, la (F) 66 Sh 43
25110* Baume-les-Dames (F) 68 Ag 43
08040 Baunei (I) 83 Ak 50
3901 Bauska (LV) 41 Ce 34
02625 Bautzen (D) 55 Be 39
Bavly (RUS) 46 Fd 36
57600 Bayat (TR) 88 Da 51
57600 Bayat (TR) 89 De 50
57600 Bayat (TR) 96 Ck 52
69000 Bayburt (TR) 91 Ea 50
14400* Bayeux (F) 52 Sk 41
16860 Bayındır (TR) 95 Ch 52
Bayırköy (TR) 96 Ci 54
56460 Baykan (TR) 99 Eb 52
17700 Bayramiç (TR) 87 Cg 51
18320 Bayramören (TR) 89 Dd 50
95444* Bayreuth (D) 55 Bb 41
83735 Bayrischzell (D) 69 Bc 43
Baz (AL) 86 Bk 49
18800 Baza (E) 93 Sh 53
Bazalija (UA) 58 Cg 41
Bazalijvka (UA) 60 Dg 41
Bazančatovo (RUS) 47 Fg 34
Bazarnaja Ken'ša (RUS) 45 Eg 37
Bazarnye Mataki (RUS) 45 Ek 36
Bazarnyi Karabulak (RUS) 62 Eg 38
Bazarnyj Syzgan (RUS) 45 Eg 37
Bazarskij (RUS) 47 Fk 37
33430 Bazas (F) 66 Sk 46
Baženiha (RUS) 46 Fb 35
Baženovo (RUS) 46 Ff 35
327366 Baziaş (RO) 71 Cb 46
HP10 Beaconsfield (GB) 52 Sk 39
Béal an Atha = Ballina (IRL) 49 Sa 36
Béal an Mhuirthead = Belmullet (IRL) 49 Rl 36
Béal Átha hAmhnais (IRL) 49 Sb 37
Béal Átha na Sluaighe = Ballinasloe (IRL) 49 Sb 37
Béal Átha Seanaidh = Ballyshannon (IRL) 49 Sb 36
Béal Easa (IRL) 49 Sa 37
Beal Tairbirt (IRL) 49 Sc 36
Beanntraí = Bantry (IRL) 49 Sa 39
20200 Beasain (E) 81 Sh 47
23280 Beas de Segura (E) 93 Sh 52
30300 Beaucaire (F) 67 Ae 47
45190 Beaugency (F) 67 Ab 43
69430 Beaujeu (F) 67 Ae 44
IV4 Beauly (GB) 50 Sf 33
LL58 Beaumaris (GB) 51 Sf 37
6500 Beaumont (B) 53 Ae 40
24440 Beaumont (F) 52 Si 41
24440 Beaumont (F) 66 Aa 46
82500 Beaumont-de-Lomagne (F) 66 Aa 47
95260 Beaumont-sur-Oise (F) 53 Ac 41
72170 Beaumont-sur-Sarthe (F) 53 Aa 42
21200* Beaune (F) 67 Ae 43
49600 Beaupréau (F) 66 Sk 43
85500 Beaurepaire (F) 68 Af 45
60000* Beauvais (F) 53 Ac 41
85230 Beauvoir-sur-Mer (F) 66 Sh 44
36179 Bebra (D) 54 Ak 40
5439 Bebrene (LV) 41 Cg 34
NR34 Beccles (GB) 53 Ab 38
05610 Becedas (E) 80 Se 50
21220* Bečej (SRB) 71 Ca 45
27640 Becerreá (E) 80 Sc 48
Bečevinka (RUS) 32 Dh 31
207060 Bechet (RO) 72 Cd 47
47670 Becilla de Valderaduey (E) 80 Se 48
59269 Beckum (D) 54 Ai 39
507010 Beclean (RO) 72 Ce 43
49370 Bécon-les-Granits (F) 66 Sk 43
DL8 Bedale (GB) 51 Si 36
34600 Bédarieux (F) 67 Ad 47
Bedeeva-Poljana (RUS) 47 Fg 35
27624 Bederkesa, Bad (D) 38 Ai 37
MK41 Bedford (GB) 52 Sk 38
58180 Bedirli (TR) 90 Dg 51
Bednodem'janovsk (RUS) 44 Ed 37
9780 Bedum (NL) 38 Ag 37
6190 Beek (NL) 54 Af 40
15848 Beeskow (D) 55 Be 38
22140 Bégard (F) 52 Sg 42
Beğendik (TR) 99 Ec 53
Begičevskij (RUS) 43 Di 37
2930 Begndal (N) 28 Ak 30
27373 Begonte (E) 80 Sc 47
Beguč (RUS) 62 Eg 38
Begunicy (RUS) 31 Ck 31
17860 Behramkale (TR) 87 Cg 51
9410* Beilen (NL) 38 Ag 38
8522 Beisfjord (N) 14 Bh 22
415200 Beiuş (RO) 71 Cc 44
7800-001* Beja (P) 92 Sc 52
37700 Béjar (E) 80 Se 50
Bejarn (N) 14 Be 23
Bekçiler (TR) 96 Ck 54
5630 Békés (H) 71 Cb 44
5600 Békéscsaba (H) 71 Cb 44
Bekeševo (RUS) 64 Fi 38
20930* Bekilli (TR) 96 Ck 52
72410 Bekirhan (TR) 99 Eb 52
Beklemiševo (RUS) 45 Eh 37
Bekovo (RUS) 61 Ed 38

Bekovo | 165

66410 Bektaşlı (TR) 98 Dg 54
Belaazërsk (BY) 58 Cf 38
26340 Bela Crkva (SRB) 71 Cb 46
Belaja Berëzka (RUS) 59 Dd 38
Belaja Cerkov' = Bila Cerkva (UA) 59 Da 41
Belaja Glina (RUS) 76 Ea 44
Belaja Holunica (RUS) 34 Fa 32
Belaja Kalitva (RUS) 61 Ea 42
Belaja Rečka (RUS) 76 Ed 47
14280 Belalcázar (E) 92 Se 52
Belanovica (SRB) 71 Ca 46
18310 Bela Palanka (SRB) 71 Cc 47
Belasovka (RUS) 45 Ee 34
3100 Bel'c' = Bălţi (MD) 73 Ch 43
Belceğiz (TR) 96 Db 52
97-400 Bełchatów (PL) 56 Bk 39
50130 Belchite (E) 82 Sk 49
58540 Belcik (TR) 90 Dg 51
Belcoo (IRL) 49 Sc 36
3100 Bel'cy = Bălţi (MD) 73 Ch 43
07985 Beldibi (TR) 96 Da 54
07985 Beldibi (TR) 96 Dc 54
Belebej (RUS) 46 Fe 36
Belebelka (RUS) 31 Da 33
31351 Belen (TR) 97 Dg 54
Belenihino (RUS) 60 Dg 40
Beleño (Ponga) (E) 80 Se 47
Belev (RUS) 43 Dg 37
BT18 Belfast (GB) 49 Se 36
NE70 Belford (GB) 51 Si 35
90000* Belfort (F) 68 Ag 43
04874 Belgern-Schildau (D) 55 Bd 39
Belgorod (RUS) 60 Dg 40
Belgorod-Dnestrovskij (UA) 73 Da 44
11133* Belgrad = Beograd (SRB) 71 Ca 46
5363 Belica (BG) 72 Cg 47
Belica (BY) 41 Cf 37
Belica (RUS) 60 Df 39
Beličaevskoe (RUS) 77 Ef 46
Belik (RUS) 42 Dc 36
Beli Manastir (HR) 71 Bi 45
3462 Belimel (BG) 71 Cc 47
33830 Belin-Béliet (F) 66 Sk 46
Belinskij (RUS) 44 Ed 38
407075 Beliş (RO) 72 Cd 44
Beljaevka (RUS) 35 Ff 33
Beljaevka (RUS) 64 Fg 39
Beljanka (RUS) 47 Fk 34
42355 Belkaya (TR) 97 Dd 53
Bel'kovo (RUS) 43 Dd 37
87300 Bellac (F) 67 Ab 44
22021 Bellagio (I) 69 Ak 45
Belleek (IRL) 49 Sb 36
45270 Bellegarde (F) 67 Ac 43
01200 Bellegarde-sur-Valserine (F) 68 Af 44
22810 Belle-Isle-en-Terre (F) 52 Sg 42
61130 Bellême (F) 53 Aa 42
01300 Belley (F) 68 Af 45
6500* Bellinzona (CH) 69 Ak 44
25250 Bellpuig (E) 82 Ab 49
32100 Belluno (I) 69 Bc 44
14240 Bélmez (E) 92 Se 52
ZE2 Belmont (GB) 50 Sk 30
16640 Belmonte (E) 80 Sd 47
16640 Belmonte (E) 81 Sh 51
6250-020* Belmonte (P) 80 Sc 50
33830 Belmonte de Miranda = Belmonte (E) 80 Sd 47
Belmullet = Béal an Mhuirthead (IRL) 49 Rl 36
Beloe (RUS) 33 Dk 32
Beloe More (RUS) 16 Dc 23
Beloe Ozero (RUS) 47 Fg 37
Beloevo (RUS) 35 Fe 31
Beloger'e (RUS) 60 Dk 40
Belogornoe (RUS) 62 Eh 38
Belogorskoe (RUS) 45 Ei 37
Belogradcik (BG) 71 Cc 47
3900 Belogradčik (BG) 71 Cc 47
Belojarka (RUS) 37 Ge 32
Belojarskij (RUS) 47 Gb 34
18424 Beloljin (SRB) 71 Cb 47
Belomorsk (RUS) 24 De 26
Beloomut (RUS) 44 Dk 36
09250 Belorado (E) 81 Sg 48
Belorečensk (RUS) 35 Fc 32
Belorečensk (RUS) 75 Dk 46
Beloreck (RUS) 47 Fi 37
Belören (TR) 89 Dd 50
Belören (TR) 96 Dc 53
Belören (TR) 98 Dh 53
9178 Beloslav (BG) 88 Ch 47
4470 Belovo (BG) 87 Cd 48
4470 Belovo (BG) 87 Ce 48
Belovod'e (RUS) 45 Eg 36
Belozersk (RUS) 32 Dh 30
DE56 Belper (GB) 51 Si 37
Belpınar (TR) 88 Db 51
Bel'skoe (RUS) 44 Ea 36
Belturbet = Beal Tairbirt (IRL) 49 Sc 36
018 61 Beluša (SK) 56 Bi 41
Beluš'e (RUS) 18 Eh 24
35263 Belušić (SRB) 71 Cb 47
20110 Belvédère-Campomoro (F) 83 Ai 49
87021 Belvedere Marittimo (I) 85 Bf 51
24170 Belvès (F) 67 Ab 46
Belye Berega (RUS) 43 De 37
Belyi Kolodez' (RUS) 60 Di 40
Belyj (RUS) 42 Dc 35
Belyj Gorodok (RUS) 43 Dh 34
Belyševo (RUS) 34 Ef 33
22-670 Bełżec (PL) 57 Cd 40
Bemyž (RUS) 46 Fb 34
22580 Benabarre (E) 82 Aa 48
11150 Benalup de Sidonia (E) 92 Se 54
22440 Benasque (E) 82 Aa 48
49600 Benavente (E) 80 Se 48
24280 Benavides de Órbigo (E) 80 Se 48
3200 Bender = Tighina (MD) 73 Ck 44
3200 Bendery = Tighina (MD) 73 Ck 44
83671 Benediktbeuern (D) 69 Bb 43
549 83 Benešov (CZ) 55 Be 41
82100 Benevento (I) 85 Be 49
67230 Benfeld (F) 54 Ah 42
66600 Bengtsfors (S) 29 Bc 31
12580 Benicarló (E) 82 Aa 50
12560 Benicasim = Benicàssim (E) 82 Aa 50
12560 Benicàssim (E) 82 Aa 50
03501* Benidorm (E) 82 Sk 52
46450 Benifaió (E) 82 Sk 51
Benkovac (HR) 70 Bf 46
Bensbyn (S) 22 Cc 25
48455 Bentheim, Bad (D) 54 Ah 38
11133* Beograd (SRB) 71 Ca 46
Berane (SRB) 86 Bk 48
Berat (AL) 86 Bk 50
Berazino (BY) 42 Ci 36
Berazino (BY) 42 Ci 37
09511 Berberana (E) 81 Sg 48
83471 Berchtesgaden (D) 69 Bc 43
62600 Berck-Plage (F) 53 Ab 40
Berdičev = Berdyčiv (UA) 58 Ci 41
Berdil (TR) 98 Dk 53
Berdjans'k (UA) 75 Dg 44
Berdjansk = Berdjans'k (UA) 75 Dg 44
Berdjaš (RUS) 64 Fh 38
Berdjauš (RUS) 47 Fk 35
Berdún (E) 82 Sk 48
Berdyčiv (UA) 58 Ci 41
Bereg (RUS) 32 Dh 30
Beregove = Berehove (UA) 57 Cc 42
Berehomet (UA) 58 Cf 42
Berehove (UA) 57 Cc 42
Bereket (TR) 91 Ed 51
Bereket (TR) 97 De 53
Bereketli (TR) 90 Dh 50
Berendeevo (RUS) 44 Dk 34
42280 Berendi (TR) 97 De 53
Berestečko (UA) 58 Cf 40
Berestove (UA) 75 Dg 43
Berettyóújfalu (H) 71 Cb 43
Berez' (RUS) 32 Dg 32
Berezan' (UA) 59 Db 40
Berezanka (UA) 74 Db 44
Berezanskaja (RUS) 75 Dk 45
Berežany (UA) 57 Ce 41
Berezdiv (UA) 58 Ch 40
Berezine (UA) 58 Cg 40
Berezivka (UA) 73 Da 43
Berezna (UA) 59 Db 39
Berežnaja (RUS) 33 Ed 29
Berezn'aky (UA) 59 Dc 41
Bereznehuvate (UA) 74 Dc 43
Bereznik (RUS) 25 Ec 28
Bereznik (RUS) 25 Ed 26
Berezniki (RUS) 35 Fg 31
Bereznjagi (RUS) 61 Eb 41
Berezova (RUS) 23 Dc 26
Berezovec, Nikolo- (RUS) 33 Ec 32
Berezovka (RUS) 34 Ef 29
Berezovka (RUS) 35 Fh 33
Berezovka (RUS) 44 Di 37
Berezovka (RUS) 47 Fi 34
Berezovo (RUS) 32 Di 30
Berëzovskij (RUS) 47 Ga 34
Berezy (RUS) 25 Eb 26
Berg (N) 14 Bh 21
08600 Berga (E) 82 Ab 48
35700 Bergama (TR) 87 Ch 51
24100* Bergamo (I) 69 Ak 45
20570 Bergara (E) 81 Sh 47
08239 Bergen (D) 38 Ak 38
5003* Bergen (N) 28 Af 30
08239 Bergen (NL) 38 Ae 38
18528 Bergen (Rügen) (D) 39 Bd 36
4600* Bergen op Zoom (NL) 53 Ae 39
24100* Bergerac (F) 66 Aa 46
Bergin (RUS) 77 Eh 44
51427* Bergisch Gladbach (D) 54 Ah 40
38502 Bergkvara (S) 40 Bg 34
Berglia (N) 21 Bd 26
08300 Bergnicourt (F) 53 Ae 41
66220 Bergö (FIN) 22 Cb 28
Bergshamra (S) 29 Bi 31
Bergsjö (S) 21 Bh 29
59380 Bergues (F) 53 Ac 40
76887 Bergzabern, Bad (D) 54 Ah 41
3580 Beringen (B) 54 Af 39
99438 Berka, Bad (D) 55 Bb 40
Berkåk (N) 20 Ba 28
3500 Berkovica (BG) 72 Cd 47
Berkovići (BIH) 85 Bi 47
06930 Berlanga (E) 92 Se 52
42360 Berlanga de Duero (E) 81 Sh 49
57319 Berleburg, Bad (D) 54 Ai 39
9980 Berlevåg (N) 15 Ck 20
10115* Berlin (D) 55 Bd 38
48370 Bermeo (E) 66 Sh 47
3000* Bern (CH) 68 Ah 44
75012 Bernalda (I) 85 Bg 50
16321 Bernau bei Berlin (D) 39 Bd 38
80370 Bernaville (F) 53 Ac 40
72240 Bernay (F) 53 Aa 41
06406 Bernburg (Saale) (D) 55 Bb 39
2560 Berndorf (A) 70 Bg 43
14990 Bernières-sur-Mer (F) 52 Sk 41
54470 Bernkastel-Kues (D) 54 Ah 41
7434 Bernstein (A) 70 Bg 43
6215 Beromünster (CH) 68 Ai 43
266 01 Beroun (CZ) 55 Be 41
2330 Berovo (MK) 86 Cc 49
13130 Berre-l'Étang (F) 68 Af 47
Beršad' (UA) 58 Ck 42
49593 Bersenbrück (D) 54 Ah 38
Bersut (RUS) 46 Fa 35
TD15 Berwick-upon-Tweed (GB) 51 Sh 35
Beryslav (UA) 74 Dd 44
Beşağıl (TR) 97 Dd 53
Besalú (E) 82 Ac 48
25000* Besançon (F) 68 Ag 43
Bešankovičy (BY) 42 Ck 35
Besarabca (MD) 73 Ci 44
Besarabjaska = Besarabca (MD) 73 Ci 44
Besedino (RUS) 46 Fd 37
Besedino (RUS) 60 Dg 39
46000 Beşenli (TR) 98 Dh 53
61800 Beşikdüzü (TR) 90 Dk 49
72200 Beşiri (TR) 99 Eb 53
Beşkonak (TR) 96 Db 53
Beslan (RUS) 91 Ee 47
Beslenej (RUS) 76 Eb 46
02300 Besni (TR) 98 Dh 53
Bešpagir (RUS) 76 Ec 45
69400 Beşpınar (TR) 99 Eb 53
6700 Bessarabka = Besarabca (MD) 73 Ci 44
Besskorbnaja (RUS) 76 Eb 46
5680* Best (NL) 54 Af 39
Bestobe (RUS) 65 Gc 39
Bestuževka (RUS) 45 Ei 37
36500 Beşyol (TR) 98 Di 53
15300 Betanzos (E) 80 Sb 47
46117 Bétera (E) 82 Sk 51
62400 Béthune (F) 53 Ac 40
Betina (HR) 70 Bf 47
Betlica (RUS) 43 Dd 36
64033 Bettna (S) 29 Bg 32
KW14 Bettyhill (GB) 50 Sf 32
LL24 Betws-y-Coed (GB) 51 Sg 37
27210 Beuzeville (F) 53 Aa 41
Bevelli (TR) 96 Ck 52
HU17 Beverley (GB) 51 Sk 37
27616 Beverstedt (D) 38 Ai 37
TN39 Bexhill (GB) 53 Aa 40
20590 Beyağaç (TR) 96 Ci 53
59600 Beyazköy (TR) 88 Ch 49
17800 Beyçayırı (TR) 87 Cg 50
17800 Beyçayırı (TR) 99 Eb 52
67980 Beycuma (TR) 88 Db 49
35790 Beydağ (TR) 95 Ci 52
Beydili (TR) 88 Da 50
34801* Beykoz (TR) 88 Ck 49
26750 Beylikova (TR) 88 Db 51
45240 Beyoba (TR) 95 Ch 52
06730 Beypazarı (TR) 88 Db 50
Beypınarı (TR) 90 Dh 51
Beypınarı (TR) 98 Dg 52
42700 Beyşehir (TR) 96 Db 53
73800 Beytüşşebap (TR) 99 Ed 53
Beyyurdu (TR) 89 Df 51
Bežanicy (RUS) 42 Ck 34
Bezbožnik (RUS) 34 Ei 31
Bežeck (RUS) 32 Dg 33
Bezenčuk (RUS) 45 Ek 38
Bezengi (RUS) 91 Ed 47
34500* Béziers (F) 67 Ad 47
Bezmenšur (RUS) 46 Fb 34
Bezopasnoe (RUS) 76 Eb 45
Bezymjannoe (RUS) 62 Eg 39
Biała, Bielsko- (PL) 56 Bk 41
12-230 Biała Piska (PL) 41 Cc 37
21-500 Biała Podlaska (PL) 57 Cd 38
78-200 Białogard (PL) 39 Bf 36
78-425 Biały Bór (PL) 40 Bg 37
15-900 Białystok (PL) 41 Cd 37
64200* Biarritz (F) 66 Si 47
52011 Bibbiena (I) 69 Bb 47
88400 Biberach an der Riß (D) 54 Ak 42
Bibirevo (RUS) 42 Dc 34
Bibrka (UA) 57 Ce 41
Bicaj (AL) 86 Ca 49
615100 Bicaz (RO) 72 Cg 44
Bicchisano, Petreto- (F) 83 Ai 49
Biçer (TR) 88 Db 51
OX26 Bicester (GB) 52 Si 39
2060* Bicske (H) 71 Bi 43
Bičurino (RUS) 46 Ff 34
64520 Bidache (F) 66 Si 47
EX39 Bideford (GB) 52 Sf 39
Bidjovagge (N) 15 Cc 21
38-340 Biecz (PL) 57 Cb 41
2500* Biel = Bienne (CH) 68 Ah 43
99-423 Bielawy (PL) 56 Bk 38
33602* Bielefeld (D) 54 Ai 38
13900 Biella (I) 68 Ai 45
22350 Bielsa (E) 82 Aa 48
09-230 Bielsk (PL) 56 Bk 38
43-300* Bielsko-Biała (PL) 56 Bk 41
17-100* Bielsk Podlaski (PL) 41 Cd 38
2500* Bienne = Biel (CH) 68 Ah 43
557045 Biertan (RO) 72 Ce 44
22630 Biescas (E) 82 Sk 48
74321 Bietigheim-Bissingen (D) 54 Ak 42
09-320 Bieżuń (PL) 40 Bk 38
17200 Biga (TR) 88 Ch 50
10440 Bigadiç (TR) 88 Ci 51
33380 Biganos (F) 66 Sk 46
ML12 Biggar (GB) 51 Sg 35
Bihać (BIH) 70 Bf 46
417050 Biharia (RO) 71 Cb 43
Bijavaš (RUS) 47 Fg 34
Bijela (BIH) 71 Bi 46
Bijeljina (BIH) 71 Bk 46
81 304 Bijelo Polje (MNE) 86 Bk 47
Bílá (SK) 56 Bi 41
Bila Cerkva (UA) 59 Da 41
48001* Bilbao = Bilbo (E) 66 Sh 47
48001 Bilbo = Bilbao (E) 66 Sh 47
465 Bíldudalur (IS) 48 Qg 25
Bileća (BIH) 85 Bi 48
Bilecik (TR) 88 Ck 50
23-400 Biłgoraj (PL) 57 Cc 40
Bilhorod-Dnistrovs'kyj (UA) 73 Da 44
Bilimbaj (RUS) 47 Fk 34
Bilisht (AL) 86 Ca 50
Biljarsk (RUS) 46 Fa 36
63160 Billom (F) 67 Ad 45
Billsta (S) 21 Bi 27
7190 Billund (DK) 38 Ak 35
41130 Billy (F) 67 Ad 44
Bil'mak (UA) 75 Dg 43
Bilohir'ja (UA) 58 Cg 40
Bilohors'k 74 De 45
Bilokurakyne (UA) 60 Di 41
Biloluc'k (UA) 60 Dk 41
Bilopil'l'a (UA) 59 De 39
Bilousivka (UA) 59 Dc 41
Bilovods'k (UA) 60 Dk 41
Bilto (N) 15 Cb 21
Biluchivka (UA) 60 Df 41
Bilyi Kolodjaz' (UA) 60 Dh 40
22500 Binéfar (E) 82 Aa 49
55411 Bingen am Rhein (D) 54 Ah 41
12000 Bingöl (TR) 99 Ea 52
18609 Binz (D) 39 Bd 36
Biograd na Moru (HR) 70 Bf 47
Biorra = Birr (IRL) 49 Sc 37
37-740 Bircza (PL) 57 Cc 41
Birecik (TR) 98 Dh 53
35775 Birgi (TR) 95 Ci 52
4760 Birkeland (N) 28 Ai 32
97834 Birkenfeld (D) 54 Ah 41
CH42 Birkenhead (GB) 51 Sg 37
3460 Birkerød (DK) 39 Bc 35
8190 Birkfeld (A) 70 Bf 43
B8 Birmingham (GB) 52 Si 38
Birr = Biorra (IRL) 49 Sc 37
Birsk (RUS) 46 Ff 35
59009 Birštonas (LT) 41 Ce 36
41001 Biržai (LT) 41 Ce 34
5214 Birži (LV) 41 Cf 34
17100 Bisbal d'Empordà, la (E) 82 Ad 49
40600* Biscarrosse (F) 66 Si 46
70052 Bisceglie (I) 85 Bg 49
5500* Bischofshofen (A) 69 Bd 43
01877 Bischofswerda (D) 55 Be 39
67240 Bischwiller (F) 54 Ah 42
Biser = Biserski (RUS) 36 Fi 32
Biserovo (RUS) 35 Fd 31
Biserski (RUS) 36 Fi 32
Bisert' (RUS) 47 Fk 34
DL14 Bishop Auckland (GB) 51 Si 36
SY9 Bishop's Castle (GB) 52 Sg 38
Bishtqethm (AL) 86 Bk 50
63040 Bisignano (I) 85 Bg 51
11-300 Biskupiec (PL) 40 Ca 37
39629 Bismark (Altmark) (D) 39 Bb 38
21500 Bismil (TR) 99 Ea 53
Bispgården (S) 21 Bg 27
207065 Bistreţ (RO) 72 Cd 47
000420* Bistriţa (RO) 72 Ce 43
427005 Bistriţa Bârgăului (RO) 72 Ce 43
11-230 Bisztynek (PL) 40 Ca 36
54634 Bitburg (D) 54 Ag 41
57230 Bitche (F) 54 Ah 41
13000 Bitlis (TR) 99 Ec 52
7000* Bitola (MK) 86 Cb 49
70032 Bitonto (I) 85 Bg 49
06749 Bitterfeld-Wolfen (D) 55 Bc 39
08021 Bitti (I) 83 Ak 50
Bižbuljak (RUS) 46 Fe 37
Bizjar (RUS) 35 Fg 33
Bjahoml' (BY) 42 Ci 36
7100 Bjala (BG) 72 Cf 47
7100 Bjala (BG) 87 Cg 48
7100 Bjala (BG) 88 Ch 48
3200 Bjala Slatina (BG) 72 Cd 47
Bjalyničy (BY) 42 Ck 37
9426 Bjarkøy (N) 14 Bg 22
Bjaroza (BY) 57 Ce 38
Bjarozavka (BY) 41 Cf 37
24601 Bjärred (S) 39 Bd 35
89300 Bjästa (S) 21 Bi 27
Bjelovar (HR) 70 Bg 45
8643 Bjerka (N) 14 Bd 24
8530 Bjerkvik (N) 14 Bh 22
8850 Bjerringbro (DK) 38 Ak 34
2676 Bjølstad (N) 28 Ak 29
78045 Björbo (S) 29 Be 30
Bjordal (N) 28 Af 29
Bjørkås (N) 14 Bk 22
1940 Bjørkelangen (N) 28 Bb 31
98193 Björkliden (S) 14 Bi 22
65870 Björköby (FIN) 22 Cb 27
Björköby (S) 29 Be 33
92041 Björksele (S) 21 Bi 26
84070 Björkvattnet (S) 21 Bd 26
2669 Bjorli (N) 20 Ai 28
Bjørn (N) 14 Bc 24
89050 Björna (S) 21 Bi 27
9910 Bjørnevatn (N) 15 Ck 21
64050 Björnlunda (S) 29 Bh 31
82700 Björsarv (S) 21 Bg 28
91601 Bjurholm (S) 22 Bk 27
79021 Bjursås (S) 29 Bf 30
26701 Bjuv (S) 39 Bc 34
18420 Blace (SRB) 71 Cb 47
AB2 Blackburn (GB) 51 Sh 37
FY1 Blackpool (GB) 51 Sg 37
59094 Blackstad (S) 29 Bg 33
Blagodarnij (RUS) 76 Ed 45
Blagodarnyj (RUS) 76 Ed 45
Blagodatovka (RUS) 63 Fa 38
2700* Blagoevgrad (BG) 87 Cd 48
Blagoevo (RUS) 25 Eh 27
Blagovar (RUS) 46 Fe 36
Blagoveščensk (RUS) 46 Ff 35
44130 Blain (F) 66 Si 43
PH10 Blairgowrie (GB) 50 Sg 34
515400 Blaj (RO) 72 Cd 44
Blakstad (N) 28 Ai 32
36300 Blanc, le (F) 67 Ab 44
DT11 Blandford Forum (GB) 52 Sh 40
17300 Blanes (E) 82 Ac 49
76340 Blangy-sur-Bresle (F) 53 Ab 41
8370 Blankenberge (B) 53 Ad 39
382 41 Blansko (CZ) 56 Bg 41
98-235 Błaszki (PL) 56 Bi 39
Blattnicksele (S) 21 Bh 25
89143 Blaubeuren (D) 54 Ak 42
33390 Blaye (F) 66 Sk 45
21354 Bleckede (D) 39 Ba 37
99752 Bleicherode (D) 55 Ba 39
8481 Bleik (N) 14 Bf 21
Bleikvassli (N) 21 Bd 25
89220 Bléneau (F) 67 Ac 43
37150 Bléré (F) 66 Aa 43
52024 Blidsberg (S) 29 Bd 33
Blinisht (AL) 86 Bk 49
41000* Blois (F) 67 Ab 43
540 Blönduós (IS) 48 Qk 25
55-330 Błonie (PL) 57 Ca 38
6700* Bludenz (A) 69 Ak 43
NE24 Blyth (GB) 51 Si 35
Blyznjuky (UA) 60 Dg 42
Bø (N) 28 Ak 31
33720 Boal (E) 80 Sd 47
PH24 Boat of Garten (GB) 50 Sg 33
71032* Böblingen (D) 54 Ak 42
76-020 Bobolice (PL) 40 Bg 37
Bobr (BY) 42 Ck 36
Bobrava (RUS) 60 Df 40
Bobrov (RUS) 60 Dk 39
Bobrovskoe (RUS) 37 Ge 33
Bobrovycja (UA) 59 Db 40
76-231 Bobrowniki (PL) 41 Cd 37
Bobrujsk = Babrujsk (BY) 42 Ck 37
Bobrynec' (UA) 59 Dc 42
Bočevo (RUS) 32 Dd 31
32-700 Bochnia (PL) 57 Ca 41

166 | Bektaşlı

46395* Bocholt (D) 54 Ag 39
364 71 Bochov (CZ) 55 Bd 40
44787* Bochum (D) 54 Ah 39
57900 Bockara (S) 29 Bg 33
457045 Bocşa (RO) 71 Cb 45
317055 Bocsig (RO) 71 Cb 44
Boda (S) 29 Bf 29
38075 Böda (S) 29 Bh 33
96100* Boden (S) 22 Cb 25
Bod'ja, Jaškur- (RUS) 35 Fd 33
PL31 Bodmin (GB) 52 Sf 40
8003* Bodø (N) 14 Be 23
48400 Bodrum (TR) 95 Ch 53
Bodsjö (S) 21 Be 28
88051 Bodum (S) 21 Bg 27
48-340 Bodzanów (PL) 57 Ca 38
42130 Boën (F) 67 Ae 45
Boeve (RUS) 60 Dk 39
Bogatiščevo (RUS) 43 Di 36
Bogatoe (RUS) 46 Fb 37
Bogatye Saby (RUS) 46 Fa 35
Bogatyr' (RUS) 46 Fa 37
Bogazi 97 Dd 55
35135 Boğaziçi (TR) 95 Ch 52
19310 Boğazkale (TR) 89 De 50
Boğazkaya (TR) 89 Df 49
Boğazköprü (TR) 97 Df 52
66400 Boğazlıyan (TR) 89 Df 51
Bogdanovka (RUS) 46 Fa 37
Bogdanovka (RUS) 63 Fa 38
Bogdanovka (RUS) 63 Fc 38
Bogdanovo (RUS) 43 Dg 37
Bogdanovo (RUS) 47 Fg 35
Bogdanovskoe (RUS) 64 Fk 38
49-200 Bogdanów (PL) 56 Bk 39
Böğecik (TR) 97 Dd 53
8533 Bogen (N) 14 Bg 22
5400 Bogense (DK) 39 Ba 35
PO21 Bognor Regis (GB) 52 Sk 40
Bogoljubovo (RUS) 44 Ea 34
1415 Bogomila (MK) 86 Cb 49
1482 Bogorodica (MK) 86 Cc 49
Bogorodick (RUS) 43 Di 37
Bogorodsk (RUS) 26 Fc 28
Bogorodsk (RUS) 44 Ed 34
Bogorodsk (RUS) 47 Fh 34
Bogorodskoe (RUS) 32 Dh 33
Bogorodskoe (RUS) 34 Fa 33
Bogorodskoe (RUS) 46 Ff 38
Bogovarovo (RUS) 34 Eh 32
Bogučar (RUS) 61 Ea 41
Bögürtlen (TR) 98 Di 53
Boguslav' (RUS) 32 Dg 32
02110 Bohain-en-Vermandois (F) 53 Ad 41
4264 Bohinjska Bistrica (SLO) 69 Bd 44
Bohoduchiv (UA) 60 Df 40
10320 Bohonal de Ibor (E) 80 Se 51
8719 Böhönye (H) 70 Bh 44
Bohorodčany (UA) 57 Ce 42
Bohušèvsk (BY) 42 Da 36
Bohuslav (UA) 59 Da 41
19258 Boizenburg (Elbe) (D) 39 Ba 37
1226 Bojane (MK) 86 Cb 48
86021 Bojano (I) 85 Be 49
63-940 Bojanowo (PL) 56 Bg 39
Bojarkeros (RUS) 34 Fb 29
Bojaščina (RUS) 24 Df 28
3430 Bojčinovci (BG) 72 Cd 47
3840 Bojnica (BG) 71 Cc 47
16205 Bojnik (SRB) 71 Cb 47
23252 Boka (SRB) 71 Ca 45
Bokovskaja (RUS) 61 Eb 41
Boksitogorsk (RUS) 32 Dd 31
Bol (HR) 70 Bg 47
Bol'šaja Vereika (RUS) 60 Di 38
13260 Bolaños de Calatrava (E) 93 Sg 52
17350 Bolayır (TR) 87 Cg 50
76210 Bolbec (F) 53 Aa 41
217080 Bolboşi (RO) 72 Cd 46
105300 Boldeşti-Scăeni (RO) 72 Cg 45
Boldovo (RUS) 45 Ee 36
Bolechiv (UA) 57 Cd 41
59-700 Bolesławiec (PL) 56 Bf 39
Bolhov (RUS) 43 Dg 37
Bolhrad (UA) 73 Ci 45
93601 Boliden (S) 22 Ca 26
085100 Bolintin-Vale (RO) 72 Cf 46
Boljanići (MNE) 71 Bk 47
8720 Boljarovo (BG) 87 Cg 48
19370 Boljevac (SRB) 71 Cb 47
84500 Bollène (F) 67 Ae 46
82100* Bollnäs (S) 29 Bg 29
87320 Bollstabruk (S) 21 Bh 28
Bollullos Par del Convado (E) 92 Sd 53
Bolmsö (S) 39 Bd 33
40100* Bologna (I) 69 Bb 46
Bologoe (RUS) 32 De 33
Bologovo (RUS) 42 Db 34
Bološnevo (RUS) 44 Ea 36
Bolotovskoe (RUS) 36 Gc 32
Bol'šaja (RUS) 33 Dk 30
Bol'šaja Atnja (RUS) 45 Ek 34
Bol'šaja Budnica (RUS) 42 Da 35
Bol'šaja Černigovka (RUS) 63 Fa 38
Bol'šaja Dergunovka (RUS) 63 Fa 38
Bol'šaja Doroga (RUS) 44 Ea 37
Bol'šaja Džalga (RUS) 76 Ec 45
Bol'šaja Glušica (RUS) 63 Fa 38
Bol'šaja Gora (RUS) 25 Eb 27
Bol'šaja Kamenka (RUS) 46 Fa 37
Bol'šaja Kandala (RUS) 45 Ek 36
Bol'šaja Karpuniha (RUS) 34 Ef 33
Bol'šaja Kaskan (RUS) 34 Eh 31
Bol'šaja Kiselenka (RUS) 32 De 33
Bol'šaja Martynovka = S'loboda Bol'šaja Martynovka (RUS) 76 Eb 43
Bol'šaja Nisogora (RUS) 25 Ef 26
Bol'šaja Orlovka (RUS) 76 Eb 43
Bol'šaja Poljana (RUS) 60 Di 38
Bol'šaja Privalovka (RUS) 60 Dk 39
Bol'šaja Rečka (RUS) 34 Eg 31
Bol'šaja Šludka (RUS) 34 Eg 29
Bol'šaja Šonoma (RUS) 26 Ei 29
Bol'šaja Sosnovka (RUS) 35 Fe 33
Bol'šaja Tavoložka (RUS) 62 Ek 38
Bol'šaja Tovra (RUS) 25 Eb 26
Bol'šaja Usa (RUS) 46 Ff 34
Bol'šakovo (RUS) 40 Cb 36
Bol'šečernihivka (UA) 60 Dk 42
Bol'šekrepinskaja (RUS) 75 Dk 43
Bol'šelug (RUS) 26 Fc 28
01023 Bolsena (I) 84 Bb 48
Bol'šenabatovskij (RUS) 61 Ed 42
Bol'šetroickoe (RUS) 60 Dh 40
Bol'šeustinskoe (RUS) 47 Fi 35
Bol'ševik (RUS) 61 Ed 40
Bol'šie Berezniki (RUS) 45 Ef 36
Bol'šie Kajbicy (RUS) 45 Ei 35
Bol'šie Ključi (RUS) 45 Ei 34
Bol'šie Ključišči (RUS) 45 Ei 36
Bol'šie Medveki (RUS) 43 Dh 37
Bol'šie Ozerki (RUS) 62 Eg 38
Bol'šie Suslovy (RUS) 34 Ei 32
Bol'šie Tarhany (RUS) 45 Ei 36
Bol'šinka (RUS) 61 Eb 42
Bol'šoe Boldino (RUS) 45 Ef 36
Bol'šoe Gorodišče (RUS) 60 Dh 40
Bol'šoe Ignatovo (RUS) 45 Ef 35
Bol'šoe Muraškino (RUS) 45 Ee 35
Bol'šoe Nagatkino (RUS) 45 Ei 36
Bol'šoe Pole (RUS) 31 Ci 30
Bol'šoe Pole (RUS) 45 Ef 34
Bol'šoe Selo (RUS) 32 Di 33
Bol'šoe Šemjakino (RUS) 45 Ei 35
Bol'šoe Šeremetovo (RUS) 44 Ec 37
Bol'šoe Tokarevo (RUS) 33 Ec 31
Bol'šoe Zaborov'e (RUS) 32 Dd 32
Bol'šoe Žirovo (RUS) 60 Df 39
Bol'šoj (RUS) 61 Ec 41
Bol'šoj Čurki (RUS) 25 Eh 27
Bol'šoj Dvor (RUS) 32 De 31
Bol'šoj Lučak (RUS) 61 Ed 40
Bol'šoj Melik (RUS) 61 Ed 39
Bol'šoj Ramen' (RUS) 45 Eh 34
Bol'šoj Sabsk (RUS) 31 Ck 31
Bol'šoj Ut (RUS) 47 Fi 33
Bol'šoj V'jas (RUS) 45 Ef 37
Bol'šoj V''jas (RUS) 45 Ef 37
Bolsward (NL) 38 Af 37
22340 Boltaña (E) 82 Aa 48
BL1 Bolton (GB) 51 Sh 37
Bolturino (RUS) 42 Dc 36
14000* Bolu (TR) 88 Db 50
Bölükyazı (TR) 99 Ec 52
415 Bolungarvík (IS) 48 Qg 24
03300 Bolvadin (TR) 96 Db 52
39100 Bolzano = Bozen (I) 69 Bb 44
01020 Bomarzo (I) 84 Bc 48
24850 Boñar (E) 80 Se 48
IV24 Bonar Bridge (GB) 50 Sf 33
Bondari (RUS) 44 Ec 38
46023 Bondeno (I) 69 Bb 46
Bondjug (RUS) 35 Fg 30
Bonga (RUS) 32 Dh 30
20169 Bonifacio (F) 83 Ak 49
02610 Bonillo, El (E) 81 Sh 52
53111* Bonn (D) 54 Ah 40
72110 Bonnétable (F) 53 Aa 42
28800 Bonneval (F) 53 Ab 42
74130 Bonneville (F) 68 Ag 44
45420 Bonny-sur-Loire (F) 67 Ac 43
07011 Bono (I) 83 Ak 50
07012 Bonorva (I) 83 Ai 50
7150 Bonyhád (H) 71 Bi 44
56154 Boppard (D) 54 Ah 40
348 02 Bor (CZ) 55 Bc 41
Bor (RUS) 32 De 32
Bor (RUS) 37 Gh 33
Bor (RUS) 45 Ee 34
19210* Bor (SRB) 71 Cc 46
51700 Bor (TR) 97 De 53
50110* Borås (S) 29 Bc 33
7150-101* Borba (P) 92 Sc 52
08400 Borçka (TR) 91 Eb 49
33000* Bordeaux (F) 66 Sk 46
8005-423* Bordeira (P) 92 Sb 53
370 Borðeyri (IS) 48 Qi 25
59030 Borensberg (S) 29 Bf 32
06500* Borgå = Porvoo (FIN) 30 Cf 30
□ Borgarfjörður (IS) 48 Rg 25
310 Borgarnes (IS) 48 Qi 26
9530 Borger (NL) 38 Ag 38
25400 Borges Blanques, les (E) 82 Aa 49
38701 Borgholm (S) 40 Bg 34
28021 Borgomanero (I) 68 Ai 45
12011 Borgo San Dalmazzo (I) 68 Ah 46
50032 Borgo San Lorenzo (I) 69 Bb 47
43043 Borgo Val di Taro (I) 69 Ak 46
38051 Borgo Valsugana (I) 69 Bb 44
51370 Borgstena (S) 29 Bd 33
6854 Borgund (N) 28 Ah 29
4824 Borino (BG) 87 Ce 49
Borinskoe (RUS) 60 Dk 38
Borisogleb (RUS) 44 Ec 35
Borisoglebovka (RUS) 62 Eh 39
Borisoglebsk (RUS) 61 Ec 39
Borisoglebskij (RUS) 33 Dk 33
Borisov = Barysav (BY) 42 Ci 36
Borisovka (RUS) 60 Dg 40
Borisovo (RUS) 33 Dk 31
Borisovo (RUS) 33 Ee 31
Borisovo-Sudskoe (RUS) 32 Dg 31
Borivs'ke (UA) 60 Di 42
Börjelsbyn (S) 22 Cc 25
Borkavičy (BY) 42 Ci 35
04916 Borken (D) 54 Ag 39
9475 Borkenes (N) 14 Bg 22
78100* Borlänge (S) 29 Bf 30
6854 Borlaug (N) 28 Ah 29
45940 Borlu (TR) 96 Ci 52
23032 Bormio (I) 69 Ba 44
04552 Borna (D) 55 Bc 39
43350 Borne (F) 67 Ad 45
Borodinskoe (RUS) 31 Ck 29
Borodjanka (UA) 58 Ck 40
Borodki (RUS) 45 Ee 34
Borodulino (RUS) 35 Fe 33
Borodyno (UA) 73 Ck 44
Borok (RUS) 31 Da 32
Borok (RUS) 31 Dc 32
Borok (RUS) 32 Dg 30
Borok (RUS) 32 Dh 32
Borok-Suležskij (RUS) 32 Dg 33
Boromlja (UA) 60 Df 40
42-283 Boronów (PL) 56 Bi 40
Borova (UA) 60 Dh 41
3240 Borovan (BG) 72 Cd 47
Borove (UA) 58 Ch 39
2626 Borovec (BG) 87 Cd 48
Borovenka (RUS) 32 Dd 32
Boroviči (RUS) 31 Ck 33
Boroviči (RUS) 32 Dd 32
Borovina (RUS) 25 Ee 28
2904 Borovo (BG) 72 Cf 47
Borovo (RUS) 26 Ek 27
Borovoe (RUS) 65 Ga 38
Borovoj (RUS) 23 Dc 26
Borovsk (RUS) 43 Dg 35
Borovskij (RUS) 37 Gf 33
27621 Borrby (S) 39 Be 35
Borre (DK) 39 Bc 36
12530 Borriana (E) 82 Sk 51
Borrisokane = Buiríos Uí Chéin (IRL) 49 Sb 38
Börrum (S) 29 Bg 32
707592 Borşa (RO) 72 Ce 43
Borščiv (UA) 58 Cg 42
9716 Børselv (N) 15 Cf 20
Borskoe (RUS) 46 Fb 38
19110 Bort-les-Orgues (F) 67 Ac 45
84035 Börtnan (S) 21 Bd 28
IV51 Borve (GB) 50 Sd 33
Boryslav (UA) 57 Cd 41
Boryspil' (UA) 59 Da 40
Borzna (UA) 59 Dc 39
08013 Bosa (I) 83 Ai 50
Bosanska Gradiška (BIH) 70 Bh 45
Bosanska Krupa (BIH) 70 Bg 46
Bosanski Brod = Brod (BIH) 70 Bi 45
Bosanski Novi (BIH) 70 Bg 45
Bosanski Petrovac (BIH) 70 Bg 46
Bosanski Šamac (BIH) 71 Bi 45
Bosansko Grahovo (BIH) 70 Bg 46
PL35 Boscastle (GB) 52 Sf 40
Bosinska Dubica (BIH) 70 Bg 45
680 01 Boskovice (CZ) 56 Bg 41
10680 Bostancı (TR) 99 Ec 53
Bostanlı (TR) 99 Eb 53
PE21 Boston (GB) 51 Sk 38
88195 Boteå (S) 21 Bh 27
2140 Botevgrad (BG) 87 Cd 48
5460-502 Boticas (P) 80 Sc 49
7140 Botngård (N) 20 Ak 27
000710* Botoşani (RO) 72 Cg 43
92276 Botsmark (S) 22 Ca 26
64340 Boucau (F) 66 Si 47
Bougado (P) 80 Sb 49
6830 Bouillon (B) 54 Af 41
57220 Boulay-Moselle (F) 54 Ag 41
92100* Boulogne-Billancourt (F) 53 Ac 42
31350 Boulogne-sur-Gesse (F) 66 Aa 47
62200* Boulogne-sur-Mer (F) 53 Ab 40
71140 Bourbon-Lancy (F) 67 Ad 44
03160 Bourbon-l'Archambault (F) 67 Ad 44
59630 Bourbourg (F) 53 Ac 40
33710 Bourg (F) 66 Sk 45
23400 Bourganeuf (F) 67 Ab 45
42220 Bourg-Argental (F) 67 Ae 45
26300 Bourg-de-Péage (F) 68 Af 45
01000* Bourg-en-Bresse (F) 68 Af 44
18000* Bourges (F) 67 Ac 43
63760 Bourg-Lastic (F) 67 Ac 45
66760 Bourg-Madame (F) 82 Ab 48
44580 Bourgneuf-en-Retz (F) 66 Si 43
38300 Bourgoin-Jallieu (F) 68 Af 45
07700 Bourg-Saint-Andéol (F) 67 Ae 46
73700 Bourg-Saint-Maurice (F) 68 Ag 45
37140 Bourgueil (F) 66 Aa 43
BH1 Bournemouth (GB) 52 Si 40
85480 Bournezeau (F) 66 Si 44
33110 Bouscat, le (F) 66 Sk 46
23600 Boussac (F) 67 Ac 44
7300 Boussu (B) 53 Ad 40
57320 Bouzonville (F) 54 Ag 41
89034 Bovalino Marina (I) 84 Bg 52
45047 Bovallstrand (S) 28 Bb 32
89035 Bova Marina (I) 84 Bf 53
5230 Bovec (SLO) 69 Bd 44
49155 Bóveda de Toro, La (E) 80 Se 49
2690 Bøverdal (N) 28 Ai 29
PA44 Bowmore (GB) 49 Sd 35
59010 Boxholm (S) 29 Bf 32
5830 Boxmeer (NL) 54 Af 39
5280* Boxtel (NL) 54 Af 39
57200 Boyabat (TR) 89 De 49
Boyalı (TR) 89 Dd 49
Boyalı (TR) 97 Dd 52
16870 Boyalıca (TR) 88 Ck 50
34232 Boyalık (TR) 88 Ci 49
Boyle = Mainistir na Búille (IRL) 49 Sb 37
Bozan (TR) 96 Ck 52
48710 Bozburun (TR) 96 Ci 54
17680 Bozcaada (TR) 87 Cg 51
Bozd g (TR) 96 Ci 52
09760 Bozdoğan (TR) 96 Ci 53
39100 Bozen = Bolzano (I) 69 Bb 44
Bozkaya (TR) 98 Dg 53
Bozkır (TR) 89 Dd 50
Bozkır (TR) 96 Dc 53
Bozkır (TR) 97 De 52
37660 Bozkurt (TR) 96 Ck 53
17200 Bozlar (TR) 88 Ch 50
Bozoğlak (TR) 90 Di 51
12340 Bozouls (F) 67 Ac 46
63850 Bozova (TR) 96 Da 53
63850 Bozova (TR) 98 Di 53
Boztepe (TR) 89 Df 50
11300 Bozüyük (TR) 88 Da 51
Bozyaka (TR) 96 Ck 54
33830* Bozyazı (TR) 97 Dd 54
12042 Bra (I) 68 Ah 46
00062 Bracciano (I) 84 Bc 48
41250 Bracieux (F) 67 Ab 43
84060 Bräcke (S) 21 Bf 28
NN13 Brackley (GB) 52 Si 38
RG12 Bracknell (GB) 52 Sk 39
Braclav (UA) 58 Ci 42
Braclavka (RUS) 65 Ga 39
335200 Brad (RO) 71 Cc 44
BD9 Bradford (GB) 51 Si 37
7568 Bradvari (BG) 73 Ch 47
Bradzjacin (BY) 57 Cd 39
8740 Brædstrup (DK) 38 Ak 35
AB35 Braemar (GB) 50 Sg 33
4700-001* Braga (P) 80 Sb 49
5300-001* Bragança (P) 80 Sd 49
92100* Brahestad (FIN) 22 Ce 26
Brahin (BY) 59 Da 39
000810* Brăila (RO) 73 Ch 45
CM7 Braintree (GB) 53 Aa 39
Brajiliv (UA) 58 Ci 41
26919 Brake (Unterweser) (D) 38 Ai 37
33034 Brakel (D) 54 Ak 39
37010 Bräkne-Hoby (S) 39 Bf 34
46065 Brålanda (S) 29 Bc 32
33057 Brálos (GR) 94 Cc 52
6740 Bramming (DK) 38 Ai 35
NR34 Brampton (GB) 51 Sh 36
49565 Bramsche (D) 54 Ah 38
Brånaberg (S) 21 Bg 25
89036 Brancaleone Marina (I) 84 Bg 53
Brandbu (N) 28 Ba 30
7330 Brande (DK) 38 Ak 35
14770* Brandenburg an der Havel (D) 55 Bc 38
IP27 Brandon (GB) 53 Aa 38
250 01 Brandýs nad Labem-Stará Boleslav (CZ) 55 Be 40
14-500 Braniewo (PL) 40 Bk 36
Br'anka (UA) 60 Di 42
34829 Brañosera (E) 81 Sf 48
17-120 Brańsk (PL) 41 Cc 38
24310 Brantôme (F) 66 Aa 45
Braslav (BY) 42 Ch 35
000500* Braşov (RO) 72 Cf 45
2930 Brasschaat (B) 53 Ae 39
1348 Brassus, Le (CH) 68 Ag 44
45420 Brastad (S) 28 Bb 32
810 00* Bratislava (SK) 56 Bh 42
6250 Bratja Daskalovi (BG) 87 Cf 48
Bratki (RUS) 61 Eb 39
207095 Bratovoeşti (RO) 72 Cd 46
Brats'ke (UA) 74 Db 43
6270 Brattvåg (N) 20 Ag 28
Bratunac (BIH) 71 Bk 46
5280* Braunau am Inn (A) 55 Bd 42
38700 Braunlage (D) 55 Ba 39
38100* Braunschweig (D) 55 Ba 38
Bray = Bré (IRL) 49 Sd 37
77480 Bray-sur-Seine (F) 53 Ad 42
13450 Brazatortas (E) 93 Sf 52
Brčko (BIH) 71 Bi 46
62-620 Brdów (PL) 56 Bi 38
Bré = Bray (IRL) 49 Sd 37
50370 Brécey (F) 52 Si 42
DD9 Brechin (GB) 50 Sh 34
2960 Brecht (B) 53 Ae 39
690 02* Břeclav (CZ) 56 Bg 42
LD3 Brecon (GB) 52 Sg 39
4800* Breda (NL) 53 Ae 39
33010 Bredaryd (S) 29 Bd 33
83100 Bredbyn (S) 21 Bi 27
33650 Brède, la (F) 66 Sk 46
Bredsel (S) 22 Ca 25
25821 Bredstedt (D) 38 Ai 36
Bredy (RUS) 65 Ga 38
53150 Bree (B) 54 Af 39
Bregadnaja (RUS) 76 Eb 47
6900* Bregenz (A) 69 Ak 43
6878 Bregovo (BG) 71 Cc 46
50290 Bréhal (F) 52 Si 42
Breiðavik (IS) 48 Qf 25
760 Breiðdalsvík (IS) 48 Rg 26
79206 Breisach am Rhein (D) 54 Ah 42
9593 Breivikbotn (N) 15 Cc 20
Brejtovo (RUS) 32 Dh 32
Brekken (N) 20 Bb 28
Brekkestø (N) 28 Ai 32
Brekksillan (N) 20 Bb 26
7130 Brekstad (N) 20 Ak 27
Bremangerpollen (N) 20 Ae 29
28195* Bremen (D) 38 Ai 37
27568* Bremerhaven (D) 38 Ai 37
27432 Bremervörde (D) 38 Ak 37
41310 Brenes (E) 92 Se 53
HS2 Brenish (GB) 50 Sc 32
25043 Breno (I) 69 Ba 45
CM13 Brentwood (GB) 53 Aa 39
Brescia (I) 69 Ba 45
4510 Breskens (NL) 53 Ad 39
39042 Bressanone = Brixen (I) 69 Bb 44
79300* Bressuire (F) 66 Sk 44
Brèst (BY) 57 Cd 38
29200* Brest (F) 52 Sf 42
Brest = Brèst (BY) 57 Cd 38
46130 Bretenoux (F) 67 Ab 46
60120 Breteuil (F) 53 Aa 42
60120 Breteuil (F) 53 Ac 41
75015 Bretten (D) 54 Ai 41
Brevik (N) 28 Ak 31
Breza (BIH) 71 Bi 46
8250 Brežice (SLO) 70 Bf 45
Brežnev = Nabereżnye Čelny (RUS) 46 Fc 35
2972 Breznica (BG) 87 Cd 49
Brežnica (PL) 56 Bk 39
2360 Breznik (BG) 86 Cc 48
977 01 Brezno (SK) 56 Bk 42
245500 Brezoi (RO) 72 Ce 45
28270 Brezolles (F) 53 Ab 42
906 13 Brezová pod Bradlom (SK) 56 Bh 42
5083 Brezovo (BG) 87 Cf 48

Brezovo | 167

Campo (E) 82 Aa 48
6100 Campobasso (I) 85 Be 49
2023 Campobello di Licata (I) 84 Bd 53
13610 Campo de Criptana (E) 81 Sg 51
7370-010* Campo Maior (P) 80 Sc 51
44158 Campos (E) 82 Ad 51
18565 Campotéjar (E) 93 Sg 53
15100 Câmpulung (RO) 72 Cf 45
725100 Câmpulung Moldovenesc (RO) 72 Cf 43
Çamsu (TR) 96 Ck 52
01365 Çamuzcu (TR) 97 Df 54
Čamzihka (RUS) 45 Ef 36
Čamzinka (RUS) 45 Ef 36
17400 Çan (TR) 87 Ch 50
17400 Çan (TR) 91 Ea 51
27440 Canabal (E) 80 Sc 48
28810 Çanakçı (TR) 90 Di 50
28810 Çanakçı (TR) 98 Dk 53
17000* Çanakkale (TR) 87 Cg 50
46650 Canals (E) 82 Sk 52
35260 Cancale (F) 52 Si 42
47290 Cancon (F) 66 Aa 46
Candarlı (TR) 88 Ck 50
35986 Çandarlı (TR) 95 Cg 52
33430 Candás (Carreño) (E) 80 Se 47
49440 Candé (F) 66 Si 43
71024 Candela (I) 85 Bf 49
05480 Candeleda (E) 80 Se 50
66620 Çandır (TR) 89 Dd 50
66620 Çandır (TR) 89 Df 51
66620 Çandır (TR) 96 Da 53
14053 Canelli (I) 68 Ai 46
22880* Canfranc (E) 82 Sk 48
Cangas (E) 80 Sb 48
33800 Cangas del Narcea (E) 80 Sd 47
33550 Cangas de Onís (Cangues d'Onís) (E) 80 Se 47
92024 Canicatti (I) 84 Bd 53
49440 Cañizal (E) 80 Se 49
Çankaya (TR) 89 Dc 51
18000 Çankırı (TR) 89 Dd 50
06400* Cannes (F) 68 Ah 47
IV4 Cannich (GB) 50 Sf 33
WS11 Cannock (GB) 51 Sh 38
70053 Canosa di Puglia (I) 85 Bg 49
40320 Cantalejo (E) 81 Sg 49
37405 Cantalpino (E) 80 Se 49
3060-121* Cantanhede (P) 80 Sb 50
7300 Cantemir (MD) 73 Ci 44
CT1 Canterbury (GB) 53 Ab 39
61044 Cantiano (I) 69 Bc 47
41320 Cantillana (E) 92 Se 53
22063 Cantù (I) 69 Ak 45
76450 Cany-Barville (F) 53 Aa 41
30021 Caorle (I) 69 Bc 45
84047 Capaccio (I) 85 Bf 50
Čapaevo (RUS) 77 Ei 45
Čapaevskj (RUS) 45 Ek 38
Caparde (BIH) 71 Bi 46
40130 Capbreton (F) 66 Si 47
12700 Capdenac-Gare (F) 67 Ac 46
Cape Gata (CY) 96 Dc 56
Capel'ka (RUS) 31 Ci 32
02260 Capelle, la (F) 53 Ad 41
Čapljina (BIH) 85 Bh 47
Čaplygin (RUS) 44 Dk 37
Čaplynka (UA) 74 Dd 44
25044 Capo di Ponte (I) 69 Ba 44
98071 Capo d'Orlando (I) 84 Be 52
88841 Capo Rizzuto (I) 85 Bh 52
Cappoquin = Ceapach Choinn (IRL) 49 Sc 38
Capranica (I) 84 Bc 48
217125 Căpreni (RO) 72 Cd 46
80073 Capri (I) 85 Be 50
33840 Captieux (F) 66 Sk 46
Capua (I) 85 Be 49
Čara (HR) 85 Bg 48
235200 Caracal (RO) 72 Ce 46
31460 Caraman (F) 67 Ab 47
33114 Caranga (E) 80 Sd 47
325400 Caransebeş (RO) 71 Cc 45
827061 Caraorman (RO) 73 Ck 45
32500 Carballino, O (E) 80 Sb 48
15186 Carballo (E) 80 Sb 47
09013 Carbonia (I) 83 Ai 51
31390 Carbonne (F) 67 Ab 47
17043 Carcare (I) 68 Ai 46
11000* Carcassonne (F) 82 Ac 47
83570 Carcès (F) 68 Ag 47
66320* Çardak (TR) 96 Ck 53
66320* Çardak (TR) 98 Dg 52
14445 Cardeña (E) 93 Sf 52
CF24 Cardiff (GB) 52 Sg 39
SA43 Cardigan (GB) 52 Sf 38
08261 Cardona (E) 82 Ab 49
445100 Carei (RO) 71 Cc 43
50500 Carentan (F) 52 Si 41
8260 Carevo (BG) 88 Ch 48
20130 Cargèse (F) 83 Ai 48
29270* Carhaix-Plouguer (F) 52 Sg 42
87062 Cariati (I) 85 Bg 51
33750 Caridad, La (E) 80 Sd 47

08110 Carignan (F) 54 Af 41
Çarıklıfabrıkasıköyü (TR) 99 Ea 53
Carini (I) 84 Bd 52
7280 Car Kalojan (BG) 72 Cg 47
727110 Cârlibaba (RO) 72 Cf 43
CA2 Carlisle (GB) 51 Sh 36
09014 Carloforte (I) 83 Ai 51
14100 Carlota, La (E) 93 Sf 53
Carlow = Ceatharlach (IRL) 49 Sd 38
HS2 Carloway (GB) 50 Sd 32
10022 Carmagnola (I) 68 Ah 46
SA31 Carmarthen (GB) 52 Sf 39
81400 Carmaux (F) 67 Ac 46
Cármenes (E) 80 Se 48
39558 Carmona (E) 92 Se 53
56340* Carnac (F) 66 Sg 43
Carn Domhnach (IRL) 49 Sc 35
Carndonagh = Carn Domhnach (IRL) 49 Sc 35
LA5 Carnforth (GB) 51 Sh 36
2163 Carnikava (LV) 30 Ce 33
DD7 Carnoustie (GB) 50 Sh 34
23200 Carolina, La (E) 93 Sg 52
26409 Carolinensiel (D) 38 Ah 37
Čarozero (RUS) 32 Di 30
84200 Carpentras (F) 68 Af 46
41012 Carpi (I) 69 Ba 46
307090 Cărpiniş (RO) 71 Ca 45
44470 Carquefou (F) 66 Si 43
PA28 Carradale (GB) 49 Se 35
Carraig Air (IRL) 49 Sc 35
Carraig an Chabhalfaigh (IRL) 49 Sa 38
Carraig Mhachaire Rois (IRL) 49 Sd 37
Carraig na Siúire (IRL) 49 Sc 38
Carral (E) 80 Sb 47
54033 Carrara (I) 69 Ba 46
5140-053* Carrazeda de Ansiães (P) 80 Sc 49
PH23 Carrbridge (GB) 50 Sg 33
Carrick = An Charraig (IRL) 49 Sb 36
Carrickart = Carraig Air (IRL) 49 Sc 35
BT38 Carrickfergus (GB) 49 Se 36
Carrickmacross = Carraig Mhachaire Rois (IRL) 49 Sd 37
Carrick on Shannon = Cora Droma Rúisc (IRL) 49 Sb 37
Carrick on Suir = Carraig na Siúire (IRL) 49 Sc 38
Carrigaholt = Carraig an Chabhalfaigh (IRL) 49 Sa 38
13150 Carrión de Calatrava (E) 81 Sg 51
34120 Carrión de los Condes (E) 81 Sf 48
Çarşamba (TR) 90 Dg 49
61420 Çarşıbaşı (TR) 90 Dk 49
DG7 Carsphairn (GB) 51 Sf 35
30201* Cartagena (E) 93 Sk 53
2070-003* Cartaxo (P) 80 Sb 51
21450 Cartea (E) 92 Sc 53
50270 Carteret, Barneville- (F) 52 Si 41
62220 Carvin (F) 53 Ac 40
Caryčanka (UA) 59 De 42
Casa del Puerto (E) 93 Si 52
15033 Casale Monferrato (I) 68 Ai 45
70010 Casamassima (I) 85 Bg 50
20290 Casamozza (F) 83 Ak 48
29690 Casares (E) 92 Se 54
05450 Casavieja (E) 81 Sf 50
2750-001* Cascais (P) 92 Sa 52
81100 Caserta (I) 85 Be 49
Cashel = Caiseal (IRL) 49 Sc 38
46171 Casinos (E) 82 Sk 51
Časiv Jar (UA) 60 Dh 42
286 01 Čáslav (CZ) 56 Bf 41
NP19 Casnewydd = Newport (GB) 52 Sh 39
Čašniki (BY) 42 Ck 36
Casoli (I) 85 Be 48
Časovenskoe (RUS) 32 Dd 30
Časovo (RUS) 26 Fa 28
50700 Caspe (E) 82 Sk 49
59670 Cassel (F) 53 Ac 40
03043 Cassino (I) 84 Bd 49
13260 Cassis (F) 68 Af 47
10340 Castañar de Ibor (E) 80 Se 51
3280-007* Castanheira de Pêra (P) 80 Sb 50
90013 Castelbuono (I) 84 Be 53
67031 Castel di Sangro (I) 85 Be 49
Castelfranco Veneto (I) 69 Bb 45
00040 Castel Gandolfo (I) 84 Bc 49
47700 Casteljaloux (F) 66 Aa 46

84048 Castellabate (I) 85 Be 50
Castellammare del Golfo (I) 84 Bc 52
80053 Castellammare di Stabia (I) 85 Be 50
04120 Castellane (F) 68 Ag 47
13750 Castellar de Santiago (E) 93 Sg 52
23260 Castellar de Santisteban (E) 93 Sg 52
25154 Castelldans (E) 82 Aa 49
08860 Castelldefels (E) 82 Ab 49
18740 Castell de Ferro (E) 93 Sg 54
SA11 Castell-nedd = Neath (GB) 52 Sg 39
12001 Castelló de la Plana (E) 82 Sk 51
12001 Castellón de la Plana = Castelló de la Plana (E) 82 Sk 51
44560 Castellote (E) 82 Sk 50
11400* Castelnaudary (F) 67 Ab 47
65230 Castelnau-Magnoac (F) 66 Aa 47
42035 Castelnovo ne'Monti (I) 69 Ba 46
53019 Castelnuovo Berardenga (I) 69 Bb 47
55032 Castelnuovo di Garfagnana (I) 69 Ba 46
6005-001 Castelo Branco (P) 80 Sc 51
82100* Castelsarrasin (F) 67 Ab 46
92025 Casteltermini (I) 84 Bd 53
91022 Castelvetrano (I) 84 Bc 53
40300 Castets (F) 66 Si 47
57012 Castiglioncello (I) 69 Ba 47
06061 Castiglione del Lago (I) 84 Bc 47
Castiglione della Pescaia (I) 84 Ba 48
52043 Castiglion Fiorentino (I) 69 Bb 47
06680 Castilblanco (E) 80 Se 51
41230 Castilblanco de los Arroyos (E) 92 Se 53
Castillo, O (Salvaterra de Miño) (E) 80 Sb 48
45641 Castillo de Bayuela (E) 81 Sf 50
09800 Castillon-en-Couserans (F) 82 Ab 48
33350 Castillon-la-Bataille (F) 66 Sk 46
47330 Castillonnès (F) 66 Aa 46
Castlebar = Caisleán an Bharraigh (IRL) 49 Sa 37
HS9 Castlebay (GB) 50 Sc 34
Castlebellingham = Baile an Ghearlánaigh (IRL) 49 Sd 37
Castleblayney (IRL) 49 Sd 36
BT81 Castlederg (GB) 49 Sc 36
Castleisland = Oileán Ciarrai (IRL) 49 Sa 38
Castlepollard = Baile na gCros (IRL) 49 Sc 37
Castlerea = An Caisleán Riabhach (IRL) 49 Sb 37
IM9 Castletown (GBM) 51 Sf 36
Castletown Bearhaven = Baile Chaisleáin Bhéarra (IRL) 49 Rl 39
81100* Castres (F) 67 Ac 47
1900 Castricum (NL) 53 Ae 38
18816 Castril (E) 93 Sh 53
3600-069* Castro Daire (P) 80 Sc 50
09110 Castrojeriz (E) 81 Sf 48
33760 Castropol (E) 80 Sc 47
39700 Castro-Urdiales (E) 66 Sg 47
7780-090* Castro Verde (P) 92 Sb 53
87012 Castrovillari (I) 85 Bg 51
06420 Castuera (E) 92 Se 52
Častye (RUS) 35 Ff 33
Çat (TR) 91 Ea 51
Çatak (TR) 88 Da 50
Çatak (TR) 97 Dd 54
Çatak (TR) 99 Ed 52
01790 Çatalan (TR) 97 Df 53
Çatalarmut (TR) 90 Dk 51
34540* Çatalca (TR) 88 Ci 49
Çatalçam (TR) 90 Di 51
Çatallar (TR) 96 Da 54
827076 Cataloi (RO) 73 Ci 45
95100 Catania (I) 84 Bf 53
88100 Catanzaro (I) 85 Bg 52
Catanzaro Lido (I) 85 Bg 52
59360 Cateau-Cambrésis, le (F) 53 Ad 40
94010 Catenanuova (I) 84 Be 53
Cathair na Mairt = Westport (IRL) 49 Sa 37
Catheir Saidhbhin (IRL) 49 Rk 39
Çatköy (TR) 98 Dg 54
Cattolica (I) 69 Bc 47
59540 Caudry (F) 53 Ad 40
22350 Caulnes (F) 52 Sh 42
11160 Caunes-Minervois (F) 67 Ac 47
4300 Căuşeni (MD) 73 Ck 44

82300 Caussade (F) 67 Ab 46
65110 Cauterets (F) 82 Sk 48
84300 Cavaillon (F) 68 Af 47
12230 Cavalerie, la (F) 67 Ad 46
Cavan = An Cabhán (IRL) 49 Sc 37
Čavan'ga (RUS) 24 Dh 24
30014 Cavarzere (I) 69 Bc 45
Çavdar (TR) 95 Ch 53
43710 Çavdarhisar (TR) 88 Ck 51
15900 Çavdır (TR) 96 Ck 53
Cavtat (HR) 85 Bi 48
55420 Çavuş (TR) 96 Db 53
Çavuşçugöl (TR) 96 Db 52
Çavuşköy (TR) 96 Da 54
Çavuşlar (TR) 89 Dc 49
Čavusy (BY) 42 Da 37
37270 Çay (TR) 96 Db 52
34886 Çayağzı (TR) 88 Ck 49
36500 Çayarası (TR) 91 Ec 50
Çaybağı (TR) 98 Dk 52
05300 Çaybaşı (TR) 90 Dh 49
27700 Çaybeyi (TR) 98 Dh 54
67900 Çaycuma (TR) 89 Dc 49
53200 Çayeli (TR) 91 Ea 49
80410 Cayeux-sur-Mer (F) 53 Ab 40
42335 Çayhan (TR) 97 De 53
55700 Çayır (TR) 89 Df 49
66600 Çayıralan (TR) 89 Df 51
36000 Çayırbaşı (TR) 91 Ec 50
06922 Çayırhan (TR) 88 Db 50
55300 Çayırkent (TR) 90 Dg 49
47510 Çayırlı (TR) 91 Ea 51
25900 Çayırözü (TR) 97 Df 52
Çaykara (TR) 91 Ea 50
49610 Çaylar (TR) 91 Eb 51
34520 Caylar, le (F) 67 Ad 47
Çaylarbaşı (TR) 98 Dk 53
82160 Caylus (F) 67 Ab 46
Çayönü (TR) 90 Dh 50
21560 Çaytepe (TR) 99 Ea 52
41370 Cazalla de la Sierra (E) 92 Se 53
64700 Cazaubon (F) 66 Sk 47
31220 Cazères (F) 82 Ab 47
Cazin (BIH) 70 Bf 46
Čazma (HR) 70 Bg 45
23470 Cazorla (E) 93 Sg 53
24174 Cea (E) 80 Se 48
6101 Ceadîr-Lunga (MD) 73 Ci 44
Ceanánnas (IRL) 49 Sd 37
Ceann Toirc (IRL) 49 Sb 38
Ceapach Choinn (IRL) 49 Sc 38
Ceatharlach = Carlow (IRL) 49 Sd 38
Čebarkul' (RUS) 47 Ga 35
37400 Çebeci (TR) 91 Ed 50
Čeboksary (RUS) 45 Eh 34
Čebotovka (RUS) 60 Dk 42
991 25 Čebovce (SK) 56 Bk 42
05260 Cebreros (E) 81 Sf 50
Čebsara (RUS) 32 Di 31
Čeburga (RUS) 37 Gi 33
03023 Ceccano (I) 84 Bd 49
7013 Cece (H) 71 Bi 44
Čečel'nyk (UA) 58 Ck 42
Cecimli (TR) 98 Dh 52
Cecina (I) 69 Ba 47
15350 Cedeira (E) 80 Sb 47
10513 Cedillo (E) 80 Sc 51
44147 Cedrillas (E) 82 Sk 50
90015 Cefalù (I) 84 Be 52
Čegem Pervyj (RUS) 76 Ed 47
Ceği (LV) 30 Cc 33
2700 Cegléd (H) 71 Bk 43
Ceglie Messapico (I) 85 Bh 50
1237 Čegrane (MK) 86 Ca 49
30430 Cehegín (E) 93 Si 52
Čehov (RUS) 43 Dh 35
SA45 Ceinewydd = New Quay (GB) 52 Sf 38
Čekalin (RUS) 43 Dg 36
66500 Çekerek (TR) 89 Df 50
Çekirge (TR) 89 Dc 51
Čekmaguš (RUS) 46 Fe 35
Čekšino (RUS) 33 Ea 31
Celâli (TR) 90 Dh 51
67043 Celano (I) 84 Bd 48
32800 Celanova (E) 80 Sc 48
Čelbasskaja (RUS) 75 Dk 45
Celbridge = Cill Droichid (IRL) 49 Sd 37
71810 Çelebi (TR) 89 Dd 51
Čelić (BIH) 71 Bi 46
02600 Çelikhan (TR) 98 Di 52
Čelina (RUS) 76 Eb 44
Čelinnyj (RUS) 47 Fi 37
Čelinnyj (RUS) 76 Ee 44
Čeljabinsk (RUS) 47 Gb 35
Celjachany (BY) 58 Cf 38
3000* Celje (SLO) 70 Bf 44
9500 Celldömölk (H) 70 Bh 43
29221* Celle (D) 55 Ba 38
Čelno-Veršiny (RUS) 46 Fb 36
6360-287* Celorico da Beira (P) 80 Sc 50
Çeltek (TR) 96 Db 52
Çeltik (TR) 88 Db 51

Çeltikçi (TR) 89 Dc 50
Çeltikçi (TR) 96 Da 53
Çeltikli (TR) 89 Dc 51
19050 Çemilbey (TR) 89 Df 50
50420 Çemilköy (TR) 97 De 52
62600 Çemişgezek (TR) 90 Di 51
Cé na Cille Móire (IRL) 49 Sd 38
Cengerli (TR) 90 Di 51
36500 Cengilli (TR) 91 Ec 50
33150 Cenon (F) 66 Sk 46
08540 Centelles (E) 82 Ac 49
44042 Cento (I) 69 Bb 46
Central'no-Kospašskij (RUS) 35 Fh 31
Central'nyj (RUS) 34 Fa 31
Čepeck, Kirovo- (RUS) 34 Fa 32
Čepeckij (RUS) 34 Fb 32
4850 Čepelare (BG) 87 Ce 49
Čepin (HR) 71 Bi 45
Çepni (TR) 88 Db 50
5253 Čepovan (SLO) 69 Bd 44
Čerachavka (BY) 59 Db 38
66290 Cerbère (F) 82 Ad 48
7555-101 Cercal (P) 92 Sb 53
87070 Cerchiara di Calabria (I) 85 Bg 51
Çerçiler (TR) 89 Df 49
58340 Cercy-la-Tour (F) 67 Ad 44
Čerdakly (RUS) 45 Ei 36
36130 Cerdedo (E) 80 Sb 48
45620 Cerdon (F) 67 Ac 43
Čerdyn' (RUS) 35 Fg 30
Čerelennye Buruny (RUS) 77 Ef 46
Čeremošnica (RUS) 34 Eg 31
Čeremšan (RUS) 46 Fb 36
Čeremšanka (RUS) 47 Ga 34
Čeremuhovo (RUS) 36 Ga 30
Čerencovo (RUS) 31 Dc 31
Čerenskoe (RUS) 32 Df 32
Čerepovec (RUS) 32 Dh 31
10070 Ceres (I) 68 Ah 45
66400 Céret (F) 82 Ac 48
Čerevkovo (RUS) 25 Ef 29
40591 Cerezo de Abajo (E) 81 Sg 49
71042 Cerignola (I) 85 Bf 49
03350 Cérilly (F) 67 Ac 44
79140 Cerizay (F) 66 Sk 44
Čerkas'ke (UA) 60 Dh 42
Čerkasskoe (RUS) 62 Eh 38
Čerkassy = Čerkasy (UA) 59 Dc 41
Čerkasy (UA) 59 Dc 41
18600 Çerkeş (TR) 89 Dc 50
Čerkessk (RUS) 76 Ec 46
59500 Çerkezköy (TR) 88 Ci 49
1380 Cerknica (SLO) 70 Be 45
5959 Cerkovica (BG) 72 Ce 47
Čerkutino (RUS) 44 Dk 34
317075 Cermei (RO) 71 Cb 44
Čermenino (RUS) 33 Ed 31
21600 Çermik (TR) 98 Dk 52
Čermoz (RUS) 35 Fg 32
Čern' (RUS) 43 Dg 37
827045 Cerna (RO) 73 Ci 45
Černaja, Ust'- (RUS) 35 Fc 30
Černaja Holunica (RUS) 34 Fb 32
207185 Cernătești (RO) 72 Cd 46
Černava (RUS) 44 Dk 37
Černavka (RUS) 61 Ec 38
905200 Cernavodă (RO) 73 Ci 46
68700 Cernay (F) 68 Ah 43
Cernégula (E) 81 Sg 48
Černevo (RUS) 31 Ci 32
Černigov = Černihiv (UA) 59 Db 39
Černigovskaja (RUS) 75 Dk 46
Černihiv (UA) 59 Db 39
Černivci (UA) 58 Cf 42
Černjachiv (UA) 58 Ci 40
Černjahovsk (RUS) 40 Cb 36
Černjanka (RUS) 60 Dh 40
Černoborskaja (RUS) 26 Fd 25
Černoe (RUS) 34 Eg 33
Černoe (RUS) 37 Gk 33
Černogolovka (RUS) 43 Di 34
Černoistočinsk (RUS) 36 Fk 33
Černoreč'e (RUS) 47 Ga 36
Černorečenskij (RUS) 35 Fc 30
Černovcy = Černivci (UA) 58 Cf 42
Černovskoe (RUS) 34 Eh 32
Černovskoe (RUS) 35 Fe 33
Černovskoe (RUS) 45 Ef 35
Černozer'e (RUS) 45 Ee 34
Černuška (RUS) 47 Fg 34
Černut'evo (RUS) 26 Ei 27
Černyhivka (UA) 75 Dg 43
Černyj Jar (RUS) 62 Eg 42
Černyj Otrog (RUS) 64 Fg 39
Černyškovskij (RUS) 61 Ec 42
Čerrik (AL) 86 Bk 49
50052 Certaldo (I) 69 Bb 47
Čertkovo (RUS) 44 Ec 35
Čertkovo (RUS) 61 Ea 41
Čerusti (RUS) 44 Ea 35
Červa (RUS) 26 Ei 28

A B C D E F G H I J K L M N O P Q R S T U V W X Y Z

Červa | 169

Čèrven' BY 42 Ci 37
5980 Červen Brjag BG 72 Ce 47
25200 Cervera E 82 Ab 49
34840 Cervera de Pisuerga E 81 Sf 48
00052 Cerveteri I 84 Bc 49
48015 Cervia I 69 Bc 46
33052 Cervignano del Friuli I 69 Bd 45
83012 Cervinara I 85 Be 49
20221 Cervione F 83 Ak 48
Cervo E 80 Sc 47
Červone UA 59 De 39
Červonoarmijs'k UA 58 Cf 40
Červonoarmijs'k UA 58 Ci 40
Červonoarmijs'ke UA 73 Ci 45
Červonograd = Červonohrad UA 57 Ce 40
Červonohrad UA 57 Ce 40
Červonozavods'ke UA 59 Dd 40
Červonoznam'janka UA 73 Da 43
Čèrykav BY 42 Db 37
47023 Cesena I 69 Bc 46
Cesenatico I 69 Bc 46
4101 Cēsis LV 30 Cf 33
407 21 Česká Kamenice CZ 55 Be 40
470 01* Česká Lípa CZ 55 Be 40
560 02* Česká Třebová CZ 56 Bg 41
370 01* České Budějovice CZ 55 Be 42
282 01 Český Brod CZ 55 Be 40
381 01 Český Krumlov CZ 55 Be 42
735 61* Český Těšín CZ 56 Bi 41
Česma RUS 47 Ga 37
35930 Çeşme TR 95 Cg 52
42445 Çeşmelisebil TR 96 Dc 52
31210 Cestobrodica SRB 71 Ca 47
4871 Cesvaine LV 41 Cg 34
207190 Cetate RO 72 Cd 46
81 250 Cetinje MNE 86 Bi 48
58920 Çetinkaya TR 90 Dh 51
87022 Cetraro I 85 Bf 51
Četyrman, Bala- RUS 46 Ff 37
Ceuta (Sebta) E 92 Se 55
12073 Ceva I 68 Ai 46
73400 Cevizdüzü TR 99 Ec 53
Cevizli TR 96 Db 53
Cevizlik TR 90 Dg 49
Çevizlik TR 99 Ec 52
81 258 Čevo MNE 86 Bi 48
01920* Ceyhan TR 97 Df 53
63570 Ceylanpınar TR 99 Ea 54
16150 Chabanais F 66 Aa 45
26120 Chabeuil F 68 Af 46
89800 Chablis F 67 Ad 43
36210 Chabris F 67 Ab 43
71150 Chagny F 67 Ae 44
43160 Chaise-Dieu, la F 67 Ad 45
36370 Chalais F 66 Aa 45
45120 Châlette-sur-Loing F 53 Ac 42
85300 Challans F 66 Si 44
49290 Chalonnes-sur-Loire F 66 Sk 43
51000 Châlons-en-Champagne F 53 Ae 42
Châlons-sur-Marne = Châlons-en-Champagne F 53 Ae 42
71100* Chalon-sur-Saône F 67 Ae 44
Chalopeničy BY 42 Ci 36
87230 Châlus F 66 Aa 45
93413 Cham D 55 Bc 41
73000* Chambéry F 68 Af 45
43400 Chambon-sur-Lignon, le F 67 Ae 45
41250 Chambord F 67 Ab 43
87140 Chamborêt F 67 Ab 44
74400* Chamonix-Mont-Blanc F 68 Ag 45
16350 Champagne-Mouton F 66 Aa 45
39300* Champagnole F 68 Af 44
51270 Champaubert F 53 Ad 42
1874 Champéry CH 68 Ag 44
70600 Champlitte F 68 Af 43
11020 Champoluc I 68 Ah 45
27500 Chantada E 80 Sc 48
60500 Chantilly F 53 Ac 41
Chantôme, Eguzon- F 67 Ab 44
85110 Chantonnay F 66 Si 44
18380 Chapelle-d'Angillon, la F 67 Ac 43
TA20 Chard GB 52 Sh 40
58400* Charité-sur-Loire, la F 67 Ad 43
Charkiv UA 60 Dg 41
Charkow = Charkiv UA 60 Dg 41
6000 Charleroi B 53 Ae 40
Charlestown = Baile Chathail IRL 49 Sb 37
08000* Charleville-Mézières F 53 Ae 41
67301 Charlottenberg S 29 Bc 31
88130 Charmes F 54 Ag 42
89120 Charny F 67 Ad 43
71120 Charolles F 67 Ae 44
28000* Chartres F 53 Ab 42
16260 Chasseneuil-sur-Bonnieure F 66 Aa 45
85130 Châtaigneraie, la F 66 Sk 44
04160 Château-Arnoux F 68 Ag 46
56500 Châteaubriant F 66 Si 43
58120 Château-Chinon F 67 Ad 43
1837 Château-d'Oex CH 68 Ah 44
17480 Château-d'Oléron, Le F 66 Si 45
72500 Château-du-Loir F 66 Aa 43
28200 Châteaudun F 53 Ab 42
53200* Château-Gontier F 66 Sk 43
77570 Château-Landon F 53 Ac 42
37330 Château-la-Vallière F 66 Aa 43
29150 Châteaulin F 52 Sf 42
18370 Châteaumeillant F 67 Ac 44
48170 Châteauneuf-de-Randon F 67 Ad 46
29520 Châteauneuf-du-Faou F 52 Sg 42
28170 Châteauneuf-en-Thymerais F 53 Ab 42
16120 Châteauneuf-sur-Charente F 66 Sk 45
45110 Châteauneuf-sur-Loire F 67 Ac 43
49330 Châteauneuf-sur-Sarthe F 66 Sk 43
87290 Châteauponsac F 67 Ab 44
37110 Château-Renault F 66 Aa 43
36000* Châteauroux F 67 Ab 44
57170 Château-Salins F 54 Ag 42
02400* Château-Thierry F 53 Ad 41
52120 Châteauvillain F 53 Ae 42
17340 Châtelaillon-Plage F 66 Si 44
6200 Châtelet B 53 Ae 40
86100 Châtellerault F 66 Aa 44
11024 Châtillon I 68 Ah 45
45230 Châtillon-Coligny F 67 Ac 43
58110 Châtillon-en-Bazois F 67 Ad 43
26410 Châtillon-en-Diois F 68 Af 46
01400 Châtillon-sur-Chalaronne F 67 Ae 44
36700 Châtillon-sur-Indre F 67 Ab 44
21400* Châtillon-sur-Seine F 67 Ae 43
86390 Châtre, la F 67 Ab 44
15110 Chaudes-Aigues F 67 Ad 46
71170 Chauffailles F 67 Ae 44
52000* Chaumont F 54 Af 42
52000* Chaumont F 67 Ab 44
02300* Chauny F 53 Ad 41
86300 Chauvigny F 66 Aa 44
2300* Chaux-de-Fonds, La CH 68 Ag 43
5000-215 Chaves P 80 Sc 49
350 02 Cheb CZ 55 Bc 40
79110 Chef-Boutonne F 66 Sk 44
06105 Cheles E 92 Sc 52
22-100 Chełm PL 57 Cd 39
62-660 Chełmno PL 40 Bi 37
CM2 Chelmsford GB 53 Aa 39
87-140 Chełmża PL 40 Bi 37
GL50 Cheltenham GB 52 Sh 39
46176 Chelva E 82 Sk 51
49120 Chemillé F 66 Sk 43
09111* Chemnitz D 55 Bc 40
NP16 Chepstow GB 52 Sh 39
50100 Cherbourg-Octeville F 52 Si 41
Cherman MD 73 Ch 43
89690 Chéroy F 53 Ad 42
Cherson UA 74 Dc 44
KT15 Chertsey GB 52 Sk 39
46380 Cheste E 82 Sk 51
CH1 Chester GB 51 Sh 37
CT5 Chesterfield GB 51 Si 37
03230 Chevagnes F 67 Ad 44
52170 Chevillon F 54 Af 42
45520 Chevilly F 53 Ab 42
79120 Chey F 66 Sk 44
07160 Cheylard, le F 67 Ae 46
60033 Chiaravalle I 69 Bd 47
88064 Chiaravalle Centrale I 85 Bg 52
25032 Chiari I 69 Ak 45
16043 Chiavari I 69 Ak 46
23022 Chiavenna I 69 Ak 44
PO19 Chichester GB 52 Sk 40
11130 Chiclana de la Frontera E 92 Sd 54
10023 Chieri I 68 Ah 45
66100 Chieti I 85 Be 48
6460 Chimay B 53 Ae 40
02520 Chinchilla de Monte Aragón E 93 Si 52
28370 Chinchón E 81 Sg 50
37500 Chinon F 66 Aa 43
30015 Chioggia I 69 Bc 45
Chiperceni MD 73 Ci 43
11550 Chipiona E 92 Sd 54
SN15 Chippenham GB 52 Sh 39
BS37 Chipping Sodbury GB 52 Sh 39
04825 Chirivel E 93 Sh 53
2000 Chişinău MD 73 Ci 43
315100 Chişineu-Criş RO 71 Cb 44
53043 Chiusi I 69 Bb 47
10034 Chivasso I 68 Ah 45
Chlystunivka UA 59 Db 41
Chmeliv UA 59 Dd 40
Chmel'nyc'kyj UA 58 Cg 41
Chmel'nyc'kyj, Perejaslav- UA 59 Db 40
36-016 Chmielnik PL 57 Ca 40
Chmil'nyk UA 58 Ch 41
565 01 Choceň CZ 56 Bg 41
Chocimsk BY 42 Dc 37
73-120 Chociwel PL 39 Bf 37
Chočyne UA 58 Ch 39
87-860 Chodecz PL 56 Bk 38
Chodoriv UA 57 Ce 41
64-800 Chodzież PL 40 Bg 38
74-500 Chojna PL 39 Be 38
89-600 Chojnice PL 40 Bh 37
Chojniki BY 58 Ck 39
49300* Cholet F 66 Sk 43
Cholmeč BY 59 Da 38
Cholmy UA 59 Dc 39
430 01* Chomutov CZ 55 Bd 40
05230 Chorges F 68 Ag 46
Chorol UA 59 Dd 41
06-330 Chorzele PL 40 Ca 37
41-500 Chorzów PL 56 Bi 40
73-200 Choszczno PL 39 Bf 37
583 01 Chotěboř CZ 56 Bf 41
Chotin' UA 59 De 39
Chotyn UA 58 Cg 42
Chovmy UA 59 Dc 39
Chrinivka BY 59 Db 38
Chrinivka UA 59 Db 38
BH23 Christchurch GB 52 Si 40
6070 Christiansfeld DK 38 Ak 35
537 01* Chrudim CZ 56 Bf 41
Chrysochou Bay CY 96 Dc 55
Chrystynivka UA 58 Ck 42
28-133 Chrzanów PL 56 Bk 40
7000* Chur CH 69 Ak 44
Chust UA 57 Cd 42
Chyriv UA 57 Cc 41
6101 Ciadîr-Lunga = Ceadîr-Lunga MD 73 Ci 44
Čiblega RUS 34 Fa 29
Çiçekdağı TR 89 De 51
Çiçekli TR 88 Ci 51
Çiçekli TR 91 Eb 51
Çiçekli TR 91 Ed 51
Çiçekli TR 97 Df 53
37400 Çicekyayla TR 89 De 49
06-400 Ciechanów PL 40 Ca 38
18-230 Ciechanowiec PL 41 Cc 38
28350 Ciempozuelos E 81 Sg 50
37-611 Cieszanów PL 57 Cd 40
63-435 Cieszyn PL 56 Bi 41
30530 Cieza E 93 Si 52
51910 Çiftehan TR 97 De 53
26700 Çifteler TR 88 Db 51
48700 Çiftlik TR 91 Ea 51
48700 Çiftlik TR 97 De 52
Çiftlikköy TR 89 De 49
Çiftlikköy TR 91 Ee 51
05000 Çiğdemlik TR 89 Df 50
30720 Çiğli TR 99 Ed 53
Čihačevo RUS 31 Ck 33
Cihadiye TR 97 Df 53
42850 Cihanbeyli TR 96 Dc 52
Čikman RUS 36 Fi 31
Čikola RUS 91 Ed 47
75400 Çıldır TR 91 Ed 49
Čilgar RUS 77 Ef 44
Çilhane TR 90 Dh 50
127180 Cilibia RO 73 Ch 45
237075 Cilieni RO 72 Ce 47
14360 Çilimli TR 88 Db 50
Čilipi HR 85 Bi 48
Cill Airne = Killarney IRL 49 Sa 38
Cill Bheagáin = Kilbeggan IRL 49 Sc 37
Cill Chainnigh = Kilkenny IRL 49 Sc 38
Cill Chaoi = Kilkee IRL 49 Sa 38
Cill Chuillin IRL 49 Sd 37
Cill Dalua IRL 49 Sb 38
Cill Dara = Kildare IRL 49 Sd 37
Cill Droichid IRL 49 Sd 37
Cillín Chaoimhín IRL 49 Sd 37
Cill Mhantáin = Wicklow IRL 49 Sd 38
Cill Náile IRL 49 Sc 38
Cill Orglan = Killorglin IRL 49 Sa 38
Cill Rois = Kilrush IRL 49 Sa 38
Cill Rónáin IRL 49 Sa 37
Cil'na RUS 45 Ei 36
Cilvegözü TR 98 Dg 54
4101 Cimişlia MD 73 Ci 44
Cimljansk RUS 76 Ec 43
Çimşit TR 89 Dc 51
Çınar TR 99 Ea 53
Çınarcık TR 88 Ck 50
09500 Çine TR 95 Ci 53
5590 Ciney B 54 Af 40
Cingaly RUS 37 Gk 30
62011 Cingoli I 69 Bd 47
Čin'javoryk RUS 26 Fc 27
Cinn Átha Gad IRL 49 Sc 37
Cinn Mhara IRL 49 Sb 37
927075 Ciochina RO 73 Ch 46
Cionn Sáile IRL 49 Sb 39
107160 Cioranii de Jos RO 72 Cg 46
13600 Ciotat, la F 68 Af 47
Cip'ja RUS 46 Fa 34
Ciprovci BG 71 Cc 47
3460 Čiprovci BG 71 Cc 47
58510 Çırçır TR 90 Dg 50
GL7 Cirencester GB 52 Si 39
54480 Cirey-sur-Vezouze F 54 Ag 42
10073 Ciriè I 68 Ah 45
Čirikovo RUS 43 Dh 35
88813 Cirò I 85 Bh 51
6200 Čirpan BG 87 Cf 48
Çırpı TR 95 Ch 52
127185 Cislău RO 72 Cg 45
Čišmy RUS 46 Ff 36
38-607 Cisna PL 57 Cc 41
Cista Provo HR 70 Bg 47
24800 Cistierna E 80 Se 48
Čistoe RUS 44 Ed 34
Čistopol' RUS 46 Fa 35
35013 Cittadella I 69 Bb 45
06062 Città della Pieve I 84 Bc 48
Città del Vaticano V 84 Bc 49
06012 Città di Castello I 69 Bc 47
Cittaducale I 84 Bc 48
89022 Cittanova I 85 Bg 52
407225 Ciucea RO 71 Cc 44
4114 Ciucur Mingir MD 73 Ci 44
827055 Ciucurova RO 73 Ci 46
13001* Ciudad Real E 81 Sg 52
37500 Ciudad-Rodrigo E 80 Sd 50
07760 Ciutadella E 82 Ad 51
33043 Cividale del Friuli I 69 Bd 44
Civil'sk RUS 45 Eh 35
01033 Civita Castellana I 84 Bc 48
62012 Civitanova Marche I 69 Bd 47
00053 Civitavecchia I 84 Bb 48
86400 Civray F 66 Aa 44
20600* Çivril TR 96 Ck 52
Čiža RUS 17 Ee 23
73200 Cizre TR 99 Ec 53
Cjurupyns'k = Oleškу UA 74 Dc 44
Čkalovsk RUS 44 Ed 34
Čkalovskij RUS 76 Ee 43
CO15 Clacton-on-Sea GB 53 Ab 39
58500* Clamecy F 67 Ad 43
Clár Clainne Mhuiris IRL 49 Sb 37
Claremorris = Clár Chlainne Mhuiris IRL 49 Sb 37
IV27 Clashnessie GB 50 Se 32
71800 Clayette, la F 67 Ae 44
HD9 Cleethorpes GB 51 Sk 37
087045 Clejani RO 72 Cf 46
09420 Clermont F 53 Ac 41
55120 Clermont-en-Argonne F 54 Af 41
63000* Clermont-Ferrand F 67 Ad 45
34800 Clermont-l'Hérault F 67 Ad 47
BS21 Clevedon GB 52 Sh 39
Clifden = An Clochán IRL 49 Rk 37
44190 Clisson F 66 Si 43
BB7 Clitheroe GB 51 Sh 37
Cloghan = An Clochán IRL 49 Sc 37
Cloich na Coillte IRL 49 Sb 39
Clonakilty = Cloich na Coillte IRL 49 Sb 39
Clones = Cluain Eois IRL 49 Sc 36
Clonmel = Cluain Meala IRL 49 Sc 38
49661 Cloppenburg D 38 Ai 38
BT24 Clough GB 49 Se 36
EX39 Clovelly GB 52 Sf 39
Cluain Cearbán IRL 49 Sa 37
Cluain Eois IRL 49 Sc 36
Cluainín IRL 49 Sb 36
Cluain Meala = Clonmel IRL 49 Sc 38
000400* Cluj-Napoca RO 72 Cd 44
71250 Cluny F 67 Ae 44
24023 Clusone I 69 Ak 45
G81 Clydebank GB 51 Sf 35
ML6 Coatbridge GB 51 Sf 35
907065 Cobadin RO 73 Ci 46
Cobandede TR 91 Eb 51
Çobanlar TR 96 Da 52
Cóbh = An Cóbh IRL 49 Sb 39
96450 Coburg D 55 Ba 40
56812 Cochem D 54 Ah 40
CA13 Cockermouth GB 51 Sg 36
44021 Codigoro I 69 Bc 46
507100 Codlea RO 72 Cf 45
26845 Codogno I 69 Ak 45
33033 Codroipo I 69 Bc 45
48653 Coesfeld D 54 Ah 39
7740 Coevorden NL 54 Ag 38
16100* Cognac F 66 Sk 45
11012 Cogne I 68 Ah 45
Çoğun TR 89 De 51
3000-001* Coimbra P 80 Sb 50
29100 Coín E 93 Sf 54
23320 Čoka SRB 71 Ca 45
33590 Çokak TR 98 Dg 53
Çokören TR 89 Dc 51
Çolaklı TR 98 Di 52
CO3 Colchester GB 53 Aa 39
04680 Colditz D 55 Bc 39
TD12 Coldstream GB 51 Sh 35
BT51 Coleraine GB 49 Sd 35
5313 Colibaşi MD 73 Ci 45
Colico I 69 Ak 44
28400 Collado-Villalba E 81 Sg 50
53034 Colle di Val d'Elsa I 69 Bb 47
00034 Colleferro I 84 Bd 49
57014 Collesalvetti I 69 Ba 47
Collobrières F 68 Ag 47
68000* Colmar F 54 Ah 42
29170 Colmenar E 93 Sf 54
28770 Colmenar Viejo E 81 Sg 50
32430 Cologne F 66 Aa 47
52330 Colombey-les-deux-Églises F 53 Ae 42
31770 Colomiers F 67 Ab 47
07638 Colònia de Sant Jordi E 82 Ac 51
45313 Colonia Iberia E 81 Sg 51
Čolovo RUS 31 Da 32
33320 Colunga E 80 Se 47
LL29 Colwyn Bay = Bae Colwyn GB 51 Sg 37
44022 Comacchio I 69 Bc 46
087055 Comana RO 72 Cg 46
087055 Comana RO 73 Ci 47
605200 Comăneşti RO 72 Cg 44
18400 Çomar TR 89 Dd 49
70120 Combeaufontaine F 68 Af 43
BT23 Comber GB 49 Se 36
4170 Comblain-au-Pont B 54 Af 40
35270 Combourg F 52 Si 42
28120 Combray, Illiers- F 53 Ab 42
33600 Çömelek TR 97 Dd 54
Çömlük TR 97 Df 53
03600 Commentry F 67 Ac 44
85220 Commequiers F 66 Si 44
55200* Commercy F 54 Af 42
22100 Como I 69 Ak 45
60200* Compiègne F 53 Ac 41
7570-469* Comporta P 92 Sb 52
3801 Comrat MD 73 Ci 44
29900* Concarneau F 66 Sg 43
27190 Conches-en-Ouche F 53 Aa 42
15190 Condat F 67 Ac 45
14110 Condé-sur-Noireau F 52 Sk 42
32100 Condom F 66 Aa 47
31015 Conegliano I 69 Bc 45
9261 Conevo BG 72 Cf 47
16500 Confolens F 66 Aa 44
3819 Congaz MD 73 Ci 44
CW12 Congleton GB 51 Sh 37
19243 Congostrina E 81 Sh 49
11140 Conil de la Frontera E 92 Sd 54
72240 Conlie F 52 Sk 42
CH7 Connah's Quay GB 51 Sg 37
317085 Conop RO 71 Cb 44
29217 Conquet, le F 52 Sf 42
14448 Conquista E 93 Sf 52
DH8 Consett GB 51 Si 36
000900* Constanța RO 73 Ci 46
41450 Constantina E 92 Se 53
45700 Consuegra E 81 Sg 51
41700 Contres F 67 Ab 43
88140* Contrexéville F 54 Af 42
80160 Conty F 53 Ac 41
LL32 Conwy GB 51 Sg 37
BT80 Cookstown GB 49 Sd 36
Cootehill IRL 49 Sc 36
Čop UA 57 Cc 42

170 | Čèrven'

57260 Dieuze (F) 54 Ag 42
17008 Dieveniškės (LT) 41 Cf 36
8324 Digermulen (N) 14 Bf 22
04000* Digne-les-Bains (F) 68 Ag 46
71160 Digoin (F) 67 Ae 44
36670 Digor (TR) 91 Ed 50
Digora (RUS) 91 Ee 47
Dij (RUS) 36 Fi 29
Dijaševo (RUS) 46 Fd 35
21000* Dijon (F) 68 Af 43
Dijur (RUS) 26 Fd 25
91094 Dikanäs (S) 21 Bf 25
55510 Dikbıyık (TR) 90 Dg 49
Dikili (TR) 87 Cg 51
61500 Dikkaya (TR) 90 Dk 50
57660 Dikmen (TR) 96 Db 54
57660 Dikmen (TR) 99 Ea 53
8600 Diksmuide (B) 53 Ac 39
29600 Dilekyolu (TR) 90 Dk 50
32009 Dílesi (GR) 94 Cd 52
Diljatyn (UA) 57 Ce 42
35683* Dillenburg (D) 54 Ai 40
89407 Dillingen an der Donau (D) 55 Ba 42
40003 Dímitra (GR) 86 Cc 51
Dimitrievka (RUS) 44 Ea 38
6400* Dimitrovgrad (BG) 87 Cf 48
Dimitrovgrad (RUS) 45 Ek 36
18320 Dimitrovgrad (SRB) 86 Cc 47
22007 Dimitsána (GR) 94 Cc 53
4757 Dimovo (BG) 71 Cc 47
22100* Dinan (F) 52 Sh 42
5500 Dinant (B) 53 Ae 40
03400 Dinar (TR) 96 Da 52
35800* Dinard (F) 52 Sh 42
LL16 Dinbych = Denbigh (GB) 51 Sg 37
SA70 Dinbych-y-pysgodm = Tenby (GB) 52 Sf 39
Dinek (TR) 88 Db 51
Dinek (TR) 96 Dc 53
Dinek (TR) 97 Dd 53
37351 Dingelstädt (D) 55 Ba 39
Dingle = An Daingean (IRL) 49 Rk 38
84130 Dingolfing (D) 55 Bc 42
IV15 Dingwall (GB) 50 Sf 33
91550 Dinkelsbühl (D) 55 Ba 41
Dinskaja (RUS) 75 Dk 45
46535* Dinslaken (D) 54 Ag 39
03290 Diou (F) 67 Ad 44
Dipkarpaz = Rizokarpaso 97 De 55
64009 Dipótamos (GR) 87 Ce 49
Direkli (TR) 90 Dg 51
22023 Dirráhi (GR) 94 Cc 53
7180 Disentis/Mustér (CH) 68 Ai 44
IP22 Diss (GB) 53 Ab 38
44019 Dístrato (GR) 86 Cb 50
537090 Ditrău (RO) 72 Cf 44
Diveevo (RUS) 44 Ed 35
14160* Dives-sur-Mer (F) 52 Sk 41
Div'ja (RUS) 35 Fg 32
Divnoe (RUS) 76 Ed 45
Divnogor'e (RUS) 60 Dk 40
Divo (RUS) 42 Db 35
58300 Divriği (TR) 90 Di 51
04900 Diyadin (TR) 91 Ed 51
21000* Diyarbakır (TR) 99 Ea 53
D'jakonovo (RUS) 33 Ea 31
D'jakovo, Verhovino- (RUS) 33 Ed 31
Djat'kovo (RUS) 43 De 37
Djukovo (RUS) 34 Ef 32
9108 Djulino (BG) 88 Ch 48
510 Djúpavík (IS) 48 Qi 25
765 Djúpivogur (IS) 48 Rf 26
Djupvik (N) 14 Ca 21
Djurås (S) 29 Bf 30
Djurtjuli (RUS) 46 Fe 35
Dmitrievka (RUS) 63 Fe 38
Dmitrievka (RUS) 64 Fh 38
Dmitriev-L'govskij (RUS) 60 Df 38
Dmitrievo (RUS) 44 Eb 35
Dmitrievščina (RUS) 61 Ec 38
Dmitrievskoe (RUS) 43 Di 33
Dmitrov (RUS) 43 Dh 34
Dmitrovskij Pogost (RUS) 44 Dk 35
Dmytrivka (UA) 59 Dc 40
Dmytrivka (UA) 60 Dg 42
Dmytrivka (UA) 75 Dg 44
Dneprovskoe (RUS) 43 Dd 35
3352 Dnestrovsc (MD) 73 Ck 44
Dnipro (UA) 60 Df 42
Dniprodzeržyns'k = Kamjans'ke (UA) 59 De 42
Dnipropetrovs'k = Dnipro (UA) 60 Df 42
Dniprorudne (UA) 74 De 43
Dno (RUS) 31 Ck 33
BT39 Doagh (GB) 49 Sd 36
39034 Dobbiaco = Toblach (I) 69 Bc 44
3701* Dobele (LV) 41 Cd 34
04720 Döbeln (D) 55 Bd 39
66-520 Dobiegniew (PL) 39 Bf 38
74000* Doboj (BIH) 71 Bi 46
37-530 Dobra (PL) 39 Bf 37
337215 Dobra (RO) 72 Cf 46
12224 Dobra (SRB) 71 Cb 46
11-040 Dobre Miasto (PL) 40 Ca 37
9300* Dobrič (BG) 73 Ch 47
247629 Dobriceni (RO) 72 Ce 46
Dobrinka (RUS) 61 Ea 38
Dobrino (RUS) 37 Ge 32
263 01 Dobříš (CZ) 55 Be 41
Dobrjanka (BY) 59 Db 38
Dobrjanka (RUS) 35 Fg 32
Dobrjatino (RUS) 44 Eb 35
46-380 Dobrodzień (PL) 56 Bi 40
Dobroe (RUS) 44 Db 38
Dobromyl' (UA) 57 Cc 41
Dobron' (UA) 57 Cc 42
Dobropil'l'a (UA) 60 Dh 42
Dobro Polje (BIH) 71 Bi 47
Dobroslav (UA) 73 Da 44
147115 Dobroteşti (RO) 72 Ce 46
Dobrovelyčkivka (UA) 59 Db 42
Dobrovil'l'a (UA) 60 Dg 42
Dobrovol'sk (RUS) 41 Cc 36
Dobruči (RUS) 31 Ch 32
Dobrun (BIH) 71 Bk 47
Dobruš (BY) 59 Db 38
87-610 Dobrzyń nad Wisłą (PL) 56 Bk 38
87033 Docksta (S) 21 Bi 27
45500 Dodóni (GR) 86 Ca 51
19060 Dodurga (TR) 88 Ck 51
19060 Dodurga (TR) 89 De 50
7001* Doetinchem (NL) 54 Ag 39
42980 Doğanbey (TR) 95 Cg 52
42980 Doğanbey (TR) 96 Db 53
24450 Doğanbeyli (TR) 90 Dk 51
37800 Doğanca (TR) 99 Ec 53
37800 Doğanca (TR) 99 Ed 53
47510 Doğançay (TR) 88 Da 50
26960 Doğançayır (TR) 88 Da 51
42930 Doğanhisar (TR) 96 Db 52
66740 Doğankent (TR) 90 Di 50
66740 Doğankent (TR) 97 Df 54
14370 Doğanlı (TR) 89 Df 51
26860 Doğanoğlu (TR) 88 Db 51
27920 Doğanpınar (TR) 98 Dh 54
58780 Doğanşar (TR) 90 Dh 50
44500 Doğanşehir (TR) 98 Dh 52
04530 Doğansu (TR) 91 Ec 51
05070 Doğantepe (TR) 89 Df 50
44880 Doğanyol (TR) 98 Dk 52
Doğanyurt (TR) 90 Dg 50
Döğer (TR) 88 Da 51
12063 Dogliani (I) 68 Ah 46
Doğruyol (TR) 91 Ed 49
04400 Doğubayazıt (TR) 91 Ee 51
5550 Dojrenci (BG) 72 Ce 47
2870 Dokka (N) 28 Ba 30
9100 Dokkum (NL) 38 Af 37
60800 Dökmetepe (TR) 90 Dg 50
472 01 Doksy (CZ) 55 Be 40
Dokšycy (BY) 42 Ch 36
415600 Doktor Petru Groza = Ştei (RO) 71 Cc 44
Dokučaevs'k (UA) 75 Dh 43
Dokukino (RUS) 45 Ef 34
11130 Dokuz (TR) 96 Dc 52
Dokuzyol (TR) 97 Dd 53
35120 Dol-de-Bretagne (F) 52 Si 42
39100* Dole (F) 68 Af 43
7244 Dolenci (MK) 86 Cb 49
LL40 Dolgellau (GB) 51 Sg 38
Dolgie Budy (RUS) 60 Df 39
Dolgoderevenskoe (RUS) 47 Gb 35
Dolgoe (RUS) 60 Dh 38
Dolgorukovo (RUS) 40 Ca 36
Dolgorukovo (RUS) 60 Di 38
Dolgoščel'e (RUS) 25 Ed 24
09041 Dolianova (I) 83 Ak 51
Dolina Karzanov (RUS) 76 Ec 47
Dolina Narzanov (RUS) 76 Ec 47
Doljevac (SRB) 71 Cb 47
2420 Dolna Dikanja (BG) 87 Cd 48
5855 Dolna Mitropolia (BG) 72 Ce 47
9120 Dolni Čiflik (BG) 88 Ch 48
5870 Dolni Dăbnik (BG) 72 Ce 47
3958 Dolni Lom (BG) 71 Cc 47
026 01 Dolný Kubín (SK) 56 Bk 41
Dolores (E) 93 Sk 52
Doluca (TR) 98 Dg 53
Dolyna (UA) 57 Ce 42
Dolyns'ka (UA) 59 Dc 42
Dolyns'ke (UA) 73 Ck 43
Dolžanskaja (RUS) 75 Dh 44
43850 Domaniç (TR) 88 Ck 51
Domanivka (UA) 74 Db 43
36-230 Domaradz (PL) 57 Cb 41
Domaška (RUS) 46 Fa 38
344 01 Domažlice (CZ) 55 Bc 41
Dombaj (RUS) 76 Eb 47
Dombarovka (RUS) 64 Fi 40
Dombarovskij (RUS) 64 Fk 40
2660 Dombås (N) 20 Ak 28
54110 Dombasle-sur-Meurthe (F) 54 Ag 42
7200 Dombóvár (H) 71 Bi 44
4492 Dombrád (H) 57 Cb 42
03410 Domérat (F) 67 Ac 44
61700 Domfront (F) 52 Sk 42
19303 Dömitz (D) 39 Bb 37
077090 Domneşti (RO) 72 Ce 45
Domnísta (GR) 94 Cb 52
Domodedovo (RUS) 43 Dh 35
28845 Domodossola (I) 68 Ai 44
88270 Dompaire (F) 54 Ag 42
03290 Dompierre-sur-Besbre (F) 67 Ad 44
1230 Domžale (SLO) 70 Be 44
Don (RUS) 35 Fd 29
78166 Donaueschingen (D) 68 Ai 43
86609 Donauwörth (D) 55 Ba 42
06400 Don Benito (E) 80 Se 52
DN1 Doncaster (GB) 51 Si 37
5106 Dondjušany = Donduşeni (MD) 58 Ch 42
5106 Donduşeni (MD) 58 Ch 42
Doneck (RUS) 60 Dk 42
Donec'k (UA) 75 Dh 43
Doneck = Donec'k (UA) 75 Dh 43
Doneckij, Ust'- (RUS) 76 Ea 43
Doneckoe (RUS) 63 Fe 39
Donec'kyj (UA) 60 Di 42
Donegal = Dún na nGall (IRL) 49 Sb 36
Dönemeç (TR) 99 Ed 52
Donja Brela (HR) 70 Bg 47
Donja Konjšćina (HR) 70 Bg 44
Donja Rudnica (SRB) 71 Ca 47
Donja Stupnica (HR) 70 Bg 45
Donji Lapac (HR) 70 Bf 46
Donji Miholjac (HR) 71 Bi 45
19220 Donji Milanovac (SRB) 71 Ce 46
Donji Muć (HR) 70 Bg 47
Donji Srb (HR) 70 Bg 46
Donji Vakuf (BIH) 70 Bh 46
03130 Donjon, le (F) 67 Ad 44
20001 Donostia-San Sebastián (E) 66 Si 47
Donskoe (RUS) 60 Di 38
Donskoe (RUS) 64 Fh 39
Donskoe (RUS) 76 Fe 45
Donskoj (RUS) 43 Di 37
26290 Donzère (F) 67 Ae 46
58220 Donzy (F) 67 Ad 43
7500 Doornik = Tournai (B) 53 Ad 40
Dor (RUS) 33 Eb 32
87210 Dorat, le (F) 67 Ab 44
OX10 Dorchester (GB) 52 Sh 40
3300* Dordrecht (NL) 53 Ae 39
84405 Dorfen (D) 55 Bc 42
2115 Dörfles (A) 56 Bg 42
08022 Dorgali (I) 83 Ak 50
24011 Dório (GR) 94 Cb 53
68500 Dorísko (GR) 87 Cg 50
RH4 Dorking (GB) 52 Sk 39
41539* Dormagen (D) 54 Ag 39
51700 Dormans (F) 53 Ad 41
917055 Dor Mărunt (RO) 72 Cg 46
6850* Dornbirn (A) 69 Ak 43
IV25 Dornoch (GB) 50 Sf 33
827070 Dorobanţu (RO) 73 Ci 46
Dorobino (RUS) 43 Dh 37
Dorofeevo (RUS) 44 Dk 35
Dorogobuž (RUS) 43 Dd 36
Dorogorskoe (RUS) 25 Ee 25
715200 Dorohoi (RO) 72 Cg 43
Dorohovo (RUS) 43 Dg 35
Dorošata (RUS) 34 Fb 33
91701 Dorotea (S) 21 Bg 26
46282* Dorsten (D) 54 Ag 39
Dörtdivan (TR) 89 Dc 50
44135* Dortmund (D) 54 Ah 39
05800 Dörtyol (TR) 97 Df 52
05800 Dörtyol (TR) 97 Dg 54
27632 Dorum (D) 38 Ai 37
Dorutay (TR) 99 Ee 52
Dosčatoe (RUS) 44 Ec 35
Döşemealtı (TR) 96 Da 53
41700 Dos Hermanas (E) 92 Se 53
4831 Dospat (BG) 87 Ce 49
59500 Douai (F) 53 Ad 40
29100 Douarnenez (F) 52 Sf 42
45220 Douchy (F) 67 Ad 43
76560 Doudeville (F) 53 Aa 41
49700 Doué-la-Fontaine (F) 66 Sk 43
ML12 Douglas (GB) 51 Sg 35
IM1 Douglas (GBM) 51 Sf 36
80600 Doullens (F) 53 Ac 40
KW14 Dounreay (GB) 50 Sg 32
91410 Dourdan (F) 53 Ac 42
CT16 Dover (GB) 53 Ab 39
Dovhe (UA) 57 Cd 42
2662 Dovre (N) 20 Ak 29
Dovšans'k = Sverdlovs'k (UA) 60 Dk 42
Dovsk (BY) 42 Da 37
PE38 Downham Market (GB) 53 Aa 38
BT30 Downpatrick (GB) 49 Se 36
Doxáto (GR) 87 Ce 49
Drabiv (UA) 59 Dc 41
9200* Drachten (NL) 38 Ag 37
917080 Dragalina (RO) 73 Ch 46
235400 Drăgăneşti-Olt (RO) 72 Ce 46
147135 Drăgăneşti-Vlaşca (RO) 72 Cf 46
9349 Draganovo (BG) 72 Cf 47
22000 Dragaš = Dragash (RKS) 86 Ca 48
22000 Dragash = Dragaš (RKS) 86 Ca 48
245700 Drăgăşani (RO) 72 Ce 46
31317 Draglica (SRB) 71 Bk 47
Dragoç (AL) 86 Bk 48
2210 Dragoman (BG) 86 Cc 48
617165 Dragomireşti (RO) 73 Ch 44
5285 Dragomirovo (BG) 72 Cf 47
25870 Dragsfjärd (FIN) 30 Cc 30
83300* Draguignan (F) 68 Ag 47
Dragunskoe (RUS) 60 Dg 40
807115 Drăguşeni (RO) 72 Cg 43
Drahičyn (BY) 58 Cf 38
43060 Drakótripa (GR) 86 Cb 51
66100 Dráma (GR) 87 Ce 49
3004* Drammen (N) 28 Ba 31
3750 Drangedal (N) 28 Ak 31
510 Drangsnes (IS) 48 Qi 25
78-500 Drawsko Pomorskie (PL) 39 Bf 37
06-214 Drążdżewo (PL) 40 Cb 37
3920 Drenovec (BG) 71 Cc 47
01067* Dresden (D) 55 Bd 39
Drètun' (BY) 42 Ck 35
28100* Dreux (F) 53 Ab 42
2443 Drevsjø (N) 21 Bc 29
66-530 Drezdenko (PL) 39 Bf 38
Dreznica (BIH) 69 Bd 44
YO25 Driffield (GB) 51 Sk 36
Drimó (GR) 94 Cc 54
57200 Drimós (GR) 86 Cc 50
6493 Drjanovo (BG) 87 Cf 48
Drjazgi (RUS) 60 Dk 38
Drniš (HR) 70 Bg 47
1440 Drøbak (N) 28 Ba 31
000220* Drobeta-Turnu Severin (RO) 71 Cc 46
5200 Drochia (MD) 58 Ch 42
Drogheda = Droichead Átha (IRL) 49 Sd 37
Drogobyč = Drohobyč (UA) 57 Cd 41
Drohobyč (UA) 57 Cd 41
Droichead Átha = Drogheda (IRL) 49 Sd 37
Droichead na Bandan = Bandan (IRL) 49 Sb 39
Droim Seanbho (IRL) 49 Sb 36
Dromad (IRL) 49 Sc 37
Dromod = Dromad (IRL) 49 Sc 37
BT78 Dromore (GB) 49 Sc 36
Dromore West (IRL) 49 Sb 36
12025 Dronero (I) 68 Ah 46
8250* Dronten (NL) 54 Af 38
2095 Drosendorf Stadt-Zissersdorf (A) 56 Bf 42
Droskovo (RUS) 60 Dg 38
47043 Drossopigí (GR) 86 Cb 51
Drozdyn' (UA) 58 Ch 39
Drume (SRB) 86 Bk 48
Drumshanbo = Droim Seanbho (IRL) 49 Sb 36
66001 Druskininkai (LT) 41 Cd 36
Družba (UA) 59 Dd 38
Družbivka (UA) 74 De 44
Družinino (RUS) 47 Fk 34
Družkivka (UA) 60 Dh 42
Družkovka = Družkivka (UA) 60 Dh 42
Družnyj (RUS) 47 Gb 35
Drvenik (HR) 85 Bh 47
3560-048* Duas Igrejas (P) 80 Sd 49
4500 Dubăsari (MD) 73 Ck 43
Dubec (RUS) 32 Di 32
04849 Düben, Bad (D) 55 Bc 39
Dubenki (RUS) 45 Eg 36
Dubenskij (RUS) 64 Fg 39
4500 Dubėsar' = Dubăsari (MD) 73 Ck 43
Dub"jazy (RUS) 45 Ek 34
Dubki (RUS) 62 Eg 39
Dublin = Baile Átha Cliath (IRL) 49 Sd 37
Dubna (RUS) 43 Dg 36
Dubna (RUS) 43 Dh 34
Dubno (UA) 58 Cf 40
4500 Dubossary = Dubăsari (MD) 73 Ck 43
Duboštica (BIH) 71 Bi 46
26224 Dubovac (SRB) 71 Cb 46
Dubovaja Gora (RUS) 46 Ff 34
Dubovaja Rošča (RUS) 43 Dg 37
Dubove (UA) 57 Cd 42
Dubovjazivka (UA) 59 Dd 39
Dubovka (RUS) 61 Ee 41
Dubovo (RUS) 35 Ff 33
Dubovskoe (RUS) 76 Ec 43
Dubovyj Ovrag (RUS) 61 Ee 42
Dubovyj Umet (RUS) 46 Fa 38
Dubrovino (RUS) 36 Gc 32
Dubrovka (RUS) 34 Fb 31
Dubrovka (RUS) 42 Ci 34
Dubrovka (RUS) 43 Dd 37
Dubrovka (RUS) 61 Eb 39
Dubrovki (RUS) 44 Ed 37
Dubrovna (BY) 42 Da 36
Dubrovnik (HR) 85 Bi 48
Dubrovnoe (RUS) 37 Gk 33
Dubrovo (RUS) 32 Dh 31
Dubrovo (RUS) 46 Fe 34
Dubrovycja (UA) 58 Cg 39
50220 Ducey (F) 52 Si 42
Duchanivka (UA) 59 Dd 39
419 01 Duchcov (CZ) 55 Bd 40
3401 Dudelange (L) 54 Ag 41
37115 Duderstadt (D) 55 Ba 39
817040 Dudeşti (RO) 73 Ch 46
DY3 Dudley (GB) 52 Sh 38
Dudorovskij (RUS) 43 Df 37
34210 Dueñas (E) 81 Sf 49
AB55 Dufftown (GB) 50 Sg 33
36312 Duga Poljana (SRB) 71 Ca 47
Duga Resa (HR) 70 Bf 45
Dugna (RUS) 43 Dg 36
Dugo Selo (HR) 70 Bg 45
Duhovnickoe (RUS) 62 Ei 38
Duhovščina (RUS) 42 Dc 35
74410 Duingt (F) 68 Ag 45
34013 Duino-Aurisina (I) 69 Bd 45
47051* Duisburg (D) 54 Ag 39
Dukëz (AL) 86 Bk 50
38-450 Dukla (PL) 57 Cb 41
Dukora (BY) 42 Ch 37
30042 Dūkštas (LT) 41 Cg 35
Duljapino (RUS) 33 Ea 33
48249 Dülmen (D) 54 Ah 39
7650 Dulovo (BG) 73 Ch 47
G82 Dumbarton (GB) 51 Sf 35
DG1 Dumfries (GB) 51 Sg 35
Duminiči (RUS) 43 Df 37
Dumlu (TR) 91 Eb 50
26600 Dumluca (TR) 88 Db 51
43820 Dumlupınar (TR) 96 Ck 52
7020 Dunaföldvár (H) 71 Bi 44
Dunajivci (UA) 58 Cg 41
Dunajivci (UA) 58 Cg 42
929 01 Dunajská Streda (SK) 70 Bh 43
Dunaszekcső (H) 71 Bi 44
2400 Dunaújváros (H) 71 Bi 44
6145 Dunavci (BG) 71 Cc 47
EH42 Dunbar (GB) 51 Sh 35
FK15 Dunblane (GB) 50 Sg 34
3270 Dundaga (LV) 30 Cc 33
Dundalk = Dún Dealgan (IRL) 49 Sd 36
Dún Dealgan = Dundalk (IRL) 49 Sd 36
DD3 Dundee (GB) 50 Sh 34
KY11 Dunfermline (GB) 50 Sg 34
BT71 Dungannon (GB) 49 Sd 36
Dún Gar (IRL) 49 Sb 37
Dún Garbhán = Dungarvan (IRL) 49 Sc 38
Dungarvan = Dún Garbhán (IRL) 49 Sc 38
BT47 Dungiven (GB) 49 Sd 36
Dunglow = An Clochán Liath (IRL) 49 Sb 36
7506 Dunje (MK) 86 Cb 49
Dunkeld (GB) 50 Sg 34
59140* Dunkerque (F) 53 Ac 39
Dún Laoghaire (IRL) 49 Sd 37
Dunleary = Dún Laoghaire (IRL) 49 Sd 37
Dún Mánmhaí (IRL) 49 Sa 39
Dunmanway = DúnMrínmhaí (IRL) 49 Sa 39
Dún Mor (IRL) 49 Sb 37
Dunmore = Dún Mor (IRL) 49 Sb 37
Dún na nGall (IRL) 49 Sb 36
Dún na Séad = Baltimore (IRL) 49 Sa 39
PA23 Dunoon (GB) 51 Sf 35
Dún Selachainn (IRL) 49 Sd 37
Dunshaughlin = Dún Selachainn (IRL) 49 Sd 37
18130 Dun-sur-Auron (F) 67 Ac 44
55110 Dun-sur-Meuse (F) 54 Af 41
IV55 Dunvegan (GB) 50 Sd 33
2600 Dupnica (BG) 87 Cd 48
57700 Durağan (TR) 89 Df 49
01470 Durak (TR) 88 Ci 51
48200 Durango (E) 66 Sh 47
47120 Duras (F) 66 Aa 46
3440 Durbe (LV) 40 Cb 34
Đurđenovac (HR) 71 Bi 45
Đurđevac (HR) 70 Bh 44
52349* Düren (D) 54 Ag 40
DH1 Durham (GB) 51 Si 36
Durhasan (TR) 96 Ci 52
Durlas = Thurles (IRL) 49 Sc 38
IV27 Durness (GB) 50 Sf 32
3601 Dürnstein (A) 56 Bf 42
06231 Dürrenberg, Bad (D) 55 Bc 39
Durrës (AL) 86 Bk 49
Durrow = Darú (IRL) 49 Sc 38
10800 Dursunbey (TR) 88 Ci 51
49430 Durtal (F) 66 Sk 43

172 | **Dieuze**

Eydehamn (N) 28 Ai 32
TD14 Eyemouth (GB) 51 Sh 35
19340 Eygurande (F) 67 Ac 45
24500 Eymet (F) 66 Aa 46
87120 Eymoutiers (F) 67 Ab 45
28850 Eynesil (TR) 90 Dk 49
26280 Ezcaray (E) 81 Sg 48
3891 Ezere (LV) 41 Cc 34
5692 Ezernieki (LV) 42 Ch 34
Eževo (RUS) 35 Fc 32
Ežiha (RUS) 34 Eh 32
17600 Ezine (TR) 87 Cg 51
Ezjaryšča (BY) 42 Ck 35
Ёzva (RUS) 34 Fa 29

F

5600 Faaborg = Fåborg (DK) 39 Ba 35
2625 Fåberg (N) 28 Ba 29
5600 Fåborg = Faaborg (DK) 39 Ba 35
60044 Fabriano (I) 69 Bc 47
927110 Făcăeni (RO) 73 Ch 46
48018 Faenza (I) 69 Bb 46
4820-002* Fafe (P) 80 Sb 49
505200 Făgăraş (RO) 72 Ce 45
83086 Fågelberget (S) 21 Be 26
Fågelsjö (S) 21 Be 29
2900 Fagernes (N) 28 Ak 30
2900 Fagernes (N) 14 Bk 21
73701* Fagersta (S) 29 Bf 30
607207 Făget (RO) 71 Cc 45
880 Fagurhólsmýri (IS) 48 Rd 27
Faing (IRL) 49 Sa 38
Fakel (RUS) 35 Fd 33
NR21 Fakenham (GB) 51 Aa 38
Fakılı (TR) 89 Df 51
Fakovići (BIH) 71 Bk 46
4640 Fakse (DK) 39 Bc 35
14700 Falaise (F) 52 Sk 42
Falcarragh = An Fál Carrach (IRL) 49 Sb 35
Falconara Marittima (I) 69 Bd 47
Falenki (RUS) 34 Fb 32
5901 Fălești (MD) 73 Ch 43
5901 Faleštу = Fălești (MD) 73 Ch 43
31101* Falkenberg (S) 39 Bc 34
04895 Falkenberg (Elster) (D) 55 Bd 39
14612 Falkensee (D) 55 Bd 38
52101* Falköping (S) 29 Bd 32
91501 Fällfors (S) 22 Ca 25
29683 Fallingbostel, Bad (D) 38 Ak 38
TR11 Falmouth (GB) 52 Se 40
43730 Falset (E) 82 Aa 49
725200 Fălticeni (RO) 72 Cg 43
79101* Falun (S) 29 Bf 30
Fanahammaren (N) 28 Af 30
7320 Fannrem (N) 20 Ak 27
61032 Fano (I) 69 Bd 47
Fanrem (N) 20 Ak 27
56320 Faouët, le (F) 52 Sg 42
02032 Fara in Sabina (I) 84 Bc 48
45801 Färgelanda (S) 28 Bb 32
Färila (S) 21 Bf 29
SN7 Faringdon (GB) 52 Si 39
38601 Färjestaden (S) 40 Bg 34
42031 Farkadóna (GR) 86 Cc 51
327200 Fârliug (RO) 71 Cb 45
8700-152* Faro (P) 92 Sc 53
62035 Fårösund (S) 29 Bk 33
Farrenfore = An Fearann Fuar (IRL) 49 Sa 38
40300 Fársala (GR) 86 Cc 51
4550 Farsund (N) 28 Ag 32
72015 Fasano (I) 85 Bh 50
750 Fáskrúðsfjörður (IS) 48 Rg 26
Fastiv (UA) 58 Ck 40
Fastov = Fastiv (UA) 58 Ck 40
Fatela, La (E) 80 Sd 50
Fatež (RUS) 60 Df 38
34080* Fatih (TR) 88 Ci 49
2495-551* Fátima (P) 80 Sb 51
52400 Fatsa (TR) 90 Dh 49
57380 Faulquemont (F) 54 Ag 41
815100 Făurei (RO) 73 Ch 45
8200 Fauske (N) 14 Bf 23
85460 Faute-sur-Mer, la (F) 66 Si 44
2634 Fåvang (N) 28 Ba 29
70160 Faverney (F) 68 Ag 43
ME13 Faversham (GB) 53 Aa 39
91023 Favignana (I) 84 Bc 53
SO45 Fawley (GB) 52 Si 40
52500 Fayl-la-Forêt (F) 68 Af 43
50795 Fayón (E) 82 Aa 49
Fearna (IRL) 49 Sd 38
76400 Fécamp (F) 53 Aa 41
5947 Fedje (N) 28 Ae 30
Fedjukovo (RUS) 43 Df 36
Fedorovka (RUS) 45 Ek 37
Fedorovka (RUS) 46 Ff 37
Fëdorovka (RUS) 75 Di 43
Fedorovskoe (RUS) 44 Dk 34
Fedotovo (RUS) 33 Ec 30
Fedovo (RUS) 24 Dk 28
Fehimli (TR) 89 Df 51
23769 Fehmarn (D) 39 Bb 36
16833 Fehrbellin (D) 39 Bc 38
9710 Feistritz an der Drau (A) 69 Bd 44
01660 Feke (TR) 97 Df 53
38750* Felâhiye (TR) 89 Df 51
07200 Felanitx (E) 82 Ad 51
8330 Feldbach (A) 70 Bf 44
17258 Feldberg (D) 39 Bd 37
507065 Feldioara (RO) 72 Cf 45
6800* Feldkirch (A) 69 Ak 43
9560 Feldkirchen in Kärnten (A) 70 Be 44
Fèlešt' = Falešti (MD) 73 Ch 43
IP11 Felixstowe (GB) 53 Ab 39
23500 Felletin (F) 67 Ac 45
32032 Feltre (I) 69 Bb 44
10060 Fenestrelle (I) 68 Ah 45
Fenevyči (UA) 59 Da 40
Feodosija 74 Df 45
Ferapontovo (RUS) 32 Di 31
02800 Fère, la (F) 53 Ad 41
51230 Fère-Champenoise (F) 53 Ad 42
02130 Fère-en-Tardenois (F) 53 Ad 41
03013 Ferentino (I) 84 Bd 49
70000* Ferizaj = Uroševac (RKS) 86 Cb 48
54110 Ferizli (TR) 88 Da 50
9170* Ferlach (A) 70 Be 44
25001 Ferma (LT) 41 Ce 35
63023 Fermo (I) 69 Bd 47
49220 Fermoselle (E) 80 Sd 49
Fermoy = Mainistir Fhear Maí (IRL) 49 Sb 38
Ferns = Fearna (IRL) 49 Sd 38
75013 Ferrandina (I) 85 Bg 50
44100 Ferrara (I) 69 Bb 46
7900-195* Ferreira do Alentejo (P) 92 Sb 52
07750 Ferreries (E) 83 Ae 51
29024 Ferriere (I) 69 Ak 46
15510 Ferrol (E) 80 Sb 47
Feršampenuaz (RUS) 47 Fk 37
72400 Ferté-Bernard, la (F) 53 Aa 42
61600 Ferté-Macé, la (F) 52 Sk 42
45240 Ferté-Saint-Aubin, la (F) 67 Ab 43
77260 Ferté-sous-Jouarre, la (F) 53 Ad 42
Festvåg (N) 14 Be 23
925100 Fetești (RO) 73 Ch 46
48300 Fethiye (TR) 96 Ck 54
48300 Fethiye (TR) 98 Di 52
1900 Fetsund (N) 28 Bb 31
91555 Feuchtwangen (D) 55 Ba 41
42110 Feurs (F) 67 Ae 45
4870 Fevik (N) 28 Ai 32
27830 Fevzipaşa (TR) 98 Dg 53
LL41 Ffestiniog (GB) 51 Sg 38
62035 Fiastra (I) 84 Bd 47
05016 Ficulle (I) 84 Bc 48
43036 Fidenza (I) 69 Ba 46
137100 Fieni (RO) 72 Cf 45
Fier (AL) 86 Bk 50
Fierzë (AL) 86 Ca 48
3984 Fiesch (CH) 68 Ai 44
50014 Fiesole (I) 69 Bb 47
20114 Figari (F) 83 Ak 49
46100* Figeac (F) 67 Ac 46
57205 Figeholm (S) 29 Bg 33
Figgjo, Ålgård- (N) 28 Af 32
59100 Figline (I) 69 Bb 47
3080-011* Figueira da Foz (P) 80 Sb 50
6440-100* Figueira de Castelo Rodrigo (P) 80 Sd 50
3260-305* Figueiró dos Vinhos (P) 80 Sb 51
17600 Figueres (E) 82 Ac 48
Fil'čenki (RUS) 42 Dc 35
Filevo (BG) 87 Cf 48
YO14 Filey (GB) 51 Sk 36
13601 Filí (GR) 94 Cd 52
205300 Filiași (RO) 72 Cd 46
24300 Filiatrá (GR) 94 Cb 53
Filimonovo (RUS) 47 Ga 36
Filinskoe (RUS) 44 Ec 35
Filippovka (RUS) 45 Ek 36
Filippovka (RUS) 65 Gc 39
68201 Filipstad (S) 29 Be 31
7240 Fillan (N) 20 Ai 27
17024 Finale Ligure (I) 68 Ai 46
04500 Fiñana (E) 93 Sh 53
22530 Finby (AX) 30 Ca 30
Fındık (TR) 99 Eb 53
Fındıkköyü (TR) 98 Dg 52
05000 Fındıklı (TR) 87 Cg 50
05000 Fındıklı (TR) 91 Eb 49
33730 Fındıkpınarı (TR) 97 De 54
07740 Finike (TR) 96 Da 54
24006 Finikounda (GR) 94 Cb 54
57413 Finnentrop (D) 54 Ah 39
Finnskog (N) 29 Bc 30
9300 Finnsnes (N) 14 Bh 21
61201* Finspång (S) 29 Bf 32
03238 Finsterwalde (D) 55 Bd 39
Fintown (IRL) 49 Sb 36
PA76 Fionnphort (GB) 50 Sd 34
50100* Firenze (I) 69 Bb 47
50033 Firenzuola (I) 69 Bb 46
42700 Firminy (F) 67 Ae 45
Firovo (RUS) 32 Dd 33
SA65 Fishguard (GB) 52 Sf 39
4122 Fiskå (N) 20 Af 28
Fiskebøl (N) 14 Be 22
51170 Fismes (F) 53 Ad 41
30009 Fíties (GR) 94 Cb 52
03014 Fiuggi (I) 84 Bd 49
54013 Fivizzano (I) 69 Ba 46
6848 Fjærland (N) 28 Ag 29
45071 Fjällbacka (S) 28 Bb 32
84098 Fjällnes (S) 21 Bc 28
5856 Fjellerup (DK) 39 Ba 34
9690 Fjerritslev (DK) 38 Ak 33
Fjordgård (N) 14 Bh 21
3539 Flå (N) 28 Ak 30
Flakstad (N) 14 Bd 22
5743 Flåm (N) 28 Ah 30
425 Flateyri (IS) 48 Qg 24
Flatval (N) 20 Ai 27
72200* Flèche, la (F) 66 Sk 43
FY7 Fleetwood (GB) 51 Sg 37
4400 Flekkefjord (N) 28 Ag 32
Flen (S) 29 Bg 31
24937* Flensburg / Flensborg (D) 38 Ak 36
61100 Flers (F) 52 Sk 42
3620 Flesberg (N) 28 Ak 31
32500 Fleurance (F) 66 Aa 47
CH6 Flint (GB) 51 Sg 37
2270 Flisa (N) 29 Bc 30
43750 Flix (E) 82 Aa 49
52040 Floby (S) 29 Bd 32
Floda (S) 29 Bc 33
09557 Flöha (D) 55 Bd 40
48400 Florac (F) 67 Ad 46
50100 Florenz = Firenze (I) 69 Bb 47
Florešt' = Florești (MD) 73 Ci 43
5000 Florești (MD) 73 Ci 43
5000 Floreštу = Florești (MD) 73 Ci 43
96014 Floridia (I) 84 Bf 53
53100 Flórina (GR) 86 Cb 50
7525 Flornes (N) 20 Bb 27
6900 Florø (N) 28 Af 29
Foča (BIH) 71 Bi 47
35680 Foça (TR) 95 Cg 52
IV32 Fochabers (GB) 50 Sg 33
000620* Focșani (RO) 73 Ch 45
71100 Foggia (I) 85 Bf 49
09000* Foix (F) 82 Ab 48
Fojnica (BIH) 70 Bh 47
Foki (RUS) 46 Fe 34
Fokino (RUS) 43 De 37
7985 Foldereid (N) 21 Bc 26
84011 Folégandros (GR) 94 Ce 54
06034 Foligno (I) 84 Bc 48
CT18 Folkestone (GB) 53 Ab 39
7796 Follafoss (N) 20 Bb 27
2580 Folldal (N) 20 Ak 28
2656 Follebu (N) 28 Ba 29
83060 Föllinge (S) 21 Be 27
Follonica (I) 84 Ba 48
Fominki (RUS) 44 Ec 35
Fomino (RUS) 43 De 36
Fominskij (RUS) 47 Fk 36
Fominskoe (RUS) 33 Eb 32
Fominskoe (RUS) 33 Ec 31
36012 Fondi (I) 84 Bd 49
08023 Fonni (I) 83 Ak 50
27100 Fonsagrada, A (E) 80 Sc 47
77300* Fontainebleau (F) 53 Ac 42
Fontanka (UA) 73 Da 44
85200 Fontenay-le-Comte (F) 66 Sk 44
05310 Fontiveros (E) 81 Sf 50
Fontur (IS) 48 Rf 24
8640 Fonyód (H) 70 Bh 44
76596 Forbach (F) 54 Ag 41
04300 Forcalquier (F) 68 Af 47
91301 Forchheim (D) 55 Bb 41
6826 Førde (N) 28 Af 29
6826 Førde (N) 28 Af 31
85-900 Fordon (PL) 40 Bi 37
09083 Fordongianus (I) 83 Ai 51
DD8 Forfar (GB) 50 Sh 34
76440 Forges-les-Eaux (F) 53 Ab 41
Forli (I) 69 Bc 46
L37 Formby (GB) 51 Sg 37
04023 Formia (I) 84 Bd 49
Forminskij (RUS) 34 Ei 29
Fornells (E) 83 Ae 50
43045 Fornovo di Taro (I) 69 Ak 46
Foros 74 Dd 46
IV36 Forres (GB) 50 Sg 33
66701 Forshaga (S) 29 Bd 31
Forshällan (S) 14 Bk 24
88101 Forsmo (S) 21 Bh 27
7246 Forsnes (N) 20 Ai 27
32003 Forssa (FIN) 30 Cd 30
03149 Forst (Lausitz) (D) 55 Be 39
PH32 Fort Augustus (GB) 50 Sf 33
IV1 Fort George (GB) 50 Sf 33
30620 Fortuna (E) 93 Si 52
PH33 Fort William (GB) 50 Se 34
Forvik (N) 21 Bc 25
6090 Fosnavåg (N) 20 Af 28
12045 Fossano (I) 68 Ah 46
9350 Fossbakken (N) 14 Bh 22
61034 Fossombrone (I) 69 Bc 47
60100 Fotiná (GR) 86 Cc 50
29170 Fouesnant (F) 66 Sf 43
35300* Fougères (F) 52 Si 42
70220 Fougerolles (F) 68 Ag 43
58600 Fourchambault (F) 67 Ad 43
59610 Fourmies (F) 53 Ae 40
Fourni (GR) 95 Cg 53
Foxford = Béal Easa (IRL) 49 Sa 37
Foynes = Faing (IRL) 49 Sa 38
27780 Foz (E) 80 Sc 47
22520 Fraga (E) 82 Aa 49
Fragiista (GR) 94 Cb 52
6690 Fraiture (B) 54 Af 40
72021 Francavilla Fontana (I) 85 Bh 50
85034 Francavilla in Sinni (I) 85 Bg 50
47600 Francescas (F) 66 Aa 46
96015 Francofonte (I) 84 Be 53
Franeker = Frjentsjer (NL) 38 Af 37
35066 Frankenberg (Eder) (D) 54 Ai 39
67227 Frankenthal (Pfalz) (D) 54 Ai 41
15230* Frankfurt (Oder) (D) 55 Be 38
60311* Frankfurt am Main (D) 54 Ai 40
83051 Frankrike (S) 21 Bd 27
84012 Frånsta (S) 21 Bg 28
18461 Franzburg (D) 39 Bc 36
00044 Frascati (I) 84 Bc 49
AB43 Fraserburgh (GB) 50 Sh 33
8500* Frauenfeld (CH) 68 Ai 43
7000 Fredericia (DK) 38 Ak 35
9900 Frederikshavn (DK) 28 Ba 33
3600 Frederikssund (DK) 39 Bc 35
3300 Frederiksværk (DK) 39 Bc 35
91050 Fredrika (S) 21 Bi 26
77010 Fredriksberg (S) 29 Be 30
1604* Fredrikstad-Sarpsborg (N) 28 Ba 31
06340 Fregenal de la Sierra (E) 92 Sd 52
09599 Freiberg (D) 55 Bd 40
1700* Freiburg = Fribourg (CH) 68 Ah 44
79098* Freiburg im Breisgau (D) 68 Ah 43
16259 Freienwalde, Bad (D) 39 Be 38
3183 Freiland (A) 70 Bf 43
83395 Freilassing (D) 69 Bc 43
85354* Freising (D) 55 Bb 42
4240* Freistadt (A) 55 Be 42
01705 Freital (D) 55 Bd 40
83600* Fréjus (F) 68 Ag 47
Frenchpark = Dún Gar (IRL) 49 Sb 37
744 01 Frenštát pod Radhoštěm (CZ) 56 Bi 41
Fresno-Alhándiga (E) 80 Se 50
42311 Fresno de Caracena (E) 81 Sg 49
6896 Fresvik (N) 28 Ag 29
41160 Fréteval (F) 67 Ab 43
70130 Fretigney-et-Velloreille (F) 68 Af 43
72250 Freudenstadt (D) 54 Ai 42
62270 Frévent (F) 53 Ac 40
94078 Freyung (D) 55 Bd 42
85800 Frí (GR) 95 Cg 55
1700* Fribourg = Freiburg (CH) 68 Ah 44
86316 Friedberg (A) 70 Bg 43
61169 Friedberg (Hessen) (D) 54 Ai 40
37133 Friedland (D) 39 Bd 37
88045* Friedrichshafen (D) 69 Ak 43
74177 Friedrichshall, Bad (D) 54 Ak 41
25840 Friedrichstadt (D) 38 Ak 36
9360 Friesach (A) 70 Be 44
26169 Friesoythe (D) 38 Ah 37
82700 Friggesund (S) 21 Bg 29
Frikes (GR) 94 Ca 52
51300 Fristad (S) 29 Bd 33
51110 Fritsla (S) 29 Bc 33
34560 Fritzlar (D) 54 Ak 39
Frjanovo (RUS) 43 Di 34
Frjentsjer = Franeker (NL) 38 Af 37
Frološči (RUS) 44 Ec 34
Frolovo (RUS) 32 Dh 31
Frolovo (RUS) 61 Ed 41
BA11 Frome (GB) 52 Sh 39
34440 Frómista (E) 81 Sf 48
34110* Frontignan (F) 67 Ad 47
03100 Frosinone (I) 84 Bd 49
Frösö (S) 21 Be 27
86095 Frosolone (I) 85 Be 49
Frossíni (GR) 86 Ca 51
7633 Frosta (N) 20 Ba 27
Frostviksbränna (S) 21 Bd 26
147140 Frumoasa (RO) 72 Cf 44
917100 Frumușani (RO) 72 Cg 46
Frunze (UA) 74 De 44
Frunzivka = Zacharivka (UA) 73 Ck 43
3714 Frutigen (CH) 68 Ah 44
738 01* Frýdek-Místek (CZ) 56 Bi 41
464 01 Frýdlant (CZ) 56 Bf 40
29640 Fuengirola (E) 93 Sf 54
02651 Fuente-Álamo (E) 93 Si 53
39588 Fuente Dé (E) 66 Sf 47
06240 Fuente de Cantos (E) 92 Sd 52
06980 Fuente del Arco (E) 92 Se 52
29315 Fuente del Fresno (E) 81 Sg 51
Fuente de San Esteban, La (E) 80 Sd 50
14290 Fuente Obejuna (E) 92 Se 52
49400 Fuentesaúco (E) 80 Se 49
50740 Fuentes de Ebro (E) 82 Sk 49
34337 Fuentes de Nava (E) 81 Sf 48
4250 Fuglebjerg (DK) 39 Bb 35
36037* Fulda (D) 54 Ak 40
Fulunäs (S) 29 Bd 29
47500 Fumel (F) 66 Aa 46
84095 Funäsdalen (S) 21 Bc 28
6100-820* Fundão (P) 80 Sc 50
915200 Fundulea (RO) 72 Cg 46
147145 Furculești (RO) 72 Cf 47
Furmanov (RUS) 33 Eb 33
8630 Furnes = Veurne (B) 53 Ac 39
49584 Fürstenau (D) 54 Ah 38
16798 Fürstenberg (Havel) (D) 39 Bd 37
8280 Fürstenfeld (A) 70 Bf 43
82256 Fürstenfeldbruck (D) 55 Bb 42
15517 Fürstenwalde (Spree) (D) 55 Be 38
64658 Fürth (D) 55 Ba 41
93437 Furth im Wald (D) 55 Bc 41
78120 Furtwangen im Schwarzwald (D) 54 Ai 42
79070 Furudal (S) 29 Bf 29
9062 Furuflaten (N) 14 Ca 21
81491 Furuvik (S) 29 Bh 30
5641 Fusa (N) 28 Af 30
5672 Fusch an der Großglocknerstraße (A) 69 Bc 43
Fushë-Arrëz (AL) 86 Ca 48
Fushë-Krujë (AL) 86 Bk 49
87629 Füssen (D) 69 Ba 43
6440 Fynshav (DK) 38 Ak 36
3870 Fyresdal (N) 28 Ai 31

G

3265 Gabare (BG) 72 Cd 47
Gabovo (RUS) 35 Fd 30
2557 Gabreševci (BG) 86 Cc 48
Gabrica (RKS) 86 Cb 48
5300* Gabrovo (BG) 87 Cf 48
61230 Gacé (F) 53 Aa 42
Gacko (BIH) 85 Bi 47
83090 Gäddede (S) 21 Be 26
19205 Gadebusch (D) 39 Bb 37
Gadja (RUS) 35 Fh 29
Gadjač = Hadjač (UA) 59 Dd 40
135200 Găeşti (RO) 72 Cf 46
04024 Gaeta (I) 84 Bd 49
Gagarin (RUS) 43 De 35
Gagino (RUS) 45 Ef 35
Gagrino (RUS) 32 De 31
Gagšor (RUS) 34 Fa 30
3872 Gaiķi (LV) 41 Cc 34
74405 Gaildorf (D) 54 Ak 41
81600* Gaillac (F) 67 Ab 47
Gaillimh = Galway (IRL) 49 Sa 37
DN21 Gainsborough (GB) 51 Sk 37
Gaïou (GR) 86 Ca 51
IV21 Gairloch (GB) 50 Se 33
Gaj (HR) 70 Bh 45
Gaj (RUS) 64 Fi 39
Gajny (RUS) 35 Fe 30
Gajutino (RUS) 32 Di 32
Gakugsa (RUS) 32 Dg 29
2784 Gâlâbovo (BG) 87 Cf 48
Galanovo (RUS) 46 Fe 34
TD1 Galashiels (GB) 51 Sh 35
2827 Galata (CY) 96 Dc 55
Galatás (GR) 94 Cd 53
000800* Galați (RO) 73 Ci 45
73013 Galatina (I) 85 Bi 50
63073 Galátista (GR) 87 Cd 50
18840 Galera (E) 93 Sh 53
Galeria (F) 83 Ai 48
457140 Gâlgău (RO) 72 Cd 43
Galiakberovo (RUS) 47 Fh 37

174 I Eydehamn

Galič (RUS) 33 Ec 32
'47205 Galicea (RO) 72 Ce 46
'1256 Galičnik (MK) 86 Ca 49
Galkino (RUS) 37 Ge 32
'1013 Gallarate (I) 68 Ai 45
'3014 Gallipoli (I) 85 Bh 50
'8201 Gällivare (S) 14 Ca 23
'4050 Gällö (S) 21 Bf 28
Galway = Gaillimh (IRL) 49 Sa 37
Gam (RUS) 26 Ek 28
'0220 Gamaches (F) 53 Ab 41
'9401 Gamleby (S) 29 Bg 33
'7100 Gammelstaden (S) 22 Cc 25
'775 Gamvik (N) 15 Ci 19
'4290 Gan (F) 66 Sk 47
'000 Gand = Gent (B) 53 Ad 39
27777 Ganderkesee (D) 38 Ai 37
37581 Gandersheim, Bad (D) 55 Ba 39
43780 Gandesa (E) 82 Aa 49
46700 Gandía (E) 82 Sk 52
237185 Găneasa (RO) 72 Ce 46
34190 Ganges (F) 67 Ad 47
03800 Gannat (F) 67 Ad 44
2230 Gänserndorf (A) 56 Bg 42
Gapkin (RUS) 76 Eb 43
Gar' (RUS) 34 Ei 30
9780 Gara Hitrino (BG) 72 Cg 47
30823* Garbsen (D) 54 Ak 38
37016 Garda (I) 69 Ba 45
13120 Gardanne (F) 68 Af 47
38701 Gardby (S) 40 Bg 34
39638 Gardelegen (D) 55 Bb 38
46200 Gardíki (GR) 86 Cb 51
46200 Gardíki (GR) 94 Cb 52
83086 Gärdnäs (S) 21 Bf 26
Gardone Val Trompia (I) 69 Ba 45
Gärdsjö (S) 29 Bf 30
Garešnica (HR) 70 Bg 45
24400 Gargaliáni (GR) 94 Cb 53
92073 Gargnäs (S) 21 Bh 25
96001 Gargždai (LT) 40 Cb 35
Gari (RUS) 36 Gc 31
Gar'inskij (RUS) 34 Fa 29
27026 Garlasco (I) 68 Ai 45
53030 Garliava (LT) 41 Cd 36
64330 Garlin (F) 66 Sk 47
82467 Garmisch-Partenkirchen (D) 69 Bb 43
2685 Garmo (N) 20 Ai 29
10940 Garrovillas (E) 80 Sd 51
04630 Garrucha (E) 93 Si 53
27203 Gärsnäs (S) 39 Be 35
16307 Gartz (Oder) (D) 39 Be 37
Garusovo (RUS) 32 Df 33
Gårva (N) 15 Cf 21
7670-121* Garvão (P) 92 Sb 53
08-400 Garwolin (PL) 57 Cb 39
17419 Garz (D) 39 Bd 36
Gaškovo (RUS) 36 Fi 31
307185 Gătaia (RO) 71 Cb 45
Gatčina (RUS) 31 Da 31
DG7 Gatehouse of Fleet (GB) 51 Sf 36
NE11 Gateshead (GB) 51 Si 36
13045 Gattinara (I) 68 Ai 45
29480 Gaucín (E) 92 Se 54
6868 Gaupne (N) 28 Ah 29
65120 Gavarnie (F) 82 Sk 48
6050-201 Gavião (P) 80 Sc 51
80002* Gävle (S) 29 Bh 30
50450 Gavray (F) 52 Si 42
Gavrilkovo (RUS) 33 Ea 31
Gavrilov-Jam (RUS) 33 Dk 33
Gavrilov Posad (RUS) 44 Ea 34
84501 Gávrio (GR) 94 Ce 53
91060 Gavsele (S) 21 Bh 26
Gävunda (S) 29 Be 30
Gazi Antep (TR) 98 Dh 53
Gaziler (TR) 91 Ec 50
Gaziler (TR) 91 Ed 50
Gazimagusa = Ammochostos 97 Dd 55
Gazipaşa (TR) 96 Dc 54
Gazlıgöl (TR) 96 Da 52
Gazlıkuyu (TR) 98 Dk 54
80-009* Gdańsk (PL) 40 Bi 36
Gdov (RUS) 31 Ch 32
81-004* Gdynia (PL) 40 Bi 36
46420 Geben (TR) 98 Dg 53
07540 Gebiz (TR) 96 Da 53
41400* Gebze (TR) 88 Ck 50
Geçitli (TR) 99 Ed 53
Gedikbaşı (TR) 90 Di 51
24860 Gedikdere (TR) 91 Ea 51
62630 Gedikler (TR) 90 Di 51
Gedikli (TR) 97 Df 52
05910 Gediksaray (TR) 89 Df 50
5575 Gedinne (B) 53 Ae 41
43600 Gediz (TR) 96 Ck 52
4874 Gedser (DK) 39 Bb 36
2440 Geel (B) 54 Af 39
52511 Geilenkirchen (D) 54 Ag 40
3580 Geilo (N) 28 Ai 30
85290 Geisenfeld (D) 55 Bb 42
73312 Geislingen an der Steige (D) 54 Ak 42
Geiterygghytta (N) 28 Ah 30
3360 Geithus, Åmot- (N) 28 Ai 31
93012 Gela (I) 84 Be 53
47608 Geldern (D) 54 Ag 39
Gelembe (TR) 88 Ch 51
32900 Gelendost (TR) 96 Db 52
Gelendžik (RUS) 75 Di 46
Gelenler (TR) 99 Ee 52
48700 Gelibolu (TR) 87 Cg 50
63571 Gelnhausen (D) 54 Ak 40
45879* Gelsenkirchen (D) 54 Ah 39
24395 Gelting (D) 38 Ak 36
5030 Gembloux (B) 53 Ae 40
58840 Gemerek (TR) 90 Dg 51
16600 Gemlik (TR) 88 Ck 50
33013 Gemona del Friuli (I) 69 Bd 44
17260 Gémozac (F) 66 Sk 45
97737 Gemünden am Main (D) 54 Ak 40
12500 Genç (TR) 99 Ea 52
42482 Gencek (TR) 96 Db 53
Generalovskij (RUS) 76 Ed 43
9500 General Toševo (BG) 73 Ci 47
1200* Genève (CH) 68 Ag 44
1200* Genf = Genève (CH) 68 Ag 44
3600 Genk (B) 54 Af 40
21110 Genlis (F) 68 Af 43
6590 Gennep (NL) 54 Ag 39
49350 Gennes (F) 66 Sk 43
16100 Genova (I) 68 Ai 46
9000 Gent (B) 53 Ad 39
39307 Genthin (D) 55 Bc 38
Genua = Genova (I) 68 Ai 46
85013 Genzano di Lucania (I) 85 Bg 50
Georgievka (RUS) 46 Fa 37
Georgievsk (RUS) 76 Ed 46
Georgievskoe (RUS) 32 Dg 31
Georgievskoe (RUS) 34 Ef 32
Georgiu-Dež = Liski (RUS) 60 Dk 40
07545* Gera (D) 55 Bc 40
9500 Geraardsbergen (B) 53 Ad 40
89040 Gerace (I) 85 Bg 52
23070 Gérakas (GR) 94 Cd 54
23058 Geráki (GR) 94 Cc 54
88400* Gérardmer (F) 54 Ag 42
Gerasimovka (RUS) 37 Gf 32
72300 Gercüş (TR) 99 Eb 53
14900 Gerede (TR) 89 Dc 50
41860 Gerena (E) 92 Sd 53
04550 Gérgal (E) 93 Sh 53
Gerger (TR) 98 Dk 52
07635 Geriş (TR) 96 Db 54
09700 Germencik (TR) 95 Ch 53
76726 Germersheim (D) 54 Ai 41
48300 Gernika-Lumo (E) 66 Sh 47
23071 Gerolimėnas (GR) 94 Cc 54
17001 Gerona = Girona (E) 82 Ac 49
59590 Geseke (D) 54 Ai 39
Gesunda (S) 29 Be 30
22340 Geta (AX) 30 Bk 30
28901* Getafe (E) 81 Sg 50
31044 Getinge (S) 39 Bc 34
65700 Gevaş (TR) 99 Ed 52
1480* Gevgelija (MK) 86 Cc 49
01170 Gex (F) 68 Ag 44
61500 Geyikli (TR) 87 Cg 51
Geyikpınar (TR) 99 Eb 52
09385 Geyre (TR) 96 Ci 53
54700 Geyve (TR) 88 Da 50
38180 Gezi (TR) 97 Df 52
Gezin (TR) 98 Dk 52
Gëziq (AL) 86 Bk 49
3542* Gföhl (A) 56 Bf 42
25016 Ghedi (I) 69 Ba 45
000601* Gheorghe Gheorghiu-Dej = Onești (RO) 72 Cg 44
535500 Gheorgheni (RO) 72 Cf 44
405300 Gherla (RO) 72 Cd 43
09074 Ghilarza (I) 83 Ai 50
087095 Ghimpați (RO) 72 Cf 46
20240 Ghisonaccia (F) 83 Ak 48
Giaginskaja (RUS) 75 Ea 46
06540 Giandola, la (F) 68 Ah 47
58100 Giannitsá (GR) 86 Cc 50
95014 Giarre (I) 84 Bf 53
63620 Giat (F) 67 Ac 45
04010 Giba (I) 83 Ai 51
9372 Gibostad (N) 14 Bi 21
21500 Gibraleón (E) 92 Sd 53
Gibraltar (GBZ) 92 Se 54
89037 Gideå (S) 22 Bk 27
45500* Gien (F) 67 Ac 43
38610 Gières (F) 68 Af 45
35390* Gießen (D) 54 Ai 40
9460 Gieten (NL) 38 Ag 37
8355 Giethoorn (NL) 38 Ag 38
38518 Gifhorn (D) 55 Ba 38
Gigant (RUS) 76 Eb 44
6553 Giggl (A) 69 Ba 43
207285 Gighera (RO) 72 Cd 47
Giglio Castello (I) 84 Ba 48
34150 Gignac (F) 67 Ad 47
03200* Gijón = Xixón (E) 80 Se 47
407310 Gilău (RO) 72 Cd 44
99460 Gilbbesjavri = Kilpisjärvi (FIN) 14 Ca 21
3250 Gilleleje (DK) 39 Bc 34
Gillesnuole (S) 21 Bg 25
SP8 Gillingham (GB) 53 Aa 39
74702 Gimo (S) 29 Bi 30
Gimoly (RUS) 23 Dc 28
32200 Gimont (F) 66 Aa 47
70023 Gioia del Colle (I) 85 Bg 50
89013 Gioia Tauro (I) 84 Bf 52
Giokaréika (GR) 94 Cc 53
Gir, Saraj- (RUS) 46 Fd 37
28000* Giresun (TR) 90 Di 50
88024 Girifalco (I) 85 Bg 52
47330 Girmeli (TR) 99 Eb 53
Girne = Keryneia 97 Dd 55
17001 Girona (E) 82 Ac 49
08680 Gironella (E) 82 Ab 48
617210 Girov (RO) 72 Cg 44
KA26 Girvan (GB) 51 Sf 35
Girvas (RUS) 23 Dd 28
Girvas (RUS) 16 Da 23
33201 Gislaved (S) 29 Bd 33
27140 Gisors (F) 53 Ab 41
23200 Githio (GR) 94 Cc 54
Gittun (S) 14 Bi 24
207290 Giubega (RO) 72 Cd 46
64021 Giulianova (I) 84 Bd 48
927135 Giurgeni (RO) 73 Ch 46
000080* Giurgiu (RO) 72 Cf 47
5318 Giurgiulești (MD) 73 Ci 45
7323 Give (DK) 38 Ak 35
08600 Givet (F) 53 Ae 40
69700 Givors (F) 67 Ae 45
Gizel' (RUS) 91 Ee 48
37340 Gizeux (F) 66 Aa 43
11-500* Giżycko (PL) 40 Cb 36
4980 Gjerstad (N) 28 Ak 32
Gjersvik (N) 21 Bd 26
9765 Gjesvær (N) 15 Cf 19
60000* Gjilan = Gnjilane (RKS) 86 Cb 48
Gjirokastër (AL) 86 Ca 50
476 Gjógv (FO) 50 Sd 28
Gjormë (AL) 86 Bk 50
476 Gjøv = Gjógv (FO) 50 Sd 28
Gjøvik (N) 28 Ba 30
Glad' (RUS) 31 Dc 31
Gladstad (N) 20 Bb 25
Glamoč (BIH) 70 Bg 46
7372 Glåmos (N) 20 Bb 28
5620 Glamsbjerg (DK) 39 Ba 35
8750 Glarus (CH) 69 Ak 43
G40 Glasgow (GB) 51 Sf 35
BA16 Glastonbury (GB) 52 Sh 39
08371 Glauchau (D) 55 Bc 40
Glaumbær (IS) 48 Ql 25
Glavace (HR) 70 Bf 46
Glavatićevo (BIH) 71 Bi 47
4409 Glavinica (BG) 72 Cg 47
Glazaniha (RUS) 24 Di 27
Glazov (RUS) 35 Fc 32
Glazunovka (RUS) 60 Dg 38
Gleann Beithe (IRL) 49 Rl 38
8200* Gleisdorf (A) 70 Bf 43
Glenamoy (IRL) 49 Sa 36
BT44 Glenariff (GB) 49 Sd 35
BT44 Glenarm (GB) 49 Se 36
BT29 Glenavy (GB) 49 Sd 36
Glenbeigh = Gleann Beithe (IRL) 49 Rl 38
Glengarriff = An Glean Garbh (IRL) 49 Sa 39
DG8 Glenluce (GB) 51 Sf 36
KY6 Glenrothes (GB) 50 Sg 34
Glenties = Na Gleannta (IRL) 49 Sb 36
35013 Glifa (GR) 94 Cc 52
28064 Glimåkra (S) 39 Be 34
Glina (HR) 70 Bg 45
Glinka (RUS) 42 Dc 36
06-450 Glinojeck (PL) 40 Ca 38
44-100* Gliwice (PL) 56 Bi 40
Gllavë (AL) 86 Bk 50
4900 Glodeni (MD) 73 Ch 43
2640* Gloggnitz (A) 70 Bf 43
67-200* Głogów (PL) 56 Bg 39
8160 Glomfjord (N) 14 Bd 24
93081 Glommersträsk (S) 22 Bk 25
SK13 Glossop (GB) 51 Si 37
Glotovka (RUS) 45 Eg 37
Glotovo (RUS) 26 Ek 27
GL2 Gloucester (GB) 52 Sh 39
76-220 Główczyce (PL) 40 Bh 36
11-040 Głowno (PL) 56 Bk 39
48-100 Głubczyce (PL) 56 Bh 40
Glubokij (RUS) 61 Ea 42
48-340 Głuchołazy (PL) 56 Bh 40
25348 Glückstadt (D) 38 Ak 37
Gluhovo (RUS) 44 Ed 35
Gluša (BY) 42 Ci 37
Gluškovo (RUS) 59 De 39
Gmelinka (RUS) 62 Eg 40
9853 Gmünd (A) 55 Be 42
9853 Gmünd (A) 69 Bd 44
4810* Gmunden (A) 55 Bd 43
82077 Gnarp (S) 21 Bh 28
27442 Gnarrenburg (D) 38 Ak 37
83-140 Gniew (PL) 40 Bi 37
88-140 Gniewkowo (PL) 40 Bi 38
62-200* Gniezno (PL) 56 Bh 38
60000* Gnjilane = Gjilan (RKS) 86 Cb 48
17179 Gnoien (D) 39 Bc 37
35700 Göçbeyli (TR) 88 Ch 51
2900 Goce Delčev (BG) 87 Cd 49
47574 Goch (D) 54 Ag 39
560 Goðdali (IS) 48 Ql 25
2240 Godeč (BG) 72 Cc 47
76110 Goderville (F) 53 Aa 41
84-218 Godętowo (PL) 40 Bh 36
Gödöllő (H) 71 Bk 43
83-209 Godziszewo (PL) 40 Bi 36
Goes (NL) 53 Ad 39
Gofickoe (RUS) 76 Ed 45
18586 Göhren (D) 39 Bd 36
36750 Goián (E) 80 Sb 49
3330-209* Góis (P) 80 Sb 50
Gojani i Sipërm (AL) 86 Bk 49
67670 Gökçebey (TR) 89 Dc 49
Gökçedağ (TR) 88 Ci 51
Gökçekent (TR) 90 Di 50
27700 Gökçeli (TR) 90 Dg 50
Gökçen (TR) 95 Ch 52
18800 Gökçeören (TR) 96 Ci 52
25500 Gökçeşeyh (TR) 91 Ea 51
Gökçesu (TR) 88 Db 50
60030 Gökdere (TR) 90 Dg 50
60030 Gökdere (TR) 96 Ck 52
33321 Gökkuşağı (TR) 97 De 54
25000 Gökoğlan (TR) 91 Eb 51
Gökova (TR) 95 Ci 53
Göksu (TR) 91 Ec 51
46600 Göksun (TR) 98 Dg 52
Göktepe (TR) 96 Ci 53
Göktepe (TR) 96 Dc 54
Gökyurt (TR) 96 Dc 53
3570 Gol (N) 28 Ai 30
Golaj (AL) 86 Ca 48
13800 Gölbaşı (TR) 89 Dc 51
13800 Gölbaşı (TR) 98 Dh 53
07350 Gölcük (TR) 88 Ch 51
07350 Gölcük (TR) 88 Ck 50
07350 Gölcük (TR) 97 De 52
07350 Gölcük (TR) 98 Dk 53
72-410 Golczewo (PL) 39 Be 37
19-500* Gołdap (PL) 41 Cc 36
19399 Goldberg (D) 39 Bc 37
Göldüzü (TR) 99 Ed 52
Goldyrevskij (RUS) 35 Fh 33
75700 Göle (TR) 91 Ec 50
2150-120* Golegã (P) 80 Sb 51
72-100* Goleniów (PL) 39 Be 37
97-320 Golesze (PL) 56 Bk 39
07020 Golfo Aranci (I) 83 Ak 50
15400 Gölhisar (TR) 96 Ck 53
Golicino (RUS) 45 Ee 37
Golicyno (RUS) 43 Dg 35
62-590 Golina (PL) 56 Bi 38
5726 Goliševa (LV) 42 Ch 34
Golitcino (RUS) 16 Df 21
5670 Goljama Železna (BG) 87 Ce 48
8624 Goljam Manastir (BG) 87 Cg 48
8729 Goljamo Kruševo (BG) 87 Cg 48
Gölköy (TR) 90 Dh 50
5440 Golling an der Salzach (A) 69 Bd 43
Göllü (TR) 89 De 51
45580 Gölmarmara (TR) 95 Ch 52
4204 Golnik (SLO) 70 Be 44
Gölören (TR) 97 Dd 53
07350 Gölova (TR) 90 Di 50
07350 Gölova (TR) 96 Da 54
Golovcevo (RUS) 45 Eg 37
Golovinka (RUS) 75 Dk 47
11130 Gölpazarı (TR) 88 Da 50
KW10 Golspie (GB) 50 Sg 33
12223 Golubac (SRB) 71 Cb 46
14380 Gölyaka (TR) 88 Da 50
49510 Gölyanı (TR) 99 Ec 52
Gölyazı (TR) 97 Dd 52
Golynki (RUS) 42 Db 36
14778 Golzow (D) 55 Bc 38
10700 Gömeç (TR) 87 Cg 51
Gomel' = Homel' (BY) 59 Db 38
Gomorovići (RUS) 32 De 30
Gončarovka (RUS) 60 Dk 40
3550-125* Gondomar (P) 80 Sb 49
10900 Gönen (TR) 88 Ch 50
10900 Gönen (TR) 96 Da 53
40004 Góni (GR) 86 Cc 51
DN14 Goole (GB) 51 Sk 37
7470 Goor (NL) 54 Ag 38
73033* Göppingen (D) 54 Ak 42
95-047 Góra (PL) 56 Bg 39
95-047 Góra (PL) 57 Ca 38
Gora (RUS) 33 Dk 29
Goragorskij (RUS) 77 Ef 47
05-530 Góra Kalwaria (PL) 57 Cb 39
73000* Goražde (BIH) 71 Bi 47
Gorbunovskij (RUS) 47 Fk 37
Gorčuha (RUS) 33 Ed 33
79091 Gördalen (S) 29 Bc 29
45750 Gördes (TR) 96 Ci 52
Gordino (RUS) 35 Fd 32
28800 Görele (TR) 90 Dk 49
Gorelki (RUS) 43 Dh 36
50000 Göreme (TR) 97 De 52
Gorevaja (RUS) 34 Ef 31
Gorey = Guaire (IRL) 49 Sd 38
Goricy (RUS) 32 Dg 33
Goricy (RUS) 44 Eb 33
4200* Gorinchem (NL) 53 Ae 39
34170 Gorizia (I) 69 Bd 45
Gorjačevodskij (RUS) 76 Ed 46
Gorjačij Ključ (RUS) 75 Dk 46
Gorjainovka (RUS) 62 Ei 38
Gorka (RUS) 32 Dd 33
Gor'kij = Nižnij Novgorod (RUS) 44 Ed 34
Gor'kovskij (RUS) 61 Ee 42
4281 Gørlev (DK) 39 Bb 35
38-300* Gorlice (PL) 57 Cb 41
02826* Görlitz (D) 55 Be 39
Gorlovka = Horlivka (UA) 60 Di 42
Gorlovo (RUS) 44 Dk 37
5100 Gorna Orjahovica (BG) 87 Cf 47
5294 Gorna Studena (BG) 72 Cf 47
Gorneckoe (RUS) 31 Dc 32
Gornjackij (RUS) 61 Ea 42
Gornjak (RUS) 44 Dk 37
32300* Gornji Milanovac (SRB) 71 Ca 46
Gornji Vakuf-Uskoplje (BIH) 70 Bh 47
Gornoslinkino (RUS) 37 Gi 32
Gornozavodsk (RUS) 36 Fi 32
Gornručej (RUS) 32 Df 30
Gornyj (RUS) 62 Ei 39
Gorodec (RUS) 44 Ed 34
Gorodeck (RUS) 25 Ef 27
Gorodišče (RUS) 31 Ck 32
Gorodišče (RUS) 45 Ef 37
Gorodišče (RUS) 45 Eh 36
Gorodišče (RUS) 63 Fe 39
Gorodišče, Krestovo- (RUS) 45 Ei 36
Gorodnja (RUS) 43 Dg 34
Gorodovikovsk (RUS) 76 Eb 44
Gorohovec (RUS) 44 Ec 34
Górowo Iławieckie (PL) 40 Ca 36
53120 Gorron (F) 52 Sk 42
Goršečnoe (RUS) 60 Di 39
6865 Gorski Izvor (BG) 87 Cf 48
Goršok (RUS) 25 Ec 25
Gort = An Gort (IRL) 49 Sb 37
Göründü (TR) 99 Ec 52
Görvik (S) 21 Bf 27
66-400* Gorzów Wielkopolski (PL) 39 Bf 38
38640* Goslar (D) 55 Ba 39
Gospić (HR) 70 Bf 46
9202 Gossau (SG) (CH) 69 Ak 43
1230* Gostivar (MK) 86 Ca 49
72-405 Gostyń (PL) 56 Bh 39
09-500 Gostynin (PL) 56 Bk 38
40010* Göteborg (S) 28 Bb 33
53301 Götene (S) 29 Bd 32
99867 Gotha (D) 55 Ba 40
62030 Gothem (S) 29 Bi 33
37073* Göttingen (D) 54 Ak 39
Gottskär (S) 29 Bc 33
Gotval'd = Zmijiv (UA) 60 Dg 41
2801* Gouda (NL) 53 Ae 38
20014 Goúra (GR) 94 Cc 53
46300 Gourdon (F) 67 Ab 46
56110 Gourin (F) 52 Sg 42
76220 Gournay-en-Bray (F) 53 Ab 41
2705-409* Gouveia (P) 80 Sc 50
Gouvia (GR) 86 Bk 51
23230 Gouzon (F) 67 Ac 44
05900 Göynücek (TR) 89 Df 50
50500 Göynük (TR) 88 Da 50
50500 Göynük (TR) 91 Ea 51
50500 Göynük (TR) 96 Da 52
Gözeli (TR) 98 Dk 52
27800 Gözkaya (TR) 98 Dg 54
33400 Gözne (TR) 97 De 54
Gräbo (S) 29 Bc 33
19300 Grabow (D) 39 Bb 37
63-520 Grabów nad Prosną (PL) 56 Bi 39
Gračac (HR) 70 Bf 46
Gračanica (BIH) 71 Bi 46
18310 Graçay (F) 67 Ab 43
Gračevka (RUS) 46 Fc 38
Gračevka (RUS) 61 Ea 38
Gračevka (RUS) 76 Ec 45
Gračev Kust (RUS) 62 Ek 39
Gradac (HR) 85 Bh 47
84 215 Gradac (MNE) 71 Bk 47
Gradačac (BIH) 71 Bi 46
8990 Gradec (BG) 71 Cc 46
8990 Gradec (BG) 87 Cg 48
24160 Gradefes (E) 80 Se 48
9362 Grades (A) 70 Be 44
237205 Grădinari (RO) 72 Ce 46
077110 Grădiștea (RO) 73 Ch 46
9498 Gradnica (BG) 87 Ce 48
34073 Grado (I) 69 Bd 45
Grado, El (E) 82 Aa 48

Grado, El | 175

33820 Grado (Grau) (E) 80 Sd 47
1420 Gradsko (MK) 86 Cb 49
82166 Gräfelfing (D) 55 Bb 42
94481 Grafenau (D) 55 Bd 42
06773 Gräfenhainichen (D) 55 Bc 39
4198 Graf Ignatievo (BG) 87 Ce 48
85567 Grafing bei München (D) 55 Bb 42
Grahovo (RUS) 46 Fc 34
81 420 Grahovo (MNE) 86 Bi 48
Graig na Managh (IRL) 49 Sd 38
Graiguenamanagh = Graig na Managh (IRL) 49 Sd 38
19-200 Grajewo (PL) 41 Cc 37
Grajvoron (RUS) 60 Df 40
6510 Gram (DK) 38 Ak 35
3830 Gramada (BG) 71 Cc 47
46500 Gramat (F) 67 Ab 46
9500 Grammont = Geraardsbergen (B) 53 Ad 40
Gramsh (AL) 86 Ca 50
17291 Gramzow (D) 39 Be 37
2750 Gran (N) 28 Ba 30
18001* Granada (E) 93 Sg 53
03738 Granadella, la (E) 82 Aa 49
Granard (IRL) 49 Sc 37
33730 Grandas (Grandas de Salime) (E) 80 Sd 47
30110 Grand-Combe, la (F) 67 Ae 46
34280 Grande-Motte, la (F) 67 Ae 47
35390 Grand-Fougeray (F) 66 Si 43
72150 Grand-Lucé, le (F) 66 Aa 43
7570-112* Grândola (P) 92 Sb 52
60210 Grandvilliers (F) 53 Ab 41
22260 Grañén (E) 82 Sk 49
Grange = An Ghrainseach (IRL) 49 Sb 36
77201 Grängesberg (S) 29 Bf 30
88295 Graninge (S) 21 Bg 27
06910 Granja de Torrehermosa (E) 92 Se 52
38075 Grankullavik (S) 29 Bh 33
56301 Gränna (S) 29 Be 32
92397 Grannäs (S) 21 Bg 25
92295 Granö (S) 22 Bk 26
08400* Granollers (E) 82 Ac 49
16775 Gransee (D) 39 Bd 37
Gränssjö (S) 21 Be 25
NG31 Grantham (GB) 51 Sk 38
PH26 Grantown-on-Spey (GB) 50 Sg 33
50400* Granville (F) 52 Si 42
5736 Granvin (N) 28 Ag 30
06130* Grasse (F) 68 Ag 47
6300 Gråsten (DK) 38 Ak 36
46701 Grästorp (S) 29 Bc 32
81300* Graulhet (F) 67 Ab 47
22430 Graus (E) 82 Aa 48
5360 Grave (NL) 54 Af 39
59820 Gravelines (F) 53 Ac 40
2554* Gravenhage, ,s- = Den Haag (NL) 53 Ae 38
70022 Gravina di Puglia (I) 85 Bg 50
70100* Gray (F) 68 Af 43
8010* Graz (A) 70 Bf 43
16220 Grdelica (SRB) 86 Cc 48
TS9 Great Ayton (GB) 51 Si 36
WR14 Great Malvern (GB) 52 Sh 38
NR30 Great Yarmouth (GB) 53 Ab 38
45702 Grebbestad (S) 28 Bb 32
Grebinka = Hrebimka (BY) 59 Dc 40
Grebnevo (RUS) 44 Dk 36
PA16 Greenock (GB) 51 Sf 35
SE10 Greenwich (GB) 53 Aa 39
17489* Greifswald (D) 39 Bd 36
4360* Grein (A) 55 Be 42
07973 Greiz (D) 55 Bc 40
Gremiha (RUS) 17 Dk 22
Gremjač'e (RUS) 60 Dk 39
Gremjačevo (RUS) 44 Ed 35
Gremjačinsk (RUS) 35 Fh 32
8500 Grenå = Grenaa (DK) 39 Ba 34
8500 Grenaa = Grenå (DK) 39 Ba 34
31330 Grenade (F) 67 Ab 47
40270 Grenade-sur-l'Adour (F) 66 Sk 47
2540 Grenchen (CH) 68 Ah 43
610 Grenivík (IS) 48 Rb 25
38000* Grenoble (F) 68 Af 45
Grense Jakobselv (N) 16 Da 21
Gressåmoen (N) 21 Bd 26
DG16 Gretna (GB) 51 Sg 36
88630 Greux (F) 54 Af 42
50022 Greve in Chianti (I) 69 Bb 47
48268 Greven (D) 54 Ah 38
51100 Grevená (GR) 86 Cb 50
41515* Grevenbroich (D) 54 Ag 39
44014 Greveníti (GR) 86 Cb 51
Greystones = Na Clocha Liatha (IRL) 49 Sd 37
Gribanovskij (RUS) 61 Eb 39
Gridino (RUS) 24 De 25
94086 Griesbach im Rottal, Bad (D) 55 Bd 42
Grigor'evka (RUS) 64 Ff 39
Grigor'evskaja (RUS) 35 Ff 32
Grigor'evskoe (RUS) 33 Ed 33
4500 Grigoriopol (MD) 73 Ck 43
Grigoropolisskaja (RUS) 76 Eb 45
04668 Grimma (D) 55 Bc 39
18507 Grimmen (D) 39 Bd 36
L3 Grimsby (GB) 51 Sk 37
660 Grímsstaðir (IS) 48 Rd 25
4876 Grimstad (N) 28 Ai 32
4700 Grimstrup (DK) 38 Ai 35
531 Grimstunga (IS) 48 Qk 25
240 Grindavík (IS) 48 Qh 27
3818 Grindelwald (CH) 68 Ai 44
7200 Grindsted (DK) 38 Ai 35
57300 Gripenberg (S) 29 Be 33
71041 Griškabūdis (LT) 41 Cd 36
Griškino (RUS) 45 Eh 34
82170 Grisolles (F) 67 Ab 47
76045 Grisslehamn (S) 29 Bi 30
Griva (RUS) 34 Fa 30
Grivenskaja (RUS) 75 Di 45
927145 Grivița (RO) 73 Ch 46
Grjadcy (RUS) 42 Db 34
Grjady (RUS) 31 Db 32
Grjazi (RUS) 60 Dk 38
Grjaznovskij, Ust'- (RUS) 61 Ec 42
Grjazovec (RUS) 33 Ea 32
6612 Grøa (N) 20 Ai 28
3430 Grobiņa (LV) 40 Cb 34
8962 Gröbming (A) 69 Bd 43
11306 Grocka (SRB) 71 Ca 46
6763 Grodås (N) 20 Ag 29
49-200 Grodków (PL) 56 Bh 40
Grodno = Hrodna (BY) 41 Cd 37
08-825 Grodzisk Mazowiecki (PL) 57 Ca 38
62-065 Grodzisk Wielkopolski (PL) 56 Bg 38
7140 Groenlo (NL) 54 Ag 38
56590 Groix (F) 66 Sg 43
05-600 Grójec (PL) 57 Ca 39
23743 Grömitz (D) 39 Ba 36
Gromovo (RUS) 40 Cb 36
7870 Grong (N) 21 Bc 26
9700* Groningen (NL) 38 Ag 37
57993 Grönskåra (S) 29 Bf 33
27624 Großenhain (D) 55 Bd 39
58100 Grosseto (I) 84 Bb 48
3920 Großgerungs (A) 55 Be 42
9423 Grøtavær (N) 14 Bg 22
2625 Grov (N) 14 Bh 22
36980 Grove, O (E) 80 Sb 48
Groznyj (RUS) 77 Ef 47
2742 Grua (N) 28 Ba 30
Grubišno Polje (HR) 70 Bh 45
8300 Grudovo = Sredec (BG) 88 Ch 48
06-460 Grudusk (PL) 40 Ca 37
86-300 Grudziądz (PL) 40 Bi 37
227240 Gruia (RO) 71 Cc 46
Grumantbyen (N) 14 I Svalbard
66401 Grums (S) 29 Bd 31
4645* Grünau im Almtal (A) 69 Bd 43
35305 Grünberg (D) 54 Ai 40
350 Grundarfjörður (IS) 48 Qg 26
82201 Gruvberget (S) 29 Bg 29
34230 Gruža (SRB) 71 Ca 47
81024 Gruzdžiai (LT) 41 Cd 34
33-330 Grybów (PL) 57 Ca 41
72-300 Gryfice (PL) 39 Bf 37
74-100 Gryfino (PL) 39 Be 37
59-620 Gryfów Śląski (PL) 56 Bf 39
Grykë (AL) 86 Bk 50
9380 Gryllefjord (N) 14 Bh 21
1882 Gryon (CH) 68 Ah 44
61042 Gryt (S) 29 Bg 32
19001* Guadalajara (E) 81 Sg 50
41390 Guadalcanal (E) 92 Se 52
10140 Guadalupe (E) 80 Se 51
Guadisa (E) 80 Se 51
Guaire (IRL) 49 Sd 38
06023 Gualdo Tadino (I) 69 Bc 47
3240-671* Guarda (P) 80 Sc 50
36780 Guarda, A (E) 80 Sb 49
03140 Guardamar del Segura (E) 93 Sk 52
45760 Guardia, La (E) 81 Sg 51
66016 Guardiagrele (I) 85 Be 48
82034 Guardia Sanframondi (I) 85 Be 49
34880 Guardo (E) 81 Sf 48
05540 Guareña (E) 92 Sd 52
42016 Guastalla (I) 69 Ba 46
Guba Dolgaja (RUS) 19 Fi 20
Gubaha (RUS) 35 Fh 32
06024 Gubbio (I) 69 Bc 47
92070 Gubbträsk (S) 21 Bh 25
03172 Guben (D) 55 Be 39
66-620 Gubin (PL) 55 Be 39
03172 Gubin = Guben (D) 55 Be 39
Gubkin (RUS) 60 Dh 39
32230 Guča (SRB) 71 Ca 47
46300 Gücük (TR) 98 Db 52
Gudbor (RUS) 35 Fg 30
3760 Gudhjem (DK) 39 Be 35
32540 Gudiña, A (E) 80 Sc 48
29650 Güdül (TR) 89 Dc 50
5747 Gudvangen (N) 28 Ag 30
68500* Guebwiller (F) 68 Ah 43
56160 Guémené-sur-Scorff (F) 52 Sg 42
56380 Guer (F) 66 Sh 43
44350 Guérande (F) 66 Sh 43
35130 Guerche-de-Bretagne, la (F) 66 Si 43
23000* Guéret (F) 67 Ab 44
58130 Guérigny (F) 67 Ad 43
71130 Gueugnon (F) 67 Ae 44
86034 Guglionesi (I) 85 Be 49
35580 Guichen (F) 66 Si 43
37770 Guijuelo (E) 80 Se 50
06470 Guillaumes (F) 68 Ag 46
05600 Guillestre (F) 68 Ag 46
4800-001* Guimarães (P) 80 Sb 49
22200* Guingamp (F) 52 Sg 42
02120 Guise (F) 53 Ad 41
25210 Guissona (E) 82 Ab 49
27300 Guitiriz (E) 80 Sc 47
4401 Gulbene (LV) 30 Cg 33
Güldere (TR) 97 Dd 53
33590 Gülek (TR) 97 De 53
5960 Guljanci (BG) 72 Ce 47
Gul'keviči (RUS) 76 Ea 45
8400 Gullesfjordbotn (N) 14 Bf 22
54700 Gullspång (S) 29 Be 32
Güllü (TR) 91 Ec 51
Güllü (TR) 96 Ck 52
48200 Güllük (TR) 95 Ch 53
33700 Gülnar (TR) 97 Dd 54
17600 Gülpınar (TR) 87 Cg 51
50900 Gülşehir (TR) 97 De 52
Gumarino (RUS) 23 Dd 28
09370 Gumiel de Hizán (E) 81 Sg 49
51643* Gummersbach (D) 54 Ah 39
Gümüşakar (TR) 90 Di 51
Gümüşdere (TR) 99 Ed 52
05700 Gümüşhacıköy (TR) 89 Df 50
29000 Gümüşhane (TR) 90 Dk 50
50900 Gümüşkent (TR) 97 De 52
Gümüşsu (TR) 95 Ch 52
Gümüşsu (TR) 96 Da 52
29800 Gündoğdu (TR) 88 Ch 50
Gündoğmuş (TR) 96 Dc 54
73200 Güneşli (TR) 88 Ci 51
73200 Güneşli (TR) 97 Df 52
Güney (TR) 96 Ck 52
53350 Güneysu (TR) 91 Ea 50
Güneyyurt (TR) 96 Dc 54
92051 Gunnarn (S) 21 Bh 25
96197 Gunnarsbyn (S) 22 Cb 24
Gunnilbo (S) 29 Bf 31
Günyüzü (TR) 89 Dc 51
89312 Günzburg (D) 55 Ba 42
91710 Gunzenhausen (D) 55 Ba 41
317145 Gurahonț (RO) 71 Cc 44
725300 Gura Humorului (RO) 72 Cf 43
127280 Gura Teghii (RO) 72 Cg 45
Gürbulak (TR) 91 Ee 51
10305 Güre (TR) 96 Ck 52
Gur'evka (RUS) 46 Fb 34
52610 Gürgentepe (TR) 90 Dh 50
9342* Gurk (A) 70 Be 44
9644 Gurkovo (BG) 87 Cf 48
13800 Güroymak (TR) 99 Ec 52
65900 Gürpınar (TR) 99 Ed 52
Gürsu (TR) 88 Ck 50
58800 Gürün (TR) 98 Dh 52
Gusev (RUS) 41 Cc 36
Gusevo (RUS) 43 Dd 34
Gus'-Hrustal'nyj (RUS) 44 Ea 35
Gusino (RUS) 42 Db 36
Gusmar (AL) 86 Bk 50
09036 Guspini (I) 83 Ai 51
7540* Güssing (A) 70 Bg 43
13400 Gustavsberg (S) 29 Bi 31
66693 Gustavsfors (S) 29 Bd 30
18273 Güstrow (D) 39 Bc 37
Gus'-Železnyj (RUS) 44 Eb 35
ZE2 Gutcher (GB) 50 Si 30
2770* Gutenstein (A) 70 Bf 43
33330* Gütersloh (D) 54 Ai 39
Guvåg (N) 14 Be 22
06890 Güvem (TR) 89 Dc 50
07645 Güzelbağ (TR) 96 Db 54
35311 Güzelbahçe (TR) 95 Cg 52
33730 Güzeloluk (TR) 97 De 54
13800 Güzelsu (TR) 96 Db 54
13800 Güzelsu (TR) 99 Ed 52
25000 Güzelyurt (TR) 97 De 52
Gvardejsk (RUS) 40 Cb 36
3810 Gvarv (N) 28 Ak 31
Gyakovë = Đakovica (RKS) 86 Ca 48
Gybdan (RUS) 46 Fb 34
Gyljen (S) 15 Cc 24
5500 Gyoma (H) 71 Ca 44
3200 Gyöngyös (H) 71 Bk 43
9010* Győr (H) 70 Bh 43
81021 Gysinge (S) 29 Bg 30
5700 Gyula (H) 71 Cb 44

H

86001 Häädemeeste (EST) 30 Ce 32
2554* Haag, Den = ,s-Gravenhage (NL) 53 Ae 38
83527 Haag in Oberbayern (D) 55 Bc 42
7480 Haaksbergen (NL) 54 Ag 38
54270 Haapajärvi (FIN) 22 Cf 27
86601 Haapavesi (FIN) 22 Cf 26
90502* Haapsalu (EST) 30 Cd 32
2011* Haarlem (NL) 53 Ae 38
Habariha (RUS) 26 Fc 25
73300 Haberli (TR) 99 Eb 53
Habez (RUS) 76 Eb 46
56601 Habo (S) 29 Be 33
50800 Hacıbektaş (TR) 97 De 52
39000 Hacıfakılı (TR) 96 Db 52
19910 Hacıhamza (TR) 89 De 49
71480 Hacılar (TR) 89 Dd 51
71480 Hacılar (TR) 96 Da 53
71480 Hacılar (TR) 97 Df 52
Hacıömer (TR) 91 Eb 51
83023 Hackås (S) 21 Be 28
6100 Haderslev (DK) 38 Ak 35
42830 Hadım (TR) 96 Dc 53
34232 Hadımköy (TR) 88 Ci 49
Hadjač (UA) 59 Dd 40
8370 Hadsten (DK) 39 Ba 34
9560 Hadsund (DK) 39 Ba 34
Hadyžensk (RUS) 75 Dk 46
4720 Hægeland (N) 28 Ah 32
58760 Hafik (TR) 90 Dh 51
220* Hafnarfjörður (IS) 48 Qi 26
230 Hafnir (IS) 48 Qh 27
58089* Hagen (D) 54 Ah 39
19230 Hagenow (D) 39 Bb 37
40700 Hagetmau (F) 66 Sk 47
68301 Hagfors (S) 29 Bd 30
83030 Häggenås (S) 21 Be 27
83090 Häggnäset (S) 21 Be 26
Häggsjöbränna (S) 21 Bc 27
801 Hagi (IS) 48 Qg 25
67500* Haguenau (F) 54 Ah 42
Hahaly (RUS) 45 Ee 34
8771 Hahót (H) 70 Bg 44
90480 Hailuoto (FIN) 22 Ce 25
3170 Hainfeld (A) 56 Bf 42
09661 Hainichen (D) 55 Bd 40
4220 Hajdúböszörmény (H) 71 Cb 43
4080 Hajdúnánás (H) 71 Cb 43
4200 Hajdúszoboszló (H) 71 Cb 43
17-200 Hajnówka (PL) 41 Cd 38
Hajsyn (UA) 58 Ck 42
30000 Hakkâri (TR) 99 Ed 53
98041 Hakkas (S) 15 Cb 24
9532 Hakkstabben (N) 15 Cd 20
25008 Halandrítsa (GR) 94 Cb 52
38820* Halberstadt (D) 55 Bb 39
1763* Halden (N) 28 Bb 31
39340 Haldensleben (D) 55 Bb 38
IP19 Halesworth (GB) 53 Ab 38
63950 Halfeti (TR) 98 Dh 53
HX2 Halifax (GB) 51 Si 37
25900 Halilkaya (TR) 91 Ea 50
Halilovo (RUS) 47 Fi 37
Halilovo (RUS) 64 Fi 39
Halitçavuş (TR) 91 Eb 51
45850 Halitpaşa (TR) 95 Ch 52
45301 Haljala (EST) 30 Cg 31
42280 Halkapınar (TR) 97 De 53
40009 Hálki (GR) 95 Ch 54
Halkiádes (GR) 86 Cc 51
34100 Halkída (GR) 94 Cd 52
Halkidó (GR) 86 Cc 50
91060 Hälla (S) 21 Bh 27
37620 Halle (B) 53 Ae 40
06108* Halle (Saale) (D) 55 Bb 39
33790 Halle (Westfalen) (D) 54 Ai 38
71201 Hällefors (S) 29 Be 31
5400* Hallein (A) 69 Bd 43
53304 Hällekis (S) 29 Bd 32
83001 Hallen (S) 21 Be 27
Hällestad (S) 29 Bf 32
6060 Hall in Tirol (A) 69 Bb 43
Hällnäs (S) 22 Bk 26
Hallormsstaður (IS) 48 Rf 25
69401 Hallsberg (S) 29 Bf 31
76300 Hallstavik (S) 29 Bi 30
30004* Halmstad (S) 39 Bc 34
9370 Hals (DK) 39 Ba 33
8178 Halsa (N) 20 Ai 27
Hal'šany (BY) 41 Cg 36
69510 Halsua (FIN) 22 Ce 27
45721 Haltern am See (D) 54 Ah 39
Halturin (RUS) 34 Ei 32
NE49 Haltwhistle (GB) 51 Sh 36
Halyč (UA) 57 Ce 41
80400 Ham (F) 53 Ad 41
Hamam (TR) 98 Dg 54
05700 Hamamözü (TR) 89 Df 50
2315* Hamar (N) 28 Bb 30
20099* Hamburg (D) 39 Ba 37
45070 Hamburgsund (S) 28 Bb 32
19600 Hamdi (TR) 89 De 50
39101 Hämeenkyrö (FIN) 30 Cd 29
13100* Hämeenlinna (FIN) 30 Ce 29
31785* Hameln (D) 54 Ak 38
Hamidiye (TR) 87 Cg 49
Hamidiye (TR) 88 Da 51
Hamilton (GB) 51 Sf 35
49461 Hamina (FIN) 31 Ch 30
59063* Hamm (D) 54 Ah 39
84070 Hammarstrand (S) 21 Bg 27
82200* Hammaslahti = Pyhäselkä (FIN) 23 Ck 28
8450 Hammel (DK) 38 Ak 34
97762 Hammelburg (D) 54 Ak 40
83070 Hammerdal (S) 21 Bf 27
9600 Hammerfest (N) 15 Cd 20
9460 Hammershøj (DK) 38 Ak 34
9181 Hamneidet (N) 14 Ca 21
3930 Hamont-Achel (B) 54 Af 39
82051 Hamra (S) 29 Be 29
Hamrånge (S) 29 Bh 30
04850 Hamur (TR) 91 Ec 51
Hamyski (RUS) 75 Ea 46
Hamzalar (TR) 91 Eb 51
50900 Hamzalı (TR) 99 Eb 52
75900 Hanak (TR) 91 Ec 49
63450* Hanau (D) 54 Ai 40
Hancavičy (BY) 41 Cg 38
Handen (S) 29 Bi 31
83019 Handöl (S) 21 Bc 27
2478 Hanestad (N) 20 Ba 29
10900* Hangö (FIN) 30 Cc 31
21800 Hani (TR) 99 Ea 52
73101 Haniá (GR) 94 Ce 55
Hanino (RUS) 43 Dg 36
41521 Hankasalmen asema (FIN) 22 Cg 28
23130 Hankendi (TR) 98 Dk 52
10900* Hanko = Hangö (FIN) 30 Cc 31
Hanköy (TR) 97 Dg 52
34346 Hann. Münden (D) 54 Ak 39
30159* Hannover (D) 54 Ak 38
Han Pijesak (BIH) 71 Bi 46
Hanskaja (RUS) 75 Dk 46
7730 Hanstholm (DK) 28 Ai 33
Hanty-Mansijsk (RUS) 37 Gk 29
094 31 Hanušovce nad Topl'ou (SK) 57 Cb 41
95301 Haparanda (S) 22 Ce 25
Håra (N) 28 Ag 31
Harabali (RUS) 77 Eh 43
Harabeköy (TR) 96 Dc 52
Harabekri = Knidos Harabekri (TR) 95 Ch 54
48980 Harabeleri (TR) 95 Ch 54
Haradok (BY) 42 Ck 35
Haradok, Davyd- (BY) 58 Ch 38
Haradzeja (BY) 41 Cg 37
Haradzišča (BY) 41 Cg 37
50200 Haravgí (GR) 86 Cb 50
Harborø (DK) 38 Ai 34
21073* Harburg (D) 38 Ak 37
86655 Harburg (Schwaben) (D) 55 Ba 42
6924 Hardbakke (N) 28 Ae 29
7770 Hardenberg (NL) 54 Ag 38
3840* Harderwijk (NL) 54 Af 38
6060 Hareid (N) 20 Ag 28
49733 Haren (Ems) (D) 38 Ah 38
2743 Harestua (N) 28 Ba 30
Harino (RUS) 33 Ed 31
Haritonovo (RUS) 34 Eh 29
7815 Harkány (H) 71 Bi 45
Har'kov = Charkiv (UA) 60 Dg 41
Har'kovka (RUS) 64 Fg 40
Harlamovskaja (RUS) 32 Dh 32
705100 Hârlău (RO) 72 Cg 43
IP20 Harleston (GB) 53 Ab 38
4652 Hårlev (DK) 39 Bc 35
Harlingen = Harns (NL) 38 Af 37
Harlovka (RUS) 16 Dh 22
Harlovskoe (RUS) 36 Gd 33
CM17 Harlow (GB) 53 Aa 39
507085 Hărman (RO) 72 Cf 45
Harmancık (TR) 88 Ck 51
Harmancık (TR) 90 Dh 51
82075 Harmånger (S) 21 Bh 29
Härmänkylä (FIN) 23 Ck 26
6450 Harmanli (BG) 87 Cf 49
Harmanlı (TR) 98 Dh 53
87101* Härnösand (S) 21 Bh 28
Harns = Harlingen (NL) 38 Af 37
26200 Haro (E) 81 Sh 48
ZE2 Haroldswick (GB) 50 Sk 30
Harovsk (RUS) 33 Ea 31
27243 Harpstedt (D) 38 Ai 38
23140 Harput (TR) 98 Dk 52
7873 Harran (N) 21 Bc 26
Harran (TR) 98 Dk 54
HG3 Harrogate (GB) 51 Si 37
21698 Harsefeld (D) 38 Ak 37
Hârşova (RO) 73 Ch 46
9402* Harstad (N) 14 Bg 22
Harsvik (N) 20 Ba 26
8230* Hartberg (A) 70 Bf 43
TS24 Hartlepool (GB) 51 Si 36
19601 Hartola (FIN) 30 Cg 29
Harun (TR) 89 De 50

176 I Grado (Grau)

CO12 Harwich (GB) 53 Ab 39
38667 Harzburg, Bad (D) 55 Ba 39
06493 Harzgerode (D) 55 Bb 39
Hasanağa (TR) 88 Ci 50
44420 Hasançelebi (TR) 98 Dh 52
72350 Hasankeyf (TR) 99 Eb 53
06850 Hasanoğlan (TR) 89 Dd 50
66670 Hasbek (TR) 89 Df 51
49740 Haselünne (D) 38 Ah 38
6300* Haskovo (BG) 87 Cf 49
22500 Hasköy (TR) 87 Cg 49
22500 Hasköy (TR) 91 Ec 50
GU27 Haslemere (GB) 52 Sk 39
4690 Haslev (DK) 39 Bb 35
64240 Hasparren (F) 66 Si 47
31700 Hassa (TR) 98 Dg 54
82078 Hassela (S) 21 Bg 28
3500 Hasselt (B) 54 Af 40
97437 Haßfurt (D) 55 Ba 40
08112 Haßlau, Wilkau- (D) 55 Bc 40
28101* Hässleholm (S) 39 Bd 34
TN34 Hastings (GB) 53 Aa 40
28023 Hästveda (S) 39 Bd 34
9590 Hasvik (N) 15 Cc 20
Hatay (Antakya) (TR) 97 Dg 54
335500 Haţeg (RO) 71 Cc 45
AL9 Hatfield (GB) 52 Sk 39
42215 Hatip (TR) 96 Dc 53
Hatlestrand (N) 28 Af 30
8690 Hattfjelldal (N) 21 Bd 25
81950 Hattuselkonen (FIN) 23 Da 27
81650 Hattuvaara (FIN) 23 Db 28
42220 Hatunsaray (TR) 96 Dc 53
3000* Hatvan (H) 71 Bk 43
5514* Haugesund (N) 28 Af 31
Haugland (N) 28 Ae 30
14700 Hauho (FIN) 30 Ce 29
810 Haukadalur (IS) 48 Qk 26
Haukeligrend (N) 28 Ah 31
90840 Haukipudas (FIN) 22 Cf 25
51601 Haukivuori (FIN) 23 Ch 28
57874 Haurida (S) 29 Be 33
12520 Hausjärvi (FIN) 30 Ce 30
98995 Hautajärvi (FIN) 15 Ck 24
Hautavaara (RUS) 23 Dc 28
94051 Hauzenberg (D) 55 Bd 42
Havaalanı (TR) 90 Dg 51
PO9 Havant (GB) 52 Sk 40
39539 Havelberg (D) 39 Bc 38
SA61 Haverfordwest (GB) 52 Sf 39
CB9 Haverhill (GB) 53 Aa 38
580 01 Havlíčkův Brod (CZ) 56 Bf 41
9690 Havøysund (N) 15 Ce 19
10560 Havran (TR) 88 Ch 51
76600 Havre, Le (F) 53 Aa 41
Havrylivka (UA) 60 Dg 42
22500 Havsa (TR) 87 Cg 49
83081 Havsnäs (S) 21 Bf 26
58940 Havuz (TR) 90 Dh 51
55700 Havza (TR) 89 Df 50
DL8 Hawes (GB) 51 Sh 36
TD9 Hawick (GB) 51 Sh 35
57700 Hayange (F) 54 Ag 41
03480 Haydarlı (TR) 96 Da 52
Haydere (TR) 96 Ci 53
50250 Haye-du-Puits, La (F) 52 Si 41
06860 Haymana (TR) 89 Dc 51
59400 Hayrabolu (TR) 88 Ch 49
61450 Hayrat (TR) 91 Ea 50
TR21 Haywards Heath (GB) 52 Sk 39
Hazar (TR) 98 Dk 52
59190 Hazebrouck (F) 53 Ac 40
Hazine (TR) 99 Ed 52
21560 Hazro (TR) 99 Ea 52
Headfort = Áth Cinn (IRL) 49 Sa 37
8411* Hearrenfean, It = Heerenveen (NL) 38 Af 38
74401 Heby (S) 29 Bg 31
72379 Hechingen (D) 54 Ai 42
2930 Hedal (N) 28 Ak 30
Hede (S) 21 Bd 28
77601 Hedemora (S) 29 Bf 30
95795 Hedenäset (S) 22 Cd 24
8722 Hedensted (DK) 38 Ak 35
81040 Hedesunda (S) 29 Bg 30
84092 Hedeviken (S) 21 Bd 28
HU12 Hedon (GB) 51 Sk 37
8411* Heerenveen = It Hearrenfean (NL) 38 Af 38
6400* Heerlen (NL) 54 Af 40
9222 Hegyeshalom (H) 70 Bh 43
25746 Heide (D) 38 Ak 36
69115* Heidelberg (D) 54 Ai 41
89518* Heidenheim an der Brenz (D) 55 Ba 42
3860* Heidenreichstein (A) 56 Bf 42
27511 Heikkilä (FIN) 23 Ck 25
IV27 Heilam (GB) 50 Sf 32
37308 Heilbad Heiligenstadt (D) 55 Ba 39
74072* Heilbronn (D) 54 Ak 41
9844* Heiligenblut am Großglockner (A) 69 Bc 43
23774 Heiligenhafen (D) 39 Ba 36
37308 Heiligenstadt, Heilbad (D) 55 Ba 39
1850 Heiloo (NL) 38 Ae 38
7072 Heimdal (N) 20 Ba 27
79701 Heinävesi (FIN) 23 Ci 28
18200 Heinola (FIN) 30 Cg 29
8300 Heist, Knokke- (B) 53 Ad 39
2220 Heist-op-den-Berg (B) 53 Ae 39
54770 Heituinlahti (FIN) 31 Ch 29
62020 Hejde (S) 29 Bi 33
Hekimdağ (TR) 88 Da 51
44400 Hekimhan (TR) 98 Dh 52
84-150 Hel (PL) 40 Bi 36
84035 Helagsstugorna (S) 21 Bc 28
1783 Helder, Den (NL) 38 Ae 38
G84 Helensburgh (GB) 50 Sf 34
88293 Helgum (S) 21 Bg 27
850 Hella (IS) 48 Qk 27
Helle, Vadfoss- (N) 28 Ak 32
4376 Helleland (N) 28 Ag 32
Hellemobotn (N) 14 Bg 23
Hellesvik (N) 20 Ai 27
6218 Hellesylt (N) 20 Ag 28
3220* Hellevoetsluis (NL) 53 Ae 39
02400 Hellín (E) 93 Si 52
360 Hellisandur (IS) 48 Qg 26
Hellnessund (N) 14 Be 23
5700* Helmond (NL) 54 Af 39
KW8 Helmsdale (GB) 50 Sg 32
YO62 Helmsley (GB) 51 Si 36
38350 Helmstedt (D) 55 Ba 38
25002* Helsingborg (S) 39 Bc 34
00002* Helsingfors = Helsinki (FIN) 30 Ce 30
3000 Helsingør (DK) 39 Bc 34
23311 Helsinki (FIN) 30 Ce 30
TR13 Helston (GB) 52 Se 40
Hemavan (S) 21 Bf 25
HP1 Hemel Hempstead (GB) 52 Sk 39
57830 Heming (F) 54 Ag 42
89051 Hemling (S) 21 Bi 27
94493 Hemmingsmark (S) 22 Cb 25
1970 Hemnes (N) 28 Bb 31
8640 Hemnesberget (N) 14 Bd 24
62012 Hemse (S) 29 Bi 33
3560 Hemsedal (N) 28 Ai 30
87010 Hemsö (S) 21 Bi 28
47301 Henån (S) 28 Bb 32
64700* Hendaye (F) 66 Si 47
54300 Hendek (TR) 88 Da 50
7255* Hengelo (NL) 54 Ag 38
Heničes'k (UA) 74 De 44
RG9 Henley-on-Thames (GB) 52 Sk 39
56700 Hennebont (F) 66 Sg 43
16761 Hennigsdorf (D) 55 Bd 38
Henningsvær (N) 14 Be 22
2415 Heradsbygd (N) 28 Bb 30
41190 Herbault (F) 67 Ab 43
85500 Herbiers, les (F) 66 Si 44
44410 Herbignac (F) 66 Sh 43
42-284 Herby (PL) 56 Bi 40
85 340 Herceg-Novi (MNE) 85 Bi 48
Hercegovačka Goleša = Pribojska Goleša (SRB) 71 Bk 47
4766 Herefoss (N) 28 Ai 32
41800 Hereke (TR) 88 Ck 50
Herfell (IS) 48 Rf 25
32049* Herford (D) 54 Ai 38
70400 Héricourt (F) 68 Ag 43
9100* Herisau (CH) 69 Ak 43
37293 Herleshausen (D) 55 Ba 39
9620 Hermagor-Pressegger See (A) 69 Bd 44
29320 Hermannsburg (D) 39 Ba 38
6863 Hermansverk (N) 28 Ag 29
7400 Herning (DK) 38 Ai 34
Herøy (N) 21 Bc 25
3965 Herre (N) 28 Ak 31
71083 Herrenberg (D) 54 Ai 42
06670 Herrera del Duque (E) 80 Se 51
34400 Herrera de Pisuerga (E) 81 Sf 48
10560 Herreruela (E) 80 Sd 51
Herringbotn (N) 21 Bd 25
52401 Herrljunga (S) 29 Bd 32
91217 Hersbruck (D) 55 Bb 41
36251 Hersfeld, Bad (D) 54 Ak 40
Herson = Cherson (UA) 74 Dc 44
5248 Hertogenbosch, ,s- (NL) 54 Af 39
04916 Herzberg (Elster) (D) 55 Bd 39
37412 Herzberg am Harz (D) 55 Ba 39
62140 Hesdin (F) 53 Ac 40
Hessfjord (N) 14 Bk 21
37235 Hessisch Lichtenau (D) 54 Ak 39
400 Hesteyri (IS) 48 Qh 24
91300 Hetekylä (FIN) 22 Cg 25
Hetolambina (RUS) 16 Dd 24
Hetovo (RUS) 25 Ec 27
3360 Heves (H) 71 Ca 43
671 69 Hevlín (CZ) 56 Bg 42
NE46 Hexham (GB) 51 Sh 36
LA3 Heysham (GB) 51 Sh 36
Hibiny (RUS) 16 Dd 23
3876 Hidasnémeti (H) 57 Cb 42
18565 Hiddensee (D) 39 Bd 36
8920* Hieflau (A) 70 Be 43
88901 Hietapera (FIN) 23 Ck 26
HP12 High Wycombe (GB) 52 Sk 39
51520 Hiirola (FIN) 23 Ch 29
44530 Híjar (E) 82 Sk 49
98646 Hildburghausen (D) 55 Ba 40
31134* Hildesheim (D) 54 Ak 38
20008 Hiliomódi (GR) 94 Cc 53
2180 Hillegom (NL) 53 Ae 38
3400 Hillerød (DK) 39 Bc 35
33033 Hillerstorp (S) 29 Bd 33
ZE2 Hillswick (GB) 50 Si 30
63900 Hilvan (TR) 98 Di 53
1200* Hilversum (NL) 54 Af 38
68100 Himanka (FIN) 22 Cd 26
Himarë (AL) 86 Bk 50
Himki (RUS) 43 Dh 35
38420 Himmetdede (TR) 97 Df 52
3400 Hînceşti (MD) 73 Ci 44
LE10 Hinckley (GB) 52 Si 38
43063 Hindås (S) 29 Bc 33
25600 Hınıs (TR) 91 Eb 51
27600 Hinnerjoki (FIN) 30 Cb 30
14270 Hinojosa del Duque (E) 92 Se 52
82100 Híos (GR) 95 Cg 52
59581 Hirschberg (D) 55 Bb 40
35320 Hirsilä (FIN) 30 Ce 29
02500 Hirson (F) 53 Ae 41
Hîrtop (MD) 73 Ci 44
9850 Hirtshals (DK) 28 Ak 33
97130 Hirvas (FIN) 15 Cf 24
73400 Hisar (TR) 89 Dd 51
43780 Hisarcık (TR) 88 Ck 51
4180 Hisarja (BG) 87 Ce 48
Hislaviči (RUS) 42 Dc 36
9433 Hitovo (BG) 73 Ch 47
13600 Hizan (TR) 99 Ec 52
9320 Hjallerup (DK) 28 Ba 33
5259 Hjellestad (N) 28 Af 30
Hjellset (N) 20 Ah 28
Hjelmeland (N) 28 Ag 31
2661 Hjerkinn (N) 20 Ak 28
54401 Hjo (S) 29 Be 32
9800 Hjørring (DK) 28 Ba 33
69793 Hjortkvarn (S) 29 Bf 32
Hlavani (UA) 73 Ck 45
7280 Hlebarovo = Car Kalojan (BG) 72 Cg 47
Hlepen' (RUS) 43 De 35
Hlevacha (UA) 59 Da 40
370 01 Hlinsko (CZ) 56 Bf 41
Hlobyne (UA) 59 Dd 41
920 01 Hlohovec (SK) 56 Bh 42
Hluchiv (UA) 59 Dd 39
Hluša (BY) 42 Ci 37
Hlusk (BY) 42 Ci 38
Hluškavičy (BY) 58 Ch 39
Hlyboka (UA) 58 Cf 42
Hlybokae (BY) 42 Ch 35
Hlyns'k (UA) 59 Dc 42
Hlystalovo (RUS) 34 Ek 31
Hmelevka (RUS) 34 Eg 32
Hmelita (RUS) 43 Dd 35
Hmel'nickij = Chmel'nyc'kyj (UA) 58 Cg 41
Hnivan' (UA) 58 Ci 41
981 01 Hnúšt'a (SK) 56 Bk 42
9500 Hobro (DK) 38 Ak 34
Hocabey (TR) 90 Dg 51
03530 Hocalar (TR) 96 Ck 52
91315 Höchstadt an der Aisch (D) 55 Ba 41
Hódmezővásárhely (H) 71 Ca 44
695 01 Hodonín (CZ) 56 Bh 42
Hodovariha (RUS) 18 Fd 22
3150 Hoek van Holland (NL) 53 Ae 39
04758 Hof (D) 55 Bb 40
Höfðakaupstaður = Skagaströnd (IS) 48 Qk 25
34369 Hofgeismar (D) 54 Ak 39
780 Höfn (IS) 48 Re 26
81301 Hofors (S) 29 Bg 30
565* Hofsós (IS) 48 Ql 25
7470* Hof van Twente (NL) 54 Ag 38
26300* Höganäs (S) 39 Bc 34
38075 Högby (S) 29 Bh 33
83081 Högbynäs (S) 21 Bf 26
91494 Högland (S) 21 Bf 26
83001 Höglekardalen (S) 21 Bd 27
Högsäter (S) 29 Bc 32
57900 Högsby (S) 29 Bg 33
Høgstadgård (N) 14 Bk 22
Hőgyész (H) 71 Bi 44
6845* Hohenems (A) 69 Ak 43
24594 Hohenwestedt (D) 38 Ak 36
Hoholiv (UA) 59 Db 40
Hohol'skij (RUS) 60 Di 39
6280 Højer (DK) 38 Ai 36
3300 Hokksund (N) 28 Ak 31
3576 Hol (N) 28 Ai 30
Hol, Ulan- (RUS) 77 Eg 45
Hola Prystan' (UA) 74 Dc 44
551 Hólar (IS) 48 Ql 25
8950 Holbæk (DK) 39 Bb 35
769 01 Holešov (CZ) 56 Bh 41
783 71 Holice (CZ) 56 Bf 40
68065 Höljes (S) 29 Bc 30
2020* Hollabrunn (A) 56 Bg 42
Hollandstrom (GB) 50 Sh 31
Høllen (N) 28 Ah 32
3176 Hollókő (H) 71 Bk 43
23601 Höllviken (S) 39 Bc 35
Hollywood = Cillín Chaoimhín (IRL) 49 Sd 37
25488 Holm (FIN) 22 Cc 27
25488 Holm (RUS) 31 Db 33
30279 Holm (S) 21 Bg 28
Holmajärvi (S) 14 Bk 23
510* Hólmavík (IS) 48 Qi 25
Holmeči (RUS) 59 De 38
6982 Holmedal (N) 28 Af 29
0010* Holmenkollen (N) 28 Ba 31
3080 Holmestrand (N) 28 Ba 31
Holmogorskaja (RUS) 24 Ea 27
Holmogory (RUS) 25 Eb 26
Holmskij (RUS) 75 Di 46
91301 Holmsund (S) 22 Ca 27
82392 Holmsveden (S) 29 Bg 29
Holm-Žirkovskij (RUS) 43 Dd 35
Holoby (UA) 58 Cf 39
Holovkivka (UA) 59 Dc 41
2540 Holøydal (N) 20 Bb 28
7500 Holstebro (DK) 38 Ai 34
6670 Holsted (DK) 38 Ai 35
EX22 Holsworthy (GB) 52 Sf 40
Holtobino (RUS) 43 Di 36
Holwerd (NL) 38 Af 37
LL65 Holyhead (GB) 51 Sf 37
TD15 Holy Island (GB) 51 Si 35
83607 Holzkirchen (D) 69 Bb 43
37603 Holzminden (D) 54 Ak 39
35315 Homberg (Ohm) (D) 54 Ak 40
66424 Homburg (D) 54 Ah 41
61348* Homburg vor der Höhe, Bad (D) 54 Ai 40
Homel' (BY) 59 Db 38
8960 Hommelstø (N) 21 Bc 25
7550 Hommelvik (N) 20 Ba 27
Homutovka (RUS) 59 De 39
Homutovo (RUS) 43 Dh 38
20330* Honaz (TR) 96 Ck 53
20280 Hondarribia (E) 66 Si 47
3510* Hønefoss (N) 28 Ba 30
14600 Honfleur (F) 53 Aa 41
EX14 Honiton (GB) 52 Sg 40
38951 Honkajoki (FIN) 22 Cc 29
53557 Hönningen, Bad (D) 54 Ah 40
9750 Honningsvåg (N) 15 Cf 20
7900* Hoogeveen (NL) 38 Ag 38
9615 Hoogezand-Sappemeer (NL) 38 Ag 37
24301 Höör (S) 39 Bd 35
1620* Hoorn (NL) 38 Af 38
08600 Hopa (TR) 91 Eb 49
Hopen (N) 20 Ai 27
Hopen Radio (N) 14 I Svalbard
Hopseidet (N) 15 Ch 20
24600 Hóra (GR) 94 Cb 53
25800 Horasan (TR) 91 Ec 50
341 01 Horažďovice (CZ) 55 Bd 41
24201 Hörby (S) 39 Bd 35
13110 Horcajo de los Montes (E) 81 Sf 51
16410 Horcajo de Santiago (E) 81 Sh 51
Hordyšče (UA) 60 Dk 41
Horej-Ver (RUS) 19 Fh 23
Horki (BY) 42 Da 36
Horlivka (UA) 60 Di 42
3580* Horn (A) 56 Bf 42
Horn (N) 21 Bc 25
59042 Horn (S) 29 Bf 33
06228 Hornachos (E) 92 Sd 52
14740 Hornachuelos (E) 92 Se 53
32805 Horn-Bad Meinberg (D) 54 Ai 39
LN9 Horncastle (GB) 51 Sk 37
77404 Horndal (S) 29 Bg 30
21640 Horneburg (D) 38 Ak 37
91020 Hörnefors (S) 22 Bk 27
756 12 Horní Lideč (CZ) 56 Bi 41
8900 Horning (DK) 39 Ba 34
HU18 Hornsea (GB) 51 Sk 37
91495 Hörnsjö (S) 22 Bk 27
8543 Hornslet (DK) 39 Ba 34
Hornum (DK) 38 Ak 34
25997 Hörnum (Sylt) (D) 38 Ai 36
Horochiv (UA) 57 Ce 40
Horodec (UA) 58 Cg 39
Horodenka (UA) 58 Cf 42
Horodnja (UA) 59 Db 39
Horodnycja (UA) 58 Ch 40
Horodok (UA) 57 Cd 41
Horodok (UA) 58 Cg 41
Horodyšče (UA) 59 Db 41
51900 Horred (S) 29 Bc 33
8700 Horsens (DK) 38 Ak 35
RH13 Horsham (GB) 52 Sk 39
2970 Hørsholm (DK) 39 Bc 35
Horslunde (DK) 39 Bb 36
346 01 Horšovský Týn (CZ) 55 Bc 41
09950 Horsunlu (TR) 96 Ci 53
3181* Horten (N) 28 Ba 31
Horticy (RUS) 32 Dd 31
4071 Hortobágy (H) 71 Cb 43
Hory (BY) 42 Db 36
Hošča (UA) 58 Cg 40
Hoševtovo (RUS) 77 Eh 44
84050 Hosjö (S) 29 Bf 30
43890 Hospitalet de l'Infant, l' (E) 82 Aa 50
08901 Hospitalet de Llobregat, l' (E) 82 Ac 49
09390 Hospitalet-près-l'Andorre, l' (F) 82 Ab 48
89999 Hossa (FIN) 23 Ck 25
40510 Hossegor, Soorts- (F) 66 Si 47
Hosta (RUS) 75 Dk 47
17450 Hostalric (E) 82 Ac 49
Hostomel' (UA) 59 Da 40
42405 Hotamış (TR) 97 Dd 53
087125 Hotarele (RO) 72 Cg 46
83080 Hoting (S) 21 Bg 26
Hotynec (RUS) 43 Df 37
ZE2 Houbie (GB) 50 Sk 30
33990 Hourtin (F) 66 Si 45
21770 Houtskär (FIN) 30 Cb 30
7700 Hov (DK) 39 Ba 35
2862 Hov (N) 28 Ba 30
54800 Hova (S) 29 Be 32
Hovden (N) 28 Ah 31
36051 Hovmantorp (S) 39 Bf 34
Hovotrojic'ke (UA) 75 Dh 43
6993 Høyanger (N) 28 Ag 29
02977 Hoyerswerda (D) 55 Be 39
7977 Høylandet (N) 21 Bc 26
62400 Hozat (TR) 90 Dk 51
Hrabjani (BY) 58 Ci 39
500 02* Hradec Králové (CZ) 56 Bf 40
Hradyz'k (UA) 59 Dd 41
Hradzjanka (BY) 42 Ci 37
351 24 Hranice (CZ) 56 Bh 41
1430 Hrastnik (SLO) 70 Bf 44
545 Hraun (IS) 48 Qk 24
Hrebinka (UA) 59 Dc 40
Hrebinky (UA) 59 Da 41
Hresivs'ke 74 De 45
630 Hrísey (IS) 48 Rb 25
64200 Hrissoúpoli (GR) 87 Ce 50
Hrjaščevka (RUS) 45 Ek 37
Hrodna (BY) 41 Cd 37
966 53 Hronský Beňadik (SK) 56 Bi 42
22-500 Hrubieszów (PL) 57 Cd 40
Hrušuvacha (UA) 60 Dg 41
Hryhorivka (UA) 59 Db 41
Hubynycha (UA) 60 Df 42
41836 Hückelhoven (D) 54 Ag 39
HD2 Huddersfield (GB) 51 Si 37
82400* Hudiksvall (S) 21 Bh 29
Huduk, Naryn- (RUS) 77 Eg 45
405400 Huedin (RO) 72 Cd 44
29690 Huelgoat (F) 52 Sg 42
23560 Huelma (E) 93 Sg 53
21001* Huelva (E) 92 Sd 53
04600 Huércal-Overa (E) 93 Si 53
22001* Huesca (E) 82 Sk 48
18830 Huéscar (E) 93 Sh 53
16500 Huete (E) 81 Sh 50
32701 Huittinen (FIN) 30 Cc 29
Hukovo (UA) 60 Dk 42
Hul'ajpole (UA) 75 Dg 43
Hulhuta (RUS) 77 Eg 44
4560 Hulst (NL) 53 Ae 39
57498 Hultanäs (S) 29 Bf 33
57701 Hultsfred (S) 29 Bf 33
Hum (BIH) 86 Bi 47
09124 Humada (E) 81 Sf 48
19220 Humanes (E) 81 Sg 50
066 01 Humenné (SK) 57 Cb 42
396 01 Humpolec (CZ) 56 Bf 41
31641 Humppila (FIN) 30 Cd 30
3390 Hundested (DK) 39 Bb 35
000331* Hunedoara (RO) 71 Cc 45
36088 Hünfeld (D) 54 Ak 40
35410 Hungen (D) 54 Ai 40
45046 Hunnebostrand (S) 28 Bb 32
PE36 Hunstanton (GB) 51 Aa 38
PE29 Huntingdon (GB) 52 Sk 38
AB54 Huntly (GB) 50 Sh 33
14520 Huppain, Port-en-Bessin- (F) 52 Sk 41
2090 Hurdal (N) 28 Bb 30
217260 Hurezani (RO) 72 Cd 46
Hurivka (UA) 59 Dd 42
Hurki (BY) 42 Da 35
7760 Hurup (DK) 38 Ai 34
Hurzuf 74 De 46
Hurzuk (RUS) 76 Ec 47
311 Húsafell (IS) 48 Qk 26
720 Húsavík (IS) 48 Rc 24
Husby (S) 29 Bg 30
7113 Husbysjøen (N) 20 Ba 27
HS3 Hushinish (GB) 50 Sc 33
735100 Huşi (RO) 73 Ci 44
Husjatyn (UA) 58 Cg 41
56101* Huskvarna (S) 29 Be 33
5460 Husnes (N) 28 Af 31
Hustad (N) 20 Ah 28
31632 Husum (D) 38 Ak 36
89035 Husum (S) 22 Bk 27
Husvallgölen (S) 29 Bd 29
8883 Husvika (N) 21 Bc 25

Husvika | 177

Hutovo (BIH) 85 Bh 48
35625 Hüttenberg (A) 70 Be 44
99950 Huutoniemi (FIN) 15 Cg 21
4500 Huy (B) 54 Af 40
Hüyük (TR) 96 Db 53
Hvalovo (RUS) 31 Dc 31
Hvalpsund (DK) 38 Ak 34
Hvalynsk (RUS) 62 Ei 38
531 Hvammstangi (IS) 48 Qk 25
Hvar (HR) 85 Bg 47
Hvardijs'ke 74 De 45
Hvastoviči (RUS) 43 Df 37
810 Hveragerði (IS) 48 Qi 26
640 Hveravellir (IS) 48 Ql 26
6960 Hvide Sande (DK) 38 Ai 34
3647 Hvittingfoss (N) 28 Ba 31
Hvojnaja (RUS) 32 De 32
850 Hvolsvöllur (IS) 48 Qk 27
Hvorostjanka (RUS) 61 Ea 38
Hvorostjanka (RUS) 62 Ei 38
SA61 Hwlfordd = Haverfordwest (GB) 52 Sf 39
59042 Hycklinge (S) 29 Bf 33
6829 Hyen (N) 20 Af 29
83400* Hyères (F) 68 Ag 47
31401 Hyltebruk (S) 39 Bd 33
3400 Hynčešt' = Hînceşti (MD) 73 Ci 44
89401 Hyrynsalmi (FIN) 23 Ci 26
44220 Hytölä (FIN) 22 Cg 28
05950 Hyvinkää (FIN) 30 Ce 30

I

727315 Iacobeni (RO) 72 Cf 43
Ialissos (GR) 96 Ci 54
6801 Ialoveni (MD) 73 Ci 44
815200 Ianca (RO) 73 Ch 45
6321 Iargara (MD) 73 Ci 44
000700* Iaşi (RO) 73 Ch 43
Ib (RUS) 34 Fa 29
Iba (RUS) 25 Eh 27
Ibakibka = Ivanivka (UA) 57 Cc 42
49477* Ibbenbüren (D) 54 Ah 38
İbek (TR) 89 Df 50
9419 Ibestad (N) 14 Bh 22
03440 Ibi (E) 93 Sk 52
07800 Ibiza = Eivissa (E) 82 Ab 52
Ibragimovo (RUS) 46 Ff 36
Ibresi (RUS) 45 Eh 35
22410 İbriktepe (TR) 87 Cg 49
Ibrjaevo (RUS) 46 Fc 36
İçel (Mersin) (TR) 97 De 54
42970 İçeriçumra (TR) 96 Dc 53
23150 İçme (TR) 98 Dk 52
Ičnja (UA) 59 Dc 40
6060-100* Idanha-a-Nova (P) 80 Sc 51
55743 Idar-Oberstein (D) 54 Ah 41
Idel' (RUS) 24 De 26
Idel'bakovo (RUS) 64 Fh 39
73300 İdil (TR) 99 Eb 53
Idivuoma (S) 15 Cc 22
15351 Ídra (GR) 94 Cd 53
79091 Idre (S) 21 Bc 29
5280 Idrija (SLO) 69 Bd 45
65510 Idstein (D) 54 Ai 40
3913 Iecava (LV) 41 Ce 34
8900 Ieper (B) 53 Ac 40
72200 Ierápetra (GR) 95 Cf 55
545100 Iernut (RO) 72 Ce 44
Ievlevo (RUS) 37 Gh 33
9742 Ifjord (N) 15 Ch 20
7275 Igal (H) 70 Bh 44
38655 Iğdecik (TR) 88 Db 51
Iğdeli (TR) 90 Dh 51
76000 Iğdir (TR) 89 Dd 49
76000 Iğdir (TR) 89 Df 50
76000 Iğdır (TR) 91 Ee 51
82500 Iggesund (S) 29 Bh 29
09016 Iglesias (I) 83 Ai 51
Iglino (RUS) 47 Fg 36
30001 Ignalina (LT) 41 Cg 35
Ignatovo (RUS) 32 Dh 30
39650 İğneada (TR) 88 Ch 49
Igodovo (RUS) 33 Ec 32
46100 Igoumenitsa (GR) 86 Ca 51
Igra (RUS) 35 Fd 33
08700 Igualada (E) 82 Ab 49
Igüeña (E) 80 Sd 48
Igumhovskaja (RUS) 25 Ee 28
Igumnovskaja (RUS) 33 Ed 30
68570 Ihlara (TR) 97 De 52
37250 İhsangazi (TR) 89 Dd 49
41650 İhsaniye (TR) 88 Da 51
2050 Ihtiman (BG) 87 Cd 48
41101 Iisaku (EST) 31 Ch 31
74130 Iisalmi (FIN) 23 Ch 27
1970* IJmuiden (NL) 53 Ae 38
39510 Ikaalinen (FIN) 30 Cd 29
7430 Ikast (DK) 38 Ak 34
Iki-Burul (RUS) 76 Ee 45
İkikuyu (TR) 99 Ea 52
Iki Manlan (RUS) 77 Ef 43
İkizce (TR) 89 Dc 51
İkizdere (TR) 91 Ea 50
18900 İkizören (TR) 89 Dd 50
Ikrjanoe (RUS) 77 Eh 44
Ikša (RUS) 43 Dh 34
Ikšķile (LV) 41 Ce 34
019 01 Ilava (SK) 56 Bi 42
Ildır (TR) 95 Cg 52
Ileck, Sol'- (RUS) 63 Fe 39
Ilek (RUS) 63 Fd 39
Ileksinskaja (RUS) 32 Dh 29
20220 Île-Rousse, L' (F) 83 Ai 48
EX34 Ilfracombe (GB) 52 Sf 39
18400 Ilgaz (TR) 89 Dd 50
42600 Ilgın (TR) 96 Db 52
İlhanköy (TR) 88 Ch 50
3830-024* Ílhavo (P) 80 Sb 50
337270 Ilia (RO) 71 Cc 45
Ilıbaşı (TR) 88 Da 51
Iliç (TR) 90 Di 51
Il'iča (RUS) 35 Fg 33
37620 Ilıca (TR) 88 Ch 51
Ilica (TR) 88 Ci 51
37620 Ilıca (TR) 89 Dc 51
37620 Ilıca (TR) 91 Eb 51
37620 Ilıca (TR) 95 Cg 52
37620 Ilıca (TR) 96 Dc 54
37620 Ilıca (TR) 98 Dg 53
Ilıcalar (TR) 99 Ea 52
Ilidža (BIH) 71 Bi 47
Ilim (RUS) 36 Fi 33
Il'inka (RUS) 61 Eb 38
Il'inka (RUS) 64 Fh 39
Il'inka (RUS) 77 Eh 44
Il'ino (RUS) 42 Db 35
Il'inskaja (RUS) 76 Ea 45
Il'inskij (RUS) 31 Dc 29
Il'inskij (RUS) 35 Fe 32
Il'inskoe (RUS) 32 Di 33
Il'inskoe (RUS) 43 Dh 34
Il'inskoe (RUS) 46 Fc 34
Il'inskoe- Hovanskoe (RUS) 44 Dk 34
Il'insko-Podomskoe (RUS) 34 Eh 29
Il'insko-Zaborskoe (RUS) 33 Ee 33
6250 Ilirska Bistrica (SLO) 70 Be 45
Il'ja (BY) 42 Ch 36
Iljuhinskaja (RUS) 33 Eb 30
Il'kino (RUS) 44 Eb 35
LS29 Ilkley (GB) 51 Si 37
66130 Ille-sur-Têt (F) 82 Ac 48
Illičivs'k = Čornomors'k (UA) 73 Da 44
28120 Illiers-Combray (F) 53 Ab 42
Illinci (UA) 58 Ck 41
60801 Ilmajoki (FIN) 22 Cc 28
Il'men' (RUS) 61 Ee 40
98693 Ilmenau (D) 55 Ba 40
Il'men'-Suvorovskij (RUS) 61 Ed 42
82901 Ilomantsi (FIN) 23 Da 28
Ilovajs'k (UA) 75 Di 43
Ilovatka (RUS) 62 Ef 40
Ilovka (RUS) 60 Di 40
Ilovlja (RUS) 61 Ee 41
68-120 Iłowa (PL) 56 Bf 39
5447 Ilūkste (LV) 41 Cg 35
Ilyaspaşa (TR) 88 Db 51
27-100 Iłża (PL) 57 Cb 39
37400 İmamoğlu (TR) 97 Df 53
Imandra (RUS) 16 Dd 23
55100* Imatra (FIN) 31 Ci 29
07350 İmecik (TR) 96 Da 54
Imena Babuškina (RUS) 33 Ed 31
Imeni Michai-
la Ivanoviča Kalinina (RUS) 34 Ef 33
Imjanlikuevo (RUS) 46 Fe 35
87509 Immenstadt im Allgäu (D) 69 Ba 43
DN40 Immingham (GB) 51 Sk 37
40026 Imola (I) 69 Bb 46
Imotski (HR) 70 Bh 47
18100 Imperia (I) 68 Ai 47
58160 Imphy (F) 67 Ad 44
58980 İmranlı (TR) 90 Di 51
İmroz (TR) 87 Cf 50
6460* Imst (A) 69 Ba 43
99871 Inari (FIN) 15 Ch 22
07300 Inca (E) 82 Ac 51
İncesu (TR) 97 Dd 52
İncesu (TR) 97 Df 52
İncetarla (TR) 97 Df 53
İncidere (TR) 98 Di 54
İncirli (TR) 98 Di 53
01340 İncirlik (TR) 97 Df 53
09600 İncirliova (TR) 95 Ch 53
Incy (RUS) 24 Ea 25
86040 Indal (S) 21 Bh 28
827150 Independenţa (RO) 73 Ck 45
Indiga (RUS) 18 Ek 23
22319* Inđija (SRB) 71 Ca 45
9710 Indre Billefjord (N) 15 Cf 20
39050 İnece (TR) 88 Ch 49
İnecik (TR) 88 Ch 50
16400 İnegöl (TR) 88 Ck 50
315300 Ineu (RO) 71 Cb 44
33530 Infiesto (E) 80 Se 47
10160 Ingå (FIN) 30 Ce 30
57031 Ingatorp (S) 29 Bf 33
8770 Ingelmunster (B) 53 Ad 40
85049* Ingolstadt (D) 55 Bb 42
11640 İnhisar (TR) 88 Da 50
Ínio (GR) 95 Cf 55
Inis = Ennis (IRL) 49 Sb 38
BT74 Inis Ceithleann = Enniskillen (GB) 49 Sc 36
Inis Córthaidh = Enniscorthy (IRL) 49 Sd 38
10160 Inkoo = Ingå (FIN) 30 Ce 30
İnlice (TR) 96 Dc 53
Innbygda (N) 29 Bc 29
8140 Inndyr (N) 14 Be 23
EH44 Innerleithen (GB) 51 Sg 35
3862 Innertkirchen (CH) 68 Ai 44
6020* Innsbruck (A) 69 Bb 43
Innset (N) 14 Bi 22
Innset (N) 20 Ba 28
İnönü (TR) 88 Da 51
88-100 Inowrocław (PL) 40 Bi 38
Inozemcevo (RUS) 76 Ed 46
Insar (RUS) 45 Ee 37
79304 Insjön (S) 29 Bf 30
Inta (RUS) 27 Ga 24
17060 İntepe (TR) 87 Cg 50
3800* Interlaken (CH) 68 Ah 44
PA32 Inveraray (GB) 50 Se 34
AB30 Inverbervie (GB) 50 Sh 34
PH35 Invergarry (GB) 50 Sf 33
IV3 Inverness (GB) 50 Sf 33
AB51 Inverurie (GB) 50 Sh 33
Inza (RUS) 45 Eg 37
Inžavino (RUS) 61 Ec 38
Inzer (RUS) 47 Fh 36
45001* Ioánnina (GR) 86 Ca 51
Ionava (LT) 41 Ce 35
Ios (GR) 95 Cf 54
Ipatovo (RUS) 76 Ec 45
22400 İpsala (TR) 87 Cg 50
IP4 Ipswich (GB) 53 Ab 38
Ira (RUS) 46 Ff 38
Iraël' (RUS) 26 Ff 26
62400 Iráklia (GR) 87 Cd 49
71001* Iráklio (GR) 95 Cf 55
Irbit (RUS) 36 Gd 33
Irgakly (RUS) 76 Ee 46
Irgizly (RUS) 47 Fh 38
Iriklinskij (RUS) 64 Fi 39
Irklievskaja (RUS) 75 Dk 45
Irklijiv (UA) 59 Dc 41
Iron-Bridge (GB) 52 Sh 38
Iršava (UA) 57 Cd 42
75022 Irsina (I) 85 Bg 50
Irta (RUS) 26 Ei 28
20301 Irún (E) 66 Si 47
31730 Irurita (E) 81 Si 47
KA12 Irvine (GB) 51 Sf 35
BT94 Irvinestown (GB) 49 Sc 36
31417 Isaba (E) 82 Sk 48
825200 Isaccea (RO) 73 Ci 45
415 Ísafjörður (IS) 48 Qg 24
Isajeve (UA) 73 Da 43
Isakly (RUS) 46 Fb 36
Isakovo (RUS) 43 De 35
207340 Isalniţa (RO) 72 Cd 46
ZE2 Isbister (GB) 50 Si 30
47420 Íscar (E) 81 Sf 49
03750 İscehisar (TR) 96 Da 52
Ischia (I) 69 Bb 44
80077 Ischia (I) 84 Bd 50
Išeevka (RUS) 45 Ei 36
25049 Iseo (I) 69 Ba 45
Isergapovo (RUS) 46 Fd 36
58636* Iserlohn (D) 54 Ah 39
86170 Isernia (I) 85 Be 49
6320 Isfjorden (N) 20 Ah 28
Isfjord Radio (N) 14 I Svalbard
14230 Isigny-sur-Mer (F) 52 Si 41
31330 Işıklı (TR) 96 Ck 52
31330 Işıklı (TR) 99 Ed 53
08033 Isili (I) 83 Ak 51
Išimbaj (RUS) 47 Fg 37
Isjangulovo (RUS) 64 Fg 38
Iska (RUS) 37 Gf 33
Iškeevo (RUS) 46 Fb 35
09290 İskele (TR) 96 Ci 53
31200* İskenderun (TR) 98 Dg 54
Iske-Rjazap (RUS) 45 Ek 36
19400 İskilip (TR) 89 De 50
7580 Iskra (BG) 87 Cf 49
Iskušta (RUS) 47 Fh 36
53350 İslahiye (TR) 98 Dg 53
147160 Islaz (RO) 72 Ce 47
31230 Isle-en-Dodon, l' (F) 66 Aa 47
86150 Isle-Jourdain, l' (F) 67 Ab 47
84800 Isle-sur-la-Sorgue, l' (F) 68 Af 47
Išlja (RUS) 47 Fh 37
Išly (RUS) 46 Ff 36
Išma (RUS) 24 Ea 26
85737 Ismaning (D) 55 Bb 42
İsmetpaşa (TR) 89 Dc 50
İsmil (TR) 97 Dd 53
Išmurzino (RUS) 64 Fi 38
88316 Isny im Allgäu (D) 69 Ba 43
64901 Isojoki (FIN) 22 Cb 28
76940 Isokylä (FIN) 15 Ch 24
61501 Isokyrö (FIN) 22 Cc 27
64045 Isola del Gran Sasso d'Italia (I) 84 Bd 48
48320 Ispagnac (F) 67 Ad 46
32000 Isparta (TR) 96 Da 53
7400 Isperih (BG) 72 Cg 47
25900 İspir (TR) 91 Ea 50
Issa (RUS) 45 Ee 37
63500 Issoire (F) 67 Ad 45
36100 Issoudun (F) 67 Ab 44
21120 Is-sur-Tille (F) 68 Af 43
34000* İstanbul (TR) 88 Ci 49
34200 Istiéa (GR) 94 Cd 52
Istobnoe (RUS) 60 Di 39
31000 Istog = Istok (RKS) 86 Ca 48
31000 Istok = Istog (RKS) 86 Ca 48
Istra (RUS) 43 Dg 35
13800 Istres (F) 67 Ae 47
907155 Istria (RO) 73 Ci 46
44220 Istunmäki (FIN) 22 Cg 28
İstuzu (TR) 96 Ci 54
95370 Itäkoski (FIN) 22 Ce 25
33200 Itéa (GR) 86 Cc 51
33200 Itéa (GR) 94 Cc 52
28300 Itháki (GR) 94 Ca 52
07044 Ittiri (I) 83 Ai 50
25524 Itzehoe (D) 38 Ak 37
Ivacėvičy (BY) 41 Cf 38
6570 Ivajlovgrad (BG) 87 Cg 49
99801 Ivalo (FIN) 15 Ch 22
Ivanava (BY) 58 Cf 38
664 91 Ivančice (CZ) 56 Bg 41
Ivanec (HR) 70 Bg 44
Ivangorod (RUS) 31 Ci 31
84 300 Ivangrad = Berane (MNE) 86 Bk 48
Ivanhorod (UA) 59 Dc 39
Ivanić Grad (HR) 70 Bg 45
Ivanišči (RUS) 44 Ea 35
Ivaniši (RUS) 43 Df 34
Ivanivka (UA) 57 Cc 42
Ivanivka (UA) 60 Di 42
Ivanivka (UA) 74 De 44
32250 Ivanjica (SRB) 71 Ca 47
Ivanjska (BIH) 70 Bh 46
Ivankiv (UA) 58 Ck 40
Ivan'kovo (RUS) 43 Dh 36
Ivano-Frankivs'k (UA) 57 Ce 42
Ivano-Frankove (UA) 57 Cd 41
Ivano-Frankovsk = Ivano-Frankivs'k (UA) 57 Ce 42
Ivano-Kuvalat (RUS) 64 Fh 38
Ivanopil' (UA) 58 Ci 41
Ivanovka (RUS) 46 Fd 38
Ivanovka (RUS) 46 Fe 36
6465 Ivanovo (BG) 72 Cf 47
Ivanovo (RUS) 42 Da 34
Ivanovo (RUS) 44 Ea 34
Ivanovsk, Katav- (RUS) 47 Fi 36
Ivanovskaja (RUS) 75 Di 45
Ivanovskoe (RUS) 33 Ee 32
Ivanovskoe (RUS) 35 Ff 32
Ivanovskoe, Usen'- (RUS) 46 Fe 36
9810 Ivanski (BG) 73 Ch 47
Ivanteevka (RUS) 62 Ek 38
Ivanteevo (RUS) 32 Dd 33
Ivaševo (RUS) 33 Ec 33
Iv'e (BY) 41 Cf 37
737320 Iveşti (RO) 73 Ch 45
Ivjanec (BY) 41 Cg 37
Ivlevskaja (RUS) 25 Ec 28
Ivnja (RUS) 60 Dg 39
Ivot Star' (RUS) 43 De 37
10015 Ivrea (I) 68 Ah 45
10770 İvrindi (TR) 88 Ch 51
53600 İyidere (TR) 91 Ea 49
Ižberdino (RUS) 64 Fg 38
87-865 Izbica Kujawska (PL) 56 Bi 38
237230 Izbiceni (RO) 72 Ce 47
Izborsk (RUS) 31 Ch 33
Izdeškovo (RUS) 43 Dd 35
5300-591* Izeda (P) 80 Sd 49
Iževsk (RUS) 46 Fd 34
Iževskoe (RUS) 44 Ea 36
Izi-Kugunur (RUS) 45 Ei 34
Izjum (UA) 60 Dh 41
Ižma (RUS) 26 Fd 25
Izmail = Izmajil (UA) 73 Ci 45
Izmajil (UA) 73 Ci 45
Izmajlovo 2-e(Vtoroe) (RUS) 32 Di 32
Izmalkovo (RUS) 60 Dh 38
35000* İzmir (TR) 95 Ch 52
İzmit = Kocaeli (TR) 88 Ck 50
16860 İznik (TR) 88 Ck 50
Iznoski (RUS) 43 De 35
Izobil'noe (RUS) 63 Fe 39
Izobil'nyj (RUS) 76 Eb 45
6310 Izola (SLO) 69 Bd 45
6070 Izsák (H) 71 Bk 44
Izumrud (RUS) 36 Gb 33
8153 Izvor (BG) 86 Cc 48
1414 Izvor (MK) 86 Cb 49
117405 Izvoru (RO) 72 Cf 46

J

81430 Jaakonvaara (FIN) 23 Da 27
47710 Jaala (FIN) 30 Cg 29
Jablan Do (BIH) 85 Bi 48
5750 Jablanica (BG) 87 Ce 47
Jablanica (BIH) 70 Bh 47
466 01* Jablonec nad Nisou (CZ) 56 Bf 40
62-067 Jabłonna (PL) 57 Ca 38
87-330 Jabłonowo Pomorskie (PL) 40 Bk 37
19304 Jabukovac (SRB) 71 Cc 46
22700 Jaca (E) 82 Sk 48
362 51 Jáchymov (CZ) 55 Bc 40
19240* Jadraque (E) 81 Sh 50
Jadrin (RUS) 45 Eg 35
23001 Jaén (E) 93 Sg 53
6167 Jagoda (BG) 87 Cf 48
35000* Jagodina (SRB) 71 Cb 47
Jagodnoe (RUS) 45 Ek 37
Jagubovka (RUS) 45 Ee 35
Jahotyn (UA) 59 Db 40
Jahren'ga (RUS) 34 Eg 30
38300 Jailleu, Bourgoin- (F) 68 Af 45
Jajce (BIH) 70 Bh 46
Jajva (RUS) 35 Fh 31
Jäkkvik (S) 14 Bg 24
68600* Jakobstad (FIN) 22 Cc 27
Jakolevo (RUS) 60 Dg 40
2790 Jakoruda (BG) 87 Cd 48
Jakovlevka (RUS) 62 Eg 38
Jakovlevo (RUS) 43 Dh 36
Jakovlevskaja (RUS) 25 Ed 28
Jakovlevskij (RUS) 43 Dh 36
Jakovo (RUS) 35 Fd 29
Jakša (RUS) 27 Fg 29
Jakšino (RUS) 26 Fc 24
Jakšino (RUS) 32 Dh 30
Jakun'ël' (RUS) 34 Ek 31
Jakunvara (RUS) 23 Db 28
Jakymivka (UA) 74 Df 44
61601 Jalasjärvi (FIN) 22 Cc 28
Jal'čiki (RUS) 45 Ei 35
Jalguba (RUS) 24 De 29
03220 Jaligny-sur-Besbre (F) 67 Ad 44
Jalta 74 De 46
Jama (UA) 60 Di 42
Jamansaz (RUS) 64 Fi 38
Jambirno (RUS) 44 Ec 36
8600* Jambol (BG) 87 Cg 48
Jamena (SRB) 71 Bk 46
38800 Jämijärvi (FIN) 22 Cc 29
37300 Jämjö (S) 39 Bf 34
Jamkino (RUS) 31 Ck 33
Jamnovo (RUS) 45 Ee 34
Jampil' (UA) 58 Cg 41
Jampil' (UA) 59 Dd 39
42120 Jämsä (FIN) 22 Cf 29
Janaul (RUS) 46 Fe 34
Janavičy (BY) 42 Da 35
Jandovka (RUS) 43 Di 37
Jangiskain (RUS) 47 Fg 37
Janiševo (RUS) 32 Dh 29
Janiskoski (RUS) 15 Ci 22
Janjina (HR) 85 Bh 48
Jänkisjärvi (S) 15 Cd 24
6440 Jánoshalma (H) 71 Bk 44
23-300 Janów Lubelski (PL) 57 Cc 40
21-505 Janów Podlaski (PL) 57 Cd 38
83051 Jänsmässholmen (S) 21 Bd 27
Jantarnyi (RUS) 40 Bk 36
Jantikovo (RUS) 45 Eh 35
35150 Janzé (F) 66 Si 43
Jar (RUS) 35 Fc 32
Jar (RUS) 37 Gf 33
10380 Jaraicejo (E) 80 Se 51
10400 Jaraiz de la Vera (E) 80 Se 50
10450 Jarandilla de la Vera (E) 80 Se 50
Jaransk (RUS) 34 Eh 33
Järbo (S) 29 Bg 30
Jarcevo (RUS) 42 Dc 35
Jarega (RUS) 26 Fd 27
Jarenga (RUS) 26 Ek 28
Jarensk (RUS) 26 Ek 28
45150 Jargeau (F) 67 Ac 43
Jarhois (S) 15 Cd 24
Jarkovo (RUS) 37 Gg 33
17126 Jarmen (D) 39 Bd 37
Jarmolynci (UA) 58 Cg 41
15300 Järna (S) 29 Bh 31
Järna, Dala- (S) 29 Be 30
16200 Jarnac (F) 66 Sk 45
91401 Järnäsklubb (S) 22 Bk 27
Jarnema (RUS) 24 Dk 28
57081 Järnforsen (S) 29 Bf 33
54800 Jarny (F) 54 Af 41
63-200 Jarocin (PL) 56 Bh 39
Jarok (RUS) 44 Ea 38
551 01 Jaroměř (CZ) 56 Bf 40
Jaroslaviči (RUS) 32 De 30
Jaroslavka (RUS) 47 Fh 35
Jaroslavl' (RUS) 33 Dk 33

178 I Hutovo

Jaroslavskaja (RUS) 76 Ea 46
37-500 Jarosław (PL) 57 Cc 40
53104 Järpås (S) 29 Bc 32
83005 Järpen (S) 21 Bd 27
73301 Järva-Jaani (EST) 30 Cf 31
79101 Järvakandi (EST) 30 Ce 32
73901 Järvenpää (FIN) 22 Cb 28
73901 Järvenpää (FIN) 30 Cf 30
82040 Järvsö (S) 29 Bg 29
Jašalta (RUS) 76 Ec 44
23230 Jaša Tomić (SRB) 71 Ca 45
Jasenivs'kyj (UA) 60 Dk 42
Jasenki (RUS) 60 Di 39
Jasenskaja (RUS) 75 Di 44
Jasinja (UA) 57 Ce 42
17038 Jašiūnai (LT) 41 Cf 36
Jaškino (RUS) 46 Fd 38
Jaškul' (RUS) 77 Ef 44
Jaškur-Bod'ja (RUS) 35 Fd 33
38-200 Jasło (PL) 57 Cb 41
Jasnaja Poljana (RUS) 43 Dh 36
Jasnogorsk (RUS) 43 Dh 36
Jasnogorskij (RUS) 63 Fd 38
Jasnoje (RUS) 40 Cb 35
Jasnyj (RUS) 64 Fk 40
84-140 Jastarnia (PL) 40 Bi 36
Jastrebarsko (HR) 70 Bf 45
64-915 Jastrowie (PL) 40 Bg 37
Jasunt (RUS) 27 Ga 26
Jasynuvata (UA) 60 Dh 42
5130 Jászapáti (H) 71 Ca 43
5123 Jászárokszállás (H) 71 Bk 43
5100 Jászberény (H) 71 Bk 43
4420 Jaungulbene (LV) 30 Cg 33
5134 Jaunjelgava (LV) 41 Cf 34
4125 Jaunpiebalga (LV) 41 Cg 33
3145 Jaunpils (LV) 41 Cd 34
Javgil'dino (RUS) 47 Fg 35
Javkyne (UA) 74 Dc 43
Javoriv (UA) 57 Cd 41
94401 Jävre (S) 22 Cb 25
53250 Javron-les-Chapelles (F) 52 Sk 42
Javzora (RUS) 25 Ef 27
56-330 Jawor (PL) 56 Bg 39
43-600 Jaworzno (PL) 56 Bk 40
Jaželbicy (RUS) 31 Dc 32
Jazevec (RUS) 25 Eg 25
Jažma (RUS) 17 Ee 24
Jazykovo (RUS) 43 Dh 38
Jazykovo (RUS) 45 Eh 36
Jazykovo (RUS) 46 Fe 36
TD8 Jedburgh (GB) 51 Sh 35
18-420 Jedwabne (PL) 41 Cc 37
5201* Jēkabpils (LV) 41 Cf 34
Jekaterinburg = Ekaterinburg (RUS) 47 Ga 34
Jektvika (N) 14 Bd 24
Jelanec' (UA) 74 Db 43
58-500 Jelenia Góra (PL) 56 Bf 40
3001* Jelgava (LV) 41 Cd 34
7300 Jelling (DK) 38 Ak 35
6630 Jels (DK) 38 Ak 35
Jelsa (HR) 85 Bg 47
049 16 Jelšava (SK) 57 Ca 42
Jelyzavethradka (UA) 59 Dc 42
Jemil'čyne (UA) 58 Ch 40
07743* Jena (D) 55 Bb 40
Jenakijeve (UA) 60 Di 42
6200* Jenbach (A) 69 Bb 43
Jenerhodar (UA) 74 De 43
66850 Jeppo (FIN) 22 Cc 27
66850 Jepua = Jeppo (FIN) 22 Cc 27
11401* Jerez de la Frontera (E) 92 Sd 54
06380 Jerez de los Caballeros (E) 92 Sd 52
12450 Jérica (E) 82 Sk 51
39319 Jerichow (D) 55 Bc 38
5315 Jersika (LV) 41 Cg 34
4270 Jesenice (SLO) 70 Be 44
790 01 Jeseník (CZ) 56 Bh 40
980 02 Jesenské (SK) 57 Ca 42
60035 Jesi (I) 69 Bd 47
30016 Jesolo (I) 69 Bc 45
06917 Jessen (Elster) (D) 55 Bc 39
2050* Jessheim (N) 28 Bb 30
59460 Jeumont (F) 53 Ae 40
26441 Jever (D) 38 Ah 37
3520 Jevnaker (N) 28 Ba 30
Jevpatorija 74 Dd 45
Jezerane (HR) 70 Bf 45
Jezero (BIH) 70 Bh 46
11-320 Jeziorany (PL) 40 Ca 37
455200 Jibou (RO) 72 Cd 43
506 01* Jičín (CZ) 56 Bf 40
59058 Jieznas (LT) 41 Ce 36
586 01 Jihlava (CZ) 56 Bf 41
03100 Jijona = Xixona (E) 82 Sk 52
514 01 Jilemnice (CZ) 56 Bf 40
Jiltjer (S) 21 Bg 25
305400 Jimbolia (RO) 71 Ca 45
11330* Jimena de la Frontera (E) 92 Se 54
377 01 Jindřichův Hradec (CZ) 56 Bf 41
431 11* Jirkov (CZ) 55 Bd 40
16247 Joachimsthal (D) 39 Bd 38
Jócar (E) 93 Sg 53
Jock (S) 15 Cc 24
80100* Joensuu (FIN) 23 Ck 28
Joesjö (S) 21 Be 25
48303* Jõgeva (EST) 30 Cg 32
08349 Johanngeorgenstadt (D) 55 Bc 40
KW1 John o'Groats (GB) 50 Sg 32
41541 Jõhvi-Ahtme (EST) 31 Ch 31
89300* Joigny (F) 53 Ad 43
52300* Joinville (F) 54 Af 42
96201 Jokkmokk (S) 14 Bk 24
22151 Jomala (AX) 30 Bk 30
5627 Jondal (N) 28 Ag 30
39027 Joniškėlis (LT) 41 Ce 34
84001 Joniškis (LT) 41 Cd 34
55001* Jönköping (S) 29 Be 33
7450 Jonkova (BG) 72 Cg 47
17700 Jonquera, La (E) 82 Ac 48
17500 Jonzac (F) 66 Sk 45
2430 Jordet (N) 29 Bc 29
Jorgastak (N) 15 Cf 21
Jorgucat (AL) 86 Ca 51
Jormlien (S) 21 Bd 26
93055 Jörn (S) 22 Ca 25
79601 Joroinen (FIN) 23 Ch 28
4100 Jørpeland (N) 28 Ag 31
Joškar-Ola (RUS) 45 Eh 34
Jospidol (HR) 70 Bf 45
Jössefors (S) 29 Bc 31
7746 Jøssund (N) 20 Ba 26
89320 Joukokylä (FIN) 23 Ch 25
19651 Joutsa (FIN) 30 Cg 29
54101 Joutseno (FIN) 31 Ci 29
98710 Joutsijärvi (FIN) 15 Ch 24
Jovik (N) 14 Bk 21
9531 Jovkovo (BG) 73 Ci 47
07260 Joyeuse (F) 67 Ae 46
73501 Juankoski (FIN) 23 Ci 27
8750* Judenburg (A) 70 Be 43
Judin (RUS) 61 Eb 42
Judinki (RUS) 43 Dh 36
Judybaevo (RUS) 64 Fh 38
7130 Juelsminde (DK) 39 Ba 35
Jug (RUS) 35 Fg 33
Jugo-Kamskij (RUS) 35 Ff 33
Jugydtydor (RUS) 26 Fd 28
Juhnevo (RUS) 33 Ec 29
Juhnov (RUS) 43 Df 36
Juhoviči (RUS) 42 Ci 34
Juhovo (RUS) 42 Da 34
215100 Jui, Bumbeşti- (RO) 72 Cd 45
19350 Juillac (F) 67 Ab 45
Jukamenskoe (RUS) 35 Fc 33
98191 Jukkasjärvi (S) 14 Ca 23
Jukseevo (RUS) 35 Fe 31
92070 Juktfors (S) 21 Bh 25
Jule (N) 21 Bd 26
52428 Jülich (D) 54 Ag 40
Jum (RUS) 35 Fe 31
Juma (RUS) 23 Dd 25
Jumaguzino (RUS) 47 Fg 38
49160 Jumelles, Longué- (F) 66 Sk 43
30520 Jumilla (E) 93 Si 52
73230 Juminen (FIN) 23 Ch 27
97870 Jumisko (FIN) 15 Ci 24
Junakivka (UA) 60 Df 39
98062 Junosuando (S) 15 Cc 23
17700 Junquera, La = La Jonquera (E) 82 Ac 48
88037 Junsele (S) 21 Bg 27
89770 Juntusranta (FIN) 23 Ck 25
Juodrantė (LT) 40 Cb 35
42063 Juodupė (LT) 41 Cf 34
95723 Juoksengi (S) 15 Cd 24
95640 Juoksenki (FIN) 15 Cd 24
91630 Juorkuna (FIN) 22 Cg 26
Juratiški (BY) 41 Cf 36
74001 Jurbarkas (LT) 41 Cc 35
Jur'evec (RUS) 33 Ed 33
Jur'evo (RUS) 34 Ei 32
Jur'ev-Pol'skij (RUS) 44 Dk 34
827115 Jurilovca (RO) 73 Ci 46
Jurino (RUS) 45 Eg 34
Jur'ja (RUS) 34 Ek 31
Jurjivka (UA) 60 Dg 42
Jurjuzan' (RUS) 47 Fi 36
Jurkino (RUS) 33 Dk 33
Jurkovka (RUS) 77 Eg 46
Jurla (RUS) 35 Fe 31
Jurlovka (RUS) 61 Ea 38
3015 Jūrmala (LV) 41 Cd 34
Juroma (RUS) 25 Ef 25
Jurovo (RUS) 33 Ed 33
Jurovo (RUS) 43 Dd 38
66301 Jurva (FIN) 22 Cb 28
Jury (RUS) 42 Dc 36
Jušala (RUS) 37 Ge 33
Jušino (RUS) 18 Fe 22
Juškozero (RUS) 23 Dc 26
70500 Jussey (F) 68 Af 43
Justa (RUS) 77 Eg 43
Justozero (RUS) 23 Dd 28
Jus'va (RUS) 35 Ff 32
14913 Jüterbog (D) 55 Bd 39
Jutuz, Ust'- (RUS) 47 Fh 34
83901 Juuka (FIN) 23 Ck 27
93850 Juuma (FIN) 15 Ck 24
23101 Juva (FIN) 23 Ch 29
53380 Juvigné (F) 52 Si 42
91200 Juvisy-sur-Orge (F) 53 Ac 42
Juža (RUS) 44 Ec 34
Južakovo (RUS) 36 Gb 33
Južno Suhokumsk (RUS) 77 Ef 46
Južno-Suhokumsk (RUS) 77 Ef 46
Južnoukrains'k (UA) 74 Db 43
Južnoural'sk (RUS) 47 Gb 36
Južnyj (RUS) 47 Ga 37
Južnyj (RUS) 63 Fb 38
Južnyj (RUS) 76 Eb 43
Južnyj (RUS) 76 Ee 45
4560 Jyderup (DK) 39 Bb 35
74380 Jyrkkä (FIN) 23 Ch 27
40100* Jyväskylä (FIN) 22 Cf 28

K

99910 Kaamanen (FIN) 15 Ch 21
99950 Kaamasmukka (FIN) 15 Cg 21
99460 Kaaresuvanto (FIN) 15 Cc 22
20781 Kaarina (FIN) 30 Cc 30
73601 Kaavi (FIN) 23 Ci 28
Kabaca (TR) 88 Db 50
Kabadüz (TR) 90 Dh 50
Kabahaydar (TR) 98 Dk 53
Kabanne (UA) 60 Di 41
96205 Kåbdalis (S) 22 Bk 24
Kabeliaj pervyj (BY) 41 Ce 37
9488 Kableškovo (BG) 88 Ch 48
Kača 74 Dd 46
Kačalino (RUS) 61 Ee 41
71000 Kaçanik = Kačanik (RKS) 86 Cb 48
71000 Kačanik = Kaçanik (RKS) 86 Cb 48
Kačanovo (RUS) 31 Ch 33
06956 Kaçarlı (TR) 89 Dd 51
Kacbahskij (RUS) 47 Fk 38
Kachovka (UA) 74 Dd 44
Kačkanar (RUS) 36 Fk 32
3900 Kačul = Cahul (MD) 73 Ci 45
432 01 Kadaň (CZ) 55 Bd 40
7530 Kadarkút (H) 70 Bh 44
Kadijivka (UA) 60 Di 42
17350 Kadiköy = Evrese (TR) 87 Cg 50
Kadıkuyusu (TR) 88 Db 51
42800 Kadınhanı (TR) 96 Dc 52
80750* Kadirli (TR) 97 Dg 53
66540 Kadışehri (TR) 89 Df 50
Kadnikov (RUS) 33 Ea 31
Kadnikovskij (RUS) 33 Ea 30
Kadom (RUS) 44 Ec 36
Kadoškino (RUS) 45 Ee 36
Kaduj (RUS) 32 Dh 31
Kadyj (RUS) 33 Ed 33
Kadžerom (RUS) 26 Ff 26
Kåfjord (N) 15 Cf 20
Kåfjordbotn (N) 14 Ca 21
Kagal'nickaja (RUS) 76 Ea 44
93401 Kåge (S) 22 Ca 26
36700 Kağızman (TR) 91 Ed 50
Kağnılı (TR) 91 Ed 51
Kaharlyk (UA) 59 Da 41
25000 Kahramanlar (TR) 91 Eb 51
46000* Kahramanmaraş (TR) 98 Dg 53
02400 Kâhta (TR) 98 Di 53
3900 Kahul = Cahul (MD) 73 Ci 45
92101 Käina (EST) 30 Cc 32
98065 Kainulasjärvi (S) 15 Cc 22
Kairovo (RUS) 47 Fh 35
67655* Kaiserslautern (D) 54 Ah 41
56001 Kaišiadorys (LT) 41 Ce 36
Kaitum (S) 14 Ca 23
87100* Kajaani (FIN) 23 Ch 26
Kajasula (RUS) 77 Ef 46
7550 Kajnardža (BG) 73 Ch 47
Kajsackoe (RUS) 62 Eg 41
Kajuki (RUS) 45 Ek 35
Kajvaksa (RUS) 32 Dd 31
Kakanj (BIH) 71 Bi 46
20340 Kaklık (TR) 96 Ck 53
06121 Kalaba (TR) 97 De 52
Kalač (RUS) 61 Eb 40
Kalač-na-Donu (RUS) 61 Ed 42
85101 Kalajoki (FIN) 22 Cd 26
Kalak (N) 15 Ch 20
61650 Kalakoski (FIN) 22 Cd 28
55101* Kalamariá (GR) 86 Cc 50
24100 Kalamáta (GR) 94 Cc 53
42200 Kalambáka (GR) 86 Cb 51
Kalamiá (GR) 86 Ca 51
63081 Kalamitsi (GR) 87 Cd 51
Kalamos (GR) 95 Cf 53
92212 Kalana (EST) 30 Cc 32
Kalančak (UA) 74 Dd 44
63077 Kalándra (GR) 87 Cd 51
4400 Kalaraš = Călăraşi (MD) 73 Ci 43
Kälarne (S) 21 Bg 28
Kalašnikov (RUS) 32 Df 33
25001 Kalávrita (GR) 94 Cc 52
1370 Kalce (SLO) 70 Be 45
9395 Kaldfarnes (N) 14 Bg 21
Kale (TR) 90 Dk 50
Kale (TR) 96 Ci 53
Kale (TR) 96 Da 54
Kale (TR) 97 Df 53
Kale (TR) 97 Df 54
Kale (TR) 98 Di 52
Kalecik (TR) 89 Dd 50
Kaleköy (TR) 89 Df 50
Kalepiiha (RUS) 34 Ef 31
Kaleste (EST) 30 Cc 32
Kalevala (RUS) 23 Db 25
880 Kálfafell (IS) 48 Rc 27
780 Kálfafellsstaður (IS) 48 Re 26
Kal'i (RUS) 25 Ec 27
20016 Kaliáni (GR) 94 Cc 53
Kalikino (RUS) 46 Fe 38
85200 Kálimnos (GR) 95 Cg 54
Kalinin = Tver' (RUS) 43 Df 34
Kaliningrad (RUS) 40 Ca 36
Kalinino (RUS) 45 Eg 35
Kalinino (RUS) 75 Di 45
Kalininsk (RUS) 61 Ee 39
Kalininskaja (RUS) 75 Di 45
Kalinkavičy (BY) 58 Ck 38
Kalinniki (RUS) 46 Ff 35
Kalino (RUS) 35 Fg 33
Kalino (RUS) 35 Fh 32
Kalinovik (BIH) 71 Bi 47
Kalinovka (RUS) 46 Fa 37
62-800 Kalisz (PL) 56 Bi 39
78-540 Kalisz Pomorski (PL) 39 Bf 37
64004 Kalíves (GR) 87 Ce 50
Kalivia (GR) 94 Cc 53
95200 Kalix (S) 22 Cd 25
Kalixforsbron (S) 14 Ca 23
Kal'ja (RUS) 36 Ga 30
Kaljazin (RUS) 32 Dh 33
Kalkan (TR) 96 Ck 54
Kalkan (TR) 99 Ea 52
53500 Kalkandere (TR) 91 Ea 50
47546 Kalkar (D) 54 Ag 39
Kalkım (TR) 88 Ch 51
83005 Kall (S) 21 Bd 27
60103* Kallaste (EST) 31 Ch 32
88403 Kalli (EST) 30 Ce 32
58810 Kallislahti (FIN) 23 Ci 29
84200 Kallonì (GR) 86 Cb 50
84200 Kalloní (GR) 87 Cg 51
99430 Kalmankaltio (FIN) 15 Ce 22
Kalmar (S) 40 Bg 34
Kalmaš (RUS) 47 Fh 35
Kalmykovskij (RUS) 61 Ec 42
19353 Kalna (SRB) 71 Cc 47
935 32 Kalná nad Hronom (SK) 56 Bi 42
Kalnciems (LV) 41 Cd 34
6300 Kalocsa (H) 71 Bi 44
Kalodna (BY) 58 Cg 39
8881 Kalojanovo (BG) 87 Ce 48
Kalonija (BY) 57 Ce 38
44004 Kalpáki (GR) 86 Ca 51
18028 Kaltanėnai (LT) 41 Cf 35
Kaltasy (RUS) 46 Fe 34
24568 Kaltenkirchen (D) 38 Ak 37
36452 Kaltennordheim (D) 55 Ba 40
75044 Kaltinėnai (LT) 41 Cc 35
Kaluga (RUS) 43 Dg 36
4400 Kalundborg (DK) 39 Bb 35
Kaluš (UA) 57 Ce 41
6729 Kalvåg (N) 20 Ae 29
69030 Kalvarija (LT) 41 Cd 36
68301 Kälviä (FIN) 22 Cd 27
14530 Kalvola (FIN) 30 Ce 29
93027 Kalvträsk (S) 22 Bk 26
8775 Kalwang (A) 70 Be 43
Kalynivka (UA) 58 Ci 41
Kalynivka (UA) 59 Da 40
Kalynivka (UA) 74 Dc 43
Kalyta (UA) 59 Db 40
40300 Kaman (TR) 89 Dd 51
70002 Kamáres (GR) 94 Ce 54
Kambarka (RUS) 46 Fe 34
85500 Kámbos (GR) 95 Cg 53
Kamčuga (RUS) 33 Ed 30
Kameevo (RUS) 47 Fg 35
59174 Kamen (BG) 72 Cf 47
Kamen' (BY) 42 Ci 35
Kamen' (RUS) 36 Fi 31
Kamenec-Podol'skij = Kam'janec'-Podil's'kyj (UA) 58 Cg 42
Kamenica (BIH) 71 Bk 47
Kamenka (RUS) 37 Gf 33
Kamenka (RUS) 42 Dc 35
Kamenka (RUS) 45 Ee 37
Kamenka (RUS) 60 Dk 40
Kamenka (RUS) 64 Ff 38
Kamenka (RUS) 18 Fa 23
Kamenki (RUS) 43 Dh 34
Kamennnyj Perebor (RUS) 34 Fb 33
Kamennobrodskaja (RUS) 76 Eb 45
Kamennoe (RUS) 25 Ee 29
Kamennoe (RUS) 34 Ef 33
Kamennogorsk (RUS) 31 Ck 30
Kamennomostskij (RUS) 75 Ea 46
8120 Kameno (BG) 88 Ch 48
Kamenskij (RUS) 62 Ef 40
Kamenskoe (RUS) 43 Dg 35
Kamensk-Šahtinskij (RUS) 61 Ea 42
Kamensk-Ural'skij (RUS) 47 Gb 34
01917 Kamenz (D) 55 Be 39
Kameškovo (RUS) 44 Eb 34
Kamešnaja (RUS) 33 Dk 30
26-100 Kamienna, Skarżysko- (PL) 57 Ca 39
58-400 Kamienna Góra (PL) 56 Bg 40
72-400 Kamień Pomorski (PL) 39 Be 37
97-360 Kamieńsk (PL) 56 Bk 39
19500 Kâmil (TR) 89 De 49
Kamin'-Kašyrs'kyj (UA) 57 Ce 39
Kaminskij (RUS) 33 Eb 33
Kamışlı (TR) 97 De 53
Kamışlık (TR) 99 Ee 53
Kamışlıkuyu (TR) 97 De 53
Kamjanec (BY) 57 Cd 38
Kam'janec'-Podil's'kyj (UA) 58 Cg 42
Kamjanka (UA) 59 Dc 41
Kam'janka (UA) 60 Dk 41
Kam'janka (UA) 73 Da 44
Kamjanka-Buz'ka (UA) 57 Ce 40
Kamjans'ka Sloboda (UA) 59 Dd 38
Kamjans'ke (UA) 59 De 42
Kam'janske (UA) 57 Ce 42
1241 Kamnik (SLO) 70 Be 44
8260* Kampen (NL) 54 Af 38
Kamskij (RUS) 35 Fd 31
Kamskoe Ust'e (RUS) 45 Ek 35
Kamyševatskaja (RUS) 75 Dh 44
Kamyšin (RUS) 62 Ef 40
Kamyšla (RUS) 46 Fc 36
Kamyšuvacha (UA) 74 Df 43
Kamyzjak (RUS) 77 Ei 44
Kanabeki (RUS) 35 Fh 33
Kanadej (RUS) 45 Eh 37
84006 Kanála (GR) 94 Ce 53
38500 Kanália (GR) 86 Cc 51
Kananikol'skij (RUS) 47 Fh 38
Kanaš (RUS) 45 Eh 35
Kanavka (RUS) 62 Ei 40
Kandalakša (RUS) 16 Dc 23
3120 Kandava (LV) 41 Cc 33
76870 Kandel (D) 54 Ai 41
25680 Kandilli (TR) 91 Ea 51
41600 Kandıra (TR) 88 Da 49
Kandry (RUS) 46 Fe 36
63101 Kanepi (EST) 30 Cg 33
Kanevka (RUS) 17 Dk 23
Kanevskaja (RUS) 75 Di 44
25200 Kangádio (GR) 94 Cb 52
58900 Kangal (TR) 90 Dh 51
79480 Kangaslampi (FIN) 23 Ci 28
51201 Kangasniemi (FIN) 22 Cg 29
98063 Kangos (S) 15 Cc 23
99360 Kangosjärvi (FIN) 15 Cd 23
Kanin Nos (RUS) 17 Ed 22
Kaniv (UA) 59 Db 41
24420 Kanjiža (SRB) 71 Ca 44
38701 Kankaanpää (FIN) 22 Cc 29
41410 Kankainen (FIN) 22 Cg 28
Kanlıavşar (TR) 98 Di 53
33730 Kanlıdivane (TR) 97 De 54
43300 Kannonkoski (FIN) 22 Cf 28
43340 Kannonsaha (FIN) 22 Cf 28
69101 Kannus (FIN) 22 Cd 27
77380 Kantala (FIN) 23 Ch 28
Kantar (TR) 99 Eb 53
Kantarma (TR) 98 Db 52
Kantemirovka (RUS) 60 Dk 41
Kantornes (N) 14 Bk 21
Kanturk = Ceann Toirc (IRL) 49 Sb 38
9960 Kaolinovo (BG) 73 Ch 47
32234 Kaona (SRB) 71 Ca 47
37256 Kaonik (SRB) 71 Cb 47
Kapatkevičy (BY) 58 Ci 38
67039 Kapčiamiestis (LT) 41 Cd 36
47608 Kapellen (B) 53 Ae 39
8605* Kapfenberg (A) 70 Bf 43
Kapini (LV) 42 Ch 34
382 41* Kaplice (CZ) 55 Be 42
7400 Kaposvár (H) 70 Bh 44
2849 Kapp (N) 28 Ba 30
55483 Kappel (D) 54 Ah 40
Kappelskär (S) 29 Bk 31
24376 Kappeln (D) 38 Ak 36
Kappelshamn (S) 29 Bi 33
30015 Kapsorráhi (GR) 94 Cb 52
53350 Kaptanpaşa (TR) 91 Ea 50
Kapustin Jar (RUS) 62 Ef 42
Kapustino (RUS) 46 Fc 34
Kapustnoe (RUS) 16 De 23
Kapustynci (UA) 59 De 40
9330 Kapuvár (H) 70 Bh 43
Kapyl' (BY) 41 Ch 37
Kara (RUS) 47 Fh 37
42950 Karaağa (TR) 96 Dc 54
Karaağaç (TR) 91 Ec 51
Karaağaç (TR) 96 Ci 54
49550 Karaağıl (TR) 91 Ec 51
Karabanovka (RUS) 46 Fb 37

Karabanovka | 179

Karabanovo (RUS) 43 Di 34
Karabaš (RUS) 46 Fc 36
Karabaš (RUS) 47 Ga 35
Karabaška (RUS) 37 Gf 32
Karabeyli (TR) 96 Ck 52
17950 Karabiga (TR) 88 Ch 50
Karabucak (TR) 97 Df 53
07350 Karabük (TR) 89 Dc 49
Karabulak (RUS) 76 Ee 47
34558 Karaburun (TR) 88 Ci 49
34558 Karaburun (TR) 95 Cg 52
16670 Karacaali (TR) 88 Ck 50
16700 Karacabey (TR) 88 Ci 50
Karacadağ (TR) 88 Ch 49
Karacadağ (TR) 98 Dk 53
Karačaevsk (RUS) 76 Eb 47
Karacagür (TR) 87 Cg 49
Karacahisar (TR) 96 Db 53
Karačaj Tereze (RUS) 76 Ec 47
48700 Karacaköy (TR) 88 Ci 49
Karacaören (TR) 90 Di 51
14020 Karacasu (TR) 96 Ci 53
19300 Karaçay (TR) 89 De 50
Karaçayır (TR) 90 Dg 51
Karačev (RUS) 43 Df 37
25620 Karaçoban (TR) 91 Ec 51
10700 Karadere (TR) 88 Ch 51
10700 Karadere (TR) 88 Da 50
03550 Karadirek (TR) 96 Da 52
Karagač (RUS) 64 Fg 39
Karagaj (RUS) 35 Ff 32
31825 Karagöl (TR) 89 Dc 50
31825 Karagöl (TR) 90 Dg 51
64700 Karahallı (TR) 96 Ck 52
52700 Karahasan (TR) 91 Ec 51
50610 Karahasanlı (TR) 89 De 51
Karaidel' (RUS) 47 Fg 35
Karaidel'skij (RUS) 47 Fh 35
33830 Karaisalı (TR) 97 Df 53
Karaja Masel'ga (RUS) 24 De 27
Karaj-Saltykovo (RUS) 61 Ec 38
Karakale (TR) 91 Ed 49
Karakaya (TR) 88 Db 50
Karakaya (TR) 96 Dc 53
63620 Karakeçi (TR) 98 Dk 53
71500 Karakeçili (TR) 89 Dd 51
Karakent (TR) 96 Da 53
Karakoç (TR) 99 Ed 52
23600 Karakoçan (TR) 99 Ea 52
05000 Karaköprü (TR) 91 Eb 51
Karaköy (TR) 88 Db 50
Karaköy (TR) 91 Eb 51
Karaköy (TR) 95 Ch 52
Karaköy (TR) 96 Ci 53
Karakoyunlu (TR) 91 Ee 51
Karakša (RUS) 45 Eh 33
24860 Karakulak (TR) 91 Ea 51
Karakulino (RUS) 46 Fd 34
Karakurt (TR) 91 Ec 50
66320 Karamağara = Saraykent (TR) 89 Df 51
70000* Karaman (TR) 97 Dd 53
46000 Karamanlı (TR) 96 Ck 53
41500 Karamürsel (TR) 88 Ck 50
Karamusa (TR) 89 Dd 50
Karamyševo (RUS) 31 Ci 33
Karaoğlan (TR) 90 Dk 51
48200 Karaova (TR) 95 Ch 53
Karapazar (TR) 89 Dc 50
9390 Karapelit (BG) 73 Ch 47
Karapınar (TR) 96 Db 52
Karapınar (TR) 97 Dd 53
Karapürçek (TR) 88 Da 50
Karaš (RUS) 44 Dk 34
18600 Karaşar (TR) 89 Dc 50
99460 Karasavvon = Kaaresuvanto (FIN) 15 Cc 22
Karasinir (TR) 96 Dc 53
9730 Karasjok (N) 15 Cf 21
54500 Karasu (TR) 88 Da 49
Karasyn (UA) 58 Cf 39
Karatajka (RUS) 19 Gb 22
Karataş (TR) 96 Ci 52
Karataş (TR) 97 Df 54
48960 Karatoprak = Turgutreis (TR) 95 Ch 54
Karats (S) 14 Bi 24
Karaul'skoe (RUS) 36 Ga 31
36520 Karaurgan (TR) 91 Ec 50
Karavaciĉy (BY) 59 Da 38
Karavās (GR) 94 Cc 54
4350 Karavelovo (BG) 87 Cg 48
60540 Karayaka (TR) 90 Dg 50
25830 Karayazı (TR) 91 Ec 51
Karayün (TR) 90 Dh 51
Karbany (RUS) 37 Gg 33
31000 Karbeyaz (TR) 97 Dg 54
82043 Kårböle (S) 21 Bf 29
7960 Karby (DK) 38 Ai 34
5300 Karcag (H) 71 Ca 43
Kardakāta (GR) 94 Ca 52
85300 Kardámena (GR) 95 Ch 54
82300 Kardámila (GR) 95 Cg 52
Kardamili (GR) 94 Cc 54
Kardeljevo = Ploče (HR) 85 Bh 47
43101 Kardítsa (GR) 86 Cb 51
92411* Kärdla (EST) 30 Cc 32
Kardymovo (RUS) 42 Dc 36
6600* Kărdžali (BG) 87 Cf 49
Kărdžali (BG) 87 Cf 49
Kardžin (RUS) 91 Ee 47
Karelakša (RUS) 23 Dc 25
Karèličy (BY) 41 Cg 37
Karelina (RUS) 37 Gi 33
Karelino (RUS) 36 Ga 32
Karelino (RUS) 46 Fa 34
Karel'skaja Masel'ga (RUS) 23 Dd 27
Karepol'e (RUS) 25 Ed 25
98016 Karesuando (S) 15 Cc 22
Kargala (RUS) 63 Fe 39
Kargali (RUS) 46 Fa 35
19900 Kargı (TR) 89 De 49
19900 Kargı (TR) 96 Ck 54
19900 Kargı (TR) 96 Da 53
48200 Kargıcak (TR) 97 Dd 54
58510 Kargın (TR) 89 De 50
58510 Kargın (TR) 96 Da 53
Kargino (RUS) 45 Eh 37
Kargopol' (RUS) 32 Di 29
66-120 Kargowa (PL) 56 Bf 38
86480 Karhukangas (FIN) 22 Cf 26
48810 Karhula (FIN) 30 Cg 30
Karian (RUS) 61 Eb 38
23067 Kariés (GR) 87 Ce 50
99950 Karigasniemi (FIN) 15 Cf 21
63501 Karilatsi (EST) 30 Cg 32
21840 Karinainen (FIN) 30 Cc 30
Karine (TR) 95 Ch 53
Karinka (RUS) 34 Fa 32
34001 Káristos (GR) 94 Ce 52
10300* Karjaa = Karis (FIN) 30 Cd 30
97890 Karjalaisenniemi (FIN) 15 Ci 24
Karjalan kirkonkylä (FIN) 30 Cc 30
Karkinágri (GR) 95 Cg 53
03620 Karkkila (FIN) 30 Ce 30
16610 Kärkölä (FIN) 30 Cd 30
69104 Karksi-Nuia (EST) 30 Cf 32
67100* Karleby = Kokkola (FIN) 22 Cd 27
78-230 Karlino (PL) 39 Bf 36
12900 Karlıova (TR) 91 Eb 51
Karlivka (UA) 60 Df 41
Karlobag (HR) 70 Bf 46
Karlo-Libknehtovsk = Soledar (UA) 60 Di 42
Karlovac (HR) 70 Bf 45
83200 Karlovássi (GR) 95 Cg 53
Karlovka (RUS) 62 Ek 39
4300 Karlovo (BG) 87 Ce 48
360 01* Karlovy Vary (CZ) 55 Bc 40
Karlsborg (S) 22 Cd 25
Karlsborg (S) 29 Be 32
37400* Karlshamn (S) 39 Be 34
69101* Karlskoga (S) 29 Be 31
37100* Karlskrona (S) 39 Bf 34
76131* Karlsruhe (D) 54 Ai 41
65001* Karlstad (S) 29 Bd 31
97753 Karlstadt (D) 54 Ak 41
Karlyhanovo (RUS) 47 Fi 35
Karma (BY) 42 Da 37
Karmanovo (RUS) 43 De 35
Karmaskaly (RUS) 47 Fg 36
4337 Kărnare (BG) 87 Ce 48
8400 Karnobat (BG) 87 Cg 48
58-540 Karpacz (PL) 56 Bf 40
93990 Kärpänkylä (FIN) 23 Ck 25
85700 Kárpathos (GR) 95 Ch 55
36100 Karpeníssi (GR) 94 Cb 52
42200 Karperó (GR) 86 Cb 51
Karpinsk (RUS) 36 Ga 31
Karpogory (RUS) 25 Ee 26
Karpuninskij (RUS) 36 Gb 32
Karpušiha (RUS) 36 Fk 33
Karpuzlu (TR) 87 Cg 50
Karpuzlu (TR) 95 Ch 53
36000* Kars (TR) 91 Ed 50
86710 Kärsämäki (FIN) 22 Cf 27
5717 Kārsava (LV) 42 Ch 34
Karsovaj (RUS) 35 Fd 32
43501 Karstula (FIN) 22 Ce 28
Karsun (RUS) 45 Eg 36
Karsy (RUS) 47 Gb 36
Kartaěl' (RUS) 26 Fd 26
Kartaly (RUS) 47 Ga 37
72101 Karttula (FIN) 22 Cg 28
83-300 Kartuzy (PL) 40 Bi 36
95393 Karungi (S) 22 Cd 24
95530 Karunki (FIN) 22 Ce 24
7470 Karup (DK) 38 Ak 34
44910 Kärväskyla (FIN) 22 Cf 27
39930 Karvia (FIN) 22 Cc 28
733 01* Karviná (CZ) 56 Bi 41
Karvio (FIN) 23 Ci 28
Karžimant (RUS) 45 Ef 38
Kaş (TR) 96 Ck 54
Kaş (TR) 97 Dg 53
07580 Kasaba (TR) 96 Ck 54
29901 Kasaböle = Kasala (FIN) 22 Cb 29
29901 Kasala (FIN) 22 Cb 29
Kašalëvo, Buda- (BY) 42 Da 38
Kašary (RUS) 61 Ea 41
Kascjanevičy (BY) 42 Ch 36
Kascjukovičy (BY) 42 Dc 37
Kascjukovka (BY) 59 Da 38
Kåseberga (S) 39 Be 35
Kašhatau (RUS) 76 Ed 47
Kasımoğlu (TR) 99 Ed 52
Kasimov (RUS) 44 Eb 36
Kašin (RUS) 32 Dh 33
42206 Kaşınhanı (TR) 96 Dc 53
Kaširа (RUS) 43 Di 36
Kaskara (RUS) 37 Gf 33
Kaškarancy (RUS) 16 Dg 24
64260 Kaskinen (FIN) 22 Cb 28
Kaškino (RUS) 47 Fh 34
64260 Kaskö = Kaskinen (FIN) 22 Cb 28
Kasli (RUS) 47 Ga 35
Kašperivka (UA) 58 Ci 41
Kaspijskij = Lagan' (RUS) 77 Eh 45
63077 Kassándria (GR) 87 Cd 50
Kassandrinó (GR) 87 Cd 50
63599 Kassel (D) 54 Ak 39
49100 Kassiópi (GR) 86 Bk 51
37000* Kastamonu (TR) 89 Dd 49
60100 Kastania (GR) 86 Cc 50
Kastéli (GR) 94 Cd 55
52100 Kastoriá (GR) 86 Cb 50
Kastornoe (RUS) 60 Di 39
Kašyrs'kyj, Kamin'- (UA) 57 Ce 39
27100 Katákolo (GR) 94 Cb 53
29090 Katastári (GR) 94 Ca 53
Katav, Ust'- (RUS) 47 Fi 36
Katav-Ivanovsk (RUS) 47 Fi 36
60100 Kateríni (GR) 86 Cc 50
Katerynopil' (UA) 59 Da 42
1044 Katlanovo (MK) 86 Cb 49
Kátō Ahaía (GR) 94 Cb 52
19012 Káto Alepohóri (GR) 94 Cd 52
27054 Káto Figália (GR) 94 Cb 53
Káto Glikóvrisi (GR) 94 Cc 54
Káto Kateliós (GR) 94 Ca 52
66033 Káto Nevrokópi (GR) 87 Cd 49
Kato Pyrgos (CY) 96 Dc 55
Káto Samikó (GR) 94 Cb 53
19500 Káto Soúnio (GR) 94 Ce 53
40-001 Katowice (PL) 56 Bk 40
64101* Katrineholm (S) 29 Bg 32
85019 Kattavía (GR) 95 Ch 55
Katterjåkk (S) 14 Bi 22
Katthammarsvik (S) 29 Bi 33
Kattilasaari (S) 22 Cd 25
92195 Kattisavan (S) 21 Bi 26
2830 Katunci (BG) 87 Cd 49
Katunino (RUS) 34 Ef 32
2225 Katwijk aan Zee (NL) 53 Ae 38
87600 Kaufbeuren (D) 69 Ba 43
61801 Kauhajoki (FIN) 22 Cc 28
62201 Kauhava (FIN) 22 Cd 27
99110 Kaukonen (FIN) 15 Ce 23
41001 Kauksi (EST) 31 Ch 32
44001* Kaunas (LT) 41 Cd 36
6854 Kaupanger (N) 28 Ah 29
4300 Kaušany = Căușeni (MD) 73 Ck 44
69601 Kaustinen (FIN) 22 Cd 27
Kautokeino (N) 15 Cd 21
Kavacık (TR) 88 Ci 51
Kavacık (TR) 89 Dc 50
1430* Kavadarci (MK) 86 Cc 49
Kavajë (AL) 86 Bk 49
Kavak (TR) 87 Cg 50
Kavak (TR) 89 De 50
Kavak (TR) 90 Dg 49
Kavak (TR) 90 Dh 51
13730 Kavakbaşı (TR) 99 Eb 52
48570 Kavaklıdere (TR) 96 Ci 53
65000 Kavála (GR) 87 Ce 50
9650 Kavarna (BG) 73 Ci 47
29021 Kavarskas (LT) 41 Ce 35
Kaverino (RUS) 44 Eb 36
24401 Kävlinge (S) 39 Bd 35
49080 Kávos (GR) 86 Ca 51
Kavra (RUS) 25 Ed 27
83051 Kaxås (S) 21 Bd 27
Kayabaşı (TR) 89 Dc 51
Kayacık (TR) 99 Ea 52
37400 Kayadibi (TR) 90 Dg 51
Kayaönü (TR) 97 Dd 53
Kayapınar (TR) 99 Eb 53
93850 Käylä (FIN) 15 Ck 24
Käymäjärvi (S) 15 Cc 23
26640 Kaymaz (TR) 88 Da 50
26640 Kaymaz (TR) 88 Db 51
38710 Kaynar (TR) 98 Dg 52
16900 Kaynarca (TR) 88 Ck 50
16900 Kaynarca (TR) 88 Da 49
01970 Kaypak (TR) 98 Dg 53
37620 Kayrak (TR) 97 Dd 54
38000* Kayseri (TR) 97 Df 52
Kazača Lopan' (UA) 60 Dg 40
Kazačka (RUS) 61 Ed 39
Kazaki (RUS) 60 Di 38
Kazakkulovo (RUS) 47 Fi 37
Kazan' (RUS) 45 Ek 35
Kazan (TR) 89 Dc 50
18400 Kazancı (TR) 96 Dc 54
18400 Kazancı (TR) 99 Ea 53
Kazanka (UA) 74 Dc 43
6100* Kazanlăk (BG) 87 Cf 48
37600 Kazanlı (TR) 97 De 54
Kazanskaja (RUS) 61 Eb 41
Kazarka (RUS) 45 Ef 37
Kazenščina (RUS) 25 Eb 27
48400 Kazıklı (TR) 95 Ch 53
Kazil'skoe (RUS) 64 Fi 38
Kâzımkarabekir (TR) 96 Dc 53
Kazinaka (RUS) 60 Dh 40
Kaz'jany (BY) 41 Cg 35
Kaz'jany (BY) 42 Ck 35
Kazlų Rūda (LT) 41 Cd 36
Kažma (RUS) 24 De 28
Kažukas = Marijampole (LT) 41 Cd 36
Kažym (RUS) 34 Fb 30
Kčevka (RUS) 62 Ei 40
89-240 Kcynia (PL) 40 Bh 38
23700 Keban (TR) 98 Di 52
Kebnekaise fjällstation (S) 14 Bi 23
6237 Kecel (H) 71 Bk 44
32700 Keçiborlu (TR) 96 Da 53
Keçiler (TR) 96 Ck 52
55810 Keçiören (TR) 89 Dc 50
6000 Kecskemét (H) 71 Bk 44
57001* Kėdainiai (LT) 41 Cd 35
36072 Kédra (GR) 86 Cb 51
43300 Kédros (GR) 86 Cc 51
Kedrozero (RUS) 24 De 28
47-200 Kędzierzyn (PL) 56 Bi 40
47-200 Kędzierzyn-Koźle (PL) 56 Bi 40
Keel = An Caol (IRL) 49 Rk 37
85301 Kéfalos (GR) 95 Cg 54
41610 Kefken (TR) 88 Da 49
415 Keflavík (IS) 48 Qh 26
77694 Kehl (D) 54 Ah 42
74305* Kehra (EST) 30 Cf 31
Kehyčivka (UA) 60 Df 41
BD21 Keighley (GB) 51 Si 37
32730 Keikyä (FIN) 30 Cc 29
76605* Keila (EST) 30 Ce 31
5062 Ķeipene (LV) 41 Cf 34
72601 Keitele (FIN) 22 Cg 27
AB55 Keith (GB) 50 Sh 33
97785 Kelankylä (FIN) 23 Ch 25
Këlcyrë (AL) 86 Ca 50
20870 Kelekçi (TR) 96 Ck 53
4400 Kėlėraš' = Călărași (MD) 73 Ci 43
16740 Keles (TR) 88 Ck 51
93309 Kelheim (D) 55 Bb 42
29600 Kelkit (TR) 90 Dk 50
25548 Kellinghusen (D) 38 Ak 37
98920 Kelloselkä (FIN) 15 Ci 24
86001 Kelmė (LT) 41 Cc 35
Kel'menci (UA) 58 Cg 42
TD5 Kelso (GB) 51 Sh 35
Kem' (RUS) 24 De 26
24400 Kemah (TR) 90 Dk 51
Kemâliye (TR) 90 Di 51
08610 Kemalpaşa (TR) 91 Eb 49
08610 Kemalpaşa (TR) 95 Ch 52
17220 Kemer (TR) 88 Ch 50
17220 Kemer (TR) 96 Ci 53
17220 Kemer (TR) 96 Ck 54
17220 Kemer (TR) 96 Da 53
17220 Kemer (TR) 96 Da 54
17220 Kemer (TR) 97 Dd 52
34075 Kemerburgaz (TR) 88 Ci 49
51730 Kemerhisar (TR) 97 De 53
94900 Kemi (FIN) 22 Ce 25
98840 Kemihaara (FIN) 15 Ci 23
98999 Kemijärvi (FIN) 15 Ch 24
94450 Keminmaa (FIN) 22 Ce 25
25701 Kemiö (FIN) 30 Cc 30
Kemlja (RUS) 45 Ef 36
95478 Kemnath (D) 55 Bb 41
90451 Kempele (FIN) 22 Cf 26
47906 Kempen (D) 54 Ag 39
87435* Kempten (Allgäu) (D) 69 Ba 43
LA9 Kendal (GB) 51 Sh 36
Kenica (RUS) 25 Eb 26
Kenmare = Neidín (IRL) 49 Sa 39
Kento (RUS) 23 Db 25
27200 Kéntro (GR) 94 Cb 53
Kenttan (N) 15 Cf 21
Kepa (RUS) 23 Dc 25
Kepino (RUS) 25 Eb 25
63-600 Kępno (PL) 56 Bh 39
10660 Kepsut (TR) 88 Ci 51
64011* Keramotí (GR) 87 Ce 50
Keräntöjärvi (S) 15 Cc 23
Kerč 75 Dg 45
Kerčëm'ja (RUS) 35 Fd 29
Kerčevskij (RUS) 35 Fg 31
Kërçukaj (AL) 86 Bk 49
3396 Kerecsend (H) 71 Ca 43
Keret' (RUS) 16 Dd 24
29092 Kerí (GR) 94 Ca 53
58201 Kerimäki (FIN) 23 Ck 29
49100 Kérkira (GR) 86 Bk 51
8870 Kermen (BG) 87 Cg 48
Keros (RUS) 35 Fc 30
50169* Kerpen (D) 54 Ag 40
Kerstinbo (S) 29 Bg 30
5300 Kerteminde (DK) 39 Ba 35
25011 Kértezi (GR) 94 Cb 53
Keryneia = Girne 97 Dd 55
59801 Kesälahti (FIN) 23 Ck 29
22800* Keşan (TR) 87 Cg 50
28900 Keşap (TR) 90 Di 50
Kesikköprü (TR) 89 Dd 51
Kesikköprü Hani (TR) 89 De 51
61680 Keskikylä (FIN) 22 Ce 26
71800 Keskin (TR) 89 Dd 51
Kesova Gora (RUS) 32 Dh 33
Kesten'ga (RUS) 23 Db 25
92700 Kestilä (FIN) 22 Cg 26
NR12 Keswick (GB) 51 Sg 36
8360 Keszthely (H) 70 Bh 44
Ketčenery (RUS) 76 Ee 43
11-401 Kętrzyn (PL) 40 Cb 36
NN15 Kettering (GB) 52 Sk 38
KW17 Kettletoft (GB) 50 Sh 31
32-650 Kęty (PL) 56 Bk 41
14669 Ketzin/Havel (D) 55 Bc 38
42721 Keuruu (FIN) 22 Ce 28
4300 Kèušen' = Căușeni (MD) 73 Ck 44
47623* Kevelaer (D) 54 Ag 39
Kevjudy (RUS) 76 Ee 45
Kez (RUS) 35 Fd 33
Kežmarok (SK) 57 Ca 41
20200 Kiáto (GR) 94 Cc 52
14610 Kıbrıscık (TR) 88 Db 50
6250* Kičevo (MK) 86 Ca 49
Kičižno (RUS) 25 Eb 26
Kicman' (UA) 58 Cf 42
Kičmengskij Gorodok (RUS) 34 Ef 31
DY10 Kidderminster (GB) 52 Sh 38
Kidekša (RUS) 44 Ea 34
SA17 Kidwelly (GB) 52 Sf 39
Kidyš (RUS) 47 Ga 36
88901 Kiekinkoski (FIN) 23 Da 26
24103* Kiel (D) 39 Ba 36
25-001 Kielce (PL) 57 Ca 40
44-187 Kieleczka (PL) 56 Bi 40
Kifino Selo (BIH) 71 Bi 47
14501 Kifissiá (GR) 94 Cd 52
12800 Kiği (TR) 91 Ea 51
Kihelkona (EST) 30 Cc 32
95950 Kihlanki (FIN) 15 Cd 23
39820 Kihniö (FIN) 22 Cd 28
25390 Kiikala (FIN) 30 Cd 30
38360 Kiikoinen (FIN) 30 Cc 29
90901 Kiiminki (FIN) 22 Cf 25
99250 Kiistala (FIN) 15 Cf 23
Kija (RUS) 17 Ee 23
Kijasovo (RUS) 46 Fd 34
24060 Kijevo = Rixhevë (RKS) 86 Ca 48
Kikerino (RUS) 31 Ck 31
23300* Kikinda (SRB) 71 Ca 45
Kiknur (RUS) 34 Eh 33
Kikvidze (RUS) 61 Ed 40
Kil (S) 29 Bd 31
Kila (S) 29 Bg 32
82301 Kilafors (S) 29 Bg 29
70120 Kılbasan (TR) 97 Dd 53
Kilbeggan = Cill Bheagáin (IRL) 49 Sc 37
Kilboghamn (N) 14 Bd 24
9402 Kilbotn (N) 14 Bg 22
Kil'čenga (RUS) 34 Eg 30
Kilcullen = Cill Chuilin (IRL) 49 Sd 37
Kildare = Cill Dara (IRL) 49 Sd 37
Kil'dinstroj (RUS) 16 Dd 22
Kilemary (RUS) 45 Eg 34
77020 Kılıç (TR) 88 Ck 50
08820 Kılıçkaya (TR) 91 Eb 50
5050 Kilifarevo (BG) 87 Cf 48
Kilija (UA) 73 Ck 45
Kilimli (TR) 88 Db 49
Kilingi-Nõmme (EST) 30 Ce 32
27068 Kilíni (GR) 94 Cb 53
Kilis (TR) 98 Dh 54
Kilkee = Cill Chaoi (IRL) 49 Sa 38
BT34 Kilkeel (GB) 49 Sd 36
Kilkenny = Cill Chainnigh (IRL) 49 Sc 38
61100 Kilkís (GR) 86 Cc 50
Killaloe = Cill Dalua (IRL) 49 Sb 38
Killarney = Cill Airne (IRL) 49 Sa 38
Killenaule = Cill Náile (IRL) 49 Sc 38
57200 Killik (TR) 96 Ci 52
Killinge (S) 14 Ca 23
34980 Killinkoski (FIN) 22 Cd 28
Killorglin = Cill Orglan (IRL) 49 Sa 38
Killybegs = Na Ceala Beaga (IRL) 49 Sb 36
KA3 Kilmarnock (GB) 51 Sf 35
PA34 Kilmelfort (GB) 50 Se 34
Kil'mez' (RUS) 46 Fb 33
Kil'mez' (RUS) 46 Fb 34
Kil'mez', Ust'- (RUS) 46 Fa 34
99460 Kilpisjärvi (FIN) 14 Ca 21
Kilp'javr (RUS) 16 Dc 21
BT51 Kilrea (GB) 49 Sd 36
Kilronan = Cill Rónáin (IRL) 49 Sa 37

180 I **Karabanovo**

Kilrush = Cill Rois (IRL) 49 Sa 38
Kilvik (N) 14 Bd 24
34003 Kími (GR) 94 Ce 52
25700* Kimito = Kemiö (FIN) 30 Cc 30
Kimovaara (RUS) 23 Db 27
Kimovsk (RUS) 43 Di 37
Kimry (RUS) 43 Dh 34
Kimža (RUS) 25 Ee 25
KW11 Kinbrace (GB) 50 Sg 32
8650* Kindberg (A) 70 Bf 43
Kindelja (RUS) 63 Fd 39
Kinel' (RUS) 46 Fa 37
Kinelahti (RUS) 31 Dc 29
Kinel'-Čerkasy (RUS) 46 Fb 37
Kinešma (RUS) 33 Ec 33
Kingisepp (RUS) 31 Ci 31
PE30 King's Lynn (GB) 51 Aa 38
HU1 Kingston upon Hull (GB) 51 Sk 37
PH21 Kingussie (GB) 50 Sf 33
Kınık (TR) 88 Ch 51
Kınık (TR) 96 Ck 54
PH16 Kinloch Rannoch (GB) 50 Sf 34
51100* Kinna (S) 29 Bc 33
52103 Kinnarp (S) 29 Bd 32
Kinnegad = Cionn Átha Gad (IRL) 49 Sc 37
43901 Kinnula (FIN) 22 Ce 27
Kinsale = Cionn Sáile (IRL) 49 Sb 39
5780 Kinsarvik (N) 28 Ag 30
Kinvarra = Cinn Mhara (IRL) 49 Sb 37
Kionia (CY) 97 Dd 56
24500 Kiparissía (GR) 94 Cb 53
Kipelovo (RUS) 33 Dk 31
Kipen' (RUS) 31 Ck 31
Kipievo (RUS) 26 Fe 25
93140 Kipinä (FIN) 22 Cg 25
51031 Kipouríou (GR) 86 Cb 51
40009 Kipséli (GR) 86 Ce 51
Kipti (UA) 59 Db 39
Kıraçtepe (TR) 91 Ea 51
Kirav (BY) 59 Da 39
Kiravsk (BY) 42 Ck 37
35890 Kiraz (TR) 95 Ci 52
Kirazlı (TR) 87 Cg 50
06733 Kırbaşı (TR) 88 Db 50
22260 Kırcasalih (TR) 87 Cg 49
91281 Kirchenthumbach (D) 55 Bb 41
35274 Kirchhain (D) 54 Ai 40
73230 Kirchheim unter Teck (D) 54 Ak 42
Kırdamı (TR) 91 Ed 50
Kirdasovo (RUS) 47 Fi 37
Kireç (TR) 88 Ci 51
Kireevsk (RUS) 43 Dh 37
42696 Kıreli (TR) 96 Db 53
Kirgišany (RUS) 47 Fk 34
Kirgiz-Mijaki (RUS) 46 Fe 37
32006 Kiriáki (GR) 94 Cc 52
39750 Kırık (TR) 89 Dd 49
39750 Kırık (TR) 91 Ea 50
31440 Kırıkhan (TR) 97 Dg 54
71000* Kırıkkale (TR) 89 Dd 51
Kirillov (RUS) 32 Di 31
Kiriši (RUS) 31 Dc 31
Kırızlı (TR) 97 Df 53
Kirja (RUS) 45 Eg 35
Kirjabinskoe (RUS) 47 Fk 36
Kir'jamo (RUS) 31 Ci 31
Kırka (TR) 88 Da 51
45700 Kırkağaç (TR) 88 Ch 51
LA6 Kirkby Lonsdale (GB) 51 Sh 36
CA17 Kirkby Stephen (GB) 51 Sh 36
KY1 Kirkcaldy (GB) 50 Sg 34
DG6 Kirkcudbright (GB) 51 Sf 36
4330 Kirke Hvalsø (DK) 39 Bb 35
2260 Kirkenær (N) 29 Bc 30
9900 Kirkenes (N) 16 Da 21
65930 Kırkgeçit (TR) 99 Ed 52
Kırkışla (TR) 96 Dc 52
880 Kirkjubæjarklaustur (IS) 48 Rb 27
39000* Kırklareli (TR) 88 Ch 49
KW15 Kirkwall (GB) 50 Sh 32
Kırmızıköprü (TR) 90 Dk 51
Kiroba (RUS) 75 Dk 47
33975 Kırobası (TR) 97 Dd 54
Kirov (RUS) 34 Ek 32
Kirov (RUS) 43 De 36
Kirovgrad (RUS) 36 Ga 33
Kirovhrad (RUS) 36 Ga 33
Kirovo-Čepeck (RUS) 34 Fa 32
Kirovohrad = Kropyvnyc'kyj (UA) 59 Dc 42
Kirovsk (RUS) 31 Db 31
Kirovsk (RUS) 16 Dd 23
Kirovskaja (RUS) 76 Ea 44
Kirovs'ke (UA) 60 Di 42
Kirovs'ke 74 Df 45
Kirovskij (RUS) 77 Ei 45
Kirovskoe (RUS) 36 Gc 32
Kirpil'skaja (RUS) 75 Dk 45
DD8 Kirriemuir (GB) 50 Sg 34
Kirs (RUS) 35 Fc 31
Kirsa (RUS) 47 Fk 37
Kirsanov (RUS) 61 Ec 38
40000* Kırşehir (TR) 89 De 51
Kirteli (RUS) 45 Ei 36
98101* Kiruna (S) 14 Ca 23
Kirušca (RUS) 61 Ea 39
Kiržač (RUS) 43 Dg 34
59040 Kisa (S) 29 Bf 33
Kısas (TR) 98 Di 53
2870 Kisbér (H) 71 Bi 43
Kiselëvka (RUS) 76 Ee 43
Kiseljak (BIH) 71 Bi 47
Kišert', Ust'- (RUS) 35 Fh 33
18-421 Kisielnica (PL) 41 Cc 37
2000 Kišinev = Chişinău (MD) 73 Ci 43
25470 Kisko (FIN) 30 Cd 30
Kiskőrös (H) 71 Bk 44
6100 Kiskunfélegyháza (H) 71 Bk 44
6400 Kiskunhalas (H) 71 Bk 44
6120 Kiskunmajsa (H) 71 Bk 44
Kışlaköy (TR) 91 Ec 50
Kisljakovskaja (RUS) 75 Dk 44
Kislovodsk (RUS) 76 Ec 47
Kissámou Kasteli (GR) 94 Cd 55
97688 Kissingen, Bad (D) 55 Ba 40
Kistanje (HR) 70 Bf 47
6760 Kistelek (H) 71 Bk 44
660 Kistufell (IS) 48 Rf 26
5310 Kisújszállás (H) 71 Ca 43
Kisvárda (H) 57 Cc 42
82501 Kitee (FIN) 23 Da 28
80100 Kíthira (GR) 94 Cc 54
84006 Kíthnos (GR) 94 Ce 53
Kitkiöjoki (S) 15 Cd 23
Kitlilä (FIN) 15 Ce 23
Kitsi (FIN) 23 Da 27
Kittelfjäll (S) 21 Bf 25
49570 Kitula (FIN) 30 Cd 30
6370 Kitzbühel (A) 69 Bc 43
97318 Kitzingen (D) 55 Ba 41
74701 Kiuruvesi (FIN) 22 Cg 27
Kiverci (UA) 58 Cf 40
Kiveriči (RUS) 32 Dg 33
88350 Kivesjärvi (FIN) 23 Ch 26
43800 Kivijärvi (FIN) 22 Cf 27
27701 Kivik (S) 39 Be 35
Kiviõli (EST) 30 Cg 31
Kıyıköy (TR) 88 Ci 49
Kizel (RUS) 35 Fh 31
Kizema (RUS) 33 Ee 29
Kızılabalı (TR) 89 De 48
Kızılağaç (TR) 99 Eb 52
Kızılburç (TR) 98 Di 53
Kızılcabölük (TR) 96 Ck 53
07820 Kızılcadağ (TR) 96 Ck 53
06890 Kızılcahamam (TR) 89 Dc 50
Kızılçakır (TR) 96 Dc 53
37400 Kızılcaören (TR) 88 Da 51
18280 Kızılırmak (TR) 89 Dd 50
Kızılkaya (TR) 96 Da 53
Kızılören (TR) 96 Da 52
Kızılören (TR) 96 Dc 53
07610 Kızılot (TR) 96 Db 54
73200 Kızılsu (TR) 99 Ec 53
Kızıltepe (TR) 99 Ea 53
Kizner (RUS) 46 Fb 34
Kızören (TR) 97 Dd 52
Kiz'va (RUS) 35 Fe 32
Kjanda (RUS) 24 Di 26
8543 Kjeldebotn (N) 14 Bg 22
8620 Kjellerup (DK) 38 Ak 34
Kjellmyra (N) 29 Bc 30
9790 Kjøllefjord (N) 15 Ch 20
8590 Kjøpsvik (N) 14 Bg 22
2500* Kjustendil (BG) 86 Cc 48
Kladanj (BIH) 71 Bi 46
Kladnica (SRB) 71 Ca 47
272 01 Kladno (CZ) 55 Be 40
19320 Kladovo (SRB) 71 Cc 46
7540 Klæbu (N) 20 Ba 27
9020* Klagenfurt am Wörthersee (A) 70 Be 44
91001* Klaipėda (LT) 40 Cb 35
700 Klaksvík (FO) 50 Sd 28
339 01 Klatovy (CZ) 55 Bd 41
Klavdijevo-Tarasove (UA) 59 Da 40
Kleck (BY) 41 Cg 37
62-540 Kleczew (PL) 56 Bi 38
23996 Kleinen, Bad (D) 39 Bb 37
3660* Klein-Pöchlarn (A) 56 Bf 42
6453 Kleive (N) 20 Ah 28
Klement'evo (RUS) 32 Di 33
Klemušino (RUS) 25 Ec 28
Klenovaja (RUS) 34 Eg 31
Klënovo (RUS) 35 Fe 33
Klenovskoe (RUS) 47 Fi 34
4352 Kleppe-Verdalen (N) 28 Af 32
Klesiv (UA) 58 Cg 39
Kletnja (RUS) 43 Dd 37
Kletskij (RUS) 61 Ed 41
Kletsko-Počtovskij (RUS) 61 Ed 41
Klevakinskoe (RUS) 47 Gb 34
47533 Kleve (D) 54 Ag 39
Kličav (BY) 42 Ck 37
Klimatino (RUS) 32 Dh 33
Klimavičy (BY) 42 Db 37
9150 Klimentovo (BG) 73 Ch 47
Klimkovka (RUS) 34 Fb 32
Klimovsk (RUS) 43 Dh 35
91298 Klimpfjäll (S) 21 Be 25
Klin (RUS) 43 Dg 34
32000 Klina (SRB) 71 Ca 47
Klincovka (RUS) 62 Ek 39
Klincy (RUS) 42 Dc 38
08248 Klingenthal (Sachsen) (D) 55 Bc 40
Klinskoe (RUS) 43 De 38
62020 Klintehamn (S) 29 Bi 33
26401 Klippan (S) 39 Bd 34
2600 Klirou (CY) 97 Dd 55
4341 Klisura (BG) 87 Cd 48
4341 Klisura (BG) 87 Ce 48
Kljavino (RUS) 46 Fc 36
Ključ (BIH) 70 Bg 46
Ključevka (RUS) 64 Ff 39
Ključevsk (RUS) 36 Ga 33
Ključi (RUS) 36 Gc 33
Ključi (RUS) 46 Fa 34
Ključišči (RUS) 44 Ed 35
Kljukino (RUS) 34 Eg 32
66-415 Kłodawa (PL) 56 Bi 38
57-300 Kłodzko (PL) 56 Bg 40
Kløfta (N) 28 Bb 30
5378 Klokkarvik (N) 28 Af 30
Klos (AL) 86 Ca 49
3400* Klosterneuburg (A) 56 Bg 42
7250 Klosters (CH) 69 Ak 44
38486 Klötze (D) 55 Bb 38
Klöverstrask (S) 22 Cb 25
84032 Klövsjö (S) 21 Be 28
46-200 Kluczbork (PL) 56 Bi 40
23948 Klütz (D) 39 Bb 37
Klymovo (RUS) 59 Dc 38
Knaben (N) 28 Ah 32
91050 Knaften (S) 21 Bi 26
31020 Knäred (S) 39 Bd 34
HG5 Knaresborough (GB) 51 Si 36
5911 Knarvik (N) 28 Af 30
5835 Kneža (BG) 72 Ce 47
34240 Knić (SRB) 71 Ca 47
48980 Knidos (TR) 95 Cg 54
LD7 Knighton (GB) 52 Sg 38
Knin (HR) 70 Bg 46
8720 Knittelfeld (A) 70 Be 43
Knjaginino (RUS) 45 Ef 35
19350 Knjaževac (SRB) 71 Cc 47
6566 Knjaževo (BG) 87 Cg 48
Knjaževo (RUS) 33 Ed 31
Knjaževo (RUS) 33 Ee 32
Knjazevo (RUS) 42 Ci 34
Knjažiha (RUS) 32 Dg 33
Knjažiha (RUS) 45 Eg 35
Knocklong (IRL) 49 Sb 38
8300 Knokke-Heist (B) 53 Ad 39
19-120 Knyszyn (PL) 41 Cc 37
5222 Kobarid (SLO) 69 Bd 44
Kobel'aky (UA) 59 De 41
1000* København (DK) 39 Bc 35
55-040 Kobierzyce (PL) 56 Bg 40
56068* Koblenz (D) 54 Ah 40
Kobleve (UA) 74 Db 44
Kobona (RUS) 31 Db 30
Koboža (RUS) 32 De 32
Koboža (RUS) 32 Df 32
Kobra (RUS) 34 Fa 30
Kobryn (BY) 57 Ce 38
54800 Kocaali (TR) 88 Da 49
15325 Kocaaliler (TR) 96 Da 53
Kocaeli (TR) 88 Ck 50
Kocakoç (TR) 90 Dk 51
Koçali (TR) 98 Di 53
2300* Kočani (MK) 86 Cc 49
33940 Kocapınar (TR) 91 Ed 51
09970 Koçarlı (TR) 95 Ch 53
Koçaş (TR) 97 Dd 52
Kocatepe (TR) 99 Ea 53
Koceljeva (SRB) 71 Bk 46
2640 Kočerinovo (BG) 87 Cd 48
Kočeriv (UA) 58 Ck 40
Kočetovka (RUS) 44 Ea 38
1330 Kočevje (SLO) 70 Be 45
Kočevo (RUS) 35 Fe 31
Kocjubyns'ke (UA) 59 Da 40
21-150 Kock (PL) 57 Cc 39
Kočkarlej (RUS) 45 Eh 37
Kočkoma (RUS) 24 De 26
Kočkurovo (RUS) 45 Ef 36
Koçoğlu (TR) 91 Ec 51
Kočubeevskoe (RUS) 76 Eb 46
Kočubej (RUS) 77 Eg 46
Kočunovo (RUS) 45 Ee 35
Kočury (RUS) 44 Dk 37
Kodino (RUS) 24 Dk 27
Kodyma (UA) 58 Ck 42
39700 Kofçaz (TR) 88 Ch 49
7735 Kofinou (CY) 97 Dd 56
8580* Köflach (A) 70 Bf 43
4600 Køge (DK) 39 Bc 35
Koğukçınar (TR) 98 Dg 53
79801 Kohila (EST) 30 Ce 31
Kohma (RUS) 44 Eb 34
30321* Kohtla-Järve (EST) 31 Ch 31
74301 Koirakosk (FIN) 23 Ch 27
95355 Koivu (FIN) 22 Cf 24
Kojanovo (RUS) 35 Fg 33
Kojda (RUS) 17 Ec 24
752 01 Kojetín (CZ) 56 Bh 41
Kojgorodok (RUS) 34 Fb 30
Kojnas (RUS) 25 Eh 26
22730 Kökar (AX) 30 Ca 31
Kokino (RUS) 34 Ek 32
34200 Kokinombléa (GR) 94 Cd 52
67100* Kokkola (FIN) 22 Cd 27
5113 Koknese (LV) 41 Cf 34
Kokornaja (RUS) 25 Ee 26
Kokovka (RUS) 24 Dk 28
Kokšajsk (RUS) 45 Eh 34
Kola (RUS) 16 Dd 22
95901 Kolari (FIN) 15 Cd 23
946 03 Kolárovo (SK) 70 Bh 43
83005 Kolåsen (S) 21 Bc 27
81 210 Kolašin (MNE) 86 Bk 48
Kolatsel'ga (RUS) 23 Dc 29
73040 Kolbäck (S) 29 Bg 31
356 Kolbeinsstaðir (IS) 48 Qh 26
05-340 Kołbiel (PL) 57 Cb 38
36-100 Kolbuszowa (PL) 57 Cb 40
Kol'covo (RUS) 47 Ga 34
Kol'čugino (RUS) 44 Dk 34
6000 Kolding (DK) 38 Ak 35
Kolenovskij, Elan'- (RUS) 61 Eb 39
94203 Kolerträsk (S) 22 Ca 25
Koležma (RUS) 24 Df 26
70301 Kolga-Jaani (EST) 30 Cf 32
5313 Kolibaşi = Colibaşi (MD) 73 Ci 45
280 02 Kolín (CZ) 56 Bf 40
Kolisne (UA) 73 Ck 44
Koljadivka (UA) 60 Dk 41
3275 Kolka (LV) 30 Cc 33
Kolkač (RUS) 32 Di 31
Kolky (UA) 58 Cf 39
99625 Kölleda (D) 55 Bb 39
780 Kollumulí (IS) 48 Rf 25
50667* Köln (D) 54 Ag 40
18-500 Kolno (PL) 40 Cb 37
97-320 Koło (PL) 56 Bi 38
97-320 Koło (PL) 56 Bk 39
Kolobovo (RUS) 44 Eb 34
78-100 Kołobrzeg (PL) 39 Bf 36
Koločava (UA) 57 Cd 42
Kolodez', Kon'- (RUS) 60 Dk 38
Kolodezne (UA) 60 Dh 41
Kolodino (RUS) 33 Dk 32
Kolodnoe (RUS) 60 Dg 39
Kologriv (RUS) 33 Ee 32
Kolokolčovka (RUS) 61 Ee 39
Kolomak (UA) 60 Df 41
Kolomna (RUS) 43 Di 35
Kolomyja (UA) 58 Cf 42
Kolpakskoe (RUS) 64 Fi 39
Kolpino (RUS) 31 Da 31
Kolpny (RUS) 60 Dh 38
Kolševo (RUS) 33 Eb 33
Kolsillre (S) 21 Bf 28
73030 Kolsva (S) 29 Bf 31
Koltubanovskij (RUS) 46 Fb 38
42805 Kolukısa (TR) 96 Dc 52
7970 Kolvereid (N) 20 Bb 26
Kolvica (RUS) 16 Dd 23
Kolyčivka (UA) 59 Db 39
Kolyšlej (RUS) 45 Ee 38
13050 Komaran = Komorane (RKS) 86 Ca 48
Komariči (RUS) 59 De 38
Komariha (RUS) 34 Eg 32
Komariha (RUS) 35 Fg 32
Komarne (UA) 57 Cd 41
945 01 Komárno (SK) 71 Bi 43
2900 Komárom (H) 71 Bi 43
Komintern (RUS) 64 Fk 38
Kominternivs'ke = Dobroslav (UA) 73 Da 44
Komiža (HR) 85 Bg 47
7300 Komló (H) 71 Bi 44
Kommuna (RUS) 26 Fc 27
Kommunar (RUS) 35 Fe 32
Kommunarsk = Alčevs'k (UA) 60 Di 42
13050 Komorane = Komaran (RKS) 86 Ca 48
Komorevo (RUS) 43 Dg 37
69101 Komotiní (GR) 87 Cf 49
Kompanijivka (UA) 59 Dc 42
3800 Komrat = Comrat (MD) 73 Ci 44
Komsomol'sk (RUS) 44 Ea 33
Komsomol'skij (RUS) 23 Dd 25
Komsomol'skij (RUS) 36 Gd 29
Komsomol'skij (RUS) 45 Ef 36
Komsomol'skij (RUS) 65 Ga 39
Komsomol'skij (RUS) 19 Gd 23
Komsomol'skij (RUS) 77 Eg 45
Komsomol'sk-na-Pečore (RUS) 27 Fg 28
Komsomol'skoe (RUS) 31 Ci 30
Komsomol'skoe (RUS) 62 Eh 40
Kömürlimanı (TR) 87 Cf 50
Kömürlü (TR) 91 Ec 50
Komyši (UA) 59 De 40
Komyšna (UA) 59 Dd 40
Konakovo (RUS) 43 Dg 34
Konakpınar (TR) 88 Ch 51
Konakpınar (TR) 98 Dh 52
Končanica (HR) 70 Bh 45
81400 Kondiás (GR) 87 Cf 51
Kondol' (RUS) 45 Ef 38
Kondopoga (RUS) 24 De 28
Kondratovskaja (RUS) 25 Ed 28
Kondrovo (RUS) 43 Df 36
Konecbor (RUS) 27 Fh 26
Konecgor'e (RUS) 25 Ed 28
Konevo (RUS) 24 Dk 28
99950 Köngäs (FIN) 15 Cf 21
9293 Kongerslev (DK) 39 Ba 34
44401 Konginkangas (FIN) 22 Cf 28
3610* Kongsberg (N) 28 Ak 31
Kongselva (N) 14 Bf 22
7976 Kongsmoen (N) 21 Bc 26
2208* Kongsvinger (N) 29 Bc 30
01936 Königsbrück (D) 55 Bd 39
97631 Königshofen im Grabfeld, Bad (D) 55 Ba 40
15711 Königs Wusterhausen (D) 55 Bd 38
62-500 Konin (PL) 56 Bi 38
Konispol (AL) 86 Ca 51
44100 Kónitsa (GR) 86 Ca 50
Konjic (BIH) 70 Bh 47
Kon'-Kolodez' (RUS) 60 Dk 38
06420 Könnern (D) 55 Bb 39
Konobeevo (RUS) 43 Di 35
Konoša (RUS) 33 Ea 30
Konotop (UA) 59 Dd 39
Konša (RUS) 34 Fb 29
26-200 Końskie (PL) 57 Ca 39
Konstantinovka (RUS) 46 Fa 34
Konstantinovka = Južnoukrains'k (UA) 74 Db 43
Konstantinovo (RUS) 43 Di 34
Konstantinovsk (RUS) 76 Eb 43
Konstantinovskij (RUS) 33 Dk 33
78462* Konstanz (D) 69 Ak 43
81101 Kontiolahti (FIN) 23 Ck 28
76150 Kontiomäki (FIN) 23 Ci 26
95760 Konttajärvi (FIN) 15 Ce 24
14450 Konuralp (TR) 88 Db 50
42000* Konya (TR) 96 Dc 53
Konyševka (RUS) 60 Df 39
Kopačevo (RUS) 25 Eb 27
Kopajhorod (UA) 58 Ch 42
Kopanovka (RUS) 77 Eg 43
Kopanskaja (RUS) 75 Di 44
671 Kópasker (IS) 48 Rd 24
200* Kópavogur (IS) 48 Qi 26
Kopejsk (RUS) 47 Gb 35
6000* Koper (SLO) 69 Bd 45
4250 Kopervik (N) 28 Af 31
73101* Köping (S) 29 Bf 31
Koplik (AL) 86 Bk 48
89302 Köpmanholmen (S) 21 Bi 27
Kopor'e (RUS) 31 Ck 31
2480 Koppang (N) 28 Bb 29
71401 Kopparberg (S) 29 Be 31
Kopparnäs (S) 22 Cb 25
99801 Koppelo (FIN) 15 Ch 22
7533 Kopperå (N) 20 Bb 27
Koprivnica (HR) 70 Bg 44
2077 Koprivštica (BG) 87 Ce 48
Köprübaşı (TR) 89 Df 49
Köprübaşı (TR) 91 Ea 50
Köprübaşı (TR) 96 Ci 52
Köprülü (TR) 96 Dc 54
Köprüören (TR) 88 Ck 51
Kopsa (RUS) 34 Ek 29
Koptevo (RUS) 43 De 35
Kopyčynci (UA) 58 Cf 41
Korablino (RUS) 44 Ea 37
Korača (RUS) 60 Dh 40
Koraj (BIH) 71 Bi 46
34497 Korbach (D) 54 Ai 39
Korbeniči (RUS) 32 De 30
Korçë (AL) 86 Ca 50
Korčula (HR) 85 Bh 48
Kordon (RUS) 35 Fh 33
Kordon (RUS) 37 Gk 33
Korec' (UA) 58 Ch 40
Korenevo (RUS) 59 De 39
Korenica (HR) 70 Bf 46
Korenovsk (RUS) 75 Dk 45
Korepino (RUS) 35 Fh 29
20004 Kórfos (GR) 94 Cd 53
52700 Korgan (TR) 90 Dh 50
8646 Korgen (N) 21 Bd 24
18260 Korgun (TR) 89 Dd 50
Körhasan (TR) 88 Db 51
Korino (RUS) 33 Ea 31
20100 Kórinthos (GR) 94 Cc 53
84002 Korissía (GR) 94 Ce 53
Korjažma (RUS) 34 Eh 29
Korjukivka (UA) 59 Dc 39
Korkino (RUS) 47 Gb 36
49740 Korkut (TR) 99 Eb 52
07800 Korkuteli (TR) 96 Da 53
48900 Körmen (TR) 95 Ch 54
9900 Körmend (H) 70 Bg 43
Kormovišče (RUS) 36 Fi 33
2100* Korneuburg (A) 56 Bg 42
62-035 Kórnik (PL) 56 Bh 38
Kornouhovo (RUS) 45 Ek 35
1796 Kornsjø (N) 28 Bb 32
Korolevskaja (RUS) 33 Ee 30
24004 Koróni (GR) 94 Cb 54
Koronissía (GR) 86 Ca 51
86-010 Koronowo (PL) 40 Bh 37

A B C D E F G H I J K L M N O P Q R S T U V W X Y Z

Koronowo | 181

Korop (UA) 59 Dc 39
Korošilovo (RUS) 60 Di 39
Korosten' (UA) 58 Ci 40
Korostyn' (RUS) 31 Da 32
Korostyšiv (UA) 58 Ck 40
Koroteckaja (RUS) 32 Di 30
Koroviha (RUS) 33 Ee 33
Korpikå (S) 22 Cd 25
41801 Korpilahti (FIN) 22 Cf 28
98060 Korpilombolo (S) 15 Cd 24
21720 Korpo (FIN) 30 Cb 30
21720 Korppoo = Korpo (FIN) 30 Cb 30
Korsberga (S) 29 Bf 33
Korševo (RUS) 61 Ea 39
Koršik (RUS) 34 Ek 32
82042 Korskrogen (S) 21 Bf 29
66201 Korsnäs (FIN) 22 Cb 28
4220 Korsør (DK) 39 Bb 35
Korsun'-Ševčenkivskyj (UA) 59 Db 41
62421 Kortesjärvi (FIN) 22 Cd 27
Kortkeros (RUS) 34 Fb 29
8500 Kortrijk (B) 53 Ad 40
57200 Korucu (TR) 88 Ch 51
Kõruse (EST) 30 Cb 32
768 05 Koryčany (CZ) 56 Bh 41
16-140 Korycin (PL) 41 Cd 37
Korževka (RUS) 45 Eg 36
85300 Kós (GR) 95 Ch 54
Kosa (RUS) 35 Ff 31
Kosaja Gora (RUS) 43 Dh 36
Kosava (BY) 41 Cf 38
64-000 Kościan (PL) 56 Bg 38
83-400 Kościerzyna (PL) 40 Bh 36
75101 Kose (EST) 30 Cf 31
29650 Köse (TR) 90 Dk 50
Köseali (TR) 96 Ci 52
Kösehasan (TR) 91 Ec 51
25500 Köseler (TR) 87 Cg 51
25500 Köseler (TR) 96 Da 53
06628 Kösen, Bad (D) 55 Bb 39
42280 Kösere (TR) 97 De 53
Košezabl' (RUS) 76 Ea 46
040 01* Košice (SK) 57 Cb 42
Kosino (RUS) 32 Di 31
Kosino (RUS) 34 Fb 32
Kosiv (UA) 58 Cf 42
31260 Kosjerić (SRB) 71 Bk 46
Köşk (TR) 96 Ci 53
07700 Koskenkylä = Forsby (FIN) 30 Cf 30
41901 Koskenpää (FIN) 22 Cf 28
16710 Koski (FIN) 30 Cd 30
Koški (RUS) 26 Fa 28
Koški (RUS) 46 Fa 36
Koškino (RUS) 46 Fa 34
Koskolovo (RUS) 31 Ci 31
Kos'kovo (RUS) 32 Dd 30
61720 Koskue (FIN) 22 Cc 28
Koskul' (RUS) 65 Gb 39
98303 Koskullskulle (S) 14 Ca 23
Koslan (RUS) 26 Ei 27
Košmaki (RUS) 36 Gc 31
Kosolapovo (RUS) 45 Ek 34
Kosorža (RUS) 60 Dg 38
Kosovska Mitrovica = Mitrovicë (RKS) 86 Ca 48
Kospašskij, Central'no- (RUS) 35 Fh 31
Kospašskij, Severo- (RUS) 35 Fh 31
Kösreli (TR) 97 Df 53
21061 Kósta (GR) 94 Cd 53
Kostajnica (HR) 70 Bg 45
Kost'antynivka = Južnoukrains'k (UA) 74 Db 43
517 41 Kostelec nad Orlicí (CZ) 56 Bg 40
2030 Kostenec (BG) 87 Cd 48
2230 Kostinbrod (BG) 87 Cd 48
Kostino (RUS) 36 Gc 33
Kostjantynivka (UA) 60 Dh 42
Kostjušino (RUS) 33 Ea 33
Kostobobriv (UA) 59 Dc 38
12208 Kostolac (SRB) 71 Cb 46
Kostomukša (RUS) 23 Da 26
Kostopil' (UA) 58 Cg 40
Kostroma (RUS) 33 Ea 33
66-470 Kostrzyn nad Odrą (PL) 55 Be 38
Kostyri (RUS) 43 Dd 36
Košuki (RUS) 37 Gf 33
75-900 Koszalin (PL) 40 Bg 36
42-286 Koszęcin (PL) 56 Bi 40
Kőszeg (H) 70 Bg 43
32-130 Koszyce (PL) 57 Ca 40
Kotë (AL) 86 Bk 50
Kötek (TR) 91 Ed 50
8970 Kotel (BG) 87 Cg 48
Kotel'nič (RUS) 34 Ei 32
Kotel'nikovo (RUS) 76 Ed 43
Kotel'nja (UA) 58 Ck 40
Kotel'va (UA) 59 De 40
06366 Köthen (Anhalt) (D) 55 Bb 39
89140 Kotila (FIN) 23 Ch 26
48100* Kotka (FIN) 30 Cg 30
Kotkino (RUS) 18 Fb 23
Kotlas (RUS) 34 Eg 29
Kotly (RUS) 31 Ci 31
85 330 Kotor (MNE) 86 Bi 48
Kotorsko (BIH) 71 Bi 46
Kotor Varoš (BIH) 70 Bh 46
Kotovo (RUS) 47 Fk 35
Kotovo (RUS) 61 Ee 40
Kotovsk (RUS) 61 Eb 38
Kotovs'k = Podil's'k (UA) 73 Ck 43
Kotovsk = Hînceşti (MD) 73 Ci 44
23066 Kótronas (GR) 94 Cc 54
9640* Kötschach-Mauthen (A) 69 Bc 44
93444 Kötzting, Bad (D) 55 Bc 41
57100 Koufália (GR) 86 Cc 50
8500 Kouklia (CY) 96 Dc 56
84005 Koutalás (GR) 94 Ce 53
72200 Koutsourás (GR) 95 Cf 55
45201 Kouvola (FIN) 30 Cg 30
26210 Kovačica (SRB) 71 Ca 45
Kovalëvo (RUS) 42 Dc 34
23850 Kovancılar (TR) 98 Dk 52
28310 Kovanlık (TR) 90 Di 50
Kovarzino (RUS) 32 Di 30
Kovda (RUS) 16 Dc 24
Kovdor (RUS) 16 Da 23
Kovel' = Kovil' (UA) 57 Ce 39
Kovera (RUS) 32 Dd 29
Kovernino (RUS) 33 Ed 33
82710 Kovero (FIN) 23 Da 28
Kovilovo (SRB) 71 Cc 46
26220 Kovin (SRB) 71 Ca 46
Kovkula (RUS) 24 Dk 27
Kovrigino (RUS) 33 Ed 33
Kovrov (RUS) 44 Eb 34
Kovylkino (RUS) 44 Ed 36
87-410 Kowalewo Pomorskie (PL) 40 Bi 37
58-530 Kowary (PL) 56 Bf 40
Köyceğiz (TR) 96 Ci 54
58660 Koyulhisar (TR) 90 Dh 50
Koyunağılı (TR) 88 Db 51
66540 Koyunculu (TR) 89 Df 50
Koyunlu (TR) 98 Dh 52
Koza (RUS) 33 Dk 32
29700 Kozağaç (TR) 90 Dk 50
35710 Kozak (TR) 87 Ch 51
50600 Kozaklı (TR) 89 De 51
54910* Kozan (TR) 97 Df 53
50100 Kozáni (GR) 86 Cb 50
42790 Kozanlı (TR) 89 Dc 51
Kozarac (BIH) 70 Bg 46
Kozcağa (TR) 89 Dc 49
Kozdinga (RUS) 25 Eh 27
Kozelec' (UA) 59 Db 40
Kozel'sk (RUS) 43 Df 36
26-900 Kozienice (PL) 57 Cb 39
Kozjatyn (UA) 58 Ci 41
47-200 Koźle, Kędzierzyn- (PL) 56 Bi 40
Kozlina (RUS) 33 Ea 30
3320 Kozloduj (BG) 72 Cd 47
Kozlovka (RUS) 45 Ei 35
Kozlovka (RUS) 61 Eb 39
Kozlovo (RUS) 33 Dk 30
67600 Kozlu (TR) 88 Db 49
67600 Kozlu (TR) 90 Dg 50
46000 Kozludere (TR) 98 Dh 53
Kozluk (TR) 99 Eb 52
Kozly (RUS) 24 Dk 25
63-720 Koźmin Wielkopolski (PL) 56 Bh 39
Koz'modem'jansk (RUS) 45 Eg 34
Kozova (UA) 58 Cf 41
67-120 Kożuchów (PL) 56 Bf 39
Kožva (RUS) 27 Fg 25
Kožym (RUS) 27 Fk 25
Kräckelbäcken (S) 29 Be 29
3770 Kragerø (N) 28 Ak 32
34000* Kragujevac (SRB) 71 Ca 46
Kraj Bor (RUS) 33 Ec 31
Kraj Gorbatka (RUS) 44 Eb 35
74-500 Krajnik Dolny (PL) 39 Be 37
Kraj Oktjabr' (RUS) 44 Eb 34
Krakovec' (UA) 57 Cd 41
Krakovo (RUS) 46 Fa 37
30-023 Kraków (PL) 56 Bk 40
561 69 Králíky (CZ) 56 Bg 40
Kraljevica (HR) 70 Be 45
36000* Kraljevo (SRB) 71 Ca 47
027 51 Kral'ovany (SK) 56 Bk 41
331 41 Kralovice (CZ) 55 Bd 41
077 01 Král'ovský Chlmec (SK) 57 Cb 42
278 01 Kralupy nad Vltavou (CZ) 55 Be 40
Kramators'k (UA) 60 Dh 42
Kramatorsk = Kramators'k (UA) 60 Dh 42
87200 Kramfors (S) 21 Bh 28
Kranéa (GR) 86 Cb 51
21300 Kranídi (GR) 94 Cd 53
4000* Kranj (SLO) 70 Be 44
4280 Kranjska Gora (SLO) 69 Bd 44
Krapina (HR) 70 Bf 44
Krapivenskaja (RUS) 42 Dc 36
Krapivna (RUS) 43 Dh 37
Krapivnovo (RUS) 44 Ea 34
47-300 Krapkowice (PL) 56 Bh 40
Krasavino (RUS) 34 Eg 30
Krasino (RUS) 18 Fe 20
Krasivoe (RUS) 44 Ea 37
5601 Krāslava (LV) 42 Ch 35
Krasnae (BY) 42 Ch 36
Krasnaja (RUS) 25 Eg 28
Krasnaja Gora (BY) 42 Db 37
Krasnaja Gorka (RUS) 47 Fg 35
Krasnaja Jaruga (RUS) 60 Df 40
Krasnaja Poljana (RUS) 46 Fb 34
Krasnaja Poljana (RUS) 75 Ea 47
Krasnaja Rečka (RUS) 34 Fb 31
Krasnapolle (BY) 42 Db 37
Krasnij Log (RUS) 60 Dk 39
Krasnij Luč = Krasnyj Luč (UA) 60 Di 42
23-200 Kraśnik (PL) 57 Cc 40
Krasninskij (RUS) 47 Fk 37
Krasni Okny (UA) 73 Ck 43
Krasnoarmejsk (RUS) 43 Di 35
Krasnoarmejsk (RUS) 62 Ef 39
Krasnoarmejskaja (RUS) 75 Di 45
Krasnoarmejskoe (RUS) 63 Fa 38
Krasnoarmijs'k = Pokrovs'k (UA) 60 Dh 42
Krasnobarskij (RUS) 32 Df 31
Krasnoborsk (RUS) 34 Ef 29
Krasnodar (RUS) 75 Di 45
Krasnodon (UA) 60 Dk 42
Krasnoe (RUS) 34 Eh 31
Krasnoe (RUS) 42 Db 36
Krasnoe (RUS) 44 Di 38
Krasnoe-na-Volge (RUS) 33 Eb 33
Krasnoe Selo (RUS) 31 Da 31
Krasnogorodskoe (RUS) 42 Ci 34
Krasnogorsk (RUS) 43 Dh 35
Krasnogorskij (RUS) 45 Ei 34
Krasnogorskij (RUS) 47 Gb 36
Krasnogorskoe (RUS) 35 Fc 33
Krasnogvardejskij (RUS) 36 Gc 33
Krasnogvardejskoe (RUS) 76 Eb 45
Krasnoholm (RUS) 63 Fe 39
Krasnoholmskij (RUS) 46 Ff 35
Krasnohorivka (UA) 60 Dh 42
Krasnohrad (UA) 60 Df 41
Krasnohvardijs'ke 74 De 45
Krasnojarka (RUS) 36 Ga 31
Krasnojarskij (RUS) 64 Fk 39
Krasnojil's'k (UA) 58 Cf 42
Krasnokamsk (RUS) 35 Ff 32
Krasnokuts'k (UA) 60 Df 40
Krasnomajskij (RUS) 32 De 33
Krasnopartizanskij (RUS) 76 Ed 44
Krasnopavlivka (UA) 60 Dg 41
Krasnoperekops'k 74 Dd 45
Krasnopil'l'a (UA) 60 Df 40
Krasnoščel'e (RUS) 16 Dh 23
Krasnoselec (RUS) 62 Ef 41
Krasnoslobodsk (RUS) 44 Ed 36
Krasnoslobodsk (RUS) 61 Ee 42
Krasnotur'insk (RUS) 36 Ga 31
Krasnoufimsk (RUS) 47 Fh 34
Krasnoural'sk (RUS) 36 Ga 32
Krasnousol'skij (RUS) 47 Fg 37
Krasnovišersk (RUS) 35 Fh 30
Krasnozatoskij (RUS) 34 Fa 29
Krasnoznamensk (RUS) 41 Cc 36
Krasnye Baki (RUS) 34 Ef 33
Krasnye Barrikady (RUS) 77 Eh 44
Krasnye Tkači (RUS) 33 Dk 33
Krasnyj (RUS) 42 Db 36
Krasnyj Bor (RUS) 46 Fd 35
Krasnyj Holm (RUS) 34 Dh 32
Krasnyj Jar (RUS) 46 Fa 37
Krasnyj Jar (RUS) 61 Ee 40
Krasnyj Jar (RUS) 77 Ei 44
Krasnyj Ključ (RUS) 47 Fg 35
Krasnyj Kut (RUS) 62 Eh 40
Krasnyj Luč (RUS) 31 Da 33
Krasnyj Luč (UA) 60 Di 42
Krasnyj Lyman (UA) 60 Dh 42
Krasnyj Manyč (RUS) 76 Eb 44
Krasnyj Oktjabr' (RUS) 62 Ef 41
Krasnyj Ostrov (RUS) 45 Eg 35
Krasnyj Steklovat (RUS) 45 Ei 34
Krasnyj Sulin (RUS) 76 Ea 43
Krasnyj Zarja (RUS) 43 Dh 38
22-300 Krasnystaw (PL) 57 Cd 40
Krasuha (RUS) 32 Dd 33
Krasuha (RUS) 32 Df 32
Krasyliv (UA) 58 Cg 41
1360 Kratovo (MK) 86 Cc 48
33700 Kravga (TR) 97 Dd 54
Krečetovo (RUS) 32 Di 30
47798* Krefeld (D) 54 Ag 39
Kremenčug = Kremenčuk (UA) 59 Dd 41
Kremenčuk (UA) 59 Dd 41
Kremenec' (UA) 58 Cf 40
7224 Kremenica (MK) 86 Cb 50
Kreminci (UA) 57 Ce 42
Kreminna (UA) 60 Di 41
31242 Kremna (SRB) 71 Bk 47
967 01 Kremnica (SK) 56 Bi 42
3500* Krems an der Donau (A) 56 Bf 42
12316 Krepoljin (SRB) 71 Cb 46
2840 Kresna (BG) 87 Cd 49
Krestcy (RUS) 31 Dc 32
Krestcy (RUS) 32 Di 32
Krestovka (RUS) 18 Fc 24
Krestovo-Gorodišče (RUS) 45 Ei 36
Kresty (RUS) 34 Eg 33
Kresty (RUS) 43 Dh 35
Kresty (RUS) 43 Di 37
97001 Kretinga (LT) 40 Cb 35
55543* Kreuznach, Bad (D) 54 Ah 41
Krėva (BY) 41 Cg 36
58300 Kría Vríssi (GR) 86 Cc 50
4220 Kričim (BG) 87 Ce 48
8670* Krieglach (A) 70 Bf 43
5743 Krimml (A) 69 Bc 43
57091 Kristdala (S) 29 Bg 33
4601* Kristiansand (N) 28 Ah 32
29100* Kristianstad (S) 39 Be 34
6507 Kristiansund (N) 20 Ah 27
64100 Kristiinankaupunki = Kristinestad (FIN) 22 Cb 28
92037 Kristineberg (S) 21 Bi 25
68101* Kristinehamn (S) 29 Be 31
64100 Kristinestad (FIN) 22 Cb 28
85108 Kritinía (GR) 95 Ch 54
Kriuša (RUS) 34 Ei 33
Kriuša (RUS) 44 Dk 36
Kriuša (RUS) 44 Ed 35
Krivača (BIH) 85 Bi 48
17543 Kriva Feja (SRB) 86 Cc 48
1330 Kriva Palanka (MK) 86 Cc 48
Krivcy (RUS) 24 Dh 29
3060 Krivodol (BG) 72 Cd 47
Krivoe (RUS) 25 Eh 27
Krivojar (RUS) 62 Eg 40
Krivoj Rog = Krivyj Rih (UA) 74 Dd 43
Krivoles (RUS) 42 Dc 37
Krivorož'e (RUS) 61 Ea 42
Krivov (RUS) 61 Ec 42
Krivuševo (RUS) 26 Ek 27
Krivyj Rih (UA) 74 Dd 43
Križevci (HR) 70 Bg 44
Krjučkovka (RUS) 64 Ff 39
Krjukovo (RUS) 35 Ff 33
Krk (HR) 70 Be 45
Krnov (CZ) 56 Bh 40
3535 Krøderen (N) 28 Ak 30
Krohalevo (RUS) 35 Ff 32
60002 Krokek (S) 29 Bg 32
6877 Kroken (N) 21 Be 25
83501 Krokom (S) 21 Be 27
84-110 Krokowa (PL) 40 Bi 36
380 Króksfjarðarnes (IS) 48 Qi 25
92276 Kroksjö (S) 21 Bh 26
Krolevec' (UA) 59 Dd 39
767 01* Kroměříž (CZ) 56 Bh 41
Kromy (RUS) 43 Df 38
96317 Kronach (D) 55 Bb 40
68500* Kronoby (FIN) 22 Cd 27
Kronštadt (RUS) 31 Ck 31
Kronstadt = Kronštadt (RUS) 31 Ck 31
Kropačevo (RUS) 47 Fh 35
Kropotkin (RUS) 76 Ea 45
Kropyvnyc'kyj (UA) 59 Dc 42
99-340 Krośniewice (PL) 56 Bk 38
38-400 Krosno (PL) 57 Cb 41
66-600 Krosno Odrzańskie (PL) 56 Bf 38
63-700 Krotoszyn (PL) 56 Bh 39
Krrabë (AL) 86 Bk 49
8270 Krško (SLO) 70 Bf 45
Kruglyži (RUS) 34 Eh 32
Kruhlae (BY) 42 Ck 36
Krujë (AL) 86 Bk 49
86381 Krumbach (Schwaben) (D) 55 Ba 42
Krumë (AL) 86 Ca 48
6900 Krumovgrad (BG) 87 Cf 49
15314 Krupanj (SRB) 71 Bk 46
963 01 Krupina (SK) 56 Bk 42
Krupki (BY) 42 Ck 36
2740 Krupnik (BG) 87 Cd 49
8877 Krušare (BG) 87 Cg 48
9410 Krušari (BG) 73 Ch 47
37000* Kruševac (SRB) 71 Cb 47
8148 Kruševec (BG) 88 Ch 48
7550 Kruševo (MK) 86 Cb 49
5860 Krušovene (BG) 72 Ce 47
Krutec (RUS) 32 De 32
68500* Kruunupyy = Kronoby (FIN) 22 Cd 27
Kryčav (BY) 42 Db 37
77525* Krylbo (S) 29 Bg 30
Krylovka, Radica- (RUS) 43 De 37
Krylovo (RUS) 40 Cb 36
Krylovskaja (RUS) 75 Dk 44
Krylovskaja (RUS) 76 Ea 44
Krymgireevskoe (RUS) 76 Ec 46
Krymne (UA) 57 Ce 39
Krymsk (RUS) 75 Dh 46
Krynica-Zdrój (PL) 57 Ca 41
27-230 Krynki (PL) 41 Cd 37
Krynyčne (UA) 73 Ci 45
Kryvče (UA) 58 Cg 42
Kryve Ozero (UA) 73 Da 43
Kryvsk (BY) 59 Da 38
Kryžopil' (UA) 58 Ci 42
66-435 Krzeszyce (PL) 56 Bf 38
06-316 Krzynowłoga Mała (PL) 40 Ca 37
89-650 Krzyż (PL) 40 Bg 38
Kšenskij (RUS) 60 Dh 39
Kstovo (RUS) 45 Ee 34
44002 Ktíssmata (GR) 86 Ca 51
Kuba (RUS) 76 Ed 47
Kubenskoe (RUS) 33 Dk 31
Kubovo (RUS) 24 Dh 29
7300 Kubrat (BG) 72 Cg 47
Kubrinsk (RUS) 43 Di 34
Kučema (RUS) 25 Ec 25
Kučerla (RUS) 76 Ed 45
12240* Kučevo (SRB) 71 Cb 46
Kučmalka (RUS) 76 Ec 47
Kuçovë (AL) 86 Bk 50
Küçükbahçe (TR) 95 Cg 52
17700 Küçükkuyu (TR) 87 Cg 51
37270 Küçüksu (TR) 99 Ec 52
Kučurhan (UA) 73 Ck 44
Kudeevskij (RUS) 47 Fg 36
Kudever' (RUS) 42 Ck 34
71049 Kudirkos Naumiestis (LT) 41 Cc 36
Kudowa-Zdrój (PL) 56 Bg 40
Kudrino (RUS) 34 Ef 31
Kudymkar (RUS) 35 Fe 31
Kueda (RUS) 46 Ff 34
54470 Kues, Bernkastel- (D) 54 Ah 41
6330* Kufstein (A) 69 Bc 43
Kuganavolok (RUS) 24 Dg 28
Kugej (RUS) 75 Dk 44
Kugesi (RUS) 45 Eh 34
Kugoevskaja (RUS) 76 Ea 44
Kugul'ta (RUS) 76 Ec 45
Kugunur, Izi- (RUS) 45 Ei 34
Kugušerga (RUS) 34 Eh 33
97701 Kuha (FIN) 22 Cg 25
18225 Kühlungsborn (D) 39 Bb 36
36880 Kuhmalahti (FIN) 30 Ce 29
88901 Kuhmo (FIN) 23 Ck 26
17801 Kuhmoinen (FIN) 30 Cf 29
Kuhtinka (RUS) 43 Di 36
99831 Kuhtur = Kuttura (FIN) 15 Cg 22
19510 Kuivajärvi (FIN) 23 Da 26
95100 Kuivaniemi (FIN) 22 Cf 25
94702 Kuivastu (EST) 30 Cd 32
Kuja (RUS) 18 Fd 23
Kujbyschew = Samara (RUS) 46 Fa 37
Kujbyšev = Bulgar (RUS) 45 Ek 36
Kujbyšev = Samara (RUS) 46 Fa 37
Kujbyševe = Bil'mak (UA) 75 Dg 43
Kujbyševe (UA) 75 Dh 43
Kujbyševka (UA) 74 Dd 43
Kujbyševo (RUS) 75 Di 43
Kujbyševskij Zaton (RUS) 45 Ek 35
Kujman' (RUS) 44 Dk 38
Kukës (AL) 86 Ca 48
Kukmor (RUS) 46 Fa 34
Kukolivka (UA) 59 Dd 42
Kukuj (RUS) 31 Dc 31
Kukuštan (RUS) 35 Fg 33
3800* Kula (BG) 71 Cc 47
25230* Kula (SRB) 71 Bk 45
45170 Kula (TR) 96 Ci 52
Kulak (TR) 97 De 54
9361 Kulata (BG) 87 Cd 49
3301 Kuldīga (LV) 40 Cb 34
Kulebaki (RUS) 44 Ec 35
Kuleši (RUS) 43 Dh 38
Kulevči (RUS) 47 Gb 37
Kulgunino (RUS) 47 Fg 37
90024 Kuliai (LT) 40 Cb 35
Kuliga (RUS) 35 Fd 32
Kulikovka (RUS) 62 Eh 38
29340 Kullaa (FIN) 30 Cc 29
Küllük (TR) 91 Ed 51
95326 Kulmbach (D) 55 Bb 40
Kulmuksa (RUS) 24 De 28
Kulmyženskaja (RUS) 61 Ec 41
97960 Kuloharju (FIN) 23 Ci 25
Kuloj (RUS) 25 Ed 26
Kuloj (RUS) 33 Ec 29
Kulotino (RUS) 32 Dd 32
Kulozera (RUS) 25 Ef 27
21900 Kulp (TR) 99 Eb 52
Kul'šit (RUS) 45 Ek 34
42770 Kulu (TR) 89 Dd 51
Kuluevo (RUS) 47 Ga 35

182 | Korop

44760 Kuluncak (TR) 98 Dh 52
Kulykivka (UA) 59 Db 39
Kumačove (UA) 75 Di 43
Kumak (RUS) 65 Ga 39
1300* Kumanovo (MK) 86 Cb 48
Kümbet (TR) 88 Da 51
Kümbetli (TR) 91 Ed 50
32440 Kumdanlı (TR) 96 Da 52
Kumeny (RUS) 34 Ek 32
Kumertau (RUS) 46 Ff 38
Kuminskij (RUS) 37 Gf 32
17600 Kumkale (TR) 87 Cg 51
17900 Kumköy (TR) 88 Ck 49
Kumla (S) 29 Bf 31
22820 Kumlinge (AX) 30 Ca 30
31520 Kumlu (TR) 97 Dg 54
Kumluca (TR) 96 Da 54
25770 Kumluyazı (TR) 91 Eb 50
Kummavuopio (S) 14 Ca 22
Kumrovec (HR) 70 Bf 44
52800 Kumru (TR) 90 Dh 50
Kumskoj (RUS) 77 Eg 46
Kumyrsa (RUS) 46 Fd 34
Kuna (RUS) 35 Fe 31
Kunakbaevo (RUS) 47 Fk 36
Kunašak (RUS) 47 Gb 35
44106* Kunda (EST) 30 Cg 31
Kundravy (RUS) 47 Ga 36
19800 Kunduzlu (TR) 88 Da 51
Kun'e (UA) 60 Dh 41
44200 Kungälv (S) 28 Bb 33
43400* Kungsbacka (S) 29 Bc 33
81203 Kungsgården (S) 29 Bg 29
45601 Kungshamn (S) 28 Bb 32
73601 Kungsör (S) 29 Bg 31
Kungur (RUS) 35 Fh 33
5340 Kunhegyes (H) 71 Ca 43
Kun'ja (RUS) 35 Fg 32
Kun'ja (RUS) 42 Da 34
5321 Kunmadaras (H) 71 Ca 43
5440 Kunszentmárton (H) 71 Ca 44
6090 Kunszentmiklós (H) 71 Bk 43
74653 Künzelsau (D) 54 Ak 41
Kuolajarvi (RUS) 15 Ck 24
93999 Kuolio (FIN) 23 Ci 25
Kuollejaur (S) 22 Bk 24
70100* Kuopio (FIN) 23 Ch 28
63101 Kuortane (FIN) 22 Cd 28
52730 Kuortti (FIN) 30 Cg 29
Kuouka (S) 14 Ca 24
Kup'ans'k (UA) 60 Dh 41
Kupanskoe (RUS) 43 Di 34
37222 Kupci (SRB) 71 Cb 47
Kupčik (RUS) 35 Fg 30
Kupino (RUS) 60 Dh 40
40001 Kupiškis (LT) 41 Ce 35
Kup'jans'k-Vuzlovyi (UA) 60 Dh 41
11000 Küplü (TR) 87 Cg 49
4582 Kuprava (LV) 31 Ch 33
Kupreevo (RUS) 44 Eb 35
Kupres (BIH) 70 Bh 47
Kupurinskaja (RUS) 25 Ec 29
Kurachove (UA) 75 Dh 43
Kural (TR) 98 Di 53
Kurašim (RUS) 35 Fg 33
Kuratovo (RUS) 34 Ek 30
Kurba (RUS) 33 Dk 33
Kurčatovo (RUS) 60 Df 39
Kurdzinovo (RUS) 76 Ea 47
Kürecik (TR) 98 Dh 52
93101 Kurenalus = Pudasjärvi (FIN) 23 Ch 25
93811* Kuressaare (EST) 30 Cc 32
Kurganinsk (RUS) 76 Ea 46
Kurgenicy (RUS) 24 Df 28
Kurgolovo (RUS) 31 Ci 31
61301 Kurikka (FIN) 22 Cc 28
Kurilovka (RUS) 62 Ei 40
Kur'ja (RUS) 35 Fh 29
Kürkçü (TR) 97 De 53
Kurkiëki (RUS) 31 Ck 29
Kurkino (RUS) 43 Di 37
Kurlin (RUS) 63 Fa 39
Kurlovskij (RUS) 44 Ea 35
Kurmanaevka (RUS) 63 Fb 38
Kurmanava (BY) 42 Db 36
Kurmyš (RUS) 45 Eg 35
Kurne (UA) 58 Ci 40
Kurortne (UA) 73 Ck 45
Kurort Schmalkalden (D) 55 Ba 40
Kurovskoe (RUS) 43 Di 35
Kurovskoj (RUS) 43 Dg 36
Kurovyči (UA) 57 Ce 41
21-404 Kurów (PL) 57 Cc 39
Kurravaara (S) 14 Ca 23
Kursavka (RUS) 76 Ec 46
81001 Kuršėnai (LT) 41 Cc 34
Kursk (RUS) 60 Dg 39
Kurskaja (RUS) 76 Ee 47
98600 Kursu (FIN) 15 Ci 24
18430* Kuršumlija (SRB) 86 Cb 47
16900 Kurşunlu (TR) 88 Ci 50
16900 Kurşunlu (TR) 89 Dd 50
Kurşunlu (TR) 98 Dh 52
95990 Kurtakko (FIN) 15 Ce 23
29600 Kurtalan (TR) 99 Eb 53
42815 Kurthasanlı (TR) 96 Dc 52
Kurtkale (TR) 91 Ed 49
33600 Kurtuluş (TR) 97 De 54
Kürtün (TR) 90 Dk 50
34301 Kuru (FIN) 22 Cd 29
06760 Kuruçay (TR) 90 Di 51
Kurumoč (RUS) 46 Fa 37
Kuša (RUS) 24 Dg 27
Kusa (RUS) 47 Fk 35
09400 Kuşadası (TR) 95 Ch 53
Kušalino (RUS) 32 Dg 33
Kuščevskaja (RUS) 75 Dk 44
Kus'e-Aleksandrovskij (RUS) 36 Fi 32
66869 Kusel (D) 54 Ah 41
Kusem (RUS) 64 Fk 39
33710 Kuskan (TR) 97 Dd 54
Kuškopola (RUS) 25 Ee 27
Kuskurgul' (RUS) 37 Gg 32
Kušnarenkovo (RUS) 46 Ff 35
Kuşsarayı (TR) 98 Di 52
6403 Küssnacht (SZ) (CH) 68 Ai 43
Kušva (RUS) 36 Fk 32
43000 Kütahya (TR) 88 Ck 51
Kutais (RUS) 75 Dk 46
Kutanovo (RUS) 47 Fh 37
Kutina (HR) 70 Bg 45
Kutjevo (HR) 70 Bh 45
Kutlu-Bukaš (RUS) 46 Fa 35
284 01* Kutná Hora (CZ) 56 Bf 41
99-300 Kutno (PL) 56 Bk 38
Kuttainen (S) 15 Cc 22
99831 Kuttura (FIN) 15 Cg 22
6800 Kutuzov = Ialoveni (MD) 73 Ci 44
Kúty (SK) 56 Bh 42
74601 Kuusalu (EST) 30 Cf 31
93999 Kuusamo (FIN) 23 Ck 25
45740 Kuusankoski (FIN) 30 Cg 30
83630 Kuusjärvi (FIN) 23 Ci 28
25330 Kuusjoki (FIN) 30 Cd 30
Kuvakino (RUS) 45 Eg 36
Kuvalat, Ivano- (RUS) 64 Fh 38
Kuvandyk (RUS) 64 Fh 39
Kuvšinovo (RUS) 32 De 33
Kuyubaşı (TR) 96 Dc 52
Kuyucak (TR) 96 Ci 53
Kuyucak (TR) 98 Di 53
80028 Kužiai (LT) 41 Cd 35
Kuz"elga (RUS) 47 Fh 36
Kuzema (RUS) 24 De 25
Kuzemino (RUS) 33 Ec 31
Kuzem'jarovo (RUS) 46 Ff 33
Kužener (RUS) 45 Ei 34
Kuženkino (RUS) 32 De 33
Kuzino (RUS) 47 Fk 33
Kuzjanovo (RUS) 47 Fg 37
37800 Kuzlam (TR) 89 Dd 49
Kuz'mijar (RUS) 45 Ef 34
Kuz'minka (RUS) 32 Dg 31
Kuz'minskaja (RUS) 32 Dh 30
Kuz'minskaja (RUS) 33 Ec 30
Kuz'minskoe (RUS) 44 Dk 36
Kuznečiha (RUS) 45 Ek 36
Kuznecivsk (UA) 58 Cf 39
Kuzneck (RUS) 45 Eg 37
Kuzneckoe (RUS) 47 Ga 35
Kuznečnoe (RUS) 31 Ck 29
Kuznecova (RUS) 36 Gc 31
Kuznecovo (RUS) 33 Ea 30
Kuzomen (RUS) 25 Ec 26
Kuzomen' (RUS) 16 Dg 24
Kužorskaja (RUS) 76 Ea 46
Kuzovatovo (RUS) 45 Eh 37
Kuzreka (RUS) 16 De 24
18000 Kuzu (TR) 89 Dd 50
33730 Kuzucubelen (TR) 97 De 54
37000 Kuzyaka (TR) 89 Dd 49
Kvænangsbotn (N) 15 Cc 21
5772 Kværndrup (DK) 39 Ba 35
9100 Kvaløysletta (N) 14 Bi 21
9620 Kvalsund (N) 15 Cd 20
6090 Kvalsvik (N) 20 Af 28
Kvarkeno (RUS) 64 Fk 38
Kvarnberg (S) 29 Be 29
Kvašinskoe (RUS) 36 Gc 33
Kvelia (N) 21 Bd 26
7243 Kvenvær (N) 20 Ai 27
96202 Kvikkjokk (S) 14 Bh 24
4480 Kvinesdal (N) 28 Ag 32
3850 Kviteseid (N) 28 Ai 31
82-500 Kwidzyn (PL) 40 Bi 37
18025 Kybartai (LT) 41 Cc 36
Kydz'vidz' (RUS) 34 Ek 30
Kyjiv (UA) 59 Da 40
696 55* Kyjov (CZ) 56 Bh 41
Kylasovo (RUS) 35 Fg 33
IV40 Kyle of Lochalsh (GB) 50 Se 33
54655 Kyllburg (D) 54 Ag 40
Kyn (RUS) 36 Fi 33
Kyrčany (RUS) 34 Fa 33
16866 Kyritz (D) 39 Bc 38
7200 Kyrksæterøra (N) 20 Ak 27
02400* Kyrkslätt = Kirkkonummi (FIN) 30 Ce 30
Kyrnasivka (UA) 58 Ci 42
Kyrnyčky (UA) 73 Ck 45
Kyrta (RUS) 27 Fh 26
Kyštym (RUS) 47 Ga 35
Kytlym (RUS) 36 Fk 31
43701 Kyyjärvi (FIN) 22 Ce 27
Kyzburun Tretij (RUS) 76 Ed 47

L

2136 Laa an der Thaya (A) 56 Bg 42
18299 Laage (D) 39 Bc 37
57334 Laasphe, Bad (D) 54 Ai 40
Labin (HR) 70 Be 45
Labinsk (RUS) 76 Ea 46
Labinsk, Ust'- (RUS) 75 Dk 45
89-210 Łabiszyn (PL) 40 Bh 38
40210 Labouheyre (F) 66 Sk 46
Labožskoe (RUS) 18 Fc 23
40420 Labrit (F) 66 Sk 46
81290 Labruguière (F) 67 Ac 47
Laç (AL) 86 Bk 49
33680 Lacanau (F) 66 Si 46
33680 Lacanau-Océan (F) 66 Si 45
46120 Lacapelle-Marival (F) 67 Ab 46
81230 Lacaune (F) 67 Ac 47
19020 Laçin (TR) 89 De 50
Läckeby (S) 40 Bg 34
Läckö (S) 29 Bd 32
Lackoe (RUS) 32 Di 32
08034 Laconi (I) 83 Ak 51
68300 Ládi (GR) 87 Cg 49
55760 Ládik (TR) 89 Df 50
00055 Ladispoli (I) 84 Bc 49
Ladovskaja Balka (RUS) 76 Eb 45
Ladožskoe (RUS) 32 Dg 32
Ladožskoe Ozero (RUS) 31 Db 30
Laduškin (RUS) 40 Ca 36
Ladva (RUS) 32 De 29
Ladyžyn (UA) 58 Ck 42
6854 Lærdalsøyri (N) 28 Ah 29
85107 Láerma (GR) 95 Ch 54
Lævvajokgiedde (N) 15 Cg 21
Lagan' (RUS) 77 Eh 45
Lagarfljót (IS) 48 Rf 25
63-740 Łagiewniki (PL) 56 Bg 40
73170 Lagnieu (F) 68 Af 45
77400 Lagny-sur-Marne (F) 53 Ac 42
8365-092 Lagoa (P) 92 Sb 53
67063 Lágos (GR) 87 Cf 49
8005-496 Lagos (P) 92 Sb 53
11220 Lagrasse (F) 82 Ac 47
12210 Laguiole (F) 67 Ac 46
24234 Laguna de Negrillos (E) 80 Se 48
Lahania (GR) 95 Ch 55
Lahdenpoh'ja (RUS) 31 Da 29
Lahišyn (BY) 58 Cf 38
Lahnajärvi (S) 15 Cc 24
Lahojsk (BY) 42 Ch 36
31200 Laholm (S) 39 Bd 34
Lahoma (RUS) 25 Ef 29
77933 Lahr/Schwarzwald (D) 54 Ah 42
Lahta (RUS) 23 Dd 29
23601 Lahti (FIN) 30 Cf 30
89150 Laichingen (D) 54 Ak 42
IV22 Laide (GB) 50 Se 33
21330 Laignes (F) 67 Ae 43
66401 Laihia (FIN) 22 Cc 28
Laimoluokta (S) 14 Bk 22
Lainio (S) 15 Cc 23
IV27 Lairg (GB) 50 Sf 32
12310 Laissac (F) 67 Ac 46
93093 Laisvall (S) 21 Bh 24
23801 Laitila (FIN) 30 Cb 30
Lajmy (RUS) 37 Gi 33
Lakaträsk (S) 15 Cb 24
4241 Lăki (BG) 87 Ce 49
Lăki (BG) 87 Ce 49
Lakí (GR) 95 Cg 53
Lakinsk (RUS) 44 Dk 34
73005 Lákki (GR) 94 Cd 55
68002 Lákkoma (GR) 87 Cf 50
Lakly (RUS) 47 Fi 35
9700 Lakselv (N) 15 Ce 20
Laktaši (BIH) 70 Bh 46
22950 Lalapaşa (TR) 87 Cg 49
36500 Lalín (E) 80 Sb 48
Lal'sk (RUS) 34 Eh 30
07270 Lamastre (F) 67 Ae 46
4650 Lambach (A) 55 Bd 42
22400* Lamballe (F) 52 Sh 42
Lambas (RUS) 25 Ef 28
Lambisel'ga (RUS) 23 Dc 29
Lamborn (S) 29 Bf 30
5100-387 Lamego (P) 80 Sc 49
35101 Lamía (GR) 94 Cc 52
16901 Lammi (FIN) 30 Cf 29
92010 Lampedusa (I) 84 Bc 55
3623 Lampeland (N) 28 Ak 31
SA48 Lampeter (GB) 52 Sf 38
Lampožnja (RUS) 25 Ee 25
22250 Lanaja (E) 82 Sk 49
ML11 Lanark (GB) 51 Sg 35
LA1 Lancaster (GB) 51 Sh 36
66034 Lanciano (I) 85 Be 48
58066 Lančiūnava (LT) 41 Ce 35
94405 Landau an der Isar (D) 55 Bc 42
76829 Landau in der Pfalz (D) 54 Ai 41
6500* Landeck (A) 69 Ba 43
29800 Landerneau (F) 52 Sf 42
29400* Landivisiau (F) 52 Sf 42
83100 Landön (S) 21 Be 27
86899 Landsberg am Lech (D) 55 Ba 42
84028* Landshut (D) 55 Bc 42
26100* Landskrona (S) 39 Bc 35
66849 Landstuhl (D) 54 Ah 41
Lanesborough = Baile Átha Liagh (IRL) 49 Sc 37
84093 Långå (S) 21 Bd 28
57200 Langadás (GR) 87 Cd 50
42320 Langa de Duero (E) 81 Sg 49
22003 Langádia (GR) 94 Cc 53
43300 Langeac (F) 67 Ad 45
37130 Langeais (F) 66 Aa 43
35480 Längelmäki (FIN) 30 Ce 29
49838 Langen (D) 38 Ai 37
6444 Längenfeld (A) 69 Ba 43
30851* Langenhagen (D) 54 Ak 38
99947 Langensalza, Bad (D) 55 Ba 39
4900* Langenthal (CH) 68 Ah 43
5550 Langeskov (DK) 39 Ba 35
3970 Langesund (N) 28 Ak 31
Langevåg (N) 20 Ag 28
880 Langholt (IS) 48 Rb 27
3550 Langnau im Emmental (CH) 68 Ah 44
9840 Langnes (N) 15 Ci 20
48300 Langogne (F) 67 Ad 46
41320 Langon (F) 66 Sk 46
33900 Langreo = Llangréu (E) 80 Se 47
52200* Langres (F) 68 Af 43
88220 Långsele (S) 21 Bh 27
Langstrand (N) 15 Cd 20
Långträsk (S) 22 Ca 25
89054 Långvattnet (S) 21 Bg 25
99-306 Łanięta (PL) 56 Bk 38
Lanivci (UA) 58 Cg 41
Länkipohja = Längelmäki (FIN) 30 Ce 29
98013 Lannavaara (S) 15 Cb 22
65300* Lannemezan (F) 82 Aa 47
29870 Lannilis (F) 52 Sf 42
22300* Lannion (F) 52 Sg 42
24270 Lanouaille (F) 67 Ab 45
95698 Lansjärv (S) 15 Cc 24
563 01 Lanškroun (CZ) 56 Bg 41
73480 Lanslebourg-Mont-Cenis (F) 68 Ag 45
41200* Lanthenay, Romorantin- (F) 67 Ab 43
08045 Lanusei (I) 83 Ak 51
02000* Laon (F) 53 Ad 41
03120 Lapalisse (F) 67 Ad 44
73101 Lapinlahti (FIN) 23 Ch 27
62601 Lappajärvi (FIN) 22 Cd 27
Läppe (S) 29 Bf 31
53006* Lappeenranta (FIN) 31 Ci 29
64320 Lappfjärd (FIN) 22 Cb 28
27260 Lappi (FIN) 30 Cb 29
10820 Lappohja (FIN) 30 Cd 31
Lappoluobbal (N) 15 Cd 21
10820 Lappvik = Lappohja (FIN) 30 Cd 31
Lapseki (TR) 87 Cg 50
Lapševo (RUS) 45 Ek 35
Laptevo (RUS) 42 Ci 34
62101 Lapua (FIN) 22 Cc 28
3431 Lăpușna (MD) 73 Ci 44
547331 Lăpușna (RO) 72 Cf 44
64320 Lapväärtti = Lappfjärd (FIN) 22 Cb 28
67100 L'Aquila (I) 84 Bd 48
15188 Laracha (E) 80 Sb 47
09651 Lara de los Infantes (E) 81 Sg 48
Laragh = An Láithreach (IRL) 49 Sd 37
05300 Laragne-Montéglin (F) 68 Af 46
62034 Lärbro (S) 29 Bi 33
19600 Larche (F) 68 Ag 46
39770 Laredo (E) 66 Sg 47
07110 Largentière (F) 67 Ae 46
KA30 Largs (GB) 51 Sf 35
35012 Lárimna (GR) 94 Cd 52
86035 Larino (I) 85 Be 49
Larino (RUS) 47 Fk 36
Larionovo (RUS) 33 Dk 32
41001* Lárissa (GR) 86 Cc 51
1560 Larkollen (N) 28 Ba 31
6010* Larnaka (CY) 97 Dd 56
BT40 Larne (GB) 49 Se 36
15150 Laroquebrou (F) 67 Ac 46
6084 Larsnes (N) 20 Af 28
64440 Laruns (F) 82 Sk 48
3256* Larvik (N) 28 Ba 31
86-320 Łasin (PL) 40 Bk 37
98-100 Łask (PL) 56 Bk 39
Lašma (RUS) 44 Eb 36
19100* La Spezia (I) 69 Ak 46
17440 Lassan (D) 39 Bd 37
Lastovo (HR) 85 Bg 48
Lastva (BIH) 85 Bi 48
74014 Laterza (I) 85 Bg 50
33260 La Teste-de-Buch (F) 66 Si 46
49762 Lathen (D) 38 Ah 38
KW5 Latheron (GB) 50 Sg 32
91294 Latikberg (S) 21 Bh 26
04100 Latina (I) 84 Bc 49
Lat'juga (RUS) 26 Ei 26
610 Látrar (IS) 48 Qh 24
01979 Lauchhammer (D) 55 Bd 39
Laudal (N) 28 Ah 32
TD2 Lauder (GB) 51 Sh 35
01400 Laudio = Llodio (E) 81 Sh 47
4862 Ļaudona (LV) 41 Cg 34
21481 Lauenburg/Elbe (D) 39 Ba 37
91207 Lauf an der Pegnitz (D) 55 Bb 41
810 Laugarvatn (IS) 48 Qk 26
04470 Laujar de Andarax (E) 93 Sh 54
Lauker (S) 22 Bk 25
9194 Lauksletta (N) 14 Ca 20
Laumes, les (F) 67 Ae 43
PL15 Launceston (GB) 52 Sf 40
88471 Laupheim (D) 54 Ak 42
AB30 Laurencekirk (GB) 50 Sh 34
85044 Lauria (I) 85 Bf 50
56330 Lauritsala (FIN) 31 Ci 29
1000* Lausanne (CH) 68 Ag 44
36341 Lauterbach (Hessen) (D) 54 Ak 40
37431 Lauterberg im Harz, Bad (D) 55 Ba 39
67742 Lauterecken (D) 54 Ah 41
53000* Laval (F) 52 Sk 42
83980 Lavandou, le (F) 68 Ag 47
68004 Lávara (GR) 87 Cg 49
81500 Lavaur (F) 67 Ab 47
09300 Lavelanet (F) 82 Ab 48
85024 Lavello (I) 85 Bf 49
21014 Laveno Mombello (I) 68 Ai 45
38601 Lavia (FIN) 30 Cc 29
6947 Lavik (N) 28 Af 29
38015 Lavis (I) 69 Bb 44
7050-467 Lavre (P) 92 Sb 52
Lavrio (GR) 94 Ce 53
Lavrovo (RUS) 32 Dh 31
Lavrovo (RUS) 32 Dh 33
Lavsja (RUS) 44 Eb 35
69501 Laxå (S) 29 Be 32
91201 Laxbäcken (S) 21 Bg 26
IM4 Laxey (GBM) 51 Sf 36
IV27 Laxford Bridge (GB) 50 Se 32
ZE2 Laxo (GB) 50 Si 30
Laž (RUS) 34 Ek 33
11550* Lazarevac (SRB) 71 Ca 46
Lazarevo (RUS) 46 Fa 34
Lazarevskaja (RUS) 33 Dk 29
Lazarevskoe (RUS) 75 Dk 47
67001 Lazdijai (LT) 41 Cd 36
4222 Lazo (MD) 73 Ci 43
6200 Lazovsk = Sîngerei (MD) 73 Ci 43
84-360 Łeba (PL) 40 Bh 36
16230 Lebane (SRB) 86 Cb 48
9280 Lebbeke (B) 53 Ae 39
Lebedino (RUS) 45 Ek 35
Lebedjan' (RUS) 44 Dk 37
Lebedyn (UA) 59 De 40
Lebjaž'e (RUS) 34 Ek 33
Lebjažsk (RUS) 35 Fe 29
84-300* Lębork (PL) 40 Bh 36
41740 Lebrija (E) 92 Sd 54
Lebskoe (RUS) 26 Ei 26
73100 Lecce (I) 85 Bi 50
23900 Lecco (I) 69 Ak 45
6764* Lech (A) 69 Ba 43
3622 Lēči (LV) 30 Cb 33
50160 Leciñena (E) 82 Sk 49
25917 Leck (D) 38 Ai 36
32700 Lectoure (F) 66 Aa 47
21-010 Łęczna (PL) 57 Cc 39
99-100 Łęczyca (PL) 56 Bk 38
37100 Ledesma (E) 80 Se 49
IV27 Ledmore Junction (GB) 50 Sf 32
Ledmozero (RUS) 23 Dc 26
Led'ozero (RUS) 25 Eb 28
LS7 Leeds (GB) 51 Si 37
ST13 Leek (GB) 51 Sh 37
26789 Leer (Ostfriesland) (D) 38 Ah 37
4140 Leerdam (NL) 54 Af 39
Leesi (EST) 30 Cf 31
8900* Leeuwarden = Ljouwert (NL) 38 Af 37
31082 Lefkáda (GR) 94 Ca 52
62100 Lefkónas (GR) 87 Cd 49
Lefkoniko 97 Dd 55
Lefkoşa = Lefkosia 97 Dd 55
1010* Lefkosia (CY) 97 Dd 55
28911 Leganés (E) 81 Sg 50
44650 Legé (F) 66 Si 44
05-118* Legionowo (PL) 57 Ca 38
Legkovo (RUS) 32 Di 32
20025 Legnano (I) 68 Ai 45

Legnano | 183

59-200 Legnica (PL) 56 Bg 39
Legrad (HR) 70 Bg 44
76600* Le Havre (F) 53 Aa 41
27053 Lehena (GR) 94 Cb 53
31275 Lehrte (D) 54 Ak 38
Lehta (RUS) 23 Dd 26
Lëhta (RUS) 34 Ei 30
63501 Lehtimäki (FIN) 22 Cd 28
8430* Leibnitz (A) 70 Bf 44
LE5 Leicester (GB) 52 Si 38
2300* Leiden (NL) 53 Ae 38
Leighlinbridge = Leithghlinn an Droichid (IRL) 49 Sd 38
LU7 Leighton Buzzard (GB) 52 Sk 39
6863 Leikanger (N) 28 Ag 29
6863 Leikanger (N) 20 Af 28
Leipojärvi (S) 15 Cb 23
04103* Leipzig (D) 55 Bc 39
7112 Leira (N) 28 Ak 30
7112 Leira (N) 20 Ai 27
Leirâmoen (N) 14 Be 24
2400-013* Leiria (P) 80 Sb 51
520 Leirvík (FO) 50 Sd 28
5411 Leirvik (N) 28 Af 29
5411 Leirvik (N) 28 Af 31
94501 Leisi (EST) 30 Cc 32
IP16 Leiston (GB) 53 Ab 38
Leithghlinn an Droichid (IRL) 49 Sd 38
Leitir Creanainn = Letterkenny (IRL) 49 Sc 36
41770 Leivonmäki (FIN) 22 Cg 29
31880 Leiza (E) 81 Si 47
64009 Lekáni (GR) 87 Ce 49
Lekbibaj (AL) 86 Bk 48
48280 Lekeitio (E) 66 Sh 47
Lekma (RUS) 34 Ek 31
8370 Leknes (N) 14 Bd 22
79301 Leksand (S) 29 Bf 30
7120 Leksvik (N) 20 Ba 27
Leland (N) 14 Bc 24
Lel'čycy (BY) 58 Ci 39
Lel'ma (RUS) 24 Ea 28
8200* Lelystad (NL) 54 Af 38
72000* Le Mans (F) 66 Aa 43
64350 Lembeye (F) 66 Sk 47
3010* Lemesos = Limassol (CY) 97 Dc 56
Lemeza (RUS) 47 Fh 36
32657 Lemgo (D) 54 Ai 38
Lem'ju (RUS) 26 Fe 26
99885 Lemmenjoki (FIN) 15 Cg 22
Lemmer (NL) 38 Af 38
53077 Lémos (GR) 86 Cb 50
37560 Lempäälä (FIN) 30 Cd 29
43410 Lempdes (F) 67 Ad 45
Lemptyboż (RUS) 27 Fg 27
7620 Lemvig (DK) 38 Ai 34
Lenavož (RUS) 26 Ff 27
5651 Lend (A) 69 Bd 43
70400 Léndas (GR) 94 Ce 56
9220 Lendava (SLO) 70 Bg 44
Lendery (RUS) 23 Db 27
49838 Lengerich (D) 54 Ah 38
83661 Lenggries (D) 69 Bb 43
36073 Lenhovda (S) 39 Bf 34
Lenina (BY) 59 Db 38
Lenine 74 Df 45
190000* Leningrad = Sankt-Peterburg (RUS) 31 Da 31
Leningradskaja (RUS) 75 Dk 44
Leninogorsk (RUS) 46 Fc 36
Leninsk (RUS) 35 Fe 32
Leninsk (RUS) 47 Fk 36
Leninsk (RUS) 62 Ef 42
Leninskij (RUS) 43 Dh 36
Leninskoe (RUS) 34 Eh 32
3775 Lenk (CH) 68 Ah 44
Lenkivci (UA) 58 Ch 40
62300 Lens (F) 53 Ac 40
Lent'evo (RUS) 32 Dg 32
88930 Lentiira (FIN) 23 Ck 26
96016 Lentini (I) 84 Be 53
25001 Lentvaris (LT) 41 Cf 36
8700* Leoben (A) 70 Bf 43
HR6 Leominster (GB) 52 Sh 38
24001* León (E) 80 Se 48
40550 Léon (F) 66 Si 47
Leonarisso 97 De 55
22021 Leondári (GR) 94 Cc 53
94013 Leonforte (I) 84 Be 53
22300 Leonídio (GR) 94 Cc 53
3970 Leopoldsburg (B) 54 Af 39
2285 Leopoldsdorf im Marchfelde (A) 56 Bg 42
6300 Leova (MD) 73 Ci 44
6300 Leovo = Leova (MD) 73 Ci 44
21440 Lepe (E) 92 Sc 53
Lepel' (BY) 42 Ci 36
43500 Leposavić (SRB) 71 Ca 47
34500 Lépoura (GR) 95 Ce 52
79101 Leppävirta (FIN) 23 Ch 28
8132 Lepsény (H) 71 Bi 44
49500 Leptokariá (GR) 86 Cc 50
90025 Lercara Friddi (I) 84 Bd 53
19032 Lerici (I) 69 Ak 46
25001 Lérida = Lleida (E) 82 Aa 49
09340 Lerma (E) 81 Sg 48
Lermontov (RUS) 76 Ed 46
Lermontovo (RUS) 44 Ed 38
6631 Lermoos (A) 69 Ba 43
44300* Lerum (S) 29 Bc 33
Lervik (N) 28 Ai 31
ZE1 Lerwick (GB) 50 Si 30
25540 Les (E) 82 Aa 48
29770 Lescoff (F) 52 Sf 42
Leshoz (RUS) 46 Fa 34
71010 Lesina (I) 85 Bf 49
2665 Lesja (N) 20 Ai 28
2668 Lesjaskog (N) 20 Ai 28
68096 Lesjöfors (S) 29 Be 31
Lesken (RUS) 91 Ed 47
38-600 Lesko (PL) 57 Cc 41
Leskovac (SRB) 86 Cb 48
Leskovik (AL) 86 Ca 50
59-820 Leśna (PL) 56 Bf 39
29260 Lesneven (F) 52 Sf 42
Lesnikovo (RUS) 44 Eb 35
Lesnoe (RUS) 32 Df 32
Lesnoe Ukolovo (RUS) 60 Di 40
Lesnoj (RUS) 35 Fc 31
Lesnoj (RUS) 44 Ea 36
Lesnoj (RUS) 47 Ga 36
Lesogorsk (RUS) 44 Ed 35
33340 Lesparre-Médoc (F) 66 Sk 45
40260 Lesperon (F) 66 Si 47
50430 Lessay (F) 52 Si 41
69440 Lestijärvi (FIN) 22 Ce 27
Lešukonskoe (RUS) 25 Ef 26
05-084 Leszno (PL) 56 Bg 39
4281 Létavértes (H) 71 Cb 43
8868 Letenye (H) 70 Bg 44
Letka (RUS) 34 Ek 31
31380 Letku (FIN) 30 Cd 30
Letneozerskij (RUS) 24 Ea 27
Letnerečenskij (RUS) 24 De 26
5570 Letnica (BG) 72 Cf 47
Letnij Navolok (RUS) 24 Dh 25
Letnjaja Zolotica (RUS) 24 Dg 26
Letterkenny = Leitir Creanainn (IRL) 49 Sc 36
Letyčiv (UA) 58 Ch 41
11370 Leucate-Plage (F) 82 Ad 48
3954 Leukerbad (CH) 68 Ah 44
Leunova (RUS) 25 Ec 26
3432 Leuşeni (MD) 73 Ci 44
88299 Leutkirch im Allgäu (D) 69 Ba 43
3000 Leuven (B) 53 Ae 40
Leuza (RUS) 47 Fi 35
7900 Leuze-en-Hainaut (B) 53 Ad 40
51310 Levä (FIN) 23 Ch 28
7600 Levanger (N) 20 Bb 27
19015 Levanto (I) 69 Ak 46
KY8 Leven (GB) 50 Sh 34
Levent (TR) 98 Dh 52
51371* Leverkusen (D) 54 Ag 39
22002 Levídi (GR) 94 Cc 53
20170 Levie (F) 83 Ak 49
25270 Levier (F) 68 Ag 44
Levino (RUS) 33 Dk 33
6540 Levka (BG) 87 Cg 49
33053 Levkadití (GR) 94 Cc 52
35003 Levkás (GR) 94 Cb 52
Levkinskaja (RUS) 26 Fb 26
054 01 Levoča (SK) 57 Ca 41
Levokumskoe (RUS) 76 Ee 46
36110 Levroux (F) 67 Ab 44
9171 Levski (BG) 72 Cf 47
Lev Tolstoj (RUS) 44 Dk 37
2817 Levunovo (BG) 87 Cd 49
SO45 Lewes (GB) 53 Aa 40
PR25 Leyland (GB) 51 Sh 37
Leždug (RUS) 18 Fc 23
Lezhë (AL) 86 Bk 49
11200 Lézignan-Corbières (F) 67 Ac 47
Lëzna (BY) 42 Da 35
Ležnevo (RUS) 44 Ea 34
63190 Lezoux (F) 67 Ad 45
L'gov (RUS) 60 Df 39
L'govskij, Dmitriev (RUS) 60 Df 38
6230 Liabygd (N) 20 Ah 28
34374 Liatorp (S) 39 Be 34
460 01* Liberec (CZ) 56 Bf 40
Libohovë (AL) 86 Ca 50
33500* Libourne (F) 66 Sk 46
Librazhd (AL) 86 Ca 49
92027 Licata (I) 84 Bd 53
21700 Lice (TR) 99 Ea 52
WS13 Lichfield (GB) 51 Si 38
35104 Lichtenfels (D) 55 Bb 40
Lida (BY) 41 Cf 37
91094 Liden (S) 21 Bg 28
34010 Lidhult (S) 39 Bd 34
53101* Lidköping (S) 29 Bd 32
00121 Lido di Ostia (I) 84 Bc 49
13-230 Lidzbark (PL) 40 Bk 37
11-100* Lidzbark Warmiński (PL) 40 Ca 36
16559 Liebenwalde (D) 39 Bd 38
04924 Liebenwerda, Bad (D) 55 Bd 39
15868 Lieberose (D) 55 Be 39
4000* Liège (B) 54 Af 40
81720 Lieksa (FIN) 23 Da 27
5070* Lielvārde (LV) 41 Ce 34
9900* Lienz (A) 69 Bc 44
3401* Liepāja (LV) 40 Cb 34
2500 Lier (B) 53 Ae 39
2500 Lierre = Lier (B) 53 Ae 39
4410 Liestal (CH) 68 Ah 43
Lietekkåbba (S) 14 Bk 23
21421 Lieto (FIN) 30 Cc 30
41401 Lievestuore (FIN) 22 Cg 28
62143 Liévin (F) 53 Ac 40
8940* Liezen (A) 70 Be 43
88350 Liffol-le-Grand (F) 54 Af 42
BT78 Lifford (GB) 49 Sc 36
Lifford (IRL) 49 Sc 36
35340 Liffré (F) 52 Si 42
33054 Lignano Sabbiadoro (I) 69 Bd 45
18160 Lignières (F) 67 Ac 44
55500 Ligny-en-Barrois (F) 54 Af 42
Ligórtinos (GR) 95 Cf 55
37240 Ligueil (F) 66 Aa 43
Lihačevo (RUS) 32 Dh 32
34300 Lihás (GR) 94 Cc 52
Lihoslavl' (RUS) 32 Df 33
Lihovskoj (RUS) 61 Ea 42
90302* Lihula (EST) 30 Cd 32
Lílea (GR) 94 Cc 52
28865 Lilienthal (D) 38 Ai 37
46301 Lilla Edet (S) 29 Bc 32
59000* Lille (F) 53 Ad 40
76170 Lillebonne (F) 53 Aa 41
2608* Lillehammer (N) 28 Ba 29
62190 Lillers (F) 53 Ac 40
4790 Lillesand (N) 28 Ai 32
2000 Lillestrøm (N) 28 Bb 31
84080 Lillhärdal (S) 21 Be 29
45870 Lillo (E) 81 Sg 51
91050 Lillögda (S) 21 Bh 26
78064 Lima (S) 29 Bd 30
Liman (RUS) 77 Eh 45
Liman (UA) 60 Dg 41
Limannvika (N) 21 Bd 26
34-600* Limanowa (PL) 57 Ca 41
3010* Limassol = Lemesos (CY) 97 Dc 56
BT49 Limavady (GB) 49 Sd 35
4001 Limbaži (LV) 30 Ce 33
65549* Limburg an der Lahn (D) 54 Ai 40
Limedsforsen (S) 29 Bd 30
Liménas Hersónissos (GR) 95 Cf 55
Limerick = Luimneach (IRL) 49 Sb 38
91901 Liminka (FIN) 22 Cf 26
51404 Limmared (S) 29 Bd 33
21055 Límnes (GR) 94 Cc 53
Límni (GR) 94 Cd 52
87000* Limoges (F) 67 Ab 45
46260 Limogne-en-Quercy (F) 67 Ab 46
12015 Limone Piemonte (I) 68 Ah 46
33770 Limonlu (TR) 97 De 54
11300 Limoux (F) 82 Ac 47
Linahamari (RUS) 16 Db 21
39580 Linares (E) 93 Sg 52
34007 Linariá (GR) 94 Ce 52
Linava (BY) 57 Ce 38
LN4 Lincoln (GB) 51 Sk 37
88131 Lindau (Bodensee) (D) 69 Ak 43
71101 Lindesberg (S) 29 Bf 31
85107 Líndos (GR) 96 Ci 54
Lindozero (RUS) 23 Dd 28
11300 Línea de la Concepción, La (E) 92 Se 54
Linec (RUS) 60 Df 38
Linejnoe (RUS) 77 Eh 44
Linevo (RUS) 61 Ee 40
49808* Lingen (Ems) (D) 54 Ah 38
58002* Linköping (S) 29 Bf 32
83046 Linkuva (LT) 41 Cd 34
EH49 Linlithgow (GB) 51 Sg 35
Linovo (RUS) 31 Ch 33
84201 Linsell (S) 21 Bd 28
8783 Linthal (CH) 69 Ak 44
53545 Linz (A) 55 Be 42
49220 Lion-d'Angers, le (F) 66 Sk 43
Lios Duin Bhearn (IRL) 49 Sa 37
Lios Mór = Lismore (IRL) 49 Sc 38
Lios Tuathail = Listowel (IRL) 49 Sa 38
082 71 Lipany (SK) 57 Ca 41
98055 Lipari (I) 84 Be 52
4706 Lipcani (MD) 58 Cg 42
Lipeck (RUS) 60 Dk 38
83101 Liperi (FIN) 23 Ck 28
6210 Lipica (SLO) 69 Bd 45
Lipicy-Zybino (RUS) 43 Dh 37
Lipin Bor (RUS) 32 Di 30
14000 Lipjan = Lipljan (RKS) 86 Cb 48
77-420 Lipka (PL) 40 Bh 37
4706 Lipkany = Lipcani (MD) 58 Cg 42
Lipki (RUS) 43 Dh 37
1307 Lipkovo (MK) 86 Cb 48
14000 Lipljan = Lipjan (RKS) 86 Cb 48
Lipnaja Gorka (RUS) 32 Dd 31
751 31 Lipník nad Bečvou (CZ) 56 Bh 41
64-111 Lipno (PL) 40 Bk 38
607275 Lipova (RO) 71 Cb 44
Lipovik (RUS) 25 Ec 27
Lipovskij (RUS) 62 Ek 39
Lipovskoe (RUS) 36 Gb 33
Lipovskoe (RUS) 36 Gd 33
59555* Lippstadt (D) 54 Ai 39
16-315 Lipsk (PL) 41 Cd 37
27-300 Lipsko (PL) 57 Cb 39
031 01 Liptovský Mikuláš (SK) 56 Bk 41
1000-001* Lisboa (P) 92 Sa 52
BT27 Lisburn (GB) 49 Sd 36
Lisdoonvarna = Lios Duin Bhearn (IRL) 49 Sa 37
Lisičansk = Lysyčans'k (UA) 60 Di 42
14100* Lisieux (F) 53 Aa 41
Lisij Nos (RUS) 31 Ck 31
Lis'ja (RUS) 35 Fe 33
PL14 Liskeard (GB) 52 Sf 40
Liski (RUS) 60 Dk 40
81310 Lisle-sur-Tarn (F) 67 Ab 47
99195 Lisma (FIN) 15 Cf 22
Lismore (IRL) 49 Sc 38
BT92 Lisnaskea (GB) 49 Sc 36
Lisskogsbrändan (S) 29 Bd 30
25992 List auf Sylt (D) 38 Ai 35
Lištica = Široki Brijeg (BIH) 70 Bh 47
Listowel = Lios Tuathail (IRL) 49 Sa 38
83030 Lit (S) 21 Be 27
Lithío (GR) 95 Cg 52
1270 Litija (SLO) 70 Be 44
60200 Litóhoro (GR) 86 Cc 50
412 01 Litoměřice (CZ) 55 Be 40
570 01 Litomyšl (CZ) 56 Bg 41
784 01 Litovel (CZ) 56 Bh 41
435 14* Litvínov (CZ) 55 Bd 40
Litvinovo (RUS) 34 Ei 29
Lityn (UA) 58 Ci 41
447180 Livada (RO) 72 Cd 43
66100 Livaderó (GR) 87 Ce 49
40002 Livádi (GR) 86 Cc 50
40002 Livádi (GR) 94 Ce 53
Livadiá (GR) 94 Cc 52
Livani (LV) 41 Cg 34
Livenka (RUS) 60 Di 40
L19 Liverpool (GB) 51 Sh 37
EH54 Livingston (GB) 51 Sg 35
Livno (BIH) 70 Bh 47
Livny (RUS) 60 Dh 38
93220 Livo (FIN) 22 Cg 25
57100* Livorno (I) 69 Ba 47
28200 Lixoúri (GR) 94 Ca 52
4425 Lizums (LV) 30 Cg 33
74020 Lizzano (I) 85 Bh 50
Ljachavičy (BY) 41 Cg 37
Ljady (RUS) 31 Ci 32
Ljali (RUS) 26 Fa 28
Ljalja-Titova (RUS) 36 Gb 31
Ljambir' (RUS) 45 Ef 36
Ljamca (RUS) 24 Dh 26
Ljamino (RUS) 35 Fh 32
Ljangasovo (RUS) 34 Ek 32
Ljaskelja (RUS) 23 Db 29
Ljasnaja (BY) 41 Cf 38
Ljavki (BY) 42 Ci 37
14240 Ljig (SRB) 71 Ca 46
Ljørdal (N) 29 Bc 29
Ljuban' (BY) 42 Ci 38
Ljuban' (RUS) 31 Db 31
Ljubar (UA) 58 Ch 41
Ljubašivka (UA) 73 Da 43
Ljubeč (UA) 59 Da 39
7534 Ljuben (BG) 87 Ce 48
Ljubercy (RUS) 43 Dh 35
Ljubešiv (UA) 58 Cf 39
Ljubickoe (RUS) 62 Ek 39
Ljubim (RUS) 33 Ea 32
6550 Ljubimec (BG) 87 Cg 49
Ljubinje (BIH) 85 Bi 48
1000* Ljubljana (SLO) 70 Be 44
Ljuboml' (UA) 57 Ce 39
15320 Ljubovija (SRB) 71 Bk 46
Ljubuški (BIH) 85 Bh 47
Ljubyc'ke (UA) 74 Df 43
Ljubymivka (UA) 59 Da 40
Ljubymivka (UA) 75 Dg 43
Ljubytino (RUS) 32 Dd 32
Ljudinovo (RUS) 43 De 37
Ljudkovo (RUS) 43 De 36
62016 Ljugarn (S) 29 Bi 33
Ljugoviči (RUS) 32 Dd 30
9525 Ljuljakovo (BG) 88 Ch 48
34101* Ljungby (S) 39 Bd 34
84035 Ljungdalen (S) 21 Bc 28
45901 Ljungskile (S) 28 Bb 32
82700 Ljusdal (S) 21 Bg 29
82020 Ljusne (S) 29 Bh 29
86040 Ljustorp (S) 21 Bh 28
17240 Llagostera (E) 82 Ac 49
SA48 Llanbedr Pont Steffan = Lampeter (GB) 52 Sf 38
SA19 Llandeilo (GB) 52 Sg 39
SA20 Llandovery (GB) 52 Sg 39
LD1 Llandrindod Wells (GB) 52 Sg 38
LL30 Llandudno (GB) 51 Sg 37
SA15 Llanelli (GB) 52 Sf 39
33500 Llanes (E) 66 Sf 47
SY21 Llanfair Caereinion (GB) 51 Sg 38
LD2 Llanfair-ym-Mualt = Buith Wells (GB) 52 Sg 38
LL77 Llangefni (GB) 51 Sf 37
LL20 Llangollen (GB) 51 Sg 38
33930 Llangréu = Langreo (E) 80 Se 47
SY18 Llangurig (GB) 52 Sg 38
SY18 Llanidloes (GB) 52 Sg 38
LD5 Llanwrtyd Wells (GB) 52 Sg 38
SA20 Llanymddyfri = Llandovery (GB) 52 Sg 39
25001* Lleida (E) 82 Aa 49
06900 Llerena (E) 92 Sd 52
46160 Llíria (E) 82 Sk 51
17527 Llívia (E) 82 Ab 48
Llodio = Laudio (E) 81 Sh 47
Lluanco = Luanco (E) 80 Se 47
Loban (RUS) 25 Ef 25
Lobanovo (RUS) 35 Fg 33
02708 Löbau (D) 55 Be 39
Lobcovo (RUS) 44 Ea 34
07356 Lobenstein, Bad (D) 55 Bb 40
24033 Löberöd (S) 39 Bd 35
73-150 Łobez (PL) 39 Bf 37
Lobnja (RUS) 43 Dh 34
Lobskoe (RUS) 24 Df 28
39279 Loburg (D) 55 Bc 38
Lobva (RUS) 36 Ga 31
6600* Locarno (CH) 68 Ai 44
31547 Loccum, Rehburg- (D) 54 Ak 38
PA34 Lochaline (GB) 50 Se 34
HS8 Lochboisdale (GB) 50 Sc 33
FK19 Lochearnhead (GB) 50 Sf 34
7240 Lochem (NL) 54 Ag 38
37600 Loches (F) 66 Aa 43
Loch Garman = Wexford (IRL) 49 Sd 38
PA31 Lochgilphead (GB) 50 Se 34
IV27 Lochinver (GB) 50 Se 32
DG11 Lochmaben (GB) 51 Sg 35
Lochmaddy (GB) 50 Sc 33
07-130 Łochów (PL) 57 Cb 38
KA27 Lochranza (GB) 51 Se 35
Lochvycja (UA) 59 Dd 40
DG11 Lockerbie (GB) 51 Sg 35
17321 Löcknitz (D) 39 Be 37
2400* Locle, Le (CH) 68 Ag 43
56240 Locmaria (F) 66 Sg 43
56500 Locminé (F) 66 Sh 43
89044 Locri (I) 85 Bg 52
08020 Lodè (I) 83 Ak 50
Lodejka (RUS) 34 Ef 30
Lodejnoe Pole (RUS) 32 Dd 30
34700 Lodève (F) 67 Ad 47
26900 Lodi (I) 69 Ak 45
8200 Løding (N) 14 Be 23
8550 Lødingen (N) 14 Bf 22
46371 Lödöse (S) 29 Bc 32
90-001* Łódź (PL) 56 Bk 39
Loev (BY) 59 Da 39
84085 Lofsdalen (S) 21 Bd 28
59095 Loftahammar (S) 29 Bg 33
5781 Lofthus (N) 28 Ag 30
Log (RUS) 61 Ed 41
4400 Loga (N) 28 Ag 32
Logačevka (RUS) 63 Fc 38
Loginovo (RUS) 47 Gb 34
Logovskij (RUS) 61 Ed 42
10120 Logrosán (E) 80 Se 51
9670 Løgstør (DK) 38 Ak 34
6240 Løgumkloster (DK) 38 Ai 35
5953 Lohals (DK) 39 Ba 35
35550 Lohéac (F) 66 Si 43
Lohguba (RUS) 23 Dc 25
58620 Lohilahti (FIN) 31 Ci 29
97420 Lohiniva (FIN) 15 Ce 23
08201 Lohja (FIN) 30 Ce 30
97816 Lohr am Main (D) 54 Ak 41
32210 Loimaa (FIN) 30 Cd 30
17121 Loitz (D) 39 Bd 37
Lojga (RUS) 33 Ee 29
Lojmola (RUS) 23 Db 29
Lojno (RUS) 35 Fc 31
Lokači (UA) 57 Ce 40
23450 Lokalahti (FIN) 30 Cb 30
1960 Løken (N) 28 Bb 31
9160 Lokeren (B) 53 Ad 39
99645 Lokka (FIN) 15 Ch 23
9480 Løkken (DK) 28 Ak 33
7327 Løkken (N) 20 Ak 27
Loknja (RUS) 42 Da 34
Lokot (RUS) 59 De 38
Lola (RUS) 76 Ee 44
3600 Lom (BG) 72 Cd 47
2686 Lom (N) 20 Ai 29
7838 Lomci (BG) 72 Cg 47

184 I Legnica

Malojaz (RUS) 47 Fi 35
Malokirsanovka (RUS) 75 Di 43
6700 Måløy (N) 20 Af 29
Maložujka (RUS) 24 Dh 27
10680 Malpartida de Plasencia (E) 80 Sd 51
15113 Malpica (E) 80 Sb 47
34845* Maltepe (TR) 95 Cg 52
YO17 Malton (GB) 51 Sk 36
78201 Malung (S) 29 Bd 30
82078 Malungen (S) 21 Bg 28
7563 Malvik (N) 20 Ba 27
Malye Derbety (RUS) 76 Ee 43
Malyj Uzen' (RUS) 62 Eh 40
Malyn (UA) 58 Ck 40
Malyns'k (UA) 58 Cg 39
Malyševa (RUS) 36 Gb 33
Malyševo (RUS) 44 Eb 35
Mamadyš (RUS) 46 Fb 35
900001 Mamaia (RO) 73 Ci 46
06261 Mamak (TR) 89 Dc 51
72600 Mamers (F) 53 Aa 42
Mamonovo (RUS) 44 Dk 37
Mamurras (AL) 86 Bk 49
Mamykovo (RUS) 46 Fa 36
07500 Manacor (E) 82 Ad 51
88340 Manamansalo (FIN) 23 Ch 26
917170 Mănăstirea (RO) 72 Cg 46
07600 Manavgat (TR) 96 Db 54
Mančaž (RUS) 47 Fi 34
M5 Manchester (GB) 51 Sh 37
58014 Manciano (I) 84 Bb 48
Mandač (RUS) 34 Fa 29
4513 Mandal (N) 28 Ah 32
09040 Mandas (I) 83 Ak 51
19600 Mándra (GR) 87 Ce 50
85303 Mandráki (GR) 95 Ch 54
74024 Manduria (I) 85 Bh 50
Manevyči (UA) 58 Cf 39
71043 Manfredonia (I) 85 Bf 49
905500 Mangalia (RO) 73 Ci 47
Mångsbodarna (S) 29 Bd 29
3530-092* Mangualde (P) 80 Sc 50
33085 Maniago (I) 69 Bc 44
Manino (RUS) 61 Eb 40
45000* Manisa (TR) 95 Ch 52
46940 Manises (E) 82 Sk 51
HS3 Manish (GB) 50 Sd 33
Man'kivka (UA) 59 Da 42
Manlan, Iki (RUS) 77 Ef 43
08560 Manlleu (E) 82 Ac 48
68159* Mannheim (D) 54 Ai 41
Manorhamilton = Cluainin (IRL) 49 Sb 36
04100 Manosque (F) 68 Af 47
08241* Manresa (E) 82 Ab 49
06343 Mansfeld (D) 55 Bb 39
NG18 Mansfield (GB) 51 Si 37
40591 Mansilla (E) 81 Sh 48
Mansilla de Burgos (E) 81 Sg 48
24210 Mansilla de las Mulas (E) 80 Se 48
16230 Mansle (F) 66 Aa 45
Mansurlu (TR) 97 Df 53
Mantamádos (GR) 87 Cg 51
Mantarlı (TR) 98 Dk 53
Mantasiá (GR) 86 Cc 51
6260-014* Manteigas (P) 80 Sc 50
78520 Mantes-la-Jolie (F) 53 Ab 42
46100 Mantova (I) 69 Ba 45
04601 Mäntsälä (FIN) 30 Cf 30
35820 Mänttä (FIN) 22 Ce 28
Manturovo (RUS) 33 Ee 32
52701 Mäntyharju (FIN) 30 Cg 29
97901 Mantyjärvi (FIN) 15 Ch 24
10470 Manyas (TR) 88 Ch 50
Manyčskoe (RUS) 76 Ed 44
13200 Manzanares (E) 93 Sg 52
07701 Maó (E) 83 Ae 51
45515 Maqueda (E) 81 Sf 50
Maradit (TR) 91 Eb 49
49500 Marans (F) 66 Si 44
625200 Mărășești (RO) 73 Ch 45
2900-001 Marateca (P) 92 Sb 52
19007 Marathónas (GR) 94 Cd 52
54820 Marbache (F) 54 Ag 42
14880 Marbella (E) 93 Sf 54
35037* Marburg (Lahn) (D) 54 Ai 40
8700 Marcali (H) 70 Bh 44
Marčata (RUS) 34 Fa 33
PE15 March (GB) 53 Aa 38
6900 Marche-en-Famenne (B) 54 Af 40
41620 Marchena (E) 92 Se 53
71110 Marcigny (F) 67 Ae 44
12330 Marcillac-Vallon (F) 67 Ac 46
65027 Marcinkonys (LT) 41 Ce 36
30384 Mar de Cristal (E) 93 Sk 53
47000* Mardin (TR) 99 Ea 53
17320 Marennes (F) 66 Si 45
24340 Mareuil (F) 66 Aa 45
Mar'evka (RUS) 62 Ek 38
Marevo (RUS) 31 Dc 33
Marfino (RUS) 77 Ei 44
Marganec = Marhanec' (UA) 74 De 43
Margaritovo (RUS) 75 Di 44
CT9 Margate (GB) 53 Ab 39
71044 Margherita di Savoia (I) 85 Bg 49
415300 Marghita (RO) 71 Cc 43
Marhanec' (UA) 74 De 43
7736 Mari (CY) 97 Dd 56
04838 María (E) 93 Sh 53
9550 Mariager (DK) 38 Ak 34
6430-081* Marialva (P) 80 Sc 50
57030 Mariannelund (S) 29 Bf 33
353 01 Mariánské Lázně (CZ) 55 Bc 41
8630 Mariazell (A) 70 Bf 43
4930 Maribo (DK) 39 Bb 36
2000* Maribor (SLO) 70 Bf 44
2044 Marica (BG) 87 Cf 48
Mariec (RUS) 45 Ek 34
64701 Mariefred (S) 29 Bh 31
22100* Mariehamn (AX) 30 Bk 30
54201* Mariestad (S) 29 Bd 32
13700 Marignane (F) 68 Af 47
Mariinsk (RUS) 47 Fk 34
Mariinskoe (RUS) 65 Gb 38
68001* Marijampolė (LT) 41 Cd 36
36900 Marín (E) 80 Sb 48
57034 Marina di Campo (I) 84 Ba 48
Marina di Gioiosa Jonica (I) 85 Bg 52
73040 Marina di Leuca (I) 85 Bi 51
56013 Marina di Pisa (I) 69 Ba 47
97010 Marina di Ragusa (I) 84 Be 54
48023 Marina di Ravenna (I) 69 Bc 46
Mar'ina Horka (BY) 42 Ci 37
Marinella (I) 84 Bc 53
90035 Marineo (I) 84 Bd 52
95640 Marines (F) 53 Ab 41
63350 Maringues (F) 67 Ad 45
2430-034* Marinha Grande (P) 80 Sb 51
Mar'insko (RUS) 31 Ci 32
Mari-Turek (RUS) 45 Ek 34
Mariupol' = Maryupol' (UA) 75 Dh 43
78301 Märjamaa (EST) 30 Ce 32
Marjans'ke (UA) 74 Dd 43
28501 Markaryd (S) 39 Bd 34
TF9 Market Drayton (GB) 51 Sh 38
LE16 Market Harborough (GB) 52 Sk 38
LN8 Market Rasen (GB) 51 Sk 37
Marki (RUS) 60 Dk 40
15748 Märkisch Buchholz (D) 55 Bd 38
Markivka (UA) 60 Dk 41
04416 Markkleeberg (D) 55 Bc 39
19003 Markópoulo (GR) 94 Cd 53
35210 Markovac (SRB) 71 Cb 46
4108 Markovo (BG) 73 Ch 47
Markovo (RUS) 32 Dg 30
Marks (RUS) 62 Eg 39
97828 Marktheidenfeld (D) 54 Ak 41
95615 Marktredwitz (D) 55 Bc 40
SN8 Marlborough (GB) 52 Si 39
02250 Marle (F) 53 Ad 41
47200* Marmande (F) 66 Aa 46
10360 Marmara (TR) 88 Ch 50
59000 Marmara Ereğlisi (TR) 88 Ch 50
59000 Marmaraereğlisi (TR) 88 Ch 50
48700 Marmaris (TR) 96 Ci 54
82300 Mármaro (GR) 95 Cg 52
Marmaskogen (S) 29 Bh 30
86160 Marnay (F) 68 Af 43
25709 Marne (D) 38 Ak 37
62250 Marquise (F) 53 Ab 40
50034 Marradi (I) 69 Bb 46
91025 Marsala (I) 84 Bc 53
Maršavicy (RUS) 31 Ci 33
06055 Marsciano (I) 84 Bc 48
13001* Marseille (F) 68 Af 47
60690 Marseille-en-Beauvaisis (F) 53 Ab 41
54800 Mars-la-Tour (F) 54 Af 41
19500* Märsta (S) 29 Bh 31
5960 Marstal (DK) 39 Ba 36
6310 Marstein (N) 20 Ah 28
Mart (TR) 89 Dd 50
73025 Martano (I) 85 Bi 50
46600 Martel (F) 67 Ab 46
70015 Mártha (GR) 95 Cf 55
35640 Martigné-Ferchaud (F) 66 Si 43
1920 Martigny (CH) 68 Ah 44
13500 Martigues (F) 68 Af 47
036 01 Martin (SK) 56 Bi 41
74015 Martina Franca (I) 85 Bh 50
3664* Martinsberg (A) 56 Bf 42
64014 Martinsicuro (I) 84 Bd 48
Mart'janovo (RUS) 42 Da 34
5390 Martofte (DK) 39 Ba 35
08760 Martorell (E) 82 Ab 49
23600 Martos (E) 93 Sg 53
98830 Martti (FIN) 15 Ci 23
21490 Marttila (FIN) 30 Cc 30
7330-339 Marvão (P) 80 Sc 51
48100 Marvejols (F) 67 Ad 46
CA15 Maryport (GB) 51 Sg 36
Maryupol' (UA) 75 Dh 43
09290 Mas-d'Azil, le (F) 82 Ab 47
19490 Masegoso de Tajuña (E) 81 Sh 50
Masel'gskaja (RUS) 24 De 27
Maševe (UA) 59 Dc 38
5994 Masfjorden (N) 28 Af 30
Masi (N) 15 Cd 21
Mašivka (UA) 59 De 41
Maškino (RUS) 43 Dg 36
21251 Masku (FIN) 30 Cc 30
Maslova (RUS) 36 Gb 31
Maslovare (BIH) 70 Bh 46
54100 Massa (I) 69 Ba 46
74016 Massafra (I) 85 Bh 50
Massa Marittima (I) 84 Ba 47
55054 Massarosa (I) 69 Ba 47
09320 Massat (F) 82 Ab 48
18120 Massay (F) 67 Ab 43
32140 Masseube (F) 66 Aa 47
15500 Massiac (F) 67 Ad 45
Masty (BY) 41 Ce 37
Masugnsbyn (S) 15 Cc 23
Måsvik (N) 14 Bi 21
72-130 Maszewo (PL) 39 Bf 37
84-315 Maszewo Lęborskie (PL) 40 Bh 36
70200 Matala (GR) 94 Ce 56
39410 Mataporquera (E) 81 Sf 48
08301 Mataró (E) 82 Ac 49
81850 Mätäsvaara (FIN) 23 Ck 27
Matčerka (RUS) 44 Ec 37
62024 Matelica (I) 69 Bd 47
75100 Matera (I) 85 Bg 50
4700 Mátészalka (H) 71 Cc 43
86401 Matfors (S) 21 Bh 28
17160 Matha (F) 66 Sk 45
22550 Matignon (F) 52 Sh 42
4210 Matīši (LV) 30 Cf 33
Matiši (LV) 41 Cg 35
DE4 Matlock (GB) 51 Si 37
Matoksa (RUS) 31 Da 30
4450-001* Matosinhos (P) 80 Sb 49
9971* Matrei in Osttirol (A) 69 Bc 44
Matrosy (RUS) 23 Dd 29
7210* Mattersburg (A) 70 Bg 43
5230 Mattighofen (A) 55 Bd 42
83002 Mattmar (S) 21 Bd 27
82050 Mattsmyra (S) 29 Bf 29
Matveeevskaja (RUS) 33 Ee 30
Matveevka (RUS) 45 Ek 36
Matveevka (RUS) 46 Fd 37
Matveev Kurgan (RUS) 75 Di 43
Matveevskoe (RUS) 33 Dk 31
Matvijivka (UA) 74 Df 43
59600 Maubeuge (F) 53 Ad 40
75433 Maulbronn (D) 54 Ai 41
79700 Mauléon (F) 66 Sk 44
49360 Maulévrier (F) 66 Sk 43
Maunu (S) 15 Cc 22
15200 Mauriac (F) 67 Ac 45
56430 Mauron (F) 52 Sh 42
15600 Maurs (F) 67 Ac 46
5570 Mauterndorf (A) 69 Bd 43
65130 Mauvezin (F) 66 Aa 47
79210 Mauzé-sur-le-Mignon (F) 66 Sk 44
Mavčadz' (BY) 41 Cf 37
62049 Mavrothálassa (GR) 87 Cd 50
66640 Maxmo (FIN) 22 Cc 27
KA19 Maybole (GB) 51 Sf 35
56727 Mayen (D) 54 Ah 40
53100* Mayenne (F) 52 Sk 42
03250 Mayet-de-Montagne, le (F) 67 Ad 44
Maynooth = Maigh Nuad (IRL) 49 Sd 37
47680 Mayorga (E) 80 Se 48
6290* Mayrhofen (A) 69 Bb 43
Mazagón (E) 92 Sd 53
81200 Mazamet (F) 67 Ac 47
91026 Mazara del Vallo (I) 84 Bc 53
30870 Mazarrón (E) 93 Si 53
89001* Mažeikiai (LT) 41 Cc 34
62800 Mazgirt (TR) 90 Dk 51
48200 Mazı (TR) 95 Ch 53
47700 Mazıdağı (TR) 99 Ea 53
3273 Mazirbe (LV) 30 Cc 33
4215 Mazsalaca (LV) 30 Cf 33
Mazyr (BY) 58 Ck 38
Mcensk (RUS) 43 Dg 37
Mdina (M) 84 Be 55
3050-006* Mealhada (P) 80 Sb 50
Meathas Troim (IRL) 49 Sc 37
77100 Meaux (F) 53 Ac 42
Mečetinskaja (RUS) 76 Ea 44
Mečetka (RUS) 61 Ea 40
Mečetlino (RUS) 47 Fh 35
2800 Mechelen (B) 53 Ae 39
19700 Mecitözü (TR) 89 Df 50
5843 Mečka (BG) 72 Ce 47
Medank (HR) 70 Bf 46
1670 Medemblik (NL) 38 Af 38
Medena Selišta (BIH) 70 Bg 46
Medet (TR) 96 Ck 53
Medevi (S) 29 Be 32
905600 Medgidia (RO) 73 Ci 46
000551* Mediaş (RO) 72 Ce 44
40059 Medicina (I) 69 Bb 46
47400 Medina del Campo (E) 81 Sf 49
09500 Medina de Pomar (E) 81 Sg 48
47800 Medina de Ríoseco (E) 80 Se 49
11170 Medina-Sidonia (E) 92 Se 54
13019 Medininkai (LT) 41 Cf 36
Medjanka (RUS) 35 Fh 33
93100 Medle (S) 22 Ca 26
Mednoe (RUS) 43 Df 34
Mednogorsk (RUS) 64 Fh 39
Međugorje (BIH) 85 Bh 47
16240 Medveđa (SRB) 86 Cb 48
Medvedka (RUS) 36 Fk 32
Medvedok (RUS) 34 Fa 33
Medvenka (RUS) 60 Dg 39
Medvež'egorsk (RUS) 24 De 28
Medvežka (RUS) 18 Fc 24
Medvežskaja (RUS) 27 Fh 26
37-732 Medyka (PL) 57 Cc 41
Medyn' (RUS) 43 Df 36
3461 Medze (LV) 40 Cb 34
068 01 Medzilaborce (SK) 57 Cb 41
Medžybiž (UA) 58 Ch 41
65302 Meeksi (EST) 31 Ch 32
Megalí Panagía (GR) 87 Cd 50
84005 Méga Livádi (GR) 94 Ce 53
Megálo Horío (GR) 95 Ch 54
22200 Megalópoli (GR) 94 Cc 53
Megara (GR) 94 Cd 53
7760 Megard (N) 21 Bc 26
74120 Megève (F) 68 Ag 45
Megorskij Pogost (RUS) 32 Df 30
Megra (RUS) 25 Eb 24
Megrozero (RUS) 32 Dd 29
9770 Mehamn (N) 15 Ch 19
01970 Mehmetli (TR) 98 Dg 53
Mehun-sur-Yéyre (F) 67 Ac 43
32805 Meinberg, Horn-Bad (D) 54 Ai 39
98617 Meiningen (D) 55 Ba 40
27240 Meira (E) 80 Sc 47
01662 Meißen (D) 55 Bd 39
8445 Melbu (N) 14 Be 22
ZE2 Melby Ho (GB) 50 Si 30
7336 Meldal (N) 20 Ak 27
25704 Meldorf (D) 38 Ak 36
20077 Melegnano (I) 69 Ak 45
Melehina (RUS) 35 Ff 31
Melehovo (RUS) 44 Eb 34
23269* Melenci (SRB) 71 Ca 45
Melenki (RUS) 44 Eb 35
Melent'evo (RUS) 26 Ei 27
Meleuz (RUS) 46 Ff 38
85025 Melfi (I) 85 Bf 50
8182 Melfjordbotn (N) 14 Bd 24
4960-578* Melgaço (P) 80 Sb 48
09100 Melgar de Fernamental (E) 81 Sf 48
Melgraseyri (IS) 48 Qh 24
7224 Melhus (N) 20 Ba 27
15800 Melide (E) 80 Sb 48
7570-600* Melides (P) 92 Sb 52
59031 Melíki (GR) 86 Cc 50
Melîlia = Melilla (E) 93 Sh 55
52001 Melilla (E) 93 Sh 55
207385 Melineşti (RO) 72 Cd 46
89063 Melito di Porto Salvo (I) 84 Bf 53
Melitopol' (UA) 74 Df 44
40003 Melívia (GR) 86 Cc 51
3390 Melk (A) 56 Bf 42
95690 Mellakoski (FIN) 15 Ce 24
89042 Mellansel (S) 21 Bi 27
93092 Mellanström (S) 21 Bi 25
49324* Melle (D) 54 Ai 38
49324* Melle (F) 66 Sk 44
46401 Mellerud (S) 29 Bc 32
Melliera (M) 84 Be 55
32300 Mellilä (FIN) 30 Cc 30
97638 Mellrichstadt (D) 55 Ba 40
276 01 Mělník (CZ) 55 Be 40
Mel'nycja-Podil's'ka (UA) 58 Cg 42
Melovatka (RUS) 61 Ea 40
97340 Meltaus (FIN) 15 Cf 24
LE14 Melton Mowbray (GB) 51 Sk 38
95675 Meltosjärvi (FIN) 15 Ce 24
77000 Melun (F) 53 Ac 42
Membrío (E) 80 Sc 51
87700 Memmingen (D) 69 Ba 43
Mena (UA) 59 Dc 39
48000 Mende (F) 67 Ad 46
Mendeleevo (RUS) 37 Gi 32
Mendeleevsk (RUS) 46 Fc 35
35470 Menderes (TR) 95 Ch 52
35660 Menemen (TR) 95 Ch 52
8930 Menen (B) 53 Ad 40
99880 Menesjärvi (FIN) 15 Cg 22
24700 Ménestérol, Momtpon- (F) 66 Aa 45
92013 Menfi (I) 84 Bc 53
05131 Mengamuñoz (E) 81 Sf 50
14840 Mengen (TR) 89 Dc 50
23620 Mengíbar (E) 93 Sg 53
30016 Menídi (GR) 86 Cb 51
99880 Menisjärvi = Menesjärvi (FIN) 15 Cg 22
38710 Mens (F) 68 Af 46
Men'šikovo (RUS) 59 De 39
06500* Menton (F) 68 Ah 47
Menzelinsk (RUS) 46 Fd 35
7940 Meppel (NL) 38 Ag 38
49716 Meppen (D) 38 Ah 38
50170 Mequinenza (E) 82 Aa 49
41500 Mer (F) 67 Ab 43
7530 Meråker (N) 20 Bb 27
39012 Meran = Merano (I) 69 Bb 44
39012 Merano = Meran (I) 69 Bb 44
07740 Mercadal, Es (E) 83 Ae 51
49090 Mercimekkale (TR) 99 Eb 52
22230 Merdrignac (F) 52 Sh 42
Merefa (UA) 60 Dg 41
9820 Merelbeke (B) 53 Ad 40
97980 Mergentheim, Bad (D) 54 Ak 41
22600 Meriç (TR) 87 Cg 49
6430 Meričleri (BG) 87 Cf 48
06800 Mérida (E) 92 Sd 52
33700 Mérignac (F) 66 Sk 46
86220 Merijärvi (FIN) 22 Ce 26
29901 Merikarvia (FIN) 22 Cb 29
21160 Merimasku (FIN) 30 Cb 30
117455 Merişani (RO) 72 Ce 46
65035 Merkinė (LT) 41 Ce 36
61240 Merlerault, le (F) 53 Aa 42
Mermer (TR) 99 Ea 52
7453 Mernye (H) 70 Bh 44
7409* Mersch (L) 54 Ag 41
06217 Merseburg (D) 55 Bb 39
Mersin = İçel (TR) 97 De 54
3284 Mērsrags (LV) 30 Cd 33
CF47 Merthyr Tydfil (GB) 52 Sg 39
7750-320* Mértola (P) 92 Sc 53
60110 Méru (F) 53 Ac 41
Mëry (BY) 42 Ch 35
05300 Merzifon (TR) 89 Df 50
66663 Merzig (D) 54 Ag 41
72023 Mesagne (I) 85 Bh 50
19005 Mesagrós (GR) 94 Cd 53
59872 Meschede (D) 54 Ai 39
Meščovsk (RUS) 43 Df 36
Meseda (RUS) 47 Fi 36
91060 Meselefors (S) 21 Bg 26
33590 Meşelik (TR) 97 De 53
Mesjagutovo (RUS) 47 Fi 35
Meškovskaja (RUS) 61 Eb 41
53170 Meslay-du-Maine (F) 66 Sk 43
Meşndiye (TR) 90 Dh 50
Mešnik (SRB) 71 Bk 47
6563 Mesocco (CH) 69 Ak 44
8280 Mesogi (CY) 96 Dc 56
Mesohóri (GR) 86 Cc 51
44026 Mesola (I) 69 Bc 46
48062 Mesopótamo (GR) 86 Ca 51
98100* Messina (I) 84 Bf 52
24200 Messíni (GR) 94 Cc 53
84035 Messlingen (S) 21 Bc 28
30200 Messolóngi (GR) 94 Cb 52
82102 Mestá (GR) 95 Cf 52
13592 Mestanza (E) 93 Sf 52
68100 Mésti (GR) 87 Cf 50
30175* Mestre (I) 69 Bc 45
Mešura (RUS) 26 Fa 27
75010 Metaponto (I) 85 Bg 50
18030 Méthana (GR) 94 Cd 53
60066 Methóni (GR) 94 Cb 54
Metković (HR) 85 Bh 47
8330 Metlika (SLO) 70 Bf 45
Metóhi (GR) 94 Cd 53
56730 Metsäkylä (FIN) 23 Ci 25
64440 Metsälä = Ömossa (FIN) 22 Cb 28
32270 Metsämaa (FIN) 30 Cd 30
44200 Métsovo (GR) 86 Cb 51
5640 Mettet (B) 53 Ae 40
57000* Metz (F) 54 Ag 41
45130 Meung-sur-Loire (F) 67 Ab 43
01800 Meximieux (F) 68 Af 45
Meydan (TR) 99 Eb 52
Meydancık (TR) 91 Ec 49
16945 Meyenburg (D) 39 Bc 37
19250 Meymac (F) 67 Ac 45
48150 Meyrueis (F) 67 Ad 46
Mežador (RUS) 34 Fa 29
3100 Mezdra (BG) 87 Cd 47
Meždurečensk (RUS) 45 Ek 37
Mezen' (RUS) 25 Ee 25
Mezenivka (UA) 60 Df 40
Meževoj (RUS) 47 Fi 35
Mezga (RUS) 32 Dg 32
Mézier, Charleville- (F) 53 Ae 41
87330 Mézières-sur-Issoire (F) 66 Aa 44
47170 Mézin (F) 66 Aa 46
Mežog (RUS) 26 Ek 28
Mezőkövesd (H) 71 Ca 43
40170 Mézos (F) 66 Si 46
Mezőtúr (H) 71 Ca 43
Mežova (UA) 60 Dg 42
Mežozernyj (RUS) 47 Fk 36

186 I Malojaz

Morygino (RUS) 42 Dc 36
Mosal'sk (RUS) 43 De 36
74821 Mosbach (D) 54 Ak 41
4619 Mosby (N) 28 Ah 32
Mošćenička Draga (HR) 70 Be 45
Moseevo (RUS) 25 Eg 25
Moseevo (RUS) 33 Ec 30
62-050 Mosina (PL) 56 Bg 38
Mosino (RUS) 47 Fh 34
8655* Mosjøen (N) 21 Bd 25
Moskakasy (RUS) 45 Eg 34
Moški (RUS) 43 Df 34
93086 Moskosel (S) 22 Bk 25
Moskovo (RUS) 46 Ff 35
Moskva (RUS) 43 Dh 35
Mošnikovskaja (RUS) 32 Dg 30
Mošny (UA) 59 Db 41
39013 Moso in Passiria = Moos in Passeier (I) 69 Bb 44
Mošok (RUS) 44 Eb 35
Mosonmagyaróvár (H) 70 Bh 43
1511* Moss (N) 28 Ba 31
434 01* Most (CZ) 55 Bd 40
Most (RUS) 24 Dk 28
88000* Mostar (BIH) 70 Bh 47
147410 Moşteni, Trivalea- (RO) 72 Cf 46
28931 Móstoles (E) 81 Sg 50
Mostovaja (RUS) 35 Fe 33
Mostovskoj (RUS) 76 Ea 46
Mostys'ka (UA) 57 Cd 41
16630 Mota del Cuervo (E) 81 Sh 51
47120 Mota del Marqués (E) 80 Se 49
Motal' (BY) 58 Cf 38
59100* Motala (S) 29 Bf 32
85150 Mothe-Achard, la (F) 66 Si 44
ML1 Motherwell (GB) 51 Sg 35
18600 Motril (E) 93 Sg 54
215200 Motru (RO) 71 Cc 46
74017 Mottola (I) 85 Bh 50
1510 Moudon (CH) 68 Ag 44
Moúdros (GR) 87 Cf 51
06250 Mougins (F) 68 Ag 47
38460 Mouhijärvi (FIN) 30 Cc 29
35680 Moulins (F) 67 Ad 44
Mount Bellew Bridge = An Creagán (IRL) 49 Sb 37
Mountmellick = Móinteach Mílic (IRL) 49 Sc 37
Mountrath = Maighean Rátha (IRL) 49 Sc 37
7860-001* Moura (P) 92 Sc 52
7885-011 Mourão (P) 92 Sc 52
64150 Mourenx (F) 66 Sk 47
37001 Mourési (GR) 87 Cd 51
04360 Moustiers-Sainte-Marie (F) 68 Ag 47
73600 Moûtiers (F) 68 Ag 45
85540 Moutiers-les-Mauxfaits (F) 66 Si 44
84302 Moutsoúna (GR) 95 Cf 53
60250 Mouy (F) 53 Ac 41
43060 Mouzáki (GR) 86 Cb 51
927175 Movila (RO) 73 Ch 46
817100 Movila Miresii (RO) 73 Ch 45
927180 Movilița (RO) 72 Cg 46
Moville (IRL) 49 Sc 35
32200 Movríki (GR) 94 Cd 52
57250 Moyeuvre-Grande (F) 54 Ag 41
50143 Moyuela (E) 82 Sk 49
Možaisk (RUS) 43 Dg 35
Mozdok (RUS) 76 Ee 47
Možga (RUS) 46 Fc 34
Mozyr' = Mazyr (BY) 58 Ck 38
11-700* Mrągowo (PL) 40 Cb 37
Mrakovo (RUS) 64 Fg 38
32210 Mrčajevci (SRB) 71 Ca 47
7508 Mrežičko (MK) 86 Cb 49
Mrjasimovo (RUS) 47 Fg 35
Mrkalji (BIH) 71 Bi 46
Mrkonjić Grad (BIH) 70 Bh 46
72-330 Mrzeżyno (PL) 39 Bf 36
Mscislav (BY) 42 Db 36
Msciž (BY) 42 Ci 36
Mšinskaja (RUS) 31 Ck 31
Msta (RUS) 32 De 33
Mstera (RUS) 44 Eb 34
96-320 Mszczonów (PL) 57 Ca 39
Mučkapskij (RUS) 61 Ec 39
Mučkas (RUS) 26 Ei 26
40500 Mucur (TR) 89 De 51
16940 Mudanya (TR) 88 Ci 50
Mud'juga (RUS) 24 Dk 27
14800 Mudurnu (TR) 88 Db 50
Muezerskij (RUS) 23 Dc 27
Muftjuga (RUS) 25 Eg 26
Muggia (I) 69 Bd 45
48000 Muğla (TR) 96 Ci 53
Mugreevskij (RUS) 44 Ec 34
75417 Mühlacker (D) 54 Ai 42
84453 Mühldorf am Inn (D) 55 Bc 42
Mühlen in Taufers = Molini di Tures (I) 69 Bb 44
99974 Mühlhausen/Thüringen (D) 55 Ba 39
91501 Muhos (FIN) 22 Cg 26
Muhtolovo (RUS) 44 Ed 35
Muinchille (IRL) 49 Sc 36
Muineachán = Monaghan (IRL) 49 Sd 36
IV6 Muir of Ord (GB) 50 Sf 33
Mukačeve (UA) 57 Cc 42
Mukačevo = Mukačeve (UA) 57 Cc 42
30170 Mula (E) 93 Si 52
68050* Mulhouse (F) 68 Ah 43
Mullach Íde (IRL) 49 Sd 37
79379 Müllheim (D) 68 Ah 43
Mullingar = An Muileann-gCearr (IRL) 49 Sc 37
Mullovka (RUS) 45 Ek 36
56501 Mullsjö (S) 29 Bd 33
42601 Multia (FIN) 22 Ce 28
Mumra (RUS) 77 Eh 45
95213 Münchberg (D) 55 Bb 40
15374 Müncheberg (D) 55 Be 38
80331* München (D) 55 Bb 42
34346 Münden = Hann Münden (D) 54 Ak 39
NR11 Mundesley (GB) 51 Ab 38
48100 Mungía (E) 66 Sh 47
44780 Muniesa (E) 82 Sk 49
26620 Munka-Ljungby (S) 39 Bc 34
45501 Munkedal (S) 28 Bb 32
68401 Munkfors (S) 29 Bd 31
72525 Münsingen (CH) 68 Ah 44
29633 Munster (D) 39 Ba 38
48143* Münster (D) 54 Ah 39
29633 Munster (F) 54 Ah 42
7537 Münster = Müstair (CH) 69 Ba 44
83090 Munsvattnet (S) 21 Be 26
547505 Munți, Rușii- (RO) 72 Ce 44
98495 Muodoslompolo (S) 15 Cd 23
99301 Muonio (FIN) 15 Cd 23
65500 Muradiye (TR) 95 Ch 52
65500 Muradiye (TR) 99 Ed 52
Muraši (RUS) 34 Ei 31
15300 Murat (F) 67 Ac 45
Murat (TR) 91 Ed 51
63570 Muratlı (TR) 88 Ch 49
20239 Murato (F) 83 Ak 48
81320 Murat-sur-Vèbre (F) 67 Ac 47
8850 Murau (A) 70 Be 43
09043 Muravera (I) 83 Ak 51
5090-101* Murça (P) 80 Sc 49
30001* Murcia (E) 93 Si 53
12600 Mur-de-Barrez (F) 67 Ac 46
Mur-de-Bretagne (F) 52 Sh 42
38350 Mure, la (F) 68 Af 46
8480* Mureck (A) 70 Bf 44
59800 Mürefte (TR) 88 Ch 50
Mureșenii Bârgăului (RO) 72 Ce 43
31600* Muret (F) 67 Ab 47
737370 Murgeni (RO) 73 Ci 44
Murgul (TR) 91 Eb 49
Murino (RUS) 47 Gb 34
96033 Murjek (S) 14 Ca 24
Murmansk (RUS) 16 Dd 22
Murmaši (RUS) 16 Dc 22
Murmino (RUS) 44 Ea 36
07440 Muro (E) 82 Ad 51
Muro del Acoy = Muro del Comtat (E) 82 Sk 52
34410 Murole (FIN) 22 Cd 29
85054 Muro Lucano (I) 85 Bf 50
Murom (RUS) 44 Ec 35
Murom (RUS) 60 Dg 40
33138 Muros (E) 80 Sa 48
Murovani Kurylivci (UA) 58 Ch 42
62-095* Murowana Goślina (PL) 56 Bh 38
71540 Murrhardt (D) 54 Ak 42
Mursal (TR) 90 Dh 51
Mursalimkino (RUS) 47 Fi 35
Mürşitpınar (TR) 98 Di 54
9000* Murska Sobota (SLO) 70 Bg 44
81810 Murtovaara (FIN) 23 Ck 25
Murygino (RUS) 34 Ek 32
8680* Mürzzuschlag (A) 70 Bf 43
49000* Muş (TR) 99 Eb 52
Muša (RUS) 34 Ei 33
Musabeyli (TR) 89 De 51
Musabeyli (TR) 98 Dg 54
Musljumkino (RUS) 46 Fa 35
Musljumovo (RUS) 46 Fd 35
Musljumovo (RUS) 47 Gb 35
Musorka (RUS) 45 Ek 37
EH15 Musselburgh (GB) 51 Sg 35
24400 Mussidan (F) 66 Aa 45
Mustaevo (RUS) 63 Fd 39
Mustafakemalpaşa (TR) 88 Ci 50
7537 Müstair = Münster (CH) 69 Ba 44
7180 Mustér, Disentis/ (CH) 68 Ai 44
93601 Mustjala (EST) 30 Cc 32
69701 Mustla (EST) 30 Cf 32
49603* Mustvee (EST) 30 Cg 32
33-370 Muszyna (PL) 57 Ca 41
33600 Mut (TR) 97 Dd 54
13700 Mutki (TR) 99 Eb 52
Mutnyj Materik (RUS) 26 Ff 25
26555 Muttalıp (TR) 88 Da 51
Mutyn (UA) 59 Dd 39
44880 Muurasjärvi (FIN) 22 Cf 27
49760 Muurola (FIN) 15 Cf 24
73460 Muuruvesi (FIN) 23 Ci 27
15124 Muxía (E) 80 Sa 47
Mužič'e (RUS) 61 Eb 40
56190 Muzillac (F) 66 Sh 43
Muzyvalen (RUS) 45 Eg 34
Mychajlivka (UA) 60 Df 42
Mychajlivka (UA) 74 Df 43
Mychajlivka (UA) 75 Di 43
37034 Myckelgensjö (S) 21 Bh 27
Myeldino (RUS) 26 Fe 29
907 01 Myjava (SK) 56 Bh 42
Mykland (N) 28 Ai 32
Mykolajiv (UA) 57 Cd 41
Mykolajiv (UA) 74 Db 44
Mykolajivka (UA) 59 De 42
Mykolajivka 74 Dd 46
Myla (RUS) 26 Fa 25
23101 Mynämäki (FIN) 30 Cb 30
5718 Myrdal (N) 28 Ah 30
8430 Myre (N) 14 Bf 22
Myrheden (S) 22 Ca 25
Myrhorod (UA) 59 Dd 41
660 Mýri (IS) 48 Rc 25
Myrne (UA) 74 Dd 44
Myronivka (UA) 59 Da 41
07601 Myrskylä (FIN) 30 Cf 30
Myrtou 96 Dc 55
Myrviken (S) 21 Be 28
Mys (RUS) 35 Fe 30
1850 Mysen (N) 28 Bb 31
Myškin (RUS) 32 Di 33
Myškino = Myškin (RUS) 32 Di 33
32-400 Myślenice (PL) 56 Bk 41
74-300 Myślibórz (PL) 39 Be 38
41-400* Mysłowice (PL) 56 Bk 40
07-430 Myszyniec (PL) 40 Cb 37
Myt (RUS) 44 Ec 34
Mytišči (RUS) 43 Dh 35
Mytišino (RUS) 43 De 36

N

21110 Naantali (FIN) 30 Cc 30
76851 Naarajärvi (FIN) 23 Ch 28
1410 Naarden (NL) 54 Af 38
81470 Naarva (FIN) 23 Db 27
Naas = An Nás (IRL) 49 Sd 37
99940 Näätämö (FIN) 15 Ck 21
92507 Nabburg (D) 55 Bc 41
Naberežnye Čelny (RUS) 46 Fc 35
Načalovo (RUS) 77 Ei 44
Na Ceala Beaga (IRL) 49 Sb 36
390 01 Náchod (CZ) 56 Bg 40
Na Clocha Liatha (IRL) 49 Sd 37
Nadeždinka (RUS) 62 Ei 38
315500 Nădlac (RO) 71 Ca 44
Nadporož'e (RUS) 32 Di 31
Nadvirna (UA) 57 Ce 42
Nadvojcy (RUS) 24 De 27
4365 Nærbø (N) 28 Af 32
4700 Næstved (DK) 39 Bb 35
30300 Náfpaktos (GR) 94 Cb 52
21100 Náfplio (GR) 94 Cc 53
Nagaevo (RUS) 47 Fg 36
Nagajbakovo (RUS) 46 Fd 35
Nagavskaja (RUS) 76 Ec 43
84013 Naggen (S) 21 Bf 28
72202 Nagold (D) 54 Ai 42
Nagor'e (RUS) 43 Di 34
Nagornskij (RUS) 35 Fh 32
Nagorsk (RUS) 34 Fa 31
Nagutskoe (RUS) 76 Ee 46
7500 Nagyatád (H) 70 Bh 44
Nagygéc (H) 71 Cc 43
4320 Nagykálló (H) 71 Cb 43
8800 Nagykanizsa (H) 70 Bg 44
2760 Nagykáta (H) 71 Bk 43
Nagykőrös (H) 71 Bk 43
5931 Nagyszénás (H) 71 Ca 44
95119 Naila (D) 55 Bb 40
86530 Naintré (F) 66 Aa 44
IV12 Nairn (GB) 50 Sg 33
12270 Najac (F) 67 Ab 46
26300 Nájera (E) 81 Sh 48
Najstenjarvi (RUS) 23 Dc 28
89-100* Nakło nad Notecią (PL) 40 Bh 37
4900 Nakskov (DK) 39 Bb 36
827160 Nalbant (RO) 73 Ci 45
Nal'čik (RUS) 76 Ed 47
Nalibaki (BY) 41 Cg 37
89670 Näljänkä (FIN) 23 Ci 25
06920 Nallıhan (TR) 88 Db 50
5000 Namen = Namur (B) 53 Ae 40
029 01 Námestovo (SK) 56 Bk 41
7800 Namsos (N) 20 Bb 26
7890 Namsskogan (N) 21 Bd 26
Namsvassgardan (N) 21 Bd 26
5000 Namur (B) 53 Ae 40
46-100 Namysłów (PL) 56 Bh 39
54000* Nancy (F) 54 Ag 42
77370 Nangis (F) 53 Ad 42
Nannestad (N) 28 Bb 30
12230 Nant (F) 67 Ad 46
92000 Nanterre (F) 53 Ac 42
44000* Nantes (F) 66 Si 43
60440 Nanteuil-le-Haudouin (F) 53 Ac 41
CW5 Nantwich (GB) 51 Sh 37
84401 Náousa (GR) 95 Cf 53
59200 Náoussa (GR) 86 Cc 50
000400* Napoca, Cluj- (RO) 72 Cd 44
80100* Napoli (I) 85 Be 50
Narač (BY) 41 Cg 36
Naratasty (RUS) 46 Fd 36
Naratasty (RUS) 46 Fe 36
SA67 Narberth (GB) 52 Sf 39
11100* Narbonne (F) 82 Ac 47
2540 Narbuvoll (N) 20 Bb 28
73048 Nardo (I) 85 Bi 50
4239 Narečenski Bani (BG) 87 Ce 49
Narezka (RUS) 31 Dc 33
Narimanov (RUS) 77 Eh 44
02440 Narince (TR) 98 Di 53
Nar'jan-Mar (RUS) 18 Fc 23
10510 Narlı (TR) 98 Dh 53
10510 Narlı (TR) 99 Ec 53
13040 Narlıdere (TR) 99 Eb 52
19600 Narlık (TR) 97 Df 54
25530 Narman (TR) 91 Eb 50
05035 Narni (I) 84 Bc 48
Narodyči (UA) 58 Ck 39
Naro-Fominsk (RUS) 43 Dg 35
Narovčat (RUS) 44 Ed 37
Narovlja (BY) 58 Ck 39
64260 Närpes (FIN) 22 Cb 28
64260 Närpiö = Närpes (FIN) 22 Cb 28
Nartkala (RUS) 76 Ed 47
Naruksovo (RUS) 45 Ee 36
20103* Narva (EST) 31 Ci 31
37370 Narva (FIN) 30 Cd 29
29021* Narva-Jõesuu (EST) 31 Ci 31
8514* Narvik (N) 14 Bh 22
Naryn-Huduk (RUS) 77 Eg 45
Naryškino (RUS) 43 Df 38
Nasafjäll (S) 14 Bf 24
88030 Näsåker (S) 21 Bg 27
425200 Năsăud (RO) 72 Ce 43
Na Sceirí (IRL) 49 Sd 37
Našice (HR) 71 Bi 45
Naşidiye (TR) 97 Df 53
05-190 Nasielsk (PL) 57 Ca 38
Naslednickoe (RUS) 65 Ga 38
6465 Nassereith (A) 69 Ba 43
88041 Nässjö (S) 29 Be 33
91201 Nastansjö (S) 21 Bg 26
15561 Nastola (FIN) 30 Cf 30
Nasva (RUS) 42 Da 34
Natal'in Jar (RUS) 63 Fa 39
Natal'ino (RUS) 45 Ek 38
98206 Nattavaara (S) 14 Ca 24
39025 Naturno = Naturns (I) 69 Ba 44
39025 Naturns = Naturno (I) 69 Ba 44
12800 Naucelle (F) 67 Ac 46
Naučnyj 74 De 46
14641 Nauen (D) 55 Bc 38
85001 Naujoji Akmenė (LT) 41 Cc 34
06618 Naumburg (Saale) (D) 55 Bb 39
Naumovskaja (RUS) 33 Ed 30
Naumovskij (RUS) 76 Eb 43
Nausta (S) 14 Bk 24
6817 Naustdal (N) 28 Af 29
Nautijaur (S) 14 Bk 24
Nautsi (RUS) 15 Ck 21
33520 Nava (E) 80 Se 47
Navacëlki (BY) 58 Ci 38
40450 Nava de la Asunción (E) 81 Sf 49
47500 Nava del Rey (E) 80 Se 49
45670 Nava de Ricomalillo, La (E) 81 Sf 51
06486 Nava de Santiago, La (E) 80 Sd 51
Navael'nja (BY) 41 Cf 37
45150 Navahermosa (E) 81 Sf 51
Navahrudak (BY) 41 Cf 37
28600 Navalcarnero (E) 81 Sf 50
40280 Navalmanzano (E) 81 Sf 49
10300 Navalmoral de la Mata (E) 80 Se 51
45140 Navalmorales, Los (E) 81 Sf 51
06760 Navalvillar de Pela (E) 80 Se 51
Navan = An Uaimh (IRL) 49 Sd 37
Navapolack (BY) 42 Ci 35
46823 Navarrés (E) 82 Sk 51
41460 Navas de la Concepción, Las (E) 92 Se 53
10930 Navas del Madroño (E) 80 Sd 51
Navasëlki (BY) 41 Cg 38
Navašino (RUS) 44 Ec 35
Navesnoe (RUS) 60 Dh 38
33710 Navia (E) 80 Sd 47
Navlja (RUS) 43 De 38
905700 Năvodari (RO) 73 Ci 46
Navoloki (RUS) 33 Eb 33
84300 Náxos (GR) 95 Cf 53
64800 Nay-Bourdettes (F) 82 Sk 47
2450-100* Nazaré (P) 80 Sa 51
Nazija (RUS) 31 Db 31
09800* Nazilli (TR) 96 Ci 53
62950 Nazimiye (TR) 90 Dk 51
Néa Apolonía (GR) 87 Cd 50
63080 Néa Kalikrátia (GR) 87 Cd 50
19005 Néa Mákri (GR) 94 Cd 52
57004 Néa Mihanióna (GR) 86 Cc 50
Néa Moudania (GR) 87 Cd 50
000610* Neamț, Piatra- (RO) 72 Cg 44
Neapel = Napoli (I) 85 Be 50
23053 Neápoli (GR) 86 Cb 50
23053 Neápoli (GR) 94 Cd 54
23053 Neápoli (GR) 95 Cf 55
Néa Potídea (GR) 87 Cd 50
SA11 Neath (GB) 52 Sg 39
62042 Néa Zíhni (GR) 87 Cd 49
35980 Nebiler (TR) 87 Cg 51
Nebolči (RUS) 32 Dd 31
Nečaevka (RUS) 45 Ee 37
Nechvoroša (UA) 59 De 41
69151 Neckargemünd (D) 54 Ai 41
15510 Neda (E) 80 Sb 47
4990 Nedelino (BG) 87 Cf 49
Nedel'noe (RUS) 43 Dg 36
Nedobojivci (UA) 58 Cg 42
Nedryhajliv (UA) 59 Dd 40
5560 Nedstrand (N) 28 Af 31
Nedvigouka (RUS) 75 Dk 43
Neftegorsk (RUS) 46 Fb 38
Neftegorsk (RUS) 75 Dk 46
Neftekamsk (RUS) 46 Fe 34
Neftekumsk (RUS) 76 Ee 46
Neftekumsk (RUS) 77 Ef 46
Negonovo (RUS) 43 De 34
19300* Negotin (SRB) 71 Cc 46
1235 Negotino (MK) 86 Cc 49
117535 Negrași (RO) 72 Cf 46
15830 Negreira (E) 80 Sb 48
82800 Nègrepelisse (F) 67 Ab 46
445200 Negrești-Oaș (RO) 72 Cd 43
905800 Negru Vodă (RO) 73 Ci 47
Nehaevskij (RUS) 61 Eb 40
125100 Nehoiu (RO) 72 Cg 45
9930 Neiden (N) 15 Ck 21
Neidín = Kenmare (IRL) 49 Sa 39
Neja (RUS) 33 Ed 32
Nejvinskij, Verh- (RUS) 36 Ga 33
Nejvo-Rudjanka (RUS) 36 Ga 33
Nekljudovo (RUS) 32 Dh 33
Nekljudovo (RUS) 44 Ed 34
Nekrasovo (RUS) 47 Gb 34
Nekrasovskoe (RUS) 33 Ea 33
Neksø (DK) 39 Bf 35
3505-172* Nelas (P) 80 Sc 50
Nelidovo (RUS) 42 Dc 34
99860 Nellim (FIN) 15 Ci 22
Nema (RUS) 34 Fa 33
Neman (RUS) 41 Cc 35
20500 Neméa (GR) 94 Cc 53
15019 Nemenčinė (LT) 41 Cf 36
Nemnjuga (RUS) 25 Ee 27
77140* Nemours (F) 53 Ac 42
Nemyriv (UA) 57 Cd 40
Nemyriv (UA) 58 Ci 42
Nenagh = An tAonach (IRL) 49 Sb 38
82103 Nenitoúria (GR) 95 Cf 52
Nenoksa (RUS) 24 Dk 26
68200 Neohóri (GR) 86 Ca 51
68200 Neohóri (GR) 86 Cb 51
68200 Neohóri (GR) 94 Cb 52
62043 Néo Petrítsi (GR) 87 Cd 49
Néos Marmarás (GR) 87 Cd 50
Nepljuevo (RUS) 43 Dg 38
335 01 Nepomuk (CZ) 55 Bd 41
47600 Nérac (F) 66 Aa 46
43100 Neraída (GR) 86 Cb 51
277 11 Neratovice (CZ) 55 Be 40
Nerdva (RUS) 35 Ff 32
Nerehta (RUS) 33 Ea 33
12242 Neresnica (SRB) 71 Cb 46
5118 Nereta (LV) 41 Cf 34
Nerl' (RUS) 43 Dh 33
Nerl' (RUS) 44 Ea 34
18350 Nérondes (F) 67 Ac 44
21670 Nerva (E) 92 Sd 53
7630 Nes (N) 28 Ak 30
Nes' (RUS) 17 Ee 24
3540 Nesbyen (N) 28 Ak 30
8230 Nesebăr (BG) 88 Ch 48
4244 Nesflaten (N) 28 Ag 31
740 Neskaupstaður (IS) 48 Rg 25
8700 Nesna (N) 14 Bd 24
1450 Nesoddtangen (N) 28 Ba 31
5131 Nesseby (N) 15 Ci 20

188 I Morygino

Nesterov (RUS) 41 Cc 36
Nesterov = Žovkva (UA) 57 Cd 40
Nesterovka (RUS) 63 Fd 38
Nestiary (RUS) 45 Ef 34
52051 Nestório (GR) 86 Cb 50
Nesvetajskaja, Rodionovo- (RUS) 75 Dk 43
17033* Neubrandenburg (D) 39 Bd 37
18233 Neubukow (D) 39 Bb 36
86633 Neuburg an der Donau (D) 55 Bb 42
2000* Neuchâtel (CH) 68 Ag 43
53474 Neuenahr-Ahrweiler, Bad (D) 54 Ah 40
2000* Neuenburg = Neuchâtel (CH) 68 Ag 43
15366 Neuenhagen bei Berlin (D) 55 Bd 38
49828 Neuenhaus (D) 54 Ag 38
68600 Neuf-Brisach (F) 54 Ah 42
6840 Neufchâteau (B) 54 Af 41
88300 Neufchâteau (F) 54 Af 42
76270 Neufchâtel-en-Bray (F) 53 Ab 41
02190 Neufchâtel-sur-Aisne (F) 53 Ae 41
98724 Neuhaus am Rennweg (D) 55 Bb 40
37360 Neuillé-Pont-Pierre (F) 66 Aa 43
23992 Neukloster (D) 39 Bb 37
Neum (BIH) 85 Bh 48
4720 Neumarkt im Hausruckkreis (A) 55 Bd 42
92318 Neumarkt in der Oberpfalz (D) 55 Bb 41
24534* Neumünster (D) 38 Ak 36
41210 Neung-sur-Beuvron (F) 67 Ab 43
66538* Neunkirchen (A) 70 Bg 43
66538* Neunkirchen (D) 54 Ah 41
16816 Neuruppin (D) 39 Bc 38
2183 Neusiedl an der Zaya (A) 56 Bg 42
41460* Neuss (D) 54 Ag 39
16845 Neustadt (Dosse) (D) 39 Bc 38
07806 Neustadt (Orla) (D) 55 Bb 40
79822 Neustadt, Titisee- (D) 68 Ai 43
31535 Neustadt am Rübenberge (D) 54 Ak 38
91413 Neustadt an der Aisch (D) 55 Ba 41
93333 Neustadt an der Donau (D) 55 Bb 42
67433* Neustadt an der Weinstraße (D) 54 Ai 41
23730 Neustadt in Holstein (D) 39 Ba 36
17235 Neustrelitz (D) 39 Bd 37
89231* Neu-Ulm (D) 55 Ba 42
27330 Neuve-Lyre, la (F) 53 Aa 42
24190 Neuvic (F) 67 Ac 45
86170 Neuville-de-Poitou (F) 66 Aa 44
69250 Neuville-sur-Saône (F) 67 Ae 45
36230 Neuvy-Saint-Sépulchre (F) 67 Ab 44
18330 Neuvy-sur-Barangeon (F) 67 Ac 43
56564* Neuwied (D) 54 Ah 40
Nevel' (RUS) 42 Ck 34
58000* Nevers (F) 67 Ad 44
Nevesinje (BIH) 71 Bi 47
2595 Nevestino (BG) 86 Cc 48
Nevinnomyssk (RUS) 76 Eb 46
Nev'jansk (RUS) 36 Ga 33
50000* Nevşehir (TR) 97 De 52
Nevskij, Aleksandro (RUS) 44 Ea 37
NG24 Newark on Trent (GB) 51 Sk 37
NE64 Newbiggin-by-the-Sea (GB) 51 Si 35
BT22 Newcastle (GB) 49 Se 36
NE2 Newcastle upon Tyne (GB) 51 Si 36
Newcastle West = An Caisleán Nua (IRL) 49 Sa 38
DG7 New Galloway (GB) 51 Sf 35
CT11 Newhaven (GB) 53 Aa 40
CB8 Newmarket (GB) 53 Aa 38
CB11 Newport (GB) 51 Sh 38
CB11 Newport (GB) 52 Sh 39
CB11 Newport (GB) 52 Si 40
TR7 Newquay (GB) 52 Se 40
SA45 New Quay (GB) 52 Sf 38
TN28 New Romney (GB) 53 Aa 40
New Ross = Ros Mhic Thriúin (IRL) 49 Sd 38
BT34 Newry (GB) 49 Sd 36
HS2 New Tolsta (GB) 50 Sd 32
IV27 Newton (GB) 50 Sc 33
TQ12 Newton Abbot (GB) 52 Sg 40
DG8 Newton Stewart (GB) 51 Sf 36
SY16 Newtown (GB) 52 Sg 38
BT37 Newtownabbey (GB) 49 Se 36
BT23 Newtownards (GB) 49 Se 36
BT78 Newtownsteward (GB) 49 Sc 36
87800 Nexon (F) 67 Ab 45
Nezamaevskaja (RUS) 76 Ea 44
Nežin = Nižyn (UA) 59 Db 39
Nežinka (RUS) 64 Ff 39
Neznanovo (RUS) 44 Ea 36
Nežnurskij (RUS) 45 Eg 34
Nezvys'ko (UA) 58 Cf 42
23060 Niáta (GR) 94 Cc 54
9240 Nibe (DK) 38 Ak 34
Nicaj-Shalë (AL) 86 Bk 48
88046 Nicastro (I) 85 Bg 52
06000* Nice (F) 68 Ah 47
Nicinskoe, Ust'- (RUS) 37 Ge 33
Nicolo-Berezovec (RUS) 33 Ec 32
94014 Nicosia (I) 84 Be 53
1010* Nicosia = Lefkosia (CY) 97 Dd 55
89844 Nicotera (I) 84 Bf 52
93012 Nida (LT) 40 Cb 35
12-220 Nida, Ruciane- (PL) 40 Cb 37
31084 Nídri (GR) 94 Ca 52
13-100 Nidzica (PL) 40 Ca 37
25899 Niebüll (D) 38 Ai 36
72-350 Niechorze (PL) 39 Bf 36
67110 Niederbronn-les-Bains (F) 54 Ah 42
14823 Niemegk (D) 55 Bc 38
95595 Niemisel (S) 22 Cc 24
31582 Nienburg (Weser) (D) 54 Ak 38
02906 Niesky (D) 55 Be 39
8620 Nieuwpoort (B) 53 Ac 39
51000* Niğde (TR) 97 De 52
62200 Nigríta (GR) 87 Cd 50
04100 Níjar (E) 93 Sh 54
Nijemci (HR) 71 Bk 45
3860 Nijkerk (NL) 54 Af 38
6500* Nijmegen (NL) 54 Af 39
7440 Nijverdal (NL) 54 Ag 38
Nikel' (RUS) 16 Da 21
Nikifarovo (RUS) 46 Fe 37
Nikiforovo (RUS) 32 Di 29
Nikitino (RUS) 33 Ee 33
Nikitovka (RUS) 60 Di 40
Nikkaluokta (S) 14 Bi 23
Nikolaev = Mykolajiv (UA) 74 Db 44
Nikolaevka (RUS) 42 Dc 37
Nikolaevka (RUS) 45 Eh 37
Nikolaevka (RUS) 46 Ff 37
Nikolaevka (RUS) 62 Ei 38
Nikolaevo (RUS) 31 Ck 32
Nikolaevsk (RUS) 62 Ef 40
Nikoliskoe (RUS) 33 Ee 32
Nikologry (RUS) 44 Ec 34
Nikolo-Pavlovskoe (RUS) 36 Ga 33
Nikolo-Šanga (RUS) 34 Ef 32
Nikol'sk (RUS) 34 Ef 31
Nikol'sk (RUS) 45 Eg 37
Nikol'skaja (RUS) 46 Fd 37
Nikol's'ke (UA) 75 Dh 43
Nikol'skij Toržok (RUS) 32 Di 31
Nikol'skoe (RUS) 33 Ec 31
Nikol'skoe (RUS) 33 Ee 31
Nikol'skoe (RUS) 45 Ee 38
Nikol'skoe (RUS) 60 Dg 38
Nikol'skoe (RUS) 60 Dk 38
Nikol'skoe (RUS) 63 Fe 39
Nikol'skoe (RUS) 64 Ff 38
Nikol'skoe (RUS) 76 Ee 46
Nikol'skoe (RUS) 77 Eg 43
Nikol'skoe-na-Čeremšane (RUS) 45 Ek 36
5940 Nikopol (BG) 72 Ce 47
Nikopol' (UA) 74 De 43
60600* Niksar (TR) 90 Dg 50
81 400* Nikšić (MNE) 86 Bi 48
Nikulino (RUS) 33 Ee 32
Nikuljata (RUS) 34 Ei 33
Nikul'skoe (RUS) 33 Dk 33
Nilivaara (S) 15 Cb 23
Nil'maguba (RUS) 23 Dc 25
73301 Nilsiä (FIN) 23 Ci 27
Nimen'ga (RUS) 24 Dh 27
30000* Nîmes (F) 67 Ae 47
Nin (HR) 70 Bf 46
79000* Niort (F) 66 Sk 44
18101* Niš (SRB) 71 Cb 47
6050-302* Nisa (P) 80 Sc 51
93015 Niscemi (I) 84 Be 53
37-400 Nisko (PL) 57 Cc 40
6400 Nisporen' = Nisporeni (MD) 73 Ci 43
6400 Nisporeni (MD) 73 Ci 43
6400 Nisporeny = Nisporeni (MD) 73 Ci 43
3854 Nissedal (N) 28 Ai 31
74250 Nissilä (FIN) 22 Cg 27
Nitaure (LV) 41 Cf 33
031 01* Nitra (SK) 56 Bi 42
972 13 Nitrianske Pravno (SK) 56 Bi 42
89310 Nitry (F) 67 Ad 43
Nittedal (N) 28 Ba 30
85540 Nivala (FIN) 22 Ce 27
Nivenskoe (RUS) 40 Ca 36
Nivšera (RUS) 26 Fc 28
Nivskij (RUS) 16 Dc 23
Niz (RUS) 25 Eb 28
Niz (RUS) 32 Df 31
Niža (RUS) 17 Ed 24
27700 Nizip (TR) 98 Dh 53
Nižmozero (RUS) 24 Dh 26
Nižnee Al'keevo (RUS) 46 Fa 36
Nižnee Ust'e (RUS) 24 Di 28
Nižneirginskoe (RUS) 47 Fh 34
Nižneivkino (RUS) 34 Ek 32
Nižnekamsk (RUS) 46 Fb 35
Nižnepavlovka (RUS) 63 Fe 39
Nižnetroickij (RUS) 46 Fd 36
Nižnie Kigi (RUS) 47 Fi 35
Nižnie Sergi (RUS) 47 Fk 34
Nižnie Vjazovye (RUS) 45 Ei 35
Nižnij Bajgora (RUS) 60 Dk 39
Nižnij Baskunčak (RUS) 62 Eg 42
Nižnij Čir (RUS) 61 Ec 42
Nižnij Duvanka (UA) 60 Di 41
Nižnij Enagsk (RUS) 34 Eg 31
Nižnij Kisljaú (RUS) 61 Ea 40
Nižnij Lomov (RUS) 44 Ed 37
Nižnij Luh (RUS) 35 Fg 32
Nižnij Novgorod (RUS) 44 Ed 34
Nižnij Odes (RUS) 26 Fe 27
Nižnij Tagil (RUS) 36 Fk 33
Nižnij Takanyš (RUS) 46 Fb 35
Nižnij Ufalej (RUS) 47 Fk 35
Nižnij Veduga (RUS) 60 Di 39
Nižnij Voč' (RUS) 35 Fe 29
Nižnij Zaramag (RUS) 91 Ee 48
Nižnjaja (RUS) 25 Eg 26
Nižnjaja Maktama (RUS) 46 Fc 36
Nižnjaja Mgla (RUS) 17 Ee 24
Nižnjaja Mondoma (RUS) 32 Dh 30
Nižnjaja Omra (RUS) 26 Ff 28
Nižnjaja Peša (RUS) 18 Eh 24
Nižnjaja Pokrovka (RUS) 63 Fa 39
Nižnjaja Salda (RUS) 36 Ga 32
Nižnjaja Sanarka (RUS) 47 Gb 36
Nižnjaja Stanovaja (RUS) 33 Ec 31
Nižnjaja Tavda (RUS) 37 Gg 33
Nižnjaja Tura (RUS) 36 Fk 32
Nižnjaja Zolotica (RUS) 24 Ea 25
Nižyn (UA) 59 Db 39
Njalinskoe (RUS) 37 Gk 29
Njandoma (RUS) 33 Ea 29
230 Njarðvik (IS) 48 Qh 27
Njašabož (RUS) 26 Fd 25
Njasviž (BY) 41 Cg 37
Njazepetrovsk (RUS) 47 Fk 34
99860 Njellim = Nellim (FIN) 15 Ci 22
Njučpas (RUS) 34 Fb 30
Njuhča (RUS) 24 Dg 27
Njuhča (RUS) 25 Eg 27
Njuksenica (RUS) 33 Ee 30
99430 Njunnas = Nunnanen (FIN) 15 Ce 22
99990 Njuorggam = Nuorgam (FIN) 15 Ch 20
86202 Njurunda (S) 21 Bh 28
Njuvčim (RUS) 34 Fa 29
10080 Noasca (I) 68 Ah 45
84014 Nocera Inferiore (I) 85 Be 50
06025 Nocera Umbra (I) 69 Bc 47
4645 Nodeland (N) 28 Ah 32
06173 Nogales (E) 92 Sd 52
Nogaylar (TR) 98 Dg 53
52800 Nogent (F) 54 Af 42
28210 Nogent-le-Roi (F) 53 Ab 42
28400* Nogent-le-Rotrou (F) 53 Aa 42
10400* Nogent-sur-Seine (F) 53 Ad 42
Nogersund (S) 39 Be 34
Noginsk (RUS) 43 Di 35
15200 Noia (E) 80 Sb 48
42440 Noirétable (F) 67 Ad 45
85330 Noirmoutier-en-l'Île (F) 66 Sh 43
37150 Nokia (FIN) 30 Cd 29
44911 Nol (S) 29 Bc 33
80035 Nola (I) 85 Be 50
Nolinsk (RUS) 34 Fa 33
Nolvik (S) 21 Bf 25
27320 Nonancourt (F) 53 Ab 42
Nonburg (RUS) 26 Fa 25
24300 Nontron (F) 66 Aa 45
2202 Noordwijk aan Zee (NL) 53 Ae 38
29601 Noormarkku (FIN) 30 Cb 29
86040 Nora (S) 29 Bf 31
Norberg (N) 20 Ai 29
73801 Norberg (S) 29 Bf 30
06046 Norcia (I) 84 Bd 48
6430 Nordborg (DK) 38 Ak 35
6720 Nordby (DK) 39 Ba 35
6214 Norddal (N) 28 Af 29
26506 Norden (D) 38 Ah 37
26954 Nordenham (D) 38 Ai 37
Norderhov (N) 28 Ba 30
26548 Norderney (D) 38 Ah 37
Norderö (S) 21 Be 27
22844* Norderstedt (D) 38 Ak 37
Nordfjord (N) 16 Da 20
6770 Nordfjordeid (N) 20 Af 29
8286 Nordfold (N) 14 Bf 23
99734 Nordhausen (D) 55 Ba 39
48527* Nordhorn (D) 54 Ah 38
9040 Nordkjosbotn (N) 14 Bk 21
7882 Nordli (N) 21 Bd 26
86720 Nördlingen (D) 55 Ba 42
91401 Nordmaling (S) 22 Bk 27
Nordmark (S) 29 Be 31
8489 Nordmela (N) 14 Bf 21
Nordneidet (N) 14 Bk 21
Nordovka (RUS) 46 Ff 37
Nordreisa (N) 15 Cb 21
82011 Nordsjö (S) 29 Bg 29
510 Norðurflörður (IS) 48 Qi 24
Nord-Vågsøy (N) 20 Af 29
3629 Nore (N) 28 Ak 30
3536 Noresund (N) 28 Ak 30
5600 Norheimsund (N) 28 Ag 30
Norra Fjällnäs (S) 21 Bf 25
56201* Norrahammar (S) 29 Be 33
83081 Norråker (S) 21 Bf 26
Norra Ny (S) 29 Bd 30
Norrby (S) 21 Bi 26
4840 Nørre Alslev (DK) 39 Bb 36
6830 Nørre Nebel (DK) 38 Ai 35
9400 Nørresundby (DK) 38 Ak 33
7700 Nørre Vorupør (DK) 38 Ai 34
91493 Norrfors (S) 21 Bi 27
36042 Norrhult-Klavreström (S) 29 Bf 33
60002* Norrköping (S) 29 Bg 32
64530 Norrnäs (FIN) 22 Cb 28
76100* Norrtälje (S) 29 Bi 31
61021 Norsholm (S) 29 Bf 32
93501 Norsjö (S) 22 Bk 26
DL6 Northallerton (GB) 51 Si 36
NN1 Northampton (GB) 52 Sk 38
KY11 North Berwick (GB) 50 Sh 34
37154 Northeim (D) 54 Ak 39
NE68 North Sunderland (GB) 51 Si 35
NR28 North Walsham (GB) 51 Ab 38
CW9 Northwich (GB) 51 Sh 37
24589 Nortorf (D) 38 Ak 36
44390 Nort-sur-Erdre (F) 66 Si 43
NR4 Norwich (GB) 53 Ab 38
Nosivka (UA) 59 Db 40
Nosly (RUS) 46 Fa 34
Nosovaja (RUS) 34 Ef 33
Nosovaja (RUS) 18 Fe 22
Nosovskaja (RUS) 25 Ed 29
46501 Nossebro (S) 29 Bc 32
Nošul' (RUS) 34 Ek 30
96017 Noto (I) 84 Bf 54
3674 Notodden (N) 28 Ak 31
NG1 Nottingham (GB) 51 Si 38
37460 Nouans-les-Fontaines (F) 67 Ab 43
Nova Astrachan (UA) 60 Di 41
Nova Basan' (UA) 59 Db 40
Nova Borova (UA) 58 Ci 40
2147 Novačene (BG) 87 Cd 48
7211 Novaci (MK) 86 Cb 49
Novafeltria (I) 69 Bc 47
Nova Gradiška (HR) 70 Bh 45
Nova Haleščyna (UA) 59 Dd 41
Novaja (RUS) 25 Eb 29
Novaja Kahovka = Nova Kachovka (UA) 74 Dd 44
Novaja Kalitva (RUS) 61 Ea 40
Novaja Kriuša (RUS) 61 Eb 40
Novaja Ladoga (RUS) 31 Dc 30
Novaja Lavela (RUS) 25 Ef 27
Novaja Ljada (RUS) 61 Eb 38
Novaja Ljalja (RUS) 36 Ga 31
Novaja Majna (RUS) 45 Ek 36
Novaja Poltavka (RUS) 62 Eg 40
Novaja Porubežka (RUS) 62 Ek 39
Novaja Usman' (RUS) 60 Dk 39
Nova Kachovka (UA) 74 Dd 44
Novalukoml' (BY) 42 Ck 36
Nova Majačka (UA) 74 Dd 44
Nova Odesa (UA) 74 Db 43
28100 Novara (I) 68 Ai 45
Nova Radča (UA) 58 Ck 39
98058 Novara di Sicilia (I) 84 Bf 52
Nova Rjabyna (UA) 60 Df 40
Nova Sloboda (UA) 59 De 39
23025 Novate Mezzola (I) 69 Ak 44
Nova Topola (BIH) 70 Bh 45
Nova Ušycja (UA) 58 Ch 42
31320 Nova Varoš (SRB) 71 Bk 47
Nova Vodolaha (UA) 60 Df 41
Nova Zagora (BG) 87 Cg 48
592 31 Nové Město nad Moravě (CZ) 56 Bg 41
915 01 Nové Mesto nad Váhom (SK) 56 Bh 42
940 51* Nové Zámky (SK) 71 Bi 43
Novgorod (RUS) 31 Db 32
Novgorodka (RUS) 42 Ci 33
Novhorodka (UA) 59 Dc 42
Novhorod-Siver'skyj (UA) 59 Dd 38
Novhorods'ke, Znob'- (UA) 59 Dd 38
23272 Novi Bečej (SRB) 71 Ca 45
Novi Belokorovyči (UA) 58 Ci 39
Novigrad (HR) 69 Bd 45
1280 Novi Iskăr (BG) 87 Cd 48
Novi Jarylovyči (BY) 59 Db 38
Novi Jarylovyči (UA) 59 Db 38
Novikbož (RUS) 27 Fg 24
15067 Novi Ligure (I) 68 Ai 46
6710 Novi Pazar (BG) 73 Ch 47
36300* Novi Pazar (SRB) 86 Ca 47
21101* Novi Sad (SRB) 71 Bk 45
Novi Sanžary (UA) 59 De 41
Novi Vinodolski (HR) 70 Be 45
Novlenskoe (RUS) 33 Dk 31
Novoadjar (UA) 60 Dk 42
Novoaleksandrovka (RUS) 63 Fc 38
Novoaleksandrovsk (RUS) 76 Eb 45
Novoalekseevskaja (RUS) 76 Ea 46
Novoanninskij (RUS) 61 Ec 40
Novoaptula (RUS) 37 Gi 33
Novoarchanhel's'k (UA) 59 Da 42
Novoarhangelovka (RUS) 46 Ff 38
Novoazovs'k (UA) 75 Di 43
Novobaltačevo (RUS) 46 Fe 35
Novobelokataj (RUS) 47 Fi 35
Novoborovyci (UA) 75 Dk 43
Novočeboksarsk (RUS) 45 Eh 34
Novočeremšansk (RUS) 46 Fa 36
Novočerkassk (RUS) 64 Fg 39
Novočerkassk (RUS) 76 Ea 43
Novocimljanskaja (RUS) 76 Ec 43
Novodevič'e (RUS) 45 Ei 37
Novodugino (RUS) 43 De 35
Novodvinsk (RUS) 24 Ea 26
Novoe Bajbatyrevo (RUS) 45 Eh 35
Novoe Ermakovo (RUS) 46 Fb 36
Novoe Mansurkino (RUS) 46 Fb 37
Novoe Mašozero (RUS) 23 Dd 26
Novofedorivka (UA) 74 Dc 44
Novogornyj (RUS) 47 Ga 35
Novograd-Volynskij = Novohrad-Volyns'kyj (UA) 58 Ch 40
Novohoperskij (RUS) 61 Eb 39
Novohrad-Volyns'kyj (UA) 58 Ch 40
Novoil'inskij (RUS) 35 Ff 33
Novojantuzovo (RUS) 46 Ff 35
Novokašpirskij (RUS) 45 Ei 37
Novokubansk (RUS) 76 Eb 45
Novokujbyševsk (RUS) 45 Ek 37
Novol'vovsk (RUS) 43 Di 37
Novomalorossijskaja (RUS) 75 Dk 45
Novomar'evka (RUS) 64 Ff 40
8000* Novo Mesto (SLO) 70 Bf 45
Novomičurinsk (RUS) 44 Dk 36
Novomihajlovskij (RUS) 75 Di 46
Novominskaja (RUS) 75 Di 44
Novomoskovsk (RUS) 43 Di 36
Novomoskovs'k (UA) 60 Df 42
Novomoskovsk = Novomoskovs'k (UA) 60 Df 42
Novomuraptalovo (RUS) 64 Ff 38
Novomusino (RUS) 46 Fe 38
Novomykolajivka (UA) 74 Dc 44
Novomykolajivka (UA) 74 Df 43
Novomyrhorod (UA) 59 Db 42
Novonikolaevka (RUS) 62 Eg 42
Novonikolaevskaja (RUS) 75 Di 45
Novonikolaevskij (RUS) 61 Ec 40
Novooleksijivka (UA) 74 De 44
Novoorenburg (RUS) 64 Fk 38
Novoorsk (RUS) 64 Fk 39
Novopavlivka (UA) 60 Dg 42
Novopavlovsk (RUS) 76 Ed 47
Novopetrivka (UA) 75 Dg 44
Novopetrovo (RUS) 37 Gk 33
Novopetrovskoe (RUS) 43 Dg 35
Novopetrykivka (UA) 75 Dg 43
Novopokrovka (RUS) 64 Fh 39
Novopokrovka (UA) 59 De 42
Novopokrovskaja (RUS) 76 Ea 45

Novopokrovskaja I 189

Novopokrovskoe (RUS) 61 Ed 39
Novopolevodino (RUS) 62 Eh 39
Novopoljan'e (RUS) 44 Dk 37
Novopolock = Navapolack (BY) 42 Ci 35
Novopskov (UA) 60 Dk 41
Novorepnoe (RUS) 62 Ei 39
Novorossijsk (RUS) 75 Dh 46
Novorossošanskij (RUS) 76 Eb 43
Novoržev (RUS) 42 Ck 33
Novosadkovskij (RUS) 76 Eb 43
Novošahtinsk (RUS) 75 Dk 43
Novoščerbinovskaja (RUS) 75 Di 44
Novosel'cy (RUS) 31 Db 32
Novoselë (AL) 86 Bk 50
Novosel'e (RUS) 31 Ci 32
8958 Novoselec (BG) 87 Cg 48
Novoselickoe (RUS) 76 Ed 46
Novoselivs'ke 74 Dd 45
Novoselka (RUS) 46 Ff 38
2434* Novo Selo (MK) 86 Cc 49
Novosel'skoe (RUS) 61 Ed 39
Novoselycja (UA) 58 Cg 42
Novosemejkino (RUS) 46 Fa 37
Novosergievka (RUS) 63 Fd 38
Novošešminsk (RUS) 46 Fb 35
Novosil' (RUS) 43 Dh 38
Novosil'skoe (RUS) 60 Di 39
Novosineglazovskij (RUS) 47 Gb 35
Novosokol'niki (RUS) 42 Da 34
Novospasskoe (RUS) 45 Eh 37
Novospasskoe (RUS) 63 Fe 38
Novosvitlivka (UA) 60 Dk 42
Novotaimasovo (RUS) 46 Ff 38
Novotitarovskaja (RUS) 75 Di 45
Novot'jalovo (RUS) 37 Gg 33
Novotroick (RUS) 64 Fi 39
Novotroickaja (RUS) 76 Eb 45
Novotroickoe (RUS) 34 Eh 32
Novotroickoe (RUS) 45 Ee 36
Novotroji'cke (UA) 74 De 44
Novotulka (RUS) 62 Eh 40
Novoukrajinka (UA) 59 Db 42
Novoul'janovsk (RUS) 45 Ei 36
Novouspenskoe (RUS) 34 Eg 33
Novoutkinsk (RUS) 47 Fk 34
Novouzensk (RUS) 62 Ei 40
Novovasylivka (UA) 74 Df 44
Novov'azivs'ke (UA) 60 Df 42
Novovil'venskij (RUS) 36 Fi 32
Novovjatsk (RUS) 34 Ek 32
Novovladimirovskaja (RUS) 76 Ea 45
Novovolyns'k (UA) 57 Ce 40
Novovolynsk = Novovolyns'k (UA) 57 Ce 40
Novovoroncovka (UA) 74 Dd 43
Novozavidovskij (RUS) 43 Dg 34
Novožedrino (RUS) 46 Fd 37
Novozizevka (RUS) 62 Ei 40
Novozybkov (BY) 59 Db 38
Novska (HR) 70 Bg 45
473 01 Nový Bor (CZ) 55 Be 40
504 01 Nový Bydžov (CZ) 56 Bf 40
6500 Novye Aneny = Anenii Noi (MD) 73 Ck 44
Novye Burasy (RUS) 62 Eg 38
Novye Ljady (RUS) 35 Fg 32
Novye Selo (RUS) 32 Dd 31
Novye Zjatcy (RUS) 35 Fc 33
Novyi Oskol (RUS) 60 Dh 40
Novyj (RUS) 77 Ef 45
Novyj Bor (RUS) 18 Fc 24
Novyj Buh (UA) 74 Dc 43
Novyj Bujan (RUS) 46 Fa 37
Novyj Byt (RUS) 44 Eb 35
Novyj Egorlyk (RUS) 76 Eb 44
741 01* Nový Jičín (CZ) 56 Bi 41
Novyj Karačaj (RUS) 76 Eb 47
Novyj Kiner (RUS) 45 Ek 34
Novyj Multan (RUS) 35 Fc 33
Novyj Nekouz (RUS) 32 Di 33
Novyj Rozdol (UA) 57 Ce 41
Novyj Sinec (RUS) 43 Dg 37
Novyj Skrebel' (RUS) 32 Dd 33
Novyj Subaj (RUS) 47 Fh 35
Novyj Tap (RUS) 37 Gh 33
Novyj Tor''jal (RUS) 34 Ei 33
Novy Pahost (BY) 42 Ch 35
83-404 Nowa Karczma (PL) 40 Bi 36
57-400* Nowa Ruda (PL) 56 Bg 40
67-100* Nowa Sól (PL) 56 Bf 39
86-170 Nowe (PL) 40 Bi 37
32-120 Nowe Brzesko (PL) 57 Ca 40
67-124 Nowe Miasteczko (PL) 56 Bf 39
13-300 Nowe Miasto Lubawskie (PL) 40 Bk 37
26-420 Nowe Miasto nad Pilicą (PL) 57 Ca 39
72-022 Nowe Warpno (PL) 39 Be 37
72-200 Nowogard (PL) 39 Bf 37
66-010 Nowogród Bobrzański (PL) 56 Bf 39
82-100 Nowy Dwór Gdański (PL) 40 Bk 36
05-100* Nowy Dwór Mazowiecki (PL) 57 Ca 38
33-300 Nowy Sącz (PL) 57 Ca 41
34-400* Nowy Targ (PL) 57 Ca 41
64-300 Nowy Tomyśl (PL) 56 Bg 38
49490 Noyant (F) 66 Aa 43
89310 Noyers (F) 67 Ad 43
60400 Noyon (F) 53 Ad 41
44170 Nozay (F) 66 Si 43
Nudol' (RUS) 43 Dg 34
24900 Nuevo Riaño (E) 81 Sf 48
Nuguš (RUS) 47 Fg 37
21700 Nuits-Saint-Georges (F) 67 Ae 43
12520 Nules (E) 82 Sk 51
CV10 Nuneaton (GB) 52 Si 38
99430 Nunnanen (FIN) 15 Ce 22
8070 Nunspeet (NL) 54 Af 38
99990 Nuorgam (FIN) 15 Ch 20
08100 Nuoro (I) 83 Ak 50
531 Núpsdalstunga (IS) 48 Qk 25
Nur, Cagan- (RUS) 77 Ef 43
46370 Nurhak (TR) 98 Dh 53
Nurlat (RUS) 46 Fa 36
Nurlaty (RUS) 45 Ei 35
75531 Nurmes (FIN) 23 Ck 27
81950 Nurmijärvi (FIN) 23 Ck 27
81950 Nurmijärvi (FIN) 30 Ce 30
90402* Nürnberg (D) 55 Bb 41
72622 Nürtingen (D) 54 Ak 42
47300 Nusaybin (TR) 99 Eb 53
Nuvvus = Nuuvos (FIN) 15 Cg 21
91494 Nyåker (S) 22 Bk 27
9173 Ny Ålesund (N) 14 I Svalbard
2422 Nybergsund (N) 29 Bc 29
Nybor (RUS) 35 Fg 30
5800 Nyborg (DK) 39 Ba 35
95281 Nyborg (S) 22 Cd 25
38201* Nybro (S) 39 Bf 34
3433 Nyékládháza (H) 71 Ca 43
77014 Nyhammar (S) 29 Be 30
Nyirád (H) 70 Bh 43
4254 Nyíradony (H) 71 Cb 43
4300 Nyírbátor (H) 71 Cc 43
4400 Nyíregyháza (H) 71 Cb 43
66900 Nykarleby (FIN) 22 Cc 27
3180 Nykirke (N) 28 Ba 30
4800 Nykøbing Falster (DK) 39 Bb 36
7900 Nykøbing Mors (DK) 38 Ai 34
4500 Nykøbing Sjælland (DK) 39 Bb 35
61100* Nyköping (S) 29 Bh 32
68090 Nykroppa (S) 29 Be 31
87052 Nyland (S) 21 Bh 27
Nylga (RUS) 46 Fc 34
288 02 Nymburk (CZ) 56 Bf 40
Nymoen (N) 21 Be 25
14900* Nynäshamn (S) 29 Bh 32
7870 Nyneset (N) 21 Bc 26
1260 Nyon (CH) 68 Ag 44
26110 Nyons (F) 68 Af 46
Nyr (RUS) 34 Eh 33
Nyrud (RUS) 15 Ck 21
48-300* Nysa (PL) 56 Bh 40
Nyša (RUS) 46 Fb 34
Nysäter (S) 29 Bc 31
4880 Nysted (DK) 39 Bb 36
Nytva (RUS) 35 Ff 33
Nyvoll (N) 15 Cd 20
Nyžankovyči (UA) 57 Cc 41
Nyžni Sirohozy (UA) 74 De 44
Nyžni Torhaji (UA) 74 De 44
Nyžni Vorota (UA) 57 Cd 42
Nyžn'ohirs'kyj 74 De 45

O

LE15 Oakham (GB) 51 Sk 38
807235 Oancea (RO) 73 Ci 45
Obal' (BY) 42 Ck 35
PA34 Oban (GB) 50 Se 34
91341 Obbola (S) 22 Ca 27
29650 Öbektaş (TR) 97 Dd 53
42006 Obeliai (LT) 41 Cf 35
82487 Oberammergau (D) 69 Bb 43
9781 Oberdrauburg (A) 69 Bc 44
46045* Oberhausen (D) 54 Ag 39
77704 Oberkirch (D) 54 Ai 42
67210 Obernai (F) 54 Ah 42
5110 Oberndorf bei Salzburg (A) 55 Bc 43
7350 Oberpullendorf (A) 70 Bg 43
87561 Oberstdorf (D) 69 Ba 43
55743 Oberstein, Idar- (D) 54 Ah 41
9821 Obervellach (A) 69 Bd 44
7400* Oberwart (A) 70 Bg 43
8832 Oberwölz Stadt (A) 70 Be 43
8762 Oberzeiring (A) 70 Be 43
2510-001* Óbidos (P) 80 Sa 51
Obil'noe (RUS) 76 Ee 43
Ob''jačevo (RUS) 34 Ek 30
Oblastnaja (RUS) 46 Fc 34
Obninsk (RUS) 43 Dg 35
5922 Obnova (BG) 72 Ce 47
Obodivka (UA) 58 Ck 42
Obojan (RUS) 60 Dg 39
Obolensk (RUS) 43 Dh 36
Obolon' (UA) 59 Dc 41
Obón (E) 82 Sk 50
64-600* Oborniki (PL) 56 Bg 38
55-120 Oborniki Śląskie (PL) 56 Bg 39
Obozerskij (RUS) 24 Ea 27
11500* Obrenovac (SRB) 71 Ca 46
9630 Obročište (BG) 73 Ci 47
Obrovac (HR) 70 Bf 46
Obručevka (RUS) 64 Fk 38
Obruk (TR) 97 Dd 52
Obšarovka (RUS) 45 Ei 37
Obuchiv (UA) 59 Da 40
Obval (RUS) 44 Ed 38
Obvinsk (RUS) 35 Fe 32
Obža (RUS) 31 Dc 30
Obzon (BG) 88 Ch 48
Očakiv (UA) 74 Db 44
25500 Ocaklı (TR) 91 Ed 50
45300 Ocaña (E) 81 Sg 51
Očer (RUS) 35 Fe 33
Očeretuvate (UA) 74 Df 43
Očevlje (BIH) 71 Bi 46
97199 Ochsenfurt (D) 55 Ba 41
48607 Ochtrup (D) 54 Ah 38
Ochtyrka (UA) 59 De 40
81601 Ockelbo (S) 29 Bg 30
515700 Ocna Mureş (RO) 72 Cd 44
555600 Ocna Sibiului (RO) 72 Ce 45
Octeville, Cherbourg- (F) 52 Si 41
Octovcy (RUS) 43 Dd 34
5750 Odda (N) 28 Ag 30
8300 Odder (DK) 39 Ba 35
8670-320* Odeceixe (P) 92 Sb 53
8950-351* Odeleite (P) 92 Sc 53
7630-121* Odemira (P) 92 Sb 53
18000 Ödemiş (TR) 95 Ch 52
71501 Odensbacken (S) 29 Bf 31
5000* Odense (DK) 39 Ba 35
31046 Oderzo (I) 69 Bc 45
Odesa (UA) 73 Da 44
59901 Ödeshög (S) 29 Be 32
Odessa = Odesa (UA) 73 Da 44
Odincovo (RUS) 43 Dh 35
137345 Odobeşti (RO) 73 Ch 45
Odoev (RUS) 43 Dg 37
Odomlja (RUS) 32 Df 33
535600 Odorheiu Secuiesc (RO) 72 Cf 44
26-425 Odrzywół (PL) 57 Ca 39
Odunboğazı (TR) 89 Dd 51
25250 Odžaci (SRB) 71 Bk 45
Odžak (BIH) 71 Bi 45
39646 Oebisfelde-Weferlingen (D) 55 Ba 38
2780-001* Oeiras (P) 92 Sa 52
08606 Oelsnitz (D) 55 Bc 40
86732 Oettingen in Bayern (D) 55 Ba 42
1779 Oever, Den (NL) 38 Af 38
61830 Of (TR) 91 Ea 50
63065* Offenbach am Main (D) 54 Ai 40
77652* Offenburg (D) 54 Ah 42
76550 Offranville (F) 53 Ab 41
Ogarkovo (RUS) 32 Di 32
Öğdem (TR) 91 Eb 50
Ogorelyši (RUS) 24 Df 27
5001* Ogre (LV) 41 Ce 34
Oğulcak (TR) 89 Df 51
Ogulin (HR) 70 Bf 45
420 Ögur (IS) 48 Qh 24
Öğütlü (TR) 99 Eb 53
Oğuz (TR) 90 Di 51
Oğuz (TR) 99 Eb 53
Ohansk (RUS) 35 Ff 33
Ohlebinino (RUS) 47 Fg 36
Ohotino (RUS) 32 Di 33
6000* Ohrid (MK) 86 Ca 49
Ohtoma (RUS) 33 Eb 29
99981 Ohtsejohka = Utsjoki (FIN) 15 Ch 21
95160 Oijärvi (FIN) 22 Cf 25
97610 Oikarainen (FIN) 15 Cg 24
Oileán Ciarrai (IRL) 49 Sa 38
76350 Oissel (F) 53 Ab 41
68550 Öja (FIN) 22 Cc 27
78061 Öje (S) 29 Bd 30
82801 Öjung (S) 29 Bf 29
EX20 Okehampton (GB) 52 Sf 40
Okladnevo (RUS) 32 Dd 32
7680 Okorš (BG) 73 Ch 47
Oksajärvi (S) 15 Cc 23
6430 Oksbøl (DK) 38 Ai 35
6857 Oksby (DK) 38 Ai 35
9550 Øksfjord (N) 15 Cc 20
Oksino (RUS) 18 Fc 23
Oksovskij (RUS) 24 Dk 28
Oktarbr'skij (RUS) 60 Dg 40
Oktjabr'sk (RUS) 45 Ei 37
Oktjabr'skaja (RUS) 24 Dg 28
Oktjabr'skaja (RUS) 75 Dk 44
Oktjabr'skij (RUS) 32 Dg 29
Oktjabr'skij (RUS) 33 Ed 29
Oktjabr'skij (RUS) 43 Di 36
Oktjabr'skij (RUS) 44 Dk 37
Oktjabr'skij (RUS) 45 Ei 34
Oktjabr'skij (RUS) 45 Ei 36
Oktjabr'skij (RUS) 46 Fd 36
Oktjabr'skij (RUS) 47 Fh 34
Oktjabr'skij (RUS) 16 De 23
Oktjabr'skij (RUS) 76 Ed 43
Oktjabr'skoe (RUS) 61 Eb 39
Oktjabr'skoe (RUS) 64 Ff 38
Oktjabr'skoe (RUS) 76 Ec 45
Okučami (HR) 70 Bh 45
Okuklje (HR) 85 Bh 48
Okulovka (RUS) 32 Dd 32
Okulovo (RUS) 25 Ee 24
Okulovo (RUS) 47 Gb 34
Okulovskaja (RUS) 33 Ed 30
Okunev Nos (RUS) 18 Fc 24
07415 Okurcalar (TR) 96 Db 54
Ola, Joškar- (RUS) 45 Eh 34
□ Ólafsfjörður (IS) 48 Rb 24
355 Ólafsvík (IS) 48 Qg 26
2114 Olaine (LV) 41 Cd 34
34390 Olargues (F) 67 Ac 47
55-200 Oława (PL) 56 Bh 40
09526 Olbernhau (D) 55 Bd 40
07026 Olbia (I) 83 Ak 50
6788 Olden (N) 20 Ag 29
26121* Oldenburg (D) 38 Ai 37
23758 Oldenburg (Holstein) (D) 39 Ba 36
9146 Olderdalen (N) 14 Ca 21
Olderfjord (N) 15 Cf 20
9034 Oldervik (N) 14 Bk 21
OL1 Oldham (GB) 51 Sh 37
AB51 Oldmeldrum (GB) 50 Sh 33
19-400 Olecko (PL) 41 Cc 36
Oleiros (E) 80 Sb 47
6160-011 Oleiros (P) 80 Sc 51
Oleksandrivka, Lozno- (UA) 60 Di 41
Oleksandrivka (UA) 59 Db 42
Oleksandrivka (UA) 59 Dc 42
Oleksandrivka (UA) 59 Dd 42
Oleksandrivka (UA) 60 Dg 42
Oleksandrivka (UA) 74 Db 43
Oleksandrivka (UA) 74 Dc 44
Oleksandrivka (UA) 75 Dh 43
Olema (RUS) 25 Eg 26
5580 Ølen (N) 28 Af 31
Olenica (RUS) 16 Df 24
Olenino (RUS) 43 Dd 34
Olenivka (UA) 74 Dc 45
Olenivka (UA) 75 Dh 43
Olenogorsk (RUS) 16 Dd 22
Oles'ko (UA) 57 Ce 41
Olešky (UA) 74 Dc 44
28-220* Oleśnica (PL) 56 Bh 39
33-210 Olesno (PL) 56 Bi 40
Olevs'k (UA) 58 Ch 39
Ol'ginka (RUS) 75 Di 46
Ol'gino (RUS) 44 Ea 36
6870 Ølgod (DK) 38 Ai 35
8700-152* Olhão (P) 92 Sc 53
91140 Olhava (FIN) 22 Cf 25
Ol'hi (RUS) 44 Eb 37
Ol'hovatka (RUS) 60 Dk 40
Ol'hovatka (UA) 60 Dh 40
Ol'hovka (RUS) 61 Ee 41
Olib (HR) 70 Be 46
08025 Oliena (I) 83 Ak 50
27065 Olimbía (GR) 94 Cb 53
85700 Olimbos (GR) 95 Ch 55
Olingskog (S) 29 Be 29
46780 Oliva (E) 82 Sk 52
06120 Oliva de la Frontera (E) 92 Sd 52
3720-001* Oliveira de Azeméis (P) 80 Sb 50
3400-056* Oliveira do Hospital (P) 80 Sc 50
06100 Olivenza (E) 92 Sc 52
32-300 Olkusz (PL) 56 Bk 40
NG22 Ollerton (GB) 51 Sk 37
47410 Olmedo (E) 81 Sf 49
Olmillos de Sasamón (E) 81 Sf 48
29300 Olofström (S) 39 Be 34
771 00* Olomouc (CZ) 56 Bh 41
Olonec (RUS) 31 Dc 30
34210 Olonzac (F) 67 Ac 47
64400* Oloron-Sainte-Marie (F) 82 Sk 47
17800 Olot (E) 82 Ac 48
Olovo (BIH) 71 Bi 46
57462 Olpe (D) 54 Ah 39
Ol'ša (RUS) 42 Db 36
Ol'šanka (RUS) 60 Dh 40
10-900 Olsztyn (PL) 40 Ca 37
11-015 Olsztynek (PL) 40 Ca 37
Olt, Drăgăneşti (RO) 72 Ce 46
4333 Oltedal (N) 28 Ag 32
4600* Olten (CH) 68 Ah 43
915400 Oltenița (RO) 72 Cg 46
907215 Oltina (RO) 73 Ch 46
25400 Oltu (TR) 91 Ec 50
Olüdeniz (TR) 96 Ck 54
66300 Oluközü (TR) 89 Df 51
Olukpınar (TR) 96 Dc 54
25650 Olur (TR) 91 Ec 50
Olymskij (RUS) 60 Di 39
Oma (RUS) 18 Eg 24
BT79 Omagh (GB) 49 Sc 36
28887 Omegna (I) 68 Ai 45
Omel'nyk (UA) 59 Dd 41
Ömerli (TR) 88 Ck 49
Ömerli (TR) 99 Ea 53
Omiš (HR) 70 Bg 47
Omitrovsk-Orlovskij (RUS) 60 Df 38
7730 Ommen (NL) 54 Ag 38
40007 Omólio (GR) 86 Cc 51
26230 Omoljica (SRB) 71 Ca 46
64930 Ömossa (FIN) 22 Cb 28
7900 Omurtag (BG) 87 Cg 47
Omutninsk (RUS) 35 Fc 32
09530 Oña (E) 81 Sg 48
20560 Oñati (E) 81 Sh 47
Onbirnisan (TR) 98 Di 53
12200 Onda (E) 82 Sk 51
48700 Ondarroa (E) 66 Sh 47
55420 Ondokuzmayıs (TR) 90 Dg 49
Ondozero (RUS) 23 Dd 27
Onega (RUS) 24 Di 27
000601* Oneşti (RO) 72 Cg 44
Onež'e (RUS) 26 Fa 28
82360 Onkamo (FIN) 23 Da 28
Onolva, Ust'- (RUS) 35 Fe 31
46870 Ontinyent (E) 82 Sk 52
88640 Ontojoki (FIN) 23 Ci 26
02652 Ontur (E) 93 Si 52
8400 Oostende (B) 53 Ac 39
4900* Oosterhout (NL) 53 Ae 39
7840 Opaka (BG) 72 Cg 47
Opanözü (TR) 88 Ck 51
Oparino (RUS) 34 Ei 31
Opatija (HR) 70 Be 45
42-152 Opatów (PL) 57 Cb 40
Opava (CZ) 56 Bh 41
Opečenskij Posad (RUS) 32 De 32
Opejica (MK) 86 Ca 49
Opišn'a (UA) 59 De 41
Opočka (RUS) 42 Ci 34
26-300 Opoczno (PL) 57 Ca 39
45-076 Opole (PL) 56 Bh 40
24-300 Opole Lubelskie (PL) 57 Cb 39
7340 Oppdal (N) 20 Ak 28
55276 Oppenheim (D) 54 Ai 41
Oppstryn (N) 20 Ah 29
Opsa (BY) 41 Cg 35
39040 Ora = Auer (I) 69 Bb 44
000410* Oradea (RO) 71 Cb 43
21000* Orahovac = Rahovec (RKS) 86 Ca 48
Orahov Do (BIH) 85 Bh 48
Orahovica (HR) 70 Bh 45
84100* Orange (F) 67 Ae 46
08026 Orani (I) 83 Ak 50
16515 Oranienburg (D) 39 Bd 38
Oran Mór (IRL) 49 Sb 37
Oranmore = Oran Mór (IRL) 49 Sb 37
Oranžeri (RUS) 77 Eh 45
Orašje (BIH) 71 Bi 45
335700 Orăştie (RO) 72 Cd 45
Orativ (UA) 58 Ck 41
66800 Oravainen = Oravais (FIN) 22 Cc 27
66800 Oravais (FIN) 22 Cc 27
325600 Oravița (RO) 71 Cb 45
63619 Orb, Bad (D) 54 Ak 40
5853 Ørbæk (DK) 39 Ba 35
147237 Orbeasca de Jos (RO) 72 Cf 46
14290 Orbec (F) 53 Aa 41
58015 Orbetello (I) 84 Bb 48
59310 Orchies (F) 53 Ad 40
Orda (RUS) 35 Fg 33
Ördekçi (TR) 96 Db 52
15680 Ordes (E) 80 Sb 47
52000* Ordu (TR) 90 Dh 50
48460 Orduña (E) 81 Sg 48
Ordžonikidze = Pokrov (UA) 74 De 43
Ordžonikidze = Vladikavkaz (RUS) 91 Ee 48
Ordžonikidzevskij (RUS) 76 Eb 47
Orebić (HR) 85 Bh 48
70002* Örebro (S) 29 Bf 31
Oredež (RUS) 31 Da 32
74071 Öregrund (S) 29 Bi 30
Orehovka (RUS) 65 Ga 39
Orehovo-Zuevo (RUS) 43 Di 35
Orel (RUS) 35 Fg 31
Orel (RUS) 43 Dg 38
06740 Orellana la Vieja (E) 80 Se 51
28850 Ören (TR) 95 Ch 53
Orenburg (RUS) 64 Ff 39
Örencik (TR) 88 Ck 51
Örenköy (TR) 98 Dh 52
32001 Orense = Ourense (E) 80 Sc 48
Örenşehir (TR) 98 Dg 51
68200 Orestiáda (GR) 87 Cg 49
64008 Orfáni (GR) 87 Cd 50
IP12 Orford (GB) 53 Ab 38
69500 Orgáni (GR) 87 Cf 49
Organyà (E) 82 Ab 48

190 | Novopokrovskoe

Pavlovac (HR) 70 Bh 45
Pavlov Huter (RUS) 43 Di 37
Pavlovka (RUS) 47 Fg 35
Pavlovka (RUS) 62 Eh 38
Pavlovo (RUS) 44 Ed 35
Pavlovsk (RUS) 31 Da 31
Pavlovsk (RUS) 61 Ea 40
Pavlovskaja (RUS) 75 Dk 44
Pavlovskij Posad (RUS) 43 Di 35
Pavlovskoe (RUS) 44 Eb 34
Pavlovskoe, Nikolo- (RUS) 36 Ga 33
Pavlyš (UA) 59 Dd 42
41026 Pavullo nel Frignano (I) 69 Bb 46
Payamlı (TR) 98 Di 53
1530 Payerne (CH) 68 Ag 44
21560 Paymogo (E) 92 Sc 53
06893 Pazar (TR) 89 Dc 50
06893 Pazar (TR) 90 Dg 50
06893 Pazar (TR) 91 Ea 49
Pazarcık (TR) 90 Dg 51
Pazarcık (TR) 91 Ed 50
Pazarcık (TR) 98 Dh 53
Pazardzik (BG) 87 Ce 48
4400* Pazardžik (BG) 87 Ce 48
Pazarköy (TR) 89 Dc 50
43350 Pazarlar (TR) 88 Ck 51
Pazarören (TR) 97 Dg 52
11800 Pazaryeri (TR) 88 Ck 50
25900 Pazaryolu (TR) 91 Ea 50
52000 Pazin (HR) 69 Bd 45
6561 Paznaun (A) 69 Ba 43
23460 Peal de Becerro (E) 93 Sg 53
30000* Peć = Pejë (RKS) 86 Ca 48
06742 Peçenek (TR) 89 Dc 50
Pečenga (RUS) 16 Db 21
Pečengskoe, Ust'- (RUS) 33 Ec 31
Pečeničino (RUS) 42 Dc 35
16251 Pečenjevce (SRB) 86 Cb 47
Pečerniki (RUS) 44 Dk 36
14207 Pecka (SRB) 71 Bk 46
Pečmen' (RUS) 47 Fg 34
Pečora (RUS) 27 Fh 25
Pečory (RUS) 31 Ch 33
7600* Pécs (H) 71 Bi 44
27670 Pedrafita do Cebreiro (E) 80 Sc 48
40172 Pedraza de la Sierra (E) 81 Sg 49
10630 Pedro Muñoz (E) 81 Sh 51
16660 Pedroñeras, Las (E) 81 Sh 51
41360 Pedroso, El (E) 92 Se 53
EH45 Peebles (GB) 51 Sg 35
IM5 Peel (GBM) 51 Sf 36
17449 Peenemünde (D) 39 Bd 36
Peganovo (RUS) 34 Eg 30
04523 Pegau (D) 55 Bc 39
91257 Pegnitz (D) 55 Bb 41
03780 Pego (E) 82 Sk 52
Pegyš (RUS) 26 Fa 27
2326 Pehčevo (MK) 86 Cc 49
39210 Pehlivanköy (TR) 87 Cg 49
31224* Peine (D) 55 Ba 38
32810 Peipohja (FIN) 30 Cc 29
03185 Peitz (D) 55 Be 39
30000* Pejë = Peć (RKS) 86 Ca 48
Peklino (RUS) 43 Dd 37
Pektubaevo (RUS) 45 Ei 33
35013 Pelasgía (GR) 94 Cc 52
350 02 Pelhřimov (CZ) 56 Bf 41
55700 Pelitbükü (TR) 89 Df 49
98500 Pelkosenniemi (FIN) 15 Ch 23
95701 Pello (FIN) 15 Cd 24
5870 Pelovo (BG) 72 Ce 47
99420 Peltovuoma (FIN) 15 Ce 22
Pelym (RUS) 35 Fe 31
33700 Pembecik (TR) 97 Dd 54
SA71 Pembroke (GB) 52 Sf 39
47300 Peñafiel (E) 81 Sf 49
4560-450* Penafiel (P) 80 Sb 49
33829 Peñaflor (E) 92 Se 53
6090-508* Penamacor (P) 80 Sc 50
37300 Peñaranda de Bracamonte (E) 80 Se 50
09410 Peñaranda de Duero (E) 81 Sg 49
14200 Peñarroya-Pueblonueva (E) 92 Se 52
CF64 Penarth (GB) 52 Sg 39
02120 Peñas de San Pedro (E) 93 Si 52
49178 Peñausende (E) 80 Se 49
15236 Pendéli (GR) 94 Cd 52
3230-249* Penela (P) 80 Sb 50
SA71 Penfro = Pembroke (GB) 52 Sf 39
2520-200* Peniche (P) 80 Sa 51
09322 Penig (D) 55 Bc 40
Peninga (RUS) 23 Dc 27
Penkino (RUS) 44 Ea 34
29760 Penmarc'h (F) 66 Sf 43
65017 Penne (I) 84 Bd 48
Peno (RUS) 42 Dc 34
CA11 Penrith (GB) 51 Sh 36
TR10 Penryn (GB) 52 Se 40
50007 Pentálofos (GR) 86 Cb 50
Penza (RUS) 45 Ef 37
TR18 Penzance (GB) 52 Se 40
82377 Penzberg (D) 69 Bb 43
Peqin (AL) 86 Bk 49
9099 Pér (H) 70 Bh 43
Pêra (P) 92 Sb 53
20300 Perahóra (GR) 94 Cc 52
10335 Peraleda de la Mata (E) 80 Se 51
06919 Peraleda de Zaucejo (E) 92 Se 52
74052 Pérama (GR) 94 Ce 55
89770 Peranka (FIN) 23 Ci 25
24429 Peranzanes (E) 80 Sd 48
97820 Perä-Posio (FIN) 15 Ch 24
61101 Peräseinäjoki (FIN) 22 Cd 28
46100 Pérdika (GR) 86 Ca 51
46100 Pérdika (GR) 94 Cd 53
Perečyn (UA) 57 Cc 42
Perehins'ke (UA) 57 Ce 42
Perejaslav-Chmel'nyc'kyj (UA) 59 Db 40
Perejaslovskaja (RUS) 75 Dk 45
Perekopka (RUS) 61 Ed 41
Perelešinskij (RUS) 61 Ea 39
Pereljub (RUS) 63 Fa 39
Peremoha (UA) 59 Db 40
Peremyšl' (RUS) 43 Dg 36
Peremyšljany (UA) 57 Ce 41
Pereščepyne (UA) 60 Df 41
3541 Peresecina (MD) 73 Ci 43
Pereslavl'-Zalesskij (RUS) 43 Di 34
Peresypkino Pervoe (RUS) 44 Ec 38
Per'evo (RUS) 33 Dk 31
Perevolockij (RUS) 63 Fe 39
Perevoz (RUS) 45 Ee 35
38057 Pergine Valsugana (I) 69 Bb 44
Pergola (I) 69 Bc 47
31140 Perho (FIN) 22 Ce 27
307315 Periam (RO) 71 Ca 44
50190 Périers (F) 52 Si 41
927190 Perieţi (RO) 73 Ch 46
24000* Périgueux (F) 66 Aa 45
917195 Perişoru (RO) 73 Ch 46
19348 Perleberg (D) 39 Bb 37
Perlevka (RUS) 60 Di 39
Perm' (RUS) 35 Fg 32
Permas (RUS) 34 Ef 31
Përmet (AL) 86 Ca 50
2300* Pernik (BG) 87 Cd 48
25501 Perniö (FIN) 30 Cd 30
80200 Péronne (F) 53 Ac 41
Përparim (AL) 86 Bk 51
66000* Perpignan (F) 82 Ac 48
22700 Perros-Guirec (F) 52 Sg 42
Persåsen (S) 21 Be 28
52750 Perşembe (TR) 90 Dh 49
Peršinskaja (RUS) 33 Ea 30
Peršotravneve = Mokvin (UA) 75 Dh 43
Peršotravnevoe = Mokvin (UA) 75 Dh 43
28401 Perstorp (S) 39 Bd 34
Pertek (TR) 98 Dk 52
PH1 Perth (GB) 50 Sg 34
Pertjugskij (RUS) 34 Eg 31
Pertominsk (RUS) 24 Di 26
84120 Pertuis (F) 68 Af 47
52730 Pertunmaa (FIN) 30 Cg 29
06100 Perugia (I) 84 Bc 47
Perušić (HR) 70 Bf 46
56700 Pervari (TR) 99 Ec 53
Pervoavgustovskij (RUS) 60 Df 38
Pervomaiskyj (UA) 60 Dg 41
Pervomajsk (RUS) 44 Ed 36
Pervomajs'k (UA) 59 Da 42
Pervomajs'k (UA) 60 Di 42
Pervomajsk = Pervomajs'k (UA) 59 Da 42
Pervomajs'ke (UA) 74 Dc 43
Pervomajs'ke 74 Dd 45
Pervomajskij (RUS) 33 Ee 29
Pervomajskij (RUS) 44 Ea 37
Pervomajskij (RUS) 46 Fb 37
Pervomajskij (RUS) 47 Gb 36
Pervomajskij (RUS) 61 Ee 38
Pervomajskij (RUS) 62 Ei 39
Pervomajskij (RUS) 63 Fb 39
Pervomajskoe (RUS) 31 Ck 30
Pervomajskoe (RUS) 61 Eb 42
Pervomajskoe (RUS) 62 Eh 39
Pervoural'sk (RUS) 47 Fk 34
61100 Pesaro (I) 69 Bc 47
Pesčanoe (RUS) 24 Df 28
Pesčanokopskoe (RUS) 76 Eb 44
65100* Pescara (I) 85 Be 48
Peščera (RUS) 35 Fc 31
71010 Peschici (I) 85 Bg 49
37019 Peschiera del Garda (I) 69 Ba 45
67057 Pescina (I) 84 Bd 48
Pescočnja (RUS) 43 Dd 37
Pesenec (RUS) 25 Ec 28
Peshkëpi (AL) 86 Bk 50
Peshkopi (AL) 86 Ca 49
89640 Pesiökylä (FIN) 23 Ci 26
Peski (RUS) 43 Di 35
Peski (RUS) 61 Ea 40
Peskovka (RUS) 35 Fc 31
Peškovo (RUS) 60 Dh 38
6342 Pesočani (MK) 86 Ca 49
Pesočnja (RUS) 44 Ea 36
Pesocnoe (RUS) 31 Ck 30
5050-208* Peso da Régua (P) 80 Sc 49
33600 Pessac (F) 66 Sk 46
6323 Peštani (MK) 86 Ca 49
4754 Peštera (BG) 87 Ce 48
Pestjaki (RUS) 44 Ec 34
Pestovo (RUS) 32 Df 32
Pestravka (RUS) 62 Ek 38
75930 Petäiskylä (FIN) 23 Ck 27
41901 Petäjävesi (FIN) 22 Cf 28
66240 Petalax (FIN) 22 Cb 28
24005 Petalidi (GR) 94 Cb 54
PE3 Peterborough (GB) 52 Sk 38
Peterculter (GB) 50 Sh 33
AB42 Peterhead (GB) 50 Si 33
SR8 Peterlee (GB) 51 Si 36
GU32 Petersfield (GB) 52 Sk 39
3250 Pétervására (H) 57 Ca 42
Petín (E) 80 Sc 48
76140 Petit-Quevilly, le (F) 53 Ab 41
99670 Petkula (FIN) 15 Cg 23
66240 Petolahti = Petalax (FIN) 22 Cb 28
60100 Pétra (GR) 87 Cg 51
20140 Petreto-Bicchisano (F) 83 Ai 49
2850 Petrič (BG) 87 Cd 49
335800 Petrila (RO) 72 Cd 45
Petrinja (HR) 70 Bg 45
Petriščevo (RUS) 42 Dc 35
Petrivka (UA) 59 Db 40
Petrivka (UA) 60 Dk 42
Petrivka (UA) 73 Da 44
Petrivka (UA) 74 De 44
Petrjaevskij (RUS) 34 Ef 31
Petrodvorec (RUS) 31 Ck 31
Petrokamenskoe (RUS) 36 Ga 33
Petrokrepost' = Šlissel'burg (RUS) 31 Db 31
2404 Petronell-Carnuntum (A) 56 Bg 42
Petropavlika (UA) 60 Dh 41
Petropavlivka (UA) 60 Dg 42
Petropavlovka (RUS) 47 Fk 35
Petropavlovka (RUS) 61 Ea 40
Petropavlovka (RUS) 62 Eh 40
Petropavlovsk (RUS) 35 Fe 33
Petropavlovsk (RUS) 47 Fh 34
Petropavlovskij (RUS) 47 Fk 36
Petropavlovskoe (RUS) 76 Ee 45
000332* Petroşani (RO) 72 Cd 45
Petrova (RUS) 25 Ed 26
Petrova Buda (BY) 42 Db 38
12300 Petrovac (SRB) 71 Cb 46
85 300 Petrovac na moru (MNE) 86 Bi 48
Petrovcy (RUS) 35 Fd 32
Petrove (UA) 59 Dd 42
Petroviči (RUS) 42 Dc 37
Petrovka (RUS) 46 Fb 37
Petrovka (RUS) 61 Ea 40
Petrovo (RUS) 32 Df 32
Petrovsk (RUS) 62 Ef 38
Petrovskaja (RUS) 75 Dh 45
Petrovskij (RUS) 44 Ea 34
Petrovskoe (RUS) 44 Dk 33
Petrovskoe (RUS) 47 Fg 37
Petrovskoe (RUS) 61 Ea 38
Petrov Val (RUS) 62 Ef 40
Petrozavodsk (RUS) 24 De 29
Petrušino (RUS) 44 Dk 35
Petrykav (BY) 58 Ci 38
Petrykivka (UA) 59 De 42
Petuški (RUS) 44 Dk 35
4722 Peuerbach (A) 55 Bd 42
40300 Peyrehorade (F) 66 Si 47
Pezë e Vogël (AL) 86 Bk 49
34120 Pézenas (F) 67 Ad 47
Pezinok (SK) 56 Bh 42
Pezmog (RUS) 26 Fb 29
84066 Pfaffenberg, Mallersdorf- (D) 55 Bc 42
84347 Pfarrkirchen (D) 55 Bc 42
75172* Pforzheim (D) 54 Ai 42
88630 Pfullendorf (D) 69 Ak 43
6542 Pfunds (A) 69 Ba 44
57370* Phalsbourg (F) 54 Ah 42
5600 Philippeville (B) 53 Ae 40
29100 Piacenza (I) 69 Ak 45
26034 Piadena (I) 69 Ba 45
40065 Pianoro (I) 69 Bb 46
57036 Pianosa (I) 84 Ba 48
7860-001 Pias (P) 92 Sc 52
74-110 Piaseczno (PL) 57 Cb 38
63-820 Piaski (PL) 57 Cc 39
99-120 Piątek (PL) 56 Bk 38
907197 Piatra (RO) 72 Cf 47
000610* Piatra-Neamţ (RO) 72 Cg 44
94015 Piazza Armerina (I) 84 Be 53
24014 Piazza Brembana (I) 69 Ak 45
Pičaevo (RUS) 44 Ec 37
Pičiha (RUS) 33 Dk 30
YO18 Pickering (GB) 51 Sk 36
Pičkirjaevo (RUS) 44 Ec 36
03185 Picnjo = Peitz (D) 55 Be 39
80310 Picquigny (F) 53 Ac 41
Pidhajci (UA) 58 Cf 41
Pid'ma (RUS) 32 De 30
81016 Piedimonte Matese (I) 85 Be 49
13100 Piedrabuena (E) 81 Sf 51
Piedrahita (E) 80 Se 50
76150 Pieksämäki (FIN) 23 Ch 28
72430 Pielavesi (FIN) 22 Cg 27
14-520 Pieniężno (PL) 40 Ca 36
59-930 Pieńsk (PL) 56 Bf 39
53026 Pienza (I) 84 Bb 47
KW17 Pierowall (GB) 50 Sh 31
15230 Pierrefort (F) 67 Ac 46
26700 Pierrelatte (F) 67 Ae 46
Piešt'any (SK) 56 Bh 42
68600* Pietarsaari = Jakobstad (FIN) 22 Cc 27
Pietra Ligure (I) 68 Ai 46
55045 Pietrasanta (I) 69 Ba 47
147250 Pietroşani (RO) 72 Cf 47
18026 Pieve di Teco (I) 68 Ah 46
Pigari (RUS) 62 Ek 39
42910 Pihlajavesi (FIN) 22 Ce 28
44801 Pihtipudas (FIN) 22 Cf 27
92620 Piippola (FIN) 22 Cf 26
97630 Piittisjärvi (FIN) 15 Cg 24
Pikalevo (RUS) 32 De 31
Pikasilla (EST) 30 Cg 32
64-920 Piła (PL) 40 Bg 37
Pil'na (RUS) 45 Ef 35
51100 Pilorí (GR) 86 Cb 50
24001 Pílos (GR) 94 Cb 54
3620 Piltene (LV) 30 Cb 33
39-220 Pilzno (PL) 57 Cb 41
Pınarbaşı (TR) 97 Dd 53
Pınarbaşı (TR) 98 Dg 52
Pınarbaşı (TR) 99 Ea 53
Pınarcık (TR) 95 Ch 53
20144 Pinarellu (F) 83 Ak 49
39300 Pınarhisar (TR) 88 Ch 49
Pınarlar (TR) 98 Dk 52
28-400 Pińczów (PL) 57 Ca 40
Pinduši (RUS) 24 De 28
Pinega (RUS) 25 Ed 26
10064 Pinerolo (I) 68 Ah 46
64025 Pineto (I) 85 Be 48
10220 Piney (F) 53 Ae 42
4485-431 Pinhel (P) 80 Sc 50
Pinjug (RUS) 34 Eh 30
25421 Pinneberg (D) 38 Ak 37
03650 Pinoso (E) 93 Si 52
Pinsk (BY) 58 Cg 38
93290 Pintamo (FIN) 23 Ch 25
28320 Pinto (E) 81 Sg 50
57025 Piombino (I) 84 Ba 48
Pionerskij (RUS) 40 Ca 36
97-300 Piotrków Trybunalski (PL) 56 Bk 39
35028 Piove di Sacco (I) 69 Bc 45
35550 Pipriac (F) 66 Si 43
Piqeras (AL) 86 Bk 50
28340 Piraziz (TR) 90 Di 50
18547 Pireás (GR) 94 Cd 53
82102 Pirgí (GR) 95 Cf 52
70010 Pírgos (GR) 94 Cb 53
70010 Pírgos (GR) 95 Cf 55
53400 Pirinçlik (TR) 99 Ea 53
Pirinem (RUS) 25 Ee 26
Pirki (UA) 59 Da 39
95470 Pirkkiö (FIN) 22 Ce 25
3641 Pîrliţa (MD) 73 Ch 43
66953* Pirmasens (D) 54 Ah 41
01796 Pirna (D) 55 Bd 40
18300* Pirot (SRB) 71 Cc 47
Pirovac (HR) 70 Bf 47
44015 Pirsógiani (GR) 86 Ca 50
14450 Pirttikoski (FIN) 15 Ch 24
56100* Pisa (I) 69 Ba 47
Pisarovina (HR) 70 Bf 45
Pišča (UA) 57 Cd 39
Piščane (UA) 59 Db 41
Piščanka (UA) 58 Ci 42
Piščanyj Brid (UA) 59 Dc 42
Piscovo (RUS) 33 Ea 33
207455 Piscu Vechi (RO) 72 Cd 47
397 01 Písek (CZ) 55 Be 41
Piski-Rad'kivis'ki (UA) 60 Dh 41
Piskivka (UA) 58 Ck 40
Pišnur (RUS) 34 Eh 33
Pisses (GR) 94 Ce 53
40410 Pissos (F) 66 Sk 46
75015 Pisticci (I) 85 Bg 50
Pistoia (I) 69 Ba 47
12-200 Pisz (PL) 40 Cb 37
94101* Piteå (S) 22 Cb 25
Pitelino (RUS) 44 Eb 36
Piterka (RUS) 62 Eh 40
110323 Piteşti (RO) 72 Ce 46
83103 Pithagório (GR) 95 Cg 53
45300 Pithiviers (F) 53 Ac 42
58017 Pitigliano (I) 84 Bb 48
Pitítsa (GR) 94 Cb 52
Pitkjaranta (RUS) 31 Db 29
Pitkul' (RUS) 16 Dd 23
PH16 Pitlochry (GB) 50 Sg 34
Pitomača (HR) 70 Bh 45
6257 Pivka (SLO) 70 Be 45
Piwniczna-Zdrój (PL) 57 Ca 41
Pižanka (RUS) 34 Ei 33
Pižma (RUS) 34 Eh 33
89812 Pizzo (I) 85 Bg 52
Pjalica (RUS) 24 Dk 24
Pjalka (RUS) 17 Ea 24
Pjal'ma (RUS) 24 Df 28
Pjanda (RUS) 25 Ec 28
Pjanteg (RUS) 35 Fg 30
Pjaozerskij (RUS) 23 Db 25
Pjašnica (RUS) 32 Dg 31
Pjatigorsk (RUS) 76 Ed 46
Pjatychatky (UA) 59 Dd 42
Pjažel'ka (RUS) 32 Df 30
81401 Pláka (GR) 87 Cf 50
81401 Pláka (GR) 94 Cc 53
Plana (BIH) 85 Bi 48
22940 Plancoët (F) 52 Sh 42
26360 Plandište (SRB) 71 Cb 45
Planers'ke 74 Df 46
Plasë (AL) 86 Ca 50
10600 Plasencia (E) 80 Sd 50
Plaški (HR) 70 Bf 45
2427 Plassen (N) 29 Bc 29
Plast (RUS) 47 Ga 36
Plastmass (RUS) 43 Dh 36
34001 Platanistós (GR) 94 Ce 52
94447 Plattling (D) 55 Bc 42
19395 Plau am See (D) 39 Bc 37
08523* Plauen (D) 55 Bc 40
84 325 Plav (MNE) 86 Bk 48
Plavinas (LV) 41 Cf 34
Plavsk (RUS) 43 Dh 37
15700 Pleaux (F) 67 Ac 45
Ples (RUS) 33 Eb 33
Plešanovo (RUS) 46 Fd 38
Pleščanicy (BY) 42 Ch 36
Pleseck (RUS) 24 Ea 28
Pleški (RUS) 43 De 34
Plëso (RUS) 32 Df 31
63-300 Pleszew (PL) 56 Bh 39
Pleternica (HR) 70 Bh 45
5800* Pleven (BG) 72 Ce 47
29190 Pleyben (F) 52 Sg 42
Plisa (BY) 42 Ch 35
Plitvica (HR) 70 Bf 46
84 210* Pljevlja (MNE) 71 Bk 47
Pljussa (RUS) 31 Ck 32
Ploče (HR) 85 Bh 47
09-400 Płock (PL) 56 Bk 38
56800 Ploërmel (F) 66 Sh 43
000100* Ploieşti (RO) 72 Cg 46
81200 Plomári (GR) 95 Cg 52
24306 Plön (D) 39 Ba 36
09-100 Płońsk (PL) 57 Ca 38
Ploska (RUS) 33 Ee 33
Ploskoe (RUS) 43 Df 36
Ploskoš' (RUS) 42 Db 34
Plotniki (RUS) 32 Dg 33
72-310 Płoty (PL) 39 Bf 37
22420 Plouaret (F) 52 Sg 42
56240 Plouay (F) 66 Sg 43
29830 Ploudalmézeau (F) 52 Sf 42
22470 Plouézec (F) 52 Sh 42
29270 Plouguer, Carhaix- (F) 52 Sg 42
22580 Plouha (F) 52 Sh 42
4000* Plovdiv (BG) 87 Ce 48
29710 Plozévet (F) 52 Sf 43
BT79 Plumbridge (GB) 49 Sc 36
90001 Plungė (LT) 40 Cb 35
56330 Pluvigner (F) 66 Sg 43
PL9 Plymouth (GB) 52 Sf 40
301 00* Plzeň (CZ) 55 Bd 41
62-045 Pniewy (PL) 56 Bg 38
8679 Pobeda (BG) 87 Cg 48
Pobeda (RUS) 44 Ec 34
Pobedino (RUS) 41 Cc 36
08696 Pobla de Lillet, la (E) 82 Ab 48
25500 Pobla de Segur, la (E) 82 Aa 48
Poboišče (RUS) 64 Fh 38
Pobuz'ke (UA) 59 Da 42
Poča (RUS) 24 Di 28
Počajiv (UA) 58 Cf 40
Počapynci (UA) 59 Da 41
Počep (RUS) 43 Dd 38
Počiniki (RUS) 45 Ee 36
Počinok (RUS) 32 De 33
Počinok (RUS) 42 Dc 36
Počitelj (BIH) 85 Bh 47
YO42 Pocklington (GB) 51 Sk 37
Počtovskij, Kletsko- (RUS) 61 Ed 41
207465 Podari (RO) 72 Cd 46
Podbel'sk (RUS) 46 Fb 37
Podberez'e (RUS) 31 Db 32
Podberez'e (RUS) 42 Da 34
Podbolot'e (RUS) 33 Ee 31
441 01 Podbořany (CZ) 55 Bd 40
Podborka (RUS) 24 Ea 26
Podborov'e (RUS) 31 Cf 33
Podbožur (MNE) 86 Bi 48

192 | Pavlovac

36074 Proussós (GR) 94 Cb 52
9200 Provadija (BG) 88 Ch 47
77160* Provins (F) 53 Ad 42
Prozor (BIH) 70 Bh 47
Prozorovo (RUS) 34 Ek 33
Prudentov (RUS) 62 Eg 41
Prudišči (RUS) 45 Ef 34
Prudki (RUS) 43 Dg 36
48-200 Prudnik (PL) 56 Bh 40
54595 Prüm (D) 54 Ag 40
087180 Prundu (RO) 72 Cg 46
227390 Prunişor (RO) 71 Cc 46
83-000* Pruszcz Gdański (PL) 40 Bi 36
6522* Prutz (A) 69 Ba 43
Pružany (BY) 57 Ce 38
Pružinki (RUS) 44 Dk 38
Pryazovs'ke (UA) 74 Df 44
Pryluky (UA) 59 Dc 40
Prymors'k (UA) 75 Dg 44
Prymors'ke (UA) 75 Dh 44
Pryp'jat' (UA) 59 Da 39
Pryvitne 74 De 46
06-300 Przasnysz (PL) 40 Ca 37
97-570 Przedbórz (PL) 56 Bk 39
37-700 Przemyśl (PL) 57 Cc 41
06-126 Przewodowo, Parcele- (PL) 40 Ca 38
37-200 Przeworsk (PL) 57 Cc 40
68-132 Przewóz (PL) 55 Be 39
34400 Psahná (GR) 94 Cd 52
82104 Psará (GR) 95 Cf 52
53077 Psarádes (GR) 86 Cb 50
20500 Psári (GR) 94 Cc 53
Psebaj (RUS) 76 Ea 46
72052 Psihro (GR) 95 Cf 55
Pskov (RUS) 31 Ci 33
43-200 Pszczyna (PL) 56 Bi 41
50200 Ptolemaída (GR) 86 Cb 50
2250 Ptuj (SLO) 70 Bf 44
Pucarevo (BIH) 70 Bh 46
Pūceskrogs (LV) 41 Cc 34
Pučež (RUS) 44 Ed 34
107485 Puchenii Mari (RO) 72 Cg 46
Puchivka (UA) 59 Da 40
135400 Pucioasa (RO) 72 Cf 45
46530 Puçol (E) 82 Sk 51
93101 Pudasjärvi (FIN) 23 Ch 25
Pudem (RUS) 35 Fc 32
Pudož (RUS) 24 Dg 29
06630 Puebla de Alcocer (E) 80 Se 52
18820 Puebla de Don Fadrique (E) 93 Sh 53
13109 Puebla de Don Rodrigo (E) 81 Sf 51
21550 Puebla de Guzmán (E) 92 Sc 53
24855 Puebla de Lillo (E) 80 Se 47
41130 Puebla del Río, La (E) 92 Sd 53
Puebla de Montalbán (E) 81 Sf 51
49300 Puebla de Sanabria (E) 80 Sd 48
44450 Puebla de Valverde, La (E) 82 Sk 50
45570 Puente del Arzobispo, El (E) 80 Se 51
14500 Puente-Genil (E) 93 Sf 53
11500 Puerto de Santa María, El (E) 92 Sd 54
13500 Puertollano (E) 93 Sf 52
30890 Puerto Lumbreras (E) 93 Si 53
11510 Puerto Real (E) 92 Sd 54
Pugačev (RUS) 62 Ei 38
Pugačevo (RUS) 46 Fd 34
Pugačevskij (RUS) 64 Ff 39
67406 Pühajärve (EST) 30 Cg 32
Puhnovo (RUS) 42 Db 35
93350 Puhos (FIN) 23 Ch 25
93350 Puhos (FIN) 23 Ck 28
Puiatu (EST) 30 Cf 32
737425 Puieşti (RO) 73 Ch 44
17520 Puigcerdà (E) 82 Ab 48
08692 Puig-Reig (E) 82 Ab 49
08692 Puigreig = Puig-Reig (E) 82 Ab 49
37520 Pukavik (S) 39 Be 34
Pukë (AL) 86 Bk 48
Pukšen'ga (RUS) 25 Eb 27
Pula (HR) 69 Bd 46
09010 Pula (I) 83 Ai 51
Pulaj (AL) 86 Bk 49
24-100 Puławy (PL) 57 Cb 39
17320 Pulkkila (FIN) 22 Cf 26
Pulonga (RUS) 17 Dk 24
Pulozero (RUS) 16 Dd 22
04640 Pulpí (E) 93 Si 53
Pulsujärvi (S) 15 Cb 22
06-100 Pułtusk (PL) 40 Cb 38
Pülümür (TR) 90 Dk 51
Pummanki (RUS) 16 Db 21
39012 Pumpėnai (LT) 41 Ce 35
58501 Punkaharju (FIN) 31 Ck 29
31901 Punkalaidun (FIN) 30 Cd 29
58450* Punkasalmi = Punkaharju (FIN) 31 Ck 29
21100 Punta Umbría (E) 92 Sd 53
99981 Puoddopohki = Patoniva (FIN) 15 Ch 21
91750 Pukio (FIN) 23 Ch 26
89201 Puolanka (FIN) 23 Ch 26
Puoltikasvaara (S) 15 Cb 23
Puottaure (S) 22 Ca 24
04870 Purchena (E) 93 Sh 53
Purdoški (RUS) 44 Ed 36
Pureh (RUS) 44 Ed 34
1440* Purmerend (NL) 53 Ae 38
Purnema (RUS) 24 Dh 26
38950 Pusatlı (TR) 97 Df 52
Puščino (RUS) 43 Dh 36
Puškin (RUS) 31 Da 31
Puškino (RUS) 43 Df 34
Puškino (RUS) 43 Dh 34
Puškino (RUS) 62 Eh 39
Puškinskie Gory (RUS) 42 Ci 33
Pušlahta (RUS) 24 Dg 26
Pušnoj (RUS) 24 De 26
4150 Püspökladány (H) 71 Cb 43
Pustaja Guba (RUS) 16 Dd 23
Pusterno (I) 69 Bb 45
Pustoška (RUS) 42 Ck 34
18581 Putbus (D) 39 Bd 36
145200 Putineiu (RO) 72 Ce 47
Putjanino (RUS) 44 Eb 36
Putjaševo (RUS) 35 Fd 30
16949 Putlitz (D) 39 Bc 37
23769 Puttgarden (D) 39 Bb 36
Putyvl' (UA) 59 Dd 39
95255 Puukkokumpu (FIN) 22 Cf 25
52201 Puumala (FIN) 31 Ci 29
43000* Puy-en-Velay, le (F) 67 Ad 45
46700 Puy-L'Evêque (F) 67 Ab 46
Puzači (RUS) 60 Dh 39
LL53 Pwllheli (GB) 51 Sf 38
Pyčas (RUS) 46 Fc 34
98510 Pyhäjärvi (FIN) 22 Cf 27
98510 Pyhäjärvi (FIN) 15 Ch 23
27920 Pyhäjoki (FIN) 22 Ce 26
89770 Pyhäkylä (FIN) 23 Ci 25
92930 Pyhäntä (FIN) 22 Cg 26
23950 Pyhäranta (FIN) 30 Cb 30
82200* Pyhäselkä (FIN) 23 Ck 28
49270 Pyhtää (FIN) 30 Cg 30
Pylema (RUS) 25 Ef 26
Pylemec (RUS) 18 Fc 23
43440 Pylkönmäki (FIN) 22 Ce 28
9179 Pyramiden (N) 14 I Svalbard
Pyrižky (UA) 58 Ck 40
Pyrjatyn (UA) 59 Dc 40
31812 Pyrmont, Bad (D) 54 Ak 39
74-200 Pyrzyce (PL) 39 Be 37
Pyščyg (RUS) 34 Ef 32
Pyš'ja, Ust'- (RUS) 35 Ff 31
44-120 Pyskowice (PL) 56 Bi 40
Pys'menne (UA) 60 Df 42
Pyšna (BY) 42 Ci 36
Pytalovo = Abrene (RUS) 41 Ch 33
Pytalovo = Abrene (RUS) 42 Ch 33
49270 Pyttis = Pyhtää (FIN) 30 Cg 30
62-310 Pyzdry (PL) 56 Bh 38

Q

Qaf-Mollë (AL) 86 Bk 49
Qeparo (AL) 86 Bk 50
49610 Quakenbrück (D) 38 Ah 38
8125-001* Quarteira (P) 92 Sb 53
09045 Quartu Sant'Elena (I) 83 Ak 51
06484 Quedlinburg (D) 55 Bb 39
EH30 Queensferry (GB) 51 Sg 35
53360 Quelaines-Saint-Gault (F) 66 Sk 43
06268 Querfurt (D) 55 Bb 39
50630 Quettehou (F) 52 Si 41
56170* Quiberon (F) 66 Sg 43
25451 Quickborn (D) 38 Ak 37
11500 Quillan (F) 82 Ac 48
29000* Quimper (F) 52 Sf 43
29300 Quimperlé (F) 66 Sg 43
24397 Quintana del Castillo (E) 80 Sd 48
45800 Quintanar de la Orden (E) 81 Sg 51
09348 Quintanilla del Coco (E) 81 Sg 49
22800 Quintin (F) 52 Sh 42
50770 Quinto (E) 82 Sk 49
30260 Quissac (F) 67 Ae 47
Qukës-Skënderbej (AL) 86 Ca 49
Qyrsaç (AL) 86 Bk 48
Qyteti Stalin = Kuçovë (AL) 86 Bk 50

R

3820 Raabs an der Thaya (A) 56 Bf 42
92150 Raahe (FIN) 22 Ce 26
82301 Rääkkylä (FIN) 23 Ck 28
8100 Raalte (NL) 54 Ag 38
97250 Raanujärvi (FIN) 15 Ce 24
99340 Raattama (FIN) 15 Ce 22
Rab (HR) 70 Be 46
417400 Răbăgani (RO) 71 Cc 44
Rabat (M) 84 Be 55
Rabat = Victoria (M) 84 Be 54
34-700 Rabka-Zdrój (PL) 56 Bk 41
Rabočeostrovsk (RUS) 24 De 26
12254 Rabrovo (SRB) 71 Cb 46
607480 Răcăciuni (RO) 72 Cg 44
327315 Răcăşdia (RO) 71 Cb 46
Rachiv (UA) 57 Ce 42
09-140 Raciąż (PL) 40 Ca 38
47-400 Racibórz (PL) 56 Bi 40
Radaškovičy (BY) 42 Ch 36
725400 Rădăuţi (RO) 72 Cf 43
01454 Radeberg (D) 55 Bd 39
1433 Radeče (SLO) 70 Bf 44
Radechiv (UA) 57 Ce 40
Radica-Krylovka (RUS) 43 De 37
Radiščevo (RUS) 45 Eg 37
Radiščevo (RUS) 45 Eh 38
Rad'kivis'ki, Piski- (UA) 60 Dh 41
6260 Radnevo (BG) 87 Cf 48
Radohova (BIH) 70 Bh 46
78315 Radolfzell am Bodensee (D) 68 Ai 43
26-600 Radom (PL) 57 Cb 39
2400 Radomir (BG) 86 Cc 48
237365 Radomireşti (RO) 72 Ce 46
97-500 Radomsko (PL) 56 Bk 39
Radomyšl' (UA) 58 Ck 40
207485 Radovan (RO) 72 Cd 46
6564 Radovec (BG) 87 Cg 49
2420* Radoviš (MK) 86 Cc 49
5550 Radstadt (A) 69 Bd 43
82001 Radviliškis (LT) 41 Cd 35
37-550 Radymno (PL) 57 Cc 41
88-200 Radziejów (PL) 56 Bi 38
87-220 Radzyń Chełmiński (PL) 40 Bi 37
21-300 Radzyń Podlaski (PL) 57 Cc 39
46348 Raesfeld (D) 54 Ag 39
Raevskij (RUS) 46 Fe 36
92015 Raffadali (I) 84 Bd 53
19009 Rafína (GR) 94 Ce 52
2144 Ragana (LV) 30 Ce 33
Raglicy (RUS) 31 Da 32
Raguli (RUS) 76 Ed 45
97100 Ragusa (I) 84 Be 54
Rahačav (BY) 42 Da 37
32369 Rahden (D) 54 Ai 38
Rah'ja (RUS) 31 Da 30
Rahmanovka (RUS) 62 Ek 38
Rahmanovka (RUS) 62 Ek 39
2070 Råholt (N) 28 Bb 30
21000* Rahovec = Orahovac (RKS) 86 Ca 48
86641 Rain (D) 55 Ba 42
21280 Raisio (FIN) 30 Cc 30
39610 Raivala (FIN) 22 Cc 29
99801 Raja-Jooseppi (FIN) 15 Ci 22
99650 Rajala (FIN) 15 Cg 23
Rajhorodka (UA) 60 Di 42
Rakav (BY) 42 Ch 37
4640 Rakitovo (BG) 87 Ce 49
1890 Rakkestad (N) 28 Bb 31
3820 Rakovica (BG) 71 Cc 47
269 01* Rakovník (CZ) 55 Bd 40
Rakovskaja (RUS) 25 Eb 28
4150 Rakovski (BG) 87 Ce 48
44306* Rakvere (EST) 30 Cg 31
Rakytne (UA) 59 Da 41
11233 Ralja (SRB) 71 Ca 46
Ralppaluoto = Repolt (FIN) 22 Cb 27
39800 Ramales de la Victoria (E) 66 Sg 47
Ramasuha (RUS) 43 Dd 38
88700 Rambervillers (F) 54 Ag 42
78120* Rambouillet (F) 53 Ab 42
Ramen'e (RUS) 32 Df 33
Ramen'e (RUS) 33 Ea 32
Ramenskoe (RUS) 43 Di 35
3231 Rammersdorf (A) 56 Bf 42
73060 Ramnäs (S) 29 Bg 31
3175 Ramnes (N) 14 Bg 22
Ramni (BY) 42 Da 35
907073 Râmnicu de Jos (RO) 73 Ci 46
125300 Râmnicu Sărat (RO) 73 Ch 45
000240* Râmnicu Vâlcea (RO) 72 Ce 45
Ramon' (RUS) 60 Dk 39
71198 Ramsberg (S) 29 Bf 31
88037 Ramsele (S) 21 Bg 27
IM8 Ramsey (GB) 51 Sf 36
CT11 Ramsgate (GB) 53 Ab 39
82700 Ramsjö (S) 21 Bf 28
84097 Ramundberget (S) 21 Bc 28
Ramuševo (RUS) 31 Db 33
87016 Ramvik (S) 21 Bh 28
38031 Ramygala (LT) 41 Ce 35
Rancevo (RUS) 43 Dd 34
BT41 Randalstown (GB) 49 Sd 36
95036 Randazzo (I) 84 Be 53
84093 Rånddalen (S) 21 Bd 28
8900 Randers (DK) 39 Ba 34
Randijaur (S) 14 Bk 24
95501 Råneå (S) 22 Cc 25
Ranemsletta (N) 20 Bb 26
HS2 Ranish (GB) 50 Sd 32
Rannee (RUS) 63 Fc 39
Rånön (S) 22 Cc 25
Rantajärvi (S) 15 Cd 24
58901 Rantasalmi (FIN) 23 Ci 28
92501 Rantsila (FIN) 22 Cf 26
97701 Ranua (FIN) 22 Cg 25
16035 Rapallo (I) 69 Ak 46
64503* Räpina (EST) 31 Ch 32
79512* Rapla (EST) 30 Ce 31
8640 Rapperswil-Jona (CH) 68 Ai 43
Raša (HR) 70 Be 45
60001 Raseiniai (LT) 41 Cd 35
36350* Raška (SRB) 71 Ca 47
Rasna (BY) 42 Db 37
505400 Râşnov (RO) 72 Cf 45
Rasony (BY) 42 Ci 35
907250 Rasova (RO) 73 Ch 46
Rasskazovo (RUS) 61 Eb 38
Rassypnaja (RUS) 63 Fd 39
76437 Rastatt (D) 54 Ai 42
26180 Rastede (D) 38 Ai 37
457202 Răstoci (RO) 72 Cd 43
84030 Rätansbyn (S) 21 Be 28
Ratčino (RUS) 44 Dk 37
Ráth Caola (IRL) 49 Sb 38
Ráth Droma (IRL) 49 Sd 38
Rathdrum = Ráth Droma (IRL) 49 Sd 38
14712 Rathenow (D) 55 Bc 38
BT34 Rathfriland (GB) 49 Sd 36
Rathkeale = Ráth Caola (IRL) 49 Sb 38
Rath Luirc (IRL) 49 Sb 38
40878* Ratingen (D) 54 Ag 39
Ratne (UA) 57 Ce 39
8673* Ratten (A) 70 Bf 43
6240* Rattenberg (A) 69 Bb 43
79501 Rättvik (S) 29 Bf 30
23909 Ratzeburg (D) 39 Ba 37
74057 Raudonė (LT) 41 Cd 35
675 Raufarhöfn (IS) 48 Re 24
2830 Raufoss (N) 28 Ba 30
3864 Rauland (N) 28 Ai 31
27003 Rauma (FIN) 30 Cb 29
77701 Rautalampi (FIN) 22 Cg 28
73901 Rautavaara (FIN) 23 Ci 27
Rautjärvi (FIN) 31 Ck 29
Rava-Rus'ka (UA) 57 Cd 40
36023 Rävemåla (S) 39 Bf 34
48100 Ravenna (I) 69 Bc 46
88212* Ravensburg (D) 69 Ak 43
96-200 Rawa Mazowiecka (PL) 57 Ca 39
63-900 Rawicz (PL) 56 Bg 39
7727 Razeni (MD) 73 Ci 44
Razgort (RUS) 26 Ei 27
7200* Razgrad (BG) 72 Cg 47
2760 Razlog (BG) 87 Cd 49
RG2 Reading (GB) 52 Sk 39
07042 Reale, la (I) 83 Ai 49
81120 Réalmont (F) 67 Ac 47
Reboly (RUS) 23 Da 27
5320-164 Rebordelo (P) 80 Sc 49
2294 Rebrovo (BG) 87 Cd 48
Rečane (RUS) 42 Db 34
307340 Recaş (RO) 71 Cb 45
21290 Recey-sur-Ource (F) 67 Ae 43
Rečica = Rèčyca (BY) 59 Da 38
49509 Recke (D) 54 Ah 38
45657* Recklinghausen (D) 54 Ah 39
6800 Recogne (B) 54 Af 41
Rèčyca (BY) 59 Da 38
73-210 Recz (PL) 39 Bf 37
84-240 Reda (PL) 40 Bi 36
TS10 Redcar (GB) 51 Si 36
B97 Redditch (GB) 52 Si 38
8978 Rédics (H) 70 Bg 44
Redkino (RUS) 43 Dg 34
Red'kino (RUS) 46 Fe 35
35600* Redon (F) 66 Sh 43
Redondela (E) 80 Sb 48
7005-760 Redondo (P) 92 Sc 52
TR15 Redruth (GB) 52 Se 40
24300 Refahiye (TR) 90 Di 51
33021 Reftele (S) 29 Bd 33
Reftinskij (RUS) 36 Gb 33
94209 Regen (D) 55 Bd 42
93047* Regensburg (D) 55 Bc 41
93128 Regenstauf (D) 55 Bc 41
89100 Reggio di Calabria (I) 84 Bf 52
42100 Reggio nell'Emilia (I) 69 Ba 46
545300 Reghin (RO) 72 Ce 44
Regna (S) 29 Bf 32
Reguby (FIN) 30 Cc 31
Reguengos de Monsaraz (P) 92 Sc 52
95111 Rehau (D) 55 Bc 40
31547 Rehburg-Loccum (D) 54 Ak 38
19217 Rehna (D) 39 Bb 37
RH2 Reigate (GB) 52 Sk 39
51100* Reims (F) 53 Ae 41
21465 Reinbek (D) 39 Ba 37
8390 Reine (N) 14 Bd 23
39200 Reinosa (E) 66 Sf 47
2840 Reinsvoll (N) 28 Ba 30
42580 Reis (TR) 96 Db 52
85900 Reisjärvi (FIN) 22 Ce 27
97-310 Rękoraj (PL) 56 Bk 39
35260 Rekovac (SRB) 71 Cb 47
03578 Relleu (E) 82 Sk 52
61110 Rémalard (F) 53 Aa 42
Remennikovo (RUS) 42 Ci 34
74940 Remeskylä (FIN) 22 Cg 27
88200* Remiremont (F) 54 Ag 42
Remontnoe (RUS) 76 Ed 44
42853* Remscheid (D) 54 Ah 39
2450 Rena (N) 28 Bb 29
9600 Renaix = Ronse (B) 53 Ad 40
82064 Renålandet (S) 21 Bf 26
4232 Rencēni (LV) 30 Cf 33
3319 Renda (LV) 30 Cc 33
24768 Rendsburg (D) 38 Ak 36
Reni (UA) 73 Ci 45
7391 Rennebu (N) 20 Ak 28
35000* Rennes (F) 52 Si 42
88041 Rensjön (S) 14 Bk 22
43068 Rentína (GR) 86 Cb 51
43068 Rentína (GR) 87 Cd 50
33190* Réole, la (F) 66 Sk 46
9653 Répcelak (H) 70 Bh 43
Rep'evka (RUS) 60 Di 39
Repino (RUS) 31 Ck 30
65930 Replot (FIN) 22 Cb 27
Reppen (N) 14 Bd 24
9768 Repvåg (N) 15 Cf 20
12170 Réquista (F) 67 Ac 46
Reşadiye (TR) 90 Dh 50
Reşadiye (TR) 99 Ec 52
Resanovci (BIH) 70 Bg 46
35237 Resavica (SRB) 71 Cb 46
5060 Resen (BG) 72 Cf 47
7310 Resen (MK) 86 Cb 49
4660-211* Resende (P) 80 Sc 49
Rešetnikovo (RUS) 43 Dg 34
Rešetylivka (UA) 59 De 41
000320* Reşiţa (RO) 71 Cb 45
72-315 Resko (PL) 39 Bf 37
11-440 Reszel (PL) 40 Cb 36
08300* Rethel (F) 53 Ae 41
74100 Réthimno (GR) 94 Ce 55
35240 Retiers (F) 66 Si 43
43130 Retournac (F) 67 Ae 45
13194 Retuerta del Bullaque (E) 81 Sf 51
2070* Retz (A) 56 Bf 42
43201* Reus (E) 82 Ab 49
Reutec (RUS) 60 Df 39
17153 Reuterstadt Stavenhagen (D) 39 Bc 37
72760* Reutlingen (D) 54 Ak 42
Revda (RUS) 47 Fk 34
Revda (RUS) 16 De 23
31250 Revel (F) 67 Ac 47
55800 Revigny-sur-Ornain (F) 53 Ae 42
08170 Revin (F) 53 Ae 41
Reyðarfjörður (IS) 48 Rf 25
31500 Reyhanlı (TR) 98 Dg 54
380 Reykhólar (IS) 48 Qh 25
311 Reykholt (IS) 48 Qi 26
Reykjahlíð (IS) 48 Rd 25
150* Reykjavík (IS) 48 Qi 26
Rež (RUS) 36 Gb 33
44400 Rezé (F) 66 Si 43
4601* Rēzekne (LV) 42 Ch 34
5400 Rezina (MD) 73 Ci 43
8281 Rezovo (BG) 88 Ch 48
19214 Rgotina (SRB) 71 Cc 46
LD6 Rhayader (GB) 52 Sg 38
33378 Rheda-Wiedenbrück (D) 54 Ai 39
48429* Rheine (D) 54 Ah 38
79618 Rheinfelden (Baden) (D) 68 Ah 43
16831 Rheinsberg (D) 39 Bc 37
IV27 Rhiconich (GB) 50 Sf 32
14728 Rhinow (D) 39 Bc 38
20017 Rho (I) 69 Ak 45
CF41 Rhondda (GB) 52 Sg 39
SA18 Rhydaman = Ammanford (GB) 52 Sg 39
LL18 Rhyl (GB) 51 Sg 37
60100 Riákia (GR) 86 Cc 50
40500 Riaza (E) 81 Sg 49
32400 Ribadavia (E) 80 Sb 48
27700 Ribadeo (E) 80 Sc 47
33560 Ribadesella (E) 80 Se 47
37259 Ribare (SRB) 71 Cb 47
5720 Ribarica (BG) 87 Ce 48
36309 Ribariće (SRB) 86 Ca 48
6760 Ribe (DK) 38 Ai 35
68150* Ribeauvillé (F) 54 Ah 42
4870-150* Ribeira de Pena (P) 80 Sc 49
92016 Ribera (I) 84 Bd 53
24600 Ribérac (F) 66 Aa 45
17534 Ribes de Freser (E) 82 Ac 48
Ribnica (BIH) 71 Bi 46
6240 Ribnica (SLO) 70 Be 45
5500 Rîbniţa (MD) 73 Ck 43

194 I Proussós

A B C D E F G H I J K L M N O P Q R S T U V W X Y Z

Šahar, Erken- (RUS) 76 Eb 46
Şahin (TR) 87 Cg 49
36790 Şahnalar (TR) 91 Ed 50
Šahovskaja (RUS) 43 Df 34
Šahta (RUS) 35 Fh 31
Šahtinskij, Kamensk- (RUS) 61 Ea 42
Šahtnyj (RUS) 35 Fh 32
Šahty (RUS) 76 Ea 43
Šahun'ja (RUS) 34 Eg 33
936 01 Šahy (SK) 56 Bi 42
98950 Saija (FIN) 15 Ci 23
26340 Saillans (F) 68 Af 46
01740 Saimbeyli (TR) 97 Dg 52
12400 Saint-Affrique (F) 67 Ac 47
41110 Saint-Aignan (F) 67 Ab 43
AL3 Saint Albans (GB) 52 Sk 39
58310 Saint-Amand-en-Puisaye (F) 67 Ad 43
59230* Saint-Amand-les-Eaux (F) 53 Ad 40
18200* Saint-Amand-Montrond (F) 67 Ac 44
39160 Saint-Amour (F) 68 Af 44
33240 Saint-André-de-Cubzac (F) 66 Sk 46
KY16 Saint Andrews (GB) 50 Sh 34
35140 Saint-Aubin-du-Cormier (F) 52 Si 42
24410 Saint-Aulaye (F) 66 Aa 45
PL25 Saint Austell (GB) 52 Sf 40
57500 Saint-Avold (F) 54 Ag 41
31440 Saint-Béat (F) 82 Aa 48
22000* Saint-Brieuc (F) 52 Sh 42
72120 Saint-Calais (F) 66 Aa 43
46400 Saint-Céré (F) 67 Ab 46
42400 Saint-Chamond (F) 67 Ae 45
48200 Saint-Chély-d'Apcher (F) 67 Ad 46
34360 Saint-Chinian (F) 67 Ac 47
42670 Saint-Claude (F) 68 Af 44
16190 Saint-Cybard, Montmoreau- (F) 66 Aa 45
SA62 Saint David's (GB) 52 Se 39
93200* Saint-Denis (F) 53 Ac 42
88100* Saint-Dié (F) 54 Ag 42
52100* Saint-Dizier (F) 53 Ae 42
33220 Sainte-Foy-la-Grande (F) 66 Aa 46
85210 Sainte-Hermine (F) 66 Si 44
63700 Saint-Eloy-les-Mines (F) 67 Ac 44
37800 Sainte-Maure-de-Touraine (F) 66 Aa 43
83120 Sainte-Maxime (F) 68 Ag 47
51800* Sainte-Menehould (F) 53 Ae 41
17100* Saintes (F) 66 Sk 45
13460 Saintes-Maries-de-la-Mer (F) 67 Ae 47
42100 Saint-Étienne (F) 67 Ae 45
89170 Saint-Fargeau (F) 67 Ad 43
BT24 Saintfield (GB) 49 Se 36
45600 Saint-Florent (F) 83 Ak 48
89570 Saint-Florentin (F) 67 Ad 43
18400 Saint-Florent-sur-Cher (F) 67 Ac 44
15100* Saint-Flour (F) 67 Ad 45
31800* Saint-Gaudens (F) 82 Aa 47
36800 Saint-Gaultier (F) 67 Ab 44
71330 Saint-Germain-du-Bois (F) 68 Af 44
87380 Saint-Germain-les-Belles (F) 67 Ab 45
63390 Saint-Gervais-d'Auvergne (F) 67 Ac 44
46330 Saint-Géry (F) 67 Ab 46
35590 Saint-Gilles (F) 67 Ae 47
85800 Saint-Gilles-Croix-de-Vie (F) 66 Si 44
1898 Saint-Gingolph (CH) 68 Ag 44
74500 Saint-Gingolph (F) 68 Ag 44
09200 Saint-Girons (F) 82 Ab 48
56220 Saint-Gravé (F) 66 Sh 43
WA10 Saint Helens (GB) 51 Sh 37
JE1 Saint-Helier (GBJ) 52 Sh 41
44800 Saint-Herblain (F) 66 Si 43
85440 Saint-Hilaire, Talmont- (F) 66 Si 44
87260 Saint-Hilaire-Bonneval (F) 67 Ab 45
50600 Saint-Hilaire-du-Harcouët (F) 52 Si 42
30170 Saint-Hippolyte-du-Fort (F) 67 Ad 47
6870 Saint-Hubert (B) 54 Af 40
PE17 Saint Ives (GB) 52 Se 40
PE17 Saint Ives (GB) 52 Sk 38
17400 Saint-Jean-d'Angély (F) 66 Sk 45
38440 Saint-Jean-de-Bournay (F) 68 Af 45
21170 Saint-Jean-de-Losne (F) 68 Af 43
64500 Saint-Jean-de-Luz (F) 66 Si 47
85160 Saint-Jean-de-Monts (F) 66 Sh 44
64220 Saint-Jean-Pied-de-Port (F) 81 Si 47
DL13 Saint John's Chapel (GB) 51 Sh 36
81990 Saint-Juéry (F) 67 Ac 47
87200 Saint-Junien (F) 66 Aa 45
60130 Saint-Just-en-Chaussée (F) 53 Ac 41
42170 Saint-Just-Saint-Rambert (F) 67 Ae 45
65170 Saint-Lary-Soulan (F) 82 Aa 48
66250 Saint-Laurent-de-la-Salanque (F) 82 Ac 48
39150 Saint-Laurent-en-Grandvaux (F) 68 Af 44
33112 Saint-Laurent-Médoc (F) 66 Sk 45
87400 Saint-Léonard-de-Noblat (F) 67 Ab 45
50000* Saint-Lô (F) 52 Si 41
70800 Saint-Loup-sur-Semouse (F) 68 Ag 43
79400 Saint-Maixent-l'École (F) 66 Sk 44
35400* Saint-Malo (F) 52 Sh 42
15220 Saint-Mamet-la-Salvetat (F) 67 Ac 46
38160 Saint-Marcellin (F) 68 Af 45
34380 Saint-Martin-de-Londres (F) 67 Ad 47
17410 Saint-Martin-de-Ré (F) 66 Si 44
06670 Saint-Martin-du-Var (F) 68 Ah 47
88560 Saint-Maurice-sur-Moselle (F) 68 Ag 43
83470 Saint-Maximin-la-Sainte-Baume (F) 68 Af 47
35290 Saint-Méen-le-Grand (F) 52 Sh 42
73450 Saint-Michel-de-Maurienne (F) 68 Ag 45
55300 Saint-Mihiel (F) 54 Af 42
44600* Saint-Nazaire (F) 66 Sh 43
Saint Neots (GB) 52 Sk 38
54210 Saint-Nicolas-de-Port (F) 54 Ag 42
62500* Saint-Omer (F) 53 Ac 40
64120 Saint-Palais (F) 66 Si 47
66220 Saint-Paul-de-Fenouillet (F) 82 Ac 48
40990 Saint-Paul-lès-Dax (F) 66 Si 47
07130 Saint-Péray (F) 67 Ae 46
GY1 Saint Peter Port (GBG) 52 Sh 41
44310 Saint-Philbert-de-Grand-Lieu (F) 66 Si 43
17310 Saint-Pierre-d'Oléron (F) 66 Si 45
58240 Saint-Pierre-le-Moûtier (F) 67 Ad 44
14170 Saint-Pierre-sur-Dives (F) 52 Sk 41
29250 Saint-Pol-de-Léon (F) 52 Sg 42
62130 Saint-Pol-sur-Ternoise (F) 53 Ac 40
34220 Saint-Pons-de-Thomières (F) 67 Ac 47
03500 Saint-Pourçain-sur-Sioule (F) 67 Ad 44
02100* Saint-Quentin (F) 53 Ad 41
26140 Saint-Rambert-d'Albon (F) 67 Ae 45
83700* Saint-Raphaël (F) 68 Ag 47
13210* Saint-Rémy-de-Provence (F) 67 Ae 47
58330 Saint-Saulge (F) 67 Ad 43
Saint-Saveur-sur-Tinée (F) 68 Ah 46
33920 Saint-Savin (F) 66 Aa 44
40500* Saint-Sever (F) 66 Sk 47
81370 Saint-Sulpice (F) 67 Ab 47
33113 Saint-Symphorien (F) 66 Sk 46
3800 Saint-Trond = Sint-Truiden (B) 54 Af 40
83990* Saint-Tropez (F) 68 Ag 47
50550 Saint-Vaast-la-Hougue (F) 52 Si 41
Saint-Valéry-en-Caux (F) 53 Aa 41
80230 Saint-Valery-sur-Somme (F) 53 Ab 40
26240 Saint-Vallier (F) 67 Ae 44
26240 Saint-Vallier (F) 67 Ae 45
23320 Saint-Vaury (F) 67 Ab 44
40230 Saint-Vincent-de-Tyrosse (F) 66 Si 47
4780 Saint-Vith (B) 54 Ag 40
33590 Saint-Vivien-de-Médoc (F) 66 Si 45
87500 Saint-Yrieix-la-Perche (F) 67 Ab 45
11310 Saissac (F) 67 Ac 47
Saitbaba (RUS) 47 Fg 36
Saittarova (S) 15 Cc 23
Saja (RUS) 35 Fh 33
Šajduriha (RUS) 36 Ga 33
Šajgino (RUS) 34 Eg 33
Šajince (SRB) 86 Cc 48
3770 Sajószentpéter (H) 57 Ca 42
18800 Sakaevi (TR) 89 Dd 50
38610 Sakaltutan (TR) 97 Df 52
46090 Sakarya (TR) 88 Da 50
Sakçagöz (TR) 98 Dg 53
71001 Šakiai (LT) 41 Cd 36
Šakin (RUS) 61 Ec 41
57200 Sakız (TR) 88 Ch 49
Sakmara (RUS) 64 Ff 39
Sakony (RUS) 44 Ed 35
4990 Sakskøbing (DK) 39 Bb 36
Saky 74 Dd 45
Sakyatan (TR) 96 Dc 53
27920 Säkylä (FIN) 30 Cc 29
73301* Sala (S) 29 Bg 31
927 01* Šal'a (SK) 56 Bh 42
Salačgriva (LV) 30 Ce 33
84036 Sala Consilina (I) 85 Bf 50
85106 Sálakos (GR) 95 Ch 54
Šalakuša (RUS) 24 Ea 28
37001* Salamanca (E) 80 Se 50
Salamat (RUS) 47 Gb 37
18900 Salamína (GR) 94 Cd 53
97035 Salantai (LT) 40 Cb 34
33860 Salas (E) 80 Sd 47
09600 Salas de los Infantes (E) 81 Sg 48
09140 Salau (F) 82 Ab 48
Salavat (RUS) 46 Ff 37
01780 Salbaş (TR) 97 Df 53
41300 Salbris (F) 67 Ac 43
17001 Šalčininkai (LT) 41 Cf 36
34100 Saldaña (E) 81 Sf 48
Šaldež (RUS) 45 Ee 34
3801 Saldus (LV) 41 Cc 34
Salema (P) 92 Sb 53
91018 Salemi (I) 84 Bc 53
78067 Sälen (S) 29 Bd 29
83690 Salernes (F) 68 Ag 47
84100* Salerno (I) 85 Be 50
Salgan (RUS) 45 Ef 35
3100 Salgótarján (H) 56 Bk 42
Šalgovaara (RUS) 23 Dd 27
Sali (HR) 70 Bf 47
Šali (RUS) 45 Ek 35
64270 Salies-de-Béarn (F) 66 Sk 47
17600 Salihler (TR) 87 Cg 51
17600 Salihler (TR) 88 Db 51
Salihli (TR) 95 Ci 52
Salihorsk (BY) 42 Ch 38
Salino (RUS) 43 De 34
39110 Salins-les-Bains (F) 68 Af 44
55530 Salıpazarı (TR) 89 De 49
SP1 Salisbury (GB) 52 Si 39
557225 Săliște (RO) 72 Cd 45
Šalja (RUS) 36 Fi 33
Sal'kove (UA) 58 Ck 42
98901 Salla (FIN) 15 Ci 24
74700 Sallanches (F) 68 Ag 45
08650 Sallent (E) 82 Ab 49
33770 Salles (F) 66 Sk 46
66910 Salmanlı (TR) 89 De 51
Salmi (RUS) 31 Db 29
25003 Salo (FIN) 30 Cd 30
25087 Salò (I) 69 Ba 45
13300 Salon-de-Provence (F) 68 Af 47
415500 Salonta (RO) 71 Cb 44
61670 Şalpazarı (TR) 90 Dk 50
7960 Salsbruket (N) 20 Bb 26
66600 Salses (F) 82 Ac 48
Sal'sk (RUS) 76 Eb 44
Sal'skij (RUS) 24 Dg 29
43039 Salsomaggiore Terme (I) 69 Ak 46
PL12 Saltash (GB) 52 Sf 40
Saltburn- by-the-Sea (GB) 51 Sk 36
LN11 Saltfleet (GB) 51 Aa 37
Saltoluokta fjällstation (S) 14 Bi 23
13300 Saltsjöbaden (S) 29 Bi 31
22430 Saltvik (AX) 30 Ca 30
Šalty (RUS) 46 Fd 36
Šalty (RUS) 46 Fd 37
Saltyki (RUS) 44 Dk 37
Saltykovo, Karaja- (RUS) 61 Ec 38
Salur (TR) 98 Dk 53
12037 Saluzzo (I) 68 Ah 46
427255 Salva (RO) 72 Ce 43
2120-051* Salvaterra de Magos (P) 80 Sb 51
06175 Salvatierra de los Barros (E) 92 Sd 52
46340 Salviac (F) 67 Ab 46
Saly, Sultan- (RUS) 75 Dk 43
Šalyhyne (UA) 59 De 39
5020* Salzburg (A) 69 Bd 43
38226* Salzgitter (D) 55 Ba 38
36433 Salzungen, Bad (D) 55 Ba 40
29410 Salzwedel (D) 39 Bb 38
Sama (Langreo) (E) 80 Se 47
Samachvalavičy (BY) 42 Ch 37
Samailli (TR) 96 Ci 52
31770 Samandağ (TR) 97 Df 54
Samandere (TR) 88 Db 50
Samara (RUS) 46 Fa 37
Samarkovo (RUS) 76 Ed 47
Samarskoe (RUS) 64 Fi 39
Samarskoe (RUS) 75 Dk 44
Šamary (RUS) 36 Fi 33
32130 Samatan (F) 66 Aa 47
02340 Şambayat (TR) 98 Di 53
Sambir (UA) 57 Cd 41
Sambir (UA) 59 Dd 39
7503 Samedan (CH) 69 Ak 44
28080 Sámi (GR) 94 Ca 52
Samino (RUS) 34 Ei 29
10180 Şamlı (TR) 88 Ch 51
Samobor (HR) 70 Bf 45
Samoded (RUS) 24 Ea 27
Samofalovka (RUS) 61 Ee 42
Samojlovka (RUS) 61 Ed 39
2000 Samokov (BG) 87 Cd 48
931 01 Šamorín (SK) 56 Bh 42
83100 Sámos (GR) 95 Cg 53
68002 Samothráki (GR) 87 Cf 50
Samovol'no-Ivanovka (RUS) 63 Fa 38
12020 Sampeyre (I) 68 Ah 46
Sampur (RUS) 61 Eb 38
55000* Samsun (TR) 90 Dg 49
09086 Samugheo (I) 83 Ai 51
Samylovo (RUS) 33 Ee 32
21510 San Bartolomé de la Torre (E) 92 Sc 53
82028 San Bartolomeo in Galdo (I) 85 Bf 49
63039 San Benedetto del Tronto (I) 84 Bd 48
46027 San Benedetto Po (I) 69 Ba 45
37047 San Bonifacio (I) 69 Bb 45
12300 Sancak (TR) 91 Ea 51
18300 Sancerre (F) 67 Ac 43
05290 Sanchidrián (E) 81 Sf 50
18600 Sancoins (F) 67 Ac 44
Sancti-Spíritus (E) 80 Sd 50
Sančursk (RUS) 45 Eh 34
4230 Sand (N) 28 Ag 31
4230 Sand (N) 28 Bb 30
6823 Sandane (N) 20 Ag 29
2800 Sandanski (BG) 87 Cd 49
51820 Sandared (S) 29 Bc 33
Sandata (RUS) 76 Eb 44
Sandbukta (N) 15 Cb 21
26452 Sande (D) 38 Ai 37
Sande (N) 28 Af 29
Sande (N) 28 Ba 31
3208* Sandefjord (N) 28 Ba 31
245 Sandgerði (IS) 48 Qh 26
Sandhammaren (S) 39 Be 35
03500 Sandıklı (TR) 96 Da 52
84040 Sandnäset (S) 21 Bg 28
Sandnes (N) 28 Af 32
Sandneshamn (N) 14 Bi 21
8800 Sandnessjøen (N) 14 Bc 24
27-600* Sandomierz (PL) 57 Cb 40
30027 San Donà di Piave (I) 69 Bc 45
Sandovo (RUS) 32 Dg 32
Šandrivka (UA) 60 Df 42
91050 Sandsjö (S) 29 Be 29
Sandstad (N) 20 Ak 27
4735 Sandvig (DK) 39 Be 35
59010 Sandvik (S) 29 Bg 33
83015 Sandvika (S) 21 Bc 27
81100* Sandviken (S) 29 Bg 30
42330 San Esteban de Gormaz (E) 81 Sg 49
04017 San Felice Circeo (I) 84 Bd 49
37270 San Felices de los Gallegos (E) 80 Sd 50
37492 San Fernando (E) 92 Sd 54
Šanga, Nikola- (RUS) 34 Ef 32
06526 Sangerhausen (D) 55 Bb 39
Sângeru (RO) 72 Cg 45
53037 San Gimignano (I) 69 Bb 47
62026 San Ginesio (I) 84 Bd 47
91620 Sanginkylä (FIN) 22 Cg 26
74027 San Giorgio Ionico (I) 85 Bh 50
87055 San Giovanni in Fiore (I) 85 Bg 51
40017 San Giovanni in Persiceto (I) 69 Bb 46
71013 San Giovanni Rotondo (I) 85 Bf 49
95272 Sangis (S) 22 Cd 25
40100 San Ildefonso o La Granja (E) 81 Sf 50
San Janvier (E) 93 Sk 53
San José (E) 93 Sh 54
San Juan de Alacant (E) 93 Sk 52
San Juan de Alicante = San Juan de Alacant (E) 93 Sk 52
Sankok (TR) 96 Db 53
3193 Sankt Aegyd am Neuwalde (A) 70 Bf 43
8560 Sankt Anton am Arlberg (A) 69 Ba 43
9000* Sankt Gallen (CH) 69 Ak 43
5340 Sankt Gilgen (A) 69 Bd 43
56329 Sankt Goar (D) 54 Ah 40
5600* Sankt Johann im Pongau (A) 69 Bd 43
25693 Sankt Michaelisdonn (D) 38 Ak 37
7500* Sankt Moritz (CH) 69 Ak 44
190000* Sankt-Peterburg (RUS) 31 Da 31
25826 Sankt Peter-Ording (D) 38 Ai 36
3100* Sankt Pölten (A) 56 Bf 42
9300* Sankt Veit an der Glan (A) 70 Be 44
4780 Sankt-Vith = Saint-Vith (B) 54 Ag 40
66606 Sankt Wendel (D) 54 Ah 41
42140 San Leonardo de Yagüe (E) 81 Sg 49
Şanlıca (TR) 91 Eb 51
Şanlı Urfa (TR) 98 Di 53
28200 San Lorenzo (E) 81 Sf 50
13779 San Lorenzo de Calatrava (E) 93 Sg 52
11540 Sanlúcar de Barrameda (E) 92 Sd 54
21595 Sanlúcar de Guadiana (E) 92 Sc 53
41800 Sanlúcar la Mayor (E) 92 Sd 53
09025 Sanluri (I) 83 Ai 51
51028 San Marcello Pistoiese (I) 69 Ba 46
47890 San Marino (RSM) 69 Bc 47
San Martín de Castañeda (E) 80 Sd 48
45165 San Martín de Montalbán (E) 81 Sf 51
28680 San Martín de Valdeiglesias (E) 81 Sf 50
38058 San Martino di Castrozza (I) 69 Bb 44
03193 San Miguel de Salinas (E) 93 Sk 53
Sänna (S) 29 Be 32
305600 Sânnicolau Mare (RO) 71 Ca 44
09-540 Sanniki (PL) 56 Bk 38
38-500 Sanok (PL) 57 Cc 41
30740 San Pedro del Pinatar (E) 93 Sk 53
18038 Sanremo (I) 68 Ah 47
11360 San Roque (E) 92 Se 54
San Sadurniño = Avenida do Marqués de Figueroa (E) 80 Sb 47
20001 San Sebastián = Donostia (E) 66 Si 47
28700 San Sebastián de los Reyes (E) 81 Sg 50
52037 Sansepolcro (I) 69 Bc 47
62027 San Severino Marche (I) 69 Bd 47
71016 San Severo (I) 85 Bf 49
Šanskij Zavod (RUS) 43 Df 35
Sanski Most (BIH) 70 Bg 46
San Stino di Livenza (I) 69 Bc 45
06410 Santa Amalia (E) 80 Sd 51
21570 Santa Bárbara de Casa (E) 92 Sc 53
09078 Santa Caterina di Pittinuri (I) 83 Ai 50
73020 Santa Cesarea Terme (I) 85 Bi 50
7665-880* Santa Clara-a-Velha (P) 92 Sb 53
17430 Santa Coloma de Farners (E) 82 Ac 49
3440-313* Santa Comba Dão (P) 80 Sb 50
39047 Santa Cristina Valgardena = Sankt Christina in Gröden (I) 69 Bb 44
97017 Santa Croce Camerina (I) 84 Be 54
13730 Santa Cruz de Mudela (E) 93 Sg 52
87020 Santa Domenica Talao (I) 85 Bf 51
14491 Santa Eufemia (E) 93 Sf 52
Santa Eugenia (Ribeira) (E) 80 Sb 48
7450-101 Santa Eulália (P) 80 Sc 51
Santa Eulària del Riu (E) 82 Ab 52
18320 Santa Fé (E) 93 Sg 53
Sant'Agata di Militelo (I) 84 Be 52
16038 Santa Margherita Ligure (I) 69 Ak 46
81055 Santa Maria Capua Vetere (I) 85 Be 49
Santa Maria de Arzua (E) 80 Sb 48
07320 Santa Maria del Camí (E) 82 Ac 51
24240 Santa María del Páramo (E) 80 Se 48
Santa Marta (E) 92 Sd 52
Santana (E) 81 Sf 48

196 | Šahar, Erken-

Sergač (RUS) 45 Ef 35
Sergeevsk (RUS) 46 Fb 37
Sergeevskij (RUS) 35 Fe 30
63700 Sergen (TR) 88 Ch 49
63700 Sergen (TR) 98 Dk 53
Sergievka (RUS) 63 Fb 39
Sergievo (RUS) 24 Dg 28
Sergiev Posad (RUS) 43 Di 34
Sergievskoe (RUS) 76 Ec 46
Serhijivka (UA) 60 Dh 42
Serhijivka (UA) 73 Da 44
07500 Serik (TR) 96 Db 54
20430* Serinhisar (TR) 96 Ck 53
13200 Serinkum (TR) 99 Ec 52
31120 Serinyol (TR) 97 Dg 54
Šer'jag (RUS) 35 Fe 29
Serkova (RUS) 36 Gc 33
Sermenevo (RUS) 47 Fi 37
3640-209* Sernancelhe (P) 80 Sc 50
Sernovodsk (RUS) 46 Fb 37
Sernur (RUS) 45 Ek 34
05-140 Serock (PL) 57 Cb 38
Seroglazka (RUS) 77 Eh 44
Serón (E) 93 Sh 53
Serov (RUS) 36 Ga 31
7830-320* Serpa (P) 92 Sc 53
Serpejsk (RUS) 43 De 36
Serpuhov (RUS) 43 Dh 36
Serra de Outes, A (Outes) (E) 80 Sb 48
10530 Serradilla (E) 80 Sd 51
89822 Serra San Bruno (I) 85 Bg 52
84200 Serres (F) 68 Af 46
6100-598* Sertã (P) 80 Sb 51
12510 Servi (TR) 99 Ea 52
50500 Sérvia (GR) 86 Cc 50
2970-041* Sesimbra (P) 92 Sa 52
95394 Seskarö (S) 22 Cd 25
81037 Sessa Aurunca (I) 84 Bd 49
Šestakovo (RUS) 34 Fa 32
Šestovoe (RUS) 37 Gi 33
10058 Sestriere (I) 68 Ag 46
16039 Sestri Levante (I) 69 Ak 46
Sestroreck (RUS) 31 Ck 30
Šešurga (RUS) 34 Eh 33
34600 Séta (GR) 94 Cd 52
58005 Šeta (LT) 41 Ce 35
34200* Sète (F) 67 Ad 47
Setermoen (N) 14 Bi 22
Setraki (RUS) 61 Ea 41
10036 Settimo Torinese (I) 68 Ah 45
BD24 Settle (GB) 51 Sh 36
2900-001* Setúbal (P) 92 Sb 52
25700 Seu d'Urgell, la (E) 82 Ab 48
08037 Seui (I) 83 Ak 51
Sevastopol' 74 Dd 46
Ševčenkivskyj, Korsun'- (UA) 59 Db 41
Ševčenkovo (UA) 60 Dh 41
Ševelevskaja (RUS) 33 Ee 30
TN13 Sevenoaks (GB) 53 Aa 39
Sever (RUS) 35 Fd 32
12150 Sévérac-le-Château (F) 67 Ad 46
Severka (RUS) 47 Ga 34
Severnoe (RUS) 46 Fc 36
Severnoe (RUS) 76 Ec 46
Severnyj (RUS) 23 Dc 26
Severnyj (RUS) 19 Gd 23
Severnyj (RUS) 77 Ef 43
Severnyj Kolčim (RUS) 35 Fh 30
Severodonec'k = Sjevjerodonec'k (UA) 60 Di 42
Severodvinsk (RUS) 24 Dk 26
Severo-Kospaškij (RUS) 35 Fh 31
Severomorsk (RUS) 16 Dd 21
Severoural'sk (RUS) 36 Ga 30
Severo-Zadonsk (RUS) 43 Di 36
99930 Sevettijärvi (FIN) 15 Ci 21
Sevgáraki (GR) 94 Cb 52
41001* Sevilla (E) 92 Se 53
41795 Sevindikli (TR) 88 Ck 50
Şevketiye (TR) 88 Ch 50
5400 Sevlievo (BG) 72 Cf 47
8290 Sevnica (SLO) 70 Bf 44
Sevrjukovo (RUS) 43 Dg 36
Sevsk (RUS) 59 De 38
7400 Sevštari (BG) 72 Cg 47
19110 Seydim (TR) 89 De 50
42360* Seydişehir (TR) 96 Db 53
Seyðisfjörður (IS) 48 Rf 25
Seyfeköy (TR) 89 De 51
Şeyhali (TR) 89 Dc 51
Şeyhli (TR) 90 Dg 50
47510 Şeyhmehmet (TR) 99 Eb 53
26950 Seyitgazi (TR) 88 Da 51
Seyitoba (TR) 95 Ch 52
83500* Seyne-sur-Mer, la (F) 68 Af 47
74910 Seyssel (F) 68 Af 45
6210 Sežana (SLO) 69 Bd 45
51120* Sézanne (F) 53 Ad 42
04018 Sezze (I) 84 Bd 49
Sfakia (GR) 94 Ce 55
000520* Sfântu Gheorghe (RO) 72 Cf 45
000520* Sfântu Gheorghe (RO) 73 Ck 46
73014 Sfinári (GR) 94 Cd 55
2491* 's-Gravenhage = Den Haag (NL) 53 Ae 38
HS2 Shader (GB) 50 Sd 32
SP7 Shaftesbury (GB) 52 Sh 39
Shannon = Sionainn (IRL) 49 Sb 38
ME12 Sheerness (GB) 53 Aa 39
S5 Sheffield (GB) 51 Si 37
IV27 Shegra (GB) 50 Se 32
Shëngjin (AL) 86 Bk 49
Shënmëri = Buçimas (AL) 86 Ca 49
DT9 Sherborne (GB) 52 Sh 40
NR26 Sheringham (GB) 51 Ab 38
5200* 's-Hertogenbosch (NL) 54 Af 39
Shijak (AL) 86 Bk 49
Shkodër (AL) 86 Bk 48
SY5 Shrewsbury (GB) 51 Sh 38
72000 Shtime = Štimlje (RKS) 86 Cb 48
76-004 Sianów (PL) 40 Bg 36
82043 Šiaulėnai (LT) 41 Cd 35
76001* Šiauliai (LT) 41 Cd 35
Sibaj (RUS) 64 Fi 38
87070 Sibari (I) 85 Bg 51
Šibenik (HR) 70 Bf 47
000550* Sibiu (RO) 72 Ce 45
Šičuga (RUS) 34 Eg 29
22239* Šid (SRB) 71 Bk 45
Sidaravičy (BY) 42 Da 37
07330 Side (TR) 96 Db 54
Sidel'kino (RUS) 46 Fb 36
3960 Siders = Sierre (CH) 68 Ah 44
Sidira (GR) 94 Cb 52
62300 Sidirókastro (GR) 87 Cd 49
Sidlyšče (UA) 58 Cf 39
EX10 Sidmouth (GB) 52 Sg 40
Sidorovo (RUS) 32 Di 33
Sidorovo (RUS) 34 Fa 30
Šidrovo (RUS) 25 Ec 28
08-100* Siedlce (PL) 57 Cc 38
53721 Siegburg (D) 54 Ah 40
57072* Siegen (D) 54 Ai 40
17-300 Siemiatycze (PL) 57 Cc 38
53100 Siena (I) 69 Bb 47
95800 Sieppijärvi (FIN) 15 Cd 23
98-200 Sieradz (PL) 56 Bi 39
42-790 Sieraków (PL) 56 Bg 38
09-200 Sierpc (PL) 40 Bk 38
3960 Sierre (CH) 68 Ah 44
85410 Sievi (FIN) 22 Ce 27
Sig (RUS) 24 De 25
Sigdal (N) 28 Ak 30
11130 Sigean (F) 82 Ac 47
8400 Sigerfjord (N) 14 Bf 22
435500 Sighetu Marmaţiei (RO) 72 Cd 43
545400 Sighişoara (RO) 72 Ce 44
Siglufjörður (IS) 48 Rb 24
72488 Sigmaringen (D) 54 Ak 42
Šigony (RUS) 45 Ei 37
81103 Sígri (GR) 87 Cf 51
19300 Sigtuna (S) 29 Bh 31
2150 Sigulda (LV) 30 Ce 33
Šihany (RUS) 62 Eh 38
Šihtovo (RUS) 42 Dc 35
29811 Siikainen (FIN) 22 Cb 29
71801 Siilinjärvi (FIN) 23 Ch 27
56000* Siirt (TR) 99 Eb 53
93350 Siivikko (FIN) 23 Ch 25
Sikfors (S) 22 Cb 25
Sikia (GR) 87 Cd 50
84010 Sikinos (GR) 95 Cf 54
7800 Siklós (H) 71 Bi 45
75001 Šilalė (LT) 41 Cc 35
Silandro = Schlanders (I) 69 Ba 44
Šil'da (RUS) 64 Fk 39
34981* Şile (TR) 88 Ck 49
Šilega (RUS) 25 Ee 26
Šilekša (RUS) 33 Ec 33
33940* Silifke (TR) 97 Dd 54
Silikatnyj (RUS) 45 Ei 37
09010 Siliqua (I) 83 Ai 51
907290 Siliştea (RO) 72 Cf 46
817177 Silistraru (RO) 73 Ch 45
34570* Silivri (TR) 88 Ci 49
3748 Siljan (N) 28 Ak 31
Silkeborg (DK) 38 Ak 34
46460 Silla (E) 82 Sk 51
40231* Sillamäe (EST) 31 Ch 31
42240 Sille (TR) 96 Dc 53
36540 Silleda (E) 80 Sb 48
72140 Sillé-le-Guillaume (F) 52 Sk 42
Silli (GR) 87 Ce 49
9920 Sillian (A) 69 Bc 44
73400 Silopi (TR) 99 Ec 53
Šilovo (RUS) 43 Di 37
Šilovo (RUS) 44 Ea 36
9303 Silsand (N) 14 Bh 21
99001 Šilutė (LT) 40 Cb 35
Silván (E) 80 Sd 48
21640* Silvan (TR) 99 Eb 52
8300-100* Silves (P) 92 Sb 53
Sim (RUS) 35 Fh 31
Sim (RUS) 47 Fh 35
Sima (RUS) 44 Dk 34
Simakivka (UA) 58 Ci 40
47130 Simancas (E) 81 Sf 49
317335 Şimand (RO) 71 Cb 44
43500 Simav (TR) 88 Ci 51
Simbirsk (RUS) 45 Ei 36
Simejkyne (UA) 60 Dk 42
335900 Simeria (RO) 72 Cd 45
Simferopol' 74 De 46
Simi (GR) 95 Ch 54
85600 Sími (GR) 95 Ch 54
2730 Simitli (BG) 87 Cd 49
Simkaičiai (LT) 41 Cc 35
455300 Şimleu Silvaniei (RO) 71 Cc 43
64037 Simnas (LT) 41 Cd 36
95201 Simo (FIN) 22 Cf 25
7081 Simontornya (H) 71 Bi 44
56610 Simpele = Rautjärvi (FIN) 31 Ck 29
27200 Simrishamn (S) 39 Be 35
Šimsk (RUS) 31 Da 32
46401 Simuna (EST) 30 Cg 31
53048 Sinalunga (I) 69 Bb 47
Sinan (TR) 99 Ea 53
03850 Sinanpaşa (TR) 96 Da 52
58365 Sincan (TR) 89 Dc 51
58365 Sincan (TR) 90 Dh 51
Sincik (TR) 98 Di 52
9870 Sindal (DK) 28 Ba 33
71063* Sindelfingen (D) 54 Ai 42
86703* Sindi (EST) 30 Ce 32
08018 Sindia (I) 83 Ai 50
10330 Sındırgı (TR) 88 Ci 51
Sindor (RUS) 26 Fb 28
Sinegor'e (RUS) 34 Fa 31
Sinegorskij (RUS) 36 Fk 33
Sinegorskij (RUS) 61 Ea 42
17260 Sinekçi (TR) 88 Ch 50
Sinekli (TR) 88 Ci 49
7520-001* Sines (P) 92 Sb 53
247595 Sineşti (RO) 72 Cd 46
97220 Sinettä (FIN) 15 Cf 24
07510 Sinéu (E) 82 Ad 51
Sinezerki (RUS) 43 De 37
78224 Singen (Hohentwiel) (D) 68 Ai 43
6200 Sîngerei (MD) 73 Ci 43
Singilej (RUS) 45 Ei 37
Singistugorna (S) 14 Bi 23
7387 Singsås (N) 20 Ba 28
Sinie Lipjagi (RUS) 60 Di 39
Sinirli (TR) 95 Ch 52
08029 Siniscola (I) 83 Ak 50
Sinj (HR) 70 Bg 47
Sinjavka (BY) 41 Cg 38
Sinjavka (RUS) 61 Ea 39
Sinodskoe (RUS) 62 Eg 39
57000 Sinop (TR) 89 Df 48
74889 Sinsheim (D) 54 Ai 41
9100 Sint-Niklaas (B) 53 Ae 39
2710-204* Sintra (P) 80 Sa 52
3800 Sint-Truiden (B) 54 Af 40
8600 Siófok (H) 71 Bi 44
1950* Sion (CH) 68 Ah 44
Sionainn = Shannon (IRL) 49 Sb 38
Šipicyno (RUS) 34 Eg 29
6150 Šipka (BG) 87 Cf 48
Šipunovskaja (RUS) 25 Ec 28
4438 Sira (N) 28 Ag 32
96100 Siracusa (I) 84 Bf 53
29700 Şiran (TR) 90 Dk 50
Sırcalı (TR) 89 Df 51
Širega (RUS) 33 Eb 30
725500 Siret (RO) 72 Cg 43
4364 Sirevåg (N) 28 Af 32
Širinguši (RUS) 44 Ec 37
Sirkeli (TR) 89 Dc 50
99131 Sirkka (FIN) 15 Ce 23
73000 Şırnak (TR) 99 Ec 53
Širocina (BY) 42 Ck 35
Široki Brijeg (BIH) 70 Bh 47
Širokij Karamyš (RUS) 62 Ef 39
Širokij Ustup (RUS) 61 Ee 39
Širokovskij (RUS) 35 Fh 32
Sirotinskaja (RUS) 61 Ed 41
22770 Sırpsındığı (TR) 87 Cg 49
Sırtköy (TR) 96 Db 53
Sirvan (TR) 99 Ec 52
19001 Širvintos (LT) 41 Ce 35
Sisak (HR) 70 Bg 45
Šiškeevo (RUS) 45 Ee 36
4450 Sissach (CH) 68 Ah 43
71001 Sísses (GR) 94 Ce 55
04200 Sisteron (F) 68 Af 46
08870 Sitges (E) 82 Ab 49
72300 Sitía (GR) 95 Cg 55
Sitojaurestugorna (S) 14 Bi 23
Šitovo (RUS) 34 Fa 32
6130* Sittard (NL) 54 Af 39
1950* Sitten = Sion (CH) 68 Ah 44
Siuč (RUS) 32 Dg 31
Siva (RUS) 35 Fe 32
25223 Sivac (SRB) 71 Bk 45
88901 Sivakka (FIN) 23 Ck 27
58000* Sivas (TR) 90 Dh 51
Sivaslı (TR) 96 Ck 52
63600 Siverek (TR) 98 Dk 53
Siverskij (RUS) 31 Da 31
Siver'skyj, Novhorod- (UA) 59 Dd 38
Sivomaskinskij (RUS) 19 Gc 24
23900 Sivrice (TR) 98 Dk 52
26600 Sivrihisar (TR) 88 Db 51
58880 Sızır (TR) 90 Df 51
Siz'ma (RUS) 32 Di 31
42208 Sızma (TR) 96 Dc 52
29450 Sizun (F) 52 Sf 42
Sjamža (RUS) 33 Eb 30
Sjanno (BY) 42 Ck 36
Sjas'stroj (RUS) 31 Dc 30
Sjava (RUS) 34 Eg 32
36310 Sjenica (SRB) 71 Ca 47
Sjevjerodonec'k (UA) 60 Di 42
27500 Sjöbo (S) 39 Bd 35
6260 Sjøholt (N) 20 Ag 28
Sjoneidet (N) 14 Bd 24
54066 Sjötorp (S) 29 Bd 32
Sjoutnäs (S) 21 Be 26
9350 Sjøvegan (N) 14 Bh 22
Sjumsi (RUS) 34 Fb 33
02580 Sjundeå = Siuntio (FIN) 30 Ce 30
Sjursvik (N) 14 Bg 21
Sjus'ma (RUS) 24 Dk 26
Sjuzva (RUS) 35 Fd 31
Skadovs'k (UA) 74 Dc 44
4230 Skælskør (DK) 39 Bb 35
7400 Skærbæk (DK) 38 Ai 35
880 Skaftafell (IS) 48 Rc 26
545 Skagaströnd (IS) 48 Qk 25
Skagaströnd = Höfðakaupstaður (IS) 48 Qk 25
9990 Skagen (DK) 28 Ba 33
89035 Skagshamn (S) 22 Bk 27
Skaidi (N) 15 Ce 20
KW17 Skaill (GB) 50 Sg 31
KW17 Skaill (GB) 50 Sh 32
84025 Skaistgirys (LT) 41 Cd 34
3924 Skaistkalne (LV) 41 Ce 34
23051 Skála (GR) 94 Cc 54
Skala Eressós (GR) 87 Cf 51
Skaláni (GR) 95 Cf 55
19017 Skála Oropoú (GR) 94 Cd 52
Skala-Podil'ska (UA) 58 Cg 42
220 Skálavík (FO) 50 Sd 29
Skålevik (N) 28 Ai 32
810 Skálholt (IS) 48 Qk 26
Skalía (GR) 95 Cg 53
Skaljap (RUS) 27 Fg 27
Skal'nyj (RUS) 36 Fi 32
52200 Skalohóri (GR) 86 Cb 50
Skaloti (GR) 87 Ce 49
8660 Skanderborg (DK) 38 Ak 34
Skånes-Fagerhult (S) 39 Bd 34
5593 Skånevik (N) 28 Af 31
59601 Skänninge (S) 29 Bf 32
Skanör med Falsterbo (S) 39 Bc 35
Skansnäs (S) 21 Bh 25
Skanvik (N) 16 Da 21
53201* Skara (S) 29 Bd 32
Skarberget (N) 14 Bg 22
5763 Skare (N) 28 Ag 31
Skåre (S) 29 Bd 31
2100 Skarnes (N) 28 Bb 30
81065 Skärplinge (S) 29 Bh 30
9763 Skarsvåg (N) 15 Cf 19
7742 Skårup (DK) 39 Ba 35
91201 Skarvsjöby (S) 21 Bh 26
26-100* Skarżysko-Kamienna (PL) 57 Ca 39
65671 Skattkärr (S) 29 Bd 31
7510 Skatval (N) 20 Ba 27
73028 Skaudvilė (LT) 41 Cc 35
Skaulo (S) 15 Cb 23
Skavšyn (BY) 58 Ch 38
Skebrobuk (S) 29 Bi 31
PE25 Skegness (GB) 51 Aa 37
7711 Skei (N) 28 Ag 29
6640 Skei-Surnadalsøra (N) 20 Ai 28
93100* Skellefteå (S) 22 Ca 26
93201 Skelleftehamn (S) 22 Cb 26
Skender Vakuf (BIH) 70 Bh 46
87-630 Skępe (PL) 40 Bk 38
Skerries = Na Sceiri (IRL) 49 Sd 37
1400* Ski (N) 28 Ba 31
37002 Skíathos (GR) 87 Cd 51
Skibbereen = An Sciobairin (IRL) 49 Sa 39
4050 Skibby (DK) 39 Bb 35
9143 Skibotn (N) 14 Ca 21
58500 Skidra (GR) 86 Cc 50
3701* Skien, Porsgrunn- (N) 28 Ak 31
96-100* Skierniewice (PL) 57 Ca 39
56820 Skillingaryd (S) 29 Be 33
27603 Skillinge (S) 39 Be 35
BD23 Skipton (GB) 51 Sh 37
1816 Skiptvet (N) 28 Bb 31
34007 Skíros (GR) 94 Ce 52
7800 Skive (DK) 38 Ak 34
9771 Skjånes (N) 15 Ci 20
6900 Skjern (DK) 38 Ai 35
Skjerstad (N) 14 Bf 23
9180 Skjervøy (N) 14 Ca 20
6876 Skjolden (N) 28 Ah 29
8514 Skjomen (N) 14 Bh 22
Šklo (UA) 57 Cd 41
Šklov (BY) 42 Da 36
43-430 Skoczów (PL) 56 Bi 41
4220 Škofja Loka (SLO) 70 Be 44
82392 Skog (S) 29 Bg 29
Skoganvarra (N) 15 Cf 21
861 Skógar (IS) 48 Qi 27
Skogfoss (N) 15 Ck 21
66301* Skoghall (S) 29 Bd 31
Skole (UA) 57 Cd 41
3618 Skollenborg (N) 28 Ak 31
69774 Sköllersta (S) 29 Bf 31
37003 Skópelos (GR) 87 Cd 51
Skopin (RUS) 44 Dk 37
1000* Skopje (MK) 86 Cb 48
64009 Skopos (GR) 87 Ce 49
240 Skopun (FO) 50 Sd 29
83-220 Skórcz (PL) 40 Bi 37
Skorlyvanovo (RUS) 33 Ec 33
Skorodnoe (RUS) 60 Df 39
Skorodnoe (RUS) 60 Dh 39
7893 Skorovatn (N) 21 Bd 26
89597 Skorped (S) 21 Bh 27
Skosyrskaja (RUS) 61 Eb 42
2230 Skotterud (N) 29 Bc 31
47044 Skoulikariá (GR) 86 Cb 51
54101* Skövde (S) 29 Bd 32
Skrad (HR) 70 Be 45
Skradin (HR) 70 Bf 47
Skradnik (HR) 70 Bf 45
93701 Skråmträsk (S) 22 Ca 26
2848 Skreia (N) 28 Ba 30
Skriveri (LV) 41 Cf 34
Skrúður (IS) 48 Rg 26
3326 Skrunda (LV) 41 Cc 34
Skrydleva (BY) 42 Da 35
4280 Skudeneshavn (N) 28 Af 31
Skulgam (N) 14 Bk 21
Skuljabiha (RUS) 34 Ef 33
Skull = An Scoil (IRL) 49 Sa 39
54101 Skultorp (S) 29 Bd 32
73050 Skultuna (S) 29 Bg 31
Škunovka (RUS) 64 Ff 40
98001 Skuodas (LT) 40 Cb 34
Škuratovskij (RUS) 43 Dh 36
Škurinskaja (RUS) 75 Dk 44
27401 Skurup (S) 39 Bd 35
8290 Skutvik (N) 14 Bf 22
Skvyra (UA) 58 Ck 41
66-440 Skwierzyna (PL) 56 Bf 38
83076 Skyttmon (S) 21 Bh 27
4200 Slagelse (DK) 39 Bb 35
93091 Slagnäs (S) 21 Bi 25
Šlancy (RUS) 31 Ci 31
Šlanga (RUS) 45 Ei 36
Slano (HR) 85 Bh 48
274 01 Slaný (CZ) 55 Be 40
117543 Slatina (RO) 72 Ce 46
1480 Slattum (N) 28 Ba 30
Slautino (RUS) 31 Dc 33
Slavharad (BY) 42 Da 37
Slavhorod (UA) 60 Df 42
Slavinja (SRB) 71 Cc 47
6473 Slavjanovo (BG) 72 Cg 47
Slavjansk = Slovjans'k (UA) 60 Dh 42
Slavjansk-na-Kubani (RUS) 75 Di 45
Slavkoviči (RUS) 31 Ck 33
684 01 Slavkov u Brna (CZ) 56 Bg 41
Slavnoe (RUS) 43 Dg 34
378 81 Slavonice (CZ) 56 Bf 42
Slavonska Požega (HR) 70 Bh 45
Slavonski Brod (HR) 71 Bi 45
Slavsk (RUS) 40 Cb 35
Slavuta (UA) 58 Cg 40
Slavutyč (UA) 59 Da 39
21-515 Sławatycze (PL) 57 Cd 39
78-450 Sławno (PL) 40 Bg 36
NG34 Sleaford (GB) 51 Sk 38
YO21 Sleights (GB) 51 Sk 36
62-561 Ślesin (PL) 56 Bi 38
Slevik (N) 28 Ba 31
Sligeach = Sligo (IRL) 49 Sb 36
Sligo = Sligeach (IRL) 49 Sb 36
Šlissel'burg (RUS) 31 Db 31
62030 Slite (S) 29 Bi 33
8800* Sliven (BG) 87 Cg 48
2844 Slivnica (BG) 87 Cd 48
7060 Slivo Pole (BG) 72 Cg 47
Slížany (CZ) 56 Bh 41
Sloboda (RUS) 61 Ea 39
Sloboda (UA) 59 Dd 38
Slobodskoj (RUS) 34 Fa 32
000920* Slobozia (RO) 73 Ch 46
147355 Slobozia Mândra (RO) 72 Ce 47
32-090 Słomniki (PL) 57 Ca 40
Slonim (BY) 41 Cf 37
Slonovka (RUS) 60 Dh 40
SL1 Slough (GB) 52 Sk 39
Slovečne (UA) 58 Ci 39
2380 Slovenj Gradec (SLO) 70 Bf 44
2310 Slovenska Bistrica (SLO) 70 Bf 44

198 | Sergač

3210 Slovenske Konjice (SLO) 70 Bf 44
Slovinka (RUS) 33 Ed 32
Slov'janohirs'k (UA) 60 Dh 41
Slovjanoserbs'k (UA) 60 Di 42
Slovjans'k (UA) 60 Dh 42
Slovjans'ke 74 Dd 45
09-533 Słubice (PL) 55 Be 38
Sluck (BY) 42 Ch 37
39020 Sluderno = Schluderns (I) 69 Ba 44
Sludka (RUS) 35 Fg 32
4524 Sluis (NL) 53 Ad 39
Slunj (HR) 70 Bf 45
62-400 Słupca (PL) 56 Bh 38
76-201* Słupsk (PL) 40 Bh 36
92397 Slussfors (S) 21 Bg 25
33301 Smålandsstenar (S) 29 Bd 33
74009 Smalininkai (LT) 41 Cc 35
Smaljany (BY) 42 Da 36
147360 Smârdioasa (RO) 72 Cf 47
Smarhon' (BY) 41 Cg 36
11300* Smederevo (SRB) 71 Ca 46
11420* Smederevska Palanka (SRB) 71 Ca 46
77701 Smedjebacken (S) 29 Bf 30
Smedsbyn (S) 22 Cc 25
Smela = Smila (UA) 59 Db 41
Smila (UA) 59 Db 41
Smilavičy (BY) 42 Ci 37
9422 Smilde (NL) 38 Ag 38
4729 Smiltene (LV) 30 Cf 33
7074 Smirnenski (BG) 72 Cg 47
Smirnovo (RUS) 45 Ee 35
9820 Smjadovo (BG) 87 Cg 47
Smokvica (MK) 86 Cc 49
Smolenec (RUS) 25 Ef 26
919 04 Smolenice (SK) 56 Bh 42
Smolensk (RUS) 42 Dc 36
Smolevičі (BY) 42 Ci 36
4700 Smoljan (BG) 87 Ce 49
055 66 Smolník (SK) 57 Ca 42
Smolyn (UA) 59 Da 39
Smolyno (UA) 59 Db 42
Smotryč (UA) 58 Cg 42
23105 Smygehamn (S) 39 Bd 35
Smyrnove (UA) 75 Dg 43
Smyšljaevsk (RUS) 46 Fa 37
7760 Snåsa (N) 21 Bc 26
Sneek = Snits (NL) 38 Af 37
Sneem = An Snaidhm (IRL) 49 Rl 39
Snihurivka (UA) 74 Dc 43
069 01 Snina (SK) 57 Cc 42
Snižne (UA) 60 Di 42
Snjatyn (UA) 58 Cf 42
Snøfjord (N) 15 Ce 20
Snopa (RUS) 18 Eh 24
55566 Sobernheim, Bad (D) 54 Ah 41
392 01 Soběslav (CZ) 55 Be 41
Sobinka (RUS) 44 Ea 35
Sobolevo (RUS) 43 Di 35
Sobolevo (RUS) 44 Ea 36
96-500* Sochaczew (PL) 57 Ca 38
Soči (RUS) 75 Dk 47
13630 Socuéllamos (E) 81 Sh 51
99601 Sodankylä (FIN) 15 Cg 23
82661 Söderala (S) 29 Bh 29
81504 Söderfors (S) 29 Bh 30
82601* Söderhamn (S) 29 Bh 29
61401 Söderköping (S) 29 Bg 32
15100* Södertälje (S) 29 Bh 31
Södra Möckleby (S) 40 Bg 34
65930 Södra Vallgrund (FIN) 22 Cb 27
59494 Soest (D) 54 Ai 39
Sofádes (GR) 86 Cc 51
1000* Sofija (BG) 87 Cd 48
Sofijivka (UA) 59 Dd 42
Sofporog (RUS) 23 Db 25
55780 Soğanlı (TR) 96 Da 53
49751 Sögel (D) 38 Ah 38
Sogndal (N) 28 Ah 29
4640 Søgne (N) 28 Ah 32
Sogra (RUS) 25 Eg 28
Soğukpınar (TR) 88 Ck 50
41520 Soğuksu (TR) 88 Da 50
Söğüt (TR) 88 Da 50
Söğüt (TR) 96 Ck 53
Söğüt (TR) 96 Ck 54
Söğütalan (TR) 88 Ci 50
Söğütlü (TR) 88 Da 50
Söğütlü (TR) 99 Ea 52
57002 Sohós (GR) 87 Cd 50
7060 Soignies (B) 53 Ae 40
63801 Soini (FIN) 22 Ce 28
02200* Soissons (F) 53 Ad 41
Sojala (RUS) 25 Ed 26
Sojana (RUS) 25 Ed 25
Sojju (RUS) 27 Fg 27
Šojna (RUS) 17 Ee 23
Sokal' (UA) 57 Ce 40
09200 Söke (TR) 95 Ch 53
3534 Sokna (N) 28 Ak 30
7288 Soknedal (N) 20 Ba 28
18230 Soko Banja (SRB) 71 Cb 47
Sokol (RUS) 33 Ea 31
16-100 Sokółka (PL) 41 Cd 37
Sokolka (RUS) 46 Fb 35
Sokol'nikovo (RUS) 33 Dk 30
356 01* Sokolov (CZ) 55 Bc 40
08-300* Sokołów Podlaski (PL) 57 Cc 38
Sokol'skoe (RUS) 33 Ed 33
18-520 Sokoły (PL) 41 Cc 37
Sokrutovka (RUS) 77 Eg 43
Šokša (RUS) 32 Df 29
Sokur (RUS) 62 Ef 39
Sokyrjany (UA) 58 Ch 42
13593 Solana, La (E) 93 Sg 52
13593 Solana del Pino (E) 93 Sf 52
39710 Solares (E) 66 Sg 47
Solberg (S) 21 Bh 27
725600 Solca (RO) 72 Cf 43
Sol'cy (RUS) 31 Da 32
Soldato Aleksandrovskoe (RUS) 76 Ed 46
Soldatskaja (RUS) 76 Ed 47
Soldatskaja Tašla (RUS) 45 Ei 37
Soldatskoe (RUS) 60 Di 39
Soldatsko-Stepnoe (RUS) 62 Ef 41
Soledar (UA) 60 Di 42
Solem (N) 20 Bb 26
Solënoe (RUS) 76 Ec 44
Solënoe Zajmišče (RUS) 77 Eg 43
Solënyj (RUS) 77 Eg 44
20145 Solenzara (F) 83 Ak 49
59730 Solesmes (F) 53 Ad 40
4500* Soleure = Solothurn (CH) 68 Ah 43
Solginskij (RUS) 33 Eb 29
12700 Solhan (TR) 99 Eb 52
5353 Solheim (N) 28 Af 30
Solidars'k = Soledar (UA) 60 Di 42
Soligalič (RUS) 33 Ec 31
Soligorsk = Salihorsk (BY) 42 Ch 38
B91 Solihull (GB) 52 Si 38
Solikamsk (RUS) 35 Fg 31
Sol'-Ileck (RUS) 63 Fe 39
Solin (HR) 70 Bg 47
42651* Solingen (D) 54 Ah 39
Soljanka (RUS) 63 Fa 39
46601 Sollebrunn (S) 29 Bc 32
Sollefteå (S) 21 Bh 27
19100* Sollentuna (S) 29 Bh 31
07100 Sóller (E) 82 Ac 51
79205 Sollerön (S) 29 Be 30
5620 Søllested (DK) 39 Bb 36
Solncevo (RUS) 60 Dg 39
Solnečnogorsk (RUS) 43 Dg 34
9122 Solnik (BG) 88 Ch 48
Solodča (RUS) 61 Ee 41
Solodniki (RUS) 62 Ef 42
Solohaul (RUS) 75 Dk 47
Soloh-Aul (RUS) 75 Dk 47
Šolohovskij (RUS) 61 Eb 42
Solone (UA) 59 De 42
Solotča (RUS) 44 Dk 36
4500* Solothurn (CH) 68 Ah 43
Solovatovo (RUS) 33 Ed 33
Soloveckie (RUS) 24 Df 25
Soloveckoe (RUS) 34 Eh 31
Soloveckoe (RUS) 34 Ei 32
Sölöz (TR) 88 Ck 50
Solozero (RUS) 24 Di 26
Solsem (N) 20 Bb 25
25280 Solsona (E) 82 Ab 49
Solsvik (N) 28 Ae 30
6320 Solt (H) 71 Bk 44
Soltanovo (RUS) 33 Ed 32
29614 Soltau (D) 38 Ak 38
29400 Sölvesborg (S) 39 Be 34
Sol'vyčegodsk (RUS) 34 Eg 29
Solynieve (E) 93 Sg 53
Solza (RUS) 24 Dk 26
45500 Soma (TR) 88 Ch 51
25101* Sombor (SRB) 71 Bk 45
Šombozero (RUS) 23 Dc 25
31401 Somero (FIN) 30 Cd 30
Somino (RUS) 32 Df 31
57302 Sommen (S) 29 Be 32
51600 Sommepy-Tahure (F) 53 Ae 41
99610 Sömmerda (D) 55 Bb 39
30250 Sommières (F) 67 Ae 47
827210 Somova (RO) 73 Ci 45
62-610 Sompolno (PL) 56 Bi 38
09572 Soncillo (E) 81 Sg 48
4990 Søndeled (N) 28 Ak 32
6400 Sønderborg (DK) 38 Ak 36
7260 Sønder Omme (DK) 38 Ai 35
99706 Sondershausen (D) 55 Ba 39
Søndersø (DK) 39 Ba 35
6950 Søndervig (DK) 38 Ai 34
23100 Sondrio (I) 69 Ak 44
Šonga (RUS) 34 Ef 31
4909 Songe (N) 28 Ak 32
74301 Sonkajärvi (FIN) 23 Ch 27
Sonkovo (RUS) 32 Dh 33
96515 Sonneberg (D) 55 Bb 40
6611 Sonogno (CH) 68 Ai 44
Šonoša, Ust'- (RUS) 33 Eb 29
Sonostrov (RUS) 24 De 24
45100 Sonseca (E) 81 Sg 51
87527 Sonthofen (D) 69 Ba 43
40150 Soorts-Hossegor (F) 66 Si 47
Sopki (RUS) 31 Da 33
Sopoha (RUS) 23 Dd 28
81-701* Sopot (PL) 40 Bi 36
9400 Sopron (H) 70 Bg 43
Šopša (RUS) 33 Dk 33
03039 Sora (I) 84 Bd 49
86035 Söråker (S) 21 Bh 28
04270 Sorbas (E) 93 Sh 53
Sørbøvåg (N) 28 Af 29
84067 Sörbygden (S) 21 Bg 28
40430 Sore (F) 66 Sk 46
5357 Sør-Flatanger (N) 20 Ba 26
91135 Sörfors (S) 22 Ca 27
08038 Sorgono (I) 83 Ak 50
06843 Sorgun (TR) 89 Df 51
06843 Sorgun (TR) 97 De 54
Sørgutvik (N) 20 Bb 25
01038 Soriano nel Cimino (I) 84 Bc 48
11-731 Sorkwity (PL) 40 Ca 37
7884 Sørli (N) 21 Bd 26
91020 Sörmjöle (S) 22 Bk 27
7663 Sørmoen (N) 21 Bc 27
4180 Sorø (DK) 39 Bb 35
3000 Soroca (MD) 58 Ci 42
Soroč'i Gory (RUS) 46 Fa 35
Soročinsk (RUS) 63 Fd 38
3000 Soroka = Soroca (MD) 58 Ci 42
3000 Soroki = Soroca (MD) 58 Ci 42
Sorokino (RUS) 31 Ck 33
Sorokovaja (RUS) 35 Ff 31
Sorokyne = Krasnodon (UA) 60 Dk 42
9310 Sørreisa (N) 14 Bi 21
80067 Sorrento (I) 85 Be 50
92070 Sorsele (S) 21 Bh 25
07037 Sorso (I) 83 Ai 50
9162 Sørstraumen (N) 15 Cb 21
25560 Sort (E) 82 Ab 48
Sortavala (RUS) 31 Da 29
8400 Sortland (N) 14 Bf 22
Sør Tverrfjord (N) 15 Cb 20
14802 Sorunda (S) 29 Bh 31
Sørværøy (N) 14 Bc 23
8392 Sørvågen (N) 14 Bd 23
380 Sørvágur (FO) 50 Sc 28
7374 Sørvika (N) 20 Bb 28
Sosedka (RUS) 44 Ec 37
Sosenskij (RUS) 43 Df 36
Soskovo (RUS) 43 Df 38
Sosnivka (UA) 57 Ce 40
Sosnogorsk (RUS) 26 Fd 27
Sosnovaja Maza (RUS) 45 Eh 38
Sosnove (UA) 58 Ch 40
Sosnovec (RUS) 24 De 26
Sosnovice (PL) 56 Bk 40
Sosnovka (RUS) 44 Eb 37
Sosnovka (RUS) 46 Fb 34
Sosnovka (RUS) 46 Fb 37
Sosnovka (RUS) 17 Fe 24
Sosnovka (RUS) 61 Ed 38
Sosnovoborsk (RUS) 45 Eg 37
Sosnovskoe (RUS) 44 Ed 35
Sosnovyj (RUS) 23 Dc 24
Sosnovyj Bor (RUS) 31 Ck 31
Sosnovyj Bor (RUS) 35 Ff 33
Sosnovyj Solonec (RUS) 45 Ek 37
Sosnycja (UA) 59 Dc 39
06380 Sospel (F) 68 Ah 47
Šostka (UA) 59 Dd 39
Sos'va (RUS) 36 Gb 31
88601 Sotkamo (FIN) 23 Ci 26
Sotnicyno (RUS) 44 Eb 36
Sotnikov Oskoe (RUS) 76 Ed 46
Sotnikovskoe (RUS) 76 Ed 45
Soto (E) 80 Sd 47
Soudozero (RUS) 23 Dd 28
Soufli (GR) 87 Cg 49
73004 Soúgia (GR) 94 Cd 55
17270 Souillac (F) 67 Ab 46
33780 Soulac-sur-Mer (F) 66 Si 45
7470-201* Sousel (P) 80 Sc 52
40140 Soustons (F) 66 Si 47
23300 Souterraine, la (F) 67 Ab 44
SO17 Southampton (GB) 52 Si 40
SS0 Southend-on-Sea (GB) 53 Aa 39
PR8 Southport (GB) 51 Sg 37
NE29 South Shields (GB) 51 Si 35
545500 Sovata (RO) 72 Cf 44
Sov'e (RUS) 34 Ek 32
88068 Soverato (I) 85 Bg 52
88049 Soveria Mannelli (I) 85 Bg 51
Sovetsk (RUS) 34 Ei 33
Sovetsk (RUS) 40 Cb 35
Sovetskaja (RUS) 61 Ec 42
Sovetskaja (RUS) 76 Eb 46
Sovetskaja (RUS) 76 Ee 47
Sovetskij (RUS) 31 Ci 30
Sovetskij (RUS) 36 Gd 29
Sovetskij (RUS) 45 Ei 34
Sovetskoe (RUS) 44 Eb 37
Sovetskoe (RUS) 46 Fc 37
Sovetskoe (RUS) 60 Di 40
Sovetskoe (RUS) 63 Fb 38
Sovetskoe (RUS) 64 Fg 39
Sovetskoe = Kašhatau (RUS) 91 Ed 47
Sovhoz Zilairskij (RUS) 64 Fi 38
Sovpol'e (RUS) 25 Ee 25
Söylemez (TR) 91 Eb 51
Sozga (RUS) 34 Ei 29
Sozonovo (RUS) 37 Gg 33
8130 Sozopol (BG) 88 Ch 48
4900 Spa (B) 54 Af 40
Spakojnaja (RUS) 76 Eb 46
Špakovskoe (RUS) 76 Ec 45
Spalding (GB) 51 Sk 38
91174 Spalt (D) 55 Ba 41
7710 Sparbu (N) 20 Bb 27
23101 Spárti (GR) 94 Cc 53
Spas (RUS) 33 Ea 33
Spas-Demensk (RUS) 43 De 36
Spas-Klepiki (RUS) 44 Ea 35
6249 Spasovo (BG) 73 Ci 47
Spasporub (RUS) 34 Ek 30
Spasskaja Guba (RUS) 23 Dd 28
Spasskij (RUS) 47 Fk 37
Spasskoe (RUS) 34 Eg 31
Spasskoe (RUS) 45 Ef 35
Spasskoe (RUS) 64 Fg 38
Spasskoe-Lutovino (RUS) 43 Dg 37
Spassk-Rjazanskij (RUS) 44 Ea 36
PH34 Spean Bridge (GB) 50 Sf 34
67346 Speyer (D) 54 Ai 41
87019 Spezzano Albanese (I) 85 Bg 51
Spiddal = An Spidéal (IRL) 49 Sa 37
8471* Spielfeld (A) 70 Bf 44
3700* Spiez (CH) 68 Ah 44
Spilimbergo (I) 69 Bc 44
70058 Spinazzola (I) 85 Bg 50
543 51 Špindlerův Mlýn (CZ) 56 Bf 40
Spirovo (RUS) 32 De 33
052 01 Spišská Nová Ves (SK) 57 Ca 42
053 04 Spišské Podhradie (SK) 57 Ca 42
9800* Spittal an der Drau (A) 69 Bd 44
Splavnoj (RUS) 25 Ee 28
Split (HR) 70 Bg 47
7435 Splügen (CH) 69 Ak 44
Spóa (GR) 95 Ch 55
5900 Spodsbjerg (DK) 39 Ba 36
Špogi (LV) 42 Ch 34
Špola (UA) 59 Db 41
06049 Spoleto (I) 84 Bc 48
03130 Spremberg (D) 55 Be 39
31832 Springe (D) 54 Ak 38
7750 Sprova (N) 20 Bb 26
1820 Spydeberg (N) 28 Bb 31
Špykiv (UA) 58 Ci 42
73018 Squinzano (I) 85 Bi 50
Sraid na Cathrach (IRL) 49 Sa 38
Šramkivka (UA) 59 Dc 40
41000 Srbica (RKS) 86 Ca 48
21480 Srbobran (SRB) 71 Bk 45
Srebrenica (BIH) 71 Bk 46
Sred Apočki (RUS) 60 Dh 39
8300 Sredec (BG) 87 Cf 48
Sredneivkino (RUS) 34 Ek 32
Sredneural'sk (RUS) 47 Ga 33
Srednij Bugalyš (RUS) 47 Fh 34
Srednij Egorlyk (RUS) 76 Ea 44
Srednij Ikorec (RUS) 60 Dk 39
Srednjaja Tereška (RUS) 45 Eh 38
Srednjaja Us'va (RUS) 36 Fk 32
Srednogorie = Pirdop + Zlatica (BG) 87 Ce 48
63-100* Śrem (PL) 56 Bh 38
22000* Sremska Mitrovica (SRB) 71 Bk 46
Sretenskoe (RUS) 35 Ff 32
Sribne (UA) 59 Dc 40
63-000* Środa Wielkopolska (PL) 56 Bh 38
11-420 Srokowo (PL) 40 Cb 36
Stachanov = Kadijivka (UA) 60 Di 42
21680* Stade (D) 38 Ak 37
Stadskanaal (NL) 38 Ag 38
07646 Stadtroda (D) 55 Bb 40
24501 Staffanstorp (S) 39 Bd 35
ST16 Stafford (GB) 51 Sh 38
Stahanov = Kadijivka (UA) 60 Di 42
4043 Staicele (LV) 30 Ce 33
TW20 Staines (GB) 52 Sk 39
8510* Stainz (A) 70 Bf 44
067 61 Stakčín (SK) 57 Cc 42
4151 Stalbe (LV) 30 Cf 33
Staloluoktastugorna (S) 14 Bg 23
4210 Stambolijski (BG) 87 Ce 48
PE9 Stamford (GB) 52 Sk 38
5727 Stamnes (N) 28 Af 30
8340 Stamsund (N) 14 Bd 22
2335 Stange (N) 28 Bb 30
DL13 Stanhope (GB) 51 Sh 36
Stanilovo (RUS) 32 Dh 32
2600 Stanke Dimitrov = Dupnica (BG) 87 Cd 48
DH9 Stanley (GB) 51 Si 36
Stanovoe (RUS) 60 Di 38
Stanovoj Kolodez' (RUS) 43 Dg 38
6370* Stans (CH) 68 Ai 44
Stanyčno-Luhans'ke (UA) 60 Dk 42
NG9 Stapleford, Beeston and (GB) 51 Si 38
Staraja Belogorka (RUS) 63 Fd 38
Staraja Ivanovka (RUS) 46 Fa 36
Staraja Kalitva (RUS) 60 Dk 40
Staraja Kulatka (RUS) 45 Eh 38
Staraja Ljalja (RUS) 36 Fk 31
Staraja Majna (RUS) 45 Ek 36
Staraja Matveevka (RUS) 46 Fd 35
Staraja Poltavka (RUS) 62 Eg 40
Staraja Račejka (RUS) 45 Ei 37
Staraja Russa (RUS) 31 Db 33
Staraja Sahča (RUS) 46 Fa 36
Staraja Toropa (RUS) 42 Db 34
Staraja Vičuga (RUS) 33 Eb 33
064 01 Stará L'ubovňa (SK) 57 Ca 41
Stara Novalja (HR) 70 Be 46
Stara Oržyc'a (UA) 59 Dc 41
8841 Stara Reka (BG) 87 Cg 48
Stara Synjava (UA) 58 Ch 41
7214 Staravina (MK) 86 Cb 49
Stara Vyživka (UA) 57 Ce 39
6000* Stara Zagora (BG) 87 Cf 48
73-100* Stargard Szczeciński (PL) 39 Bf 37
6777 Stårheim (N) 20 Af 29
85 354 Stari Bar (MNE) 86 Bk 48
Starica (RUS) 43 De 34
Starica (RUS) 43 Df 37
Starica (RUS) 62 Ef 42
Starickoe (RUS) 64 Ff 39
Starie Saviny (RUS) 60 Dh 39
Starigrad (HR) 85 Bg 47
Starigrad-Paklenica (HR) 70 Bf 46
Stari Mikanovci (HR) 71 Bi 45
Starkovo (RUS) 44 Ea 35
82319 Starnberg (D) 55 Bb 42
Starobaltačevo (RUS) 46 Ff 34
Starobeševe (UA) 75 Di 43
Starobil's'k (UA) 60 Di 41
Starobin (BY) 42 Ch 38
Staročerkasskaja (RUS) 76 Ea 43
Starodub (RUS) 59 Dc 38
Staroe (RUS) 44 Dk 35
Staroe Bajsarovo (RUS) 46 Fd 35
Staroe Šajgovo (RUS) 45 Ee 36
Staroe Šajmyrzino (RUS) 45 Eh 36
Staroe Slavkino (RUS) 62 Ef 38
Staroe Soljakovo (RUS) 46 Fd 34
83-200* Starogard Gdański (PL) 40 Bi 37
Starogol'skoe (RUS) 43 Dh 37
Starojur'evo (RUS) 44 Ea 37
Starokostjantyniv (UA) 58 Ch 41
Starokozače (UA) 73 Ck 44
Starokuručevo (RUS) 46 Fe 35
Starominskaja (RUS) 75 Dk 44
Staronikol'skoe (RUS) 60 Di 39
Staronižesteblievskaja (RUS) 75 Di 45
9110 Staro Orjahovo (BG) 88 Ch 47
Staroščerbinovskaja (RUS) 75 Di 44
Starosel'e (RUS) 43 Dg 37
Starošešminsk (RUS) 46 Fb 35
Starosubhangulovo (RUS) 47 Fh 37
Starotimoškino (RUS) 45 Eh 37
Starotitarovskaja (RUS) 75 Dh 45
Staroutkinsk (RUS) 36 Fk 33
Staroverčeskaja (RUS) 34 Ei 31
Starovo (RUS) 32 Dd 33
Starožilovo (RUS) 44 Dk 36
Staryca (BY) 42 Ch 37
Staryči (UA) 57 Cd 41
Starye Maklauši (RUS) 45 Eh 36
Starye Tukmakly (RUS) 46 Ff 36
Starye Zjatcy (RUS) 35 Fc 33
Staryi Oskol (RUS) 60 Dh 39
Staryja Darohi (BY) 42 Ci 37
Staryj Dvor (RUS) 44 Ea 34
Staryj Krym 74 Df 45
Staryj Kurdym (RUS) 46 Ff 34
Staryj Lesken (RUS) 76 Ed 47
Staryj Ostropil' (UA) 58 Ch 41
Staryj Rjab (RUS) 32 De 32
Staryj Sambir (UA) 57 Cc 41

A B C D E F G H I J K L M N O P Q R S T U V W X Y Z

Staryj Sambir I 199

33-230 Szczucin (PL) 57 Cb 40
19-230 Szczuczyn (PL) 41 Cc 37
12-100 Szczytno (PL) 40 Ca 37
3170 Szécsény (H) 56 Bk 42
6700* Szeged (H) 71 Ca 44
5520 Szeghalom (H) 71 Cb 43
8000 Székesfehérvár (H) 71 Bi 43
7100 Szekszárd (H) 71 Bi 44
Szendrő (H) 57 Ca 42
Szentendre (H) 71 Bk 43
6600 Szentes (H) 71 Ca 44
9970 Szentgotthárd (H) 70 Bg 44
Szentlőrinc (H) 70 Bh 44
Szigetvár (H) 70 Bh 44
3761 Szin (H) 57 Ca 42
67-407 Szlichtyngowa (PL) 56 Bg 39
5000 Szolnok (H) 71 Ca 43
9700 Szombathely (H) 70 Bg 43
67-300 Szprotawa (PL) 56 Bf 39
16-310 Sztabin (PL) 41 Cd 37
82-400 Sztum (PL) 40 Bk 37
82-110 Sztutowo (PL) 40 Bk 36
89-200 Szubin (PL) 40 Bh 37

T

25860 Taalintehdas = Dalsbruk (FIN) 30 Cc 30
54500* Taavetti = Luumäki (FIN) 31 Ch 30
1308* Tabanovce (MK) 86 Cb 48
49140 Tábara (E) 80 Se 49
56202 Taberg (S) 29 Be 33
390 01 Tábor (CZ) 55 Be 41
Tabory (RUS) 37 Ge 32
18300* Täby (S) 29 Bi 31
Tabynskoe (RUS) 47 Fg 36
347 01 Tachov (CZ) 55 Bc 41
Tacinskij (RUS) 61 Eb 42
407565 Taga (RO) 72 Ce 44
Tagaj (RUS) 45 Eh 36
Taganrog (RUS) 75 Di 43
18018 Taggia (I) 68 Ah 47
45019 Taglio di Po (I) 69 Bc 45
Tahanča (UA) 59 Db 41
04620 Tahir (TR) 91 Ec 51
Tahta (RUS) 76 Ec 45
16900 Tahtaköprü (TR) 88 Ck 51
69000 Tahtköy (TR) 91 Ea 50
Taibeart = Tarbert (IRL) 49 Sa 38
KW14 Tain (GB) 50 Sf 33
Taiševo (RUS) 47 Fi 35
93401 Taivalkoski (FIN) 23 Ci 25
23311 Taivassalo (FIN) 30 Cb 30
Tajmeevo (RUS) 47 Fh 35
Takazlı (TR) 89 Dd 51
32304 Takovo (SRB) 71 Ca 46
Talačyn (BY) 42 Ck 36
Talakivka (UA) 75 Dh 43
Talalajivka (UA) 59 Dd 40
06640 Talarrubias (E) 80 Se 51
38280* Talas (TR) 97 Df 52
45600 Talavera de la Reina (E) 81 Sf 51
Taldom (RUS) 43 Dh 34
33400 Talence (F) 66 Sk 46
Talica (RUS) 34 Fb 32
Talica (RUS) 36 Gc 33
Talica (RUS) 36 Gd 33
Talickij (RUS) 61 Ea 38
10111* Tallinn (EST) 30 Ce 31
91050 Tallsjö (S) 21 Bi 26
71640 Talluskylä (FIN) 22 Cg 27
Tally (RUS) 46 Fd 37
555700 Tălmaciu (RO) 72 Ce 45
85440 Talmont-Saint-Hilaire (F) 66 Si 44
Tal'ne (UA) 59 Da 42
Talovaja (RUS) 61 Ea 39
3201 Talsi (LV) 30 Cc 33
Taly (RUS) 61 Ea 41
Tamala (RUS) 61 Ed 38
37600 Tamames (E) 80 Sd 50
Taman (RUS) 35 Fg 31
Taman' (RUS) 75 Dg 45
Tamarë (AL) 86 Bk 48
07769 Tamarinda (E) 82 Ad 51
22550 Tamarite de Litera (E) 82 Aa 49
7090 Tamási (H) 71 Bi 44
Tambicy (RUS) 24 Df 28
Tambov (RUS) 44 Eb 38
Tambovka (RUS) 77 Eh 43
Tamdysaj (RUS) 64 Ff 40
Tamica (RUS) 24 Di 26
10600* Tammisaari = Ekenäs (FIN) 30 Cd 31
33002* Tampere (FIN) 30 Cd 29
46106* Tamsalu (EST) 30 Cg 31
5580 Tamsweg (A) 69 Bd 43
B78 Tamworth (GB) 52 Si 38
9840 Tanabru (N) 15 Ci 20
925200 Ţăndărei (RO) 73 Ch 46
Tandsjöborg (S) 29 Be 29
2337 Tangen (N) 28 Bb 30
39517 Tangerhütte (D) 55 Bb 38
39590 Tangermünde (D) 55 Bb 38
99640 Tanhua (FIN) 15 Ch 23
46560 Tanır (TR) 98 Dg 52
99695 Tankavaara (FIN) 15 Ch 22
36142 Tann (Rhön) (D) 55 Ba 40
84094 Tännäs (S) 21 Bc 28
84098 Tänndalen (S) 21 Bc 28
91240 Tannila (FIN) 22 Cf 25
217535 Ţântăreni (RO) 72 Cd 46
45700 Tanumshede (S) 28 Bb 32
Tanyeri (TR) 90 Dk 51
Tanyeri (TR) 91 Ec 51
Tanyolu (TR) 91 Ed 51
98039 Taormina (I) 84 Bf 53
45106* Tapa (EST) 30 Cf 31
33740 Tapia de Casariego (E) 80 Sd 47
Tapiau = Gvardejsk (RUS) 40 Cb 36
Tápiószecső (H) 71 Bk 43
8300 Tapolca (H) 70 Bh 44
7400 Taraclia (MD) 73 Ck 44
54750 Taraklı (TR) 88 Da 50
Taraksu (TR) 98 Dk 52
16400 Tarancón (E) 81 Sg 50
Taranivka (UA) 60 Dg 41
74100 Taranto (I) 85 Bh 50
69170 Tarare (F) 67 Ae 45
Tarašča (UA) 59 Da 41
13150* Tarascon (F) 67 Ae 47
Tarasiha (RUS) 45 Ee 34
Tarasivka (UA) 75 Dg 43
Tarasove, Klavdijevo- (UA) 59 Da 40
Tarasovo (RUS) 18 Eg 24
Tarasovskij (RUS) 61 Ea 42
Taratuhino (RUS) 43 Dg 37
PA60 Tarbert (GB) 50 Sd 33
Tarbert (IRL) 49 Sa 38
65000* Tarbes (F) 66 Aa 47
33017 Tarcento (I) 69 Bd 44
Tarčin (BIH) 71 Bi 47
09130 Tardajos (E) 81 Sg 48
98061 Tärendö (S) 15 Cc 23
Târgovište (BG) 72 Cg 47
000130* Târgovişte (RO) 72 Cf 46
805200 Târgu Bujor (RO) 73 Ch 45
215500 Târgu Cărbuneşti (RO) 72 Cd 46
705300 Târgu Frumos (RO) 73 Ch 43
000210* Târgu Jiu (RO) 72 Cd 45
435600 Târgu Lăpuş (RO) 72 Cd 43
000540* Târgu Mureş (RO) 72 Ce 44
615200 Târgu Neamţ (RO) 72 Cg 43
525400 Târgu Secuiesc (RO) 72 Cg 44
Tarhany (RUS) 45 Eh 35
11380 Tarifa (E) 92 Se 54
Tarkazy (RUS) 46 Fd 37
Tarlakovo (RUS) 43 Dg 34
6880 Tarm (DK) 38 Ai 35
92064 Tärnaby (S) 21 Bf 25
545600 Târnăveni (RO) 72 Ce 44
39-400 Tarnobrzeg (PL) 57 Cb 40
23-420 Tarnogród (PL) 57 Cc 40
Tarnogskij Gorodok (RUS) 33 Ed 30
33-100 Tarnów (PL) 57 Ca 40
74045 Tärnsjö (S) 29 Bg 30
Tårnvik (N) 14 Bf 23
3610-001* Tarouca (P) 80 Sc 49
01016 Tarquinia (I) 84 Bb 48
43001* Tarragona (E) 82 Ab 49
Tårrajaur (S) 14 Bk 24
25300 Tàrrega (E) 82 Ab 49
9830 Tårs (DK) 39 Bb 36
33400* Tarsus (TR) 97 De 54
40400 Tartas (F) 66 Sk 47
137435 Tărtăşeşti (RO) 72 Cf 46
50103* Tartu (EST) 30 Cg 32
Tarumovka (RUS) 77 Eg 46
Tarusa (RUS) 43 Dh 36
Tarutino (RUS) 47 Ga 37
Tarutyne (UA) 73 Ck 44
Tarxien (M) 84 Be 55
Taşağıl (TR) 96 Db 54
Taşağıl (TR) 97 Dd 53
Tašan' (UA) 59 Db 40
Taşbaşı (TR) 91 Ed 50
48700 Taşbükü (TR) 96 Ci 54
Taşburun (TR) 91 Ee 51
Taşçapı (TR) 91 Ed 51
Taşdelen (TR) 98 Di 52
Taşevi (TR) 96 Da 52
83081 Tåsjö (S) 21 Bf 26
42960 Taşkent (TR) 96 Dc 54
37400 Taşköprü (TR) 96 Db 52
Tašla (RUS) 63 Fc 39
Taşlıçay (TR) 91 Ed 51
445300 Tăşnad (RO) 71 Cc 43
25530 Taşoluk (TR) 90 Dg 50
25530 Taşoluk (TR) 96 Da 52
05800 Taşova (TR) 90 Dg 50
25900 Taşpınar (TR) 97 De 52
69005 Tassin-la-Demi-Lune (F) 67 Ae 45
Taštimerovo (RUS) 47 Fi 37
Tastuba (RUS) 47 Fh 35
33900 Taşucu (TR) 97 Dd 54
2890 Tata (H) 71 Bi 43
2800 Tatabánya (H) 71 Bi 43
Tatal (RUS) 77 Eg 43
Tatanovo (RUS) 44 Eb 38
Tatarbunary (UA) 73 Ck 45
Tatarinka (RUS) 43 Dd 35
Tatarino (RUS) 60 Dk 40
Tatarka (BY) 42 Ci 37
Tatarka (RUS) 76 Eb 46
Tatarlı (TR) 96 Da 52
Tatarlı (TR) 97 De 53
Tatarskaja Dymskaja (RUS) 46 Fc 36
Tatarskaja Karabolka (RUS) 47 Gb 35
Tatarskaja Kargala (RUS) 64 Ff 39
Tatarskij Sajman (RUS) 45 Eh 37
Tataurovo (RUS) 33 Ed 32
Tataurovo (RUS) 34 Ek 33
Tatiščevo (RUS) 47 Ga 37
Tatiščevo (RUS) 62 Ef 39
Tatköy (TR) 96 Da 53
Tatlıkuyu (TR) 97 Dd 53
13200 Tatvan (TR) 99 Ec 52
4120 Tau (N) 28 Af 31
97941 Tauberbischofsheim (D) 54 Ak 41
04425 Taucha (D) 55 Bc 39
TA1 Taunton (GB) 52 Sg 39
72001* Tauragė (LT) 41 Cc 35
60061 Tautušiai (LT) 41 Cd 35
17600 Tavaklı İskele (TR) 87 Cg 51
20500* Tavas (TR) 96 Ck 53
Tavda (RUS) 37 Gf 32
92261 Tavelsjö (S) 22 Ca 26
46760 Tavernes de la Valldigna (E) 82 Sk 51
8800-209* Tavira (P) 92 Sc 53
PL19 Tavistock (GB) 52 Sf 40
42780 Tavşançalı (TR) 97 Df 52
Tavşanlı (TR) 88 Ck 51
34003 Taxiárhes (GR) 94 Ce 52
66700 Tayfur (TR) 87 Cg 50
83-100 Tczew (PL) 40 Bi 36
427345 Teaca (RO) 72 Ce 44
81057 Teano (I) 85 Be 49
1224 Tearce (MK) 86 Cb 48
29327 Teba (E) 93 Sf 54
Teberda (RUS) 76 Eb 47
01890 Tecirli (TR) 97 Dg 53
805300 Tecuci (RO) 73 Ch 45
15600 Tefenni (TR) 96 Ck 53
5930 Tegelen (NL) 54 Ag 39
89501 Tegelträsk (S) 21 Bh 27
83684 Tegernsee (D) 69 Bb 43
Tëgrozëro (RUS) 33 Eb 29
Tehumardi (EST) 30 Cc 32
42240 Teil, le (F) 67 Ae 46
34260 Teisko (FIN) 30 Cd 29
515900 Teiuş (RO) 72 Cd 44
Tejkovo (RUS) 44 Ea 34
Teke (TR) 88 Ck 49
Tekeli (TR) 99 Ee 53
59000* Tekirdağ (TR) 88 Ch 50
Tekke (TR) 90 Dg 50
55300 Tekkeköy (TR) 90 Dg 49
55300 Tekkeköy (TR) 90 Dh 51
52330 Tekkiraz (TR) 90 Dh 50
25560 Tekman (TR) 91 Eb 51
31825 Teknepınar (TR) 97 Df 54
Tekun (RUS) 33 Ed 33
Tekun (RUS) 45 Ef 34
588 56 Telč (CZ) 56 Bf 41
Tel'č'e (RUS) 43 Dg 37
427355 Telciu (RO) 72 Ce 43
5800 Teleneşt' = Teleneşti (MD) 73 Ci 43
5800 Teleneşti (MD) 73 Ci 43
5800 Telenešty = Teleneşti (MD) 73 Ci 43
TF3 Telford (GB) 51 Sh 38
48291 Telgte (D) 54 Ah 39
Teljak, Ulu- (RUS) 47 Fg 36
Tel'manove (UA) 75 Di 43
87001* Telšiai (LT) 41 Cc 35
14513 Teltow (D) 55 Bd 38
37340 Tembleque (E) 81 Sg 51
06909 Temelli (TR) 89 Dc 51
21235* Temerin (SRB) 71 Bk 45
Temjasovo (RUS) 47 Fi 38
91950 Temmes (FIN) 22 Cf 26
Temnikov (RUS) 44 Ed 36
07029 Tempio Pausania (I) 83 Ak 50
Templemore = An Teampall Mór (IRL) 49 Sc 38
17268 Templin (D) 39 Bd 37
Temrjuk (RUS) 75 Dh 45
9140 Temse (B) 53 Ae 39
18355 Temska (SRB) 71 Cc 47
01970 Tenay (F) 68 Af 44
SA70 Tenby (GB) 52 Sf 39
06430 Tende (F) 68 Ah 46
10520 Tenhola = Tenalo (FIN) 30 Cd 30
56027 Tenhult (S) 29 Be 33
Tenja (HR) 71 Bi 45
Ten'ki (RUS) 45 Ek 35
Tennäng (S) 29 Bd 29
9465 Tennevoll (N) 14 Bh 22
TN30 Tenterden (GB) 53 Aa 39
Teofipol' (UA) 58 Cg 41
99150 Tepasto (FIN) 15 Ce 23
21520 Tepe (TR) 99 Ea 53
Tepecik (TR) 96 Da 53
Tepecikören (TR) 97 Df 53
44860 Tepehan (TR) 98 Di 52
Tepelenë (AL) 86 Ca 50
364 61 Teplá (CZ) 55 Bc 41
Teplaja Gora (RUS) 36 Fk 32
415 01* Teplice (CZ) 55 Bd 40
Tepljaki (RUS) 46 Ff 34
Teploe (RUS) 43 Dh 37
Teplyj Stan (RUS) 46 Fa 36
Teplyk (UA) 58 Ck 42
99280 Tepsa (FIN) 15 Cf 23
64100 Teramo (I) 84 Bd 48
9560 Ter Apel (NL) 38 Ah 38
22-510 Teratyn (PL) 57 Cd 40
Terbuny (RUS) 60 Di 38
24800 Tercan (TR) 91 Ea 51
Terebovlja (UA) 58 Cf 41
Terebuš (RUS) 43 Di 36
327390 Teregova (RO) 71 Cc 45
Terek (RUS) 91 Ee 47
Terekli-Mekteb (RUS) 77 Ef 46
Teren'ga (RUS) 45 Ei 37
Terensaj (RUS) 64 Fk 39
21-550 Terespol (PL) 57 Cd 38
Teresva (UA) 57 Cd 42
Tereze (RUS) 76 Ec 47
Teriberka (RUS) 16 Df 21
Terjaevo (RUS) 43 Dg 34
50230 Terlemez (TR) 97 De 52
Termachivka (UA) 58 Ck 39
55600 Terme (TR) 90 Dg 49
90018 Termini Imerese (I) 84 Bd 53
86039 Termoli (I) 85 Be 48
4452* Ternberg (A) 70 Be 43
4530* Terneuzen (NL) 53 Ad 39
05100 Terni (I) 84 Bc 48
Ternivka (UA) 60 Dg 42
Ternivka (UA) 74 Dc 43
Ternopil' (UA) 58 Cf 41
Ternopol' = Ternopil' (UA) 58 Cf 41
Ternovka (RUS) 61 Eb 39
Ternovka (RUS) 61 Ec 39
Ternuvate (UA) 75 Dg 43
Terny (UA) 59 Dd 39
Terpinn'a (UA) 74 Df 44
04019 Terracina (I) 84 Bd 49
7980 Terråk (N) 21 Bc 25
09098 Terralba (I) 83 Ai 51
85030 Terranova di Pollino (I) 85 Bg 51
08221* Terrassa (E) 82 Ac 49
24120 Terrasson-la-Villedieu (F) 67 Ab 45
Tersa (RUS) 62 Eh 38
Tersi (RUS) 46 Fc 34
08047 Tertenia (I) 83 Ak 51
9769 Tervel (BG) 73 Ch 47
3728 Tērvete (LV) 41 Cd 34
72211 Tervo (FIN) 22 Cg 28
95300 Tervola (FIN) 22 Ce 24
Tešanj (BIH) 71 Bi 46
Teslić (BIH) 70 Bh 46
Tesovo (RUS) 43 De 35
Tesovo-Netyl'skij (RUS) 31 Db 32
18195 Tessin (D) 39 Bc 36
33260 Teste-de-Buch, La (F) 66 Si 46
9100 Tét (H) 70 Bh 43
17166 Teterow (D) 39 Bc 37
5700 Teteven (BG) 87 Ce 48
Tetijiv (UA) 58 Ck 41
Tetjuši (RUS) 45 Ei 36
Tetjušskoe (RUS) 45 Ei 36
Tëtkino (RUS) 59 De 39
7044 Tetovo (BG) 72 Cg 47
1200* Tetovo (MK) 86 Ca 48
Tetrino (RUS) 24 Di 24
Teučežsk = Adygejsk (RUS) 75 Dk 46
09019 Teulada (I) 83 Ai 52
64701 Teuva (FIN) 22 Cb 28
GL20 Tewkesbury (GB) 52 Sh 39
35010 Thafmakó (GR) 86 Cc 51
06502 Thale (D) 55 Bb 39
OX9 Thame (GB) 52 Sk 39
88150 Thaon-les-Vosges (F) 54 Ag 42
21520 Tharsis (E) 92 Sc 53
64004 Thássos (GR) 87 Ce 50
24210 Thenon (F) 67 Ab 45
35001 Theológos (GR) 87 Ce 50
30008 Thérmo (GR) 94 Cb 52
62129 Thérouanne (F) 53 Ac 40
54625* Thessaloníki (GR) 86 Cc 50
IP24 Thetford (GB) 53 Aa 38
Theth (AL) 86 Bk 48
36016 Thiene (I) 69 Bb 45
470* Þingeyri (IS) 48 Qg 25
Þingvellir (IS) 48 Qi 26
57100* Thionville (F) 54 Ag 41
Thiorihia Milou (GR) 94 Ce 54
84700 Thíra (GR) 95 Cf 54
YO7 Thirsk (GB) 51 Si 36
Thísbi (GR) 94 Cc 52
7700 Thisted (DK) 38 Ai 34
32200 Thíva (GR) 94 Cd 52
24800 Thiviers (F) 66 Aa 45
69550 Thizy (F) 67 Ae 44
01140 Thoissey (F) 67 Ae 44
84008 Tholária (GR) 95 Cf 54
Thomastown = Baile Mhic Andáin (IRL) 49 Sc 38
74200* Thonon-les-Bains (F) 68 Ag 44
04170 Thorame-Haute (F) 68 Ag 46
DN8 Thorne (GB) 51 Sk 37
DG3 Thornhill (GB) 51 Sg 35
100 Thorshavn = Tórshavn (FO) 50 Sd 28
680* Þórshöfn (IS) 48 Re 24
79100 Thouars (F) 66 Sk 44
35134 Thourie (F) 66 Si 43
8820 Thourout = Torhout (B) 53 Ad 39
□ Þrándarjökull (IS) 48 Rf 26
3600* Thun (CH) 68 Ah 44
Thurles = Durlas (IRL) 49 Sc 38
KW14 Thurso (GB) 50 Sg 32
14220 Thury-Harcourt (F) 52 Sk 42
7680 Thyborøn (DK) 38 Ai 34
880 Þykkvibær (IS) 48 Qk 27
97540 Tiainen (FIN) 15 Cg 24
073 01 Tibava (SK) 57 Cc 42
54301 Tibro (S) 29 Be 32
817170 Tichileşti (RO) 73 Ch 45
52201 Tidaholm (S) 29 Bd 32
54920 Tidan (S) 29 Be 32
47870 Tiedra (E) 80 Se 49
7450 Tiefencastel (CH) 69 Ak 44
4000* Tiel (NL) 54 Af 39
3390 Tielt (B) 53 Ad 40
3300 Tienen (B) 53 Ae 40
79761 Tiengen, Waldshut- (D) 68 Ai 43
81500 Tierp (S) 29 Bh 30
HS6 Tigharry (GB) 50 Sc 33
3200 Tighina (MD) 73 Ck 44
Tignăşi (RO) 71 Cc 46
8237 Tihany (H) 70 Bh 44
Tihoreck (RUS) 76 Ea 45
Tihvin (RUS) 32 Dd 31
Tihvin Bor (RUS) 24 Df 28
Tiinsk (RUS) 45 Ek 36
62165 Tiistenjoki (FIN) 22 Cd 28
Tikša (RUS) 23 Dc 26
5000* Tilburg (NL) 54 Af 39
RM18 Tilbury (GB) 53 Aa 39
71001 Tílisos (GR) 95 Cf 55
4572 Tilža (LV) 42 Ch 34
Tim (RUS) 60 Dh 39
Timar (TR) 99 Ed 52
Timaševsk (RUS) 75 Di 45
70200 Timbáki (GR) 94 Ce 55
000300* Timişoara (RO) 71 Cb 45
23669 Timmendorfer Strand (D) 39 Ba 37
Timohino (RUS) 32 Dg 31
Timonino (RUS) 33 Eb 29
Timošino (RUS) 32 Dg 30
Timošino (RUS) 33 Ee 33
Timrå (S) 21 Bh 28
HS2 Timsgarry (GB) 50 Sc 32
417595 Tinca (RO) 71 Cb 44
61800 Tinchebray (F) 52 Sk 42
Tineo = Tinéu (E) 80 Sd 47
6360 Tinglev (DK) 38 Ak 36
36200 Tingsryd (S) 39 Be 34
62033 Tingstäde (S) 29 Bi 33
6630 Tingvoll (N) 20 Ai 28
84200 Tínos (GR) 95 Cf 53
35190 Tinténiac (F) 52 Si 42
Tiobraid Árann = Tipperary (IRL) 49 Sb 38
38079 Tione di Trento (I) 69 Ba 44
Tipperary = Tiobraid Árann (IRL) 49 Sb 38
Tiranë (AL) 86 Bk 49
23037 Tirano (I) 69 Ba 44
3300 Tiraspol (MD) 73 Ck 44
35900 Tire (TR) 95 Ch 52
28500 Tirebolu (TR) 90 Di 49
Tirljanskij (RUS) 47 Fi 36
40100 Tírnavos (GR) 86 Cc 51
5140 Tîrnova (MD) 58 Ch 42
99871 Tirro (FIN) 15 Cg 22
95643 Tirschenreuth (D) 55 Bc 41
8400 Tirstrup (DK) 39 Ba 34
Tišanka (RUS) 61 Ea 39
Tiškovo (RUS) 77 Ei 44
666 01* Tišnov (CZ) 56 Bg 41
5430 Tiszaföldvár (H) 71 Ca 44
6060 Tiszakécske (H) 71 Ca 44
4440 Tiszavasvári (H) 71 Cb 43
Titaševo (RUS) 46 Fb 37
21240 Titel (SRB) 71 Ca 45
79822 Titisee-Neustadt (D) 68 Ai 43
Titograd = Podgorica (SRB) 86 Bk 48
Titova, Ljalja- (RUS) 36 Gb 31
40000* Titova Mitrovica = Kosovska Mitrovica = Mitrovicë (RKS) 86 Ca 48

Titova Mitrovica | 201

Titov Drvar (BIH) 70 Bg 46
Titovo (RUS) 44 Ed 37
Titovo Užice = Užice (SRB) 71 Cb 47
Titov Veles = Veles (MK) 86 Cb 49
7268 Titran (N) 20 Ai 27
84529 Tittmoning (D) 55 Bc 42
135500 Titu (RO) 72 Cf 46
64250 Tiukka = Tjöck (FIN) 22 Cb 28
85 320 Tivat (MNE) 86 Bi 48
EX16 Tiverton (GB) 52 Sg 40
Tivoli (I) 84 Bc 49
Tjahynka (UA) 74 Dc 44
59030 Tjällmö (S) 29 Bf 32
Tjälme (S) 14 Ca 22
Tjåmotis (S) 14 Bi 24
Tjarnir (IS) 48 Rb 25
Tjater-Araslanovo (RUS) 46 Fe 37
Tjautjas (S) 14 Ca 23
Tjentište (BIH) 71 Bi 47
64250 Tjöck (FIN) 22 Cb 28
3145 Tjøme (N) 28 Ba 31
620 Tjörn (IS) 48 Qk 25
8860 Tjøtta (N) 21 Bc 25
83005 Tjourenstugorna (S) 21 Bd 27
Tjubuk (RUS) 47 Ga 34
Tjul'gan (RUS) 64 Fg 38
Tjuli (RUS) 37 Gk 30
Tjuljači (RUS) 46 Fa 35
Tjuljuk (RUS) 47 Fi 36
Tjul'kino (RUS) 35 Fg 31
Tjumen' (RUS) 37 Gf 33
Tjunevo (RUS) 37 Gf 33
Tjurjuševo (RUS) 46 Fe 36
Tkon (HR) 70 Bf 47
Tljaumbetovo (RUS) 64 Fg 38
Tlumač (UA) 58 Cf 42
Tobar an Choire (IRL) 49 Sb 36
02500 Tobarra (E) 93 Si 52
Tobercurry = Tobar an Choire (IRL) 49 Sb 36
PA75 Tobermory (GB) 50 Sd 34
39034 Toblach = Dobbiaco (I) 69 Bc 44
Tobol'sk (RUS) 37 Gi 32
Tobol'skij (RUS) 65 Gb 39
Toboltura (RUS) 37 Gi 33
Tobseda (RUS) 18 Fc 22
Tobys' (RUS) 26 Fc 27
67010 Töcksfors (S) 28 Bb 31
Todal (N) 20 Ai 28
06059 Todi (I) 84 Bc 48
79674 Todtnau (D) 68 Ah 43
Tofickoe (RUS) 76 Ed 45
ZE2 Toft (GB) 50 Si 30
Tofte (N) 28 Ba 31
Toftlia (N) 14 Be 24
6520 Toftlund (DK) 38 Ak 35
69301 Toholampi (FIN) 22 Ce 27
Tohumluk (TR) 90 Di 50
37801 Toijala (FIN) 30 Cd 29
97701 Toivakka (FIN) 22 Cg 28
70901 Toivala (FIN) 23 Ch 28
Tokaj (H) 57 Cb 42
Tokarevka (RUS) 61 Eb 38
Tokari (RUS) 32 De 29
Tokari (RUS) 35 Fe 33
60000* Tokat (TR) 90 Dg 50
38960 Toklar (TR) 97 Dg 52
Tokluman (TR) 89 Dd 51
Tokmak (UA) 74 Df 43
80750 Tokmaklı (TR) 98 Dg 53
Toksovo (RUS) 31 Da 30
Tolbazy (RUS) 46 Ff 36
9300* Tolbuhin = Dobrič (BG) 73 Ch 47
45001* Toledo (E) 81 Sf 51
00059 Tolfa (I) 84 Bb 48
Tol'jatti = Stavropol'-na-Volgi (RUS) 45 Ek 37
82-340 Tolkmicko (PL) 40 Bk 36
29010 Tollarp (S) 39 Bd 35
Tolmači (RUS) 32 Df 33
Tolmačovo (RUS) 31 Ck 32
33028 Tolmezzo (I) 69 Bc 44
5220 Tolmin (SLO) 69 Bd 44
7130 Tolna (H) 71 Bi 44
20400 Tolosa (E) 81 Sh 47
97925 Tolva (FIN) 15 Ci 24
Tolvojarvi (RUS) 23 Db 28
Tolvuja (RUS) 24 Df 28
83646 Tölz, Bad (D) 69 Bb 43
Tomakivka (UA) 74 De 43
2300-303* Tomar (P) 80 Sb 51
Tomarovka (RUS) 60 Dg 40
38900* Tomarza (TR) 97 Df 52
Tomaševka (BY) 57 Cd 39
Tomašpil' (UA) 58 Ci 42
22-600 Tomaszów Lubelski (PL) 57 Cd 40
97-201* Tomaszów Mazowiecki (PL) 56 Bk 39
27301 Tomelilla (S) 39 Bd 35
13700 Tomelloso (E) 81 Sg 51
AB35 Tomintoul (GB) 50 Sg 33
6590 Tømmervåg (N) 20 Ah 27
TN11 Tonbridge (GB) 53 Aa 39
3460-519* Tondela (P) 80 Sb 50
6270 Tønder (DK) 38 Ai 36
3700 Tongeren (B) 54 Af 40
IV27 Tongue (GB) 50 Sf 32
Tonkino (RUS) 34 Eg 33
98710 Tonkopura (FIN) 15 Ci 24
17430 Tonnay-Charente (F) 66 Sk 45
47400 Tonneins (F) 66 Aa 46
89700 Tonnerre (F) 67 Ad 43
25832 Tönning (D) 38 Ai 36
Tonšaevo (RUS) 34 Eg 33
3101* Tønsberg (N) 28 Ba 31
4440 Tonstad (N) 28 Ag 32
61500 Tonya (TR) 90 Dk 50
Tõostamaa (EST) 30 Cd 32
50880 Topaklı (TR) 89 De 51
Topalki (RUS) 32 Dg 32
52910 Topçam (TR) 90 Dh 50
535700 Toplița (RO) 72 Cf 44
34310 Topola (SRB) 71 Ca 46
7512 Topolčani (MK) 86 Cb 49
955 01* Topol'čany (SK) 56 Bi 42
827220 Topolog (RO) 73 Ci 46
115500 Topoloveni (RO) 72 Cf 46
6560 Topolovgrad (BG) 87 Cg 48
4260 Topolovo (BG) 87 Cf 49
087225 Toporu (RO) 72 Cf 46
907285 Topraisar (RO) 73 Ci 46
Toprakkale (TR) 91 Ec 51
Toprakkale (TR) 97 Dg 53
Topsakal (TR) 99 Ee 52
36000 Toptaş (TR) 91 Ec 50
Torà (E) 82 Ab 49
Torbalı (TR) 95 Ch 52
TQ2 Torbay (GB) 52 Sg 40
Torbeevo (RUS) 44 Ed 36
2429 Tørberget (N) 29 Bc 29
47830 Tordehúmos (E) 80 Se 49
47100 Tordesillas (E) 80 Se 49
95040 Töre (S) 22 Cc 25
54501 Töreboda (S) 29 Be 32
Torec'k (UA) 60 Dh 42
26093 Torekov (S) 39 Bc 34
08570 Torelló (E) 82 Ac 48
24450 Toreno (E) 80 Sd 48
04860 Torgau (D) 55 Bc 39
17358 Torgelow (D) 39 Be 37
37042 Torhamn (S) 39 Bf 34
8820 Torhout (B) 53 Ad 39
50160 Torigni-sur-Vire (F) 52 Sk 41
19190 Torija (E) 81 Sg 50
10100* Torino (I) 68 Ah 45
93101 Törmänen (FIN) 15 Ch 22
Tormosin (RUS) 61 Ec 42
982 01 Tornal'a (SK) 57 Ca 42
Tornesträsk (S) 14 Bk 22
95450 Tornio (FIN) 22 Ce 25
32621 Toro (E) 80 Se 49
5200 Törökszentmiklós (H) 71 Ca 43
Toropec (RUS) 42 Db 34
Torošino (RUS) 31 Ci 33
3579 Torpo (N) 28 Ai 30
84013 Torpshammar (S) 21 Bg 28
7580-001 Torrão (P) 92 Sb 52
25746 Torreblanca (E) 82 Aa 50
14410 Torrecampo (E) 93 Sf 52
Torre de la Higuera (E) 92 Sd 53
80059 Torre del Greco (I) 85 Be 50
5160-003* Torre de Moncorvo (P) 80 Sc 49
23650 Torredonjimeno (E) 93 Sg 53
3870-301* Torreira (P) 80 Sb 50
28850 Torrejón de Ardoz (E) 81 Sg 50
28180 Torrelaguna (E) 81 Sg 50
39300 Torrelavega (E) 66 Sf 47
47134 Torrelobatón (E) 80 Se 49
10184 Torremocha (E) 80 Sd 51
29620 Torremolinos (E) 93 Sf 54
34305 Torremormojón (E) 81 Sf 49
46900 Torrent (E) 82 Sk 51
30700 Torre-Pacheco (E) 93 Sk 53
10066 Torre Pellice (I) 68 Ah 46
2350-409* Torres Novas (P) 80 Sb 51
2560-230* Torres Vedras (P) 80 Sa 51
03180 Torrevieja (E) 93 Sk 53
IV22 Torridon (GB) 50 Se 33
16029 Torriglia (I) 69 Ak 46
44421 Torrijas (E) 82 Sk 50
45500 Torrijos (E) 81 Sf 51
Tørring (DK) 38 Ak 35
17257 Torroella de Montgrí (E) 82 Ad 48
38501 Torsås (S) 40 Bg 34
Torsby (S) 29 Bd 30
100 Tórshavn (FO) 50 Sd 28
09312 Tórtoles de Esgueva (E) 81 Sf 49
08048 Tortolì (I) 83 Ak 51
15057 Tortona (I) 68 Ai 46
43500 Tortosa (E) 82 Aa 50
25430 Tortum (TR) 91 Eb 50
29800 Torul (TR) 90 Dk 50
87-100 Toruń (PL) 40 Bi 37
31403 Torup (S) 39 Bd 34
68604* Tõrva (EST) 30 Cf 32
Toržok (RUS) 43 De 33
66-235 Torzym (PL) 56 Bf 38
Tosbotn (N) 21 Bc 25
Toškurovo (RUS) 47 Fg 34
Tosno (RUS) 31 Da 31
17320 Tossa de Mar (E) 82 Ac 49
21255 Tostedt (D) 38 Ak 37
Tošviska (RUS) 18 Fc 23
37300 Tosya (TR) 89 De 49
30850 Totana (E) 93 Si 53
76890 Tôtes (F) 53 Ab 41
5940 Tótkomlós (H) 71 Ca 44
Tot'ma (RUS) 33 Ec 31
TQ9 Totnes (GB) 52 Sg 40
89130 Toucy (F) 67 Ad 43
54200* Toul (F) 54 Af 42
83000* Toulon (F) 68 Af 47
31000* Toulouse (F) 67 Ab 47
62520 Touquet-Paris-Plage, le (F) 53 Ab 40
59200 Tourcoing (F) 53 Ad 40
38110 Tour-du-Pin, la (F) 68 Af 45
7500 Tournai (B) 53 Ad 40
07300 Tournon-sur-Rhône (F) 67 Ae 45
71700 Tournus (F) 67 Ae 44
61190 Tourouvre (F) 53 Aa 42
37000* Tours (F) 66 Aa 43
28390 Toury (F) 53 Ab 42
Tova (RUS) 24 Ea 25
Tovarkovskij (RUS) 43 Di 37
Tovste (UA) 58 Cf 42
Tøymskardia (N) 21 Bd 25
63600 Töysä (FIN) 22 Cd 28
37173 Trabanca (E) 80 Sd 49
61000* Trabzon (TR) 90 Dk 50
Tracino (I) 84 Bc 54
12330 Traiguera (E) 82 Aa 50
3153 Traisen (A) 56 Bf 42
2514* Traiskirchen (A) 70 Bg 43
76580 Trait, le (F) 53 Aa 41
21001 Trakai (LT) 41 Ce 36
Trakt (RUS) 26 Fb 28
Tralee = Trá Li (IRL) 49 Sa 38
Trá Li = Tralee (IRL) 49 Sa 38
SY21 Trallwng = Welshpool (GB) 52 Sg 38
07040 Tramariglio (I) 83 Ai 50
Trá Mhór (IRL) 49 Sc 38
Tramore = Trá Mhór (IRL) 49 Sc 38
2460 Trăn (BG) 86 Cc 48
57300* Tranås (S) 29 Be 32
85360 Tranche-sur-Mer, la (F) 66 Si 44
6420-623 Trancoso (P) 80 Sc 50
8305 Tranebjerg (DK) 39 Ba 35
51400 Tranemo (S) 29 Bd 33
70059 Trani (I) 85 Bg 49
8297 Tranøy (N) 14 Bf 22
78068 Transtrand (S) 29 Bd 29
91100 Trapani (I) 84 Bc 52
7092 Trăstenik (BG) 72 Ce 47
8128 Trăstikovo (BG) 88 Ch 48
4050 Traun (A) 55 Be 42
4801 Traunkirchen (A) 69 Bd 43
83278 Traunstein (D) 69 Bc 43
23570 Travemünde (D) 39 Ba 37
8105 Travers (CH) 68 Ag 44
72270* Travnik (BIH) 70 Bh 46
1420 Trbovlje (SLO) 70 Be 44
674 01 Třebíč (CZ) 56 Bf 41
89000* Trebinje (BIH) 85 Bi 48
87075 Trebisacce (I) 85 Bg 51
8210 Trebnje (SLO) 70 Be 45
379 01 Třeboň (CZ) 55 Be 42
NP22 Tredegar (GB) 52 Sg 39
LD7 Trefyclawdd = Knighton (GB) 52 Sg 38
NP25 Trefynwy = Monmouth (GB) 52 Sh 39
SY25 Tregaron (GB) 52 Sg 38
22220 Tréguier (F) 52 Sg 42
89054 Trehörningsjö (S) 21 Bi 27
19260 Treignac (F) 67 Ab 45
49800 Trélazé (F) 66 Sk 43
23102* Trelleborg (S) 39 Bd 35
17390 Tremblade, la (F) 66 Si 45
08230 Tremblois-lès-Rocroi (F) 53 Ae 41
25620 Tremp (E) 82 Aa 48
914 01 Trenčianska Teplá (SK) 56 Bi 42
911 01 Trenčín (SK) 56 Bi 42
38100 Trento (I) 69 Bb 44
Trepça = Trepča (RKS) 86 Ca 48
Trepča = Trepça (RKS) 86 Ca 48
76470 Tréport, Le (F) 53 Ab 40
6391 Tresfjord (N) 20 Ah 28
09540 Trespaderne (E) 81 Sg 48
Třešť (CZ) 56 Bf 41
Trestino (RUS) 32 Dd 33
Trestna (RUS) 32 Df 33
Tretnica (RUS) 33 Ee 30
13530 Trets (F) 68 Af 47
Tretten (N) 28 Ba 29
91757 Treuchtlingen (D) 55 Ba 42
14929 Treuenbrietzen (D) 55 Bc 38
24047 Treviglio (I) 69 Ak 45
31100 Treviso (I) 69 Bc 45
01600 Trévoux (F) 67 Ae 45
34613 Treysa (D) 54 Ak 40
17525 Trgovište (SRB) 86 Cc 48
Triánda = Ialissos (GR) 96 Ci 54
18465 Tribsees (D) 39 Bc 36
75019 Tricarico (I) 85 Bg 50
73039 Tricase (I) 85 Bi 51
8784* Trieben (A) 70 Be 43
54290* Trier (D) 54 Ag 41
34100 Triest = Trieste (I) 69 Bd 45
34100* Trieste (I) 69 Bd 45
65220 Trie-sur-Baïse (F) 66 Aa 47
53076 Trígono (GR) 86 Cb 50
59032 Tríkala (GR) 86 Cb 51
37009 Trikéri (GR) 87 Cd 51
Trilj (HR) 70 Bg 47
Trim = Baile Átha Troim (IRL) 49 Sd 37
86290 Trimouille, la (F) 67 Ab 44
13039 Trino (I) 68 Ai 45
22101 Trípoli (GR) 94 Cc 53
27063 Tripótama (GR) 94 Cb 53
85700 Tristomo (GR) 95 Ch 55
147410 Trivalea-Moşteni (RO) 72 Cf 46
86029 Trivento (I) 85 Be 49
5350 Trjavna (BG) 87 Cf 48
917 01* Trnava (SK) 56 Bh 42
Trnovo (BIH) 71 Bi 47
Trockoe (RUS) 63 Fc 38
Trödje (S) 29 Bh 30
Troekurovo (RUS) 43 Dh 37
Troekurovo (RUS) 44 Dk 37
8680 Trofors (N) 21 Bd 25
Trogir (HR) 70 Bg 47
71029 Troia (I) 85 Bf 49
Troick (RUS) 47 Gb 36
Troick (RUS) 63 Fe 40
Troickaja (RUS) 75 Dk 46
Troickij (RUS) 36 Gd 33
Troickij Sungur (RUS) 45 Eh 37
Troickoe (RUS) 36 Gc 31
Troickoe (RUS) 46 Fc 37
Troickoe (RUS) 63 Fd 38
Troickoe (RUS) 64 Fg 38
Troickoe (RUS) 76 Ee 44
Troicko-Pečorsk (RUS) 27 Fg 28
94018 Troina (I) 84 Be 53
53840* Troisdorf (D) 54 Ah 40
4980 Trois-Ponts (B) 54 Af 40
7506 Trojaci (MK) 86 Cb 49
6491 Trojan (BG) 87 Ce 48
Trojic'ke (UA) 60 Di 41
Trojic'ke (UA) 73 Da 43
Trojic'ko-Safonove (UA) 74 Dc 43
46100* Trollhättan (S) 29 Bc 32
9006* Tromsø (N) 14 Bk 21
9107 Tromvik (N) 14 Bi 21
7010* Trondheim (N) 20 Ba 27
Trönninge (S) 39 Bc 34
7120 Tronvik (N) 28 Af 29
89861 Tropea (I) 84 Bf 52
Tropojë (AL) 86 Ca 48
61901 Trosa (S) 29 Bh 31
29033 Troškūnai (LT) 41 Ce 35
Trosna (RUS) 60 Df 38
Trostan' (RUS) 59 Dc 38
Trostjanec' (UA) 58 Ck 42
Trostjanec' (UA) 59 De 40
Trostjanskij (RUS) 61 Ed 40
14360 Trouville-sur-Mer (F) 53 Aa 41
BA14 Trowbridge (GB) 52 Sh 39
10000* Troyes (F) 53 Ae 42
Trpanj (HR) 85 Bh 47
81 437 Trsa (MNE) 86 Bi 47
Trstenik (HR) 85 Bh 48
37240* Trstenik (SRB) 71 Cb 47
37240* Trstenik (SRB) 86 Ca 48
Trsteno (HR) 85 Bh 48
Trubčevsk (RUS) 59 Dd 38
Trubetčino (RUS) 44 Dk 38
33100 Trubia (E) 80 Se 47
Trudfront (RUS) 77 Eh 45
Trufanova (RUS) 25 Ee 26
10200 Trujillo (E) 80 Se 51
TR1 Truro (GB) 52 Se 40
717400 Truşeşti (RO) 73 Ch 43
Truskavec' (UA) 57 Cd 41
Trusovo (RUS) 26 Fb 25
541 01* Trutnov (CZ) 56 Bf 40
88011 Tryškiai (LT) 41 Cc 34
64-980 Trzcianka (PL) 40 Bg 37
64-980 Trzcianka (PL) 57 Cb 39
66-320 Trzciel (PL) 56 Bf 38
73-100 Trzebiatów (PL) 39 Bf 36
55-100 Trzebnica (PL) 56 Bh 39
62-240 Trzemeszno (PL) 56 Bh 38
Tsamantás (GR) 86 Ca 51
Tscheljabinsk = Čeljabinsk (RUS) 47 Gb 35
Tschernobyl = Čornobyl' (UA) 59 Da 39
Tuaim = Tuam (IRL) 49 Sb 37
Tuam = Tuaim (IRL) 49 Sb 37
Tuapse (RUS) 75 Dk 46
72070* Tübingen (D) 54 Ak 42
Tubinskij (RUS) 47 Fi 38
11350 Tuchan (F) 82 Ac 48
89-500 Tuchola (PL) 40 Bh 37
Tuchol'ka (UA) 57 Cd 42
Tučkovo (RUS) 43 Dg 35
78-640 Tuczno (PL) 40 Bg 37
47320 Tudela de Duero (E) 81 Sf 49
46606 Tudu (EST) 30 Cg 31
72160 Tuffé (F) 53 Aa 42
9670 Tufjord (N) 15 Cd 19
Tugolukovo (RUS) 61 Eb 39
Tugulym (RUS) 37 Ge 33
Tugustemir (RUS) 64 Fg 38
88120 Tuhkakylä (FIN) 23 Ci 26
Tuhkala (RUS) 23 Da 25
36700 Tui (E) 80 Sb 48
Tuilsce (IRL) 49 Sb 37
Tujmazy (RUS) 46 Fd 36
Tukan (RUS) 47 Fh 37
Tukmačevo (RUS) 35 Ff 31
3101* Tukums (LV) 41 Cd 34
Tula (RUS) 43 Dh 36
Tulach Mhór = Tullamore (IRL) 49 Sc 37
000820* Tulcea (RO) 73 Ci 45
Tul'čyn (UA) 58 Ci 42
537330 Tulgheş (RO) 72 Cf 44
Tullamore = Tulach Mhór (IRL) 49 Sc 37
19000* Tulle (F) 67 Ab 45
38210 Tullins (F) 68 Af 45
3430 Tulln (A) 56 Bg 42
Tullow = An Tulach (IRL) 49 Sd 38
Tulos (RUS) 23 Da 27
Tulpan (RUS) 35 Fh 29
98840 Tulppio (FIN) 15 Ck 23
Tul'skij (RUS) 75 Ea 46
Tuma (RUS) 44 Ea 35
Tumak (RUS) 77 Ei 44
Tumannyj (RUS) 16 Df 22
Tumanovo (RUS) 43 De 35
14700* Tumba (S) 29 Bh 31
Tumbotino (RUS) 44 Ed 35
Tumutuk (RUS) 46 Fd 35
Tuna-Hästberg (S) 29 Bf 30
43900 Tunçbilek (TR) 88 Ck 51
62000 Tunceli (TR) 90 Dk 51
Tundra (RUS) 24 Ea 26
Tungozero (RUS) 23 Db 25
Tunnhovd (N) 28 Ai 30
98960 Tuntsa (FIN) 15 Ck 23
46110 Tuohikotti (FIN) 31 Ch 29
Turav (BY) 58 Ch 38
76201 Turba (EST) 30 Ce 31
Turbe (BIH) 70 Bh 46
Turbiv (UA) 58 Ci 41
000401* Turda (RO) 72 Cd 44
40370 Turégano (E) 81 Sf 49
62-700 Turek (PL) 56 Bi 38
Turek, Mari- (RUS) 45 Ek 34
Turgenevo (RUS) 44 Eb 35
Turgut (TR) 96 Ci 53
Turgut (TR) 96 Db 52
Turgutlu (TR) 95 Ch 52
48960 Turgutreis (TR) 95 Ch 54
60030* Turhal (TR) 90 Dg 50
72210* Türi (EST) 30 Cf 32
Turijs'k (UA) 57 Ce 39
10100 Turin = Torino (I) 68 Ah 45
Turinsk (RUS) 36 Gd 32
Turinskaja Sloboda (RUS) 37 Ge 33
46389 Turís (E) 82 Sk 51
Turiščevo (RUS) 43 De 38
Tur'ja (RUS) 26 Fa 28
8796 Türje (H) 70 Bh 44
Turka (UA) 57 Cd 41
Turki (RUS) 61 Ed 39
Türkmen (TR) 89 Df 49
46800 Türkoğlu (TR) 98 Dg 53
Turksad (RUS) 76 Ee 45
Turku (FIN) 30 Cc 30
Turlu (TR) 98 Dh 53
32004 Turmantas (LT) 41 Cg 35
Turnaeva (RUS) 37 Gg 33
Turnagöl (TR) 91 Ec 51
2300 Turnhout (B) 53 Ae 39
511 01 Turnov (CZ) 56 Bf 40
Turnovo (RUS) 44 Eb 36
145200 Turnu Măgurele (RO) 72 Ce 47
8864 Turrach, Predlitz- (A) 69 Bd 44
AB53 Turriff (GB) 50 Sh 33
023 54 Turzovka (SK) 56 Bi 41
Tuscania (I) 84 Bb 48
02350 Tut (TR) 98 Dh 53
Tutaev (RUS) 33 Dk 33
Tutak (TR) 91 Ec 51
36320 Tutin (SRB) 86 Ca 47
7600 Tutrakan (BG) 72 Cg 46
78532 Tuttlingen (D) 68 Ai 43
71201 Tuusniemi (FIN) 23 Ci 28
04380 Tuusula (FIN) 30 Cf 30
Tuutisjarvi (RUS) 15 Ck 24
36000 Tuygun (TR) 91 Ec 50
Tuža (RUS) 34 Eh 33
81 101 Tuzi (MNE) 86 Bk 48
75000* Tuzla (BIH) 71 Bi 46
907295 Tuzla (RO) 73 Ci 46
01915 Tuzla (TR) 97 De 52

202 | Titov Drvar

32610 Vampula (FIN) 30 Cc 29
65000* Van (TR) 99 Ed 52
Vanda (RUS) 32 Dg 31
01002* Vanda = Vantaa (FIN) 30 Ce 30
87701 Vändra (EST) 30 Cf 32
Vandyš (RUS) 34 Ei 29
46200 Vänersborg (S) 29 Bc 32
Vang (N) 28 Ai 29
2136 Vangaži (LV) 30 Ce 33
88050 Vängel (S) 21 Bg 27
6894 Vangsnes (N) 28 Ag 29
225400 Vânju Mare (RO) 71 Cc 46
9136 Vannareid (N) 14 Bk 20
91101 Vännäs (S) 22 Bk 27
91135 Vännäsby (S) 22 Bk 27
56000* Vannes (F) 66 Sh 43
Vannvikan (N) 20 Ba 27
07140 Vans, les (F) 67 Ae 46
78050 Vansbro (S) 29 Be 30
4560 Vanse (N) 28 Ag 32
01002* Vantaa (FIN) 30 Ce 30
97625 Vanttauskoski (FIN) 15 Cg 24
Vapna (RUS) 25 Ee 27
Vapnjarka (UA) 58 Ci 42
53401 Vara (S) 29 Bc 32
74670 Varaaslahti (FIN) 22 Cg 27
44370 Varades (F) 66 Si 43
13019 Varallo (I) 68 Ai 45
Varandej (RUS) 19 Fi 22
9840 Varangerbotn (N) 15 Ci 20
Varapaeva (BY) 42 Ch 35
Varaždin (HR) 70 Bg 44
17019 Varazze (I) 68 Ai 46
43200* Varberg (S) 39 Bc 33
5845 Vărbica (BG) 72 Cg 47
Vårby (S) 29 Bh 31
6800 Varde (DK) 38 Ai 35
9950 Vardø (N) 16 Db 20
Varegovo (RUS) 33 Dk 33
95300 Varejoki (FIN) 22 Ce 24
26316 Varel (D) 38 Ai 37
65001 Varėna (LT) 41 Ce 36
Varenikovskaja (RUS) 75 Dh 45
Varenikovskij (RUS) 76 Ee 46
Varenikovskoe (RUS) 76 Ee 46
03150 Varennes-sur-Allier (F) 67 Ad 44
Vareš (BIH) 71 Bi 46
21100 Varese (I) 68 Ai 45
717450 Vârfu Câmpului (RO) 72 Cg 43
317390 Vârfurile (RO) 71 Cc 44
44700 Vårgårda (S) 29 Bc 32
Vargiádes (GR) 86 Ca 51
46821 Vargön (S) 29 Bc 32
4360 Varhaug (N) 28 Af 32
09120 Varilhes (F) 82 Ab 47
83660 Varislahti (FIN) 23 Ci 28
78900 Varkaus (FIN) 23 Ch 28
Varlamovo (RUS) 47 Ga 36
560 Varmahlíð (IS) 48 Ql 25
9000* Varna (BG) 73 Ch 47
Varna (RUS) 47 Gb 37
33101* Värnamo (S) 29 Be 33
Varnavino (RUS) 34 Ef 33
Varnek (RUS) 19 Ga 21
53273 Varnhem (S) 29 Bd 32
88050 Varniai (LT) 41 Cc 35
60302 Varnja (EST) 31 Ch 32
Varnjany (BY) 41 Cg 36
460 05 Varnsdorf (CZ) 55 Be 40
Varntresk (N) 21 Be 25
73201 Varpaisjärvi (FIN) 23 Ch 27
8100 Várpalota (H) 71 Bi 43
3540 Văršec (BG) 72 Cd 47
6170 Vartdal (N) 20 Ag 28
71150 Vartiala (FIN) 23 Ci 28
49600 Varto (TR) 91 Eb 51
147428 Vârtoapele de Sus (RO) 72 Cf 46
Varva (UA) 59 Dc 40
37260 Varvarin (SRB) 71 Cb 47
27057 Varzi (I) 69 Ak 46
Varzino (RUS) 17 Di 22
Varzuga (RUS) 16 Dg 24
58210 Varzy (F) 67 Ad 43
65100* Vasa = Vaasa (FIN) 22 Cb 27
4800 Vásárosnamény (H) 57 Cc 42
Väsby (S) 29 Bh 31
Vasilevičy (BY) 58 Ck 38
Vasil'evka (RUS) 61 Ea 40
Vasil'evo (RUS) 31 Ch 33
Vasilevo (RUS) 43 Dd 35
Vasil'evo (RUS) 45 Ei 35
Vasil'evskoe (RUS) 44 Eb 34
Vasil'evskoe (RUS) 45 Ef 34
Vasiljata (RUS) 35 Fd 32
Vasil'ki (RUS) 32 Dh 32
Vasil'ki (RUS) 32 Di 33
Vasil'kovo (RUS) 34 Ei 33
Vasil'sursk (RUS) 45 Eg 34
Vasiščeve (UA) 60 Dg 41
39034 Vaškai (LT) 41 Ce 34
Vaskelovo (RUS) 31 Da 30
Vaškivci (UA) 58 Cf 42
41001 Vasknarva (EST) 31 Ch 31
Vas'kovo (RUS) 24 Ea 26
Vas'kovyči (UA) 58 Ci 39
000730* Vaslui (RO) 73 Ch 44
Vassarás (GR) 94 Cc 53
34010 Vassiliká (GR) 87 Cd 50
34010 Vassiliká (GR) 94 Cd 52
38891 Vassmolösa (S) 40 Bg 34
86040 Västansjö (S) 21 Bf 25
Västbacka (S) 29 Be 29
72001* Västerås (S) 29 Bg 31
62020 Västergarn (S) 29 Bi 33
13700* Västerhaninge (S) 29 Bi 31
59300* Västervik (S) 29 Bg 33
66054 Vasto (I) 85 Be 48
68695 Västra Ämtervik (S) 29 Bd 31
Västra Ritjemjåkk (S) 14 Bh 23
9800 Vasvár (H) 70 Bg 43
Vasylivka (UA) 74 Df 43
Vasyl'kiv (UA) 59 Da 40
Vasyl'kivka (UA) 60 Dg 42
36150 Vatan (F) 67 Ab 43
Vathí (GR) 94 Ce 54
84003 Vathí (GR) 95 Cg 53
84003 Vathí (GR) 95 Cg 54
51100 Vatólakos (GR) 86 Cb 50
725700 Vatra Dornei (RO) 72 Cf 43
74319 Vattholma (S) 29 Bh 30
Vatutine (UA) 59 Db 42
55140 Vaucouleurs (F) 54 Af 42
30600 Vauvert (F) 67 Ae 47
Vavkalata (BY) 42 Ch 36
Vavkavysk (BY) 41 Ce 37
Vavož (RUS) 46 Fb 34
35002* Växjö (S) 39 Be 34
31207 Våxtorp (S) 39 Bd 34
Vazerki (RUS) 45 Ef 37
Važgort (RUS) 25 Eh 26
Včorajše (UA) 58 Ck 41
99981 Veähtøsaknjarga = Vetsikko (FIN) 15 Ch 21
49377 Vechta (D) 38 Ai 38
37450 Vecinos (E) 80 Se 50
4122 Vecpiebalga (LV) 41 Cf 33
Vecumnieci (LV) 41 Ce 34
Vedavågen, Åkrahamn- (N) 28 Af 31
43020 Veddige (S) 29 Bc 33
Vede (LV) 30 Cb 33
117815 Vedea (RO) 72 Ce 46
117815 Vedea (RO) 72 Cf 47
71172 Vedevåg (S) 29 Bf 31
9355 Vedrina (BG) 73 Ch 47
Vedrovo (RUS) 33 Ec 33
9640* Veendam (NL) 38 Ag 37
3900 Veenendaal (NL) 54 Af 38
33770 Vegadeo (A Veiga) (E) 80 Sc 47
24132 Vegarienza (E) 80 Sd 48
5460* Veghel (NL) 54 Af 39
73010 Veglie (I) 85 Bh 50
23210 Vehmaa (FIN) 30 Cb 30
Veidholmen (N) 20 Ah 27
Veidnes (N) 15 Cg 20
32360 Veiga, A (E) 80 Sc 48
67043 Veisiejai (LT) 41 Cd 36
95230 Veitsiluoto (FIN) 22 Ce 25
69026 Veiviržėnai (LT) 40 Cb 35
26083 Vejbystrand (S) 39 Bc 34
Vejdelevka (RUS) 60 Di 40
6600 Vejen (DK) 38 Ak 35
11150 Vejer de la Frontera (E) 92 Se 54
5672 Vejle (DK) 38 Ak 35
Vejno (RUS) 43 Df 37
Vekike Gradište (SRB) 71 Cb 46
Vekšino (RUS) 31 Db 33
Vela Luka (HR) 85 Bg 48
23053 Velanídia (GR) 94 Cd 54
Veldor'ja (RUS) 34 Ek 30
Veldozero (RUS) 31 Dc 29
4415 Velēna (LV) 30 Cg 33
3320* Velenje (SLO) 70 Bf 44
1400* Veles (MK) 86 Cb 49
04830 Vélez Blanco (E) 93 Sh 53
04820 Vélez Rubio (E) 93 Sh 53
18469 Velgast (D) 39 Bc 36
Veličaevskoe (RUS) 77 Ef 46
Velika (HR) 70 Bh 45
Velika Gorica (HR) 70 Bg 45
Velikaja (RUS) 18 Eh 23
Velikaja Guba (RUS) 24 Df 28
Velika Kladuša (BIH) 70 Bf 45
18403 Velika Plana (SRB) 71 Cb 47
Velikie Luki (RUS) 42 Da 34
Velikij Dvor (RUS) 32 De 31
Velikij Topal' (RUS) 59 Dc 38
Velikij Ustjug (RUS) 34 Eg 30
9850 Veliki Preslav (BG) 87 Cg 47
Velikodvorskij (RUS) 44 Ea 35
Velikoe (RUS) 32 Dh 31
Velikoe Selo (RUS) 33 Dk 32
Velikomihajlovka (RUS) 60 Dh 40
11320 Veliko Plana (SRB) 71 Cb 46
5000* Veliko Tărnovo (BG) 87 Cf 47
Velikovskoe (RUS) 45 Ef 34
Veliköy (TR) 91 Ec 49
81 428 Velimlje (MNE) 85 Bi 48
4600 Velingrad (BG) 87 Cd 48
Velíž (RUS) 42 Db 35
079 01 Veľké Kapušany (SK) 57 Cc 42
Velké Meziříčí (CZ) 56 Bg 41
932 01 Veľký Meder (SK) 70 Bh 43
00049 Velletri (I) 84 Bc 49
23501 Vellinge (S) 39 Bd 35
Velošel'e (RUS) 25 Eg 26
Velsen (NL) 53 Ae 38
Vel'sk (RUS) 33 Ec 29
50400 Velventós (GR) 86 Cc 50
Velyka Bahačka (UA) 59 Dd 41
Velyka Bilozerka (UA) 74 De 43
Velyka Hluša (UA) 58 Cf 39
Velyka Lepetycha (UA) 74 Dd 43
Velyka Mychajlivka (UA) 73 Ck 43
Velyka Novosilka (UA) 75 Dg 43
Velyka Oleksandrivka (UA) 74 Dd 43
Velyka Pysarivka (UA) 60 Df 40
Velyka Rublivka (UA) 59 De 41
Velyka Vil'šanka (UA) 59 Da 40
Velyka Vil'šanycja (UA) 57 Ce 41
Velyka Zahorivka (UA) 59 Dc 39
Velyki Dederkaly (UA) 58 Cg 40
Velykij Bereznyj (UA) 57 Cc 42
Velykij Byčkiv (UA) 57 Ce 42
Velykij Dobron' = Dobron' (UA) 57 Cc 42
Velyki Krynky (UA) 59 Dd 41
Velyki Mosty (UA) 57 Ce 40
Velyki Soročynci (UA) 59 Dd 40
Velykodolyns'ke (UA) 73 Da 44
Velykyj Ljubin' (UA) 57 Cd 41
Velykyj Burluk (UA) 60 Dh 40
84091 Vemhån (S) 21 Be 28
Vemsdalen (S) 21 Bd 28
57701 Vena (S) 29 Bf 33
86079 Venafro (I) 85 Be 49
06140 Vence (F) 68 Ah 47
7080-011* Vendas Novas (P) 92 Sb 52
Vendinga (RUS) 25 Eh 27
41100* Vendôme (F) 67 Ab 43
43700 Vendrell, el (E) 82 Ab 49
9751 Venec (BG) 87 Cg 48
Venedig = Venezia (I) 69 Bc 45
Venev (RUS) 43 Di 36
30100* Venezia (I) 69 Bc 45
69200* Vénissieux (F) 67 Ae 45
79293 Venjan (S) 29 Bd 30
5900* Venlo (NL) 54 Ag 39
4700 Vennesla (N) 28 Ah 32
85029 Venosa (I) 85 Bf 50
5800 Venray (NL) 54 Af 39
85019 Venta (LT) 41 Cc 34
45127 Ventas con Peña Aguilera, Las (E) 81 Sf 51
18039 Ventimiglia (I) 68 Ah 47
PO38 Ventnor (GB) 52 Si 40
3601* Ventspils (LV) 30 Cb 33
Vepryk (UA) 59 De 40
Ver, Horej- (RUS) 19 Fh 23
04620 Vera (E) 93 Si 53
Verba (UA) 57 Ce 40
Verbania (I) 68 Ai 45
13100 Vercelli (I) 68 Ai 45
Verchivceve (UA) 59 De 42
Verchnéfilatovo (RUS) 37 Gi 32
Verchne Syn'ovydne (UA) 57 Cd 41
Verchnij Rohačyk (UA) 74 De 43
Verchnjadzvimsk (BY) 42 Ch 35
Verchn'odniprovs'k (UA) 59 De 42
Verchovyna (UA) 57 Ce 42
Verdalen, Kleppe- (N) 28 Af 32
7600 Verdalsøra (N) 20 Bb 27
27283 Verden (Aller) (D) 38 Ak 38
33123 Verdon-sur-Mer, le (F) 66 Si 45
55100* Verdun (F) 54 Af 41
Vereb'e (RUS) 31 Dc 32
Vereja (RUS) 43 Dg 35
Vereščagino (RUS) 35 Fe 32
45501 Vergi (EST) 30 Cg 31
24380 Vergt (F) 66 Aa 45
Verhnečirskij (RUS) 61 Eb 41
Verhnečirskij (RUS) 61 Ed 42
Verhnečusovskie Gorodki (RUS) 35 Fh 32
Verhnee Nil'dino (RUS) 27 Gb 27
Verhnee Šilovo (RUS) 34 Ef 29
Verhnee Talyzino (RUS) 45 Ef 35
Verhnejarkeevo (RUS) 46 Fe 35
Verh-Nejvinskij (RUS) 36 Ga 33
Verhnekardil'skij (RUS) 61 Ec 39
Verhnelal'sk (RUS) 34 Eh 30
Verhnelebjaž'e (RUS) 77 Eh 44
Verhnespasskoe (RUS) 34 Ef 32
Verhnetulomskij (RUS) 16 Db 22
Verhneturovo (RUS) 60 Di 39
Verhneural'sk (RUS) 47 Fk 37
Verhnie Kigi (RUS) 47 Fi 35
Verhnie Sergi (RUS) 47 Fk 34
Verhnie Tatyšly (RUS) 46 Ff 34
Verhnie Važiny (RUS) 32 Dd 29
Verhnij Avzjan (RUS) 47 Fh 37
Verhnij Baskunčak (RUS) 62 Eg 42
Verhnij Čegem (RUS) 91 Ed 47
Verhnij Fiagdon (RUS) 91 Ee 48
Verhnij Lomov (RUS) 44 Ed 37
Verhnij Mamon (RUS) 61 Ea 40
Verhnij Tagil (RUS) 36 Fk 33
Verhnij Ufalej (RUS) 47 Ga 34
Verhnij Uslon (RUS) 45 Ek 35
Verhnij Vjalozerskij (RUS) 16 Df 24
Verhnjaja Baksan (RUS) 76 Ec 47
Verhnjaja Balkarija (RUS) 91 Ed 48
Verhnjaja Buzinovka (RUS) 61 Ed 41
Verhnjaja Čegem (RUS) 91 Ed 47
Verhnjaja In'va (RUS) 35 Fe 32
Verhnjaja Jus'va (RUS) 35 Fe 32
Verhnjaja Mara (RUS) 76 Ec 47
Verhnjaja Maza (RUS) 45 Eh 37
Verhnjaja Orljanka (RUS) 46 Fb 37
Verhnjaja Osljanka (RUS) 36 Fi 33
Verhnjaja Palen'ga (RUS) 25 Ec 26
Verhnjaja Peša (RUS) 18 Eh 24
Verhnjaja Pyšma (RUS) 47 Ga 34
Verhnjaja Salda (RUS) 36 Ga 32
Verhnjaja Sanarka (RUS) 47 Ga 36
Verhnjaja Sinjačiha (RUS) 36 Gb 32
Verhnjaja Storona (RUS) 33 Ea 31
Verhnjaja Tojma (RUS) 25 Ef 28
Verhnjaja Tura (RUS) 36 Fk 32
Verhnjaja Vollmanga (RUS) 34 Eh 31
Verhnjaja Zolotica (RUS) 24 Ea 25
Verhokam'e (RUS) 35 Fd 32
Verholuz'e (RUS) 34 Ei 31
Verhoramen'e (RUS) 34 Ei 31
Verhošižem'e (RUS) 34 Ek 32
Verhosun'e (RUS) 34 Fb 32
Verhotur'e (RUS) 36 Ga 32
Verhovaž'e (RUS) 33 Ec 30
Verhov'e (RUS) 43 Dh 38
Verhovino (RUS) 33 Ee 31
Verhovino-D'jakovo (RUS) 33 Ed 31
Verhovskij (RUS) 24 Ea 27
Verhozim (RUS) 45 Eg 38
59100 Véria (GR) 86 Cc 50
Verigino (RUS) 44 Ea 35
32600 Verín (E) 80 Sc 49
Verkola (RUS) 25 Ef 27
89270 Vermenton (F) 67 Ad 43
Vernadovka (RUS) 44 Ec 37
49390 Vernantes (F) 66 Aa 43
059 17 Vernár (SK) 57 Ca 42
127675 Vernești (RO) 72 Cg 45
27130 Verneuil-sur-Avre (F) 53 Aa 42
27200* Vernon (F) 53 Ab 41
37100* Verona (I) 69 Ba 45
11029 Verrès (I) 68 Ah 45
78000* Versailles (F) 53 Ac 42
Veršiny, Čelno- (RUS) 46 Fb 36
33775 Versmold (D) 54 Ai 38
Vertelim (RUS) 45 Ee 36
Vertijievka (UA) 59 Db 39
Vertjačij (RUS) 61 Ed 42
Vërtop (AL) 86 Ca 50
44120 Vertou (F) 66 Si 43
4800 Verviers (B) 54 Af 40
02140 Vervins (F) 53 Ad 41
72301 Vesanto (FIN) 22 Cg 28
Veščevo (RUS) 31 Ck 30
Ves'egonsk (RUS) 32 Dh 32
Veselaja (RUS) 44 Ec 37
Veselaja (RUS) 60 Di 40
Vesele (UA) 74 De 43
391 81* Veselí nad Lužnicí (CZ) 55 Be 41
Veselí nad Moravou (SK) 56 Bh 42
Veselovka (RUS) 47 Fk 35
Vesëlyj (RUS) 76 Ea 43
Veselynove (UA) 74 Db 43
Vešenskaja (RUS) 61 Eb 41
Veškajma (RUS) 45 Eh 36
Veškoma (RUS) 25 Ed 26
Vesljana (RUS) 26 Fa 27
99280 Vesmajärvi (FIN) 15 Cf 23
70000* Vesoul (F) 68 Ag 43
82102 Véssa (GR) 95 Cg 52
4550 Vestbygd (N) 28 Ag 32
Vesterli (N) 14 Bf 23
9940 Vesterø Havn (DK) 28 Ba 33
350 Vestmanhavn = Vestmanna (FO) 50 Sc 28
350 Vestmanna (FO) 50 Sc 28
900* Vestmannaeyjar (IS) 48 Qk 27
6390 Vestnes (N) 20 Ah 28
25078 Vestone (I) 69 Ba 45
Vestre Gausdal (N) 28 Ba 29
9802 Vestre Jakobselv (N) 15 Ck 20
8200 Veszprém (H) 70 Bh 43
8438 Veszprémvarsány (H) 70 Bh 43
Vésztő (H) 71 Cb 44
69701 Veteli (FIN) 22 Cd 27
Vet'ju (RUS) 26 Fa 28
Vetka (BY) 59 Db 38
57400* Vetlanda (S) 29 Bf 33
Vetluga (RUS) 34 Ef 33
Vetlužskij (RUS) 34 Ef 33
7080 Vetovo (BG) 72 Cg 47
01019 Vetralla (I) 84 Bc 48
9220 Vetrino (BG) 73 Ch 47
Vetryna (BY) 42 Ci 35
99981 Vetsikko (FIN) 15 Ch 21
8630 Veurne = Furnes (B) 53 Ac 39
1800* Vevey (CH) 68 Ag 44
53074 Vévi (GR) 86 Cb 50
05400 Veynes (F) 68 Af 46
Veža (RUS) 33 Ed 29
Vezdino (RUS) 26 Ek 28
89450 Vézelay (F) 67 Ad 43
55900 Vezirköprü (TR) 89 Df 49
86501 Vi (S) 21 Bh 28
7090-220* Viana do Alentejo (P) 92 Sb 52
32550 Viana do Bolo (E) 80 Sc 48
4900-001* Viana do Castelo (P) 80 Sb 49
55049 Viareggio (I) 69 Ba 47
34450 Vias (F) 67 Ad 47
8800 Viborg (DK) 38 Ak 34
89900 Vibo Valentia (I) 85 Bg 52
72320 Vibraye (F) 53 Aa 42
08500 Vic (E) 82 Ac 49
09220 Vicdessos (F) 82 Ab 48
Vicebck (BY) 42 Da 35
65500* Vic-en-Bigorre (F) 66 Aa 47
36100 Vicenza (I) 69 Bb 45
32190 Vic-Fezensac (F) 66 Aa 47
03200* Vichy (F) 67 Ad 44
20160 Vico (F) 83 Ai 48
727610 Vicovu de Sus (RO) 72 Cf 43
15800 Vic-sur-Cère (F) 67 Ac 46
Victoria (M) 84 Be 54
505700 Victoria (RO) 72 Ce 45
Vičuga (RUS) 33 Eb 33
Vidamlja (BY) 57 Cd 38
750 Viðareiði (FO) 50 Sd 28
6920 Videbæk (DK) 38 Ai 34
145300 Videle (RO) 72 Cf 46
750 Vidhareidhi = Viðareiði (FO) 50 Sd 28
7960-421 Vidigueira (P) 92 Sc 52
3700* Vidin (BG) 71 Cc 47
Vidlica (RUS) 31 Dc 29
627415 Vidra (RO) 72 Cg 45
627415 Vidra (RO) 72 Cg 46
94295 Vidsel (S) 22 Ca 25
60037 Vidukle (LT) 41 Cc 35
Vidzy (BY) 41 Cg 35
94234 Viechtach (D) 55 Bc 41
2430-592* Vieira de Leiria (P) 80 Sb 51
89094 Viekšniai (LT) 41 Cc 34
25530 Vielha e Mijaran (E) 82 Aa 48
25530 Viella-Mitg Arán = Vielha e Mijaran (E) 82 Aa 48
38690 Vienenburg (D) 55 Ba 39
38200 Vienne (F) 67 Ae 45
74200 Vieremä (FIN) 23 Ch 27
19120 Vierumäki (FIN) 30 Cf 29
18100* Vierzon (F) 67 Ac 43
Viesite (LV) 41 Cf 34
71019 Vieste (I) 85 Bg 49
Vietas (S) 14 Bi 23
21058 Vievis (LT) 41 Ce 36
38450 Vif (F) 68 Af 45
4560 Vig (DK) 39 Bb 35
30120 Vigan, le (F) 67 Ad 47
Vigeland (N) 28 Ah 32
27029 Vigevano (I) 68 Ai 45
80650 Vignacourt (F) 53 Ac 40
41058 Vignola (I) 69 Ba 46
36201 Vigo (E) 80 Sb 48
4362 Vigrestad (N) 28 Af 32
86401 Vihanti (FIN) 22 Ce 26
49310 Vihiers (F) 66 Sk 43
79940 Vihtari (FIN) 23 Ci 28
03401 Vihti (FIN) 30 Ce 30
37831 Viiala (FIN) 30 Cd 29
41661 Viisanmäki (FIN) 22 Cg 28
44501 Viitasaari (FIN) 22 Cf 27
45202 Viitna (EST) 30 Cg 31
30321* Viivikonna (EST) 31 Ch 31
Vijtivci (UA) 58 Cg 41
Vík (IS) 48 Rb 27
6894 Vik (N) 28 Ag 29
6894 Vik (N) 21 Bc 25

204 I **Vampula**

97510 Vikajärvi (FIN) 15 Cg 24
5994 Vikanes (N) 28 Af 30
Vikastir (S) 29 Be 30
6470 Vike (N) 28 Af 30
87194 Viksjö (S) 21 Bh 28
6894 Viksøyri (N) 28 Ag 29
6100-598 Vila de Rei (P) 80 Sb 51
8650-405* Vila do Bispo (P) 92 Sb 53
4480-001* Vila do Conde (P) 80 Sb 49
5360-301* Vila Flor (P) 80 Sc 49
08720 Vilafranca del Penedès (E) 82 Ab 49
2600-002* Vila Franca de Xira (P) 92 Sb 52
36600 Vilagarcía de Arousa (E) 80 Sb 48
03570 Vila Joiosa, la (E) 82 Sk 52
4583 Viļaka (LV) 31 Ch 33
27800 Vilalba (E) 80 Sc 47
4650 Viļāni (LV) 41 Cg 34
4920-201* Vila Nova de Cerveira (P) 80 Sb 49
4760-019* Vila Nova de Famalicão (P) 80 Sb 49
Vila Nova de Foz Côa (P) 80 Sc 49
4400-001* Vila Nova de Gaia (P) 80 Sb 49
7645-211* Vila Nova de Milfontes (P) 92 Sb 53
2435-019 Vila Nova de Ourém (P) 80 Sb 51
3650-194* Vila Nova de Paiva (P) 80 Sc 50
08800 Vilanova i la Geltrú (E) 82 Ab 49
5450-001* Vila Pouca de Aguiar (P) 80 Sc 49
12540 Vila-real (E) 82 Sk 51
5000-047* Vila Real (P) 80 Sc 49
8900-201* Vila Real de Santo António (P) 92 Sc 53
6355-201* Vilar Formoso (P) 80 Sd 50
6030-001* Vila Velha de Ródão (P) 80 Sc 51
7830-480* Vila Verde de Ficalho (P) 92 Sc 53
7160-050 Vila Viçosa (P) 92 Sc 52
23220 Vilches (E) 93 Sg 52
Vilejka (BY) 41 Cg 36
Vil'gort (RUS) 35 Fg 30
91201 Vilhelmina (S) 21 Bg 26
71003* Viljandi (EST) 30 Cf 32
70001 Vilkaviškis (LT) 41 Cd 36
54015 Vilkija (LT) 41 Cd 35
24100 Villablino (E) 80 Sd 48
20150 Villabona (E) 80 Se 47
45860 Villacañas (E) 81 Sg 51
39640 Villacarriedo (E) 66 Sg 47
23300 Villacarrillo (E) 93 Sg 52
40150 Villacastín (E) 81 Sf 50
9500* Villach (A) 69 Bd 44
09039 Villacidro (I) 83 Ai 51
34340 Villada (E) 81 Sf 48
14640 Villa del Río (E) 93 Sf 53
09120 Villadiego (E) 81 Sf 48
24500 Villafranca del Bierzo (E) 80 Sd 48
Villafranca del Cid (E) 82 Sk 50
06220 Villafranca de los Barros (E) 92 Sd 52
45730 Villafranca de los Caballeros (E) 81 Sg 51
08720 Villafranca del Panadés = Vilafranca del Penedès (E) 82 Ab 49
37069 Villafranca di Verona (I) 69 Ba 45
09344 Villafruela (E) 81 Sg 49
14210 Villaharta (E) 93 Sf 52
13332 Villahermosa (E) 93 Sh 52
09343 Villahoz (E) 81 Sg 48
53700 Villaines-la-Juhel (F) 52 Sk 42
Villajoyosa = Vila Joiosa, la (E) 93 Sk 52
47600 Villalón de Campos (E) 80 Se 48
49630 Villalpando (E) 80 Se 49
13343 Villamanrique (E) 93 Sg 52
11650 Villamartín (E) 92 Se 54
05380 Villamayor (E) 80 Se 49
16415 Villamayor de Santiago (E) 81 Sh 51
33730 Villandraut (F) 66 Sk 46
07019 Villanova Monteleone (I) 83 Ai 50
47620 Villanubla (E) 81 Sf 49
14440 Villanueva de Córdoba (E) 93 Sf 52
50830 Villanueva de Gállego (E) 82 Sk 49
13330 Villanueva de la Fuente (E) 93 Sh 52
06700 Villanueva de la Serena (E) 80 Se 52
49580 Villanueva de la Sierra (E) 80 Sd 50
49100 Villanueva del Campo (E) 80 Se 49
06110 Villanueva del Fresno (E) 92 Sc 52
21540 Villanueva de los Castillejos (E) 92 Sc 53
47174 Villanueva de los Infantes (E) 93 Sg 52
14230 Villanueva del Rey (E) 92 Se 52
41350 Villanueva del Río y Mina (E) 92 Se 53
08800 Villanueva y Geltrú = Vilanova i la Geltrú (E) 82 Ab 49
7773 Villány (H) 71 Bi 45
09550 Villarcayo (E) 81 Sg 48
05480 Villar-d'Arène (F) 68 Ag 45
38190 Villard-Bonnet (F) 68 Af 45
38250 Villard-de-Lans (F) 68 Af 45
49562 Villardeciervos (E) 80 Sd 49
46170 Villar del Arzobispo (E) 82 Sk 51
06192 Villar del Rey (E) 80 Sd 51
16432 Villarejo de Fuentes (E) 81 Sh 51
28590 Villarejo de Salvanés (E) 81 Sg 50
Villarente (E) 80 Se 48
12540 Villarreal de los Infantes = Vila-real (E) 82 Sk 51
49137 Villarrín de Campos (E) 80 Se 49
13670 Villarrubia de los Ojos (E) 81 Sg 51
28150 Villars (F) 53 Ab 42
06678 Villarta de los Montes (E) 81 Sf 51
09580 Villasana de Mena (E) 81 Sg 47
33029 Villa Santina (I) 69 Bc 44
09049 Villasimius (I) 83 Ak 51
33300 Villaviciosa (E) 80 Se 47
14300 Villaviciosa de Córdoba (E) 92 Se 52
67220 Villé (F) 54 Ah 42
50800 Villedieu-les-Poêles (F) 52 Si 42
31290 Villefranche-de-Lauragais (F) 67 Ab 47
12200* Villefranche-de-Rouergue (F) 67 Ac 46
69400* Villefranche-sur-Saône (F) 67 Ae 45
03400 Villena (E) 93 Sk 52
10370 Villenauxe-la-Grande (F) 53 Ad 42
33121 Villeneuve (F) 67 Ac 46
40190 Villeneuve-de-Marsan (F) 66 Sk 47
89190 Villeneuve-l'Archevêque (F) 53 Ad 42
30400* Villeneuve-lès-Avignon (F) 67 Ae 47
47300* Villeneuve-sur-Lot (F) 66 Aa 46
89500 Villeneuve-sur-Yonne (F) 53 Ad 42
02600* Villers-Cotterêts (F) 53 Ad 41
54190 Villerupt (F) 54 Af 41
69100* Villeurbanne (F) 67 Ae 45
78048* Villingen-Schwenningen (D) 54 Ai 42
6985 Vilnes (N) 28 Ae 29
01001* Vilnius (LT) 41 Cf 36
Vil'njans'k (UA) 74 Df 43
Vil'nohirs'k (UA) 59 De 42
35701 Vilppula (FIN) 22 Ce 28
Vil'šana (UA) 59 Dd 40
Vil'šanka (UA) 59 Da 42
Vil'šany (UA) 60 Df 40
84137 Vilsbiburg (D) 55 Bc 42
94474 Vilshofen (D) 55 Bd 42
81 423 Vilusi (MNE) 85 Bi 48
Vil'va (RUS) 36 Fi 32
1800* Vilvoorde (B) 53 Ae 40
15129 Vimianzo (E) 80 Sa 47
7040-010 Vimieiro (P) 92 Sc 52
5230-300* Vimioso (P) 80 Sd 49
59801 Vimmerby (S) 29 Bf 33
61120 Vimoutiers (F) 53 Aa 42
62800 Vimpeli (FIN) 22 Cd 27
385 01 Vimperk (CZ) 55 Bd 41
12500 Vinaròs (E) 82 Aa 50
18879 Viñas, Las (E) 93 Sg 53
707575 Vinători (RO) 71 Cc 46
50059 Vinci (I) 69 Ba 47
92201 Vindeln (S) 22 Bk 26
7830 Vinderup (DK) 38 Ai 34
Vindrej (RUS) 44 Ec 36
317400 Vinga (RO) 71 Cb 44
64301 Vingåker (S) 29 Bf 31
Vinhais (P) 80 Sc 49
2310 Vinica (MK) 86 Cc 49
3890 Vinje (N) 28 Ag 30
Vin'kivci (UA) 58 Ch 41
Vinkovci (HR) 71 Bi 45
Vinnica = Vinnycja (UA) 58 Ci 41
Vinnicy (RUS) 32 De 30
Vinnycja (UA) 58 Ci 41
Vinogradnoe (RUS) 76 Ee 47
83560 Vinon-sur-Verdon (F) 68 Af 47
28820 Vinslöv (S) 39 Bd 34
2640 Vinstra (N) 28 Ak 29
Vintjärn (S) 29 Bg 30
42150 Vinuesa (E) 81 Sh 49
Viny (RUS) 31 Dc 32
39049 Vipiteno = Sterzing (I) 69 Bb 44
Vira (HR) 70 Bg 47
Virandozero (RUS) 24 Dg 26
Viranşehir (TR) 91 Ea 51
Viranşehir (TR) 97 De 54
Viranşehir (TR) 98 Dk 53
14500 Vire (F) 52 Sk 42
4355 Vireši (LV) 30 Cg 33
Virga (RUS) 45 Ee 37
Virginia = Achadhan Iúir (IRL) 49 Sc 37
Virma (RUS) 24 Df 26
56210 Virmutjoki (FIN) 31 Ci 29
49900* Virojoki = Virolahti (FIN) 31 Ch 30
49901 Virolahti (FIN) 31 Ch 30
Virovitica (HR) 70 Bh 45
81 305 Virpazar (MNE) 86 Bk 48
34801 Virrat (FIN) 22 Cd 28
57080 Virserum (S) 29 Bf 33
99860 Virtaniemi (FIN) 15 Ci 22
6760 Virton (B) 54 Af 41
90101 Virtsu (EST) 30 Cd 32
32560 Virttaa (FIN) 30 Cc 30
Vis (HR) 85 Bg 47
Vis (RUS) 26 Fe 27
31001 Visaginas (LT) 41 Cg 35
62100* Visby (S) 29 Bi 33
4600 Visé (B) 54 Af 40
Višegrad (BIH) 71 Bk 47
3500-001* Viseu (P) 80 Sc 50
435700 Vişeu de Sus (RO) 72 Ce 43
Visim (RUS) 36 Fk 33
137515 Vişina (RO) 72 Ce 47
137515 Vişina (RO) 72 Cf 46
Visjučij Bor (RUS) 31 Dc 33
51520 Viskafors (S) 29 Bc 33
Viškil' (RUS) 34 Ei 32
34030 Vislanda (S) 39 Be 34
Višneva (BY) 41 Cg 36
Višnevaja (RUS) 43 Dh 36
Višnevka (RUS) 62 Eg 41
Višnevka (RUS) 75 Dk 47
Višnevoe (RUS) 61 Ed 38
Višnevogorsk (RUS) 47 Ga 34
14470 Viso, El (E) 93 Sf 52
13770 Viso del Marqués (E) 93 Sg 52
Visoko (BIH) 71 Bi 47
3930 Visp (CH) 68 Ah 44
36060 Vissefjärda (S) 39 Bf 34
27374 Visselhövede (D) 38 Ak 38
62039 Visso (I) 84 Bd 48
Vistabella del Maestrat (E) 82 Sk 50
Vistheden (S) 22 Ca 25
70037 Vištytis (LT) 41 Cc 36
Vitanovac (SRB) 71 Ca 47
Vitebsk = Vicebck (BY) 42 Da 35
01100 Viterbo (I) 84 Bc 48
Vitez (BIH) 70 Bh 46
Vithkuq (AL) 86 Ca 50
37210 Vitigudino (E) 80 Sd 49
Vitina (BIH) 70 Bh 47
22010 Vitina (GR) 94 Cc 53
61000 Vitina (SRB) 86 Cb 48
7508 Vitolište (MK) 86 Cb 49
Vitoria = Gasteiz (E) 81 Sh 48
79370 Vitré (F) 52 Si 42
51300 Vitry-le-François (F) 53 Ae 42
94400 Vitry-sur-Seine (F) 53 Ac 42
98010 Vittangi (S) 15 Cb 23
21350 Vitteaux (F) 67 Ae 43
88800* Vittel (F) 54 Af 42
97019 Vittoria (I) 84 Be 54
31029 Vittorio Veneto (I) 69 Bc 44
20219 Vivario (F) 83 Ak 48
27850 Viveiro (E) 80 Sc 47
Vivel del Río Martín (E) 82 Sk 50
07220 Viviers (F) 67 Ae 46
86370 Vivonne (F) 66 Aa 44
Vižaj (RUS) 36 Ga 29
Vižas (RUS) 17 Ef 24
39400 Vize (TR) 88 Ch 49
38220 Vizille (F) 68 Af 45
Vizim'jary (RUS) 45 Eg 34
Vižinada (HR) 69 Bd 45
Vizinga (RUS) 34 Fa 29
817215 Viziru (RO) 73 Ch 45
763 12 Vizovice (CZ) 56 Bh 41
95049 Vizzini (I) 84 Be 53
Vjalikaja Berestavica (BY) 41 Ce 37
Vjalikie Čunavići (BY) 58 Cg 38
Vjartsilja (RUS) 23 Da 28
Vjatskie Poljany (RUS) 46 Fb 34
Vjatskoe (RUS) 33 Ea 33
Vjaz'ma (RUS) 43 De 35
Vjazniki (RUS) 44 Ec 34
Vjazovka (RUS) 45 Ei 38
Vjazovka (RUS) 62 Ef 42
Vjazovka (RUS) 62 Eg 38
Vjazovo (RUS) 44 Dk 37
Vjazovoe (RUS) 60 Dg 39
Vjazovoe (RUS) 63 Fd 39
3130* Vlaardingen (NL) 53 Ae 39
Vlad (AL) 86 Ca 48
1641 Vladaja (BG) 87 Cd 48
17510 Vladičin Han (SRB) 86 Cc 48
Vladikavkaz (RUS) 91 Ee 48
Vladimir (RUS) 44 Ea 34
85 366 Vladimir (MNE) 86 Bk 48
9379 Vladimirovo (BG) 72 Cd 47
Vladimirskoe (RUS) 43 Dd 35
917295 Vlad Tepeş (RO) 73 Ch 46
Vladyčnoe (RUS) 33 Dk 32
Vladyslavivka 74 Df 45
147135 Vlaşca, Drăgăneşti- (RO) 72 Cf 46
17507 Vlase (SRB) 86 Cb 48
Vlasenica (BIH) 71 Bi 46
258 01 Vlašim (CZ) 55 Be 41
087203 Vlaşin (RO) 72 Cf 46
16210 Vlasotince (SRB) 86 Cc 48
4380* Vlissingen (NL) 53 Ad 39
034 03 Vlkolínec (SK) 56 Bk 41
Vlorë (AL) 86 Bk 50
Vnukovo (RUS) 43 Dh 35
Voč' (RUS) 35 Fe 29
Voćin (HR) 70 Bh 45
4840* Vöcklabruck (A) 55 Bd 43
Vodice (HR) 70 Bf 47
Vodla (RUS) 24 Dh 28
389 01 Vodňany (CZ) 55 Be 41
Vodnjan (HR) 69 Bd 46
Vodnyj (RUS) 26 Fd 27
ZE2 Voe (GB) 50 Si 30
9300 Voerså (DK) 28 Ba 33
190 Vogar (IS) 48 Qh 26
52053 Vogatsikó (GR) 86 Cb 50
27058 Voghera (I) 68 Ai 46
Vogulka (RUS) 35 Fg 31
Vogulka (RUS) 36 Fi 33
Vogvazdino (RUS) 26 Fa 28
92648 Vohenstrauß (D) 55 Bc 41
Võhma (EST) 30 Cc 32
70601 Võhma (EST) 30 Cf 32
Vohma (RUS) 34 Eg 32
Vohtoga (RUS) 33 Eb 32
Vohtozero (RUS) 23 Dd 28
737300 Voineşti (RO) 72 Cf 45
38500 Voiron (F) 68 Af 45
Voja, Ust'- (RUS) 27 Fh 26
12950 Vojakkala (FIN) 30 Ce 30
6500 Vojens (DK) 38 Ak 35
Vojinka 74 Dd 45
Vojkove 74 Dd 45
Vojnić (HR) 70 Bf 45
Vojnica (RUS) 23 Da 25
Vojnovo (BG) 73 Ch 47
Vojvož (RUS) 26 Ff 28
Voknavolok (RUS) 23 Da 26
384 51 Volary (CZ) 55 Bd 42
Volčansk (RUS) 36 Ga 31
Volčki (RUS) 61 Ea 38
6100 Volda (N) 20 Ag 28
Vol'dino (RUS) 26 Fe 28
Voldozero (RUS) 23 Dd 27
Volga (RUS) 32 Di 33
Volgino (RUS) 32 Dd 32
Volgodonsk (RUS) 76 Ec 43
Volgograd (RUS) 61 Ee 42
Volgorečensk (RUS) 33 Eb 33
Volhov (RUS) 31 Dc 31
29091 Volímes (GR) 94 Ca 53
4241 Volintiri (MD) 73 Ck 44
82103 Volissós (GR) 95 Cf 52
97332 Volkach (D) 55 Ba 41
9100* Völkermarkt (A) 70 Be 44
66333 Völklingen (D) 54 Ag 41
Volkonskoe (RUS) 43 Df 37
1255 Volkovija (MK) 86 Ca 49
Vol'noe (RUS) 77 Eh 43
Volnovacha (UA) 75 Dh 43
Voločaevskij (RUS) 76 Ec 44
Voločys'k (UA) 58 Cg 41
Volodarka (UA) 58 Ck 41
Volodarsk (RUS) 44 Ed 34
Volodars'ke = Nikol's'ke (UA) 75 Dh 43
Volodarskij (RUS) 77 Ei 44
Volodars'k-Volynskyj (UA) 58 Ci 40
Volodymyrec' (UA) 58 Cg 39
Volodymyr-Volyns'kyj (UA) 57 Ce 40
Voloe (RUS) 43 De 36
Vologda (RUS) 33 Dk 31
Volohiv Jar (UA) 60 Dg 41
Volokolamsk (RUS) 43 Df 34
Volokonovka (RUS) 60 Dh 40
Volokonovka (RUS) 60 Dk 41
Volokovaja (RUS) 18 Ei 24
Volokovye (RUS) 35 Fc 32
Voloma (RUS) 23 Db 27
Volonga (RUS) 18 Eh 23
38001 Vólos (GR) 86 Cc 51
Volosovo (RUS) 31 Ck 31
Volost' (RUS) 24 Dk 26
Vološyno (RUS) 60 Dk 42
Volot (RUS) 31 Da 33
Volotovo (RUS) 60 Di 40
Volovec' (UA) 57 Cd 42
Volovo (RUS) 43 Di 37
Volovo (RUS) 60 Dh 38
Vol'sk (RUS) 62 Eh 38
56048 Volterra (I) 69 Ba 47
Volyns'kyj, Novohrad- (UA) 58 Ch 40
Volynskyj, Volodars'k- (UA) 58 Ci 40
Volyns'kyj, Volodymyr- (UA) 57 Ce 40
Volžsk (RUS) 45 Ei 35
Volžskij (RUS) 61 Ee 42
Vondanka (RUS) 34 Eh 31
Von'ga (RUS) 24 De 25
Vonga (RUS) 25 Ed 26
30002 Vónitsa (GR) 94 Ca 52
Vonozero (RUS) 32 De 30
Vopnafjörður (IS) 48 Rf 25
Voranava (BY) 41 Cf 36
Vorb'evka (RUS) 61 Ea 40
Vorčanka (RUS) 34 Ek 31
4760 Vordingborg (DK) 39 Bb 35
Vorë (AL) 86 Bk 49
Vorenža (RUS) 24 Df 27
38340 Voreppe (F) 68 Af 45
Vorga (RUS) 42 Dc 37
Vorgašor (RUS) 19 Gd 23
Vorkuta (RUS) 19 Gd 23
Vorob'ëbo (RUS) 35 Fe 31
Voroncovka (RUS) 61 Ea 40
Voron'e (RUS) 33 Ec 32
Voroneţ (RO) 72 Cf 43
Voronež (RUS) 60 Dk 39
Voronežskaja (RUS) 75 Dk 45
Voroniž (UA) 59 Dd 39
Voronovycja (UA) 58 Ci 41
Vorošilovgrad = Luhans'k (UA) 60 Dk 42
Vorotynec (RUS) 45 Ef 34
Vorožba (UA) 59 De 39
Vorožba (UA) 59 De 40
Vorožgora (RUS) 24 Df 27
Vorsma (RUS) 44 Ed 35
65603* Võru (EST) 31 Ch 33
Vorzogory (RUS) 24 Dh 27
Voshod (RUS) 44 Ec 36
Voshod (RUS) 77 Ef 43
Voskopojë (AL) 86 Ca 50
Voskresenka (UA) 74 De 44
Voskresensk (RUS) 43 Di 35
Voskresenskoe (RUS) 32 Dh 33
Voskresenskoe (RUS) 32 Di 32
Voskresenskoe (RUS) 43 Di 37
Voskresenskoe (RUS) 45 Ef 34
Voskresenskoe (RUS) 47 Fg 37
Vospuška (RUS) 44 Dk 34
5700 Voss (N) 28 Ag 30
Vostočnaja Lica (RUS) 16 Dh 22
Vostočnoe Munozero (RUS) 16 De 23
Vostočnyj (RUS) 36 Gb 32
259 01 Votice (CZ) 55 Be 41
Votkinsk (RUS) 46 Fe 34
16608 Vouliagméni (GR) 94 Cd 53
07800 Voulte-sur-Rhône, la (F) 67 Ae 46
3670-231* Vouzela (P) 80 Sb 50
08400 Vouziers (F) 53 Ae 41
Vovčans'k (UA) 60 Dg 40
Vovna (UA) 59 Dd 38
82801 Voxna (S) 29 Bf 29
Vožael' (RUS) 26 Fb 28
Vozdviženka (RUS) 46 Fe 37
Vozdviženskoe (RUS) 43 Dg 34
Vozdviženskoe (RUS) 45 Ef 34
Vožega (RUS) 33 Ea 29
Vožgaly (RUS) 34 Fa 32
Vožgora (RUS) 26 Ei 26
Voznesen'e (RUS) 32 Df 29
Voznesens'k (UA) 74 Db 43
Voznesenskaja (RUS) 76 Eb 46
Voznesenskoe (RUS) 35 Fe 32
Voznesenskoe (RUS) 44 Ec 36
Vozroždenie (RUS) 45 Ei 38
Vozsijats'ke (UA) 74 Dc 43
Vrå (S) 39 Bd 34
952 01 Vráble (SK) 56 Bi 42
3000* Vraca (BG) 72 Cd 47
Vrácevšnica (SRB) 71 Ca 46
3853 Vrådal (N) 28 Ai 31
Vradijivka (UA) 73 Da 43
Vrana (HR) 70 Bf 47
Vranduk (BIH) 70 Bh 46
9663 Vranino (BG) 73 Ci 47
17501* Vranje (SRB) 86 Cb 48
17541* Vranjska Banja (SRB) 86 Cc 48
19344 Vratarnica (SRB) 71 Cc 47
793 23 Vrbno pod Pradědem (CZ) 56 Bh 40
922 03 Vrbové (SK) 56 Bh 42
Vrbovec (HR) 70 Bg 45
Vrbovsko (HR) 70 Bf 45
543 01* Vrchlabí (CZ) 56 Bf 40

A B C D E F G H I J K L M N O P Q R S T U V W X Y Z

Vrchlabí I 205

Vrelo (SRB) 71 Cb 47
Vrginmost (HR) 70 Bf 45
Vrgorac (HR) 85 Bh 47
1386 Vrhnika (SLO) 70 Be 45
7670 Vriezenveen (NL) 54 Ag 38
57601 Vrigstad (S) 29 Be 33
81300 Vrissa (GR) 87 Cg 51
Vrlika (HR) 70 Bg 47
36210 Vrnjačka Banja (SRB) 71 Ca 47
Vrondādos (GR) 95 Cg 52
Vrondoū (GR) 86 Cc 50
Vrouhas (GR) 95 Cf 55
Vrpolje (HR) 71 Bi 45
26300* Vršac (SRB) 71 Cb 45
Vrtoče (BIH) 70 Bg 46
755 01 Vsetín (CZ) 56 Bh 41
Vsevolodo-Vil'va (RUS) 35 Fh 31
Vsevoložsk (RUS) 31 Da 30
Vshody (RUS) 43 De 36
Vtoraja Pjatiletka (RUS) 61 Ec 38
Vtorye Levye Lamki (RUS) 44 Eb 37
42000 Vučitrn = Vushtri (RKS) 86 Ca 48
5260* Vught (NL) 54 Af 39
Vukovar (HR) 71 Bi 45
Vukpalaj-Bajzë (AL) 86 Bk 48
Vuktyl (RUS) 27 Fh 27
7660 Vuku (N) 20 Bb 27
5300 Vulcăneşti (MD) 73 Ci 45
99690 Vuohčču = Vuotso (FIN) 15 Ch 22
86810 Vuohtomäki (FIN) 22 Cg 27
88610 Vuokatti (FIN) 23 Ci 26
88270 Vuolijoki (FIN) 22 Cg 26
96030 Vuollerim (S) 14 Ca 24
Vuonatjviken (S) 14 Bh 24
Vuorijarvi (RUS) 16 Da 24
98360 Vuostimo (FIN) 15 Ch 24
99690 Vuotso (FIN) 15 Ch 22
Vuottas (S) 15 Cb 24
99970 Vuovdakuoihka = Outakoski (FIN) 15 Cg 21
Vurnary (RUS) 45 Eg 35
557295 Vurpăr (RO) 72 Ce 45
42000 Vushtri = Vučitrn (RKS) 86 Ca 48
Vuzlovyj, Kup'jans'k- (UA) 60 Dh 41
Vybor (RUS) 31 Ck 33
Vyborg (RUS) 31 Ci 30
Vydropužsk (RUS) 32 De 33
Vyezdnoe (RUS) 44 Ed 35
Vygoniči (RUS) 43 De 37
Vyksa (RUS) 44 Ed 35
Vylkove (UA) 73 Ck 45
Vynnyky (UA) 57 Ce 41
Vynogradiv = Vynohradiv (UA) 57 Cd 42
Vynohradiv (UA) 57 Cd 42
Vypolzovo (RUS) 32 Dd 33
Vyra (RUS) 31 Ck 31
Vyrica (RUS) 31 Da 31
Vyrišal'ne (UA) 59 Dd 40
Vyša (RUS) 44 Ec 37
Vyšča Dubečnja (UA) 59 Da 40
Vyščetarasivka (UA) 74 De 43
Vyselki (RUS) 75 Dk 45
Vyšhorod (UA) 59 Da 40
Vyška (RUS) 34 Ef 32
Vyškiv (UA) 57 Cd 42
Vyskod' (RUS) 31 Da 33
Vyškov (BY) 59 Db 38
682 01* Vyškov (CZ) 56 Bh 41
Vyškove (UA) 57 Cd 42
Vyšnie Dereven'ki (RUS) 60 Df 39
Vyšnij Voloček (RUS) 32 De 33
Vyšnivec' (UA) 58 Cg 41
Vysokae (BY) 57 Cd 38
Vysokaja (RUS) 25 Ee 26
Vysokaja (RUS) 34 Ef 31
Vysokaja (RUS) 34 Eh 32
Vysokaja Gora (RUS) 45 Ek 35
Vysoka Pič (UA) 58 Ci 40
565 41* Vysoké Mýto (CZ) 56 Bg 41
Vysokiniči (RUS) 43 Dg 36
Vysokoe (RUS) 33 Dk 31
Vysokoe (RUS) 43 De 34
Vysokoe (RUS) 44 Eb 37
Vysokopil'l'a (UA) 74 Dd 43
Vysokovsk (RUS) 43 Dg 34
382 73 Vyšší Brod (CZ) 55 Be 42
Vytegra (RUS) 32 Dg 29
Vyučeskij (RUS) 18 Ek 23
Vyžnycja (UA) 58 Cf 42

W

5140* Waalwijk (NL) 54 Af 39
87-200 Wąbrzeźno (PL) 40 Bi 37
8820 Wädenswil (CH) 68 Ai 43
34-100 Wadowice (PL) 56 Bk 41
62-100 Wągrowiec (PL) 40 Bh 38
71332* Waiblingen (D) 54 Ak 42
3830 Waidhofen an der Thaya (A) 56 Bf 42
3340 Waidhofen an der Ybbs (A) 70 Be 43
WF1 Wakefield (GB) 51 Si 37
58-300* Wałbrzych (PL) 56 Bg 40
78-600 Wałcz (PL) 40 Bg 37
51545 Waldbröl (D) 54 Ah 40
88339 Waldsee, Bad (D) 69 Ak 43
CH44 Wallasey (GB) 51 Sg 37
74731 Walldürn (D) 54 Ak 41
WS1 Walsall (GB) 52 Si 38
29664 Walsrode (D) 38 Ak 38
99880 Waltershausen (D) 55 Ba 40
CO14 Walton-on-the-Naze (GB) 53 Ab 39
88239 Wangen im Allgäu (D) 69 Ak 43
39164 Wanzleben-Börde (D) 55 Bb 38
34414 Warburg (D) 54 Ak 39
26203 Wardenburg (D) 38 Ai 37
OX29 Ware (GB) 52 Sk 39
8790 Waregem (B) 53 Ad 40
17192 Waren (Müritz) (D) 39 Bc 37
48231 Warendorf (D) 54 Ah 39
05-660 Warka (PL) 57 Cb 39
BA12 Warminster (GB) 52 Sh 39
18119 Warnemünde (D) 39 Bc 36
WA5 Warrington (GB) 51 Sh 37
59581 Warstein (D) 54 Ai 39
00-001* Warszawa (PL) 57 Cb 38
98-290 Warta (PL) 56 Bi 39
CV34 Warwick (GB) 52 Si 38
6484 Wassen (CH) 68 Ai 44
2240* Wassenaar (NL) 53 Ae 38
83512 Wasserburg am Inn (D) 55 Bc 42
TA23 Watchet (GB) 52 Sg 39
Waterford = Port Láirge (IRL) 49 Sc 38
1410* Waterloo (B) 53 Ae 40
Waterville = An Coireán (IRL) 49 Rk 39
WD17 Watford (GB) 52 Sk 39
59143 Watten (F) 53 Ac 40
9630 Wattwil (CH) 69 Ak 43
28-411 Węchadłów (PL) 57 Ca 40
6223 Weert (NL) 54 Af 39
11-600 Węgorzewo (PL) 40 Cb 36
Węgorzynowo (PL) 39 Bf 37
07-100 Węgrów (PL) 57 Cc 38
07570 Weida (D) 55 Bc 40
92637 Weiden in der Oberpfalz (D) 55 Bc 41
97990 Weikersheim (D) 54 Ak 41
35781 Weilburg (D) 54 Ai 40
82362 Weilheim in Oberbayern (D) 69 Bb 43
99423* Weimar (D) 55 Bb 40
69469 Weinheim (D) 54 Ai 41
91781 Weißenburg in Bayern (D) 55 Ba 41
06667 Weißenfels (D) 55 Bb 39
89264 Weißenhorn (D) 55 Ba 42
02943 Weißwasser (D) 55 Be 39
3970* Weitra (A) 55 Be 42
8160 Weiz (A) 70 Bf 43
84-200 Wejherowo (PL) 40 Bi 36
TA21 Wellington (GB) 52 Sg 40
BA5 Wells (GB) 52 Sh 39
NR23 Wells-next-the-Sea (GB) 51 Aa 38
4600* Wels (A) 55 Be 42
SY21 Welshpool (GB) 51 Sg 38
14542 Werder (Havel) (D) 55 Bc 38
49757 Werlte (D) 38 Ah 38
59368 Werne (D) 54 Ah 39
38855 Wernigerode (D) 55 Ba 39
97877 Wertheim (D) 54 Ak 41
46483* Wesel (D) 54 Ag 39
25764 Wesselburen (D) 38 Ai 36
BA13 Westbury (GB) 52 Sh 39
56457 Westerburg (D) 54 Ah 40
25980 Westerland (D) 38 Ai 35
26655 Westerstede (D) 38 Ah 37
BS23 Weston-Super-Mare (GB) 52 Sh 39
Westport = Cathair na Mairt (IRL) 49 Sa 37
LS22 Wetherby (GB) 51 Si 37
9230 Wetteren (B) 53 Ad 39
35576* Wetzlar (D) 54 Ai 40
Wexford = Loch Garman (IRL) 49 Sd 38
3335 Weyer (A) 70 Be 43
DT4 Weymouth (GB) 52 Sh 40
YO21 Whitby (GB) 51 Sk 36
HP22 Whitchurch (GB) 51 Sh 38
KW17 Whitehall (GB) 50 Sh 31
CA28 Whitehaven (GB) 51 Sg 36
DG8 Whithorn, Isle of (GB) 51 Sf 36
KW1 Wick (GB) 50 Sg 32
Wicklow = Cill Mhantáin (IRL) 49 Sd 38
84-352 Wicko (PL) 40 Bh 36
89-410 Więcbork (PL) 40 Bh 37
12-160 Wielbark (PL) 40 Ca 37
64-730 Wieleń (PL) 40 Bg 38
32-020 Wieliczka (PL) 57 Ca 41
98-300 Wieluń (PL) 56 Bi 39
1010* Wien (A) 56 Bg 42
2700* Wiener Neustadt (A) 70 Bg 43
86989 Wies (A) 70 Bf 44
65183* Wiesbaden (D) 54 Ai 40
3250* Wieselburg (A) 56 Bf 42
26639 Wiesmoor (D) 38 Ah 37
29323 Wietze (D) 54 Ak 38
WN5 Wigan (GB) 51 Sh 37
6192 Wiggen (CH) 68 Ah 44
CA7 Wigton (GB) 51 Sg 36
DG8 Wigtown (GB) 51 Sf 36
9500* Wil (SG) (CH) 69 Ak 43
14-405 Wilczęta (PL) 40 Bk 36
27793 Wildeshausen (D) 38 Ai 38
26382* Wilhelmshaven (D) 38 Ai 37
4073* Wilhering (A) 55 Be 42
08112 Wilkau-Haßlau (D) 55 Bc 40
2830 Willebroek (B) 53 Ae 39
6130 Willisau (CH) 68 Ah 43
SW20 Wimbledon (GB) 52 Sk 39
BH21 Wimborne Minster (GB) 52 Si 40
SO22 Winchester (GB) 52 Si 39
LA23 Windermere (GB) 51 Sh 36
4580 Windischgarsten (A) 70 Be 43
SL4 Windsor (GB) 52 Sk 39
9670* Winschoten (NL) 38 Ah 37
21423 Winsen (Luhe) (D) 39 Ba 37
8830 Winsum (NL) 38 Ag 37
59955 Winterberg (D) 54 Ai 39
7100* Winterswijk (NL) 54 Ag 39
8400* Winterthur (CH) 68 Ai 43
51688 Wipperfürth (D) 54 Ah 39
PE14 Wisbech (GB) 53 Aa 38
ML1 Wishaw (GB) 51 Sg 35
28-160 Wiślica (PL) 57 Ca 40
23966* Wismar (D) 39 Bb 37
67160* Wissembourg (F) 54 Ah 41
21-580 Wisznice (PL) 57 Cd 39
NE29 Withernsea (GB) 51 Aa 37
OX28 Witney (GB) 52 Si 39
74-503 Witnica (PL) 39 Be 38
19322 Wittenberge (D) 39 Bb 38
19243 Wittenburg (D) 39 Bb 37
29378* Wittingen (D) 39 Ba 38
54516 Wittlich (D) 54 Ag 41
26409 Wittmund (D) 38 Ah 37
16909* Wittstock/Dosse (D) 39 Bc 37
84-120 Władysławowo (PL) 40 Bi 36
87-800 Włocławek (PL) 56 Bk 38
22-200 Włodawa (PL) 57 Cd 39
97-330 Włodzimierzów (PL) 56 Bk 39
29-100 Włoszczowa (PL) 56 Bk 40
28-330 Wodzisław (PL) 57 Ca 40
GU22 Woking (GB) 52 Sk 39
97-371 Wola Krzysztoporska (PL) 56 Bk 39
97-310 Wola Moszczenicka (PL) 56 Bk 39
97-320 Wolbórz (PL) 56 Bk 39
32-340 Wolbrom (PL) 56 Bk 40
17348 Woldegk (D) 39 Bd 37
77709 Wolfach (D) 54 Ai 42
06749 Wolfen, Bitterfeld- (D) 55 Bc 39
38300* Wolfenbüttel (D) 55 Ba 38
06536 Wolfsberg (A) 70 Be 44
38440* Wolfsburg (D) 55 Ba 38
17438 Wolgast (D) 39 Bd 36
72-510 Wolin (PL) 39 Be 37
2120 Wolkersdorf (A) 56 Bg 42
56-100 Wołów (PL) 56 Bg 39
64-200 Wolsztyn (PL) 56 Bg 38
WV6 Wolverhampton (GB) 52 Sh 38
IP12 Woodbridge (GB) 53 Ab 38
WR2 Worcester (GB) 52 Sh 38
6300* Wörgl (A) 69 Bc 43
CA14 Workington (GB) 51 Sg 36
S81 Worksop (GB) 51 Si 37
Workum (NL) 38 Af 38
67549* Worms (D) 54 Ai 41
27726 Worpswede (D) 38 Ai 37
BN11 Worthing (GB) 52 Sk 40
LL13 Wrexham (GB) 51 Sh 37
50-041* Wrocław (PL) 56 Bh 39
64-510 Wronki (PL) 40 Bg 38
62-300 Września (PL) 56 Bh 38
67-400 Wschowa (PL) 56 Bg 39
42103* Wuppertal (D) 54 Ah 39
97070* Würzburg (D) 54 Ak 41
04808 Wurzen (D) 55 Bc 39
18347 Wustrow (Fischland) (D) 39 Bc 36
25938 Wyk auf Föhr (D) 38 Ai 36
88-300 Wylatowo (PL) 56 Bh 38
89-300 Wyrzysk (PL) 40 Bh 37
72-410 Wysoka Kamieńska (PL) 39 Be 37
21-560 Wysokie (PL) 57 Cc 40
07-110 Wyszków (PL) 57 Cb 38
09-450 Wyszogród (PL) 57 Ca 38
26-242 Wyszyna Rudzka (PL) 57 Ca 39

X

46509 Xanten (D) 54 Ag 39
67300 Xánthi (GR) 87 Ce 49
46800 Xàtiva (E) 82 Sk 52
Xerokambos (GR) 95 Cg 55
12360 Xert (E) 82 Aa 50
43592 Xerta (E) 82 Aa 50
69400 Xilaganí (GR) 87 Cf 50
20400 Xilókastro (GR) 94 Cc 52
Xinóvrisi (GR) 87 Cd 51
32630 Xinzo de Limia (E) 80 Sc 48
33027 Xixón = Gijón (E) 80 Se 47

Y

66720 Yağcılar (TR) 88 Ci 51
66720 Yağcılar (TR) 99 Eb 52
Yağlıdere (TR) 90 Di 50
Yağlıdere (TR) 90 Dk 50
Yağmuralan (TR) 98 Di 54
06840 Yağmurdede (TR) 89 Dc 50
Yağmurdere (TR) 90 Dk 50
71450 Yahşihan (TR) 89 Dd 51
58950* Yahyalı (TR) 97 Df 52
Yakacık (TR) 97 Dg 54
01350 Yakapınar (TR) 97 Df 54
61400 Yakfıkebir (TR) 90 Dk 49
58510 Yakupoğlan (TR) 90 Dg 50
41550 Yalakdere (TR) 88 Ck 50
31710 Yalankoz (TR) 98 Dg 54
42470 Yalıhüyük (TR) 96 Dc 53
Yalıköy (TR) 88 Ci 49
65940 Yalınca (TR) 99 Ed 53
46300 Yalıntaş (TR) 98 Dh 52
Yalnızçam (TR) 91 Ec 49
17900* Yalova (TR) 88 Ck 50
32400 Yalvaç (TR) 96 Db 52
Yamaç (TR) 99 Ea 52
Yamak (TR) 89 Dc 51
Yamanlar (TR) 96 Ck 52
Yanarsu (TR) 99 Eb 52
66300 Yanık (TR) 89 Df 51
22400 Yapıldak (TR) 88 Da 51
Yapraklı (TR) 89 Dd 50
45910 Yarbasan (TR) 96 Ci 52
Yardımcı (TR) 98 Dk 53
Yarıkkaya (TR) 96 Db 52
Yarımca (TR) 98 Dh 52
42265 Yarma (TR) 96 Dc 53
Yarpuz (TR) 96 Db 53
Yarpuz (TR) 98 Dg 53
48500 Yatağan (TR) 95 Ci 53
BS37 Yate (GB) 52 Sh 39
Yavacık (TR) 91 Ed 51
Yavşan Tuzlası (TR) 97 Dd 52
27970 Yavuzeli (TR) 98 Dh 53
28960 Yavuzkemal (TR) 90 Di 50
Yavuzlu (TR) 98 Dh 54
49150 Yaygın (TR) 99 Eb 52
Yayla (TR) 99 Ea 52
24800 Yaylacık (TR) 96 Dc 53
31080 Yayladağı (TR) 97 Dg 55
29150 Yaylådere (TR) 91 Ea 51
66700 Yaylak (TR) 98 Di 53
Yaylakonak (TR) 98 Di 53
Yazıçayırı (TR) 89 Dd 51
Yazıhan (TR) 98 Di 52
Yazılı (TR) 97 Dd 53
Yazılı (TR) 98 Dh 54
Yazılıkaya (TR) 88 Da 51
Yazır (TR) 96 Ck 53
Yazır (TR) 96 Ck 54
60800 Yazıtepe (TR) 90 Dg 50
3341 Ybbsitz (A) 70 Be 43
SY16 Y Drenewydd = Newtown (GB) 52 Sg 38
45470 Yébenes, Los (E) 81 Sg 51
30510 Yecla (E) 93 Si 52
Yedisalkım (TR) 99 Ed 52
12830 Yedisu (TR) 91 Ea 51
31560 Yeditepe (TR) 97 Df 54
64610 Yeleğen (TR) 96 Ci 52
Yemişendere (TR) 96 Ci 53
47510 Yemişli (TR) 97 Df 54
Yenibaşak (TR) 99 Eb 52
Yenice (TR) 88 Ch 51
Yenice (TR) 89 Dc 49
Yenice (TR) 89 Dc 51
Yenice (TR) 96 Ci 53
Yenice (TR) 97 Df 54
Yenicekale (TR) 98 Dg 53
42890 Yeniceoba (TR) 96 Dc 52
42270 Yenidoğan (TR) 91 Ee 51
Yenifoça (TR) 95 Cg 52
Yenihisar (TR) 95 Ch 53
22400 Yenikarpuzlu (TR) 87 Cg 50
Yenikent (TR) 89 Dc 50
Yenikent (TR) 97 Dd 52
Yeniköy (TR) 88 Ch 50
Yeniköy (TR) 88 Ch 51
Yeniköy (TR) 95 Ci 52
Yeniköy (TR) 95 Ci 53
Yeniköy Plajı (TR) 88 Ci 50
66490 Yenipazar (TR) 88 Da 50
66490 Yenipazar (TR) 89 Df 51
66490 Yenipazar (TR) 95 Ci 53
32850 Yenişar- Bademli (TR) 96 Db 53
16900 Yenişehir (TR) 88 Ck 50
16900 Yenişehir (TR) 96 Ck 52
Yenisu (TR) 99 Ea 52
51900 Yeniyıldız (TR) 97 De 53
Yenizengen (TR) 97 De 53
BA21 Yeovil (GB) 52 Sh 40
66900 Yerköy (TR) 89 De 51
Yeşilbağ (TR) 96 Db 53
21560 Yeşilbahçe (TR) 99 Ea 52
52930 Yeşilce (TR) 90 Dh 50
42730 Yeşildağ (TR) 96 Db 53
Yeşildağ (TR) 96 Db 53
Yeşildere (TR) 97 Dd 53
Yeşilhisar (TR) 97 Df 52
07645 Yeşilköy (TR) 98 Dg 52
Yeşilköy (TR) 98 Dk 52
15500 Yeşilova (TR) 96 Ck 53
15500 Yeşilova (TR) 97 Dd 52
50900 Yeşilöz (TR) 89 Dc 51
34886 Yeşilvadı (TR) 88 Ck 49
Yeşilyazı (TR) 90 Dk 51
34151 Yeşilyurt (TR) 89 Dc 51
34151 Yeşilyurt (TR) 96 Ci 52
34151 Yeşilyurt (TR) 98 Di 52
60870 Yeşilyurt (Sulusaray) (TR) 90 Dg 51
NP7 Y-Fenni = Abergavenny (GB) 52 Sg 39
14880 Yığılca (TR) 88 Db 50
Yığınlı (TR) 99 Ed 53
Yiğitler (TR) 90 Dg 51
Yiğitler (TR) 98 Dh 53
37400 Yılanlı (TR) 98 Dg 52
Yıldızeli (TR) 90 Dg 51
98050 Ylakiai (LT) 40 Cb 34
54410 Ylämaa (FIN) 31 Ch 30
21901 Yläne (FIN) 30 Cc 30
95290 Yli-Kärppä (FIN) 22 Cf 25
91300 Ylikiiminki (FIN) 22 Cg 25
91240 Yli-Ii (FIN) 22 Cf 25
64610* Ylimarkku = Övermark (FIN) 22 Cb 28
99310 Yli-Muonio (FIN) 15 Cd 22
61401 Ylistaro (FIN) 22 Cc 28
95601 Ylitornio (FIN) 15 Cd 24
85999 Ylivieska (FIN) 22 Ce 26
95980 Ylläsjärvi (FIN) 15 Ce 23
33480 Ylöjärvi (FIN) 30 Cd 29
Yoğun (TR) 98 Dk 52
39000 Yoğuntaş (TR) 88 Ch 49
73400 Yolağzı (TR) 98 Dh 54
Yolüstü (TR) 96 Ci 53
61250 Yomra (TR) 90 Dk 50
69000 Yoncalı (TR) 90 Di 51
69000 Yoncalı (TR) 91 Ea 50
25900 Yoncalık (TR) 91 Ea 50
Yorazlar (TR) 96 Db 52
YO23 York (GB) 51 Si 37
Youghal = Eochaill (IRL) 49 Sc 39
66000* Yozgat (TR) 89 De 51
43200 Yssingeaux (F) 67 Ae 45
27100* Ystad (S) 39 Bd 35
SA9 Ystradgynlais (GB) 52 Sg 39
5265 Ytre Arna (N) 28 Af 30
Ytterån (S) 21 Be 27
68810 Ytteresse (FIN) 22 Cd 27
Ytterhogdal (S) 21 Be 28
Yttermalung (S) 29 Bd 30
Yücebağ (TR) 99 Eb 52
Yukarı Göklü (TR) 98 Dh 53
37800 Yukarı Ilıpınar (TR) 89 Dd 49
Yukarı Kızılca (TR) 91 Ec 51
08200 Yüksekoba (TR) 91 Eb 49
30300 Yüksekova (TR) 99 Ee 53
Yumrukaya (TR) 99 Ec 52
01680 Yumurtalık (TR) 97 Df 54
42530 Yunak (TR) 96 Db 52
45210 Yuncos (E) 81 Sg 50
Yuntdağ (TR) 95 Ch 52
26920 Yunusemre (TR) 88 Db 51
59040 Yürük (TR) 88 Ch 50
08800 Yusufeli (TR) 91 Eb 50
06291 Yuva (TR) 98 Dh 52
Yuvacık (TR) 90 Dk 51
Yuvacık (TR) 99 Eb 52
Yuvalı (TR) 97 Df 52
1400* Yverdon-les-Bains (CH) 68 Ag 44
76190 Yvetot (F) 53 Aa 41
Yxnö (S) 29 Bg 32

Z

1501 Zaanstad (NL) 53 Ae 38
Zabalac' (BY) 41 Ce 37
21230 Žabalj (SRB) 71 Ca 45
Zabalocce (BY) 42 Da 38
12374 Žabari (SRB) 71 Cb 46
Žabinka (BY) 57 Ce 38
57-200* Ząbkowice Śląskie (PL) 56 Bg 40
84 220 Žabljak (MNE) 86 Bk 47
Žabljano (BG) 86 Cc 48
16-060 Zabłudów (PL) 41 Cd 37

206 I Vrelo

16-060 Zabłudów (PL) 41 Cd 38
Žabno (HR) 70 Bg 45
Žabok 70 Bf 44
Zabolot'e (RUS) 43 Dd 36
Zabor'e (RUS) 32 Df 31
Zabor'e (RUS) 35 Fg 33
Zaborovka (RUS) 45 Ei 37
Zaborskoe, Il'inskoe- (RUS) 33 Ee 33
789 01 Zábřeh (CZ) 56 Bg 41
Začač'e (RUS) 25 Eb 27
Začativka (UA) 75 Dh 43
Zacharivka (UA) 73 Ck 43
Zadar (HR) 70 Bf 46
Zadnevo (RUS) 31 Dc 31
Zadonsk (RUS) 60 Di 38
Zadonsk, Severo- (RUS) 43 Di 36
Zadzeżża (BY) 42 Ci 35
Zaem'e (RUS) 33 Ea 32
95019 Zafferana Etnea (I) 84 Bf 53
06300 Zafra (E) 92 Sd 52
68-100 Żagań (PL) 56 Bf 39
Žagarė (LT) 41 Cd 34
Zagljadino (RUS) 46 Fc 37
8939 Zagorci (BG) 88 Ch 48
Zagorsk = Sergiev Posad (RUS) 43 Di 34
Zagoskino (RUS) 45 Ee 37
10000* Zagreb (HR) 70 Bf 45
12320 Žagubica (SRB) 71 Cb 46
Zagvozd (HR) 70 Bh 47
Zaharovo (RUS) 44 Dk 36
5644 Zăicani (MD) 73 Ch 43
Zainsk (RUS) 46 Fc 35
Zajač'e (RUS) 60 Dg 40
19000* Zaječar (SRB) 71 Cc 47
Zajkava (BY) 42 Da 35
Zajkovo (RUS) 36 Gc 33
Zajmišče (RUS) 34 Ef 31
Zajmišči (RUS) 32 Di 31
29100 Zákinthos (GR) 94 Ca 53
Zakobjakino (RUS) 33 Ea 32
34-500* Zakopane (PL) 56 Bk 41
Zakupne (UA) 58 Cg 41
8741 Zalaapáti (H) 70 Bh 44
8900 Zalaegerszeg (H) 70 Bg 44
Zalalövő (H) 70 Bg 44
06430 Zalamea de la Serena (E) 92 Se 52
21640 Zalamea la Real (E) 92 Sd 53
000450* Zalău (RO) 72 Cd 43
Zalazna (RUS) 35 Fc 32
Zalegošč' (RUS) 43 Dg 38
Zaleščyky (UA) 58 Cf 42
Zales'e (RUS) 32 Dg 32
Zalesskij, Pereslavl'- (RUS) 43 Di 34
14-230 Zalewo (PL) 40 Bk 37
Zalívnoj (RUS) 76 Ea 43
Založci (UA) 58 Cf 41
Zaluč'e (RUS) 31 Db 33
Žaludok (BY) 41 Ce 37
Zalukokoaže (RUS) 76 Ed 47
Zalužne (UA) 58 Ch 40
18-300* Zambrów (PL) 41 Cc 38
Zamežnoe (RUS) 26 Fc 25
Zam'jany (RUS) 77 Eh 44
49001* Zamora (E) 80 Se 49
09-204 Zamość (PL) 57 Cd 40
Zamoš'e (RUS) 31 Ci 31
2040 Zandvoort (NL) 53 Ae 38
57015 Zanglivéri (GR) 87 Cd 50
Zanul'e (RUS) 34 Ek 30
Zaockskij (RUS) 43 Dh 36
Zaovraž'e (RUS) 43 De 34
Zaozernyj (RUS) 24 Ea 29
Zapadnaja Dvina (RUS) 42 Dc 34
Zapol'e (RUS) 31 Ck 32
Zapoljarnyj (RUS) 16 Da 21
Zaporižž'a (UA) 74 Df 43
Zaporož'e = Zaporižž'a (UA) 74 Df 43
Zaporožskoe (RUS) 31 Da 30
Zaprešić (HR) 70 Bf 45
Zaprudnja (RUS) 43 Dh 34
58700 Zara (TR) 90 Dh 51
50001* Zaragoza (E) 82 Sk 49
Zarajsk (RUS) 43 Di 36
32013 Zarasai (LT) 41 Cg 35
20800 Zarautz (E) 66 Sh 47
Zarečensk (RUS) 16 Db 24
Zarečnyj (RUS) 47 Gb 34
Zarevo (RUS) 75 Ea 46
Zaričanka (UA) 58 Cg 42
Zarične (UA) 58 Cg 39
Zarizyn = Volgograd (RUS) 61 Ee 42
Zarja (RUS) 62 Ef 42
42-310 Żarki (PL) 56 Bk 40
Žarkovskij (RUS) 42 Dc 35
966 81 Žarnovica (SK) 56 Bi 42
70002 Zarós (GR) 94 Ce 55
25006 Zaroúhla (GR) 94 Cc 53
19246 Zaruba (RUS) 25 Ef 28
Zarubiha (RUS) 16 De 21
Zarubino (RUS) 32 Dd 32

68-200 Żary (PL) 56 Bf 39
Žaryn' (RUS) 43 Dd 37
10710 Zarza de Granadilla (E) 80 Sd 50
Zašeek (RUS) 16 Db 24
Zašeek (RUS) 16 Dc 23
Zašeek (RUS) 16 De 23
Žaškiv (UA) 59 Da 41
Zaslav'e (BY) 42 Ch 36
Zasosna (RUS) 60 Di 40
Zastavna (UA) 58 Cf 42
Zasul'e (RUS) 25 Eh 26
438 01 Žatec (CZ) 55 Bd 40
Zatoka (UA) 73 Da 44
84 303 Zaton (MNE) 86 Bk 48
32-640 Zator (PL) 56 Bk 41
4113 Zaube (LV) 41 Cf 34
547660 Zau de Câmpie (RO) 72 Ce 44
Zaural'skij (RUS) 47 Gb 36
7330 Zavet (BG) 72 Cg 47
Zavetnoe (RUS) 76 Ed 43
Zavidovići (BIH) 71 Bi 46
Zavitne (UA) 75 Dg 45
Zav'jalovo (RUS) 45 Eg 36
15312 Zavlaka (SRB) 71 Bk 46
Zavodčik (RUS) 35 Ff 33
Zavod Mihajlovskij (RUS) 46 Fe 34
Zavolž'e (RUS) 44 Ed 34
Zavolžsk (RUS) 33 Ec 33
Zavolžskoe (RUS) 77 Eh 44
47-120 Zawadzkie (PL) 56 Bi 40
42-400 Zawiercie (PL) 56 Bk 40
64-360 Zbąszyń (PL) 56 Bf 38
Zberoaia (MD) 73 Ci 44
83-210 Zblewo (PL) 40 Bi 37
Zboriv (UA) 58 Cf 41
Ždamirovo (RUS) 45 Eg 36
696 32 Ždánice (CZ) 56 Bh 41
Ždanov = Maryupol' (UA) 75 Dh 43
Ždanovka (RUS) 62 Eh 39
Ždanovka (RUS) 63 Fe 38
Ždanovo (RUS) 44 Eb 36
Ždany (UA) 59 Dd 40
591 01* Žd'ár nad Sázavou (CZ) 56 Bf 41
267 51 Ždice (CZ) 55 Bd 41
Zdolbuniv (UA) 58 Cg 40
57-340 Zdrój, Duszniki (PL) 56 Bg 40
57-540 Zdrój, Lądek (PL) 56 Bg 40
59-850 Zdrój, Świeradów- (PL) 56 Bf 40
8380 Zeebrugge (B) 53 Ad 39
16792 Zehdenick (D) 39 Bd 38
3700* Zeist (NL) 54 Af 38
06712 Zeitz (D) 55 Bc 39
Zelënaja Rošča (RUS) 46 Fc 36
Zelenčukskaja (RUS) 76 Eb 47
Zelencyno (RUS) 33 Ec 32
Zelenec (RUS) 26 Ff 28
Zelenik (RUS) 25 Ee 28
Zeleninskaja (RUS) 25 Ec 28
Zelenivka (UA) 75 Dg 44
Zelenoborskij (RUS) 16 Dc 24
Zelenodol'sk (RUS) 45 Ei 35
Zelenodol's'k (UA) 74 Dd 43
Zelenogorsk (RUS) 31 Ck 30
Zelenograd (RUS) 43 Dh 35
Zelenogradsk (RUS) 40 Ca 36
Zelenokumsk (RUS) 76 Ed 46
Zelenyj Mys (UA) 59 Da 39
Zelenzukskaja (RUS) 76 Eb 47
340 04 Železná Ruda (CZ) 55 Bd 41
Železnodorožnyj (RUS) 40 Cb 36
Železnogorsk (RUS) 60 Df 38
Železnovodsk (RUS) 76 Ed 46
Železnyj, Gus'- (RUS) 44 Eb 35
Zelina (HR) 70 Bg 45
1226 Želino (MK) 86 Cb 49
35200 Zélio (GR) 94 Cc 52
5700* Zell am See (A) 69 Bc 43
4345 Zeltiņi (LV) 30 Cg 33
Želtinskij (RUS) 47 Fk 37
Żeltoe (RUS) 64 Fg 39
Želtye Vody = Žovti Vody (UA) 59 Dd 42
Žel'va (BY) 41 Ce 37
20015 Želva (LT) 41 Cf 35
9060 Zelzate (B) 53 Ad 39
Žemaičiu (Varduva) (LT) 41 Cc 34
Žemaičiu Naumiestis (LT) 40 Cb 35
Zembin (BY) 42 Ci 36
Zemetčino (RUS) 44 Ec 37
3135 Zemīte (LV) 41 Cc 34
72000* Zenica (BIH) 70 Bh 46
Zenkovo (RUS) 37 Gk 29
Zenzeli (RUS) 77 Eg 45
Žepa (BIH) 71 Bk 47
Žepče (BIH) 71 Bi 46
39261 Zerbst (D) 55 Bc 39
Žerd' (RUS) 25 Ee 25
Žerdevka (RUS) 61 Eb 39
Zerklo (RUS) 46 Fe 38
3920 Zermatt (CH) 68 Ah 44

7530 Zernez (CH) 69 Ba 44
Zernograd (RUS) 76 Ea 44
Zerzjaib (RUS) 26 Ek 27
Žešart (RUS) 26 Ek 28
Žestjanka (RUS) 62 Ek 39
07937 Zeulenroda-Triebes (D) 55 Bb 40
27404 Zeven (D) 38 Ak 37
6900* Zevenaar (NL) 54 Ag 39
16970 Zeytinbağı (TR) 88 Ci 50
Zeytindağ (TR) 95 Ch 52
10305 Zeytinli (TR) 87 Cg 51
08100 Zeytinlik (TR) 91 Eb 49
45560 Zeytinliova (TR) 95 Ch 52
95-100 Zgierz (PL) 56 Bk 39
4206 Zgornje Jezersko (SLO) 70 Be 44
59-900 Zgorzelec (PL) 56 Bf 39
5234 Zguriţa (MD) 58 Ci 42
20520 Zhur = Žur (RKS) 86 Ca 48
Zhurivka (UA) 59 Db 40
965 01 Žiar nad Hronom (SK) 56 Bi 42
20132 Zicavo (F) 83 Ak 49
Ziča (SRB) 71 Ca 47
57-220 Ziębice (PL) 56 Bh 40
65-001 Zielona Góra (PL) 56 Bf 39
4300 Zierikzee (NL) 53 Ad 39
14793 Ziesar (D) 55 Bc 38
Zigaza (RUS) 47 Fh 37
Žigulevsk (RUS) 45 Ek 37
Zijančurino (RUS) 64 Fh 39
Zilair (RUS) 64 Fh 38
Zil'djarovo (RUS) 46 Fe 37
60400* Zile (TR) 89 Df 50
010 01* Žilina (SK) 56 Bi 41
Žilino (RUS) 32 Dd 33
Žilino (RUS) 33 Eb 32
53350 Zilkale (TR) 91 Ea 50
Žiloj Bor (RUS) 32 De 31
Žilotkovo (RUS) 32 De 33
5751 Žilupe (LV) 42 Ci 34
457370 Zimbor (RO) 72 Cd 43
Zimijiv (UA) 60 Dg 41
8690 Zimnicea (RO) 87 Cg 48
145400 Zimnicea (RO) 72 Cf 47
Zimnjackij (RUS) 61 Ec 41
Zimovniki (RUS) 76 Ec 43
18374 Zingst am Darß (D) 39 Bc 36
Zin'kiv (UA) 59 De 40
7060 Zinnik = Soignies (B) 53 Ae 40
17454 Zinnowitz (D) 39 Bd 36
8420 Zirc (H) 70 Bh 43
Zirgan (RUS) 46 Ff 37
Žirjakovo (RUS) 37 Gf 33
Žirjatino (RUS) 43 Dd 37
Žirkovskij, Holm- (RUS) 43 Dd 35
90513 Zirndorf (D) 55 Ba 41
Žirnov (RUS) 61 Eb 42
Žirnovsk (RUS) 61 Ee 40
Žiteli (RUS) 25 En 25
Žitni Potok (SRB) 86 Cb 48
Žitomir = Žytomyr (UA) 58 Ci 40
Žitovo Glagolevo (RUS) 43 Dh 37
02763 Zittau (D) 55 Be 40
Živajkino (RUS) 45 Eh 37
Živi Bunari (HR) 70 Be 46
Živinice (BIH) 71 Bi 46
Žizdra (RUS) 43 De 37
Zjaleny Bor (BY) 42 Ci 36
Zjukajka (RUS) 35 Fe 33
Žjuratkul' (RUS) 47 Fk 36
Žjuzjuno (RUS) 35 Fe 33
5090 Zlatarica (BG) 72 Cf 47
2080 Zlatica (BG) 87 Ce 48
516100 Zlatna (RO) 72 Cd 44
5760 Zlatna Panega (BG) 72 Ce 47
4980 Zlatograd (BG) 87 Cf 49
Zlatoust (RUS) 47 Fk 35
760 01* Zlín (CZ) 56 Bh 41
Žlobin (BY) 42 Da 38
78-520* Złocieniec (PL) 56 Bg 37
98-270 Złoczew (PL) 56 Bi 39
19215 Zlot (SRB) 71 Cb 46
59-500* Złotoryja (PL) 56 Bf 39
77-400 Złotów (PL) 40 Bh 37
Žlynka (BY) 59 Db 38
Žmerynka (UA) 58 Ci 41
Zmiev = Zimijiv (UA) 60 Dg 41
Zmievka (RUS) 60 Dg 38
55-140 Żmigród (PL) 56 Bg 39
Znamenka (RUS) 27 Fg 29
Znamenka (RUS) 34 Ei 32
Znamenka (RUS) 43 De 36
Znamenka (RUS) 61 Eb 38
Znamensk (RUS) 40 Cb 36
Znamenskoe (RUS) 36 Gd 33
Znamenskoe (RUS) 43 Df 37
Znamjanka (UA) 59 Dc 42
88-400 Znob'-Novhorods'ke (UA) 59 Dd 38
669 02* Znojmo (CZ) 56 Bg 42

Žodino = Žodzina (BY) 42 Ci 36
Žodzina (BY) 42 Ci 36
24019 Zogno (I) 69 Ak 45
Zoločiv (UA) 57 Ce 41
Zoločiv (UA) 60 Df 40
Zolotaja Step' (RUS) 62 Eg 39
Zolote (UA) 60 Di 42
Zolotonoša (UA) 59 Dc 41
Zolotuha (RUS) 77 Eg 43
Zolotuhino (RUS) 60 Dg 38
67000* Zonguldak (TR) 88 Db 49
20124 Zonza (F) 83 Ak 49
10130 Zorita (E) 80 Se 51
44-240 Żory (PL) 56 Bi 40
15806 Zossen (D) 55 Bd 38
9620 Zottegem (B) 53 Ad 40
Zovka (RUS) 31 Ci 32
Žovkva = Nesterov (UA) 57 Cd 40
Žovti Vody (UA) 59 Dd 42
Žovtneve (UA) 57 Ce 40
Žovtneve (UA) 59 De 40
Žovtneve (UA) 74 Dd 43
Žovtyj Jar (UA) 73 Ck 45
23101* Zrenjanin (SRB) 71 Ca 45
285 22 Zruč nad Sázavou (CZ) 56 Bf 41
09405 Zschopau (D) 55 Bd 40
Zubcov (RUS) 43 De 34
Zubova Poljana (RUS) 44 Ec 36
Zubovka (RUS) 46 Fb 36
Zubovo (RUS) 32 Dh 30
Zubovo (RUS) 37 Df 36
50800 Zuera (E) 82 Sk 49
Zuevka (RUS) 34 Fb 32
21210 Zufre (E) 92 Sd 53
6300* Zug (CH) 68 Ai 43
Žuklino (RUS) 43 Di 34
Zukovka (RUS) 43 Dd 37
Žukovo (RUS) 32 Dg 32
Žukovskaja (RUS) 76 Ec 43
Žukovskoe (RUS) 36 Gc 32
Zula, Ust'- (RUS) 35 Fe 31
53909 Zülpich (D) 54 Ag 40
4880 Zundert (NL) 53 Ae 39
Župrany (BY) 41 Cg 36
20520 Žur = Zhur (RKS) 86 Ca 48
Zura (RUS) 35 Fd 33
Žuravne (UA) 57 Ce 41
Žuravskoe (RUS) 76 Ed 46
8000* Zürich (CH) 68 Ai 43
09-300 Żuromin (PL) 40 Bk 37
Zurrieq (M) 84 Be 55
17495 Züssow (D) 39 Bd 37
7200* Zutphen (NL) 54 Ag 38
Zvenigorod (RUS) 43 Dg 35
Zvenigovo (RUS) 45 Ei 34
Zvenyhorodka (UA) 59 Da 41
8170 Zvezdec (BG) 88 Ch 48
6820 Zvezdel (BG) 87 Cf 49
Zvjančatka (BY) 42 Dc 37
960 01 Zvolen (SK) 56 Bk 42
18333 Zvonce (SRB) 86 Cc 48
75400* Zvornik (BIH) 71 Bk 46
66482 Zweibrücken (D) 54 Ah 41
04442 Zwenkau (D) 55 Bc 39
3910 Zwettl (A) 56 Bf 42
08056* Zwickau (D) 55 Bc 40
22-470 Zwierzyniec (PL) 57 Cc 40
94227 Zwiesel (D) 55 Bd 41
26160 Zwischenahn, Bad (D) 38 Ai 37
26-700 Zwoleń (PL) 57 Cb 39
8011* Zwolle (NL) 54 Ag 38
Zybino, Libicy- (RUS) 43 Dh 37
Żybkove (UA) 59 Dd 42
Žydačiv (UA) 57 Ce 41
Žykovo (RUS) 34 Ek 33
Žykovo, Efremo- (RUS) 46 Fd 37
96-300 Żyrardów (PL) 57 Ca 38
Žyrjanovskij (RUS) 36 Gb 33
Žytkavičy (BY) 58 Ch 38
Žytnyky (UA) 59 Da 41
Žytomyr (UA) 58 Ci 40
34-300* Żywiec (PL) 56 Bk 41

A B C D E F G H I J K L M N O P Q R S T U V W X Y Z

Photo Credit:
★ **MP Highlights** Satellitenbildaufnahme Europa (getty images/GSO Images)
☆ Mitternachtssonne, Nordkap (huber-images/M. Rellini)
☆ Dom am Senatsplatz, Helsinki (huber-images/Gräfenhain)
☆ Altstadt, Tallinn (huber-images/Gräfenhain)
☆ Tower Bridge, London (huber-images/H.-P. Merten)
☆ Leidesegracht, Amsterdam (huber-images/M. Rellini)
☆ Stadtansicht und Eiffelturm, Paris (huber-images/L. Vaccarella)
☆ Bodensee (mauritius images/Westend61)
☆ Typische Häuser, Matterhorn (huber-images/H.-P. Merten)
☆ Bucht bei Le Lavandou, Côte d'Azur (huber-images/Ch. Seba)
☆ San Gimignano, Toskana (DuMont Bildarchiv/Ch. Anzenberger-Fink, T. Anzenberger)
☆ Tara Schlucht (mauritius images/nature picture library)
☆ Hagia Sophia, Istanbul (DuMont Bildarchiv/F. Heuer)
☆ Barcelona (DuMont Bildarchiv/F. Heuer)
☆ Alhambra, Granada, Andalusien (DuMont Bildarchiv/A. F. Selbach)
☆ Santorin (huber-images/L. Vaccarella)

Design:
fpm – factor product münchen (Cover)

➜ 2022

01-30-130400-011